DYNAMIC ECONOMY

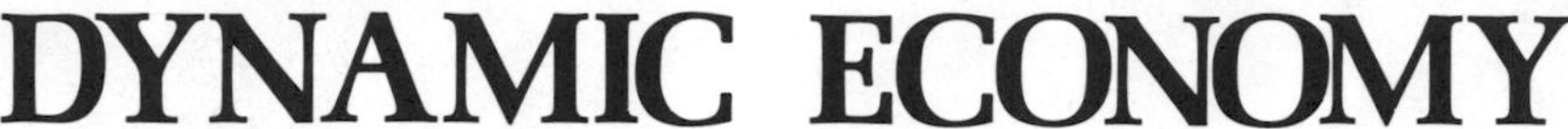

PUBLIC ASSISTANCE: RECIPIENTS

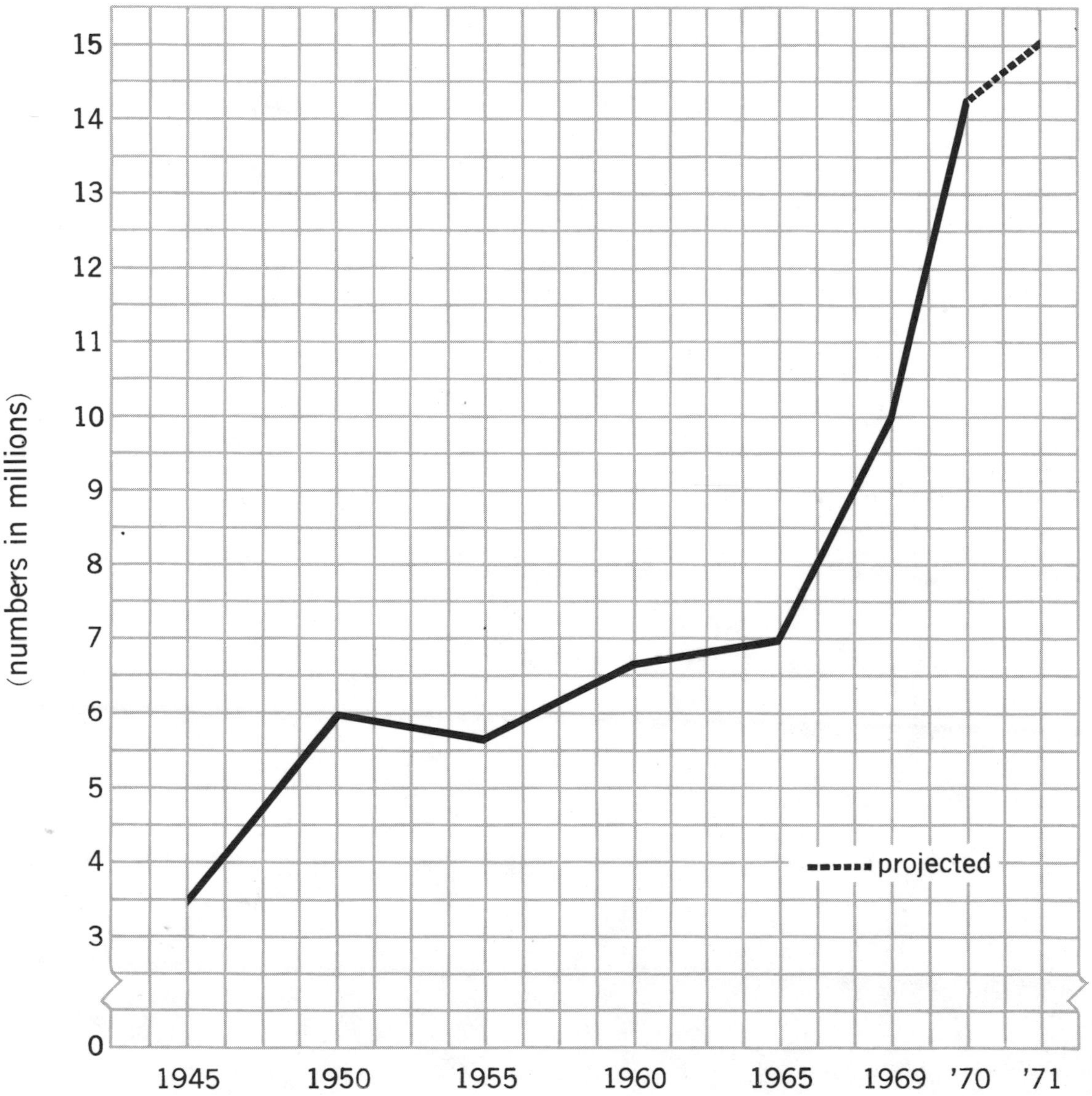

15
14
13
12
11
10
9
8
7
6
5
4
3
0
(numbers in millions)
projected
1945
1950
1955
1960
1965
1969
'70
'71

SOURCE: U.S. Department of Health, Education and Welfare, Social and Rehabilitation Service

Measure Progress?

INTRODUCTORY ECONOMICS

INTRODUCTORY ECONOMICS

Sanford D. Gordon

State University College
Oneonta, New York

George G. Dawson

Joint Council on Economic Education
New York City

D. C. HEATH AND COMPANY
Lexington, Massachusetts Toronto London

Published simultaneously in Canada.

Printed in the United States of America.

International Standard Book Number: 0-669-63537-5

Library of Congress Catalog Card Number: 75-162643

To Alice and Shirley

PREFACE

This book is written primarily for the student rather than for the instructor. It therefore contains such aids as "The Authors' Note to the Student," which provides the objectives and approach of the chapter; "A Student's Note to the Student," which offers composite reactions of actual students after they have read the chapter; materials for review; a glossary; a list of selected readings at the end of every chapter; and two acetate overlays to explain most effectively supply and demand and income determination.

Unlike most college textbooks in economics, this book is designed primarily for use in a one-semester course. If used with appropriate readings it becomes suitable for the two-semester course providing both extensive coverage of fundamental concepts and principles and practical consideration of major economic problems.

While *Introductory Economics* uses the analytical and problem-solving approach, it limits the use of mathematics to simple geometric models, bar graphs, and schedule analysis. Thus the student is given some key economist's tools without the burden of the mathematical derivation. Both the microeconomic approach (the study of the individual and of business) and the macroeconomic approach (the study of aggregates, the nation's economy as a whole) are analyzed, and each is illustrated by means of specific examples. When controversial questions are introduced, there is recognition that solutions are likely to represent a spectrum of opinion rather than a choice between two clear alternatives. In dealing with problems, a deliberate effort has been made to avoid the "either-or" approach; instead, whenever feasible, a range of possible alternatives is considered. Sufficient descriptive material is introduced to provide the background necessary for a sophisticated consideration of the major problems of contemporary economic development.

Unit I considers what economics is, what questions it seeks to answer, what the purpose of an economic system is, and how the model of classical capitalism answers the major questions of economics. The approach is analytical rather than descriptive; however, materials and examples for illustrating principles and theories are drawn from the economic environment and from experiences familiar to most individuals. At the same time that classical theory is explored, the existence of other theories and models is recognized. Chapter 3 focuses attention on major economic systems other than our own—socialism, communism, and fascism. With each of these systems care is taken to distinguish between the theory and actual practice. Recognition is given to the existence of competition in the world between these different economic systems and different ways of life, and to the fact that uncommitted nations have several alternatives from which to choose.

Unit II deals with the ways in which business maximizes profits and how it uses the factors of production: labor, natural resources, capital, and management. The roles of government and consumers are also considered. The two chapters on government stress the increasing part government plays in the economy and the ways in which its decisions affect the consumer and producer markets. A chapter on the consumer examines his role in determining production and raises questions concerning his freedom of choice.

The chapters on the factors of production are organized in similar fashion: the role of each factor in the American economy is analyzed and its part in providing answers to the basic questions of *How, What,* and *For Whom* is discussed. In relation to each factor the classical theory and its model are considered, together with certain departures from them. Finally, in the chapters on government and the consumer, some of the problems faced by our society are identified, and potential solutions are considered. Whenever possible, these solutions are evaulated in terms of the classical model.

Unit III introduces a second model, that of macroeconomic theory. In this unit fundamentals of national income accounting, income flow, money, banking, income determination, and the role of government policy as an active influence on the economy are discussed. The theories and concepts developed here are focused on the Keynesian model. The authors believe that the material included here on the fundamentals of income analysis, although by nature theoretical and abstract, provides a valuable new dimension for understanding economics. With details and qualifications held to a minimum, an adequate understanding of the national income approach can be achieved.

In Chapter 16, "Formulating Modern Economic Policy," the new model and the classical model are brought together into what economists call the *neoclassical synthesis.* The roles of modern monetary and fiscal policy, which have already been identified and evaluated, are discussed within the framework of this new model. Again, existing problems of our economy are identified, and a number of possible solutions are considered.

Unit IV views the American economy in relation to the world scene. Chapter 17 identifies the theories fundamental to international economics, the existing barriers to trade and to its future expansion, and recent developments aimed at removing such barriers. This is followed by an examination into the factors responsible for economic growth. Emphasis is placed on the emerging nations with some comparisons to the American experience.

Unit V identifies and analyzes major contemporary problems of the American economy. In this revision the economics of pollution, black economics, and the military-industrial complex are introduced. Problems faced by the farmer, the small businessman, and those economic problems associated with urban areas and in education have been revised and updated. Finally, a projection of America's economic growth in the 1970's is made for a number of important segments of our economy.

These particular problems have been selected not only because they are constantly discussed by the professional economist and the conscientious citizen but also because the traditional solutions are being questioned in the light of continuing change. An awareness of the meaning of alternative courses of action should help in the making of informed decisions.

The authors believe that the following features of *Introductory Economics* are most significant to the development of a fresh approach to the study of economics:

1. Greater emphasis is placed on the analytical than on the descriptive approach to the subject. This approach encourages understanding of economic principles instead of mere rote memorization.
2. Orientation is directed toward basic economic theory, with conscious effort to avoid endless details and qualifications. This simplification, however, does not mean oversimplification to the point of distortion; rather it represents a focus on major principles and their relation to our nation's economic system.
3. Consideration is given to the "ideal" (the model or theory) and to the "real" (actual practice as carried on in the economy).
4. The problem-solving approach is used both in the presentation of ideas and in the organization of content.
5. Recognition is given to the problems of the contemporary economic scene. Among these are questions related to economic growth, pollution, education as a factor in economic growth, and the appropriate goals of an affluent society. These problems are just beginning to receive from leaders in government, education, and economics the attention they deserve. They are likewise appropriate for consideration in the classroom.
6. Abstract ideas are explained and illustrated by means of specific examples based on familiar circumstances. In addition the classical and Keynesian models are illustrated by means of inserts, using a step-by-step visual and explanatory analysis and including transparent overlays to demonstrate conclusions. These models summarize the presentation of theory and provide a new and unique dimension for understanding abstract materials.
7. Much of the content and many of the visual materials, as well as approaches and methods, have been tested by actual use in class and have been refined by continuing experience.
8. The design is primarily for a one-semester course with opportunity for use in two semesters.

It is the sincere hope of the authors that this book provides a conceptual framework for thinking about our changing economic world. In a democratic country with a traditional emphasis on the private sector of the economy and a growing importance of the public sector, it is essential for citizens to understand the nature of economics and of the issues with which that subject is concerned, since it is their decisions that determine economic policy.

Although this book is fully the responsibility of the authors, it is, nevertheless, the product of many minds and many influences. Our first acknowledgment rightfully belongs to the thousands of students whose insights and experience have guided us. They have helped in defining the suitability of particular materials, the effectiveness of different presentations, the directions of student interest and concern, and less obvious aspects of the "new economics."

Sanford D. Gordon
George G. Dawson

CONTENTS

UNIT I

THE FRAMEWORK OF ECONOMICS

Economics—What It Is and What It Tries to Do 1

THE AUTHORS' NOTE TO THE STUDENT

Chapter 1 introduces you to the subject of economics. It explains what economics is and explores the central questions which economics seeks to answer. Furthermore, it examines the kind of economic system we have in this country. You will learn what an economic model is and what part such a model can play in answering the questions of *What? How?* and *For Whom?* Finally, you will be introduced to the approach and pattern of organization that will be followed in this study of economics.

At the beginning of each chapter there is a short introduction by the authors explaining in general terms what the chapter is about. This is followed by comments made by students like yourself who are taking an introductory course and reacting to the material contained in this chapter. Hints and evaluations are passed on to you that you may find helpful. These notes are a composite and the reaction of each student may be slightly different. Exploring new ideas is easier if you have some idea of what to expect.

As you become more deeply involved in economics, you will observe that it provides a way of looking at problems—a pattern of thought—that is not exactly like that of any other social science. As you complete each chapter try to explain the economist's approach. See if these first discoveries stand the test of time when you re-examine them later in the course. You will also be able to identify very quickly the controversy associated with economic problems. Ask yourself why economists with equally good training should disagree. Does this disagreement mean that there are no correct answers? What do we mean by "correct" answers? Many of you may emerge from this course with more questions than when you began. This curiosity is the sign of a good introduction to economics.

A STUDENT'S NOTE TO THE STUDENT

I had very little economics in high school and did not know what to expect. I heard economics is tougher than other social studies—more technical and more mathematical. This chapter made me feel more comfortable. It gave me some idea of what we are going to be covering and it was fairly easy. I hope it stays that way.

Part A
Economics as a Discipline

Why Should You Study Economics?

As you skim through the pages of this book, you will see graphs and charts, facts and figures. As you examine some sections more closely, you will probably ask the questions "Why should I study economics? Will this study help me in any way?" Psychologists have found that students are better able to learn when they can see a purpose in learning. There is good reason, then, to begin by examining possible answers to these questions.

Citizens Influence Economic Policies of Government

In a democracy we, as citizens, are expected to participate, at least indirectly, in decision making. In voting for our representatives or in supporting a political party, we are endorsing certain principles and supporting particular solutions to problems. How far should the government go in providing medical care? Should taxes be raised or lowered? Are greater curbs needed on big business and big labor? Are my tax dollars being spent wisely? Is our tariff policy in need of a change? These few questions, although they are usually asked within a political framework, have an economic nature. They are as important as the money in your pocket, and just as personal. Their answers will affect the amount of money you make and the amount of money you have to spend. There is little government activity that does not have an economic origin, and no one can avoid the influence of government in his life.

Consumers and Producers Influence Economic Policies of Business

Even though the influence of government policy on your life may seem remote at the present time, you are nevertheless deeply involved in economics. As you go shopping, you are interested in the kinds of goods you get and the prices you pay for them. When you go to work, you will be concerned about the amount of compensation you receive. The purchases you make as a consumer and the income you receive as a producer or worker help to shape the economic decisions and policies made by American businesses. Although the study of economics may not provide you with a method of earning a living, it can help you better understand your role as a consumer and a producer. It can also increase your ability to make decisions that are best for you as individual and citizen.

What Economics Is

Economics is one of the social sciences. Like political science, sociology, and geography it is concerned with the study of man's attempt to organize his environment to satisfy his needs. Economics concentrates on the satisfaction of man's material needs, such as food and shelter. Specifically, it concerns itself with *the study of production, distribution, and consumption of goods and services*.

If we picture man in an economic sense, we think of him as trying to make a living. He works to produce goods or services that people want and are willing to pay

WHAT DO ECONOMISTS DO?

Economists study man's activities devoted to satisfying human wants. They are concerned with the problems which arise in utilizing limited resources of land, raw materials, manpower, and manufactured products so as to meet, as well as possible, people's many unsatisfied wants. In this connection, they may analyze the relation between the supply of and demand for goods and services, and the ways in which goods are exchanged, produced, distributed, and consumed. Some economists are concerned with such practical problems as the control of inflation, the prevention of depression, and the development of farm, wage, tax, and tariff policies. Others develop theories to explain the causes of employment and unemployment or the ways in which international trade influences world economic conditions. Still others are engaged in the collection and interpretation of data on a wide variety of economic problems.

Economists are employed as teachers in colleges and universities, and as researchers in government agencies, private industry, and nonprofit research organizations. Through their research and analysis they may influence government and industry planning.

Employment Outlook

Employment of economists will increase very rapidly through the 1970's. Colleges and universities will need hundreds of new instructors annually to handle rapidly increasing enrollments and to replace economists who retire, die, or transfer to other fields of work. Private industry is expected to employ many more economists, as businessmen become more accustomed to relying on scientific methods of analyzing business trends, forecasting sales, and planning purchasing and production operations.

SOURCE: U.S. Department of Labor, Bureau of Labor Statistics, *Occupational Outlook Handbook*, 1968–1969 edition, pp. 172–174.

for. In return for the value he creates, he gets paid so that he can buy the things he and his family want. In the simplest society he works to produce the things he and his family want and will consume directly. In a more complex society he is more specialized and must exchange the goods or services he produces for goods and services that other people produce. This allows him to satisfy many more wants than if he himself had to create everything he needs and wants. Whether we look at man as part of a family or as part of a great nation, we know that he has material wants which he seeks to satisfy. Economics is the study of how man tries to satisfy these wants. In studying economics you may at times pause to evaluate how successful we in America have been in satisfying these wants.

The Central Problem of Economics

Though definitions are very useful in delineating the scope of an academic discipline like economics, they are sometimes weak in pointing out the purpose and direction of the discipline. In the course of living, man is faced with certain basic problems. In trying to find answers, he gathers facts, organizes them, discovers related questions, and develops methods for solving problems. Collectively, these procedures, the body of knowledge, and the attitudes developed add up to a discipline, for example, *economics*. However, the discipline develops because man is searching for answers. Let us review at this time the questions that economics seeks to answer.

For Individuals

All of us, at some time or other, allow ourselves the luxury of daydreaming. A common subject for these dreams is to picture ourselves as able to afford all the things we associate with wealth. A look through a mail-order catalogue or a visit to a large department store whets our appetite for a never-ending list of products. However, nothing can bring us back to reality sooner than reaching into our pockets and finding how little we have to work with. *The problem we are faced with is that our resources, here identified as money, are limited.* The only way we can resolve our problem is to make choices. After looking at our resources, we must examine our list of wants and identify the things that we need immediately, those that we can postpone, and those that we cannot afford. As individuals we are faced with the central problem involved in economics: *deciding just how to allocate our limited resources to fulfill as many unlimited wants as we can.*

For Nations

Nations face the same problem. As a country's population grows, the need for more goods and services grows correspondingly. Resources necessary to production may increase, but there never are enough resources to satisfy the total desires of a nation. Whether the budget meeting is taking place in the family living room, in the city hall, in the conference room of the corporation board of directors, or in the chamber of the House of Representatives in Washington, D. C., the basic problem still exists. We need to find methods of allocating our limited resources in order to satisfy our unlimited wants.

A short time ago economists divided goods into two categories, free and economic. The former, like air and water, were in such abundance that the economist had no concern for them. After all, economics is the science of scarcity and what to do about it. Today many of these "free goods" are in reality very expensive if we plan to use them. Pollution has made clean air and water expensive for the producer who has to filter his waste products, for the consumer who ultimately pays for the producer's extra cost, and for the taxpayer who pays for government's involvement in cleaning up or keeping the environment clean.

In the 1970's almost all goods are scarce. Only by effort and money can they be obtained in the form man wishes.

Meeting the needs of people and nations from the supply of resources available leads to the basic activity called *production.* In the course of trying to meet unlimited wants from limited economic goods, production leads to new problems in economics.

The Big Questions: What? How? For Whom?

There are three questions that are closely associated with the central problem of unlimited wants and limited resources. We shall call them the problems of *What? How?* and *For Whom?* Whether we study the simple subsistence economy of a South Pacific island or the complex system of an industrialized nation, we must see how the problem of *What* to produce is solved. If economics deals with the study of the satisfaction of material wants, then the student may well ask what material wants shall be met. Should the people submit an annual list? Should a central planning committee decide? How much freedom should the people have in deciding? The question of what to produce is basic and exists because we have limited resources and unlimited wants.

If we answer the question of *What,* we must then consider the question of *How:* how do we produce the goods and services we have decided upon? Production, even in a simple society, can be difficult to achieve. It involves getting the right kind and amount of "ingredients" together at the right time and place to produce the things we want. We have to be careful not to waste these ingredients, since they are usually in limited supply. Inefficient production will mean that there will not be enough resources left over to satisfy other wants. We will have more to say about these ingredients shortly.

After deciding what to produce and how to produce it, we still have a major question to answer: *For Whom* is this production meant? The *For Whom* is a question of *distribution.* Shall everyone get an equal portion? Should production be distributed according to need? If so, how do we determine need? The problem of who gets steak and who gets hamburger is as basic as the *What* and the *How.*

Factors of Production

Although nations may choose different economic systems, all must be concerned with producing. Before proceeding with our discussion of economic systems, we must first understand what we have described as the ingredients of production. All production involves four separate *factors:* natural resources, labor, capital, and management.

Natural Resources

Natural resources—the materials nature provides—are necessary to the production of the things we want. Some economists prefer to call this factor *land.* The minerals in the ground, forests, waterfalls, and fertile soil are all examples of a nation's resources; they are important in determining its production.

Labor

To adapt natural resources for human use, we must apply work. This is done by *labor,* the second factor of production. Here, too, the skill and the amount of labor will be important in determining production. India has more than twice the labor force that we have in the United States, but the greater skill of the American worker makes him far more productive. Superior education has allowed him to utilize machines.

Capital

The third factor of production is *capital.*

Production involves four factors, all of which contribute value to the final product and must be paid for.

Most people think of capital as money. To the economist *capital is any man-made instrument of production,* that is, a good used to further production. Frequently this will mean a tool or a machine. It can also mean the rolled steel that is used in automobile production. By placing great amounts of capital in skilled hands, productivity can be increased tremendously.

Management

The fourth factor of production is *management.* People engaged in this function are referred to as *entrepreneurs* (enterprisers). It is the responsibility of the manager to initiate production, to organize the other factors of production, and to operate the productive establishment. If he produces goods and services efficiently, he contributes a valuable service in satisfying people's wants. When we have the four factors mentioned previously, we have the ingredients of production.

The Need for an Economic System

In order to answer the central problem of limited resources and unlimited wants and the related questions of *What? How?* and *For Whom?* we need some rules or guiding principles. Such principles usually reflect the values that people hold. We find a broad range of values held by the American people. Most students of American history would agree that individual freedom and the sanctity of private property rank among the highest. Some people today would place equality and the general welfare high on the list. In the Soviet Union the best interests of the state and collective ownership of property are emphasized. Values such as these, and more specifically the principles that stem from them, provide the direction for answering the big questions in economics. The method a nation uses in answering these questions we call its *economic system.*

What Kind of Economic System?

An economic system must provide an answer to the question of who is to produce the goods and services. If businessmen produce all, we have an exclusively private enterprise system which we classify as *capitalism.* The emphasis of this system is on the private ownership and operation of the factors of production. If, on the other hand, the means of production and distribution are owned and operated by government, the system is labeled *socialism.*

Actually, since no country has all its production coming exclusively from either the private or the public (government) sector, all countries may be said to have more or less mixed economies. However, this does not mean they are the same. Far from it. In the United States the largest portion of our goods and services comes from businesses—private enterprises—and a much smaller, though important, portion (primarily services) comes from government. Some of these services with which we come in close contact are educational and library facilities and the postal system. Although our economy is mixed, we usually label it *capitalism, mixed capitalism, private enterprise,* or *free enterprise.* These terms are characteristic of economies in which production stems primarily from business, and in which government plays a lesser role.

In the Soviet Union most means of production are owned and operated by the government, and very little originates with private enterprise. Because of this emphasis on government production, the U.S.S.R. calls its system socialism. Most economically developed countries of the world have economic systems which are somewhere between that found in the United States and that of the Soviet Union.

Part B
An Overview of the American Economic System

Production—What?

With most of our production coming from business enterprises consisting of about 5 million privately owned firms, how do we decide what to produce? In a country with over 200,000,000 people, each of whom has a variety of wants larger than the inventory list of a supermarket, the question of *What* seems overwhelming. Even the thousands of items listed in mail-order catalogues do not begin to cover the numerous wants of people. Deciding what to produce under these circumstances would appear impossible. Yet this is being done all the time, along with decisions about how much of each product to make. Not only have we been finding answers to these questions, but the indication is that our system is working comparatively well. Americans produce and consume more goods and services than any other country in the world.

Every day businessmen throughout the country make decisions about what and how much to produce. They are very careful in their estimates because they realize that if their decisions are wrong they will lose money. They also realize that those who make the most accurate decisions will make the most money. What guidelines do we have to follow?

Individual Choices Determine Production

Businessmen watch carefully what customers buy. Every time you buy something in a store you are casting your dollar vote for that particular good. Actually you vote many hundreds of times a year for the various products you buy. If very few people buy a product, that product will be defeated at the polls; that is, it will not be produced or it will be produced in a smaller quantity. The storekeeper does not order it again, and the producer knows that he will have to cut down his production, change his product, or stop producing it. However, if a great many people buy a product, the casting of these many votes will result in the storekeeper's increasing his order and the producer's increasing the amount he manufactures. The buyers tell the sellers what they want, and the sellers in turn tell the producers.

You cast votes indicating your choice whenever you obtain something that is produced. Consider how many times you have purchased a phonograph record at your favorite music store. If you and your friends are particularly interested in a special record, the owner of the music store will have to increase his order for records to satisfy this single want of many people. You also find this same principle —of supply meeting demand—in a library. If a librarian has a number of requests for one book, she may have to order additional copies. Her second order to the book publisher tells him of an additional demand. These examples help us to see

JEREMY BENTHAM—HEDONISM AND UTILITARIANISM

Much of the philosophical basis for capitalism is found in hedonism and utilitarianism, concepts developed by an English philosopher and economist, Jeremy Bentham. Man, he said, is influenced by two forces, pain and pleasure. The basic principle of hedonism is that each man seeks his own greatest happiness. A man will continue to work until his work will no longer buy enough pleasure to offset the pain it causes. To his analysis Bentham added utilitarianism, the doctrine that all should strive for happiness for the greatest number of people. This principle minimizes self-interest and requires government to play a limited role in subordinating individualism to the common interest.

that both the kind and the amount of our production are determined by the choices which people make in buying goods and services.

Production—How?

You will recall our previous mention of the fact that all production involves four factors: natural resources, labor, capital, and management. If producers and sellers are to increase their business, they need to employ more of the factors of production —more iron ore, more machinists, more machines, and more foremen. How can these factors be obtained? They can be secured from producers facing reduced demand or from money not currently in use. Producers who are increasing their business need more of the factors; they usually take them from those whose business is declining; they do so by offering more money.

The Directing Computer: A Guide to Production

An example may help you to understand the relationships indicated in Figure 1–1. Try to imagine that floating above our country is a directing computer carrying a sensitive antenna. This instrument records every single purchase that is made by every single buyer in the entire country. It is registering the votes of people for the goods and services they want. This scientific instrument then determines whether the factors of production are going in the right amount to the places that are producing the goods and services.

Let us suppose that Americans indicate an increasing interest in new automobiles and a decreasing interest in new appliances. This change would be shown by the purchase of more automobiles and fewer appliances. Our computer, having registered this change, would indicate that some of the steel and the workers and the foremen now producing appliances should be shifted to producing cars.

Incentives Influence Production

A logical question you might ask at this point is how, in a democracy, you can shift people from one industry to another. You cannot force people to move, nor can you arbitrarily order that materials be redirected from one producer to another. This is where our wonderful instrument comes to the rescue. Signals to offer more dollars are transmitted from our computer to the factors of production. The greater the need for factors of production to move from one industry to another—as from appliances to automobiles—the more dollars will be offered to speed the change.

As a worker, you know that the more you earn, the more satisfactions you can

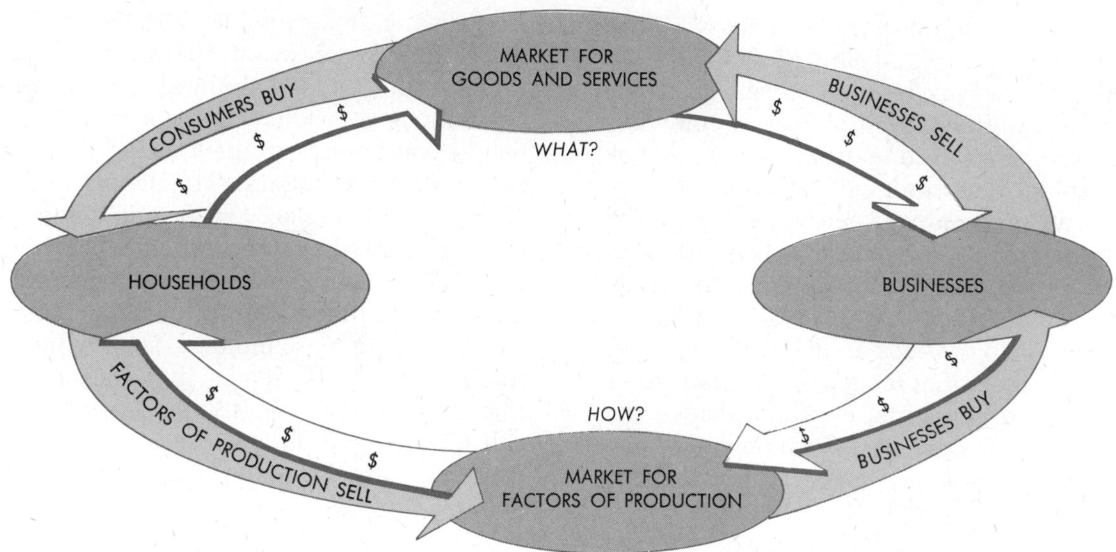

FIGURE 1–1 The Circular Flow of the Economy

This simplified circular flow model of pure capitalism shows how a free-enterprise economic system answers the questions of what to produce and how to produce. People from households go to the market as consumers to buy and they go to the market as suppliers of the factors of production to sell. Businesses go to the market to sell their production, but they must first go to the market as buyers in order to get the factors of production necessary to produce. The inner lines show the flow of money payments. The outer lines show the flow of economic resources—that is, production and factors of production. The flow of money thus determines the allocation of resources.

derive from your income. Therefore you will try to work at the job that will pay you the most. Since fewer appliances are being bought, fewer appliance workers will be needed. Some of these workers will find themselves looking for another means of earning a living. Since demand for cars has increased, thereby requiring more labor, we will find our workers following the signals—moving where more dollars are offered. The same would be true of steel and machines.

The computer, after recording the kind and quantity of our purchases, also determines the kind and amount of production needed to meet our demands. It determines whether the factors of production are going in the correct combination to the right place to produce the goods and services we want. It then suggests the necessary adjustments in the flow of our resources to the right place, in the right amounts, and at the right time. This is accomplished by directing additional resources where they are needed, and redirecting resources when they are not needed, by adjusting the amount of dollars offered. Thus, this payment provides an incentive for change.

Distribution—For Whom?

Why is our computer so successful? We are able to understand its success when we answer the question of *For Whom.* The production is there. For whom is it meant? The tall? The strong? The fair? No! With some exceptions, to be mentioned later, it will go to those who have the money—the dollars—to buy it. Businessmen want to make big profits, workers want high wages, landlords want to collect as much rent as possible, just as you want your income raised in order to buy more of the things you want.

It would be nice if everyone could have all the things he wanted. However, you will recall that we said that our needs seem unlimited—never ending—and our resources to produce are definitely limited. If we agree that everyone cannot have everything he wants, or even most of the things he wants, and we know that we have to figure out some system of distributing the production, why should it be decided on the basis of who has the most money? There are some people who have a great need for goods and services but do not have the money to obtain them.

Our System Provides Answers

American economic practices do provide us with some answers to the question of meeting our needs, although not everyone considers these the best ways of distributing goods and services. Money payments are used as incentives to reward people for making contributions to the well-being of our country. Workers may toil in order to earn money to satisfy their needs; and although they are working with their own self-interest in mind, they are also adding production that our people want. The more they produce, the better they serve society. The more their services are in demand, the higher their wages will be. Businessmen try to produce the best possible products most efficiently. As a result they will try to increase their profits by producing at as low a cost as they can and selling as much of their product as possible at the highest acceptable price. Since other businessmen are also trying to produce efficiently the things that people want, there is competition for the buyer's dollars. Those who make the best products—the products that people want most—at the lowest price will get most of the dollars. The people of the country are being served by this competition because they are getting what they want. Although the successful businessman may be doing his job for his personal gain—earning more money—society benefits by his efforts. Thus, the worker and the businessman, motivated largely by self-interest and the desire for profit, both contribute to the material growth of the country.

Adam Smith and the Theory of Classical Capitalism

Most of the theory behind classical capitalism comes from a book, *The Wealth of Nations,* published the year our country declared its political independence—1776. In it Adam Smith, a professor at the University of Glasgow, Scotland, described and advocated the system of classical capitalism. The system which Smith described and which became the basis of our economic system depends on the *market* to answer the basic economic questions. The market is the place where buyers and sellers meet and where prices placed on the goods we want to sell and buy will determine how we allocate our resources. The things we buy determine the *What*—buying the best products at the lowest prices. Those who have taken the factors of production and put them together in the most economical way to produce the goods the public wants, determine the *How.* The money that goes to those who do the jobs that we indicate we want done and do those jobs better than others, indirectly answers the question *For Whom.*

ADAM SMITH AND THE THEORY OF LAISSEZ-FAIRE

Adam Smith (1723–1790) lived at a time when England's economy was undergoing a significant transition. During the seventeenth century the Netherlands led England in commerce and France led her in manufacturing; in the next century England surpassed both.

During this time the economic philosophy dominant among the nations of western Europe was mercantilism. This system, designed to increase a nation's supply of precious metals, required extensive government controls. Monopoly privileges, subsidies, and tariff protection were granted to a select few in order to encourage investment in new business ventures bringing monetary return.

By the middle of the eighteenth century the conditions on which the mercantile system was based had begun to change in England. As businesses grew in power with the increase of trade and manufacturing, government protection was no longer so essential to them. At the same time, the Industrial Revolution was shaping a new era of production. It was on these new conditions that Adam Smith based his theories of laissez-faire.

Smith believed that individual initiative, motivated by the desire for profits, could result in a healthier national economy. If the economy was freed from the restraints of government interference, the factors of production could seek their maximum return. With supply and demand operating in a free competitive market, the problems of production and distribution could be solved most effectively. And since England was stronger than her neighbors and more efficient in production, she could afford to encourage free competition at home and overseas.

Smith is usually referred to as the father of modern economics. In giving meaning and order to the environment he lived in, he reflected the changes taking place in his day, and his ideas influenced the direction of future change and development.

The Limited Role of Government

What part does the government play in Smith's plan? The answer is: almost none. As a matter of fact we frequently refer to this system as *laissez-faire,* a French expression meaning "hands off." It is expected that government will protect us from invasion by foreign countries, and will protect our freedoms and our property. However, the original plan contemplated no interference with the free flow of the factors of production and the production itself. The directing computer—or the "invisible hand," as Smith called it—was responsible for guiding everything to the places that needed it most. Remember that need was determined by the most money offered. Only if the government stayed out of the marketplace could the questions *What, How,* and *For Whom* be answered in such a way as to insure the most good for the most people concerned.

The Classical Model: Theory and Practice

Is the economic system we now have in this country the one just described? Is the system that Adam Smith described as existing in eighteenth-century England the system we have? Do workers and businessmen determine their wages and prices in the marketplace according to the dollars suggested by the satellite? Does the government really stay out of the marketplace?

The answer to all these questions is *no.* Businessmen do not always compete with one another. Neither do workers or landlords. We must also note that the government does not always stay out of the marketplace.

This functioning system—laissez-faire, or classical capitalism—which Adam Smith and others described is what economists sometimes call a *theory* or a *model.* A model is developed to help analyze or understand the economy better. It is like models you are familiar with, a set of plans designed to work in a particular way. You have probably seen people look at a set of plans and remark, "It looks good on paper, but . . ." This means that things in real life do not seem to work out quite the way they are planned. Similarly, economists' models do not seem to work out exactly as planned. Not every situation can be anticipated, nor all details included. When theories or plans are made involving people, too many things can go wrong. This does not mean that we throw away our plans. Since we know of little involving man that is perfect, we make plans with the hope that they will be as close to perfect as possible. However, we should recognize our limitations and make changes accordingly.

The classical model as described by Adam Smith has to a great extent served as the basis for our nation's economic system. However, the model as originally set forth by Adam Smith was further defined and amplified as a result of continued study of its operation. Other economists, such as Jean Baptiste Say, a French economist writing at the beginning of the nineteenth century, and Alfred Marshall, a British professor of political economy writing at the end of the same century, took Smith's model and added to it or changed it.

The Classical Model: Practice and Change

The classical model—sometimes called capitalism, sometimes laissez-faire—developed as the private enterprise system which ultimately became characteristic of our economy. We will have to examine this model more closely. It is important to know about this model because it has guided us in the past as well as in the present, and it will probably continue to guide us in the future. In addition, we must try to answer the questions of how and why we have changed the model; we have not become slaves to blueprints, but rather have changed the blueprints somewhat to meet our needs.

There were many things that Adam Smith, writing over 180 years ago, could not have foreseen in our modern atomic age. There are times when economists expect that people will behave in certain ways and they do not. When these things happen, we need to alter our plans to allow for the unexpected or for new developments. If our model is really a good one and seems to do most of the things it is designed to do, we do not dispose of it when we have trouble. Rather, we modify it in an effort to make it a better model, one which will meet our current demands.

As an example, big business and big labor unions have at times interfered with the operation of the free market—of the directing satellite—and we have had to make adjustments. We have sometimes needed things in this country, but businessmen have either not had enough money to provide them or have not wanted to do so because of fear that they might lose money trying! At times, through no fault of their own, some people have been unable to create enough value in the marketplace to support themselves and their families. These are just a few of the examples which have influenced us to alter our model and to consider further changes.

In Chapter 13 you will be introduced to another model which uses a different approach to answer the big questions of our economy. Those who favor the new approach criticize the classical model as being too far removed from the reality of the world that is. However, the defenders of this model claim it has not been given a fair chance, and some of them say we need to return to it rather than continue altering it.

Reasons for Economic Controversy

From this discussion it is obvious that economics, like other disciplines, has unresolved problems. Just as you find disagreements about values and interpretations among physicians, biologists, historians, and art critics, so there are differences among economists. If economists disagree, how can a student who is just being introduced to the subject draw his own conclusions about economic problems? Although this question may be answered by pointing out that the same problems of disagreement exist in all subjects, there are at least two better answers. First, the tools, the method of approach, the facts, and the problems that all economists deal with are the same. Differences most frequently arise because of disagreements concerning values and judgments. These differences will be pointed out at the end of some chapters after the problems have been identified, the facts presented, and the tools given for analyzing the problem. Second, the areas of agreement are far greater than the areas of disagreement. For these reasons economists are able to function within the discipline and provide the student with the tools to make intelligent decisions as a consumer, a producer, and a citizen.

Looking Ahead

We will now take a closer look at parts of the American economy, examining the classical model, some of its modifications, and some unanswered questions. In Unit III we will look at another model—the Keynesian—and discuss its application to the American economy as a whole. Then we will see the part which the economy of our country has played and can continue to play in the world. We will conclude with a brief look at some of the economic problems we are facing in this decade.

In each instance we will try to use the following approach:

1. In what way does this answer the big questions: *What? How? For Whom?*
2. If the model applies, what does it prescribe? Has it undergone any particular changes? Does it differ appreciably from conditions in the real world?
3. Are there major problems that have to be solved? What are they, and what are some possible solutions?

REVIEW: THE HIGHLIGHTS OF THE CHAPTER

1. The study of economics helps you to understand your role as a consumer and producer and provides you with tools to make wiser decisions as a citizen.
2. Economics is a social science that concerns itself with the production, distribution, and consumption of goods and services.
3. The central problem in economics stems from the fact that there are limited

resources to satisfy man's unlimited wants. To solve this problem he must make choices.

4. Three related problems that every society must find answers to are: *What* shall we produce? *How* shall we produce it? *For Whom* shall we produce it?
5. All production involves four basic factors: natural resources, labor, capital, and management. Natural resources are the materials nature provides, labor is work applied to production, and capital is the man-made instruments used in production. Finally, management initiates and organizes the other factors.
6. An economic system provides rules and guiding principles to help answer the central and related questions. An economic system that depends primarily on private enterprise to supply production is called capitalism. When production comes mainly from government enterprise, it is socialism. Most countries have mixed economies, although they may emphasize business or government.
7. The American economy emphasizes production by private enterprise. Under this system the *What* is determined by businessmen who are influenced in their decisions by what consumers purchase in the market for goods and services. In order to produce these goods, the businessman goes to the market to buy the factors of production. Money payments are used as incentives to reward people for supplying the services that society wants.
8. Adam Smith, in *The Wealth of Nations,* set forth what has come to be known as the classical model. This model depends on a market free from government interference to answer the major questions. Government's role is to protect freedom and property and to defend against foreign invasion.
9. Many forces have worked to interfere with the freedom of the market and to cause alteration of the model. Though some disagreement exists among economists as to whether to go back to the original model, alter it further, or substitute a new model, they are in general agreement on facts, methods, and approaches to problems.

SELECTED READINGS

Andreano, Ralph L., Evan Ira Farber, and Sabron Reynolds. *The Student Economists' Handbook: A Guide to Sources.* Cambridge, Mass.: Schenkman Publishing Co., 1967.

Heilbroner, Robert L. *The Worldly Philosophers,* rev. ed. New York: Simon and Schuster, 1967.

Maher, John E. *What Is Economics.* New York: John Wiley & Sons, Inc., 1969.

Mundell, Robert A. *Man and Economics,* New York: McGraw-Hill Co., 1968.

Demand and Supply— An Answer to Resource Allocation 2

THE AUTHORS' NOTE TO THE STUDENT

In the first chapter, after identifying what economics is and what problems it seeks to solve, we sketched the model that has guided a great deal of the development of the American economy. In this and succeeding chapters we will take a closer look at this classical model and see how it provides answers to the central problem of the allocation of our resources. Since our resources are limited and our wants are not, we must make decisions as to how we use what we have. In our economic system these choices should be determined by what people want and by the efficiency of the producing unit.

The *market* is the place or condition in which buyers and sellers meet to exchange commodities for the prices they agree upon. The buyers' willingness and ability to purchase at certain prices is called *demand*. The sellers' offer to part with goods at certain prices is known as *supply*. The numbers and independence of buyers and sellers determine the kind of competition there is. In this chapter we will study our market structure and show how this method, with its price system, is used to allocate our resources. We will then consider whether this model shows how resources are actually allocated under our present system.

A STUDENT'S NOTE TO THE STUDENT

Although Part A is easy, it's starting to get tougher. Make sure you learn the graphs. Try setting up some demand and supply schedules, including changes in both, and then plot them out. The practice helps. Also make sure you understand the concept of elastic and inelastic demand and what the curve for each generally resembles. Take a few examples, plot them out, and see if you can give the reasons for the slope. It should help.

Warning! Learn the difference between a change in price and a change in demand. It's trickier than you think.

Remember that the law of diminishing marginal utility helps explain the downward sloping demand curve while the law of diminishing returns applies to the supply curve.

Finally, the acetate overlay is great for review. This tip should help you pass any test.

Part A
The Market

Price: An Important Economic Influence

Price is a primary influence in determining the allocation of resources in our free enterprise system. It determines what goods and services will be produced and in what quantity. It influences the use of the four factors of production. In addition it is most important in determining who gets what. A different way of stating this idea is to say that the price system answers the questions *What? How?* and *For Whom?*

When we think of price we often also think of value, and when we think of value we may think of usefulness or utility. The student of economics must distinguish between price, value, and utility. Although none of the three is exactly the same as the others, it is easy to see that they are closely related. *Utility* relates to the satisfaction that a good or service can provide. If, in addition to its usefulness, it is also relatively scarce, it has *economic value.* When we measure that value with other goods and services, we call it *exchange value.* When we measure its value in money we call it *price.*

Conditions of Pure Competition

A market is a place or situation where buyers and sellers meet. It can be a market for goods and services where consumers meet suppliers or a market where suppliers come to bid for the factors of production (see Fig. 2–10 on p. 33). In order for the classical model to work as planned, certain market conditions must be met:

1. There must be enough buyers and enough sellers acting independently so that the entry or exit of any one buyer or seller will not affect price.
2. The products offered for sale should be sufficiently alike so that buyers will feel free to choose the product offered by any seller.
3. New sellers should be able to enter and existing sellers should be able to leave the market freely.

When these three conditions exist, we have what economists call a *purely competitive market* or *pure competition.*

Consumers Benefit from Competitive Prices

Pure competition serves the consumer well because, if sellers are to be successful, they must offer their products at the lowest prices. Charging one penny more than any other seller will mean no sales, since it is assumed there is no difference between the quality of one product and that of another.

Society Progresses by Means of Improved Efficiency

To obtain higher profits, sellers are encouraged to improve their products and increase the efficiency of their production. The better their product and the lower their cost, the more money they will make. Their action, which at first appears to have only a selfish motive for making the greatest profit, actually serves the best interests of the consumer, too. Those who favor this classical model call the desire to make more money by increasing efficiency and improving products "incentive." They consider this a step toward a better society because it induces us to perform at our most efficient level. There are others who think that such motivation runs counter to the spirit of brotherhood, pits man against his fellowman, and is not a fair method of distributing production. The clash between several sets of values has resulted in the modification of the classical model. We will examine this synthesis after we have examined the classical model more closely and after we have taken a look at the market situations that actually exist.

Market Conditions Other Than Pure Competition

All competition which is not pure is called *imperfect competition.* There are few markets in the U.S. which meet the three conditions of pure competition. Agriculture, textiles, and certain retail fields come closest. Yet even in these areas there is some interference with the market freedom as described in the classical model.

Pure Monopoly

The opposite of pure competition is *pure monopoly.* It exists when the following conditions prevail:

1. Only one seller offers the product for sale, allowing him to exercise considerable control over price.
2. There is no close substitute to which the buyer can turn.
3. Other competing businesses may not enter the field.

A condition of pure monopoly places the consumer at the mercy of the monopolist. With no place to turn, he must deprive himself of the product or pay the price the monopolist charges. These prices are unchecked by competition, so that more of the consumer's limited resources are used. The consumer's position is further weakened in that the monopolist lacks incentive to improve his product, and the consumer has no alternative but to buy from him. In this case, monopoly interferes with progress.

Fortunately for the consumer there are today no major privately owned monopolies that are not regulated by government in our country. Thus, in *public utilities* and transportation the protective measures of the government safeguard the consumer. Public monopolies, such as the post office, mint, and fire department, are owned by the people.

Before World War II, the Aluminum Company of America had a virtual monopoly on primary aluminum. The Pullman Standard Company still makes all sleeping cars for our railroads. In some cases, government action has helped to establish competition by creating an environment which has brought additional producers into the market. We can still find businesses having a virtual monopoly in their geographic areas—television stations, newspapers, and cement plants, for instance. The effect of these local monopolies on prices is debatable.

Monopolistic Competition

Most markets are found to be somewhere between pure competition and pure monopoly. When there are a large number of sellers acting independently, with each trying to convince the buyer that his product is different from that of other sellers, we have a market condition known as *monopolistic competition.* The manufacturers of name-brand aspirin plead with buyers not to ask simply for aspirin or for a combination-of-ingredients tablet, but to ask for their aspirin by name. The implication is that their aspirin is a special product. The consumer can substitute a different brand tablet, but will he be getting the same product? Because substitution is not as easy under monopolistic competition as under pure competition, the seller has some control over price.

Oligopoly

The remaining market situations are classified as *oligopoly*. The prefix *oligo*, meaning "a few," gives us a clue to its meaning. An oligopoly exists when a few sellers have sufficient control over the market for a product so that changes in price by one will affect all other sellers. Examples of oligopolies are the "Big Three" in automobiles and the "Big Four" in rubber tires, linoleum, tin cans, and cigarettes. Although it is difficult to differentiate between products like tin cans, copper, and steel, there is an attempt to do so wherever possible. Serious barriers to entering the market exist, and little attempt is made to bring about changes in price, particularly in lowering price. The absence of pure competition does not eliminate changes in price resulting from changes in the supply of goods offered, but it does lessen such an effect. The producer, under conditions of oligopoly, must be very careful that any action he takes will not bring retaliatory action by others in the field.

Competition Among Buyers

Just as there are situations involving sellers that deviate from the classical model, so pure competition is not always found on the buyers' side. Frequently, suppliers of goods not used directly by consumers—tobacco farmers and ranchers, for instance—find themselves in market situations with few buyers or even in a condition of *monopsony*, where there is only one buyer. In some industries a few buyers meet a few sellers. Although the rubber tire industry is an oligopoly, it must sell a major share of its product to automobile manufacturers, whose industry is also oligopolistic. When large retail chain stores contract with producers to manufacture an item under the store name, they exercise considerable control over price. Though competition among buyers has not been reduced as much as it has among sellers, we cannot ignore it as a factor in influencing price.

Part B
How Demand Functions in the Classical Model

In our discussion of different market conditions we showed that prices were influenced by the number of buyers and sellers. Price is determined by the interaction of demand and supply for all market conditions. In this chapter we are concerned with the purely competitive market. It is a good starting point because:

1. Competition is a condition which most Americans consider desirable, and we have pursued a policy to make our market more competitive.

2. Imperfect competition is affected by the same forces, but in a modified way.
3. We are all consumers and are affected by price.

The Nature of Demand

In Chapter 1 we spoke about the computer's registering the wants of consumers. It did not register the daydreams that people have about the things they would buy if they had more money. Only when consumers are willing to part with their limited resources to obtain a good or service at a given price does the computer react. This willingness on the part of consumers to purchase certain amounts of a product at given prices at a particular time and place is called *demand.*

Consumers will purchase products based on (1) the urgency of their need for the product, (2) the price of the product, (3) the price of the substitutes, and (4) their income. The general rule of the *law of demand* is that the lower the price of a given product, the more of it consumers will buy. Conversely, the higher the price, the less consumers will buy.

Demand Is Subject to the Law of Diminishing Marginal Utility

Why do consumers buy products? They usually buy to satisfy a want. The utility of a product depends on its ability to satisfy wants. The greater the want-satisfaction, the greater the utility. However, the utility for a number of units of a given product, let us say bags of pretzels, is not the same. If you have eight bags of pretzels, each bagful you eat may increase your total satisfaction. However, the satisfaction you derive from the first bag of pretzels is likely to be greater than that from the second bag. The third will probably give you less satisfaction than the second, and the fourth less than the third, and so on. Even if you are particularly fond of pretzels, it is unlikely that you would wish to consume the total number of bags of pretzels that you have available. Once your hunger for pretzels is satisfied, each unit that you consume will at a certain point give you an ever-diminishing satisfaction, and therefore will have an ever-decreasing utility.

The word *marginal* is frequently used in economics. It refers to one more unit or one less unit. The marginal utility of bags of pretzels would be the degree of satisfying power—utility—of eating the last bag of pretzels you have had or the next bag you will have. The *law of diminishing marginal utility* states that as the supply of a product a consumer has increases, its satisfying power for each extra unit decreases. You may be willing to pay 35 cents for the first small bag of pretzels that usually sells for 20 cents, but you will buy additional bags only at lower prices as your desire for them declines.

Other Factors Also Influence Demand

Although the law of diminishing marginal utility explains consumer purchases based on the urgency of the need and the price of the product, the use of substitutes and the level of income of buyers also affect demand. If you are in a theater and want something to eat while watching the movie, you will probably go to the refreshment stand (a monopoly) and see what is for sale. Pretzels might be your first choice, but the 35-cent price seems too high. A small box of popcorn costs only 25 cents. While the popcorn is not quite as satisfying as the pretzels to you, it is cheaper and will last twice as long. The price of the substitute may cause you and other pretzel lovers to buy popcorn in spite of your own preference for pretzels.

Suppose that you are in the situation described above but that this time your funds are greater. Your added resources allow you to satisfy more of your wants. This phenomenon was observed on the national scene after World War II. The American consumer increased his consumption of meat and decreased his purchases of wheat, even though the price of the former had gone up considerably. Increased income made it possible to satisfy more wants. The same principle is seen to operate in the efforts of merchandisers to capture the teen-age market.

Demand Schedule

In our discussion of demand some students may have received the impression that demand referred only to how much of a product consumers would buy at a particular price. This is not the correct impression. Our definition said a "willingness" on the part of consumers to buy certain amounts of products at given prices. This means that at 35 cents only a few pretzel lovers will buy bags of pretzels that are associated with a price of 20 cents. This does not mean that many have no desire for the pretzels. They just do not want to part with that much of their limited resources. However, if the price is dropped to 30 cents, you and others who were not willing to buy before may now want to purchase pretzels. If the price is reduced to 25 cents, a greater quantity of pretzels will be sold. At a still lower price a still larger number will be sold, perhaps also to popcorn lovers buying pretzels as a substitute.

When we speak of the quantity of a product that consumers will buy at varied price levels, we are making use of the economist's concept of demand. When we list in a table the amounts consumers will buy of a product at various prices, in a particular market, and at a given point in time, we have a *demand schedule*. Table 2–1 is an example of a demand schedule.

TABLE 2–1 Demand Schedule for Bags of Pretzels for One Week

Price	Quantity
$.35	50
.30	150
.25	250
.20	350
.15	450

Increasing the price causes consumers to switch their purchases to other goods.

Demand Curve

Let us see what the demand schedule for pretzels looks like when we place it on a graph. Figure 2–1 illustrates graphically the demand schedule in Table 2–1. The vertical axis shows us the five different price levels; the horizontal axis shows us quantities at intervals of 100. We draw our demand curve (or line) by locating points on our graph for each of the different price levels. We go up the vertical axis, measuring price, until we come to 35 cents. We then follow the horizontal line to the right until we come to the right quantity for 35 cents—50. Since we have quantities identified only in intervals of 100 units, we locate our point halfway between 0 and 100. Point *A* on Figure 2–1 shows us the demand for bags of pretzels at the price of 35 cents. We now locate our points for 30 cents (*B*), 25 cents (*C*), 20 cents (*D*), and 15 cents (*E*). Now we connect points *A, B, C, D,* and *E*, and we can see what the demand schedule in Table 2–1 looks like on a graph. Can we tell how many bags of pretzels will be sold at 23 cents? Our demand schedule does not give us this information; but if we measure on the vertical axis three fifths of the way between 20 cents and 25 cents and draw a horizontal line to the right, we can get an estimate. The point at which our 23-cent price line crosses our demand curve gives us an approximation of the quantity that could be sold. Is it closest to 260, 280, or 310?

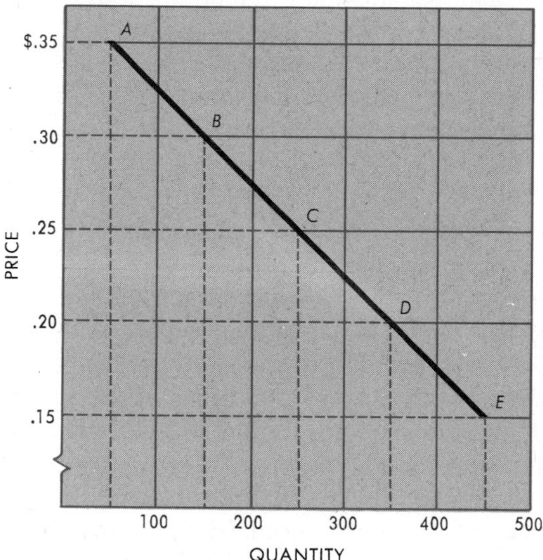

FIGURE 2–1 Demand Curve for Bags of Pretzels for One Week

The downward-sloping curve shows consumers buying more bags of pretzels as the price is reduced.

Notice how the demand curve slopes downward as we follow it to the right. This helps explain the buying habits of consumers. Can you explain the economics of a sale held by a retail merchant? As you move from left to right on our demand curve, you should be able to explain how the downward slope explains the law of diminishing marginal utility. Consider yourself buying and eating successive bags of pretzels. The diminishing utility of each (and therefore your unwillingness to pay the same price for another bag) should make diminishing marginal utility and the downward demand curve clear.

Elasticity of Demand

Not all demand curves look like the one shown in Figure 2–1. Let us look at the demand for salt rather than pretzels. The price of salt may vary from 10 cents a pound to 20 cents a pound. If your family uses between one and two pounds of salt a month, its expenditure for salt could fluctuate from 10 to 40 cents a month, depending on the extremes in the quantities used and the prices paid. Another way of looking at it is to say that the cost of satisfying your family's need for salt can fluctuate from $1/3$ cent to $1\,1/3$ cents per day, a 400 percent variation in price. There would probably be a very small decline in the sale of salt if the price increased 50 percent, or even 100 percent. The cost is so low, even at the highest price, that few people would deprive themselves. When a relatively large change in price brings about only a small change in the quantity purchased, we say that the demand for a product is *inelastic*. In other words, the demand for salt is inelastic. Another aspect to consider is what you could use in place of salt. A comparison of a curve plotted for bags of pretzels and of one for salt would show a vast difference, the latter being far steeper.

If a seller has no competition and no fear of government's controlling the price, any increase he makes in the price of an inelastic product will increase his revenue from that product. What factors might restrain such a seller from using such power excessively? What considerations will determine where the price is eventually set?

An Example of Elastic Demand

The demand curve for expensive meats is quite different from that for salt. When sirloin steak goes on sale, reduced from $1.65 a pound to $1.25 a pound, purchases are likely to increase by a far greater percentage than the percentage of the reduction in the price. Many shoppers who know that their families like steak seldom buy it because the high price would mean they would have to sacrifice too many other wants. However, a drop in price changes the whole situation. Fewer wants will have to be given up in order to obtain the satisfaction that steak provides. We can conclude that the demand for steak, being very responsive to a change in price, is elastic.

When a relatively small change in price brings about a large change in the quantity bought, we have a product with *elastic* demand. Think of elastic as stretching. A change in price that brings about little stretching (change) in the quantity bought is inelastic; a lot of stretching of quantity bought is elastic. Compare the curve of an elastic demand with that of an inelastic demand. Is it more important to have vigorous competition when a product is elastic or when it is inelastic?

A word of caution is in order before you try to analyze the elasticity of a product. In the case of most products the elasticity changes over a very broad price range. Steak may be quite elastic when its price fluctuates between $1.25 and $1.60 a pound. As the price goes above $1.50, it becomes less and less elastic. There will be a relatively small change in the quantity of steak sold when the price goes above $2.25. The relatively few who can afford to pay such a high price, or the few who feel they must have steak because of their dietary habits or the high want-satisfaction from eating steak, will probably pay the additional money no matter what the price.

The Revenue Test

The elasticity of demand for a product may be determined by noting how a change in price affects revenue. The price times the quantity sold equals total revenue. If the total revenue increases when the price decreases, the demand for a product is said to be *elastic*. When the price of steak is $2.00 a pound the butcher sells 100 pounds for a days receipts of $200 ($P \times Q = TR$) from the sale of steak. When he drops the price to $1.50 a pound his sales rise to 200 pounds per day. His revenue from steak for the day is now $300. The small change in price (−25 percent) brought about a larger change in quantity sold (+100 percent) resulting in an increase in revenue. The demand for steak is elastic.

If total revenue decreases when price decreases, the demand for the product is said to be *inelastic*. At 25 cents a grocer sells 100 cakes of bath soap a day, yielding $25 revenue. He drops the price to 20 cents and increases his sales to 110 units for a day. His total revenue decreases to $22 from the sale of soap. Additional reductions in price bring about greater decreases in total revenue. The demand for soap is inelastic.

If total revenue neither increases nor decreases with changes in price, the product is said to have a *unitary* elasticity of demand.

Factors Determining Elasticity

What makes the demand for a product inelastic? Usually the demand is inelastic when (1) it is difficult to find a substitute,

(2) it represents a small portion of an individual's budget, and (3) it is considered a necessity. Any one or a combination of these reasons will tend to make demand inelastic. Conversely, products for which there are many substitutes, which represent a large portion of the budget, and which are considered luxuries tend to be elastic in demand.

Most products will not fit neatly into either category, and what may have an elastic demand in one family may have an inelastic demand in another. Evaluate the elasticity of the demand for milk, a television set, your favorite magazine, a second car in a suburban family, and a first car for a low-income family in a metropolitan center. The influence of elasticity of demand may be seen in Cases I and II of the classical model insert following page 34.

Changes in Demand

A change in demand means an increase or a decrease in the number of units of a product that could be sold throughout the range of prices at which they are offered. It does *not,* however, mean changing the number of units sold by changing the price. An example may clarify this difference. When reports first came out linking cigarette smoking with lung cancer there was a decline in the demand for cigarettes. While the decrease was temporary, each new report brought about a change in demand. The increase or decrease in sales did not come about by a change in price. The price remained the same, but the units sold changed.

Causes for a Change in Demand

Changes in demand may be caused by a change in people's taste, a change in consumer income, and a change in the market for substitutes. An important change has taken place in the demand for butter, particularly in the last 10 years. Advertising, inventions, and style changes affect demand by changing people's tastes. How can a producer protect himself from a change in demand?

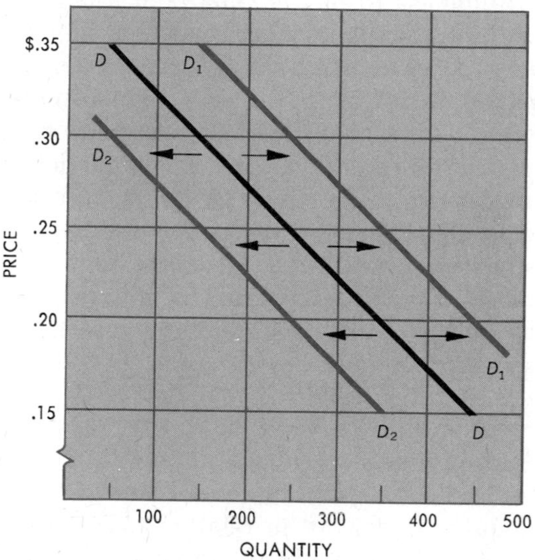

FIGURE 2–2 Changes in the Demand Curve

Changes in demand are shown by shifting the curve to the right (D_1) or to the left (D_2) from the original demand (D). Explain how you can determine which of the two curves that have shifted represents an increase in demand.

A change in demand will result in a new set of figures on the demand schedule. When we plot a new demand curve, we find the curve shifting either to the right or to the left of the original demand curve. In Figure 2–2, which curve illustrates an increase in demand? Which curve illustrates a decrease? If you follow one price level, such as 10 cents, through all three demand curves, you can easily find the answer.

Part C
How Supply Functions in the Classical Model

What Is Supply?

Just as demand deals with the consumer's willingness to buy, supply concerns itself with producers or sellers and their willingness to offer products for sale. Like demand it refers to a particular product offered in a given market at a given time and at different prices. We may define supply as the various amounts of products that a seller will offer for sale at specific prices at a specified time and place. When we have this information, we can prepare a supply schedule, just as we did for demand.

Factors Influencing Supply

Supply, like demand, is subject to change under a variety of conditions. These changes occur not in relation to price but as a response to other circumstances of the market.

Supply and the Time Factor

In considering supply, we must recognize that the time factor has an important effect on availability. For an accurate analysis of supply we must know whether reference is being made to what will be offered for sale under the following conditions:

1. The product presently available
2. The short run, where producers or sellers can utilize their present facilities to increase or decrease the amount of the product
3. The long run, where producers and sellers can increase their facilities so as to produce or sell more or less of the product, and where either additional producers or sellers or fewer producers or sellers are in the market

When bell-bottom pants were first introduced into the market, a very few firms devoted a small part of their production facilities to them. No one could possibly know how well this new style would catch on. A supply curve for the early bell-bottom pants could be drawn. When it was apparent that they were going to be very popular, the producers already involved in making them used their existing facilities to turn out more. The supply curve for this situation is for the short run. When enthusiasm continued to mount, other producers decided that they should enter the production of the new fashions, and so additional facilities were used. This last situation would call for a supply curve for the long run.

Let us once again turn back to our computer. The intensity of the demand for new-fashioned pants is picked up on the antenna and registered on the computer. This information is relayed to the businessman, who then realizes that he can earn additional dollars if he will turn his efforts to producing these pants. However, such action takes time and reflects our three possible supply situations—present, short run, and long run.

The Law of Supply

There is a direct relationship between price and the quantity supplied. When a supplier can get a higher price for his product, he has incentive to go to the market for additional factors of production so that he can offer more of his product on the goods and services market.

ALFRED MARSHALL AND HIS CONTRIBUTION TO PRICE THEORY

Alfred Marshall (1842–1924), for many years professor of economics at Cambridge University in England, is most noted for his contributions to the theory of price. Believing strongly that the best of all economic worlds is one in which the forces of supply and demand are able to operate in a free competitive market with a minimum of government interference, Marshall focused attention on the individual firm and the ways in which prices for its goods are determined. Borrowing from the classical economists Smith and Ricardo the concept of the importance of cost on the supply side, and from the marginalists, of whom he was the greatest (see p. 174), the concept of marginal utility determining demand, he created a new synthesis for interpreting price formation. An expert mathematician, he developed diagrams as an aid to economic analysis.

Perhaps the greatest contribution of Marshall was the recognition that the time element is extremely important in determining supply. For the immediate period, demand is the major factor determining price because the supply is fixed. As the time interval is lengthened, supply can be adapted to changes in demand, keeping in mind the cost of production. For the short run a business can alter its quantity by using existing facilities of production. In the long run a business is able to change its production facilities, as by adding new plant and equipment. Therefore, the supply side becomes more important as the interval of time is increased.

Marshall was not only an original thinker and a great synthesizer but also a great teacher. His most famous pupil was John Maynard Keynes, the most influential economist of the twentieth century (see p. 302).

The general rule for supply states that *producers will offer more of their product for sale as price rises and will offer less as price falls.*

Cost as a Factor Relating to Supply

In a purely competitive market the supplier of goods and services has no control over the market price, since he produces too little to influence market conditions. With no difference between his product and that of his competitors, he will sell nothing if he charges above the market price and he will sell all if he charges below the market price. However, in considering the price, he must take into account his cost of production. There are times when he may be willing to sell below his cost. This might happen when prices tumble for what he believes will be a short time. However, no businessman can afford to lose money for a prolonged period of time. He must be constantly aware of his costs in relationship to the market price if he is to compete successfully and earn a profit.

Many people are under the impression that as production increases, costs per unit decrease. Though mass production has made this true in certain industries and at certain levels of production, both logic and evidence from practical experience have shown that costs per unit begin to rise beyond a certain level of production. Some economists refer to this as the *law of increasing costs.*

The reason costs rise as production goes up is complex, and we cannot go into a complete answer to the question here. However, it is easy to recognize that, as production goes up, the need for additional factors of production will also grow. This will involve competitive bidding in the marketplace for the factors of production. If we need more skilled labor to produce more, and none of this labor is unemployed, we will have to get it from other sources. This can be done by offering higher wages. Higher bidding would also apply to the other factors of production. We should also recognize that not all labor is equally productive, just as not all land is equally fertile and not all ore is equally rich in the mineral wanted. This will be more fully explained in Chapter 5.

When output is low, producers will use the most efficient factors of production. As these factors of production grow scarcer, they will have to use the less productive factors. Only when prices rise does it pay to employ these less productive factors. Otherwise, the additional costs will be greater than the additional revenue received. We will consider the nature of cost of each factor of production in greater detail in subsequent chapters.

Supply Schedule and Supply Curve

A *supply schedule* is a table listing the amount of a product sellers will offer for sale at various prices in a particular market and at a given time. From the data in a supply schedule we can draw a supply curve. Table 2–2 shows a supply schedule for bags of pretzels for a week. Figure 2–3 shows the supply curve drawn from the supply schedule. This schedule may be compared with the demand schedule on page 22, and the supply curve compared with the demand curve on page 23.

TABLE 2–2 Supply Schedule for Bags of Pretzels for One Week

Price	Quantity
$.35	50
.30	150
.25	250
.20	350
.15	450

When the market price increases, suppliers can afford to increase the quantity they offer for sale.

Elasticity of Supply

Supply, like demand, may be *elastic* or *inelastic*. When the quantity of a product offered for sale varies little although major changes in price are made, the supply is inelastic. An inelastic supply curve appears as a steeply sloping or vertical curve because the quantity offered changes relatively little with price changes.

If the quantity of a product offered for sale varies greatly when small changes in price are made, the supply is elastic. An

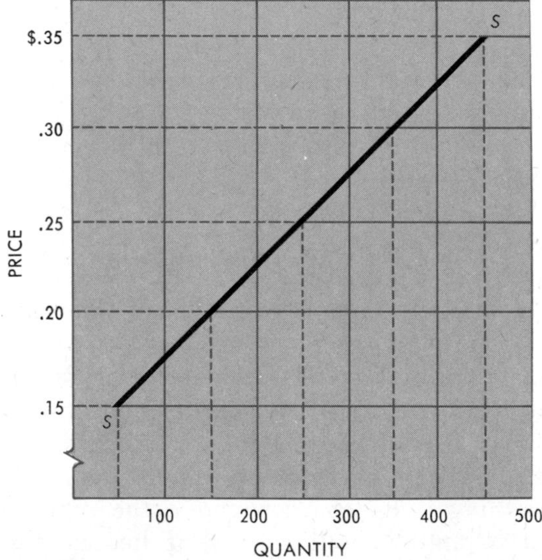

FIGURE 2–3 Supply Curve for Bags of Pretzels for One Week

The upward-sloping curve shows that the seller will offer more bags of pretzels as the price is increased.

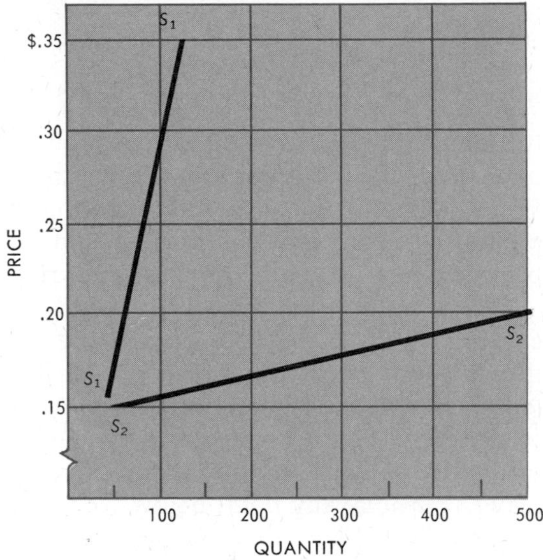

FIGURE 2–4 Elasticity of Supply

The two curves that are shown here illustrate elastic and inelastic supply. Identify each of these curves.

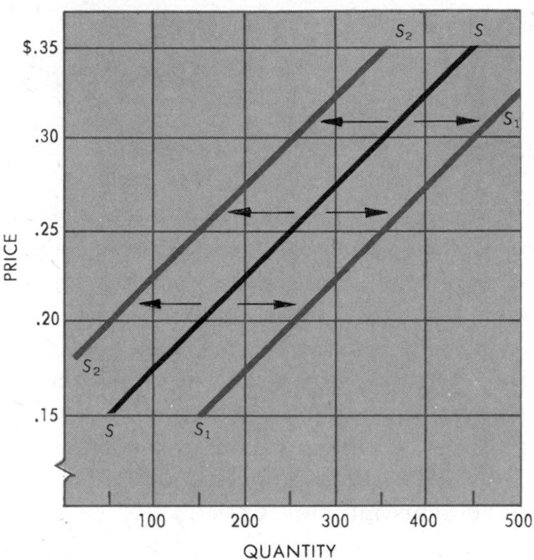

FIGURE 2–5 Changes in the Supply Curve

Changes in supply are shown by shifting the original curve (S) to the right (S_1) or to the left (S_2).

elastic curve appears as a gently sloping or horizontal curve.

The causes for elasticity of supply are complex, but as a general rule any goods whose supply can be increased in a short time is said to be elastic. If there is a longer time period producers have the opportunity of changing production facilities, and market conditions can change. Identify on Figure 2–4 the elastic and the inelastic supply curves.

Changes in Supply

A change in supply, like a change in demand, is a change in the quantity of the product at the different price levels. It is *not* a change in the quantity offered resulting from a change in price. As we have previously seen, cost is a major factor in determining supply. Changes in the cost of production, such as wage increases or technological advances in machinery, will usually result in a change in supply.

Another factor is the expectation of future prices. Businessmen do not know what prices will be; they only know what prices are. They plan their production on what they expect prices to be. If they anticipate prices to be above their costs, they produce with confidence. Falling prices will tend to discourage production.

A change in the demand for other goods can result in a change in supply. When bell-bottom pants became fashionable, the manufacturers shifted more of their facilities into the production of this popular product.

Figure 2–5 shows changes in supply. Examine the curves and note which ones show the increase. Follow one price through all curves and see what quantities are offered.

Part D
How Price Is Determined

Interaction of Supply and Demand

Supply and demand take on real significance when they are put together. Sellers offer products for sale when they anticipate demand. Buyers can convert their wants into demand only if there is supply. The two interact to create the market price and provide an answer to our basic question of allocating our resources.

Let us put our supply schedule and demand schedule side by side and see how the laws of supply and demand determine price. The illustration given assumes a purely competitive market for a given period of time. As we look at Table 2–3, we see that at prices above 25 cents dealers will offer more bags of pretzels than consumers will buy, resulting in a surplus of bags of pretzels. Having a surplus means wasting our limited resources. Sellers have a choice of cutting back their production, stopping production of pretzels for a while, or cutting their price.

Below the price of 25 cents consumers want more bags of pretzels than are offered for sale. Some who want pretzels will not be able to buy them, even if they are willing to pay more. Only at 25 cents do the number of bags of pretzels offered for sale and the number of bags of pretzels buyers wish to purchase equal each other. Where supply and demand equal each other, the market is at *equilibrium*, and the price at this point is the *equilibrium price*.

We can show the supply and demand schedules in Table 2–3 graphically by drawing the supply and demand curves (see Figure 2–6). The equilibrium point is where the supply and demand curves intersect. Any point above that would leave a surplus; any point below would be a shortage. When the forces of supply and demand are allowed to operate freely without any interference from government or groups formed to control prices, the *market will be cleared;* that is, there will be no shortage of buyers willing to pay the freely-arrived-at market price and no surplus of producers willing to sell at the freely-arrived-at market price.

Changes in Supply and Demand

Changes in price and quantity will occur when changes in supply or demand, or both, take place. This can be seen most easily in Figures 2–7, 2–8, and 2–9.

Figure 2–7 illustrates the effect of a given supply and changes in demand. An increase in demand shifts the curve to the

TABLE 2–3 Supply and Demand Schedules for Bags of Pretzels for One Week

Quantity Buyers Would Purchase	Price	Quantity Sellers Would Offer	Surplus (+) or Shortage (−)
50	$.35	450	+400
150	.30	350	+200
250	.25	250	0
350	.20	150	−200
450	.15	50	−400

What is the equilibrium price?

right, as shown by the movement of the original demand, *D*, to the increased demand, D_1. The intersection, which tells us the equilibrium price and quantity, shifts along the supply curve, showing a higher price and a greater quantity of the product bought. The broken line connecting the new intersection with the vertical axis measuring price and the horizontal axis measuring quantity shows the new market condition, 27½ cents and 300 units sold.

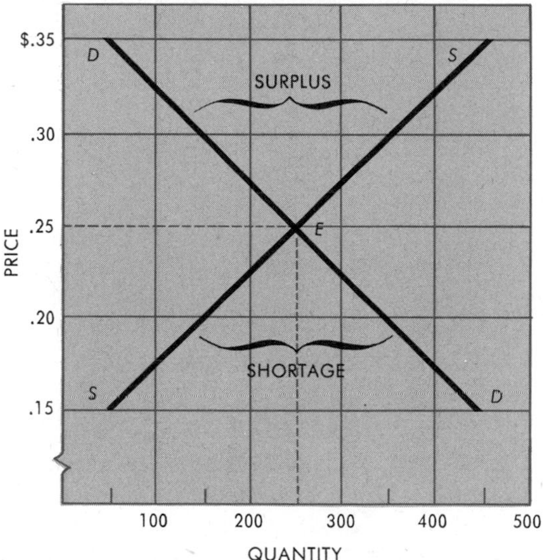

FIGURE 2–6 The Equilibrium Price and the Quantity Exchanged for Bags of Pretzels for One Week

The price of bags of pretzels for one week in a purely competitive market will be at the intersection of the supply curve and the demand curve (*E*). At this equilibrium point, the market will be cleared. Any price above *E* will leave sellers with a surplus. Any price below *E* will produce a shortage for buyers.

Both price and quantity have increased with an increase in demand. A decrease in demand is shown by D_2. What are the new equilibrium price and quantity with D_2 as demand? Compare the market situations between popular and classical records. Which of the record dealers has to be more alert to changes in demand?

Figure 2–8 illustrates the effect of a given demand and changes in supply. An increase in supply shifts the supply curve to the right, creating a new equilibrium price and quantity. The intersection of S_1 (the increased supply curve) and *D* (the unchanged demand curve) lowers the market price to 22½ cents and increases the quantity sold to 300 units. Whether we increase supply or demand, there will

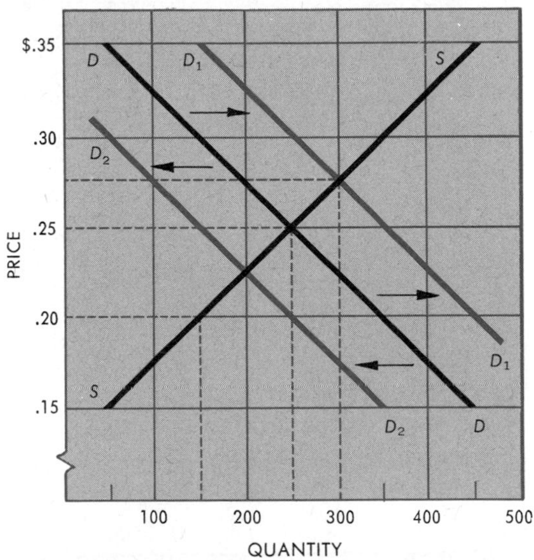

FIGURE 2–7 Change in Demand and Its Effect on Price and Quantity

An increase in demand, supply remaining the same, results in an increase in price and an increase in quantity. A decrease in demand, supply remaining the same, results in a decrease in price and a decrease in quantity. These examples show the direct relationship between changes in demand and changes in the equilibrium price and quantity exchanged.

be an increase in quantity. It is easier to learn how to draw and interpret supply and demand curves than to memorize the relationships involved. The classical model insert, following page 34, will explain further the effect of changes in supply and demand.

A decrease in supply is shown in Figure 2–8 by S_2. What influence can a new, more efficient machine have on the market? It can be seen how successful research helps both the producer and the consumer.

Figure 2–9 illustrates the effect of equal increases in supply and demand. The equal shifting of both curves to the right results in an increase in the number of units sold at the marketplace, but there is no change in price. If demand increases more than supply, both quantity and price will increase. Is the illustration in Figure 2–9 more likely to be characteristic of a short time period or a long time period? Why?

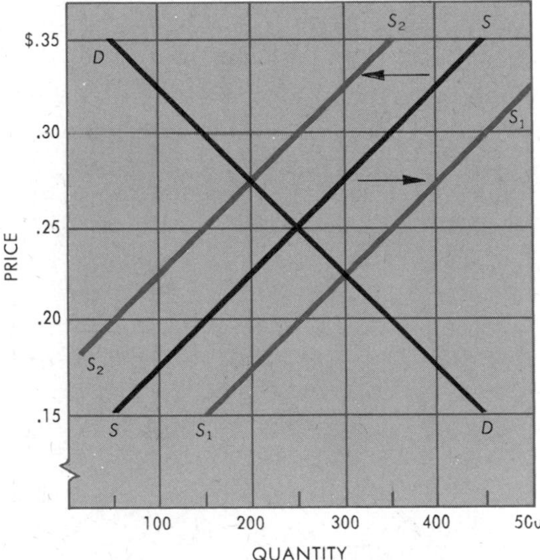

FIGURE 2–8 Change in Supply and Its Effect on Price and Quantity

An increase in supply, demand remaining the same, results in a decrease in price and an increase in quantity. A decrease in supply, demand remaining the same, results in an increase in price and a decrease in quantity. These examples show the inverse relationship between changes in supply and changes in the equilibrium price, and the direct relationship between changes in supply and changes in quantity exchanged.

Resource Allocation and the Classical Model

We are now in a better position to see how the classical model provides an answer to the allocation of our limited resources to meet our unlimited wants.

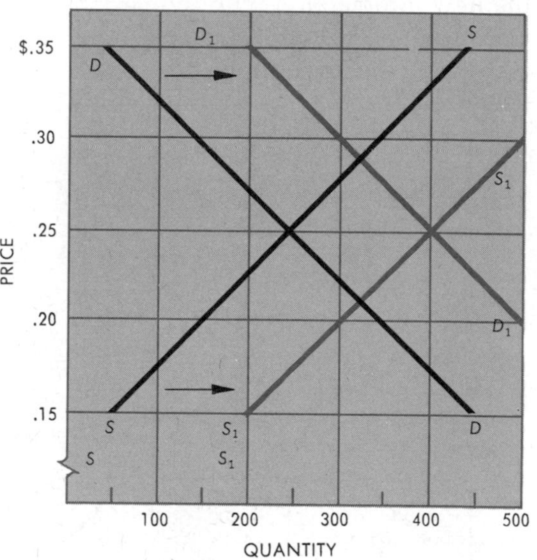

FIGURE 2–9 Change in Supply and Demand and the Effects on Price and Quantity

An increase in supply and demand will result in an increase in the quantity exchanged. The equilibrium price will change when the changes in supply and demand are not equal.

In Chapter 1, Figure 1–1, we showed a simplified model of how our economic system is supposed to operate. In Figure 2–10 we have added to the original model the forces of supply and demand in our market for goods and services and our market for the factors of production. How are resources allocated by this system? How are prices determined?

If we turn once again to our computer, we now can see that the measurements made by the computer are measurements of demand—by consumers in the marketplace for goods and services and by businesses in the marketplace for the factors of production. After figuring out demand, the computer relays the amount of dollars that would be enough to induce businesses to offer sufficient supply in the marketplace to satisfy the wants of consumers. It also tries to bring enough factors of production into the marketplace to supply the ingredients necessary for production.

In Figure 2–10 we can see how the consumers and businesses with dollars go to their respective markets representing demand. When households represent factors of production and businesses have goods to offer, they both represent supply in their respective markets. The amount of money offered—prices in the market for goods and services and payments for rent, wages, and interest for the factors of production—is the key to the allocation of our resources. Because it is the interaction of supply and demand in a purely competitive market that determines price, we can now see the importance of studying those forces.

Conditions Necessary for Making the Classical Model Work

If the classical model is to work as its creators intended, certain conditions must be met and certain assumptions must be made. If they are not, modifications in the model may be needed. What conditions and assumptions are necessary?

1. Man is primarily an economic being with an incentive to make money in order to satisfy his wants. He will take the highest paying job he can get, go into the most profitable business, sell what the public wants most and, at least in the long run, sell at the highest price that will give him the greatest profit. He will buy products at the lowest price without showing favoritism to any seller.

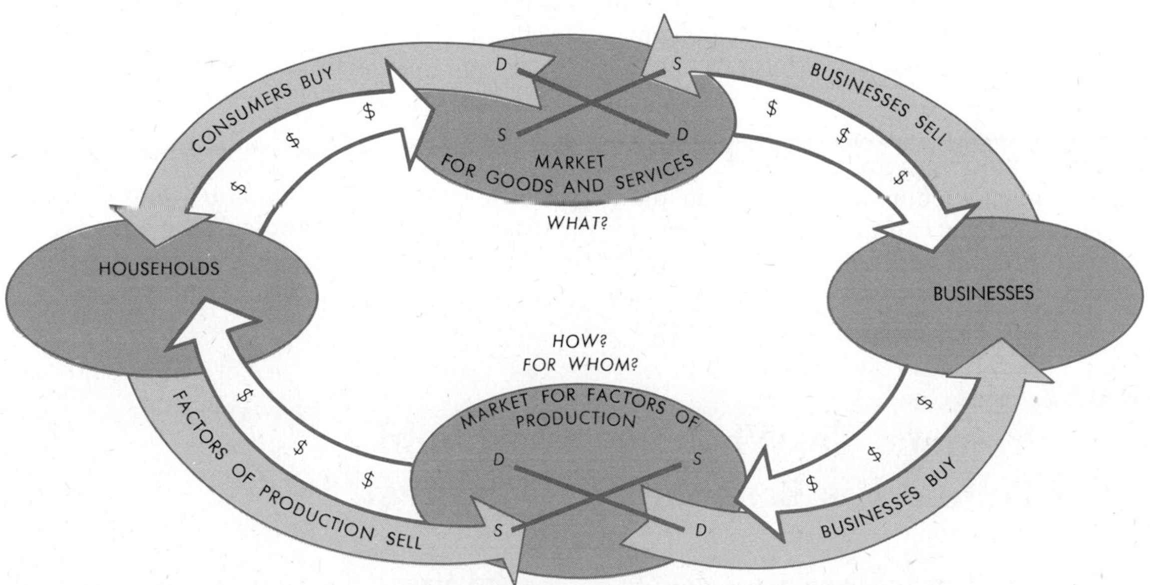

FIGURE 2–10 The Circular Flow of the Economy with Supply and Demand

The classical model's answer to resource allocation is the market mechanism. Through the interaction of supply and demand, price determines the answers to our basic questions *What? How?* and *For Whom?*

2. The factors of production, including labor, are mobile and can be readily moved to the place which will offer the highest return. As consumers' wants change, the allocation of resources must shift to meet these new needs.
3. Both the market for goods and services and the market for the factors of production are free from control whether by government, by buyers, or by sellers. Nothing must interfere with the freedom of consumers and the factors of production. Business, too, must be free to enter or leave the market and to act independently in the market.
4. Knowledge must be available to consumers so that they may determine what products can best serve their needs and can thus make wise decisions.
5. Society will achieve its maximum happiness by allowing individuals to make most of the decisions on what to produce and how to produce it. This system contrasts with one in which society, acting collectively through government, makes the decisions about production.

While the five conditions stated above do not exist in our environment in pure form, they are present to a far greater degree than in most other nations. Many people in our society think, talk, believe, and behave as if the classical model does exist in pure, or nearly pure, form. As a result the classical model influences much of our behavior as consumers, as owners of the factors of production, and as citizens trying to influence economic policy. We often refer to incentives for producing, such as commissions to salesmen, bonuses for managers, and higher pay for extra hours of work.

We have antitrust laws to keep the market competitive. Both state and national governments make information easily available to the consumer so that he can be a more effective buyer. Not only do most Americans resent the government's going into business, but loud complaints are heard when the government's budget is increased, since such action often results in individuals having fewer free choices.

The classical model, with its emphasis on a free market, cannot be dismissed merely because some controls have been instituted. Some of these controls, such as antitrust action, have helped to keep the market free. The classical model is a major factor in determining our country's answers to the big economic questions, although modifications of it and substitutions from other models have added flexibility to our economic system.

Part E
The Problem: To What Degree Should Man Follow His Economic Self-Interest?

At the end of many chapters we will present a problem involving the materials covered in the chapter. The points of view given will be those held by many people, but they must not be interpreted as being the sole truth or as necessarily being

SUPPLY AND DEMAND:

THE CLASSICAL MODEL'S ANSWER TO THE ALLOCATION OF RESOURCES

This is an exercise in the functioning of the price system: the classical model's answer to the question of allocating our limited resources. Its purpose is to review how, in a free market, the forces of supply and demand determine price and the distribution of our resources. We are going to review these concepts graphically.

Consumers make their wants known by showing a willingness and an ability to purchase certain quantities of a product at different prices. This is known as demand, and it can be shown graphically. Business offers for sale certain quantities of a product at different prices. This is known as supply, and it can also be shown graphically.

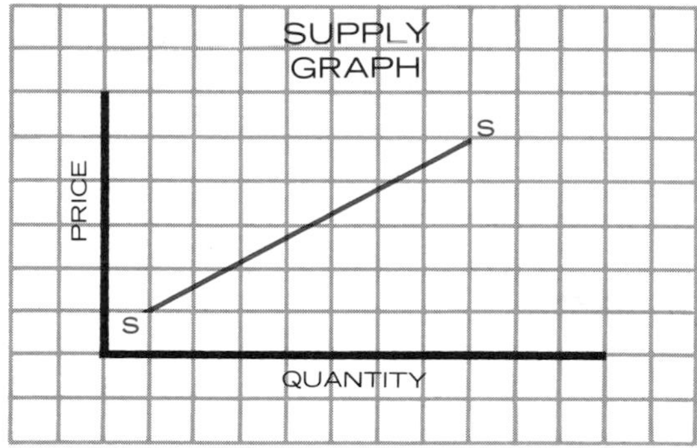

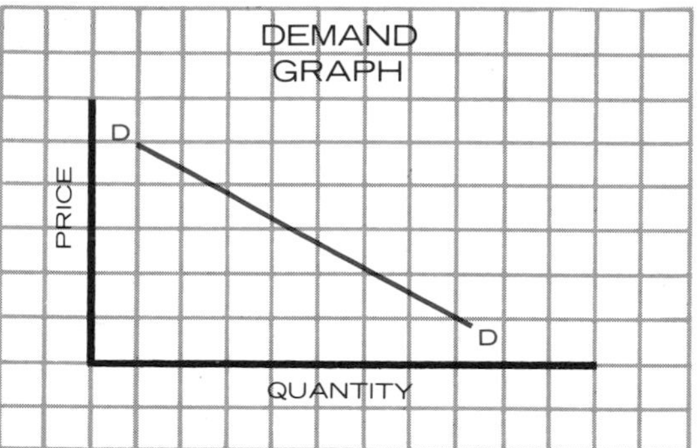

Consumers and businesses meet at the market, where the demand for goods interacts with the supply of goods. The intersection of demand and supply is the *equilibrium price.* This will clear the market. Any price higher than this will leave a surplus of goods. Any price below this point will leave consumers wanting more. Note that the intersection of demand and supply shows (1) price and (2) quantity exchanged. If we change the price we will vary the quantity exchanged, altering our resource allocation.

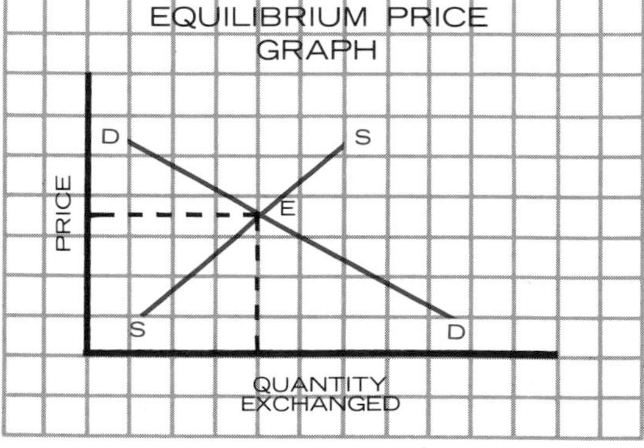

A change in demand is an increase or a decrease in the number of units that will be sold throughout the range of prices offered. It can be caused by (1) a change in consumers' income, (2) a change in taste, and (3) a change in the market for substitutes.

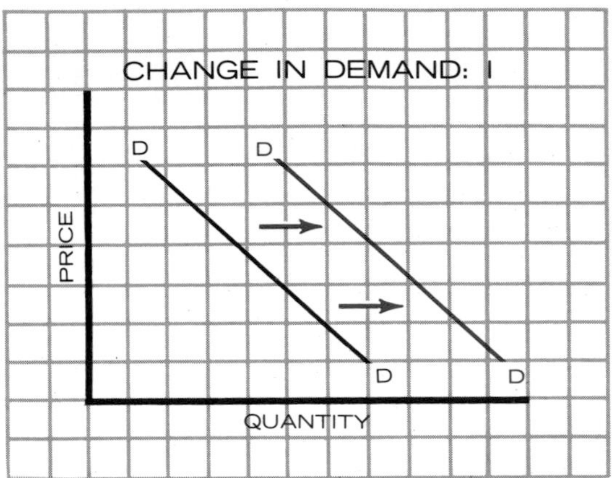

An increase in demand shifts the demand curve to the right.

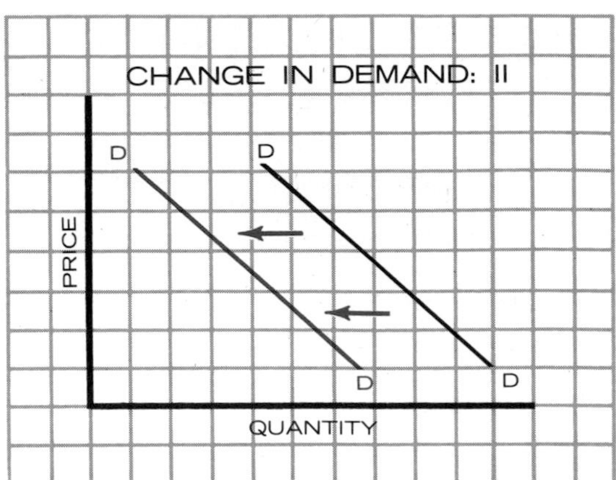

A decrease in demand shifts the demand curve to the left.

A change in supply is an increase or a decrease in the number of units offered throughout the range of prices. Changes in supply are caused by (1) changes in cost, (2) expectations of profit, and (3) changes in the demand for other goods.

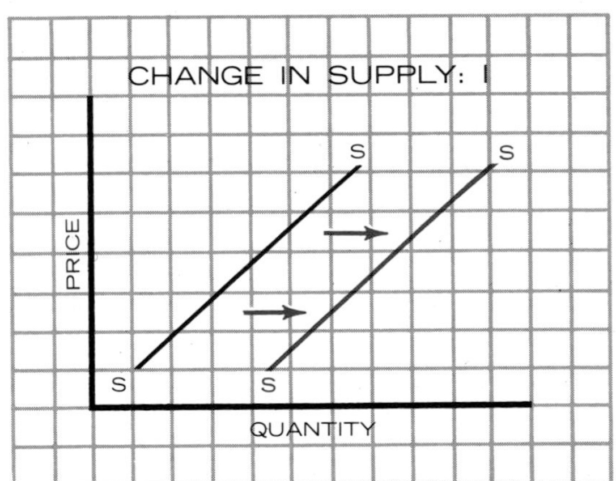

An increase in supply shifts the supply curve to the right.

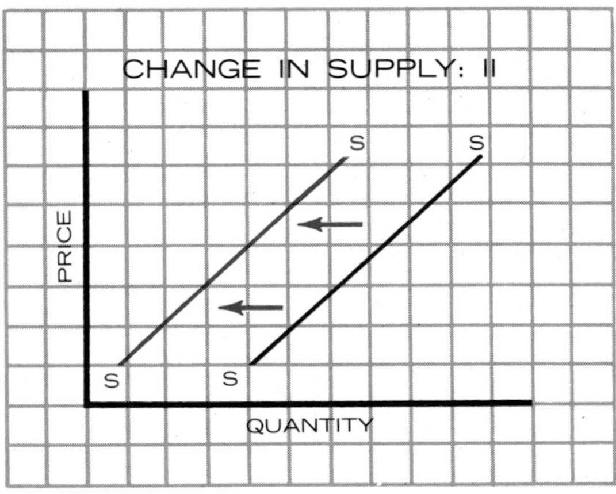

A decrease in supply shifts the supply curve to the left.

Some products are very responsive to price changes. A small change in price will bring about a major change in the quantity that is bought or offered for sale. Such products are said to have an *elastic demand* or an *elastic supply.* Shown graphically, the curves are more horizontal than vertical.

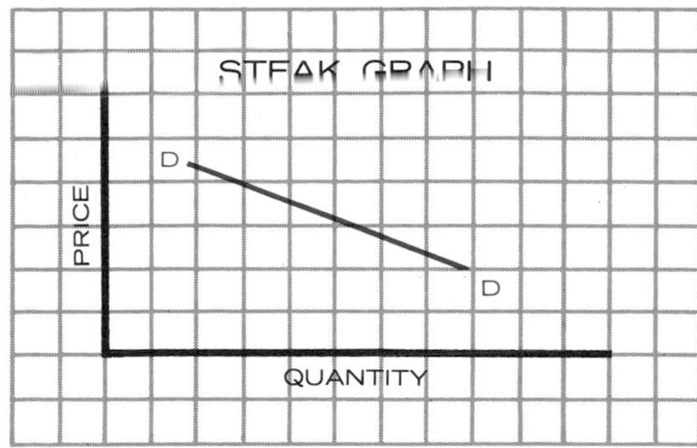

The demand for sirloin steak is highly elastic because substitutes can easily be found, it is not a necessity, and it may represent a large share of the food budget.

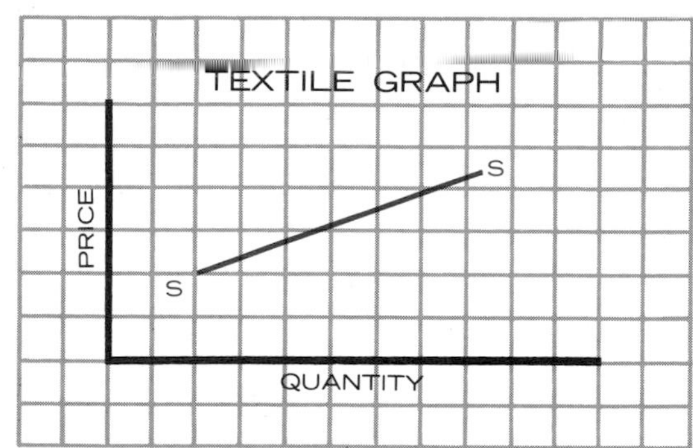

The supply of textiles is highly elastic because it is easy to increase production in a short time.

Products that respond very little to price changes are said to have an *inelastic demand* or an *inelastic supply*. Shown graphically, the curves are more vertical than horizontal.

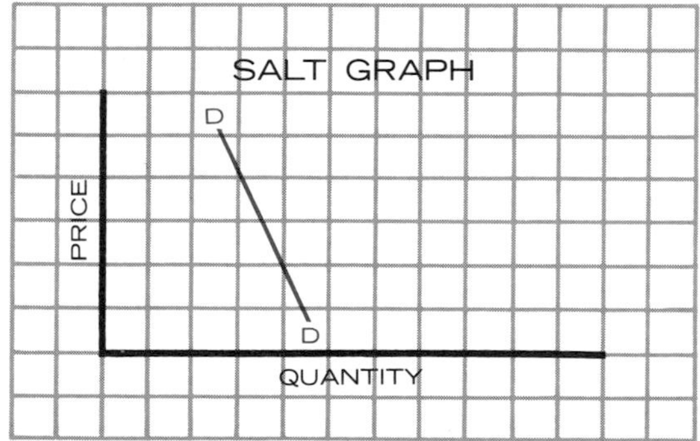

The demand for salt is highly inelastic because it represents a small share of the food budget and substitution is difficult.

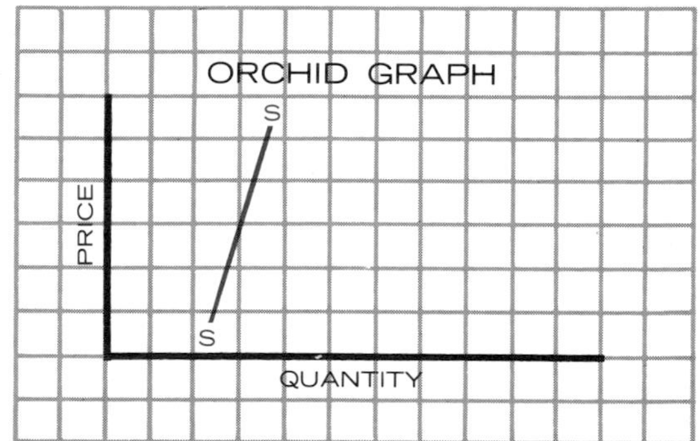

The supply of orchids is highly inelastic because of the time and difficulty involved in cultivating new plants.

Before proceeding with our case studies, a word of caution is necessary. The models that are shown above and on the transparent overlays are not accurate pictures of the real world. They are simplified in order to help you understand better how elasticity and changes in demand and supply affect distribution and price.

Few products have supply and demand schedules that fit neatly into linear patterns. Most products have schedules that are graphically expressed by curves with changing slopes, particularly at the upper and lower price ranges. This simplification does not distort the basic ideas of the functioning of the price system.

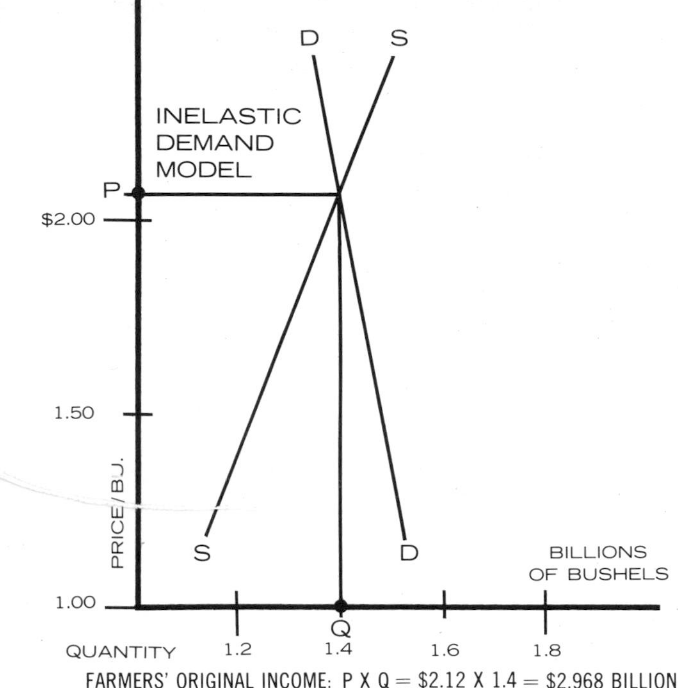

FARMERS' ORIGINAL INCOME: P X Q = $2.12 X 1.4 = $2.968 BILLION

On these pages are two case studies from "the world that is," showing graphically the importance of changes in supply and demand and of the elasticity of demand. Complete Case I on the overlay before starting Case II.

CASE I: Agriculture

The demand (D) for most agricultural products tends to be highly inelastic. Thus a change in price will make little difference in the quantity consumers buy. The point where supply (S) and demand (D) intersect is the equilibrium price (P), at which the market will be cleared (Q).

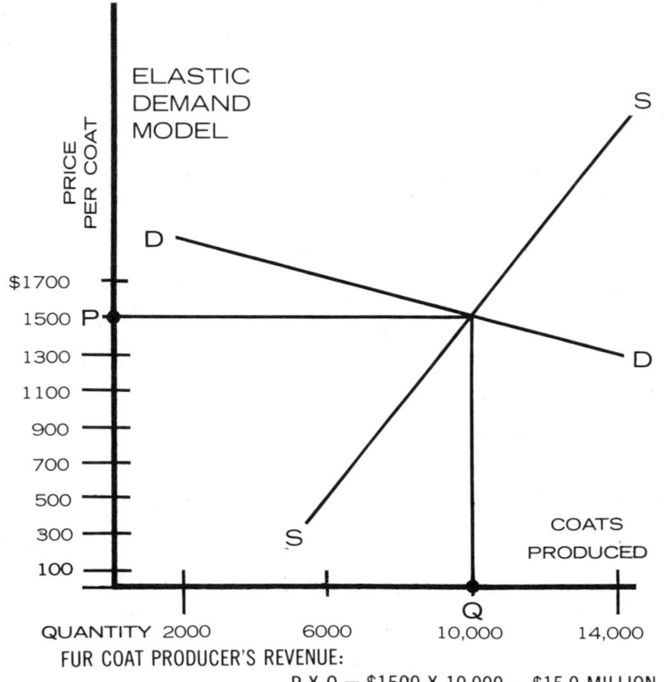

FUR COAT PRODUCER'S REVENUE:
P X Q = $1500 X 10,000 = $15.0 MILLION

CASE II: Excise tax on fur coats

The demand for many kinds of fur coats is highly elastic. A small change in price will bring about a major change in the quantity bought. The equilibrium price is P and the quantity exchanged is Q.

the right answers. There are in economics many controversial questions about which even the "experts" disagree. Using the information and the "tools" learned in the chapter and the positions stated in the problem, see if you can arrive at a conclusion which you consider best for you and the society in which you live. Let your conclusions be tentative ones, since additional information, other "tools," and different points of view will be introduced in later chapters and may cause you to change your mind.

Turning now to the problem, we may ask to what extent man should follow his economic self-interest. An observer trying to analyze the American society's system of values would encounter difficulty. He would soon find numerous examples which would be hard to explain. While we extol the virtues of individualism and independence and admire the "self-made man," we also give praise for cooperation and teamwork and show compassion for the less fortunate. Advertising frequently tries to persuade consumers to buy high-priced goods in order to show their success, and one famous economist pointed out that "keeping up with the Joneses" is part of the American way of life. At the same time we are told from the pulpit that we are too obsessed with materialism and that character is the true measure of a man.

The classical model depends on man's desire to acquire goods and services as an incentive. Is this materialistic motivation necessary? Does this kind of behavior represent only man's selfish, acquisitive motives, disregarding his altruistic and other non-material values?

The Classical Model Defended

The classical model works as intended when man pursues his own economic gain. As a producer, man is keenly aware of the effect of the computer and the number of dollars it assigns to the various jobs on the market for the factors of production. The jobs in which demand is greatest and supply the least will offer him the biggest dollar rewards. Thus, as he follows his own self-interest he is also helping to fulfill the wants of consumers.

As a consumer man also seeks his economic welfare. He tries to get the largest number of products that will satisfy his wants best and at the lowest prices. In this way his limited resources will provide him with the most want-satisfaction. When emotions and ideals that are inconsistent with the classical model are allowed to exert undue influence on man's behavior, the entire society suffers. The things men want most, as they express their wants at the market, will not be available in the kind and quantity they wish.

Every society must provide its workers and businessmen with an incentive to produce efficiently. What serves this purpose better than offering money as a reward? Money can be converted into whatever want-satisfactions the possessors wish. Acquisition of power, contributions to charities, and purchase of the things we want are all made possible by money. Workers will put forth greater effort when overtime pay is the reward. Profit spurs businessmen to produce better goods more efficiently. Everyone benefits, except those who are lazy, because society has more of the things it wants.

The Classical Model Under Attack

Many people believe that man is more than an economic animal—that he does not live by bread alone. His behavior is influenced by many things, including the fact that he is a member of society. The values that he holds cannot always be measured by a price tag. Man's primary aim in life is to seek happiness. He can do this in many ways, but few would accept mere material satisfaction as the sole, or even the primary, means. Man has a need to create, to serve, to show fellowship and compassion, to gain recognition for achievement in ways apart from financial gain.

When we consider man as a producer, we must, as the classical economist would insist, recognize incentive as a means of insuring that the things society needs will be produced. However, money need not be the only incentive. The artist or writer does not usually express himself primarily for the sake of the money he will make. Clergymen, doctors, lawyers, teachers, and social workers frequently enter their professions because they have purposes and ideals above and beyond merely earning dollars. Do the athletes on your college teams try less hard than the professionals because they are not paid for their efforts? There are many situations in society in which money is only a secondary consideration.

Does man, acting as a consumer, consider price and quality alone? An examination of shopping habits reveals conflicting evidence. Studies by consumer organizations have shown that consumers frequently fail to look at prices—that they buy at a particular place or buy a particular brand out of habit or because of location, service, or friendship. Other studies show that advertising appeals to many emotions, not all of them of an economic nature.

If we are to achieve a better society, we must curb our material considerations and encourage man to produce and achieve for human betterment. This cannot be done if man seeks only financial rewards.

Considering an Answer

What disagreements do you have with the two positions just stated? Are they different because of the facts or the values presented? Can you think of a third or fourth position? Does the favoring of one position mean that the other position is entirely wrong?

In what way does this problem relate to supply and demand? How does it relate to the questions *What? How?* and *For Whom?* How is this problem important to you?

The positions given here represent only one part of the conflict between those who believe in following the classical model closely, those who believe we should modify it, and those who want a new model. They show that economics has unresolved problems which frequently reflect conflicting values.

As you proceed with your study of economics, you will acquire additional information and learn about other tools for analyzing problems. You will also become acquainted with issues related to these problems. It will be interesting to see whether you change your conclusions about some of the problems as you consider them and other related questions.

REVIEW: THE HIGHLIGHTS OF THE CHAPTER

1. Price measures values in money. Goods and services have economic value when they satisfy want (utility) and are relatively scarce. Price plays a very important part in determining the allocation of our resources.

2. A market is a place where buyers and sellers meet. There are markets for goods and services, and markets for the factors of production. Markets can be classified as having pure competition, pure monopoly, monopolistic competition, and oligopoly. The number of buyers and sellers and their ability to influence price distinguish the type of market. Most markets fall somewhere between pure competition and pure monopoly. The classical model assumes pure competition. All competition that is not pure is called imperfect competition.
3. Demand is the willingness on the part of consumers to buy certain amounts of a product at certain prices in a given market. The general rule for demand is that the lower the price of a given product, the more of it consumers will buy. This rule is explained by the law of diminishing marginal utility. The use of substitutes and the level of buyers' income also influence demand. A demand schedule lists the quantities of a product consumers will buy at various prices, and can be plotted on a graph as a demand curve. The elasticity of demand is determined by the way price changes affect quantity. Changes in demand can be brought about in a number of ways.
4. Supply is the willingness of sellers to offer certain amounts of products at certain prices in a given market. Supply schedules will differ for products available immediately, for the short run, and for the long run. The general rule for supply states that producers will offer more of their product for sale as price rises. This is because costs, which have a great influence on supply, will begin to rise beyond a certain level of production. Supply schedules can be plotted on graphs to give supply curves. They may be elastic or inelastic and may change because of costs.
5. When we put supply and demand together we get the equilibrium price, which will clear the market of products. Changes in supply and demand will bring about changes in price and the quantity bought.
6. The classical model explains that it is the laws of supply and demand interacting at the market that determine the allocation of our resources.
7. Certain conditions must be met if the classical model is to work. They include the economic motivation of man, mobility of the factors of production, pure competition, and freedom for consumers and producers.

IN CONCLUSION: SOME AIDS TO UNDERSTANDING

Terms for Review

demand
market
supply
utility
price
monopoly
oligopoly
monopsony
elasticity
clearing the market
increasing costs
economic value
exchange value
incentive
pure competition
monopolistic competition
imperfect competition
equilibrium
change in demand
classical model
law of diminishing marginal utility

Questions for Review

1. Classical capitalism depends on the market for answers to the basic economic questions.
   (a) What is the major function of the market in the American economy?
   (b) What are the important considerations that determine the kind of competition which develops?
   (c) List and explain the various kinds of markets we have.
2. Since productive resources are usually limited, what factors determine their use and allocation? What economic principles are involved?
3. The terms *value, price,* and *utility* are all interdependent.
   (a) What is the basic economic meaning of each?
   (b) How are they interdependent?
4. The idea of competition is a keystone of the capitalist system.
   (a) What is the meaning of *competition?*
   (b) What are the various kinds of competition which may develop?
   (c) Why is competition essential to this system?
5. "Monopoly may be both a blessing and a curse to the producer and to the consumer." Give examples to demonstrate the validity of this statement.
6. In our economy, supply and demand are important factors in determining price.
   (a) Draw a graph which will show the relationship between a price increase and the quantity of an item that will be sold.
   (b) What factors besides price will determine the shape of the demand curve?
   (c) What influences are present in our economy to determine the supply of any commodity or service?
7. Some feel that maximum happiness is achieved in our democratic society if the individual is permitted to make the basic decisions on what to produce, how to produce, and so on. Give the arguments for and against this position.

Additional Questions and Problems

1. Products have value for a variety of reasons. Sometimes the value of a product will change with circumstances. We identify value in prices. Account for the prices of the following: (a) roses in February, (b) ice skates in May, (c) diamonds, (d) bread, (e) a day-old newspaper.
2. In what kind of market would you place each of the following? (a) A gas and electric company, (b) an orange grower, (c) a local automobile dealer, (d) an appliance manufacturer, (e) the Boston Symphony Orchestra.
3. Check the general rule for demand by interviewing a local merchant on the effect of a sale. What happens to demand for a product when it is no longer on sale?
4. Make a list of five products with elastic demand and five with inelastic demand. What accounts for this elasticity?
5. Over the years the demand for products changes. Can you identify some changes in consumer preferences? Explain why you think these changes have taken place.

6. The demand for a product may be elastic over one range of prices, but inelastic over another range. Why?
7. Explain the relationship between cost and supply. Why does the time period influence supply?
8. What factors are most likely to bring about a change in supply?
9. Explain how the equilibrium price is established for a product in a perfectly competitive market.
10. Draw supply and demand curves and consider them your original supply and demand. Then determine whether price and quantity will increase or decrease in the following situations:
    (a) Demand increases and supply remains the same.
    (b) Supply increases and demand remains the same.
    (c) Demand decreases and supply remains the same.
    (d) Demand and supply both decrease, but demand decreases more than supply.
11. On graph paper, plot the following supply and demand schedules. Let each interval (box) represent one cent for price (start with 20) and let each interval represent 300 cans for quantity.

Demand and Supply Schedules for 6-Ounce Cans of Frozen Orange Juice

Price per can	*Demand*	*Supply*
$ .32	1,000	5,500
.31	1,100	4,800
.30	1,200	4,300
.29	1,400	3,800
.28	1,600	3,200
.27	1,900	2,700
.26	2,300	2,300
.25	2,600	1,900
.24	3,000	1,700
.23	3,500	1,500
.22	4,100	1,300
.21	4,700	1,100
.20	5,500	1,000

(a) What is the market price for 6-ounce cans of frozen orange juice?
(b) If oranges are hurt by a frost and the supply drops 400 cans at each price level, what will be the new price?
(c) Using the revenue test, is the demand schedule for frozen orange juice above elastic or inelastic?

SELECTED READINGS

Dorfman, Robert. *The Price System.* Englewood Cliffs, N. J.: Prentice-Hall, 1964.
Haveman, Robert H., and Kenyon A. Knopf. *The Market System.* New York: John Wiley & Sons, 1966.

Leftwich, Richard H. *The Price System and Resource Allocation,* 3rd ed. New York: Holt, Rinehart & Winston, 1966.

Liebhafsky, H. H. *The Nature of Price Theory.* Homewood, Ill.: Dorsey Press, 1968.

Stern, Louis, and John R. Grabner, Jr. *Competition in the Market Place.* Glenview, Ill.: Scott, Foresman and Co., 1970.

Stigler, George J. *The Theory of Price.* New York: The Macmillan Co., 1966.

Economic Systems Other Than Capitalism 3

THE AUTHORS' NOTE TO THE STUDENT

In our study of economics we make reference to the classical model of capitalism and to variations of it. In addition to capitalism there are three major economic systems—socialism, communism, and fascism. Each of these has its own model, explaining why it offers man the greatest hope for the future; each has had sufficient appeal to win millions of followers. In these systems, as in capitalism, there is a difference between the theory (the "ought-to-be") and the practice (the "is"). Each model has critics who oppose certain of its aspects but choose to keep its framework, preferring to modify the system rather than change to another.

Before we can analyze these systems, we will separate them from their accompanying political structures and the emotional overtones often generated by isms. Once this is done, the basic differences among the systems will become apparent. These differences form a spectrum with one extreme labeled individualism and the free market and the other labeled collectivism and centralized control.

A STUDENT'S NOTE TO THE STUDENT

This has to be one of the most interesting but one of the most provocative chapters in the book. I have some very strong feelings about these politico-economic systems and I found it useful in my analysis to have the theory and practice separated as well as the political from the economic. I was surprised to find out that segments of the American and Soviet economies are moving toward each other's models, particularly "Libermanism" in the U.S.S.R.

I felt the authors showed a slight bias, but my roommate disagreed.

Part A
What Economic System? The Theory

In our present-day world there are three major economic systems competing with capitalism—*socialism, communism,* and *fascism.* Each of these has developed a model explaining the logic of its own system. Each must, like capitalism, concern itself with the problem of scarcity and the allocation of resources. Answers must be furnished for the *What, How,* and *For Whom.* Production and distribution are as important to the socialist, communist, and fascist economies as they are to the capitalist economy. We shall consider each of these systems from the point of view of its differences from capitalism or other systems, the model it follows, variations suggested for the model, and weaknesses inherent in each form.

Socialism

Socialism is found today in Norway, Sweden, Denmark, and Israel; it has existed in some degree at various times in Great Britain, Australia, New Zealand, the Netherlands, and Belgium. Most western European nations have strong socialist parties that have held political power often enough to influence the economic system strongly. To most Europeans socialism has a more favorable connotation than does capitalism, and several political parties oriented toward capitalism use the word "social" or "socialist" to make their cause more appealing to the people.

A number of underdeveloped nations, including India, have chosen socialism as their preferred system. The Socialist party in the United States has never been very successful at the polls, but it is interesting to note that many of the particular programs it has advocated have eventually become law.

Dissatisfaction with Capitalism

Modern socialist thinking has developed largely as a protest against the misery that accompanied the Industrial Revolution. Instead of looking upon the factory system as a way to improve the lot of the poor, early socialists considered it responsible for crowded slums and low wages. Most objectionable of all was the idea that laissez-faire policies would best serve the public interest. Specifically, the socialists objected to these aspects of capitalism:

1. Private ownership of the tools of production—that is, of capital—leads to increasing inequality of wealth. Having a great advantage over the worker in bargaining, the capitalist receives a larger portion of the "pie" than he deserves.
2. Profit rather than need is the motivation for production. Because of this, scarce resources may be wasted on goods and services that serve no useful purpose, whereas other goods and services that do have real utility, especially to poorer people, are in short supply.
3. Competition is often wasteful. Duplication of effort, built-in obsolescence, advertising, and shortsighted exploitation of natural resources to make a quick profit are characteristic of capitalism's wasteful methods.
4. Planning by businesses on an individual basis leads to overproduction, causing business cycles. Cycles, in turn, lead to frequent depressions, which add to the

waste of resources and the feeling of insecurity among workers.

5. The concentration of capitalistic wealth brings with it a concentration of political power. Greater concern is shown for property rights than for human rights.
6. Capitalism tends to lead to imperialism as businessmen seek raw materials, markets, and places to invest their surplus capital. When their investments abroad are threatened, they call on their government to provide protection. Such involvements may lead to war.

The Socialist Model

In a socialist economy the basic problems of scarcity and allocation of limited resources are solved by producing for use or need rather than producing for profit. By having most of the means of production owned and controlled collectively, usually by government, production can be planned and distribution organized to assure fairness for all. Socialist theory believes that instead of the market's determining what shall be produced, how it shall be produced, and for whom the production is meant, the government should provide the answers. Plans are carefully drawn so as to avoid waste, and production is aimed at improving living standards. Inequalities of income are reduced because distribution does not allow the strong to take advantage of the weak. Overproduction, duplication of effort, and depressions are avoided as competition is replaced by cooperation and planning.

Socialists believe in moving toward their goal of government ownership and control by gradual means and through democratic processes. The freedom of choice of the consumer and the producer may be curbed as the society moves from capitalism to socialism, but the decisions that citizens make as they go to the polls affect the economy even more than under capitalism. When property is *nationalized* —taken over by the government—the owners are to be compensated. Socialists claim that only by doing away with private ownership of capital and the power derived from that ownership can the state be economically and politically democratic.

Variations of the Model

Major differences exist among socialists as to how extensive government ownership and control should be. These differences are reflected in the many forms of socialism, all varying in organization, methods, or emphasis.

The oldest and most idealistic form of socialism is known as "utopian socialism." It is based on the belief that men can live together best in an environment which stresses cooperation rather than competition. Utopian socialists sought to set up communities where men would work together in harmony with little or no direction by government. Robert Owen (1771–1858), of Wales, and the followers of Charles Fourier (1772–1837), of France, set up experimental communities in the United States, hoping to show by example the superiority of their system so that other people might wish to live in the same way. The failure of these experiments and the lack of any strong formal organization, at a time when industrial organization was bringing about great changes, ruined any chances they may have had for success. A revival of communal living has become a life style for many young people throughout the world.

After the defeat of radical movements in Germany and England in the middle of the nineteenth century, a new attempt at social reform was made. Based on certain teachings of the Bible and directed primarily at workers, this movement was known as "Christian socialism." According to its teachings society should be organized on the principles of concern for humanity and belief in the brotherhood of man. Repudiating violence and class struggle, the Christian socialists advocated use of the private property of the rich for the benefit of all. They supported a broad program of reform designed to lessen the sufferings of the poor.

Some of you may already be acquainted with another form of socialism—that of Karl Marx. Marx referred to his socialism as "scientific," claiming that his analysis was based on scientific reasoning. In his two famous works, *The Communist Manifesto,* written in collaboration with Friedrich Engels, and *Das Kapital,* Marx explained his criticism of capitalism and predicted its eventual destruction and its replacement by socialism. Much of the thinking of present-day communism is based on these writings.

Marx saw history not as a meaningless succession of events but as social change resulting from the struggle of classes. With the transition from agricultural to industrial production, a change in the dominant economic class was taking place. Under capitalism economic power would become so concentrated that society would be divided between the few capitalists owning all the means of production and the masses of workers owning nothing.

Marx explained the concentration of wealth in industry by the doctrine of *surplus value.* All wealth, he argued, is produced by labor, with the other factors of production being either passive or also the result of labor. Because the worker is not paid the full value of what he produces, the capitalist is able to accumulate this reservoir of surplus value—the difference between what the worker produces and what he earns. As this process continues, the middle class disappears and the society becomes divided between the capitalist (the exploiter) and the worker (the exploited).

Since workers lack the means to buy back the goods they produce, overproduction soon leads to depressions. As this condition develops, the position of the workers becomes even more intolerable. Eventually the workers will unite and throw off capitalist domination by a revolution. With the capitalists gone, the means of production will be owned and operated by the workers. Since all people will be workers, there will be only one class. The struggle between classes will cease because the separation between owners of the means of production and workers will no longer exist. In effect, the new society will be "classless."

Toward the end of the nineteenth century a new direction in socialist thought appeared. Led by Eduard Bernstein in Germany and by Sidney and Beatrice Webb, George Bernard Shaw, H. G. Wells, and the Fabian Society in England, the new movement rejected Marx's class struggle and sudden revolution. In its place the "revisionists," as they came to be called, favored a gradual evolution to socialism. Progress for society through education and political control gained at the polls is preferred to class struggle. In extending its ownership of productive facilities, the government must proceed slowly; in some cases, such as public utilities, municipal ownership is favored over national ownership. The policies of the present British Labor party have been greatly influenced by the thinking of the

KARL MARX, THE REVOLUTIONARY

Karl Heinrich Marx (1818–1883) was born in Trier, in the German Rhineland, the son of a middle-class family. At the age of seventeen, he began his college education at the University of Bonn where, following his father's wish, he began the study of law. However, he soon changed to history and philosophy at the universities of Berlin and Jena, receiving his doctor's degree.

Marx had hoped to pursue an academic career; but when this became impossible because of his radical ideas, he turned to journalism instead. His political views soon led to the suppression of his newspaper by the government, whereupon Marx moved to Paris. There he studied political economy, particularly the writings of French utopian socialists. Although their theories interested him, his own views were more extreme. While in Paris he met Friedrich Engels, who shared his opinions and who later collaborated with him to produce the famous *Communist Manifesto.* Exiled from France at the request of the Prussian government, Marx moved to Brussels. He returned to Germany during the Revolution of 1848. Expelled again, he settled in London. There he became active in workers' organizations and continued to develop his own theories.

In his later years Marx spent most of his time in the British Museum, where he read and wrote, earning a meager living by preparing articles for the New York *Tribune.* He and his family suffered from poverty and poor health, but these circumstances did not deter him from writing his famous book, *Das Kapital,* and organizing and leading the International Workingmen's Association, later known as the First International. The second and third volumes of *Das Kapital* were edited by Engels and published after Marx's death.

The influence of Marx on the noncommunist world has been more in the fields of business cycles, stages of economic development, and interpretation of history than in the advancing of economic theory. However, the vast importance of his thinking to the development of the communist world gives his work a significance beyond its contributions to economics alone.

Fabian Society, which incorporated many revisionist ideas. However, much of Britain's production remains in private control and her government is democratic.

Socialist ideas were sometimes incorporated into political and economic movements, such as anarchism, syndicalism, and guild socialism, whose main emphasis was on ideas other than socialism. Each sought to eliminate private property, and each had strong objection to the existing organization of government. The anarchist looked at the state as the source of all evil and wished to substitute for it self-governing groups living in voluntary associations. The syndicalists wanted to organize workers into one big union which would carry out a general strike and overthrow capitalism. Each industry would then be run by workers in autonomous units, which would be federated for overall direction. Guild socialism recognized the need for government, but it wanted to organize the society into producers and consumers, each with a national association. Industry was to be run by employees organized into guilds. Though significant in their time, these groups have little influence and importance today.

Weaknesses in the Socialist Position

Just as the socialist can find fault with capitalism, so the capitalist can point to weaknesses in socialist thought. In particular, the supporters of capitalism criticize these aspects of socialist theory:

1. Socialism lacks incentives for increasing effort, whereas under capitalism, private ownership of wealth, including capital, is a motivating force. Under collective ownership unproductive members of society are subsidized by their more productive fellows, reducing incentive for both. In the system of private enterprise the individual businessman can see in a most direct way the rewards for his energy and ability.
2. Substituting production for need in place of production for profit may sound very altruistic, but who determines what need is? Even if that question could be solved to everyone's satisfaction, the fact remains that profits are as great in industries producing necessities as in those producing luxuries. In either case, profits will be made when individual consumers indicate their needs by buying what they wish. And isn't the will of the people expressed more clearly and directly by the individual vote in the marketplace than by the collective vote, even of a democratically elected government?
3. Although competition does produce some duplication and waste, it more than compensates for this by eliminating the inefficient producer and motivating those who stay in business to improve their products and reduce their costs. The cost of advertising is more than compensated by the increased market for goods resulting from the economies of large-scale production, which results from the larger market.

   Competition also yields an indirect benefit by offsetting political decisions. People frequently exercise more care in spending their own money than in evaluating the consequences of their choices in voting.
4. Overproduction and economic fluctuations can and do occur in socialist countries as well as in capitalistic countries. Modern capitalistic economic policy has greatly reduced the length and severity of recessions. Moreover capitalism, with its millions of producers, has more flexibility to adapt to changing demand.
5. Concentration of wealth has not taken place in capitalist economies as the socialists have predicted. Instead, the ownership of our giant corporations is increasingly widespread. Today millions of our workers are themselves capitalists.
6. Capitalism shows no greater tendency toward imperialism at present than does socialism. Many socialist countries have actually sought out private capital as an aid to development. Competition for raw materials and markets is more closely related to capital accumulation and trade than to the type of economic structure involved.
7. Although socialists strongly support freedom and democracy and reject communism because it ignores civil rights, the amount of regulation and central planning necessary in socialism reduces consumer sovereignty and limits the decisions of workers.

Freedom is more closely tied to the political traditions of a country than to the economic system it chooses. In such socialist countries as New Zealand, Denmark, and Israel there is great respect for civil liberties. Likewise, the socialist charge that in capitalism there can be no real freedom because economic concentration leads to political concentration seems absurd when one looks at the number of elected officials, including American presidents, who were opposed by "big business" interests.

Communism

On the surface the theories of present-day socialism and communism seem more marked by similarities than by differences. Both systems make the same criticisms of capitalism. Both received impetus from the writings of Karl Marx. Perhaps the problem of distinguishing between the two systems is one of semantics, concerning the meaning and use of the term "socialism." Both the Soviet Union and some western European nations refer to their systems as socialist states, but the informed observer knows that the socialism of western Europe and that of the communist world are two different and incompatible systems.

Analysis of the Stages Leading to Communism

Unlike most socialists, who believed in progress by peaceful evolution, Marx believed the transition from capitalism to communism would follow a particular pattern and would be accompanied by a violent revolution. Communist theoreticians have classified this process in four stages.

The first stage is marked by the workers' overthrow of capitalism, and is followed by their seizure of the government.

The second stage is characterized by the establishment of a *dictatorship of the proletariat.* A centralized authority is necessary because the majority of workers are not capable of ruling, and direction by a small, intelligent leadership—the Communist party—is required. Under the dictatorship the destruction of the capitalist class is completed, and society is reorganized along socialist lines, with private ownership and profit abolished. The state now owns and operates the means of production.

In the third stage the dictatorship of the proletariat is replaced by the establishment of a "socialist" society. The political state will still exist and, because there may still be opposition, will have considerable power; economic production is to be controlled by the workers. Because production would still be limited, output and payment would be "from each according to his ability, to each according to his work."

The fourth and highest stage is that of the true "communistic" society. Production will be in such abundance that work and payment will be made "from each according to his ability, to each according to his need." The political state will no longer be necessary because there will no longer be any antagonism between classes. Administrators will be needed, however, to supervise industrial complexes.

The communists of the U.S.S.R. claim that they have now reached the third stage—that of socialism—and they hope to have enough production to attain actual communism by the end of the 1970's.

Differences Between Socialism and Communism

As we have seen, the communists seek to end capitalism by revolution, whereas the socialists wish to do it through the ballot box, adhering to constitutional procedures. In socialism, education and persuasion are substituted for the militant class struggle advocated by the communists. For the most part, socialists believe in an orderly transfer of the means of producton from private to public ownership. This changeover can be accomplished by gradually increasing the size of the public sector, thereby allowing capitalism and socialism to live side by side during the period of transition.

One of the important differences between socialism and communism may be seen in their treatment of nationalized property. Under socialism, fair payment is to be made to the owners. Since communists look with disdain upon the capitalist, considering the property he owns as stolen from the people, they expropriate private property without any compensation. Furthermore, they do not accept a mixed economy (although they did in practice in Russia between the years 1921 and 1927) and believe in total nationalization.

Finally, socialism has a high regard for the political freedom of the individual. It does not seek to control the total way of life of the people; instead, it is responsive to popular will expressed through elections. Communism, on the other hand, is totalitarian, seeking to subject not merely economic affairs but all individual thought and activity to the good of the state.

Weaknesses of Communism

In our analysis of socialism we have already identified many of the weaknesses of communism. To these, other criticisms must be added:

1. With his materialistic interpretation of history, Marx focused attention on the role of economic forces in determining the course of history. Those people who owned wealth or the means of acquiring wealth—land in an agricultural society, boats in a maritime state, machinery in an industrial nation—also controlled the forces of government and determined their policies and direction.

   There is little doubt that Marx made a substantial contribution to the understanding of history, since too little attention had been given to economic forces before his time. At the same time he committed the error common to all those who seek a single answer—oversimplification. No single factor can possibly explain all historical development. Events occur because of multiple causes, with no one factor predominant throughout history.
2. Marx predicted that the proletarian revolution to overthrow capitalism could come only in advanced capitalistic nations. If this were true, the United States, Britain, and western Europe should have been the first to experience such revolutions. Instead, communism has developed most frequently in nations that are just beginning to emerge from feudalism into the capitalist stage.
3. Marx predicted that the polarization of classes would grow to the point where almost all people would be industrial workers and the rest would be capitalists. Writing 100 years ago, he did not anticipate the growth of the "salariat," or white-collar workers, who identify with the middle and upper classes. Today, the salariat constitute the largest percentage of workers. To them, the class struggle as envisioned by Marx is almost meaningless.
4. Marx anticipated the decline of interest rates as the accumulation of more and more capital would eventually lead to a shortage of new areas for investment. In contrast to Marx's expectations, good opportunities for investment continue to exist today, and interest rates tend to fluctuate in the same way and for the same reasons that they always have.
5. Marx predicted that only through revolution could there be any reforms for the workers. He failed to foresee the economic gains and humanitarian reforms that have been carried out by

democratic capitalistic nations without resort to force.

6. Marx and other communist theoreticians looked upon capitalist theory as a rigid doctrine incapable of solving the basic problems of a dynamic society. The capitalism of today, in theory as well as in practice, is not the same as the capitalism that Marx observed or prophesied about in the nineteenth century. Current communist theoreticians commit the same error as their predecessors, although it is more likely that they do so for propaganda purposes rather than out of sincere conviction.

Fascism

Fascism is the term associated with the economic and political system of Italy, Germany, and Japan before and during World War II. Variations of this system survive today in the governments of Spain, Portugal, and several Latin American countries. Except in these countries, fascist parties are today small and relatively lacking in power. However, the ideas of fascism are still very much alive and assume a variety of guises. Given the right stimulus, they could prove a real danger to the institutions of democracy.

Unlike capitalism, socialism, and communism, fascism does not have a clear-cut model or even a major literary work that clearly defines what it is or how it functions. Its political and economic aspects are so intertwined that separating them, as we have done with the other systems, is difficult. However, we can determine some of the major ideas and principles that set fascism apart.

Economic Aspects of Fascism

Fascism combines capitalism's private ownership of the means of production with communism's state planning. Industry, although privately owned and profit-seeking, is organized into corporations or estates under the strict regulation of the government. Membership of corporate leaders in the fascist party and participation by them in planning insures close government control of the business community. Labor unions are also severely regulated, and workers who challenge their leaders' authority suffer severe penalties. Central planning replaces the market mechanism as the means of controlling production and allocating resources.

Fascism is traditionally oriented toward a war economy. For example, when Italy, Germany, and Japan were unable to solve their serious economic problems, they turned to giant rearmament programs. Projects such as these provided swift relief for depression and unemployment. It is doubtful whether economies thus oriented could survive for long without a war.

After the outbreak of World War II the resources of conquered countries were used to support the economies of the fascist nations. Slave labor produced food for the conquerors and war materials for new conquests. Only defeat could halt the war-directed economic development of traditional fascism.

Political Aspects of Fascism

Under traditional fascism, individualism is replaced by the most extreme form of nationalism. Social and economic considerations are subordinated to the purposes of the state. For example, to expedite rearmament, the power of labor unions in fascist countries was curbed through the combined efforts of powerful industrialists and fascist political leaders. Leadership pyramids to the top so that the dictator, "Il Duce" or the "Führer," holds total authority. When Hitler was introduced to people at a Nazi demonstration with the words "Hitler is Germany, Germany is Hitler," it meant that he was the embodiment of all the glory of the German nation and that everything must give way to his will.

Unlike many other dictatorships, fascism seeks mass support for its activities and programs. Support is also won from the traditional centers of leadership—the industrialists, landowners, and especially the military leaders—who may be frightened by the prospect of labor discontent. A third source of support is the salariat, who are inclined to fear the rise of the working class and may even be jealous of higher wages paid to industrial workers. A policy of "divide and rule" enables the centralized authority to maintain control.

As a totalitarian system dominating all aspects of life, fascism employs science, literature, and the arts as instruments of political power. Emphasis on nationalism has in some cases led to belief in national and racial superiority. This supposed superiority becomes a justification for conquest of other peoples, cultures, and nations.

As we have seen, a few neofascist nations still exist. Since they are lesser powers, lacking the economic resources for political expansion, they are less threatening to other political and economic systems than the earlier, more powerful fascist nations were. Yet even in these countries the size of the armed forces and the influence of military elements are far greater than in other countries with comparable resources.

Comparison of Communism and Fascism

Communism and fascism are both totalitarian systems that have emerged in the twentieth century. But whereas communism has grown and flourished in poor and underdeveloped countries, fascism has taken hold in capitalistic and more highly industrialized nations. The major pre-World War II fascist states—Italy, Germany, Japan, and later Argentina under Perón—were capitalist states with limited experience in democratic institutions. Distrusting democracy and seemingly unable to solve their problems through existing means, they turned to fascism as an alternative. China and Russia, by contrast, were emerging from feudalism and never really developed democratic institutions. To them communism became a means of industrializing and advancing their total economic development.

Weaknesses of Fascism

The course and outcome of World War II betrayed the economic weaknesses of the fascist nations. Their dependence on a war-oriented economy, their financial instability in time of crisis, and their economic collapse at the end of the war cast serious doubts on any possible economic merits of fascism. The performance of the present fascist nations in meeting the needs of their people suffers in comparison with that of other systems. Probably the greatest weakness of fascism, at least in the long run, is its political system and the values on which it is based. Its substitution of emotion for reason, the state for the individual, might for right, violence for peace, and government by the few for government by the many conflicts with the values held by most people and most nations in the twentieth century. The record of violence and brutality built up by fascist leaders during the Second World War is too well known and too repugnant to win universal support.

The fact that fascism does not now exist in any powerful nation or that only small fascist organizations are found in major countries does not mean that fascism is no longer a danger. Fascism, intolerance, disregard for law and order, and the love of militarism did not disappear with the defeat of the Axis countries in World War II. Our best protection against any totalitarianism—communist or fascist—is the free marketplace of ideas as well as of products.

Part B
What Economic System? The Reality

Having examined the models of the three major competitors of capitalism, we are now ready to analyze the basic principles of these systems. When we speak to an adherent of any one of these systems, he will tend to exaggerate the differences among them. If, however, we can remove ourselves from the emotional involvement often associated with a discussion of isms, we can more clearly identify the real issues.

The Political and Economic Spectra

Every scientific discipline seeks to organize knowledge in such a way that it can be handled easily. Criteria are drawn up so that groups of ideas, bodies of knowledge, and systems may be categorized. When the political scientist classifies a country's political system as a democracy or an oligarchy, he has taken a number of characteristics into consideration and sees which of these categories comes closest to describing the political state he is examining. The economist does the same thing in trying to classify a nation's economic system. Actually, no nation's system, political or economic, conforms exactly to the model.

The basic issue, both politically and economically, is the degree of freedom allowed to the individual. In Figure 3–1 we can see the complete political spectrum as it moves from left to right. At the extreme left we see the complete freedom of the individual with the absence of any government coercion. Such a condition, the absence of government, is called "anarchism." At the extreme right the citizen has surrendered all his freedom to a government which has total control over every aspect of his life—totalitarianism. Absolute monarchy is listed on the extreme right because it refers to rule by one person. Constitutional monarchy, as in Britain, can be just as liberal as other democracies because the constitution guarantees the rights of the people. In an oligarchy the few would rule, whereas in a democracy rule is by the many. The political spectrum defines the extent of personal freedom the citizen has in relationship to government authority.

In Figure 3–2 we see the economic spectrum. Here the difference lies in who decides the answers to the basic economic questions of *What? How?* and *For Whom?* On the right side of the spectrum the consumer is king. His decisions, expressed by his purchases, and the response of private enterprise, expressed by supply, determine the use of our resources. It is the market mechanism at work. Laissez-faire,

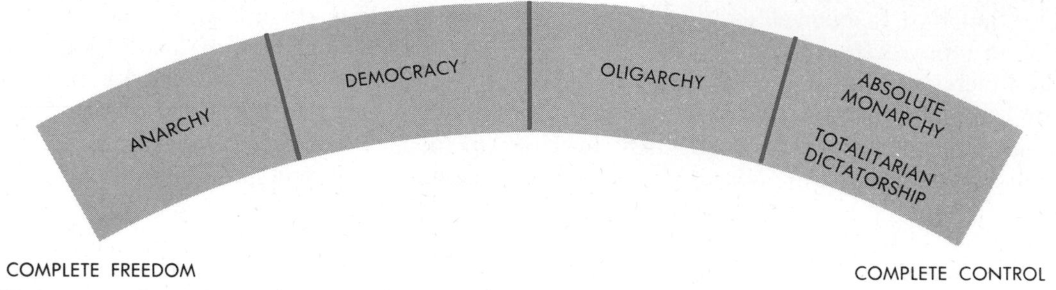

FIGURE 3–1 The Political Spectrum

Anarchy offers the individual citizen complete freedom with no government coercion. Totalitarianism subordinates the individual completely to the good of the state.

or classical capitalism, keeps the government out of decision making as much as possible.

Mixed capitalism, sometimes called *welfare capitalism,* favors decisions by the consumers but allows for some central planning. As we move toward the left from mixed socialism to socialism to communism, central planning increases and the reliance on the market mechanism declines. At the extreme left we see total central planning, where government makes almost all the decisions and consumer choices are given little attention.

Our economic spectrum is not complete unless we include the ownership of wealth. In Figure 3–3 we see complete private ownership on one side and complete collective ownership on the other. Although no countries have either of these extremes, classical capitalism calls for a maximum of private ownership and communism calls for a maximum of collective ownership, particularly of capital goods. Again we see the different degrees of stress on ownership of wealth given by mixed capitalism, mixed socialism, and socialism.

Tying the Political and Economic Spectra Together

When we try to determine where to place a particular nation on the two spectra with freedom as one of the criteria, we must consider both its political and economic systems. Although the British La-

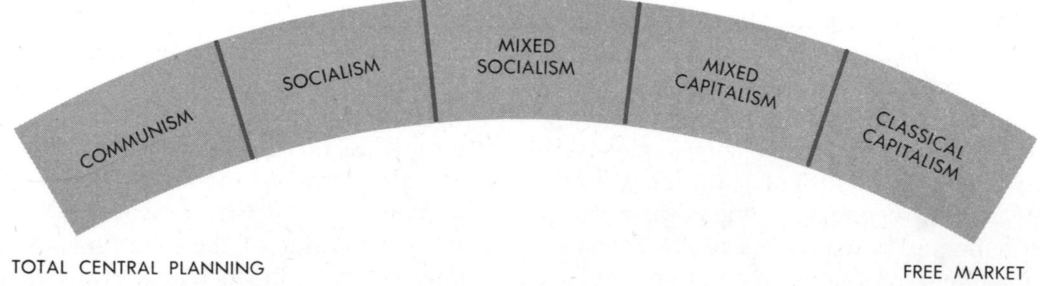

FIGURE 3–2 The Economic Spectrum

Classical capitalism makes the consumer king and the regulator of the entire market. Communism (before the state withers away) calls for the greatest amount of central planning with very little consumer sovereignty.

FIGURE 3–3 The Economic Spectrum of the Ownership of Wealth

Classical capitalism calls for a maximum of private ownership, whereas communism calls for a maximum of collective ownership.

bor party places great emphasis on central planning and believes in nationalizing some of its nation's basic industries, it can do these things only with the approval of the British electorate and with just compensation to owners whose private property is lost to collective ownership. No such limits are placed on the Soviet government.

Either democracy or totalitarianism as a political system can exist with either private or collective ownership. The Fascists in Italy and the Nazis in Germany allowed private ownership of even the basic industries, but there was little freedom, even for the owners of business. Conversely, democracy can be practiced in nations, such as our own, that rely primarily on the market mechanism for the allocation of resources, or in nations that have a great deal of central planning, such as Sweden.

Mixed Economic Systems

No major country today has wholly private ownership or collective ownership of property. No economy relies entirely on the market mechanism or on central planning for deciding the *What, How,* and *For Whom.* We may classify nations as capitalist, socialist, communist, or fascist, but even within each category there are substantial differences. The "mixture" in Israel is different from the "mixture" in New Zealand; the "mixture" in Yugoslavia differs from that in the U.S.S.R.

Instead of analyzing a nation's economic system in terms of isms, we might more appropriately inquire what part of the economy is governed by a free market and what part by central planning. When the problem is viewed in this way, we recognize that important differences exist not merely between countries but within countries. In the last 40 years one of the major differences between our Republican and Democratic parties has been the extent to which each advocated central planning by the federal government. The Republican party has generally resisted the increase in central planning and has favored reliance on the market mechanism. It has also resisted increasing collective ownership. The Democrats have gone far in supporting central planning and government ownership. These differences between parties have become less clear in the last few years, particularly after Nixon's recent wage–price freeze.

Economic Systems Evolve

Advocates of a particular economic system may preach and work to have their system take the place of what exists, but the chances of installing a completely new economic system are remote. Economic systems grow slowly, and only occasionally are changes speeded up. Under Roosevelt's New Deal policies and Labor party policies between 1945 and 1951 in Britain, significant changes occurred. In both instances the amount of central planning was accelerated. However, when opposition parties came to power, there were no great withdrawals from the major changes that had taken place. Modifications were on emphasis and degree rather than on kind.

When the Communists took control in Russia in November of 1917, they tried to replace the existing system with pure communism. Their attempt was not successful. Realizing the need for compromise, Lenin in 1921 launched the New Economic Policy (NEP), which combined elements of both communism and capitalism. For the next seven years limited private ownership and the profit motive were allowed to exist side by side with collective ownership. Gradually, central planning and collective ownership were increased, and by 1928 Stalin restored solely communist principles.

Recent Changes

Each of the political-economic systems we have considered has changed from the model as originally conceived. The reality of the present may represent a major departure from past theory. In each system recent changes have indicated new directions of development.

Trend of the American Economy

Our nation's economy today is a far cry from what the classical economists envisioned. In Chapters 9 and 10 we will learn about the changes in size and influence of our various levels of government. Today more than one fourth of the market value of all the production in the United States, called the *gross national product* (GNP), is spent by our local, state, and national governments. Additional services, particularly in health, welfare, education, and the broad field of research, are being added regularly. Other government services of long standing are being expanded rapidly. Government influence over economic groups—including labor, business, and professional groups—is being extended. Economic decisions are being made less often by individual consumers than previously, and planning is increasing at all levels of government.

Are we losing our freedom and becoming totalitarian? Most social scientists would answer with a resounding *no!* They believe that what we have done is to transfer some of our decision making as consumers to decision making as citizens. Increased specialization and interdependence have forced us, sometimes reluctantly, to give up our individual sovereignty for the common good. So long as we have a free marketplace to learn the facts and evaluate ideas, and so long as we have the power through elections to reverse the trend, we need not fear the future.

In spite of the trend toward central planning, the private sector of our economy is still almost three times as large as the public sector. Most of our economic decisions are still made by individual consumers and producers, and we continue to rely on the market mechanism to allocate most of our scarce resources. We may properly call our nation's economic system one of mixed capitalism.

Trend of the Soviet Economy

Since Stalin's death in 1953, trends in the

Soviet Union have indicated a decrease in centralized planning. Still, each year the State Planning Commission, known as the "Gosplan," makes the basic economic decisions. It does so for both short and long term and with close cooperation with party leaders. In this way economic planning reflects political decisions. Great attention is paid today to the setting of quotas and to the suggestions of regional councils and even plant managers. Although consumers appear to have relative freedom in deciding their own purchases, most consumer prices are determined not by supply and demand but by the state. If more overcoats than jackets are made, and if consumers want more jackets, a tax is placed on the jackets to discourage their purchase. The state also permits the sale of certain food products—those grown by farmers on their own time and on specially designated land—in a free market, very similar to our own.

Most Soviet workers are free to work where they wish, although some of them are required to work on special projects. Wide differences are found in the pay scale of Soviet workers, probably greater than in our own country. Scientists, plant managers, and skilled technicians have the highest incomes. The Soviet Union has adopted capitalistic incentive plans by paying *piece rates* (wages determined by output) and by offering various kinds of bonuses to managers who meet or exceed their production quotas.

A close check is maintained over the economy by the State Control Commission and the Gosbank, which handles all banking in the Soviet Union. The Gosbank works closely with the central planners, providing funds according to plan requirements. As you know, in our country the market mechanism determines the allocation of capital.

In the 1960's, first under Khrushchev and later under Brezhnev and Kosygin, the obsession with meeting production quotas and concentrating on heavy industry without regard to consumer demand changed in degree, if not in kind. Partially through the process of opening up channels for criticism (which pointed up gross inefficiencies in the system) and partially through the analysis and efforts of Y. Liberman, a Soviet professor of economics, the use of market research, of supply and demand for price adjustments, and the decentralization for managerial decisions spread to many segments of the economy. Studies revealed that, because prices and wages were fixed by a complex bureaucracy, resources were not being allocated to where they were most productive and most needed. Managers frequently operated well below their plant's capacity so as to escape the pressures of having their quotas raised regularly. Expenditures for capital investment were made without consideration to what they would yield if used in some other way. Overproduction of some parts in a truck and underproduction in others resulted in fewer trucks. Production of too many large suits and too few small suits may have filled production quotas but satisfied too few consumers. Poor quality control left unsold merchandise on counters. Rising incomes made the Soviet consumers somewhat more selective and they delayed their purchases.

Libermanism

A modified profit system was introduced in which the producing unit was charged for the materials and labor used as well as the Gosbank. Cooperation between the producer and retailer to determine consumer wants was encouraged and sales could be used to bring supply and demand into balance. The entire production process was recorded through an accounting system and profits could be determined.

Early experiments proved to be so successful in increasing efficiency and production that the plan spread to more than 12,000 enterprises in 1970. Advertising, salesmen, a bonus system, and installment buying have been used to give the Soviet Union a western flavor. Czechoslovakia and Yugoslavia have moved in this direction even faster than the U.S.S.R.

It is possible that as the Soviet economy matures and accumulates enough capital to provide a much higher standard of living for its citizens, the trend toward greater freedom may be accelerated. However, central planning and government ownership remain the key to that economic system.

Communism in China differs significantly from that in the Soviet Union. It would be unwise to attempt a comparison, since the Soviet Union is already an industrialized nation whereas China is only beginning to make the transition from an agricultural economy. Our discussion of communism is based on the present Soviet system. The recent opening up of China to American scholars may give us a more accurate picture of her economy.

Trend of Socialism

Because early socialists were discontented with great inequality of wealth, one of their major objectives was achieving greater equality in the distribution of returns from production. They hoped to accomplish this by nationalizing the means of production so that profits, the alleged cause of inequality, could be shared by everyone. They also sought to provide for all a minimum standard of living as a means to economic and social security.

As we have seen, these objectives are no longer the goals of socialists exclusively. Such goals have in fact become a reality, or close to a reality, in many of the more affluent nations. Mixed capitalism—the economic doctrine of many political parties in the Western world—has accepted many of these same objectives, but it has not considered it either desirable or necessary to do so by nationalizing industry. Social legislation providing for the poorest members of society has been passed by a Conservative government in Britain and by both Republican and Democratic administrations in the United States. Socialist nations have, like our own, used the progressive income tax and the inheritance tax to achieve greater economic equality. Greater emphasis on increasing productivity and raising the GNP so that even the smallest individual share will provide a decent living standard has replaced the desire to make the distribution of wealth more nearly equal.

Because of changes in socialism itself and in other systems, the old socialist slogans have lost some of their appeal. When the British Labor party came to power toward the end of 1964, its leader, Prime Minister Harold Wilson, sounded more like the late President Kennedy or President Johnson than the head of a party dedicated to socialism. Apart from advocating the nationalization of the steel industry, the only significant difference claimed by the Labor leaders was that they could govern better.

Conclusion

What conclusion does our study of economic systems lead us to? Economic models are important because they supply the guidelines for answering the big economic questions. They designate the direction in which a society and its people think they should be moving. However, as we have seen, there is a difference between the theory and the reality of economic systems. The basic difference between systems is largely a choice between using the market mechanism, with its emphasis on freedom and the individual, and using central planning, with its emphasis on collective decisions and collective ownership. Totalitarianism and democracy can exist with either private ownership or collective ownership.

Economic systems evolve over a period of time. Capitalistic systems are using more central planning, and communist countries are experimenting with the market mechanism. British socialism has varied according to political climate, elections, and changing economic circumstances.

What we as citizens of a democracy must remember is that we have the power and responsibility to guide our economic system in the direction we believe will best accomplish our individual and national goals. It would be unfortunate if we failed, either through ignorance or through irresponsibility, to realize the benefits of our democratic heritage.

Part C
The Problem: Progress or Weakness in the Soviet Economy?

There can be little doubt that the Soviet Union represents a distinct economic threat to the United States. Premier Khrushchev made an open challenge in 1957, calling it economic war. He claimed that the Soviet Union would soon surpass the United States in production and boasted that the Russians would "bury" us. Soviet achievements in science and technology have added substance to his claims. The underdeveloped countries of the world are aware of this challenge. Since many of them are not as yet committed to either system, they are watching the progress of the two competing systems.

In trying to evaluate Soviet economic progress, we must be aware of certain problems. We must not assume that the goals of our mixed capitalistic system are the same as those of the Soviet system. We must recognize that resources, both human and natural, are not the same. Lastly, we are not certain about the accuracy of Soviet figures. In some instances errors in comparison are made because methods and techniques in compiling statistics differ; in other instances no data are available.

The Remarkable Progress of the Soviet Economy

In the last 50 years the Soviet Union has been transformed from a largely preindustrial, feudally structured nation to the second largest industrial power in the world. It has introduced central economic planning on a scale never before attempted; its growth in production is unquestioned. Since recovering from the effects of World War II, the Soviet economic growth rate has been remarkable—about 6 percent yearly average by Soviet estimates and about 5 percent by independent Western calculations. This compares to a growth rate of less than 4 percent for the same period in the United States.

In spite of many claims that Soviet production is inefficient, most of her industrial expansion must be attributed to increases in output per worker, since the labor force has increased less rapidly than production.

Although most experts put the Soviet GNP at about one half of ours, this comparison is not a true measure of the relative economic strength of the two nations. In order for the nation to achieve such a high rate of growth, the Soviet citizen has had to forgo many consumer goods. The standard of living of the Russian people is improving, but it has gained at a slower rate than parts of the economy designated by Soviet leaders as essential. Although Soviet military power may not equal our own, it is strong enough to pose a real threat to the free world.

Any underdeveloped country wishing to become highly industrialized must sacrifice current consumption for capital investment. This is exactly what the Soviet leaders have done. Consumption as a percentage of GNP is lower in the Soviet Union than in the United States, but capital investment is far greater. It is from this additional capital investment that increased productive capacity is obtained.

Differences between the two systems in the productive capacity of heavy industry are far less than the differences in GNP would seem to indicate. In the production of new machine tools the U.S.S.R. is ahead of the United States. In steel, coal, and electricity the gap has already been closed or is being closed. The increase in the productive capacities of these basic industries may soon be reflected in higher living standards for the Russian people.

There is no doubt that borrowing from the advanced technology of Western nations has helped the Soviet Union to progress. However, she has developed a large number—and in some fields such as engineering, a greater number than our own—of highly trained specialists in the sciences, engineering, and managerial operations who provide new knowledge and techniques to sustain continuing development. In addition, the Soviet economy has been almost "depression-proof." Keeping the economy geared to full employment has eliminated the waste of resources that Western nations experience when, during a recession, they have idle labor and unused productive capacity.

Weaknesses in the Soviet Economy

If the Soviet economy is to achieve its objective of overtaking that of the United States, its economic growth rate must be twice our own. In other words, since our GNP is about twice that of the Soviets, only if their growth rate is twice the size of our own rate can they increase their total GNP as much as we do. An increase of $50 billion of GNP in the Soviet Union represents about a 10 percent gain, whereas an equal increase in our nation's GNP would be at the rate of less than 5 percent.

There is no reason to believe that the Soviet Union will be able to sustain a high growth rate. The 1960's saw fluctuations in her economic growth from below 3 percent to 8 percent. In 1962 and 1963 the American economy had higher rates of

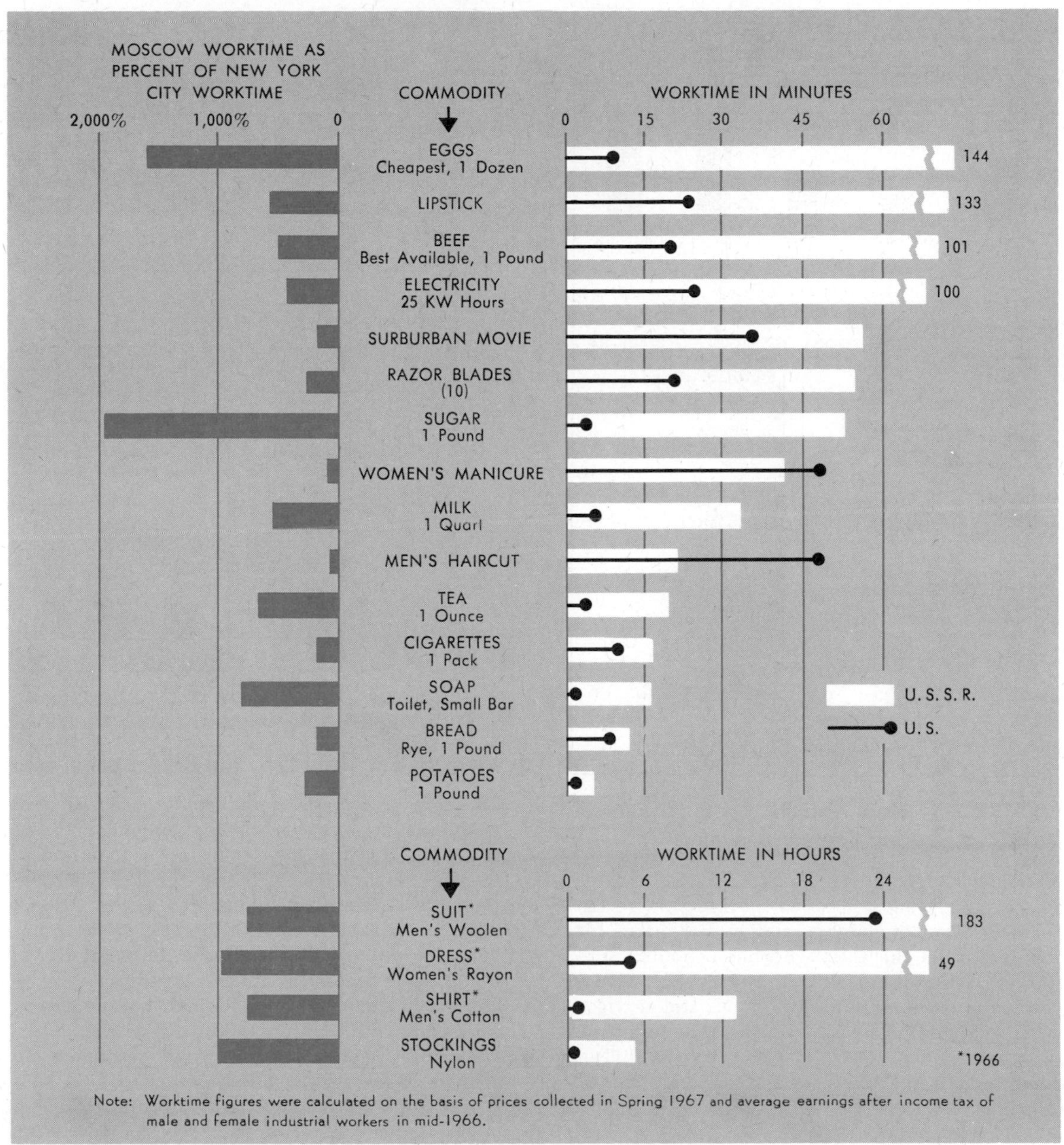

FIGURE 3–4 Worktime Required to Buy Selected Commodities and Services in Moscow and in New York City, 1967

SOURCE: National Industrial Conference Board, *Road Maps of Industry*, No. 1607.

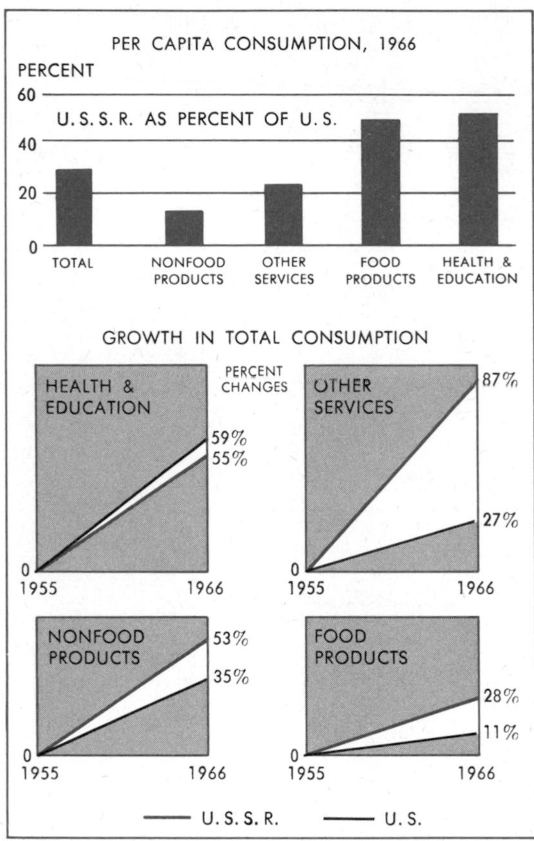

FIGURE 3–5 How Well Off Are the American and Soviet Consumers?

Although the level of welfare of the average Soviet citizen has improved markedly in recent years, it has not gained relative to that of his counterpart in the U.S., who has benefited substantially from the economic boom of the 1960's. Per capita consumption of all goods and services in the U.S. and in the U.S.S.R. increased almost 5 percent between 1964 and 1966. SOURCE: National Industrial Conference Board, *Road Maps of Industry,* No. 1607.

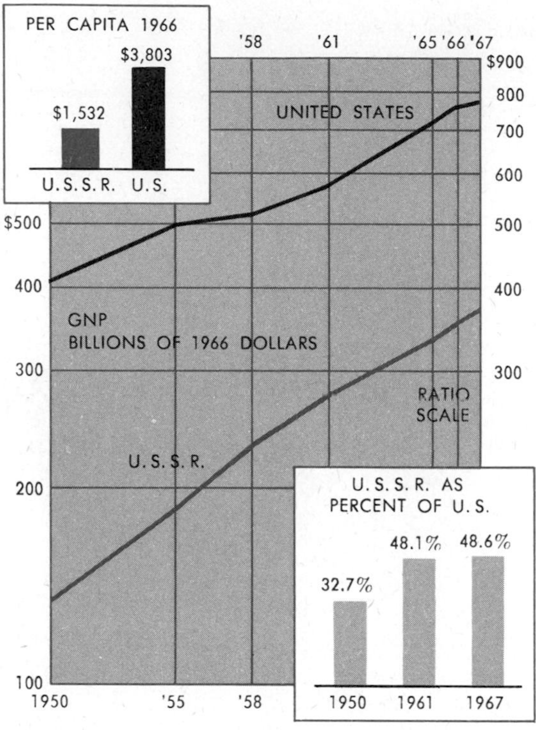

FIGURE 3–6 The U.S. and Soviet Economies

The rate of growth of the Soviet economy has been slowing, but year-to-year percent increases in output continue to exceed those of output in the U.S. Hence, real GNP in the U.S.S.R. continues to increase relative to that in the U.S., although less rapidly than in the 1950's. There has been a relative decline, however, in the ability of the Soviet Union to utilize its resources efficiently. In the 1960's, the U.S.S.R. had depended more than the U.S. on additions to its active labor force and to its plant and equipment to achieve increases in output. Agriculture continues to play a far larger and more critical role in the Soviet Union than in the U.S.; therefore, bad or good crop years affect U.S.S.R. economic growth much more. SOURCE: National Industrial Conference Board, *Road Maps of Industry,* No. 1608.

growth than the Soviet Union and in absolute rather than percentage growth, only our recession years saw the U.S. fall behind. The boast that the Soviet Union would catch up to the United States in 1970 seems empty now.

The earlier spectacular growth rate of the U.S.S.R. was accomplished at such a great sacrifice to the Soviet people that their leaders now may be changing the emphasis of production. Consumer goods seem to be receiving a higher priority than previously, and greater concern for quality may reflect consumer resistance to inferior merchandise.

There is some evidence that the best and most accessible natural resources are being depleted and that in the future such resources will be difficult and costly to obtain. It is possible that the law of diminishing returns will soon be setting in for both natural resources and technological improvements.

The modifications that have been and continue to be made in the Soviet economic system indicate that central planning may be less efficient in a maturing industrial society. Whereas high conformity of products and production methods may be satisfactory in a society that is forcing industrialization, it is less acceptable when people already have a subsistence level of living and look for something better.

Finally, the noneconomic consequences of forced industrialization and collectivization required coercion and subjection of millions of people. Although Soviet leaders have justified such ruthlessness as a means to an end—that the Soviet Union has become the second industrial power in the world—it seems unlikely that such values would ever be acceptable to people living in political democracies.

Considering an Answer

The comparison of a variety of economic systems helps to clarify the strengths and weaknesses of each one. Points of likeness and difference among systems provide a basis for evaluation and give us a more objective basis for analyzing the working of our own system. Distinguishing between economic and political aspects of these systems gives an added dimension to our analysis. Finally, making such comparisons increases our awareness of our own values as individuals and as citizens.

The following questions will guide you in evaluating Soviet economic progress:

1. What criteria are most important to you as consumer, producer, and citizen in evaluating an economy? How does Soviet progress measure up to these criteria?
2. Are the factors responsible for economic growth the same at all stages of development? What changes in these factors have taken place in the course of development in the U.S.S.R.?
3. Are the recent changes in performance trends of the Soviet and American economies likely to be temporary or permanent? Why?
4. How do your personal preferences and your own sense of values influence your evaluation and answers to the problem?

REVIEW: THE HIGHLIGHTS OF THE CHAPTER

1. The three major economic systems competing with capitalism are socialism, communism, and fascism. Each system has reasons for rejecting the other models and for choosing its own way of answering the basic economic questions.

2. Socialism rejects production for profit and private ownership of the means of production. In their place, it puts collective ownership and production for need. It prefers central planning to the free market in economic decision making. Unlike communism it can live side by side with capitalism and prefers to nationalize industry gradually through education and the ballot box. There are many forms of socialism.
3. Marx, the father of communism, believed that all history can be explained as a series of class struggles between those who own the means of production and those who seek power. Communists believe that capitalism can be overcome only by revolution. They envision society as moving into higher stages, eventually attaining communism. When that occurs, production will be so great that payment will be according to need. Much of what Marx predicted has failed to materialize.
4. Fascism, as contrasted with communism, has developed in countries already industrialized with limited experience in political democracy. Like capitalism, it allows private ownership, but it substitutes central planning for the free market. Like communism, it is a totalitarian system embracing every aspect of life; the individual is completely subservient to the state. It advocates emotionalism, racism, violence, and a regimented society.
5. No nation falls completely into any one of these three systems. The political spectrum extends from complete freedom for the individual citizen in his relation to the state to complete control by government. The economic spectra extend from a free market to total central planning and from complete private ownership to total collective ownership.
6. Systems in most countries are mixed, with differences existing within countries as well as between them. Changes in these systems tend to evolve gradually.
7. The trend in the United States has been toward more central planning; in the Soviet Union, it has been toward limited experimentation in the use of the market; and in socialist countries, it has been toward less insistence on nationalization.
8. The economic growth of the Soviet Union has posed a real challenge to the American economy. Underdeveloped countries are watching with interest the progress of the rival systems.

IN CONCLUSION: SOME AIDS TO UNDERSTANDING

Terms for Review

socialism
nationalization
scientific socialism
syndicalism
welfare capitalism
social legislation

proletariat
revisionism
utopian socialism
Christian socialism
anarchism
fascism

totalitarianism
collective ownership
communism
surplus value
salariat

Names to Know

Robert Owen
Karl Marx
Friedrich Engels
Charles Fourier
Y. Liberman
Fabian Society
Das Kapital
Communist Manifesto
Gosbank

Questions for Review

1. In considering isms, we have found close parallels between economic and political philosophies.
   (a) Explain the idea "Although there are close ties between economic and political systems, the characteristics of the two kinds of systems are not necessarily the same."
   (b) What questions does each kind of system attempt to answer?
2. Select a national economy that closely approximates each economic theory. To what extent does actual practice in each country conform to theory? Why are many of these countries unable to adhere strictly to the theories they espouse?
3. Explain socialism's appeal in other parts of the world. Why have some Americans supported socialism at various times in our history?
4. There are several variations of socialist economic philosophy. Identify four different versions and describe the ways in which they differ from one another.
5. Identify the major economic ideas set forth by Karl Marx.
   (a) What are the four stages in the development of communism from capitalism?
   (b) What proof exists that some of these stages have not fully materialized?
6. What are the essential differences in the methodology to be used by socialists and communists in achieving their goals? Illustrate these differences by referring to specific countries or historical events.
7. Explain the meaning of the following statements about fascism and evaluate their general truth:
   (a) Economically, fascism is the wedding of capitalist and communist planning.
   (b) Previous failures of fascism may not prevent its recurrence in today's troubled world filled with hungry people.
8. Explain the meaning of each of these statements:
   (a) "Communist countries are using capitalist ideas, capitalist countries are using central planning, and socialists are marking time."
   (b) "The particular conditions within each nation determine the degree of political and economic control exercised there."

Additional Questions and Problems

1. Compare one of the communities established by the utopian socialists with a modern youth commune.
2. Compare and contrast the economies of Sweden ("the middle way"), India, and Great Britain under the Labor government. How are they similar? How and why do they differ? Consider the success of each in terms of basic economic goals.
3. The Roosevelt New Deal has been called the "road to socialism" and the "savior of American capitalism." List and explain the arguments supporting each point of view.

4. Compare the ideas on the role of government expressed by F. A. Hayek in his *Road to Serfdom* with J. K. Galbraith's theories in *American Capitalism: The Concept of Countervailing Power.*
5. Discuss the statement "The political changeover in the U.S.S.R. in 1964 may have had its origin in the economic failure of the Khrushchev regime."

SELECTED READINGS

Campbell, Robert W. *Soviet Economic Power: Its Organization, Growth, and Challenge.* Boston: Houghton Mifflin Co., 1966. (Also available in paperback edition from the same publisher.)

Ebenstein, William. *Today's Isms: Communism, Fascism, Socialism, Capitalism.* Englewood Cliffs, N.J.: Prentice-Hall, 1967.

Grossman, Gregory. *Economic Systems.* Englewood Cliffs, N.J.: Prentice-Hall, 1966.

Schumpeter, Joseph A. *Capitalism, Socialism and Democracy.* New York: Harper and Row, 1962.

Schwartz, Harry. *An Introduction to the Soviet Economy.* Columbus, Ohio: Charles E. Merrill Publishing Co., 1968.

Spulber, Nicolas. *The Soviet Economy, Structure, Principles, and Problems.* New York: W. W. Norton & Co., 1969.

Turgeon, Lynn. *The Contrasting Economies.* Boston: Allyn and Bacon, 1963.

Wilcox, Clair, and others. *Economies of the World Today: Their Organization, Development, and Performance.* New York: Harcourt, Brace & World, 1966.

UNIT II

THE FACTORS RESPONSIBLE FOR PRODUCTION

Business Enterprise 4

THE AUTHORS' NOTE TO THE STUDENT

The focus of Unit II is on *microeconomics,* the study of individual units of the economy. Unit III, in turn, will deal with *macroeconomics,* the study of the nation's economy as a whole. Actually, our study of microeconomics began in Chapter 2 with an analysis of how demand and supply determine price. It continues in this unit with a consideration of how businesses maximize their profits and of the factors in the economy that are responsible for production.

In a *private enterprise* economy the decisions on what and how to produce are determined mainly by businessmen. Businessmen ascertain the probable trend of consumer wants and then proceed to organize the factors of production in order to satisfy these wants. Their motivation is profit; and if their decisions on the *What* and the *How* are correct, they will probably do well.

American businesses vary in size, organization, and product according to the many diverse needs of the consumer. Businesses are organized as single proprietorships, partnerships, or corporations, each having certain advantages and limitations. The Industrial Revolution, with its change in the methods of production, gave an impetus to the modern corporation. It also led to business combinations that changed the pattern of competition away from the classical model. Government has responded to this change by trying to keep competition as close to the original model as possible. Where competition has been impractical, the consumer has been protected by government regulation of business.

A STUDENT'S NOTE TO THE STUDENT

This chapter is very easy to follow, partly because of the example of going into business. It clarifies a number of terms and concepts and poses some interesting problems on how a businessman can raise the necessary money to start in business and later expand.

I found the brief discussion of the stock market most interesting even though our "prof" told us this was not economics. We managed to keep him on this subject by asking questions for the whole period.

Watch out when you use the word investment. The economist uses it differently than the businessman. Just remember, when you buy stock it's a transfer payment, not an investment. Strange!

Part A
Characteristics of Business Enterprise

Production in the United States

A primary concern that we, as individuals, have with economics lies in deciding how well we can afford to live. If we are to achieve a high *standard of living,* it is necessary that the production of goods and services be maintained at a high level. In 1971 the GNP was more than $1 trillion. This is equal to almost one third of the value of all the world's production. This achievement is even more remarkable when you consider that it was actually carried out by only one sixteenth of the world's population. Most of this production came from America's businesses.

The Role of Business

You will recall from the preceding chapters that the classical model calls for businessmen to go to the market for goods and services to find out what consumers want and then, spurred on by the profit motive, go to the market for the factors of production in order to produce the goods. About three fourths of the value of the total GNP resulted from the decisions made by private enterprise. Although the decisions on the remainder of our production were determined by governments at the local, state, and national levels, most of this production came from business enterprise. Our schools, our weapons of defense, and most of the purchased items in government budgets were produced by business. Throughout our history we have remained fairly consistent in favoring private enterprise over government enterprise regarding the *What* and the *How* of production.

Variety of Business Enterprises

With almost 12 million separate businesses in our country their size and organization vary greatly. The man who sells popcorn, ice cream, and hot dogs from his cart is in business, although his total sales may amount to only a few thousand dollars a year. In contrast, we have giant corporations that do more business than the value of all goods and services produced in many countries. In 1969 General Motors sold more goods and services—over $24 billion worth—than the total combined production of Greece, Ireland, Norway, and Portugal.

Both the street vendor and General Motors are producing what they think their customers want. They are both in business to make as large a profit as they can; they both must take risks, invest money, and organize the factors of production. While they have much in common, they are organized quite differently. In order to get a better understanding of business and the part that the form of organization of a business plays, we will take a hypothetical venture into business ourselves.

Starting a Business

Our chief purpose in going into business is to make a profit. This is done by supplying to consumers something they want but do not have, or something better than what they have. If there are mice but no mousetraps, build a trap. If there is a mousetrap, build a better or cheaper one.

What to Produce

First we shall call a meeting to discuss the

What. After listening to many suggestions, all of which prove unsatisfactory for one reason or another, we finally hit upon the idea for an adult game based upon urban planning. According to the latest toy trade journals, the demand has been growing for decision-making games for mature people. The game of "Monopoly" caught on years ago. A more sophisticated game should catch the educated public's interest now. Let's give it a try! After organizing ourselves into a business firm, sometimes called an enterprise, we adopt the name "Build-a-City." As the organizers of the business we are known as entrepreneurs or, more simply, managers.

How to Produce

We are now ready to consider means of producing—the *How* of business enterprise. Our responsibility is to collect the other factors of production and assemble them in the right amount, at the right time, and in the right place.

Adults are more likely to pay a higher price for a game for themselves than for their children because they reason it will be used more often over a longer period of time. We will use wooden models and will package the game in a wooden box. This being the case, the major natural resource we need is lumber. There is a mill nearby, but it is presently selling all the lumber it produces. If we are to divert the wood from its present use to our business, we must offer a slightly higher price than the present market price. We have increased the demand, but the supply of materials on hand remains the same.

In the labor market we may attract workers by offering them jobs that will pay at least as much as, if not more than, they are currently earning. However, if there is unemployment in the area—if the supply of workers is greater than the demand—labor costs may be low, and we may hire workers at the going market rate.

We will also need machinery and a factory. Usually, the more and better the machinery available to workers, the more they can produce. Because machinery is not used to satisfy the consumer's needs but rather to make the goods that the consumer wants, it is called a *capital good* or a *producer good.* Goods used directly by the consumer to satisfy his needs are called *consumer goods.*

To buy machinery and a building we obviously need money. Money, when it is used by business to buy the things needed in production, is called capital. When people ask us, "How much capital do you have?" they are not referring to the actual number of machines. They mean how much money we have for man-made instruments of production, that is, machines, buildings, and goods made by others that are necessary for production.

Raising Capital

At a meeting to discuss the cost of equipment we soon discover that we do not have enough capital. The decision is made to go to a commercial bank to see if the officials will lend us the amount of money we need. A major function of commercial banks is to provide short-term capital to businesses. If we obtain a loan, we will have to pay a price for its use, *interest.* Interest is expressed as a rate in percentage. If we borrow $100,000 at 6 percent interest for one year, it means that we pay $6,000 for the money we borrow. Although interest is paid for the money borrowed, in the long run it is for the equipment and other things needed for our business.

Money is used in many other ways in

the marketplace. The money we pay for the wood from the forest (natural resources) is called *rent,* and the money we pay our workers is called *wages.* We, the entrepreneurs, receive the money that is left, the *profits.* Payments to each of the factors of production are subject, at least in part, to supply and demand. Each of these factors of production will be discussed more fully in succeeding chapters.

Part B
Forms of Business Organization

Although we have proceeded with the initial steps in starting a business, we have neglected to answer one of the first and most important questions facing any businessman. What kind of business organization shall we choose? There are three forms of organization from which to select: a *single proprietorship,* a *partnership,* and a *corporation.* Since each form has particular advantages and disadvantages, our choice can best be made after an examination of each form.

Single Proprietorship

To illustrate the various forms of organization possible, let us suppose that you alone are the one who thought of the idea of producing "Build-a-City" sets and want to start a company by yourself. Such a business is classified as a single proprietorship, the most common type of business and the easiest to organize. Almost 80 percent of all firms use this form. You, as owner, are the boss, and need not consult with others in making your business decisions. You cannot be fired. If you fail, it will be your own fault. On the other hand, if there is a profit you will receive it all—a great incentive. Another advantage is that you do not have to pay a corporation income tax.

At first you may be happy to be the sole owner of a business. However, you soon recognize that there are serious drawbacks to such an organization. If your business is like many single proprietorships, you are likely to be bothered by a shortage of cash. This shortage may not be caused by incompetence or carelessness. Deficits are most likely to occur when you attempt to meet the constant expenditures of the business. If business had been bad, this would be easy to understand. Actually, business has been almost too good. You have had so many requests for "Build-a-City" sets that in order to meet this de-

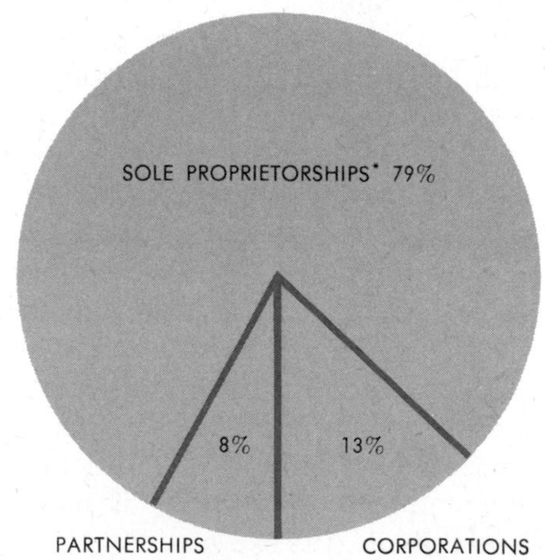

FIGURE 4–1 Legal Organization of Business Population in Percent

SOURCE: U.S. Department of Commerce.

mand, you have had to employ more of the factors of production. In addition, your financial situation has been hurt because the merchants buying your sets have been slow in paying their bills. You might solve your problem by enlarging your factory, buying a few more machines, and hiring additional men. This would allow you to increase the size of your business sufficiently to meet the demand. If only you had more capital!

As you consider enlarging your business, you may become aware of another disadvantage of the single proprietorship. It is nice to be your own boss, but it also means that all the responsibility is on your shoulders. You never seem to have any free time and are required to be a specialist in such diverse activities as buying, producing, and merchandising. You may hire a managerial assistant to help share your responsibilities, but his interest in the business is not as personal as if he were an owner. Two additional disadvantages,

TABLE 4–1 Comparison of Forms of Business Organization

	Single Proprietorship	Partnership	Corporation
Ease of organization	Easiest	Moderately difficult	Most difficult
Capital generally available for operation	Least	Intermediate	Most (best able to raise capital)
Responsibility	Centered in one person	Spread among partners	Policy set by directors; president supervises day-to-day operation
Incentive to succeed	Centered in one person	Spread among partners	Spread among many people
Flexibility	Greatest	Intermediate	Least
Ability to perform varied functions (production or purchasing, accounting, selling, etc.)	Dependent on one individual's versatility	Dependent on capabilities of two or more individuals	Best able to employ individuals with different capabilities
Possibility of conflict among those in control	None	Most prone to conflict, especially if partners have equal interest in business	Chain of command reduces internal conflict; wide ownership minimizes disagreement
Taxation	No corporate income tax	No corporate income tax	Corporate income tax
Distribution of profits or losses	All to proprietor	Distributed to partners in accordance with terms of partnership agreement	Profits retained or to stockholders as dividends; losses reduce price of stock
Liability for debts in event of failure	Unlimited	Unlimited, but spread among partners	Limited to each stockholder's investment
Length of life	Limited by one individual's life span (or until he goes out of business)	Limited (partnership is reorganized upon death or withdrawal of any partner)	Unlimited (with ownership of shares readily transferable)

After studying this table, discuss which form of organization would be best for our "Build-a-City" company. Remember that there is no single right answer. Depending on the circumstances, however, some answers will be better than others. Be sure that you consider all possibilities before you make your decision.

unlimited liability and limited life, which apply to both proprietorships and partnerships, will be considered in connection with partnerships. It occurs to you that, although a partnership also has disadvantages, perhaps it would be a better form of organization for your purposes.

Partnership

What your business needs, if it is to expand more quickly, is additional capital and perhaps additional talent. As the present owner, you might interest several people in investing their money in your business and becoming partners. A partnership might also relieve you of some of the responsibilities, and the skills of several others might be pooled to help the business develop. Like a single proprietorship, a partnership does not have to pay a corporate income tax. This is a tax which is paid to the national government on the profits of the corporation. It is in addition to the tax you pay on the income you draw from the company.

Along with their advantages, partnerships have problems. Although partners will share the profits according to a prearranged plan, you are not sure that each partner will devote his fair share of time and effort to the business. Partners do not always agree on methods and policies to be used in operating a business.

Once the decision to form a partnership is made, a competent attorney will draw up the articles of partnership. This is a necessary legal document, a *contract,* which will specify the rights and duties of all partners. With all the effort you have put into the business, you do not want to leave anything to chance.

About 8 percent of all firms in our country are partnerships. Of these, small businesses account for the largest number. Other than some professional firms—such as law, investment, accounting, and medical partnerships—the million- and multi-million-dollar firms stay away from both the proprietorship and partnership.

There are two other serious drawbacks, mentioned under proprietorships, which you must consider. Both single proprietorships and partnerships are subject to *unlimited liability* and to *limited life.* Unlimited liability would become important to you if your business were deteriorating and you found that you owed a great deal more money to your creditors than your debtors owed to you. If you thought that you could not reverse the downward trend of your business and if your creditors threatened legal action, you would probably want to dissolve your business. Unlimited liability makes this difficult. Not only are the *assets* (those things that have market value) of your business subject to loss, but your personal property could also be taken to pay your debts. In the case of a partnership each partner would be subject to this same kind of liability. Instead of your business becoming a means of supporting you, it could become a hazard capable of wiping out all your savings.

"Limited life" refers to the fact that the business will end if one of the partners leaves the company. In such an event a new partnership agreement must be drawn up. The same would apply if one partner died or if the owner of a single proprietorship died. The business and the owners are coexistent.

The Corporation

A third type of business organization is the corporation. It is usually more difficult to organize than the other two forms. First you must go to a lawyer, who draws up the necessary papers asking the state for the powers you will need to establish your business. He submits these papers to the state government, which will grant you a charter. The charter gives you the right to do business; it also makes that business separate from you before the law. Separating you from the business is an important advantage. It means that your business now has *limited liability:* you and other stockholders can lose only the money you have put into the business, and not your personal possessions. Let us suppose that a purchaser of your product injured himself because of a defective part in the "Build-a-City" set that he bought. If he decided to sue for the damages he sustained, he would not sue you or any stockholders as persons. Instead, he would file his suit against the corporation.

Unlike the single proprietorship and partnership, the corporation has *perpetual life.* No matter how many of its stockholders die, the corporation will continue to exist. Such continuity is of particular value to businesses with heavy fixed costs and capital investment.

Probably the greatest advantage of a corporate form of business organization is its great ability to raise capital. After the corporation is chartered, a primary consideration will be to determine approximately how much money your business needs and how much it is currently worth. Let us assume that you evaluate your present business at $150,000. You would like an additional $350,000 to expand your facilities and have some money to take care of your operating expenses in the transitional stage of your business. To raise this additional money you issue 50,000 shares of stock. You retain 15,000 shares and attempt to sell the remaining 35,000. A share of stock represents ownership. In your particular case each share of stock

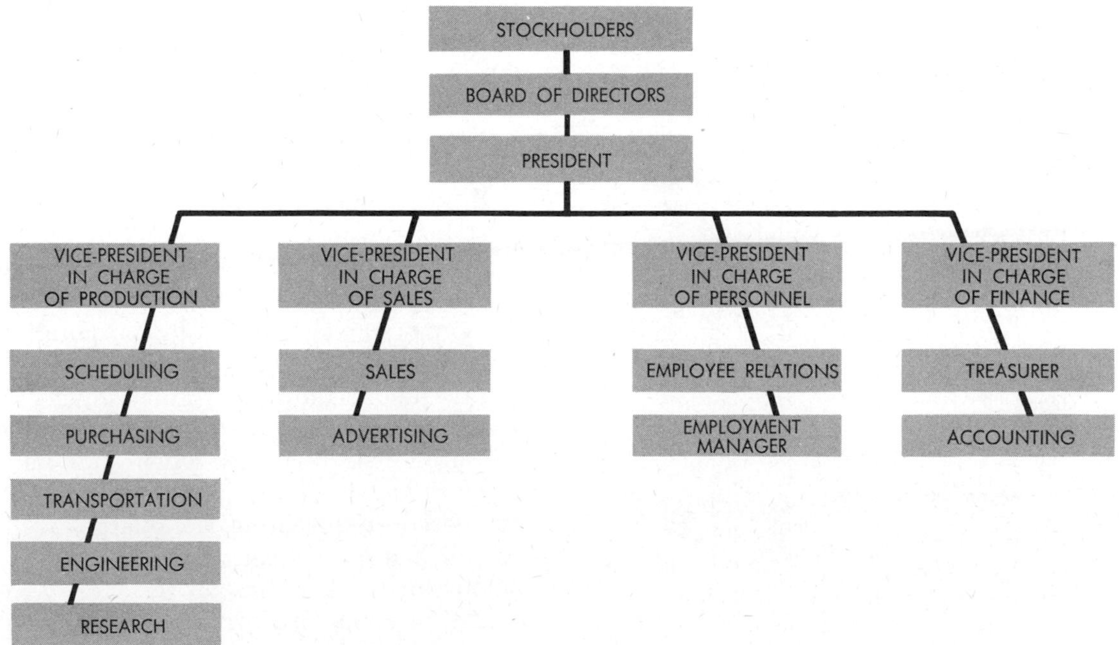

FIGURE 4–2 The Structure of a Typical Corporation

In the typical corporation the stockholders elect the board of directors. The board of directors sets general policy, makes decisions on declaring dividends, and elects the officers. The officers carry out day-to-day operations and administer policy.

will represent one fifty-thousandth ownership of the proposed corporation. If each share of stock is sold for $10 a share, the proposed corporation would now be worth $500,000. You would have the $150,000 business in addition to the $350,000 in cash for the sale of your stock for expansion and operation.

Selling Stock

How can you sell your stock? Many people will think immediately of the New York Stock Exchange as the best place. You may already be somewhat familiar with this famous stock exchange and the millions of shares of stock traded there every business day. After checking, you would soon find that only very large, long-established companies worth many millions of dollars can be listed on the New York Stock Exchange, or even on the smaller exchanges located throughout the country. A second possibility is to try to sell the stock yourself. Initially the idea might sound appealing as you think of a few people who might be able to buy stock. However, $350,000 is a great deal of money, and you soon realize that you have neither the time nor the ability to raise the money through personal sales of stock. When you talk this problem over with a business acquaintance, he tells you about an investment banker. As he explains the procedure, it sounds as if this third possibility might be your answer.

1970 High.	1970 Low.	Stocks and Div. in Dollars.	Sls. 100s.	Open.	High.	Low.	Close.	Net Chge.
		A—B—C—D						
26⅜	9¼	Abacus Fd	29	15¼	15½	15¼	15⅜	+ ⅜
78½	56¼	AbbtLb 1.10	81	75¾	77	75¾	76	+ ½
51½	35⅝	ACF Ind 2.40	28	49¼	49¼	48¾	48¾	− ⅛
24	12	AcmeClev .80	42	17⅜	17⅜	16	16¼	− ¾
46	36	Acme Mkt 2b	39	43½	44	43½	43⅝	+ ⅛
16¾	11⅛	AdmsEx .56g	16	14	14⅛	13¾	13⅞	− ¼
15½	8¼	Ad Millis .20	27	14¾	14¾	14½	14½	− ⅜
62	19½	Address .15g	280	24½	24¾	24	24½	+ ⅛
14⅞	6½	Admiral	46	9⅛	9⅜	8⅞	8⅞	− ½
50	32⅞	AetnaLfe 1.40	402	50	51½	50	51	+ 1⅜
42	33½	AetnaLf pf 2	7	42½	43⅜	42½	43	+ 1
19	6	Aguirre Co	15	10	10	9⅞	9⅞	− ⅛
42¾	19	Aileen Inc	3	41½	41½	41⅜	41⅜	− ⅛
48⅞	33⅜	Air Prod .20b	83	45⅝	46¾	45⅝	46¾	+ ⅞
127½	102½	AirPrd pf4.75	1	128	128	128	128	+ 2
23⅜	12½	Air Red .80e	113	22	22⅜	22	22⅛	.....
11½	3¼	AJ Industries	52	4	4⅛	4	4⅛	.....
37	24⅛	Akzona 1a	26	35⅛	35⅜	35	35⅛	+ ⅛
18½	14¼	Ala Gas 1.10	5	17½	17½	17½	17½	.....
27¼	9½	Alaska Inters	261	21⅞	24½	21¾	23⅞	+ 2⅛
43⅞	25¾	AlbertoC .32	64	41⅞	42	41¾	41¾	.....
13¾	8	Albertsns .36	45	13	13	12⅝	12¾	− ⅛
27⅞	19¼	AlcanAlu 1.20	326	24⅛	24¾	24⅛	24¼	+ ¼
23⅞	13	AlcoStand .30	54	19⅛	19⅜	18½	18⅝	− ½
25⅞	14½	Alexndrs .30r	10	24½	24¾	24½	24⅝	+ ½
13½	4½	Alleg Cp .20e	57	12	12	11¾	11¾	− ¼
39⅜	25⅛	AllegLud 2.40	170	32	32	31⅛	31½	− ¾
46½	35⅞	AllegLud pf 3	13	41⅛	41⅝	41	41	+ ¼
24⅜	17⅛	Alleg Pw 1.32	176	24⅛	24½	24⅛	24⅜	.....
28	16⅛	Allied Ch 1.20	448	25½	26¼	25½	25¾	+ ¼
29⅜	25¼	Alld Main .40	24	27⅛	27⅛	26¼	26½	− ⅞
43⅝	20⅛	AlldMill .75b	7	24¼	24¼	24¼	24¼	.....
32⅝	11½	Allied Pd .68	33	17⅛	17⅛	16¼	16¼	− ⅝
32¼	17⅞	AlliedStr 1.40	73	28⅞	29⅛	28½	29	+ ½
14½	4⅜	Allied Super	167	7⅞	8⅜	7⅞	8¼	+ ⅝
27	12⅞	Allis Ch .05g	296	17¼	17⅞	17⅛	17⅜	+ ¼
22¼	12⅝	AllrigtAut .60	10	21¼	21¼	21⅛	21⅛	− ¼
23¼	13	AlphaPC .40e	16	15¼	15⅜	15	15¼	+ ⅛
74	47	Alcoa 1.80	306	61	65	61	63	+ 1¾

The Investment Banker

An investment banker is in the business of selling securities. Although many people who have savings put their money in a savings account in order to receive interest, others are not satisfied with the interest that a bank pays them. They think that their money will bring a greater return if it is invested in some business. They may not want to organize a business themselves, but they might be willing to take a chance on a business that is already operating. They may buy *bonds* or *stock*.

If people buy shares of stock in a business, they become owners and share in the returns; however, they do not have to worry about day-to-day management. They may buy shares in a big corporation through a stock exchange, or they might go to investment bankers or stockbrokers to see what stock is available there. There is a bigger risk involved when one buys stock in a small company like ours as compared to investing in a large, well-established firm. Yet, there is also the chance of a big return on the money invested in a new organization. Many businesses that depend upon making money with money will frequently go to investment banks and buy stock in a growing company.

You decide to go to an *investment bank*

READING STOCK MARKET REPORTS

Most city newspapers publish daily stock market reports providing their readers with information on what is happening to the stock of major corporations of the United States. *The accompanying illustration* is an example of a report of a few New York Stock Exchange transactions. Let us see if we can learn to "read" the stock market report.

The stocks of corporations are listed alphabetically by the names of the corporations to make it easy to locate the name of the stock you are looking for. Find "Acme Mkt" on the list. At the extreme left of the name is the number 46 and next to it 36. At the top of the columns of figures you will find the labels "High" and "Low" just below "1970." This means that the highest price paid for a share of Acme Markets stock thus far in 1970 was $46 (not including the broker's commission and taxes). The lowest price paid was $36.

Just to the right of Acme Markets you find "2b." The title of this column is labeled "Stock and div in $." Stock merely means the name of the corporation. The "div in $" is an abbreviation for "dividends in dollars." The "2" means that Acme pays $2 a share as its annual rate. The *b* that follows the 2 means that you must turn to the footnote explanation, usually at the bottom of the page. The footnote reads, "Annual rate plus stock dividend," meaning that a stock dividend was paid in addition to the $2. The next column is labeled "Sales in 100s." There were 3,900 shares of Acme traded on the New York Stock Exchange for the day. "Open" (sometimes called "First") refers to the price paid for Acme when the market opened, $43.50. The price of a stock listed on the New York Stock Exchange moves in eighths of a point, a point being $1. This is followed by the highest price for the day ($44), the lowest price ($43.50), and the closing (sometimes called "Last"), 43.62^1/_2$. The last column, net change, is the difference between the closing price of the previous day's trading and the closing price of the day's trading being reported, in this case, $+^1/_8$. Thus, the price of Acme Markets has gone up 0.12^1/_2$ a share.

---

and discuss the prospect of its selling your stock. The investment bank is responsible for examining your business and deciding whether it has a reasonably good chance for future development. If the investment banker thinks it has a chance to grow, he will agree to try to sell the stock.

Let us assume that the investment bank is willing. You inform its representative that you want to get $10 a share. The bank will then try to sell your stock for as much as possible. If the stock sells for $11 a share, the bank keeps the $1 and you receive $10.

What happens if the bank cannot sell the 35,000 shares you have offered for sale? In this case you would get back the unsold shares and have to work with the capital you raised, or try to borrow the rest. Large, well-established businesses may make an arrangement with the investment bank to have it *underwrite* the stock. This means that if the investment bank cannot sell all the stock, the business would still get the agreed amount. Naturally, this is a better arrangement, but there is no way to force the bank to make such an agreement.

Transferring Ownership

People can buy or sell their ownership in the corporation quite easily. They do so by putting their stock up for sale. Suppose you decided on the corporate form for your business and it has expanded just as you have planned. The value of your business has doubled, so that it is now worth approximately 1 million dollars. Since there are still 50,000 shares, each share should be worth about double its original price. Some of the owners may think that their stock will not increase further in value and will want to sell it. There are others who admire the rapid expansion and would like to "buy in." The bigger corporations handle this exchange by having the sale of their stocks take place in the stock market.

In this case, however, the owners of "Build-a-City" stock wishing to sell would either try to arrange the sale themselves or have a brokerage house do this. A *stockbroker* is in the business of buying and selling shares of stock for others. Our stock would be an *over-the-counter* sale because it is not listed on a stock exchange. The broker differs from the investment banker in that he sells stock that is already owned, rather than new issues. Some indirect safeguards to buyers of stock, or securities, are provided by regulation through the Securities and Exchange Commission, an agency of the federal government.

Perpetual Life

If the owner of stock in a corporation dies, the stock he owns passes on to his heirs. Unlike the proprietorship or partnership, the corporation continues as if nothing had happened. This characteristic of a corporation, known as perpetual life, is possible because a corporation is considered a person in the eyes of the law. It can sue and be sued without the owners' becoming involved beyond the possible fluctuation of the value of their stock. However, the officers of the corporation, who might also be owners, may be held responsible for certain acts of the corporation specified by law. To the owner of shares of stock in the corporation, limited liability provides an important safeguard; his personal responsibility and financial liability are limited to the value of the stock that he owns.

Disadvantages of a Corporation

Before you become too impressed with the advantages of a corporation and make a hasty decision, you should consider its disadvantages. Besides having to pay a corporation income tax, you will have to consider that the corporation may fall out of your control. In your business you own 30 percent of the stock—15,000 shares of a total of 50,000. In practically none of the large corporations in this country does any single person own as much as 30 percent of the stock. Such a large block would almost certainly mean control, since most stockholders are not interested in controlling policy and give their proxy (right to vote) to the directors of the corporation. Since your corporation would be a small one with few shares of stock, there is a real possibility of several stockholders' getting together to vote you out.

You can try to avoid this difficulty in several ways. One method of keeping control would be to limit your expansion so that you always own at least 51 percent of the stock. However, such a move may not give you the money you need to develop as you have planned. Another alternative is to try to sell a different kind of stock, one that does not carry voting rights. The stock we have been referring to is known as *common stock*, and each share carries with it the right to one vote on matters concerning the control of the company. The holder of common stock also takes a chance on a return on his money because *dividends*, the money paid to the owners of this stock, are paid only after the corporation has taken care of all its other obligations. If the corporation makes a big profit, the common stockholder does well; but if business is poor, there may be no dividends. In addition, the value of the stock, which reflects the earning power of the business, may drop and discourage future buying.

Preferred Stock

A different type of stock—one having less risk but also fewer rights—is known as *preferred* stock. Although preferred stock represents ownership, it might better be called a second-class ownership. Rarely does it carry the right to vote. The corporation has an obligation to pay its preferred stockholders a stated dividend before it pays anything to those holding common stock. Therefore, if the corporation earns only a small profit, the preferred stockholder will get his dividend and the chances are that the common stockholder will be left without one. On the other hand, a large profit will not give the owner of preferred stock any additional reward, whereas the common stockholder may receive a substantial dividend.

If you are able to sell preferred stock rather than common stock to raise the capital you need, you will be sure of maintaining control. However, you will probably find that those who buy preferred stock are not willing to take great risks, and therefore they will favor large corporations that have been in business for years and have a long record of paying dividends. Still less risk is found in *cumulative preferred stock;* to holders of this kind of stock a corporation that fails to pay dividends for one or several years will have to pay accumulated dividends when profits are made.

Selling Bonds

You might also try selling bonds to raise money. A bond does not represent partial ownership of a corporation, but stands for a loan of a specified amount, often $1,000. The loan of $1,000 is referred to as the principal. The bondholder receives a specified rate of interest, usually every six months, on the principal invested. Whether the business makes money or not, the corporation must pay interest to bondholders or risk being sued. At the date of maturity the company is obligated to pay the principal to the bondholder. The bondholder runs the least risk of losing his money, but he also makes the least return on his investment if the corporation makes a substantial profit.

It would be nice if you could sell bonds, but if a person is worried about taking a risk, why should he put money into a new company? After considering the possible alternatives, you decide to go to an investment banker and ask him to sell the common stock necessary to raise the money you need.

Part C
Evolution and Concentration of Business

The Industrial Revolution Brings Changes in Methods of Production

After looking at the classical model and going through the process of organizing a business unit within the framework of this theory, we must consider a historical force that brought about a change in the real world not completely anticipated by such classical economists as Adam Smith.

One of the most important revolutions in the history of mankind was the Industrial Revolution, which occurred in western Europe and America after 1750. In the course of the Industrial Revolution waterpower, steam, and later electricity were harnessed to run new and complex machines. This in turn brought about great changes in the production and distribution of goods, involving different uses of the factors of production. Later in Chapter 7 we will examine the changes which the Industrial Revolution brought to the workingman. Here we will examine the changes it brought to ways of producing goods and services.

Fixed and Variable Costs

One change was a greater demand for capital because the businessman's costs tended to increase. These costs may be divided into two categories, *fixed costs* and *variable costs*. Fixed costs are those expenses which do not change with changes in production or sales. They pertain only to the short run, since all costs may fluctuate in the long run. The owner of the hardware store on Main Street pays his landlord $200 a month in rent. He pays that amount whether his sales are $5,000 a month or $35,000 a month. He sometimes refers to these fixed costs as his overhead.

Expenses which change with the volume of business are known as variable costs. As sales go up, variable costs will also go up. The hardware store owner will have to hire additional employees if his business gets significantly better. What other examples of variable costs can you think of?

The Effect of High Fixed Costs

Before the Industrial Revolution, fixed costs were far less important than they are today. Imagine that your "Build-a-City" business was operating in the eighteenth century. How do you think it would be organized? In all probability the actual building would be very small. In most cases the material would be distributed to workers who would return to their homes and carve the models with their own tools. Your fixed expenses would be small. You would hire workers as you needed them. If business was poor, some labor could be eliminated and your costs would decrease. If sales declined, you could close the business completely without losing much money. When economic conditions improved, you would be able to reopen your business with very little expense. The system described here operated very well for businessmen. They were able to open or close their businesses as the need for their products changed.

Now suppose that a large and costly machine is invented to produce "Build-a-City" sets. Not only would your methods of production change, but so would the basis on which you would make your decisions for the business as a whole. No longer would the workmen supply the tools. Now you would supply them. The cost of going into your kind of business would be increased considerably due to the expense of machines and a factory located in a place convenient for workers to reach. In the same way, changed methods of production led to the factory system in the course of the Industrial Revolution.

Under these new conditions, if business declined, you might still cut costs by discharging some of your employees. However, the fixed costs for the machines and the factory would remain constant. What would happen if business declined to a level at which you were losing money?

Would it pay to continue producing? If you decided to go out of business, you would lose the entire sum you invested. Also remember that if at some time you decided to come back into the business when business prospects looked better, the cost of starting again might be more than you could afford. The Industrial Revolution, by increasing fixed costs largely through the introduction of machinery and factories, greatly limited the opportunities for entering or leaving the business community. If your business has high fixed costs, the only way to pay them is to make sure your production is high enough to spread the costs over the many things you produce.

Let us suppose you have two machines, each capable of producing 100 "Build-a-City" sets an hour. You find it easy to pay for the cost of the machines and the factory when they are in operation for eight hours a day and five days a week. If business declines, however, and you have only enough orders to require the production of 800 sets a day you will have a problem. You could cut your variable costs by letting one of your machine operators go and using just one machine for the eight hours. However, the cost to cover both machines and the factory would have to come from the sale of 800 sets rather than 1,600 sets, hardly a bright prospect for making a profit.

Competition Under New Circumstances

The answer to operating a high fixed-cost business successfully is to make sure that sales are kept reasonably high at all times. After the Civil War the maturation of the American Industrial Revolution and the spread of a fine system of transportation gave American business a huge market. Producers in Boston could easily sell to buyers in St. Louis. What happened, however, when the national demand for a product declined? Each producer of that article did everything in his power to keep his sales up in order to pay for his fixed costs. This usually meant cutting his price to keep his own customers and also attract some of his competitors' customers. When his competitors followed his example, the battle to obtain a bigger portion of the market led to price wars, or "cutthroat competition." Prices fell even below the cost of production. Why? Because businessmen who spent staggering amounts of money developing their businesses could no longer afford to move. They needed to have income in order to meet their fixed costs, even if they had to dip into their past earnings or borrow money to pay for their variable costs. They would rather lose money for a short time in the hope either that business for the whole industry would improve or that some of their competitors would falter.

There were some economists, perhaps influenced by the concept of survival of the fittest, who thought that this fierce competition during a slowdown in business was beneficial in the long run. The weaker, less efficient businesses would not survive and the consumer would be left with the strongest, most efficient businessmen to serve him. Some economists still believe that this so-called social Darwinism is best. Critics of these economists point out that with fewer business opportunities and with greater requirements for capital, competition is bound to be lessened. With fewer producers it is easy to get together and agree on a price that would be higher than it would be if the market were free, with the price more affected by supply and demand. In Chapter 5 we will examine in some detail the advantages of a purely competitive market over imperfect markets.

Changes in Production Bring About Concentration of Business

If we examine the development of American industry, we find that those industries subject to high fixed costs have moved through the stages previously described. As the cost of machinery, research, and factories increased, it became difficult for new firms to enter the market. In the 1870's and 1880's, as the impact of the American Industrial Revolution made itself felt, the average size of the business unit increased. It was at this time that the corporation became more common; for as we have discovered, it was the kind of business best suited to raising large amounts of capital. Prior to this time a special act of the legislature was needed to grant a charter. Passage of general incorporation acts after 1875 simplified that process. When business conditions declined, fierce competition developed, and often only the strongest firms survived. These price wars were often disastrous for small businesses, and costly for the giants of industry as well.

Price-Fixing and Loose Combinations

To prevent the effects of excessive competition, some leaders of American industry reasoned that cooperation and agreement served their interests better than competition. What do you think would happen if all firms in an industry agreed to charge a particular price? If this price were higher than the prices of a competitive market, profits of each producer would increase. This technique, known as "price-fixing," forces the consumer to pay a higher price than he would under competition. Another technique was for producers to divide the market among themselves, with each producer having the exclusive right to sell in his portion of the market. These methods did not work well in the 1880's or 1890's because the agreements were not committed to legal documents. At a time in our history identified with "rugged individualism," when faith and trust were not relied upon, too many businessmen hedged on their agreements whenever it was possible to make more money. These oral agreements were known as *loose combinations* because they were not binding on the participants.

Closed Combinations

In time more formal agreements known as *closed combinations* developed. One kind was known as a *trust.* It was formed when producing companies surrendered their common stock and voting control in their own companies to a board of trustees of a new company. In turn the owners of the producing companies were given the equivalent of their stock in trust certificates. The new company then controlled the entire market and was usually able to make a large profit because of the high prices resulting from the absence of competition. The profit was then divided and the owners of the trust certificates received dividends.

One trust that forced people to pay artificially high prices was the sugar trust. It illustrates the harm a trust can do. Most sugarcane used in the making of sugar was imported. However, before the consumer bought it, it had to be refined. Competition among sugar refiners was intense as each struggled to gain a dominant position in the industry. Distributors and consumers benefited by the low prices that resulted. When the sugar trust was organized in 1887, there were 23 sugar companies in operation. Seventeen of these companies exchanged their stock for trust certificates, thereby coming under the single control of a giant trust called the Sugar Refineries Company. The trust certificate assured the owner dividends in the same manner as when he had common stock; but unlike the stock it was traded for, there was no voting right. The votes, and therefore the control, were in the hands of the board of trustees (the directors) of the sugar trust.

By having control over 17 of the 23 refineries, the trust was able to control the supply of sugar and thereby raise the price. The first action the trust took was to close all but four of its factories. With only a limited supply available, sugar buyers had to bid against each other to get the sugar they needed. Thus, the trust forced consumers to pay higher prices and caused workers to lose their jobs. The sugar trust was interfering with competition, an essential part of our economic system. Without competition the buyer was largely at the mercy of the seller.

Holding Companies

Another form of closed corporation that became popular after trusts started to disappear was the *holding company*. Such a company gains control by buying up enough stock of other companies to control them. In Figure 4–3 we can see how such a company can gain control of a large industrial empire with relatively little capital. Companies A through I are producing companies, each worth $10 million. Company J buys more than 50 percent of the stock of Companies A, B, and C so as to be able to control them. Company K does the same to D, E, and F; and Company L, to G, H, and I. Companies J, K, and L are holding companies. They are created not to produce but only to hold stock of other companies for the purpose of controlling A through I. For $45 million they control a $90-million industrial empire.

Company M, a higher-level holding company, is formed to gain control of Company J, K, and L. It buys up 50 percent of the stock of each of the holding companies. Company M can now control the $90-million empire for less than $23 million. If any of the producing companies or first-level holding companies have

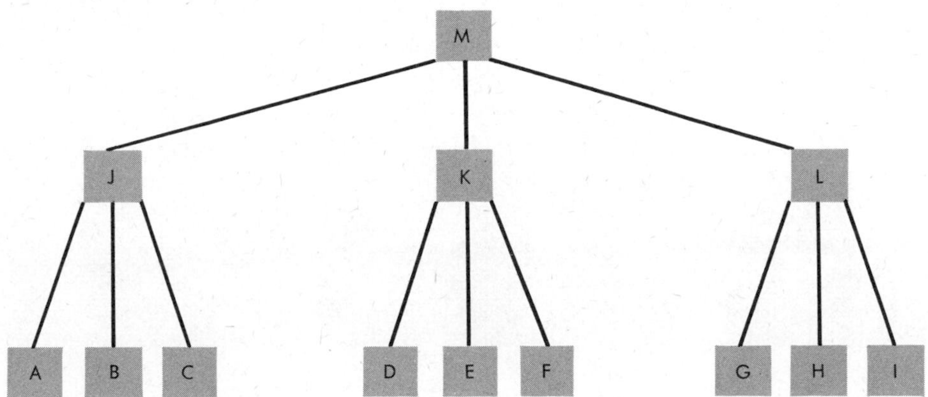

FIGURE 4–3 A Small Holding Company

Companies A through I are producing companies. Companies J, K, and L are first-level holding companies, and Company M is a second-level holding company.

preferred stock, Company M needs far less capital for control. Having holding companies at additional levels can also reduce the capital needed for control. It is also well to remember that control can almost always be achieved with far less than 50 percent ownership because of the many stockholders who have no interest in voting.

Before the passage of the Public Utility Holding Company Act of 1935, huge holding companies existed. The Associated Gas and Electric Company, a billion-dollar establishment, was controlled by a promoter who owned about $100,000 of voting stock. Samuel Insull and his associates in a giant utility holding company were able to control their producing companies with far less than one percent of the stated value of securities of their producing companies.

Mergers

The most common kind of consolidation

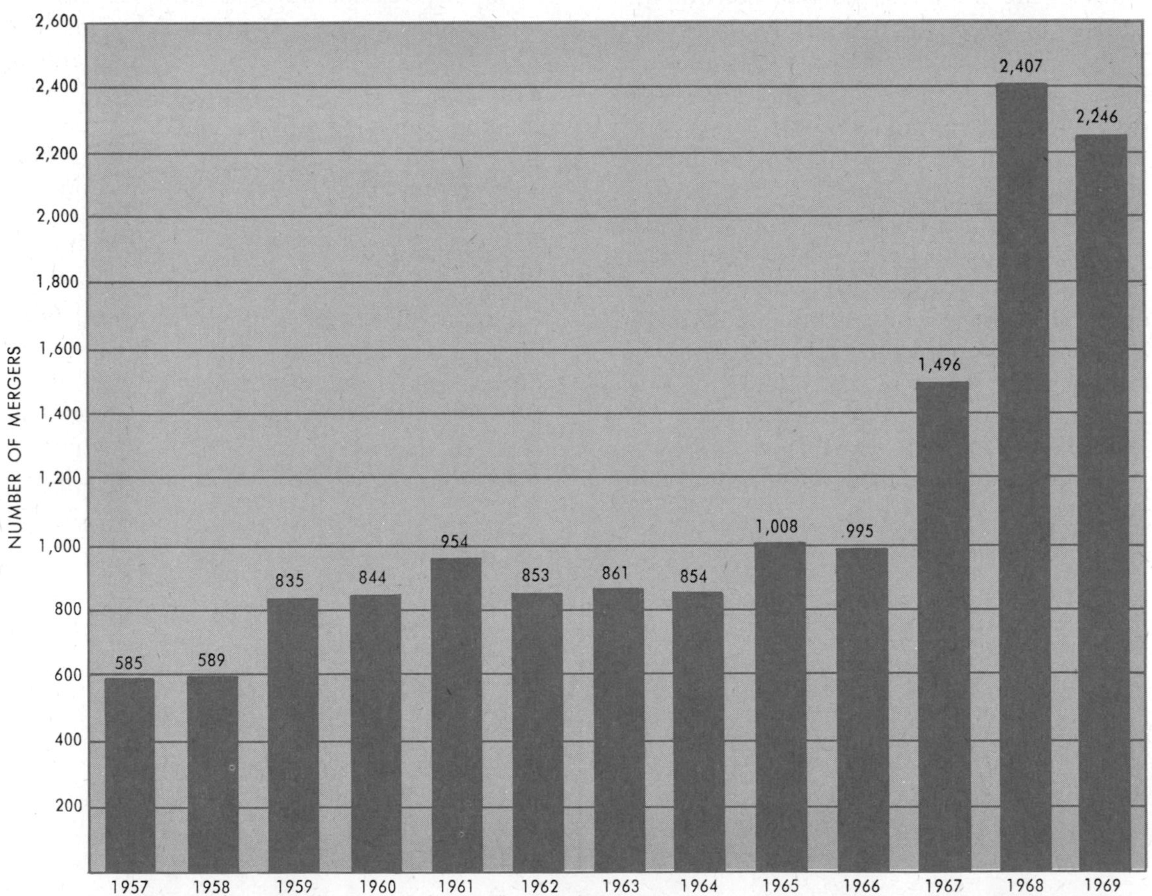

FIGURE 4–4 Mergers and Acquisitions—Manufacturing and Mining Concerns Acquired: 1957–1969

SOURCE: *Statistical Abstract, 1970.*

today is the *merger*. When two or more companies get together to form one company, a merger is created. An example is the case of the Nash and Hudson automobile companies, which joined to form the American Motors Corporation. Stockholders of each company had to approve the transaction.

"I just figured it out. It seems we're merging with ourselves."

SOURCE: Paul Peter Porges, *Saturday Review*, September 5, 1970. Copyright 1970 Saturday Review, Inc.

On occasion, mergers have been formed by smaller companies in an industry dominated by a few giant firms. These smaller companies claim that they need to merge in order to become more efficient so that they can compete more effectively against the biggest corporations. They maintain that such action increases competition rather than reducing it. The Antitrust Division of the Justice Department has not always agreed with them.

Conglomerates

The most recent type of merger movement has been characterized by giant firms in one industry diversifying their holdings by buying into unrelated industries. These are called *conglomerates*.

The most common conglomerate mergers have been large producing companies buying up consumer goods and services industries. The following acquisitions took place within a three-month period at the end of 1970: R.C.A. purchased Coronet Industries (carpets); Eli Lilly acquired Elizabeth Arden (cosmetics); American Brands, formerly American Tobacco Company, bought Andrew Jergens (toilet goods); Westinghouse took over Longines-Wittnauer (watches); National Diversified Industries purchased Dolly Madison (ice cream); and Northwest Industries, which is a holding company that owns Chicago and Northwestern Railway, was buying

Controversy continues over how vigorous an antitrust policy the government should follow.

the distribution company for Cutty Sark Scotch Whiskey.

The motivation to acquire companies in other fields is to provide some stabilization for the firm in case there is a major switch in consumer preference, an opportunity for establishing a tax loss, or for taking advantage of sharing in scarce resources that could result in real economies. The Federal Trade Commission has had a mixed reaction, since most conglomerate mergers are not likely to lessen competition. However, buying up a customer or a potential competitor is frowned upon and resulted in a slowing down of the merger movement in 1970.

Reaction to Combinations

Interfering with the trading of goods and services is contrary to the model designed by Adam Smith and other classical economists. Obstructions to the market, such as monopolies, loose combinations, trusts, holding companies, and oligopolies, brought protests from many Americans. They wanted the government to do something to insure competition and help keep prices low. In 1890 Congress passed the Sherman Antitrust Act, which outlaws monopolies, attempts to form monopolies, and combinations and conspiracies in restraint of trade. Because the Sherman Act contained no definitions, did not indicate the meaning of "restraint," and did not clearly express whether labor as well as capital was to be included, much of its meaning remained for the courts to interpret.

In 1914 Congress passed the Clayton Act. This act spelled out its purpose and meaning. Among other things, it prohibited *interlocking directorates* in competing companies, discriminatory price-cutting, tying contracts (contracts which force buyers to purchase items they may not want), and the forming of holding companies. In the same year Congress created a Federal Trade Commission to help enforce the antitrust acts. A strong effort was made to keep the market free and competitive. In subsequent years other laws have been passed, and the Supreme Court has handed down rulings relative to how much competition should exist. With few exceptions our government has expressed its approval of competition. Has this government policy worked? Do we now have the competitive society expressed in the model and sought after by our laws?

Separation of Ownership and Control

Several of our largest corporations are owned by more than a million people, and there are a great many more with over 100,000 different stockholders. In very few of these firms does any one stockholder own more than 10 percent of the outstanding stock. Studies have shown that this wide diversification of ownership has brought about a separation of ownership and control. It is rare for the entire management of such companies to own more than a fifth of all voting stock. Do you think this loss of control by the majority of the ownership in a corporation holds any danger? If so, to whom?

Natural Monopolies

There appears to be little disagreement among economists regarding the formation of natural monopolies. In some industries it is not economical to have competition. These industries—utilities and transportation companies, for instance—are usually characterized by their extremely high fixed costs. Consider how costly it would be to have three different sets of railroad tracks running side by side from New

MERGERS, LAWS, AND THE HIGH COURT: THREE VIEWPOINTS

Robert H. Bork, Associate Professor, Yale Law School:

"The laws are generally clear—but this is not to say they're good. The Court has always tried to simplify, to push toward automaticity—partly because it doesn't feel at ease dealing with economics, and partly because this Court doesn't have a firm grasp on the nature of competition and a free market. It sees anti-competitive tendencies even where they don't exist. Half the laws themselves are anti-competitive. The real problem of mergers lies with horizontal mergers. That's where the only intelligent fear lies and that's where the enforcement drive should be. Congress went too far in amending Section 7; the Supreme Court has pushed even further."

George J. Stigler, Professor, University of Chicago Graduate School of Business:

"Businessmen have always said that [the laws are confused]. It's a big game they play. They love to run behind this so-called cloud of confusion—but it's a cloud they make themselves. The antitrust laws are as good as I could expect. In general, they heighten competition—and anything that does that is good. On the other hand, when it comes to concentration in specific industries, I would not say that we're teetering on the dangerous brink. There are an immense number of fields where significantly increased concentration would not hurt. I'm not prepared to say that the Justice Department is administering the law with unbounded skill—but, in general, the laws are doing what they're supposed to be doing."

Donald F. Turner, Professor of Law and Public Administration, Harvard University:

"Any company can get competent legal advice that will indicate the outcome of a vertical or horizontal merger. But in regard to conglomerate mergers, the law is not predictable because it is in a very primitive stage. There have been no Supreme Court decisions in this area. If a company is failing, it is generally held that there are no holds barred. If the conglomerate law gets awfully tough then [competition will suffer]. In general, though, the area of industry mergers is clearly one in which there hasn't been much thinking. But I disagree with those who think the antitrust laws generally are a barrier to business growth, progress, and efficiency."

SOURCE: *Newsweek*, June 29, 1964, p. 77.

York to Chicago for three competing companies. Consider the inefficiency and inconvenience of having many competing telephone companies each with its own telephone poles, telephone books, and dial systems. Such industries are called *natural monopolies*, and an appropriate level of government grants a franchise to such businesses giving them exclusive rights to do business in a given area. If there is no competition, you may ask, how are we protected? The federal government has set up commissions, such as the Interstate Commerce Commission, to regulate those industries that engage in interstate commerce and to protect consumers. State and local governments also have commissions which regulate natural monopolies under their jurisdiction. If a company wants to increase its rate (price) it must get permission from the commission in charge. If a company does not present a good reason for raising rates, such as failing to earn a fair return on its investment, chances are slight that such increases will be granted.

Part D
The Problem: How Much Economic Competition Is Desirable?

There is a difference of opinion among economists, responsible citizens, and public officials regarding the amount of competition we should have. No other country in the world has committed itself as much as we have to promoting competition and to curbing monopolistic practices. Our sympathy has usually been for the "underdog," namely, small business, even when it could not compete effectively. However, our dependence on and support of giant corporations leaves considerable room for variation in the determination of our public policy. What follows is an examination of several points of view, each designed to show the rationale of the position taken. Each statement contains values, facts, and generalizations. This is followed by a list of facts (p. 90) which seem to lead to differing conclusions. There are, next, four groups of questions, which may be called subproblems. Answers to these subproblems should help you in arriving at an answer to the main problem: How much competition should there be? Keep in mind the material presented in this chapter that is related to the problem.

The Classical Viewpoint

We have seen that the classical economist calls for a highly competitive economy. He elevates the consumer to the highest position on the economic ladder and organizes an economic system to serve him. Production is created for the consumer, and the economy should be organized to produce the goods he wants at the lowest cost. This can be done only by having strong competition among the producers of goods and services—the businessmen. They recognize that by producing only the best goods in the most efficient way and offering them at the

TABLE 4–2 Revenues of Leading U.S. Retail Outlets (millions of dollars)

Department Stores	Revenues	Grocery Stores	Revenues
J. C. Penney Co.	4,151	Great Atlantic & Pacific Tea Co.	5,754
Federated Dept. Stores	2,092	Safeway Stores, Inc.	4,860
Allied Stores Corp.	1,212	Kroger Co.	3,736
May Dept. Stores	1,164	Food Fair	1,762
Variety Stores		**Drug Stores**	
S. S. Kresge Co.	2,559	Walgreen Co.	744
F. W. Woolworth	2,528	Sterling Drug Co.	594
Gamble-Skogmo	1,313	Thrifty Drug Stores	329
W. T. Grant	1,254		

SOURCE: *Forbes Directory*, May 15, 1971.

JOSEPH A. SCHUMPETER AND DYNAMIC CAPITALISM

Joseph A. Schumpeter (1883–1950), a professor of economics in Austria and later in the United States, is known for his studies of capitalism. Although he admired the institutions of capitalism, he prophesied their ultimate destruction. His theories on the stages of capitalism have greatly influenced subsequent economic thinking.

Schumpeter was concerned with capitalism primarily as a means of economic development. His hero was the entrepreneur, the key figure whose innovations benefit society. Driven by the desire for profit, the true entrepreneur introduces new products and methods, creates new markets, and explores new systems of organization. Schumpeter also recognized certain limitations in classical capitalism. The conditions for perfect competition are found in very few industries, and monopolistic practices are common.

Schumpeter's greatest contribution was in the analysis of capitalism as an evolutionary process. He saw that innovation, the dynamic factor in economic development, was also a source of weakness. Innovations tend to occur in clusters, creating an imbalance which leads to business cycles. Just as innovation theory explains economic development, so it also explains periodic depressions.

Eventually, in the course of business cycles, the entrepreneurial function becomes obsolete and is replaced by bureaucratic committees and teams of experts who lack the drive and imagination to move the society forward. Some of capitalism's basic institutions, such as private property, are undermined as the government comes to depend for support on inducements and popular appeal. Eventually, Schumpeter predicted, some form of "state capitalism," with its accompanying inefficiency and stagnation, will become the basis of our nation's economic system.

---

lowest prices will the consumer buy their products and allow them to make money.

If there is only one producer of a good, there is no need to improve it, to increase efficiency, or to lower price. The consumer is compelled to buy whatever product is offered. If there are only a few producers, it is a simple matter for them to cooperate with one another and to sell the product at a price high enough for the least efficient producer to make money. The more efficient producers are willing to go along at the high price, since their profits will be greater. Even if there are quite a few producers, one large company can influence the supply of the product on the market and affect the price. If the small producers try to lower the price in an effort to attract business, the giant can force them to close by lowering the price below cost for a short time. After he has destroyed them, he can raise the price to make up for his losses.

With many producers, no one business can control enough of the supply to affect the price. Only within this framework can the consumer take advantage of a free-trade market.

What would the classical economist's answer be for the little businessman who cannot compete? Does he make any special provision for him? Remember, there are millions of little businesses and only a few giants. Our defender of the classical model might remind us of the basic problem in economics: the efficient allocation of our limited resources to meet our unlimited wants. Special consideration given to any group might encourage waste. If we allow artificially high prices, we permit resources to flow to less efficient producers. In addition, we also ask the consumer to pay more and deprive him of buying other things with the money he would have had left over if he had bought in a competitive market. The inefficient producer should move into more profitable work and thereby be of greater service to society. We are all consumers, and a highly competitive society will keep prices low and allow us to get the most goods for our money. Isn't that what we all want from our economic system? Or will the elimination of the small and inefficient business eventually eliminate too much competition and result in inefficiency or exploitation of the consumer?

The Case for Limited Competition

Although economists of many different viewpoints would be eager to answer the arguments presented above and give their own pet theories, we can examine only some of the more popular positions.

Rewarding the Efficient

One of the first limitations that most critics of the classical position would point to is its self-defeating features. If we permit the existence of a free marketplace with unlimited competition, the most efficient producers will soon emerge as the victors in the economic struggle. Eventually only a few producers would be competing with one another. This in itself would not do any harm if it were easy for more producers to enter the market. This would be possible when the demand for a product increased or the producers already in the market started to make such high profits as to attract more businessmen into the field. However, with the great increase in fixed costs, businessmen cannot move in and out of an industry so easily.

Bigness Makes Progress Easier

The successful businesses acquire the best machinery for efficient production, build large research laboratories to help them improve their products, and engage in big advertising programs to help sell their products to the consumers. When new ideas are developed for better products, isn't it easier to sell them to the big, established companies than to try to compete in the field? Considering the amount of money needed to start a new business, few people are willing to take the great risk involved. Antitrust laws cannot force people to go into business to compete, and we cannot break up the big producers if we are to reward the most efficient ones.

Diversification

The most successful businesses have become so powerful and have acquired so much money that they have been able to branch out into many different industries. During World War II, General Motors went into the diesel locomotive business because of the great demand and limited supply. Within a few years General Motors was producing more diesel locomotives than any other company. It is also one of the largest manufacturers of household appliances. General Motors is not alone in diversifying its holdings. The American Motors Corporation and the Ford Motor Company also are in the appliance business. Chrysler Corporation is a large manufacturer of air conditioners. Each of these corporations is also in the finance business.

Advantages of Giant Corporations

Should we try to break up these huge corporations and penalize them for their success? If we break them up into smaller units, how will we be able to carry out costly research to improve our products? Those who favor large corporations would present the following evidence to support their viewpoint.

TABLE 4–3 Largest U.S. Corporations (millions of dollars)

Ten Largest U.S. Industrial Corporations

	Revenues	Assets
1. General Motors	18,752	14,058
2. Standard Oil (N.J.)	16,554	19,242
3. Ford Motor	14,980	9,849
4. General Electric	8,727	6,199
5. International Tel & Tel	7,611	9,002
6. International Bus. Mach.	7,504	8,539
7. Mobil Oil	7,261	7,921
8. Chrysler	7,000	4,816
9. Texaco	6,350	9,924
10. Gulf Oil	5,396	8,672

Ten Largest Corporations by Profits

	Net Profits
1. American Tel & Tel	2,189
2. Standard Oil (N.J.)	1,310
3. International Bus. Mach.	1,018
4. Texaco	822
5. General Motors	609
6. Gulf Oil	550
7. Ford Motor	516
8. Mobil Oil	483
9. Sears, Roebuck	464
10. Standard Oil (Calif.)	455

Five Largest U.S. Commercial Banks

	Assets
1. Bank America Corp.	29,740
2. First National City Corp.	25,835
3. Chase Manhattan	24,526
4. Manufacturers Hanover Corp.	12,665
5. J. P. Morgan & Co.	12,112

Five Largest U.S. Utilities Companies

	Revenues	Assets
1. American Tel & Tel	16,955	49,642
2. Consolidated Edison of N.Y.	1,128	4,449
3. Pacific Gas & Electric	1,103	4,319
4. Commonwealth Edison (Chicago)	887	3,375
5. Southern California Edison	721	3,227

Five Largest U.S. Transportation Companies

	Revenues	Assets
1. United Aircraft	2,349	1,546
2. Penn Central	1,691	4,598
3. Southern Pacific	1,272	3,066
4. Trans World Airlines	1,157	1,406
5. American Airlines	1,133	1,525

SOURCE: "Dimensions of American Business," *Forbes Annual Directory Issue,* May 15, 1971.

These corporations are owned by millions of stockholders, who are also consumers. The profits distributed by these companies help to raise the standard of living. The millions of workers employed by the giant industries earn higher wages than those in industries in which there are many producers. By providing steady employment for their millions of workers, these corporations tend to have a stabilizing effect on the entire national economy.

By diversifying their interests, large corporations do a better job of allocating resources from one product to another. Competition can and does exist among giants. When competition within an industry is largely eliminated, there may be competition between industries, as in the aluminum and stainless steel industries. Although prices have not declined, income has risen faster than prices; a high income is as important to encourage competition as a low price, particularly if it rises faster than prices.

Government action keeps big business in line and prevents it from disregarding the consumer. It would be more advantageous for the small businessman, as well as for the economy, if he worked for a large company. Finally, the American standard of living is higher than that of any other nation in the world, and it keeps getting higher. By its efficiency and its constant increasing of productivity, big business has made a significant contribution to our standard of living. Since big business has proved itself successful in meeting our economic needs and contributing to our progress, why threaten to do away with "a good thing"?

Considering an Answer

The following statements contain facts, of which some favor a policy of greater competition, some support the present condition of our economy, and some suggest the desirability of a move toward less competition. Examine these facts carefully. Identify the policy concerned and evaluate its advantages and disadvantages in each case.

The 500 largest corporations, less than one tenth of 1 percent of our total enterprises, control approximately 60 percent of the nation's assets in all fields of production.

Research now requires team effort, and only big business or government has the means to support it.

Prices have risen much faster in industries with few producers than in those with many producers.

Wages are higher in industries with few producers than in those with many.

Decision-making power in the largest corporations is in the hands of a small minority of the stockholders. Their power is so great that some might threaten our democratic way of life.

Chain stores and mail-order houses sell at lower prices than independents.

As more and more Americans own stock in large enterprises, decisions regarding those companies and earnings from them are more widely spread throughout our population.

The Senate Subcommittee on Antitrust and Monopoly in 1956 reported that giant corporations make their huge profits not from efficiency or the best allocation of the nation's resources, but rather from their great power in the marketplace.

Big corporations have given generously to support our colleges and universities in research and in scholarships to help develop human resources.

Making the Policy

With these facts and arguments in mind, try to decide what our country's economic policy ought to be regarding the amount of competition we should have. Should we:

1. Go back to our original model by having a government policy of vigorous antitrust action? Should we break up our biggest corporations and thereby increase the number of producers?
2. Allow our economic system to develop as it has in the past, making sure that government, under the watchful eye of the Federal Trade Commission, the Antitrust Division of the Justice Department, and congressional investigating committees, guards the consumers' interests from abuse?
3. Forget about competition and our classical capitalistic model? Should we encourage combinations, but give the government greater control over business —as much as it has over natural monopolies? Should we substitute government control over prices for the market control?
4. Follow different policies for different

industries? Should we use competition in industries which are most efficient producing as small units, and should we use regulation in cases in which bigness is most economical?

As a policymaker, which alternative would you select?

REVIEW: THE HIGHLIGHTS OF THE CHAPTER

1. About three fourths of the value of our goods and services results from decisions made by private enterprise. An even greater percentage of our gross national product (GNP) is produced by our businesses.
2. Sometimes a business firm is called an enterprise. Those who organize the enterprise are called entrepreneurs.
3. Collecting and organizing the factors of production is an essential function of business management.
4. Goods used to make other goods (tools) are called capital goods. Goods used directly by the consumer to satisfy his needs are called consumer goods.
5. Interest is money paid for the use of money, rent for the use of natural resources, and wages for labor performed; profit is money received for risks taken in organizing a business and operating it efficiently.
6. A business can be organized as a single proprietorship, a partnership, or a corporation. Each has advantages and disadvantages.
7. Unlimited liability and limited life are two serious drawbacks of both the single proprietorship and the partnership in contrast to the corporation.
8. The biggest advantage of a corporation form of business organization is its great ability to raise capital. Ownership in a corporation is easily transferable.
9. An investment banker is in the business of selling new issues of securities.
10. Common stock is characterized by voting rights and greater risk, while preferred stock usually carries a stated dividend and has no voting rights.
11. Bonds represent a loan rather than ownership. A corporation must pay interest to bondholders or risk being sued.
12. The Industrial Revolution was the result of the application of waterpower and steam power to the operation of machinery, largely replacing the use of man power.
13. Fixed costs are those expenses which do not change, regardless of the volume of sales. These have become more important since the Industrial Revolution.
14. Variable costs are those directly related to the volume of a particular business.
15. The cost of machinery, research, and factories makes it difficult for new firms to enter an industry. Price-fixing occurs when a group of firms agrees to charge the same price.
16. A trust is a closed combination in which producing companies exchange their control and stock for trust certificates. These certificates do not carry voting rights. A trust generally forces people to pay higher prices. Holding companies

are another form of closed combination. Conglomerate mergers are now the most common form of combination.

17. The national government attempted to solve the problem of business combinations by passing the Sherman Antitrust Act (1890), the Clayton Act (1914), and the Federal Trade Commission Act (1914). Additional legislation has been passed since then.
18. Separation of ownership and control in our largest corporations has developed because stockholders have little interest in a business other than in its dividends.
19. Natural monopolies are encouraged and regulated by the federal government.
20. A major controversy that remains unresolved is how much competition we should have in our economy.

IN CONCLUSION: SOME AIDS TO UNDERSTANDING

Terms for Review

GNP
single proprietorship
capital goods
interest
wages
factors of production
limited life
cumulative preferred stock
cutthroat competition
price-fixing
holding company
conglomerates
variable costs
fixed costs
loose combinations
corporation
partnership
consumer goods
rent
profit
liability
investment bank
common stock
bonds
social Darwinism
trusts
merger
natural monopoly
dividend
closed combinations

Names to Know

Sherman Antitrust Act
Clayton Act
Federal Trade Commission
Interstate Commerce Commission

Questions for Review

1. Imagine yourself as a businessman starting a new enterprise.
   (a) What forms of organization are available to you?
   (b) What factors will determine your choice?
   (c) What are the advantages and disadvantages of each kind of organization?
2. What form of business organization would you recommend for each of the following? Why?
   (a) a physician
   (b) an appliance manufacturer
   (c) a restaurant
   (d) a grocery store
   (e) a wheat farmer
   (f) a barbershop
   (g) an automobile repair shop
   (h) a steel mill

3. Business has found a variety of ways to gain advantage in a competitive market.
   (a) What are the historic methods used by American business to control the market?
   (b) Explain the essential differences in these methods.
   (c) What is the most common method today?
4. Since the Industrial Revolution, most large businesses have turned to the corporate form of organization.
   (a) Explain why the corporation form gained in popularity.
   (b) Describe the structure of a modern corporation.
   (c) Explain the functions of stockholders, the board of directors, officers, and creditors in controlling a corporation.
5. Explain: "The control of a giant corporation may be exercised by a well-organized group of stockholders with minor stock holdings."

Additional Questions and Problems

1. What effects do proxy votes have upon the decisions made by the management of a large corporation? Why?
2. Select five stocks from those listed on the New York Stock Exchange. Follow their daily progress in a newspaper for a period of two weeks and try to identify some of the factors that contribute to fluctuations in the stocks which you selected.
3. Why are overhead costs such as rent, taxes, interest on capital investments, and insurance considered as fixed costs whereas wages, raw materials, and freight charges are variable costs?
4. What is the difference between common stock, preferred stock, and bonds? What considerations should enter into an individual's decisions on purchasing these securities?
5. In order to check the growing power of business, the federal government has found it necessary to establish certain controls on business.
   (a) Trace the growth of federal controls over business by means of a chronological table listing the major regulatory agencies and the laws restricting corporations.
   (b) What circumstances caused the various changes in government policy?
   (c) What present business practices might require additional controls?

SELECTED READINGS

Adams, Walter, ed. *The Structure of American Industry: Some Case Studies,* 3rd ed. New York: The Macmillan Co., 1961.

Burnham, James. *The Managerial Revolution.* Bloomington: Indiana University Press, 1960.

Caves, Richard. *American Industry: Structure, Conduct, Performance.* Englewood Cliffs, N.J.: Prentice-Hall, 1967.

Chandler, Alfred D. Jr., ed. *Giant Enterprise: Ford, General Motors, and the Automobile Industry*. New York: Harcourt, Brace & World, 1964.

Cochran, Thomas C. *The American Business System: A Historical Perspective, 1900–1955*. New York: Harper & Row, 1962.

Drucker, Peter F. *The Future of Industrial Man*. New York: New American Library of World Literature, 1965.

Galbraith, John K. *The New Industrial State*. Boston: Houghton Mifflin Co., 1969.

Mansfield, Edwin, ed. *Monopoly Power and Economic Performance*. New York: W. W. Norton & Co., Inc., 1968. (Also available in paperback edition from the same publisher.)

Wilcox, Clair. *Public Policies Toward Business*, 3rd ed. Homewood, Ill.: Richard D. Irwin, 1966.

Costs, Prices, and Output in Various Markets 5

THE AUTHORS' NOTE TO THE STUDENT

In Chapter 2 we saw how the forces of demand and supply in a free market can influence the price of a good or service, and how they can affect the allocation of our resources. In analyzing the supply side of the market, we examined some of the factors which help to determine the quantity of goods produced for sale. (See the *law of increasing costs* on p. 27 for example.) In Chapter 4 we found several ways to organize a business and discussed the advantages and disadvantages of each. Using graphs, we examined changes in supply and demand, and the extremely important concept of elasticity. The student should understand all of this material before proceeding with Chapter 5.

Naturally, the businessman in a free economy is seeking profits. The intelligent businessman will not be satisfied simply with the knowledge that he is making a profit, however. He will invariably want to make the greatest profit possible—to *maximize* his profits. If, on the other hand, he should be forced to operate at a loss for a time, he will certainly attempt to incur the least loss possible—to *minimize* his losses. Whether a firm exists in a perfectly or imperfectly competitive market, it will try to maximize its profits or minimize its losses. In this chapter we shall see how this can be done. We shall examine the firm's different types of costs, how costs may change over a period of time, and how the firm adjusts to these changes.

A STUDENT'S NOTE TO THE STUDENT

I now know why they say economics is tough. Plan on reading this chapter twice, both times slowly. Here are some tips that may help.

Study each graph and don't go on until you have mastered it. You have to build one concept on top of another and if your foundation is weak, the material at the end of the chapter will mean nothing to you.

Make sure you know what the word "marginal" means. It is different than average or total and it is used many times. Under perfect competition the marginal revenue curve is demand. In imperfect markets it becomes more complicated. The demand curve and the marginal revenue curve are not the same. Try drawing some graphs until you understand them.

If you really get stuck remember that to make the most profit or suffer the least loss, production should be at the quantity where *MC* intersects *MR*. Where the *ATC* curve falls below the demand curve, profits can be made.

Finally a warning. If you think you make the most total profit at the point where the *MC* curve is farthest away from the *MR* or demand curve, you don't understand the concept "marginal." I didn't.

Part A
Fixed, Variable, and Total Costs

Although we gave some consideration to various costs in Chapter 4, we will elaborate on these important concepts here.

When the businessman wishes to determine whether or not he is making a profit, he asks two questions: How much money am I taking in? How much is it costing me to produce my output? In more technical terms, he compares his *total revenues* (*TR*—the total amount received for the sale of his goods or services) with his *total costs* (*TC*). His profit (or loss) is simply the difference between the two. If a firm's total revenues are $600,000 during a certain period of time, and its total costs of production are $570,000, then it follows that the firm's profit is $30,000—the difference between total revenues and total costs. The formula is simply: Profit = *TR* − *TC*. Obviously, if total costs should exceed total revenues, the firm would be operating at a loss. (We sometimes refer to losses as *negative profits*.)

A word of warning is in order. The economist does not always compute profits in the same fashion as the business manager or the accountant. A businessman may make the mistake of thinking of costs solely in terms of the amount of money he pays out for labor, raw materials, transportation, fuel, and the like. These are indeed part of his costs, and the economist refers to them as *explicit costs*. But we also consider the *implicit costs*—the value of productive resources which the owner supplies himself. For example, suppose that the owner of a small store owns the land and the building he uses. He does not pay himself rent, in the sense that he hands himself money each month in payment for the use of the land. But he could be renting the land to someone else for, say, $1,000. The economist will then consider $1,000 to be an implicit cost and will add this sum to the actual money payments (explicit costs) which the storeowner makes to others. Similarly, the value of any labor which the owner performs himself will be considered part of the costs. Thus, if the businessman claims a profit of $30,000, the economist may advise him that in reality a portion of that amount is not profit at all, if he has neglected to deduct from it the value of any labor which he himself has performed, the rental value of land which he himself owns, and the like. We need not concern ourselves any longer with these fine points, however. For the rest of this chapter we shall assume that all costs of doing business are accurately computed as an economist would do it.

Fixed Costs

All costs can be classified as either *fixed* or *variable*. In the short run, as we pointed out on p. 78, the firm can use only its existing facilities to increase its output. It cannot add to its plant, however, because there is not sufficient time to do so. During the short run, there are several important costs which are fixed. (In the long run, all costs can change. We shall deal with this fact later in this chapter.) *Fixed costs do not change when the firm changes its level of output.* That is, the firm may produce nothing, it may produce one unit, or it may produce 10,000 units, but its fixed costs remain unchanged. Fixed costs include such things as interest on debts of the firm, payments for rent, insurance premiums, taxes on real property owned by the firm, part of the depreciation of the firm's building and equipment, and salaries paid to important executives. These are payments which must be made, even if the firm is not producing a single unit of output. The bondholders expect to receive their interest payments on time, the insurance company demands its premiums, and so on. As Figure 5–1 shows, the total fixed cost remains the same regardless of output.

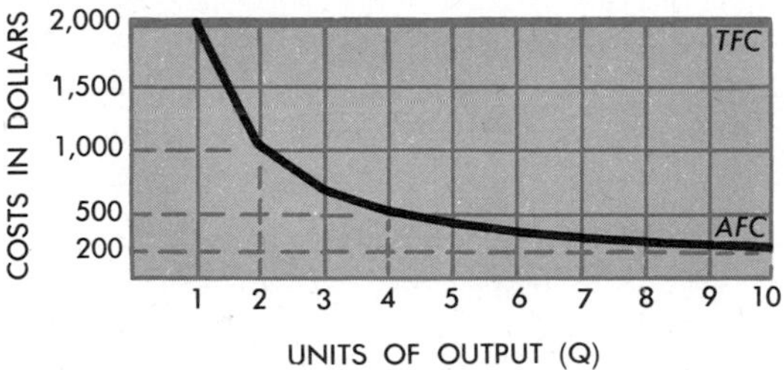

FIGURE 5–1 Total Fixed and Average Fixed Costs

The colored curve *TFC* shows the firm's total fixed costs, $2,000. Regardless of the level of output, the total fixed costs remain the same. The curve marked *AFC* shows the firm's average fixed costs at 1 to 10 units of output. Explain why the *AFC* curve will always slope downward.

Average Fixed Costs

The *average fixed cost* (*AFC*) declines, however, as the firm increases its output. Average fixed cost is determined simply by dividing total fixed cost (*TFC*) by the quantity being produced ($AFC = TFC/Q$). This is illustrated by Figure 5–1. Note that during the particular period under consideration the firm has fixed costs totaling $2,000, as shown by the horizontal solid line marked *TFC*. If this firm produces two units of output, the average fixed cost (*AFC*) drops to $1,000 (*TFC* of $2,000 divided by *Q* of *2*). When the firm increases its output to four units, the fixed costs are spread over a larger number of items, so that the *AFC* becomes $500. When the firm is producing 10 units, the *AFC* is only $200. Clearly, if a firm had nothing but fixed costs, the more it produced the lower would be its unit cost (average total cost). In such a case, a firm could continually reduce its average costs simply by increasing production to the limit permitted by its productive resources. In reality, however, the firm is also confronted by variable costs.

Variable Costs

Variable costs increase as the firm increases its output. Variable costs will decline if the firm reduces its level of output. All costs which are not fixed are variable. When a firm increases its output it must acquire more productive resources, such as additional workers and more raw material. More fuel or power will be needed in the plant, and there will be additional transportation costs. Some of the maintenance costs will rise, as the firm's plant and equipment are used more intensively. Wages and other variable costs, then, will tend to rise as the firm increases its output, and to fall as the firm reduces its output. The *total variable cost* figure will keep rising as the firm increases its output. (This is illustrated by Figure 5–3.)

Average Variable Costs and the Law of Diminishing Returns

Average variable cost is another matter. *Average variable cost* (*AVC*) is found by dividing total variable cost (*TVC*) by the firm's output. ($AVC = TVC/Q$.) Although average fixed costs decline continually as the firm increases its output, average variable costs do not. At first, average variable costs usually decline as the firm's output increases. After reaching a minimum point, however, the average variable cost begins to rise. The *AVC* curve, then, will have the general shape of the letter "U." This phenomenon is explained by the *law of diminishing returns,* also called the *law of diminishing marginal productivity.* This law states that *as more and more units of a variable factor of production* (labor, for example) *are added to a fixed factor of production* (such as capital equipment), *eventually a point will be reached where the output accounted for by each additional unit of the variable factor will decline.* A simple example will help to make this clear.

Assume that we are setting up a small factory to produce our "Build-a-City" games. Our fixed factor of production (capital, in this case) is made up of four machines. Machine number one is an electric saw which is used to cut the wood to the proper size and shape. Machine number two is a sander, which smooths the rough edges of the pieces. The third machine clamps the pieces together to form the parts of the set. Our fourth machine is a paint sprayer with which we paint the parts. At first, we hire only one worker for our factory. This one man must operate all four machines, and perform each step in the production process himself. He produces 20 sets a day.

We soon realize that we are not operating at our most efficient point. The worker is not able to become a specialist in any one job. He must go from one machine to another, and since he can operate only one machine at a time, three machines must be idle while he operates the fourth. So we decide to hire another worker. Labor, of course, is the variable factor of production which we will be adding to the fixed factor (capital). Now, with two workers in our plant, we have greater efficiency. One man operates machine number one and machine number two; the other operates number three and number four. Now we can have two machines running at the same time, and each worker can become more adept at handling his machines. As a result, we experience a marked increase in output. Our total output rises to 45 sets a day. The additional output accounted for by the fact that we have added another worker is called the *marginal product.* The marginal product resulting from hiring the second worker is 25—the difference between our total output when we had one worker and our total output after we hired the second.

The success of this move leads us to try adding still another man to our labor force. Now we can have three machines operating at once, and further specialization becomes possible. Total output rises to 80 sets. Marginal product is 35 (the difference between 45 and 80). The addition of the third worker has resulted in an increase of 35 units in our total output. It should be understood, however, that the increase in marginal product is *not* accounted for by any superiority on the part of the new worker. In fact, we assume that the workers are of equal ability. The increase stems from a more efficient combination of labor and capital.

When a fourth worker joins our labor force, total output rises to 130 sets a day. The marginal product is 50, the difference between 80 and 130. Now we have one worker for each machine. Each worker becomes a specialist in his particular phase of the operation, and all four machines can be running at once. Up to this point, we have been experiencing *increasing returns.* Each time we added a new worker, our output increased more than it did when we added the previous worker. Average output per worker has been rising—from an average of 20 sets per man when we had only one worker, to 32.5 when our labor force reached four workers. Our total variable cost has been rising, for each new worker means that our payroll will rise. However, the *average* variable cost has been going down. The benefits of specialization and the better combination of labor and capital have increased our production so that average costs have dropped. Thus, the average variable cost curve has been sloping downward.

But this situation cannot last. Suppose that we add a fifth worker to our plant, using him to relieve the others for lunch and for coffee breaks. We find that our total output rises to 160 units a day, for we do not have to shut down our machines when the workers go to lunch. The addition of the fifth man has increased our total output, but note that it has not increased it as much as the addition of the fourth man. Indeed, the marginal product is now only 30. *Now we are at the point of diminishing returns.* A sixth worker might also be useful, increasing our total output to 180. The marginal product is now only 20, however. The addition of a seventh worker might account for an increase of only 10, bringing our total output up to 190. The average output per worker has been declining since the fifth worker—and the average variable cost is *rising.* If we go on adding workers, we will even reach a point where the marginal worker adds nothing to our total output. In fact, the "crowding effect" might occur, meaning that we have so many workers in relation to our machines that they are getting in each other's way and thus reducing efficiency and lowering our output. The addition of worker number eight, then, might result in a marginal output that is negative—by hiring him we actually reduce our output instead of increasing it. Table 5–1 summarizes the situation.

Obviously, a businessman must be aware of the law of diminishing returns if his firm is to operate efficiently. We shall have occasion to refer to this law again in the next chapter, in terms of its influence on wage rates.

TABLE 5–1 An Illustration of the Law of Diminishing Returns

Machines	Workers	Total Output	Approximate Average Output	Marginal Product
4	0	0	0	0
4	1	20	20	20
4	2	45	22.5	25
4	3	80	26.6	35
4	4	130	32.5	50
	Point of Diminishing Returns			
4	5	160	32	30
4	6	180	30	20
4	7	190	27.1	10
4	8	185	23.1	–5

Total Cost

Total cost is the sum of total fixed cost and total variable cost. When a firm increases its output, total cost tends to rise. Fixed cost remains unchanged, naturally, but total cost will be pulled up by the rise in total variable cost with the rise in output. As Figure 5–2 demonstrates, *average total cost* can be found by dividing total cost by output ($ATC = TC/Q$) or by adding average fixed cost to average variable cost ($ATC = AFC$ plus AVC).

The average fixed cost curve (*AFC*), such as the one in Figure 5–1, slopes steadily downward, because average fixed cost declines as output rises. Average variable cost, on the other hand, reflects the law of diminishing returns. Average costs drop at first, because the firm is combining the variable factors with the fixed factors more efficiently. We can see that in Figure 5–2 when two units are being produced, the average variable cost is \$1,300. When output rises to three units, the curve shows us that average variable cost drops to \$1,200. Eventually, we find that new variable factors, while adding to the firm's total output, add less and less at each step. In other words, each new factor we acquire accounts for a smaller addition to total output than the factor that immediately preceded it. This is why the average variable cost curve slopes upward after the output level of four units. When seven units are being produced, the average variable cost is \$1,400. At an output level of 10 units, the *AVC* is \$1,800.

Average Total Cost

The colored-line curve shows *average total cost* (*ATC*). This is the sum of the *AFC* and *AVC* curves. For example, at an output level of one unit we note that *AFC* is \$2,000 and *AVC* is \$1,500. The sum is \$3,500, as shown by the starting point of our *ATC* curve. When four units are being produced, *AFC* is \$500, while *AVC* is \$1,200. Average total cost (*ATC*) at this point, of course, is \$1,700. When we produce 10 units, the *ATC* is \$2,000, because *AFC* is \$200 and *AVC* is \$1,800. Note that the *ATC* curve has the same general "U"

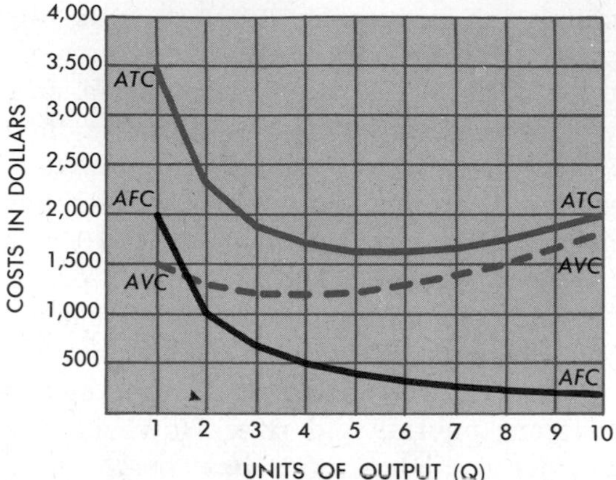

FIGURE 5–2 Average Cost Curves

The average fixed cost curve (*AFC*) is the same as the one in Figure 5–1. The dotted line shows average variable cost (*AVC*). Note that it drops at first and then rises as a result of the law of diminishing returns. The colored curve indicates average total cost (*ATC*), the sum of the other two costs. Explain why this curve declines and then rises, but does not rise as steeply as the *AVC* curve.

shape as the *AVC* curve. It drops sharply at the beginning because both *AFC* and *AVC* are dropping. It does not level off as soon as the *AVC* curve, because it is being pulled downward by the declining *AFC* curve. Eventually, it is pulled up by the rising *AVC* curve. Its ascent is not as steep, however, because it is partially offset by the *AFC* curve, which is still declining.

In Figure 5–3 we show total costs for the same firm as in the previous graphs. The colored horizontal line marked *TFC* shows total fixed cost, \$2,000. Again, it is clear that total fixed cost remains the same regardless of the level of output. By adding the total variable cost to the total fixed cost at every level of output, we get the ascending line which indicates our total cost. The *distance* between the *TFC* line and the *TC* line shows us the variable cost at each level of output. At an output level of eight units, for example, the distance between the *TFC* line and the *TC* line represents $12,000—the total variable cost at that level of output. Refer back to Figure 5–2, and you will note that the average variable cost at that level of output is $1,500. Total variable cost is obtained by multiplying $1,500 by eight (*AVC* times *Q*), which gives us our figure of $12,000. To this we add the $2,000 total fixed cost and find that total cost is $14,000 at that level of output.

The student can see the relationship between the *ATC* curve in Figure 5–2 and the *TC* line in Figure 5–3, at any level of output, by cross checking to see that $TC = ATC \times Q$. For instance, in Figure 5–2 *ATC* is $2,000 at 10 units of output. By multiplying $2,000 by 10, we get the total cost of $20,000 which appears in Figure 5–3.

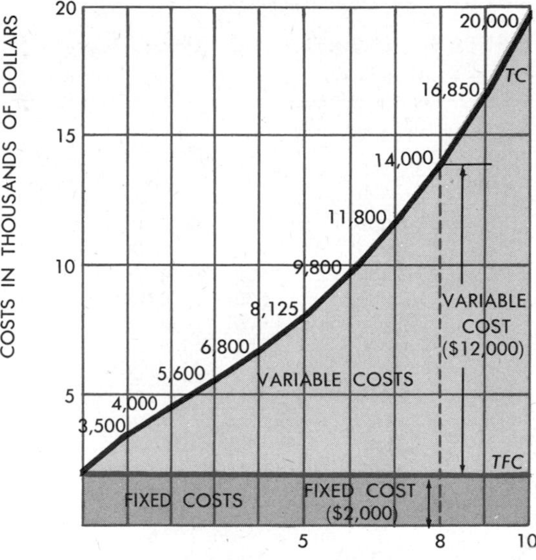

FIGURE 5–3 Total Cost

The ascending line indicates what our total cost of production (*TC*) would be at every level of output. It is the sum of total fixed cost ($2,000) and total variable cost. The dark shaded rectangle represents total fixed costs. The light shaded area shows total variable cost at each level of output. How can you determine *average* total cost, *average* fixed cost, and *average* variable cost from this graph?

Marginal Cost

The student should have a thorough understanding of the preceding parts of this chapter before tackling marginal cost. *Marginal cost* may be defined as the *additional* cost of one more unit of production. For example, suppose that a firm has been producing two units of output at a total cost of $4,600. It then decides to produce an additional unit, raising total cost to $5,600—$1,000 more than total cost at an output level of two units. The $1,000, then, is the marginal cost—the extra cost of producing an additional unit of output.

To be sure that this concept is clear, let us carry it one step further. The firm decides to increase its output to four units, and finds that total costs rise to $6,800. The difference between the total cost at this level of output and the total cost at the previous level is $1,200 ($6,800 minus $5,600). The marginal cost, then, is $1,200.

Marginal cost can also be defined as the *variable cost of the last unit produced.* We saw that the average variable cost (*AVC*) curve declines for a time, and then swings upward. This was explained by the law of diminishing returns. Because marginal cost is, in fact, *a part of* the firm's variable cost, its behavior is explained in the same way.

Using the information contained in Figure 5–3, we have constructed Table 5–2. Table 5–2 shows total fixed cost, total variable cost, total cost, and marginal cost at each level of output. Note that the marginal cost is simply the difference between

TABLE 5–2 The Determination of Marginal Cost

Total Output	Total Fixed Cost	Total Variable Cost	Total Cost	Marginal Cost
0	$2,000	$ 0	$ 2,000	$ 0
1	2,000	1,500	3,500	1,500
2	2,000	2,600	4,600	1,100
3	2,000	3,600	5,600	1,000
4	2,000	4,800	6,800	1,200
5	2,000	6,125	8,125	1,325
6	2,000	7,800	9,800	1,675
7	2,000	9,800	11,800	2,000
8	2,000	12,000	14,000	2,200
9	2,000	14,850	16,850	2,850
10	2,000	18,000	20.000	3,150

the total cost figure at one level of output, and the total cost figure at the level of output immediately preceding it.

The student should note that, in Table 5–2, the total cost figure was obtained by adding total fixed cost and total variable cost at each level of output. It can also be seen that marginal cost declines at first, and then begins to rise after a certain level of output (four units, in this case). Refer to Figure 5–4 for a graphic picture of the same information.

Figure 5–4 shows marginal cost in relation to average total cost and average variable cost. The *ATC* and *AVC* curves are identical with those in Figure 5–2. Notice that the *AVC* and *ATC* curves begin to rise as soon as they are crossed by the marginal cost (*MC*) curve. This occurs because marginal cost is a part of average variable cost and average total cost. To make this point clear, let us use an analogy. Suppose that you have been keeping a record of your test scores, and that the average is 80. Now you receive a score of 90 on your economics examination, and you add this to your previous scores. What will happen to your average score? Obviously, it must rise. If you had received a score of 70, your average would fall. Since marginal cost is added to the other costs, when the marginal cost figure is greater than the average total and average variable costs, those cost figures must begin to rise. (The mathematical rule which applies here states that whenever a number to be added to a series of numbers is *less than* their average, the average must *decline;* whenever a number to be added to a series of numbers is *larger than* their average, the average must *rise.*)

Knowledge of marginal cost is extremely important to the firm. It helps the

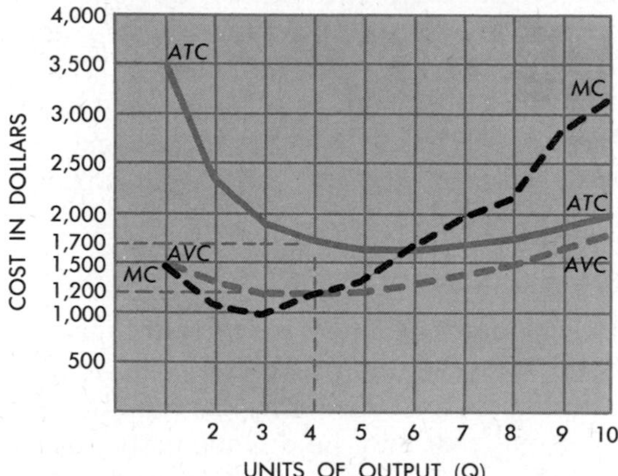

FIGURE 5–4 Marginal Cost

The *ATC* and *AVC* curves are identical to those in Figure 5–2. The broken line, representing marginal cost—the additional cost of the last unit of output—declines at first, then rises. Marginal cost is part of *AVC* and *ATC*. Why do the *ATC* and *AVC* curves begin to rise as soon as the *MC* curve crosses them?

firm to decide whether it should increase or decrease its output. Marginal cost is the cost which the firm can control most directly. As the cost which is incurred by producing one more unit, it is the cost which can be eliminated simply by reducing total production by one unit. When a firm increases its production, it naturally wants to know how much additional cost this will involve. Marginal cost indicates just how much more the firm must pay out when it produces one more unit. This cannot be learned by average cost figures alone. For example, examine Figure 5–4 again, and note that average total cost (*ATC*) at four units of output is $1,700. Marginal cost at that level, however, is only $1,200. The firm would be making a serious mistake if it assumed that by increasing its output from three to four units, it would add another $1,700 to its total costs. By examining marginal cost, it would see that it adds only $1,200. As we shall see shortly, the firm should know marginal cost in order to maximize its profit or minimize its loss.

Costs over the Long Run

Over the long run, all costs are variable. Taxes, interest rates, and other costs which are fixed in the short run can change. In the long run period there is time for the industry to build new plants, and there is time for new firms to enter the industry. Costs may decrease, stay constant, or increase in the long run.

Decreasing Costs and Economies of Scale

If unit costs fall as output rises, the firm is experiencing *decreasing costs.* When an industry is new it often lacks skilled labor and it has not yet developed efficient methods of production. As time goes on, better machines are invented, production techniques are improved, and workers become more skilled. Greater specialization becomes possible as new firms enter the industry. The improvement in efficiency leads to lower unit costs of production. The industry supply curve may actually slope downward—an exception to the law of supply. When a decrease in costs makes it possible to sell the product at lower prices, the public often benefits. A study of American economic history will show that the average consumer today enjoys many goods and services which were considered luxury items for the rich a few decades ago. This can be explained, in part, by the fact that some of our industries experienced decreasing unit costs as they increased their output.

The size of a firm can also be a factor. In some industries, large firms have lower unit costs of production than small firms. This principle is called *economies of scale.* As firms enlarge their plants, their unit costs decline because of mass production and other factors, such as:

1. *Specialization* is possible in a large firm. With a great many workers in the labor force, each man can be assigned a small but specialized task. Each worker becomes highly skilled and extremely efficient because he can concentrate on doing only one operation. In a small plant, one worker is often responsible for many tasks and is thus unable to develop skill or dexterity in any one of them. The same principle applies to management. The executive in the small firm may be responsible for personnel, production planning, selling, accounting, and several other functions. In the large firm, on the other hand, executives can hire specialists who have been trained in each of these fields, and greater efficiency results.
2. The *principle of factor substitution* can often be implemented better in a large firm. (See Chapter 8, Part A, for a discussion relevant to this concept.) Earlier, in discussing the law of diminishing returns, we saw how one factor of production (labor) was related to another factor of production (capital).

We found that in our imaginary firm there was *one point* at which labor was combined most efficiently with capital (machines). Because large firms have more machines and a larger number of workers, they are better able to experiment with various combinations of these two factors in order to find out which "mix" results in the greatest output. In fact, some firms conduct controlled experiments in which they leave one part of a plant as it is, while in another part of the plant they try various combinations of labor and capital to see which brings the greatest output at the least unit cost. The principle applies to other factors of production as well. The large firm, for example, can try substituting aluminum for steel, to see whether or not costs are reduced and profits are increased. Small firms often lack the resources to engage in this type of experimentation. Often, they must guess correctly the first time or go out of business.

3. *Better equipment* can be purchased by the large firm. Many modern machines are too costly for small firms, or are not suitable for use in small-scale enterprises. For example, it might even be wasteful for the small firm to obtain an expensive computer, for its use to the small business would be limited. The large firm, on the other hand, has so many uses for the computer that it could get its maximum utility. The very nature of some industries makes it necessary to have large plants. Steel, aluminum, motor vehicles, railroad equipment, and ocean-going vessels are but a few of the products requiring large plants and costly capital equipment.
4. *Research* is costly and difficult for the small firm, but can be carried on by large businesses. In 1968, for example, four large American firms were spending a total of nearly $3 billion on research and development. This amount, in fact, was greater than the *total* research expenditures of Italy, France, or the United Kingdom.[1] Through research, the large firm develops new and better products, improves its production methods, and reduces its costs. The large firm finds uses for materials which the small firm might discard because it does not have sufficient resources to produce by-products.
5. *Marketing advantages* often come with greater size. In the *factor market,* where firms are hiring labor, buying raw materials, obtaining capital goods, and borrowing money for investment purposes, the large firm usually has a competitive advantage. It may get a discount from a supplier because it buys in larger quantity. By offering greater stability and security, it often attracts the better workers. Because the large firm can ship its goods in great bulk, it may pay lower rates per unit. When borrowing money, the large firm often pays the prime rate. This is the lowest interest rate that commercial banks charge, the rate paid by the largest and most stable borrower. If the large firm wishes to raise capital by selling securities, it usually has a much better chance of finding buyers than does the small business. A big business can finance nationwide advertising campaigns on a large scale to broaden the market for its products.
6. *Stability* is more likely to be a feature of large businesses. That is, they are less vulnerable when recession or depression strikes the nation. While

[1] National Industrial Conference Board, *Road Maps of Industry,* January 1, 1968.

small firms are collapsing by the thousands, a large company may take huge losses on one part of its operation, but survive because other parts are profitable. The famous failure of Ford's Edsel car, for instance, was compensated for by the success of other models. A large company may even be able to operate for long periods at a loss, while small firms frequently survive almost on a day-to-day basis.

Constant Costs

Thus far we have discussed situations leading to decreasing costs. It is also possible for an industry to experience *constant costs.* This occurs when the cost per unit of output remains the same even though output is rising. The supply curve for the industry would be horizontal. An increase in demand might not result in higher prices in a competitive market, for the industry could expand its output to meet the greater demand without experiencing higher unit costs. This might be the case if raw material, labor, and other factors of production were so abundant that the industry could obtain more of them without increasing the unit cost of production. Much depends upon the nature and size of the industry as related to the factors of production it uses. For example, the manufacturers of paper clips could probably increase the output of their product many times over without causing a shortage of the metal used, and thus without increasing the unit cost of output.

There are probably few (if any) industries which can enjoy decreasing costs or constant costs forever. For a time, an industry might be characterized by decreasing costs. Industries with high fixed costs, such as railroads, telephone companies, and firms producing electric power have been decreasing cost industries. (Refer back to Figure 5–1 for a partial explanation of this.) A constant cost situation is likely to be a temporary phenomenon.

Increasing Costs and Diseconomies of Scale

Eventually, an industry will experience *increasing costs.* Increasing costs are probably the most common in America today, especially in industries that are well established. As output rises, the unit cost of production rises. The supply curve slopes upward. As an industry expands, it may have to bid against other industries for existing supplies of labor, raw materials, and capital. The result may be higher wage rates, higher prices for materials, and higher interest rates, naturally raising the average cost of producing the product. Industries which depend heavily upon natural resources are often faced by increasing costs as they expand their output. Fishing fleets must go farther out to sea to bring in larger catches. Lumbermen must go more deeply into the forests to obtain more timber. Miners often have to dig deeper, tap ores of lower quality, and use more expensive equipment to expand their output. Thus, their costs rise.

Earlier, we pointed out that a firm may enjoy *economies of scale* as it becomes larger. It is also possible, however, for a firm to exceed its optimum size. A firm can go beyond the size where it would have the lowest unit costs. If a firm becomes too large to be operated efficiently, it will experience *diseconomies of scale.* In other words, its unit cost of production will rise. When a firm becomes too vast to be managed in an orderly manner, the average total cost curve may rise. If a firm is too big, managers may lose touch with workers, with other managerial personnel, and with many important aspects of the productive operation. Vital decisions can be delayed if they must be made by the top executive, who is already occupied with too many problems. A firm producing hundreds of different products can lose track of the cost of producing each one, the market for each product, and so on.

It is difficult to say just what the optimum size of a firm should be. In some industries the optimum size may be much greater than in others. To give an extreme example, the optimum size of a firm producing automobiles is much greater than that of a firm offering a personalized service, such as haircuts. Little would be gained by having a barbershop staffed by hundreds of barbers. An automobile company, on the other hand, requires huge capital equipment, assembly lines, and a great many workers. Some large firms have attempted to meet the problem of diseconomies of scale by decentralization. One large auto company, for instance, has a number of divisions which enjoy a great deal of autonomy. In fact, the divisions actually compete with one another. Some economists feel that the American steel industry is suffering from diseconomies of scale and could be made to operate much more efficiently if the huge firms that comprise the industry would decentralize. In any event, diseconomies of scale can help to explain the rising supply curve over the long-run period.

Part B
Output and Price in Competitive Markets

In reality, it is difficult to find a market which meets the definition of pure competition. As we pointed out on p. 18, to be classified as pure competition a market must have a great many sellers who are acting independently. There may be no collusion among them, new firms may enter or leave the industry at will, and there may be no interference with the market forces which affect supply, demand, and price. The product must be standardized, so that the buyer may substitute the product of one firm for the product of another. For instance, the wheat produced by farmer Burns is no different from the wheat produced by farmer Chase. If the market is competitive, each firm is such a small part of the industry that it cannot affect the market price. That is to say, the individual firm can greatly increase its production or reduce its production without causing a change in the market price. If farmer Burns doubles the amount of wheat he raises and puts on the market, it will not cause the supply curve to shift to the right because his output is such a tiny part of the total output of wheat in the country. There will be no change in the market price if farmer Burns doubles or even triples his production of wheat. Also, in pure competition, the factors of production can be shifted from one firm to another. The seed, the workers, the fertilizer, and the machinery used on Burns' farm could be used just as well on Chase's farm. Unable to affect the existing market price, then, the firm must adjust to it. With the market price fixed (in the short run, anyway) the firm will attempt to maximize its profits or minimize its losses by adjusting its output. In this section we shall explore how a single firm in pure competition attempts to maximize its profits, how the industry as a whole adjusts to changes in the market price, and how economists evaluate pure competition. Even though pure competition is rare, there are some market situations (for example, certain agricultural industries) which come close to being pure competition. The model of pure competition enables us to compare the real life situation with the ideal—the "is" with the "ought to be."

The Short-Run Period

You will recall that in the short run, the firm does not have time to add to its plant. Thus, any adjustment that the firm wants to make will have to be done by adding or subtracting *variable* factors of production, such as raw materials and labor. Since the firm is too small a part of the industry to affect the market price by its actions, an increase or decrease in its output will not change the market price. What the firm will do, then, is attempt to produce at the point where its profits will be greatest or its losses will be minimized. There are several important factors that it must take into account.

First, *the demand curve for the individual firm in pure competition is perfectly elastic.* (See pp. 28–29 and the insert between pp. 34 and 35 for a discussion of elasticity.) A perfectly elastic demand curve is horizontal, indicating that the quantity sold will range from zero to infinity at the going market price. For the individual firm, this means that it can sell everything it can produce at the current market price. The demand curve for the industry as a whole, however, is a downward-sloping curve. If the whole industry increases its output, the extra output can be sold only at a lower market price. Figure 5–5 illustrates these points.

Graph A in Figure 5–5 shows the demand curve for the entire industry. It shows that the industry can sell 20,000 units of output at a price of $20 per unit (point x on the curve). If 100,000 units are produced, the price of the product must drop to $10 in order to clear the market (point *y* on the curve). If the industry raises its output to 200,000 units, it must accept a price of $2 in order to sell its entire output (point z). Let's assume that the market price is $10 for the period we are considering. The demand curve for an individual firm in the industry is indicated by Graph B in Figure 5–5. It shows that the individual firm can increase its output from zero to 20 without affecting price. Indeed, its output makes up much less than 1 percent of the industry's total output. It can double its production (say, from 5 to 10 units), and sell the additional output at the going market price of $10. For the individual firm, increasing output is like dumping a pail of water into the ocean—it is such a small addition to the total, that it will not cause a tidal wave (or even a ripple) on some foreign shore.

The Shutdown Point

As stated earlier, the firm compares total revenues with total costs to see what its profit or loss is. At this point, you might wonder why a firm would continue to operate if it is taking a loss. Remember that there are fixed costs and variable costs. The fixed costs must be paid anyway, even if the firm is producing nothing. Suppose that a firm's *total cost* is $300,000 at a certain level of output, $200,000 being made up of variable costs (such as labor and raw material) and $100,000 being made up of fixed costs

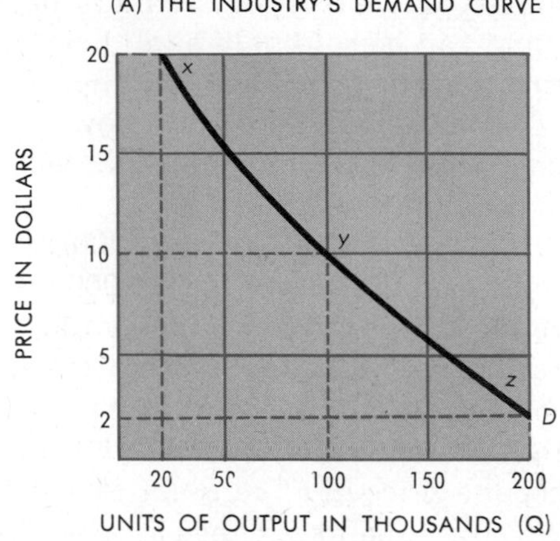

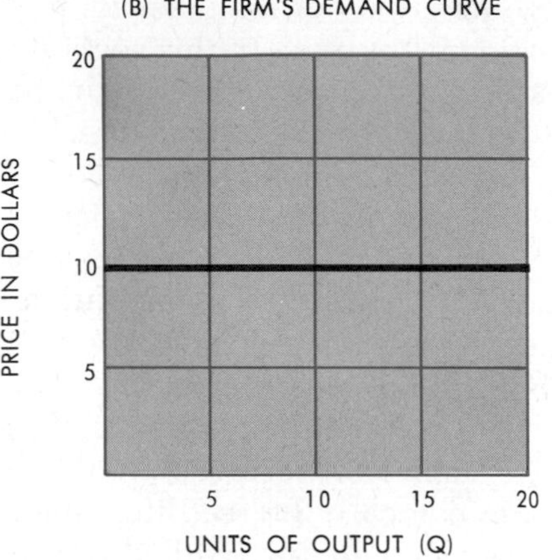

FIGURE 5–5 Demand Curves in Pure Competition

Graph A shows the demand curve for an entire industry in pure competition. Graph B shows the demand curve for the individual firm. If the industry as a whole increases its output, it must accept a lower price per unit in order to clear the market, but if an individual firm increases its output, there will be no effect upon market price. If the demand curve in graph B *did* slope downward, could we still say that pure competition existed? Why, or why not? If there were a supply curve in graph A, at what point would it cross the demand curve?

(such as interest payments, taxes, and rent). If the firm's *total revenue* is $240,000, it is clearly taking a loss. The difference between total revenue and total cost in this case is $60,000—this is its loss. But notice that the total revenue of $240,000 pays *all* of the firm's variable costs ($200,000) and also pays $40,000 of its fixed cost. If the firm were to shut down, on the other hand, its loss would total $100,000—the amount of the fixed cost. Thus, as long as a firm can cover all of its variable costs by remaining in operation it will do so. *Its shutdown point will come when total revenue no longer covers total variable cost.* For instance, if the firm's total revenue drops to $190,000, it clearly cannot cover its variable cost of $200,000, and will be better off by shutting down altogether. By shutting down it will be losing $100,000 (the toal fixed cost); by remaining in operation it will be losing $110,000 (the difference between total cost of $300,000 and total revenue of $190,000). *The shutdown point can also be defined as the point where the price is equal to the average variable cost.* Can you explain why?

The Most Profitable Point

Of course, a firm cannot go on operating at a loss forever. Many firms will operate at a loss temporarily, however, hoping that conditions will improve. The decision to operate while suffering losses will be based upon the possibility of covering all variable costs. Whether a firm is enjoying a profit or suffering a loss, however, it will try to operate at a level which maximizes the profit or minimizes the loss. Now we shall see how the firm determines this level of output.

Marginal Cost and Marginal Revenue—Profit Indices

To determine the level of output which will give it the greatest profit or the least loss, the firm must be concerned with its marginal cost and its marginal revenue. As we saw in Table 5–2 and in Figure 5–4, *marginal cost is the amount that each extra unit of output adds to total cost. Marginal revenue is the amount that each additional unit of output adds to total revenue.* Suppose that a firm has been producing 100 units of output, and selling each unit for $10. Its total revenue would be $1,000 (price of $10 times quantity of 100). When the firm increases its output to 101 units, it finds that its total revenue rises to $1,010. The marginal revenue in this case is $10. *For the firm in pure competition, marginal revenue is the same as market price.* Remember that the individual firm in pure competition can sell all that it produces at the existing market price. Refer again to Figure 5–5, Graph B. Note that the firm can sell any additional output for the market price of $10 per unit. The demand curve for the individual firm in pure competition, then, is also that firm's marginal revenue curve.

In the short run the firm does not have to worry about its marginal revenue, because it can sell each additional unit at the going market price. It *does* have to be concerned about its costs, however. Marginal cost (as shown by Table 5–2 and Figure 5–4) will change. Although it may drop as the firm increases production and approaches the point of greatest efficiency, eventually it begins to rise. *As long as marginal revenue is greater than marginal cost, it will be advantageous for the firm to increase its production.* For example, let's say that a firm can increase its output by adding another man to its labor force. After the new worker has been hired, the firm finds that its total revenues increase by $25 a day—this is the marginal revenue. If the firm has to pay the worker a daily wage of $20, it is clear that it did the right thing by hiring him. The new worker added only $20 to the firm's total costs, but accounted for an addition of $25 to its total revenues.

Figure 5–6 depicts a situation in which the firm in a purely competitive market can sell its output for the price of $10. We see that the firm's demand curve is horizontal (perfectly elastic), which means that an increase in the firm's output will *not* cause a reduction in the market price. The firm's demand curve is also its marginal revenue curve (*MR*), showing that each additional unit the firm produces and sells will add an additional $10 to its total revenues. The broken-line curve is the firm's marginal cost curve. Assume that the firm has been producing nine units, and then decides to produce a tenth. The tenth unit will add $10 to the firm's total revenues, as indicated by the demand or marginal revenue curve, and $5 to the firm's total cost, as indicated by the marginal cost curve. (Proceed upward from 10 on the horizontal axis to the *MC* curve, then move to the left to the vertical axis.) Certainly, it was advantageous for the firm to produce the tenth unit, for this added $10 to revenues but only $5 to costs.

Will the firm benefit by producing at a level of 15 units? Indeed it will. The *MR* line shows us that the firm will add $10 to its revenues by producing the fifteenth unit, while the *MC* curve shows us that it will add only $7 to its total costs. In fact, by increasing its output at any point to the left of the intersection of the curves, the firm will improve its profit position. If the nineteenth unit adds $9.99 to the firm's costs, it will still benefit the firm to produce it, for that nineteenth unit adds $10 to total revenues. Now look at the situation where the firm produces 30 units. The thirtieth unit adds $10 to total revenues, but it adds $19 to total costs. It would be foolish to produce at this level,

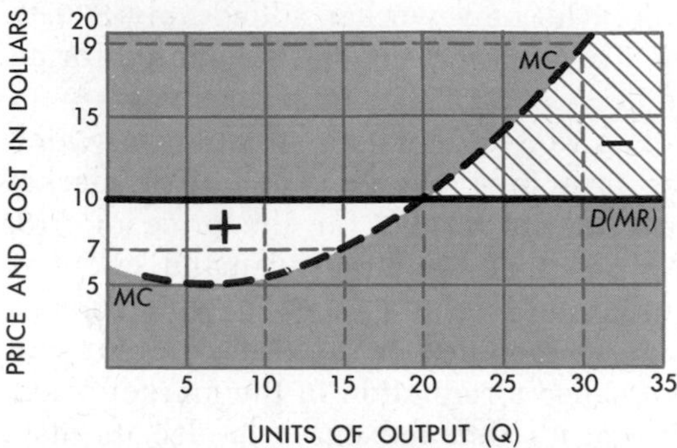

FIGURE 5–6 Marginal Cost and Marginal Revenue

For the firm in pure competition, the marginal revenue curve (*MR*) is the same as the demand curve (*D*). The firm can sell all of its output at the market price of $10 per unit. $10 is the amount that will be added to total revenue when an extra unit is sold. The marginal cost curve (*MC*) shows the amount that will be added to total cost by each additional unit of output. Any firm improves its profit position by producing up to the point where the curves intersect. Does this graph show whether or not the firm is making profits? Explain.

and the firm would benefit by reducing its output. At any point to the right of the intersection of the *MC* and *MR* curves, the firm is reducing its profits (or aggravating its losses). The rule, then, is that *the most profitable point for any firm is the point at which marginal cost equals marginal revenue.* The plus sign on the graph suggests that the firm can improve its profit position by increasing its output up to the point where *MC* crosses *MR*. The minus sign suggests that the firm will reduce its profits or increase its losses if it produces beyond the point of intersection. This rule for profit maximization applies to firms in all kinds of markets, not just to firms in pure competition. Again, profits will be maximized (or losses minimized) where marginal cost equals marginal revenue. (In Figure 5–6, profits are maximized at an output level of 20 units.)

Maximizing Profits

To prove the statement that profits are maximized where marginal cost equals marginal revenue, carefully study Figure 5–7. The firm's demand and marginal revenue are represented by the horizontal line. The going market price is $20, as this curve shows, and every time the firm sells one more unit of output it will increase its total revenues by $20. The colored line curve represents the firm's average total cost; the heavy broken-line curve is marginal cost. Notice first that the average total cost curve (*ATC*) is *below* the demand (marginal revenue) curve over a wide range of outputs. *Wherever the* ATC *curve is below the de-*

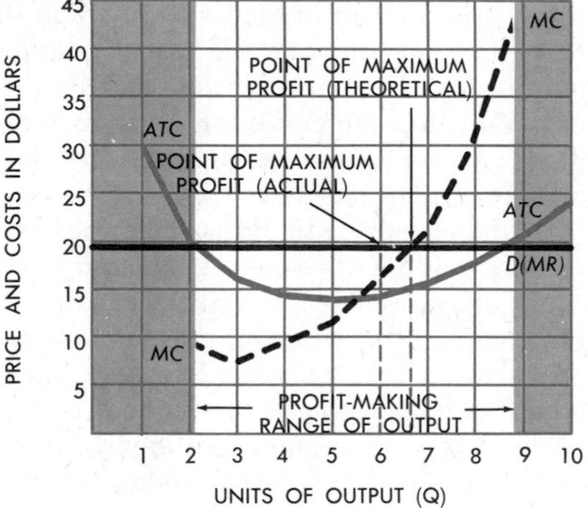

FIGURE 5–7 The Firm's Profit Position

The horizontal line, indicating a market price of $20, shows the firm's demand and marginal revenue. The firm can operate at a profit wherever the *ATC* curve is below this line. As long as it produces more than 2 units and less than 9, it will make a profit. To *maximize* its profit, it will produce as close as possible to the point where *MC* crosses *MR*, but not beyond this point. In this case, an output of 6 units will yield the greatest possible profit, for this is as close as the firm can come to equating marginal cost with marginal revenue. Compute the firm's profits at several different points to see why this is so.

mand and marginal revenue curve, the firm will make a profit. In other words, where the *ATC* curve is below the *D* curve, the *cost* of producing each unit is *less than* the price obtained for that unit.

Let us examine several possible levels of output to see where the firm can make its greatest profit. If the firm produces only one unit of output, its total cost will be $30 (*ATC* of $30 times *Q* of 1). When it sells that unit for only $20, however, it will take a loss of $10. If it produces two units, its total revenue will be $40 ($P \times Q$), and its total cost will be $40 ($ATC \times Q$). At this point, the firm will just break even. At three units of output, the firm will take in $60, and its total cost will be $48 (*ATC* of $16 times *Q* of three). Its profit will then be $12. If the firm produces five units, its total revenues will be $100, and its total cost will be $70—a profit of $30.

Now, we have maintained that the most profitable point will be where the *MC* curve crosses the *MR* curve. For any quantity beyond that intersection, the firm will be losing profits. In Figure 5–7, the *MC* curve crosses the *MR* curve somewhere between six and seven. To see if the rule is valid, we shall calculate the firm's profit position at six and at seven. At an output of seven units, the firm's total revenues will be $140, and its total cost will be $108.50 (*ATC* of $15.50 times *Q* of seven), and its profit will be $31.50. At an output of six, however, the firm's total revenue will be $120, its total cost will be $87 (*ATC* of $14.50 times *Q* of six), and its profit will be $33. While the firm in this example can make profits over a wide range, its most profitable point is an output level of six. Try computing the firm's profit position at eight (where *ATC* is $17.50) and see the results. At an output of nine, the firm will lose money, for we see that the *ATC* curve is *above* the *D* curve. At 10, the firm would be losing even more, for *ATC* at that point is $24, while marginal revenue is only $20. Our rule seems to be proven then, that the firm can maximize its profits by producing up to the point where marginal cost equals marginal revenue. (In Figure 5–7 the actual most profitable quantity falls short of the exact theoretical quantity because we must deal with whole units of output.) Table 5–3 shows the firm's profit position at various levels of output.

Minimizing Losses

Having proven that the firm can maximize its profits by producing a quantity as close as possible to the point where *MC*

TABLE 5–3 The Firm's Profit Position

Q	P (MR)	TR (P × Q)	ATC	TC (ATC × Q)	Profit or Loss
1	$20	$ 20	$30.00	$ 30.00	−$10.00 (loss)
2	20	40	20.00	40.00	breaks even
3	20	60	16.00	48.00	12.00
4	20	80	14.50	58.00	22.00
5	20	100	14.00	70.00	30.00
6	20	120	14.50	87.00	33.00 (max. profit)
7	20	140	15.50	108.50	31.50
8	20	160	17.50	140.00	20.00
9	20	180	20.50	184.50	− 4.50 (loss)
10	20	200	24.00	240.00	− 40.00 (loss)

TABLE 5–4 The Firm's Loss Position

Q	P (MR)	TR (P × Q)	ATC	TC (ATC × Q)	Loss
1	$13	$ 13	$30.00	$ 30.00	$ 17.00
2	13	26	20.00	40.00	14.00
3	13	39	16.00	48.00	9.00
4	13	52	14.50	58.00	6.00
5	13	65	14.00	70.00	5.00 (least loss)
6	13	78	14.50	87.00	9.00
7	13	91	15.50	108.50	17.50
8	13	104	17.50	140.00	36.00
9	13	117	20.50	184.50	67.50
10	13	130	24.00	240.00	110.00

equals *MR*, but not beyond that point, let us test the rule again to see if it applies to the minimizing of losses. Study Figure 5–8. The cost curves are identical with those in Figure 5–7, but the demand and marginal revenue curve has shifted downward. The market price is now only $13. We can see that the *ATC* is *above* price at *every* level of output. Thus, the firm cannot possibly operate at a profit. Since it can have no effect on the market price, it must try to adjust its output to the point where its losses will be minimized.

In Figure 5–8, the firm can come closest to equating marginal cost with marginal revenue at an output of five units. Here, the firm will have total revenues of $65 (*P* of $13 times *Q* of five). Total cost will be $70 (*ATC* of $14 times *Q* of five). The loss of only $5 is less than that at any other quantity. If the firm produces six units, for example, it will go beyond the point where *MC* equals *MR*. Its total revenues will be $78 (*P* of $13 times *Q* of six), total cost will be $87 (*ATC* of $14.50 times *Q* of six), and the loss will be $9. Table 5–4 shows the firm's losses at various levels of output.

By now, the importance of knowing marginal cost should be very clear. Any firm can maximize its profit or minimize its loss by producing a quantity up to the point where marginal cost equals marginal revenue. This rule will also apply to firms in imperfect competition.

How Does Time Influence Supply?

Up to this point, we have been considering primarily the short-run period. Now we shall examine those factors which bring about long-run equilibrium in perfectly competitive markets. On p. 26 we discussed briefly the effects of time on supply. In this chapter we shall elaborate on those points.

In analyzing a market situation, time is an extremely important consideration. Some industries can increase supply quickly in response to an increase in price, for example a manufacturing industry with much idle capacity, plenty of labor, and a productive process that is easily speeded up. Other industries need a long lapse of time before they can respond to rising prices by increasing output. For example, if the public should suddenly double its demand for peaches, the fruit-growers could not respond immediately, because it takes years for fruit trees to grow to suitable size. Time periods will differ, then, depending upon the industry in question.

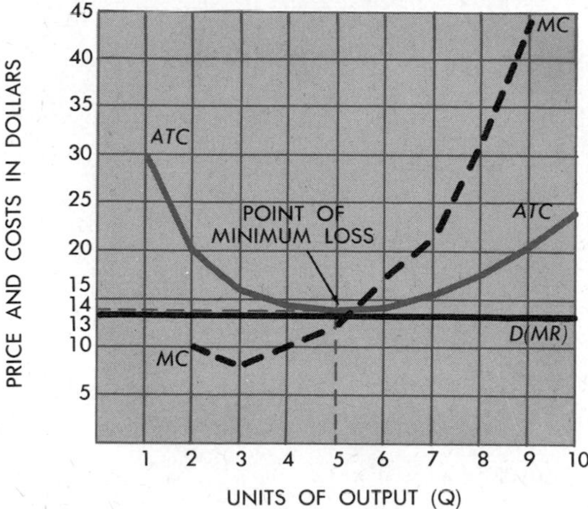

FIGURE 5–8 The Firm's Loss Position

The *MC* and *ATC* curves are identical to those in Figure 5–7, but the *D* curve has shifted downward. The firm must accept $13 as the going price for its output. With the *ATC* curve above the *D* curve at every point, the firm must operate at a loss. It will minimize its loss by operating as close as possible to the point where *MC* crosses *MR*. In this case, the firm will minimize its loss by producing 5 units of output. To test this rule, compute the firm's losses at several other levels of output.

Supply in the Market Period

It is convenient, in analyzing a market situation, to identify three time periods—the market (or momentary) period, the short-run period, and the long-run period. The *market period* in any industry is a period of time so short that the sellers cannot increase supply. The corresponding supply curve for the industry (the sum of the supply curves for each firm) is perfectly inelastic (vertical), as shown in Graph A of Figure 5–9. Suppose that a new product becomes an overnight success. The demand for the product is very great, but the sellers have no way of increasing their supply quickly: they can only sell from their existing stocks until the industry is able to increase production.

For an interesting example, remember the blackout that occurred over vast parts of the northeastern United States a few years ago. Electrical power failed, and people needed light. There was a sudden demand for candles, but sellers had very limited supplies, so candles which had been selling for a few cents commanded a price of two or three dollars.

Supply in the Short-Run Period

The *short-run period* is long enough to permit changes in the production rates in existing plants, but not long enough for the building of new plants. If demand increases, the industry can hire more workers and use its existing plant and machinery more intensively to increase output, and put more goods into the market. The corresponding supply curve for the industry slopes upward to the right (see Graph B in Figure 5–9). Supply is no longer perfectly inelastic. It might be relatively elastic or relatively inelastic, depending upon the particular situation. However, it will certainly be more elastic than the supply during the market period.

Supply in the Long-Run Period

The *long-run period* is long enough for the industry to build new plants, and for new firms to enter the industry. In a growing economy, existing firms which feel that there will be a strong demand for their product for many years to come, will build new plants, buy new machines, and use their productive resources to the fullest. Seeing that profits are being made in the industry, other businessmen will be attracted to it and will start new firms. Now, the supply curve for the industry (which is the sum of the supply curves of all the firms in the industry) will slope upward, farther to the right than the short-run supply curve. As shown by Graph C

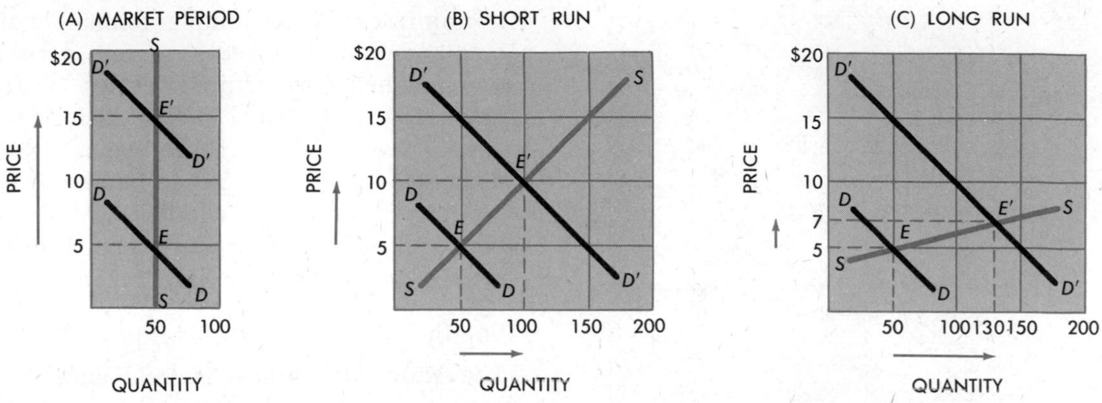

Figure 5–9 Effects of Time on Supply and Price in the Industry as a Whole

In each graph the supply curve represents the sum of the supply curves of all the firms in the industry, and the demand curves represent the sum of all their demand curves. In each graph the demand schedule has shifted upward by the same magnitude. During the market period (A), supply cannot be increased. The upward shift in demand from *DD* to *D'D'* results in a price increase from $5 to $15. In the short-run period (B), firms in the industry can increase their output by producing more intensively in their existing plants. The quantity offered for sale rises from 50 to 100 units. The new equilibrium price is $10. In the long-run period (C), existing firms have time to build new plants, and new firms enter the industry. The quantity offered for sale rises from 50 to 130 units, and price rises from $5 to $7. What would happen to price if this were a *decreasing cost industry*, with a downward-sloping *S* curve?

in Figure 5–9, it is likely to be very elastic —even perfectly elastic. (For the curve to be perfectly elastic, the industry must be increasing the supply of the product just enough to meet changes in demand without affecting the market price.)

Profits in the Long Run

If an industry is enjoying good profits, the profit position of a typical firm will be like the one in Figure 5–7. However, because there is no barrier to the entry of new firms in a competitive market situation, new firms will be attracted to a profitable industry. Let us suppose that many new firms appear on the scene and greatly increase the supply of the industry's product. Assuming no change in the market demand schedule, the market price will be forced down because of the industry's increase in supply. Figure 5–8 can be used to illustrate how this situation affects a typical firm in the industry. The firm finds that the market price has dropped (from $20 to $13, in this example). As Figure 5–8 shows, the firm now operates at a loss, because the new market price is not high enough to cover its costs at any level of output. When losses rather than profits are the typical pattern, firms will begin to *leave* the industry, thus reducing the industry's total output. When fewer goods appear on the market, the price will again be forced upward.

Long-Run Equilibrium

Where does all of this end? In theory, at least, it ends in *long-run equilibrium*—the industry settles at a point where the typical firm neither makes profits nor suffers losses. The firm's long-run equilibrium position is depicted graphically in Figure 5–10. In our analysis of Figure 5–7 and Figure 5–8, we established that the

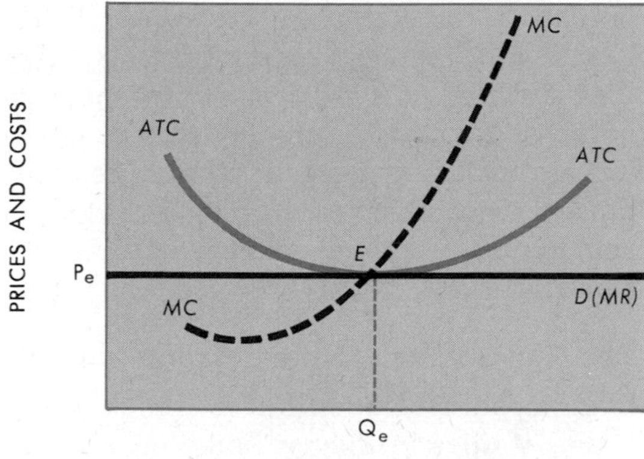

FIGURE 5–10 The Firm's Long-Run Equilibrium Position

When the typical firm in pure competition is in long-run equilibrium, price, *ATC*, *MC*, and *MR* are equal. The firm is producing Q_e units of output, for at that level *MC* crosses *MR*. It would suffer a loss by producing at any other level, for it is clear that *ATC* is above price at any other point. In what way would this situation be changed if the *D* curve remained the same, but if improvements in technology reduced the firm's average total cost?

firm can maximize profits or minimize losses only where $MC = MR$. We do not need actual figures in Figure 5–10, therefore, to see that the firm's best level of output in the long run is that point where marginal cost equals marginal revenue.

Study Figure 5–10, noting that *MC* crosses *MR* at level of output Q_e. It should be clear that if the firm operates at any other level of output it will incur a loss. If it produces fewer than Q_e units of output, it will suffer a loss because average total cost (*ATC*) will be *above* the demand curve (the market price) at every point to the left of Q_e. If it produces more than Q_e units of output, it will also operate at a loss. Again, *ATC* is above price at every level of output greater than Q_e. It seems, then, that at Q_e units of output the firm is just breaking even. It is barely covering its costs, for *ATC* at that point just equals price. At the equilibrium point *E*, then, *ATC* equals price and equals marginal cost.

Normal Profit

By now you are probably asking: "Why should a firm continue to operate in this industry if it just barely covers its costs?" The answer lies in our definition of *profit*. Earlier, we defined profit as the difference between total revenues and total costs. Wages, rents, the price of raw materials and other items were included in the total cost figure. However, *normal profit* is also considered to be a part of the total cost. By *normal profit*, we mean *the minimum amount that is necessary to keep the businessman in the industry*. When the typical firm is in equilibrium, as in Figure 5–10, the entrepreneur is making just enough of a profit to keep him in business. If he were making less he would leave the field.

Pure Profit

If the typical firm is making more than necessary to keep the entrepreneur in the field, it is making pure profits. *Pure profit*, (or economic profit), then, *is an amount above that which is necessary to keep the businessman in the industry*. It is *not* considered to be a part of total costs. It is the residual (the "left-overs") after all costs (including normal profit) have been met. When pure profits are being made, other firms will enter the industry. Normal profits are not high enough to induce other firms to enter, nor are they low enough to force existing firms to leave.

Evaluation of Pure Competition

The Advantages of Pure Competition

Some economists feel that the situation we have described is ideal. A glance at

Figure 5–10 will reveal that the firm in long-run equilibrium in a purely competitive market is producing at the most efficient point—the very bottom of the *ATC* curve. Resources are being used as efficiently as possible. The price is as low as possible, for it just covers all costs (including the modest normal profit as the reward of the entrepreneur). Indeed, the consumer is getting the product at cost.

The firm which fails to use its productive resources with maximum efficiency will not survive in this market. Again, Figure 5–10 shows that if the typical firm operates at a level where the average total cost is above the minimum point possible, it will suffer losses and will eventually be forced to leave the field. Because firms must use those productive resources which give the greatest possible return for the lowest possible cost, society benefits from maximum efficiency. There is no waste.

In pure competition the product is standardized, and thus no money is spent for advertising. The consumer will not pay a high price that reflects the cost of advertising the product. The producers will respond to the consumer's demands. If the consumer desires more of a product, he will offer a higher price, and the existing firms will make pure profits for a while. This will attract new firms to the industry, the quantity supplied will increase, and the price will be held in check. It will even be possible, in the long run, for the consumer to get more of the item at the original price. Therefore, consumer demand will help to determine what shall be produced and how the industry shall allocate the factors of production. When the consumer has obtained enough of the product, or if some other item should now appeal to him instead, he will reduce his purchases or will offer a lower price. Firms will then leave the industry (for they are taking losses) and will enter an industry which is producing a more popular product. Once again, therefore, productive resources will be reallocated in accordance with the wishes of the consumer.

The Social Costs of Pure Competition

Even if pure competition worked in real life as it does in theory, some economists would maintain that it is not always the best or most efficient system. The firm in pure competition may be forced to operate at its most efficient point in the long run, but it is often too small to pay for the research which leads to the development of new products and better technology. If it can just barely cover its costs, it can hardly devote much of its revenue to research and development. Larger firms, on the other hand, which are not operating in perfectly competitive markets do compete in another sense—to develop new products, improve production methods, and lower costs.

The equilibrium of which we spoke does not usually last very long. New adjustments always become necessary, sometimes creating considerable hardship. When losses become typical and drive firms from the industry, workers lose their jobs (at least temporarily) and capital equipment ceases to operate for a time. Unemployment of men and other productive resources is a loss to society, for we are denied the goods and services that they could be turning out.

If the firm in pure competition is in a constant battle for survival, it cannot be concerned with such problems as the pollution of our water and air or with the wasteful exploitation of our natural resources. A firm that is just barely covering its costs cannot install air pollution control devices on its smokestacks or purify the water that it has used in the productive process before returning that water to its original source. Some large firms in imperfectly competitive markets, on the other hand, do spend considerable sums to avoid polluting air and water. (Of course, many such firms are also major polluters of air and water.) Since society as a whole suffers from air and water pollution and from the wasteful exploitation of our natural resources, there are *social costs* which were not taken into account when we spoke of the great efficiency of pure competition.

In pure competition, prices act as signals to the businessman, for they reflect the effective demand of the consumer. If the price of a certain product rises, businessmen will devote more of their resources to the production of that item and less to the production of an item which commands a lower price (assuming that production costs are comparable). By *effective demand* we mean wishes or desires supported by the ability to pay. The profit-motivated businessman in pure competition, of course, must be concerned only with effective demand. He cannot concern himself with the needs or wishes of people who cannot pay for what they want. As a result, resources may be devoted to the production of yachts and other luxury items, while millions of poor persons live in dilapidated dwellings because they cannot pay for decent housing. Some of our leading economists argue that we are devoting too much of our output to luxury items while we ignore the need for schools, better roads, hospitals and other things which do not usually yield profits.

Finally, it is argued that pure competition does not provide the public with a wide choice of consumer goods. The product in a purely competitive market is standardized. Most consumers prefer to have a wide choice of products. It would be disastrous, in the eyes of the American consumer, if all women had to wear identical dresses, or if all men had to have identical cars. Some of the imperfectly competitive markets, then, offer a wide range of choices to the consumer.

In summary, while it is difficult to find a purely competitive market in America today, the model of pure competition does provide a useful yardstick against which we can measure the realities of our economic life.

Part C
Output and Price in Imperfectly Competitive Markets

If a single seller in a market can affect the market price by increasing or decreasing his output, the market is imperfectly competitive. Monopoly, oligopoly, and monopolistic competition are terms used to describe such markets (see pp. 18–20).

Monopoly

If there is only one firm selling a product, and if there is no close substitute for that product, the firm can be called a monopoly. Although there are huge business combinations in America which act like monopolies, it is difficult today to find a good example of a pure monopoly. The problem is often one of definition. If we narrowly define the market by limiting it to a single town, we might say that the man who owns the only pharmacy in that town has a monopoly. If we broaden the definition to include all the pharmacies in the county, however, we cannot say that a monopoly exists. Public utilities and other natural monopolies are special cases, which we discussed earlier (see p. 19). Most American industries today fall somewhere between the two extremes of pure competition and pure monopoly, but it will be simpler to analyze these markets if we start with the assumption that pure monopolies exist.

We found that the demand curve for a firm in pure competition is perfectly elastic (horizontal), but that the curve for the whole industry slopes downward. This implies that if the industry as a whole increased its output, it would have to accept a lower market price in order to sell the additional output. The individual firm, on the other hand, was such a small part of the total picture that it could increase its output to the limit of its capabilities without affecting the market price—thus the horizontal demand curve for the individual firm.

Demand, Marginal Revenue, and Marginal Cost

The situation is quite different for the monopoly firm. By definition, *the monopoly firm is the whole industry.* The demand curve for the industry is the same as the demand curve for the firm, and it slopes downward. Even the monopolist is unable to control demand (although he might be able to influence it through advertising). The monopolist is faced with the fact, therefore, that if he increases his output he must accept a lower price in order to sell all that he produces. The monopolist can establish any price that he chooses, and then sell whatever the consumer will purchase at that price. On the other hand, he may decide how much to produce and then sell his output at whatever price will clear the market. He must always remember, however, that if he increases his output the price will fall; if he reduces his output the price will rise.

Price alone, however, will not tell the monopolist how to make the greatest profit. He, like the producer in perfect competition, must be aware of marginal revenue and marginal cost. In pure competition, the firm's marginal revenue is the same as the market price. Thus the firm's horizontal demand curve can represent its *MR* as well as price. In the case of the monopoly firm, however, marginal revenue will *not* be the same as price. Every time the monopolist increases his output, the market price will fall, as the downward sloping demand curve indicates. For the monopolist (and for other firms in imperfectly competitive markets) *marginal revenue is below price.* That is to say, as the monopolist increases his output, the amount added to his total revenues by the last unit produced will be *less than* the amount added by the previous unit produced. Study Figure 5–11 to see why this is so.

The upper line is the monopolist's demand curve. It shows that the price will be $30 if he produces one unit. The price drops to $17 when he produces five units, and to $1 when he produces 10. When the monopolist sold one unit, his total revenue ($P \times Q$) was $30. When he in-

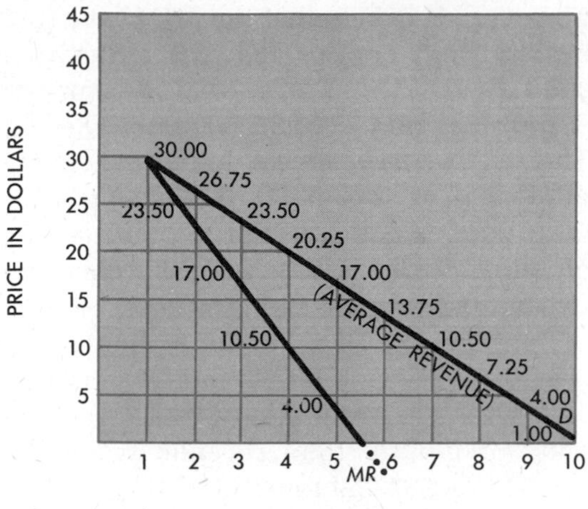

FIGURE 5–11 The Monopolist's Demand and Marginal Revenue

Because the monopolist is the only producer, the market price must fall when he increases his output. This is indicated by the downward sloping demand curve. At each point, marginal revenue is below price, as shown by the *MR* curve. What is the significance of the fact that the *MR* curve eventually goes below the horizontal axis?

creased his output to two units, the price dropped to $26.75 per unit, giving him a total revenue of $53.50 (*P* of $26.75 times *Q* of two). The *marginal revenue* (the addition to total revenue resulting from the sale of an additional unit of output) is $23.50. Remember that this is the difference between total revenue when he produced only one unit and total revenue when he produced two.

At three units of output, price is $23.50, and total revenue becomes $70.50. This is $17 more than the firm was taking in before, so marginal revenue is $17. At five units of output, the price is $17, total revenue is $85 (five times $17), and marginal revenue is only $4. Table 5–5 summarizes the situation.

The information in Table 5–5 can be checked with Figure 5–11. Note, too, that if the monopolist produces six units, the sixth unit adds nothing to total revenues —in fact it results in a *drop* in total revenue. (Marginal revenue would be negative—*minus* $2.50, and total revenues would begin to decline.)

The Most Profitable Point

The monopolist's price-output adjustment is like that of the firm in pure competition, in that it pays him to produce up to the point where marginal revenue equals marginal cost. As long as the production of one more unit adds more revenues than costs, the monopolist can increase his profits by producing the additional unit. The difference lies in the fact that the monopolist's marginal revenue schedule is not the same as his demand (average revenue) schedule. In pure competition the demand schedule did not change when the firm increased its output, but in monopoly it declines. Our analysis of Figure 5–7 and Figure 5–8 showed that the firm can maximize its profit or minimize its loss by producing at the point where *MC* equals *MR* (or as close to that point as possible, without going beyond it). We stated that the same rule applies to firms in imperfect competition. Let us test the rule just one more time by studying Figure 5–12.

TABLE 5–5 The Monopolist's Price, Total Revenue, and Marginal Revenue

Q	*P*	Total Revenue ($P \times Q$)	Marginal Revenue
1	$30.00	$30.00	$30.00
2	26.75	53.50	23.50
3	23.50	70.50	17.00
4	20.25	81.00	10.50
5	17.00	85.00	4.00
6	13.75	82.50	−2.50

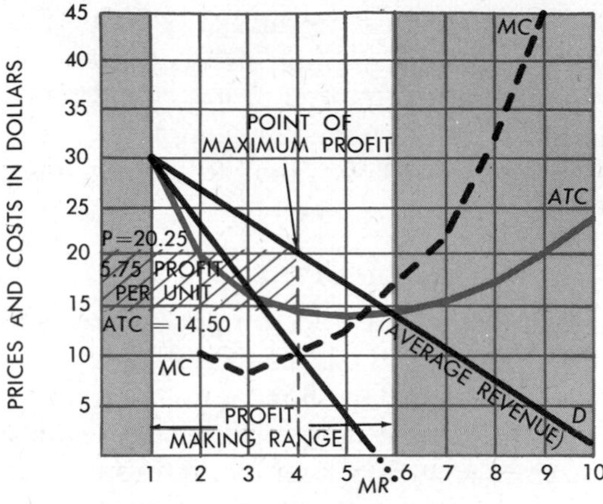

FIGURE 5–12 The Monopolist's Costs, Prices, and Profits

Although the monopolist can make a profit anywhere that the *ATC* curve lies below the *D* curve, he maximizes his profit by producing up to the point where *MC* crosses *MR* (4 units of output, in this case). The shaded area indicates his profit. At 4 units of output, his price is $5.75 above his average total cost. Total profit is $23.00—$5.75 times *Q* of 4. To test the rule, compute the firm's profits at other levels of output.

First, note that the monopolist can make a profit over a wide range of outputs. The average total cost (*ATC* curve) is below price (the *D* curve) when the firm is producing more than one unit and less than six. In this case, the firm can make a profit by producing any quantity from two to five units. Marginal cost equals marginal revenue at about four units of output, however. It is here that the *MC* curve (the broken line) crosses the *MR* curve (the solid line). The firm's total revenue is $81 at this point (*P* of $20.25 times *Q* of 4). The *ATC* curve shows us that average total cost at this point is $14.50. Total cost, then, is $58 (*ATC* of $14.50 times *Q* of four). Profit is $23, the difference between total revenue and total cost.

Suppose the firm produces five units. Here total revenue is $85, total cost is $70, and the firm's profit is only $15. At three units of output, total revenue would be $70.50 (*P* of $23.50 times *Q* of three), total cost would be $48 (*ATC* of $16 times *Q* of three), and profit would be $22.50. Obviously, the firm maximizes its profit by producing at the point where marginal cost equals marginal revenue. Table 5–6 summarizes the situation.

The same principle would apply if the monopolist were operating at a loss. He would minimize his loss by producing up to the point where *MC* equals *MR*.

The Disadvantages of Monopoly

Why do so many economists object to monopolies? A careful study of Figure 5–12 as compared with Figure 5–10 should reveal some of the reasons. In pure competition there is a very efficient allocation of productive resources in the long run. The typical firm will be producing at the lowest point on its average total cost

TABLE 5–6 The Monopolist's Profit Position

Q	P	Total Revenue (P × Q)	Total Cost (ATC × Q)	Profit or Loss
1	$30.00	$30.00	$30.00	break even
2	26.75	53.50	40.00	$13.50
3	23.50	70.50	48.00	22.50
4	20.25	81.00	58.00	23.00 (maximum)
5	17.00	85.00	70.00	15.00
6	13.75	82.50	87.00	4.50 (loss)

curve, as shown in Figure 5–10, and the price is just high enough to cover the costs of production. The firm makes no pure profit. Compare this with the monopolist's situation.

As Figure 5–12 shows, the monopolist is producing at a point (four units of output) where the average total cost curve (*ATC*) is *not* at its lowest point. The plant is not being used with maximum efficiency. (This would be at an output of five, the lowest point on the *ATC* curve.) By producing four units, the monopolist maximizes his profits. A pure profit of $5.75 per unit is made by the monopolist. Whereas the buyer would be getting the product at cost in pure competition, in the monopoly market he pays more than it cost to produce the product. The consumer gets fewer products and pays a higher price.

The monopolist does not use as many productive resources as he could be using. (Firms in imperfectly competitive markets often operate at below capacity.) Factors of production which could be employed in the monopoly firms are forced to seek employment elsewhere where they can, perhaps, be used less efficiently. It is also charged that monopolies aggravate inequalities in incomes. The monopoly firm gets a higher price than the firm in pure competition, even if that firm in pure competition has the same production costs. The owners of large firms are usually people of wealth, so that the high profits obtained because of monopoly power go to those who are already comfortably situated. Critics of monopoly power claim that the monopolist is enriched at the expense of the consuming public in general.

Oligopoly

When there are a few sellers in an industry, and when each seller is large enough to affect the market price, an oligopoly exists. The individual firm in an oligopoly market, however, must be aware of the possible effects of its own actions upon the other firms in the industry. Many major industries in the United States are oligopolies; that is, a few firms account for most of the industry's output. This is indicated by a high *ratio of concentration*. The ratio of concentration usually means the percentage of an industry's total output accounted for by the four largest firms. For example, in a recent year it was found that the four largest firms in the linoleum industry produced 87 percent of the industry's output. Thus, the ratio of concentration was 87. It is possible to find industries with a great many firms, thus creating the impression that much competition prevails. But if a few giants account for most of the industry's output, it would probably be classified as an oligopoly. Figure 5–13 shows the ratio of concentration for 10 industries.

Aside from the fact that all oligopoly markets are dominated by a few sellers, and that the sellers must recognize their mutual interdependence, it is hard to generalize about them. Some oligopolies are huge industries with a national or international market. The automobile industry is an oligopoly, for example, as is petroleum refining and steel. In 1969, a single firm in the auto industry had sales exceeding $24 billion. The power of a relatively small number of huge corporations is indicated by the fact that 200 large corporations account for over 40 percent of all value added in manufacturing. In some oligopolies, the product is not standardized. There is a difference, for example, between the automobiles produced by Ford and those produced by General Motors. In other oligopolies, product standardization is common. Steel of a certain type is pretty much the same, regardless

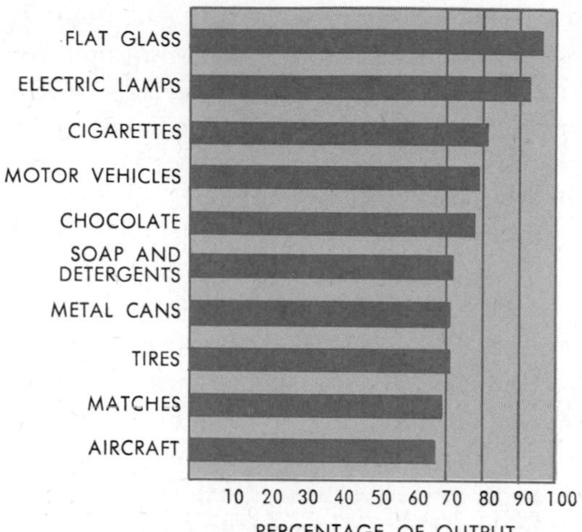

FIGURE 5–13 Concentration of Output in the First Four Companies in Each Industry

While pure monopoly is rare, oligopolies are widespread. The colored area shows what percentage of the total value of shipments is concentrated in the largest four companies of each industry. Data for 1966. SOURCE: Department of Commerce, Bureau of the Census, *Annual Survey of Manufacturers, 1966.*

of which firm produces it. While we usually think of oligopolies as huge industries which have a profound impact on the national or even on the world economy, there are some which are relatively small. Thus, if there are only a few dairies in a particular region, an oligopoly exists in the market for dairy products in that area. Many oligopolies, however, are of the type in which large-scale production is required, and it is difficult for a small firm to enter the industry.

Demand, Marginal Revenue, and Marginal Cost

In any event, one of the most important facts about oligopoly is that an individual firm cannot change its price without affecting the other firms in the industry. The demand for the industry is downward sloping, and the demand curve for each firm is downward sloping. The individual's curve is not identical with that of the industry, however. The individual firm will probably not achieve a lasting gain by cutting the price. The immediate result might be a large gain in sales at the expense of its competitors, but this gain will be temporary. Its rivals can quickly cut their prices and win back their former customers. Price cutting, then, can bring lower profits or losses to all firms in the industry.

If the individual firm raises its price, while the others continue to sell at the original market price, that firm will lose customers. Its sales will decline sharply. For these reasons, the individual firm in an oligopoly rarely raises or lowers the price.

Examine Figure 5–14, depicting the "kinked" demand curve for an oligopolistic firm. Assume that the going price in this oligopolistic market is $100, and the firm in question sells 200 units. (See Point *E*.) Its total revenue is $20,000. Now it tries raising its price to $120. The competitors continue to sell the same product for $100, however, so our firm's sales drop from 200 to 100. (See point *E′*.) Its total revenue falls to $12,000. When the oligopoly firm raises the price unilaterally, demand tends to be *elastic*—the percentage drop in sales is greater than the percentage increase in price. Now suppose that this firm attempts to undercut the competition by dropping its price to $50. Its sales rise to 220 units. (See point *E″*.) But the competitors reduce their prices accordingly, or perhaps sell for even less. Our firm's total revenues are now only $11,000 (price of $50 times quantity of 220). Thus, when the oligopoly firm attempts a price reduction, the demand for its output tends to be *inelastic*—the per-

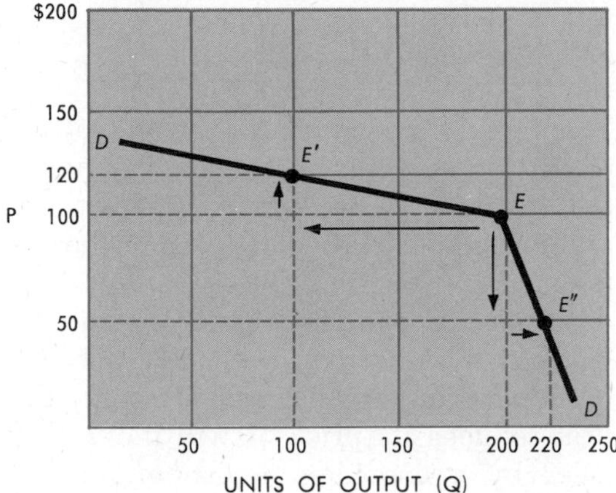

FIGURE 5–14 The "Kinked" Demand Curve of an Oligopoly Firm

When the individual firm in an oligopoly market attempts a price increase while its competitors hold the line, it can expect a more-than-proportional decline in sales. In this case, the price is increased from $100 to $120, and sales drop from 200 to 100 units. When it tries to lower the price from $100 to $50, it experiences a less-than-proportional rise in sales because its competitors also reduce their prices.

centage increase in sales is less than the percentage drop in price.

Prices in an oligopoly are often quite rigid, changing only when all of the firms in the industry change at the same time. The monopoly firm and the firm in pure competition, if they know their demand schedules, can tell what will happen to the price if they change their output. The monopoly firm does not have to worry about what competitors will do, as there are no competitors. The firm in pure competition knows that it can change its output without affecting the price. The oligopoly firm, however, can never be quite certain about what its rivals will do. He is less able to predict what his demand schedule will be, and what his marginal revenue will be. It is not so easy to find that level of output where marginal revenue equals marginal cost.

The fear of a destructive "price war" which will hurt everyone in the industry usually prevents price competition in oligopoly. There is sometimes a tacit agreement whereby everyone watches the "price leader" and charges whatever he charges. The usual result is that the price will be above the point where the *ATC* curve is at its minimum. The oligopoly firm often makes pure profits and fails to produce at its most efficient point. The price will probably be higher than it would be in pure competition, but lower than it would be if a pure monopoly existed. (Some firms in an oligopoly do better than others. Recently, one firm in the auto industry failed to pay dividends, while others were making profits.)

There are elements of competition in oligopoly. It is always possible that new firms will enter the industry if high profits are being enjoyed. Nonprice competition, in the form of attempts to provide a higher quality product, better services to customers, or advertising, may exist. Individual firms may develop better production techniques or better products in an attempt to earn high profits without touching off a disastrous price war. Oligopoly firms have often acted together in a way that has harmed the public and violated the antitrust laws, but they have also been responsible for many improvements in technology and better products which have ultimately benefited society as a whole. The oligopoly probably produces fewer goods, employs fewer factors of production, operates at a less efficient point, and charges higher prices than would be the case if the industry were purely competitive. It is quite possible, however, that some industries would perform no better as purely competitive industries than they do as oligopolies. It is hard to imagine thousands of small steel mills operating efficiently, for this is an industry in which economies are achieved through large-scale production. A few economists (such as J. M. Clark) have argued that in certain industries a degree of monopoly is preferable to cut-throat competition.

Monopolistic Competition

Monopolistic competition has many of the characteristics of pure competition. There are many firms in the industry, and the entry of new firms into the industry is often very easy. It is difficult for the firms to act in concert because of the large number and because they may not recognize mutual interdependence. Each firm accounts for only a small part of the industry's total output, with the result that it has little control over the market price. A single firm's actions may have little effect on the industry as a whole, although its influence can be greater than that of the firm in pure competition. A major difference between monopolistic competition and pure competition, is that product differentiation exists in the former. There will be some sort of difference between the products of the competing firms. The difference can be in styling (as in women's garments), quality, color, the packaging of the product, or only in the brand name. However slight these differences might be, they do suffice to remove the industry from the realm of pure competition. The product of one firm may be a close substitute for that of another firm, but the individual firm *does* have an element of monopoly control over its own product. Thus, a single firm may cause a slight change in the market price if it changes its output. A certain amount of price competition may be found, but there will also be nonprice competition in the form of advertising, services, and packaging.

Demand, Marginal Revenue, and Marginal Cost

The demand curve for the individual firm is not the same as the demand curve for the industry. The firm's demand curve will not be perfectly elastic, as in the case of pure competition, but a highly elastic demand curve is probable. Certainly the curve will be much more elastic than that of a pure monopolist. If the individual firm reduces its price, it will increase its sales by a considerable amount, for its product is very similar to the products of its competitors. If it raises price, on the other hand, it will lose sales, for its customers can easily obtain good substitutes. The few customers it retains may be accounted for by such things as preference for the firm's packaging, brand-name loyalty, habit, and the like.

As in the case of the monopoly firm, the firm in monopolistic competition will find that its marginal revenue curve lies below the demand curve. If the firm increases its output, it must expect to sell at a lower price. Again, this will mean that the amount added to the total revenue by each additional unit sold will be less than the amount added by the preceding unit. Figure 5–15 shows the firm's demand and marginal revenue curves. The entire industry's demand curve, of course, would be much steeper (less elastic).

In Figure 5–15 we have dispensed with the figures on the axes. It should no longer be necessary to prove to the reader that the firm's most profitable level of output is where *MC* crosses *MR*. *MC* crosses *MR* at output Q_e on the horizontal axis. The demand curve shows that price will be P_e. Note that the demand curve is tangent to the *ATC* curve in this case. This means that the firm is making no

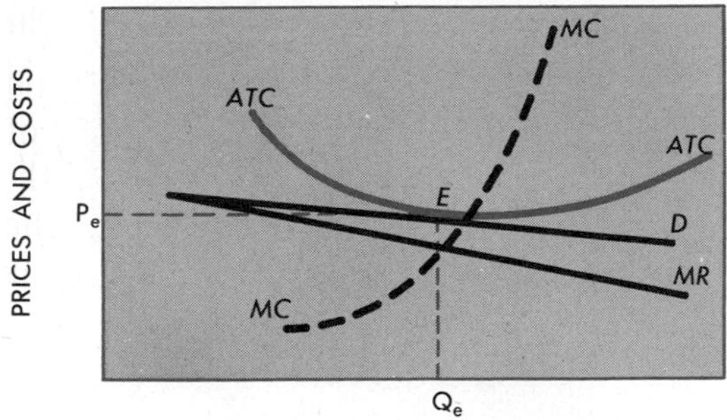

FIGURE 5–15 Price-Output Adjustment of the Firm in Monopolistic Competition

The typical firm in monopolistic competition has a highly (but not perfectly) elastic demand curve. Like the monopoly firm, it must accept a lower price if it increases its output. To maximize its profit, it produces to the point where $MC = MR$. The price (P_e) is slightly higher, and the quantity (Q_e) slightly less than in pure competition. Note that the firm is not producing at its most efficient point, which would be at the very bottom of the ATC curve. How would this diagram change if demand for the industry's product increased?

pure (or economic) profit. *ATC* just equals price at Q_e units of output, so the firm is just covering its costs. This need not always be the case.

In the short run, the typical firm in the monopolistically competitive market may enjoy pure profits. The *ATC* curve would then be *below* the demand curve, as in Figure 5–7 and Figure 5–12. But it is easy for new firms to enter the industry; businessmen would be attracted to the field by these high profits. As in the case of pure competition discussed earlier, too many firms might enter, increase the total supply, and force the market price down. Now the *ATC* curve for the typical firm might be *above* the demand curve at all points. Losses would be typical of the industry, and firms would begin to leave. Eventually, things settle at a point where the typical firm finds that the demand curve is tangent to the *ATC* curve, as in the case in Figure 5–15.

The firm is making no pure profit, but just covering its cost (which includes the *normal profit* necessary to keep the entrepreneur in the industry). A long-run equilibrium exists, and the normal profit is not high enough to induce other businessmen to enter the industry nor is it so low that it forces existing firms to leave. While this situation seems very similar to pure competition, further study of Figure 5–15 will show that the presence of an element of monopoly power *does* have an effect.

The typical firm in *pure competition*, when long-run equilibrium exists, produces at the minimum point on its average total cost curve. It will be noted in Figure 5–15 that the firm is producing slightly to the left of that point. Thus, it is not producing at its most efficient possible point. Total output is slightly below what it would be in pure competition. The price is a bit higher than would be the case in pure competition also. The firm cannot operate at any other point, however, without suffering losses. To make normal profits and to prevent losses, it is forced to produce at a level of output smaller than its point of greatest efficiency. Thus, costs and prices are higher than they would be in a purely competitive market. The consumer pays for these economic wastes.

On the other hand, the firm in monopolistic competition must often try to improve the product, or offer better service in order to compete with its rivals. It will also advertise in the hope of increasing its share of the total market. The consumer may derive some benefit from a wider variety of styles or differences in quality that result from monopolistic competition. One of the best examples of monopolistic competition is the women's garment industry, where slight differences in styling are important to the consumer. There is more choice than exists in pure competition, where the product is completely standardized. The public may benefit from improvements in the product. The consumer ultimately bears the cost of advertising, however, and although advertising plays a useful role in our economy, many economists charge that too much is spent on it. Finally, critics of monopolistic competition charge that oligopolies can develop from it, as the weaker firms fall by the wayside and as the few remaining strong firms capture increasingly large shares of the market.

REVIEW: THE HIGHLIGHTS OF THE CHAPTER

1. Profit is the difference between total cost (including implicit cost) and total revenue. Most (if not all) business firms attempt to maximize profits and minimize losses.
2. Total fixed costs (such as interest on the firm's debts) do not change with the level of output, at least in the short run. Average fixed cost declines as output rises. Variable costs (such as wages) do change as the firm's level of output changes. Average variable cost tends to decline at first, then rises because of the law of diminishing returns.
3. According to the law of diminishing returns, if we keep adding a variable factor of production to a fixed factor of production we will eventually reach a point where the output accounted for by each additional unit of the variable factor will decline.
4. Total cost is the sum of fixed and variable costs. Total cost rises as output rises. Average total cost is total cost divided by the quantity produced. Average total cost can also be found by adding average fixed cost and average variable cost.
5. Marginal cost is the additional cost of producing an extra unit of output. It is the variable cost of the last unit produced. Marginal cost tends to decline at first, then rise because of the law of diminishing returns. As soon as the marginal cost curve crosses the average total cost and average variable cost curves, those curves begin to rise. Marginal cost is very important, for it is the cost which the firm can control most directly.
6. In the long run, all costs are variable. There is time to build new plants, and new firms may enter the industry. Long run costs may be decreasing, constant, or increasing.
7. In pure competition, the individual firm is such a small part of the industry that it cannot affect the market price by increasing or decreasing its output. Its demand curve is perfectly elastic, and its marginal revenue curve is identical with the demand curve. Marginal revenue is the same as price for the firm in pure competition.
8. A firm can maximize its profit or minimize its loss by producing to the point where marginal cost equals marginal revenue. This applies both to firms in perfectly competitive markets and in imperfectly competitive markets.

9. During the market period, there is no time to increase supply. In the short-run period, supply can be increased by using existing plant more intensively. In the long-run period, new plants can be built and new firms may enter or leave the industry.
10. For a firm in imperfect competition, the demand curve slopes downward because the firm must accept a lower price if it increases its output. The marginal revenue curve will be below price (below the demand curve).
11. Firms in imperfect competition (monopolies, oligopolies, and monopolistically competitive firms) probably produce less than they could, with the result that the market price is higher than it would be in pure competition. These firms fail to produce at their most efficient possible points—the minimum point on the average total cost curve.
12. In theory, pure competition gives us the product at cost, and typical firms eventually settle at a point of maximum efficiency. Innovations and technological advances often come from firms in imperfectly competitive markets, however.

IN CONCLUSION: SOME AIDS TO UNDERSTANDING

Terms for Review

total revenue
total cost
profit
loss
explicit cost
implicit cost
fixed cost
variable cost
law of diminishing returns
marginal product
marginal cost
marginal revenue
decreasing cost
constant cost
increasing cost
economies of scale
diseconomies of scale
principle of factor substitution
perfectly elastic demand curve
shutdown point
long-run equilibrium
market period
short-run period
long-run period
normal profit
pure profit
imperfectly competitive market
monopoly
oligopoly
monopolistic competition
ratio of concentration
kinked demand curve

Questions for Review

1. Explain the difference between fixed and variable costs, giving examples by citing a firm in your area. Why does average fixed cost fall, while average variable costs fall and then rise?
2. Explain the law of diminishing returns by assuming that a potato farmer makes no change in the amount of land or capital equipment he is using, but keeps adding workers. What is the significance of this law to all producers?
3. Why does the *ATC* curve tend to resemble the *AVC* curve rather than the *AFC* curve?

4. Why must the *AVC* and *ATC* curves begin to rise as soon as they are crossed by the *MC* curve?
5. Under what conditions might an industry experience decreasing costs? Constant costs? Increasing costs?
6. Give at least four reasons why economies of scale might occur in an industry.
7. What are the characteristics of a purely competitive market? Why is the demand curve for the individual firm perfectly elastic?
8. Explain why a firm will sometimes continue to operate, even if it is operating at a loss.
9. Explain how a firm maximizes its profit or minimizes its loss.
10. Describe the possible effects of time on supply, using an actual industry to illustrate each time period.
11. How is long-run equilibrium established in a purely competitive market? How does this affect the typical firm?
12. What are the arguments for and against pure competition? Do you feel that most industry should be purely competitive? Why? Why not?
13. Why does the demand curve for the firm in imperfect competition slope downward? What is the significance of this phenomenon?
14. Why does a monopoly firm fail to produce at the minimum point on its average total cost curve?
15. Explain the statement "Firms in an oligopoly must recognize their mutual interdependence."
16. Compare and contrast monopolistic competition with pure competition and pure monopoly.

Additional Questions and Problems

1. Seventy-five percent of firm A's costs are fixed. Seventy-five percent of firm B's are variable. Other things being equal, which firm would most likely shut down first if losses are being suffered? Why?
2. Study several industries in your area and determine what constitutes the market period, the short-run period, and the long-run period for each. For example, note the difference in the short-run period for the producers of fresh fruits and vegetables and for the producers of an inexpensive manufactured item.
3. Study the industries in your area and classify them according to whether they are purely competitive, monopolistic, oligopolistic, or monopolistically competitive. Be prepared to defend your classifications by indicating how you have defined the market in each case, the ratio of concentration in each case, profits in each industry, and so on.
4. Monopoly A has a highly elastic demand curve. Monopoly B has a highly inelastic demand curve. Other things being equal, how will these differences in elasticity of demand affect each firm's decisions on determining the best level of output?
5. Refer to Figure 5–12. Draw a graph in which the monopolist's demand and marginal revenue curves are identical with these in Figure 5–12, but in which

the *ATC* curve is above the *D* curve at all points. Compute the marginal cost at each level of output and draw in the *MC* curve. Determine the level of output at which the monopolist would suffer the least possible loss.

SELECTED READINGS

Allen, Clark Lee, James M. Buchanan, and Marshall R. Colberg. *Prices, Income & Public Policy.* New York: McGraw-Hill, 1959.

Colberg, M. R., and W. C. Bradford. *Business Economics,* 3rd ed. Homewood, Ill.: Richard D. Irwin, 1964.

Dooley, Peter C. *Elementary Price Theory.* New York: Appleton-Century Crofts, 1967.

Dorfman, Robert. *The Price System.* Englewood Cliffs, N.J.: Prentice-Hall, 1964.

Galbraith, John Kenneth. *The New Industrial State.* Boston: Houghton Mifflin Co., 1967.

Grayson, Henry. *Price Theory in a Changing Economy.* New York: The Macmillan Company, 1965.

Kefauver, Estes. *In a Few Hands—Monopoly Power in America.* New York: Penguin Books, 1965.

Stigler, George J. *The Theory of Price.* New York: The Macmillan Company, 1966.

Ward, Benjamin. *Elementary Price Theory.* New York: The Free Press, 1967.

Watson, Donald S. *Price Theory in Action.* Boston: Houghton Mifflin Co., 1969.

Labor: Its Uses and Rewards 6

THE AUTHORS' NOTE TO THE STUDENT

Production of goods results from putting the factors of production together to turn out the materials and services wanted by society. We have just seen how business, when it goes to the market with goods and services, represents supply; and when it goes to the market for the factors of production, it represents demand. Here we are interested in the market concerned with the factors of production, and in one particular factor, labor.

In addition to its human value, labor represents, in dollars, our most valuable resource. Since we know from our central problem that resources are limited, we must make choices on how to allocate them. Just as price, resulting from interaction of supply and demand, helps to solve the problem of allocating our production, so wages (the price for labor) help to allocate our supply of labor. There are many factors that influence the demand and supply of labor. Some of these factors interfere with the mechanism of the classical model. In Chapter 7 we will examine the causes and the consequences of changes in the status of labor, with particular reference to the roles of government and labor unions.

A STUDENT'S NOTE TO THE STUDENT

A short, well-organized, simple chapter if you pay careful attention to the graphs. The key concept here seems to be how the productivity of labor is all-important in determining wages. If the workers' productivity increases, then the employer can increase wages without necessarily raising prices.

Make sure you understand the law of diminishing returns before tackling the marginal revenue curve, and remember that the employer cannot afford to pay the last worker (marginal cost) more than the value he creates (marginal revenue) without losing money. His alternatives seem to be to lower wages (not likely), or cut down on production and his labor force (likely), or price the cost of buying labor-saving machines (a possibility).

You should have some fun determining whether you are for or against minimum wages when you get through with all the arguments.

Part A
The Role of Labor in Production

What Is Labor?

Labor is one of the four factors of production. Its responsibility is to take natural resources and man-made instruments of production, or either of these, and fashion them into products that businessmen want for sale to consumers. It is human effort used in creating value to satisfy consumer wants. The value created by labor varies from country to country, region to region, and job to job. Value from labor can be increased by providing tools (capital) and skills (education) for workers to use. It is the human effort, shaped by the skill for producing, that businessmen bid for when they seek labor's services in the market for the factors of production.

It is important that you should not think

TABLE 6–1 Wage and Earnings Differentials: What is a man-hour of labor worth?

INDUSTRY DIFFERENTIALS

It is worth more (on the average) in one industry than in another. In 1970, the average hourly earnings of production and nonsupervisory workers in five industries were:

Construction	$5.00
Motor vehicles	4.23
Meat packing	3.78
Trucking	3.76
Farm machinery	3.45

REGIONAL DIFFERENTIALS

It is worth more in one place than in another. In 1970, for instance, the average hourly earnings of certain manufacturing production workers in five labor markets were as follows:

Michigan	$3.79
California	3.44
Connecticut	3.07
New Mexico	2.53
North Carolina	2.19

JOB DIFFERENTIALS

And everybody knows that it is worth more in one job than in another. The average hourly earnings in five occupations within one broad industrial classification in Washington, D. C. in 1970 had the following spread:

Engineer (maintenance)	$4.29
Machinist	4.00
Painter	3.54
Packer (shipping)	2.40
Janitor	1.75

Differences in the wages people receive reflect investment in their training, relative scarcity of their skill, and the influences of government, unions, and geography. Explain the reasons for the major differences between the highest and lowest wages in each of the three categories above. SOURCES: Federal Reserve Bank of Cleveland, *Economic Commentary*; *Statistical Abstract of the United States*; Reports of the U. S. Bureau of Labor Statistics.

of labor only as a factor involving physical effort. The role of labor has changed as manufactured energy, such as electricity and steam, has been substituted for human energy in producing goods.

Managers who receive salaries and people who are self-employed must also be considered labor. The economist considers that the self-employed man in effect pays himself a wage or salary, since if he performed the same work for someone else he would be paid.

The Unique Qualities of Labor

The foregoing description of labor places it in the classical model without differentiating it from other factors of production. Actually, labor has at least two characteristics that make it unique. First of all, labor stems from and cannot be separated from human beings. This means that, as a factor of production, labor has feelings and is capable of independent action. Secondly, labor has the means of buying back the goods and services produced. Machines are not sensitive to the surroundings in which they are used, and if they are not used today they can frequently make up for the lost output at some other time. The same may be said about most natural resources. Moreover, neither of these other factors is playing the additional role of consumer.

The supply of labor tends to be quite inelastic, particularly for a short period of time. This is less true for unskilled labor than for skilled labor, since several years may be needed to develop the talent necessary to perform skilled work acceptably. Another factor contributing to the inelasticity of labor is the low degree of mobility of the worker. Returning to our computer, we find that it may suggest offering the worker more dollars than he is presently earning to induce him to move from one section of the country to another. However, the worker may prefer to remain where he is because he has established roots in the community. In trying to analyze the role of labor in the classical model as well as in the actual American economy today, we must take these characteristics into consideration.

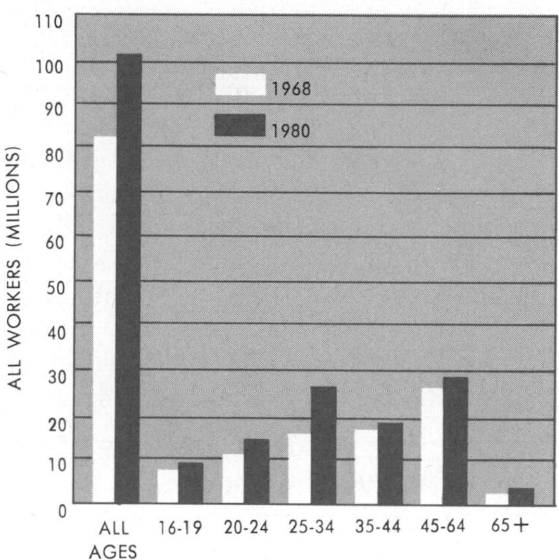

FIGURE 6–1 The Shape of the Labor Force, 1968 and 1980

The total labor force, 16 years and over, is expected to rise to 100.7 million by 1980. (The civilian labor force is made up of those persons 16 years of age and over who are employed or are looking for work.) The proportion composed of teenagers will probably decline slightly, while workers in the 25 to 34 age group will rise sharply. The proportion of the labor force accounted for by older workers, 45 to 64 years of age, will decline sharply. SOURCE: U.S. Bureau of Labor Statistics, *The U.S. Economy in 1980.*

Characteristics of the American Labor Force

Of the more than 200 million people in the United States, over 80 million were counted as members of the *labor force* in 1970. While this represents only about

40 percent of our total population, a closer look reveals that 90 percent of the men between the ages of 20 and 65 consider themselves as part of the labor force and that over 40 percent of the women in this age group do the same. The percentage of our labor force under 20 and over 65 has been growing smaller each year, and will probably continue to decline in the immediate future. This is so for our younger people because of the value placed on higher education and the difficulty they have in obtaining employment without training and skills. Our older people are retiring earlier, partially because our productivity per worker has increased sufficiently to keep our level of living high without their efforts. Our Social Security system, the additional income from pensions from both public and private employment, and savings and investments are an effect of this high productivity and allow some to retire in relative comfort. The fact that our labor force is small in proportion to our population and that our level of living is high relative to that of other nations is proof of the high productivity of American labor. Table 6–2 compares the prices of selected consumer items in Moscow and New York, in terms of work-time required to obtain them. It should be noted that the United States achieves greater output with fewer workers. In agriculture, for example, the U.S.S.R. employs about eight times as many workers but achieves lower yields per acre.

TABLE 6–2 Work Time Required to Buy Selected Goods, Moscow and New York

Item	Moscow	New York
1 lb. of white bread	23 minutes	6 minutes
1 lb. of potatoes	4.5 minutes	1.5 minutes
1 lb. of beef, rib roast	73 minutes	20 minutes
1 lb. of salted butter	163 minutes	17 minutes
1 lb. of sugar	47 minutes	2.7 minutes
1 quart of milk	28 minutes	5.9 minutes
1 dozen eggs	108 minutes	14 minutes
1 cotton shirt (men's)	13 hours	1.7 hours
1 woolen suit (men's)	183 hours	23.6 hours
1 pair of leather shoes (men's)	41 hours	6.6 hours
1 rayon dress	49 hours	5 hours
1 pair of leather shoes (women's)	38 hours	5.5 hours
1 pair of nylon stockings	5 hours	.5 hours
$3^1/_2$ oz. cake of toilet soap	21 minutes	2.7 minutes
1 fifth of vodka	8 hours	2 hours

SOURCE: Joint Economic Committee, 89th Congress, *New Directions in the Soviet Economy.*

An interesting and useful way of measuring a nation's productivity and level of living is to look at the distribution of its labor force among the categories of occupations. Figure 6–3 shows the trend since 1947. The great increase in white-collar occupations and the equally dramatic reduction in the proportion of those engaged in blue-collar work and farming shows that we have far less need for workers to engage in the physical aspects of production and far more need for those supplying mainly services rather than goods.

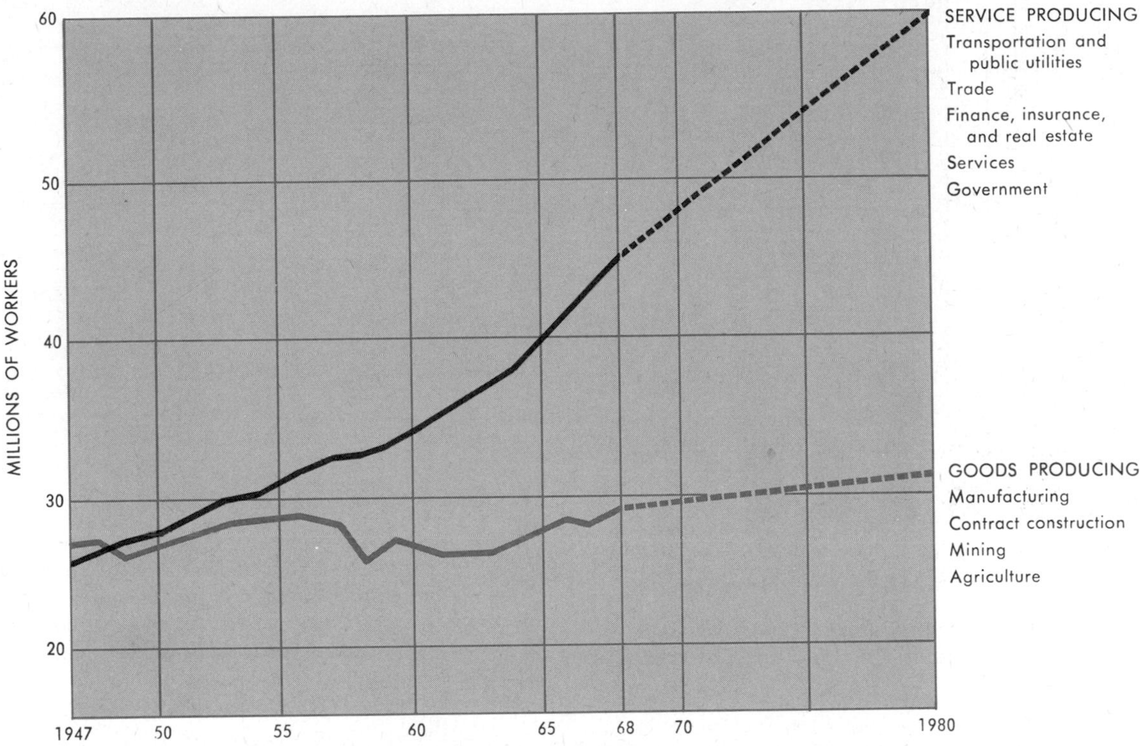

FIGURE 6–2 Employment Trends in Goods-Producing and Service-Producing Industries, 1947–1980

Although employment in the goods-producing industries is expected to rise, it will make up only about one third of total employment by 1980, as the rise will be even sharper in service-producing jobs. The goods-producing industries are manufacturing, contract construction, mining, and agriculture. (Employment will actually decline in the latter two.) The service-producing industries are transportation and public utilities; trade; finance, insurance, and real estate; services; and government. (Data from 1947 to 1968 are actual; from 1968 to 1980, projected.) SOURCE: U.S. Bureau of Labor Statistics, *The U.S. Economy in 1980.*

Importance of Capital to Labor Productivity

In countries which are underdeveloped, most workers must use a large amount of their energy in providing for the physical necessities of life. Without modern equipment (capital) to work with or the skills for using such tools, few workers can be freed to provide luxury goods or extra services associated with a high standard of living. With over 35 percent of the Soviet Union's labor force engaged in agriculture and little of the total output available for export, it is easy to see why their level of living and average productivity of workers are so much lower than ours. (Although using less land and labor, the United States uses many more tractors, trucks, grain combines, and other such equipment, as well as much more electricity on its farms.)

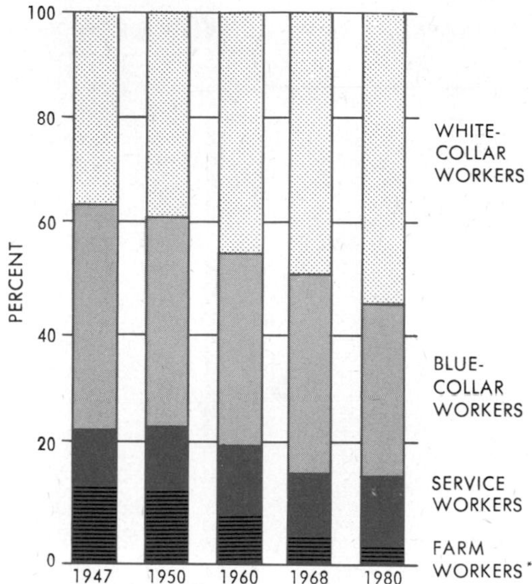

FIGURE 6–3 Employment Trends Among Major Occupational Categories

White-collar employment is expected to grow at an annual rate of 2.6 percent (assuming only 3 percent unemployment), while blue-collar jobs grow by only 1 percent and farm workers decline at a rate of 3.4 percent. What are the implications of these changes for the United States economy? SOURCE: U.S. Bureau of Labor Statistics, *The U.S. Economy in 1980.*

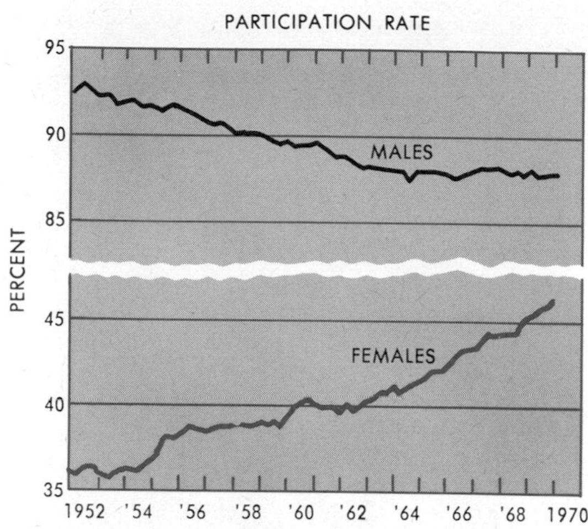

FIGURE 6–4 Labor Force Rates by Sex

The labor force participation rate is the percentage of all those age 16 and over who are able to work. (The employment rate, on the other hand, is the percentage of those in the labor force who are actually employed.) Largely because of earlier retirements, the participation rate for males has been declining since 1952. The rate for men in their 30's and 40's is about 98 percent and has changed very little. The increasing rate for women can be accounted for by educational gains made by women and the increasing demand for white-collar workers. The rates shown above represent men and women as proportions of the number potentially available for employment. SOURCE: First National City Bank, *Monthly Economic Letter,* July 1970.

FIGURE 6–5 Capital Invested per Employee in Manufacturing, 1967

Capital invested per employee in the manufacturing sector rose 3 percent in 1967 to $19,811. The petroleum industry, as in the past, had the highest capital invested per employee, $136,178; this was an increase of 13 percent over 1966. Investment per employee showed the largest annual increase in the "other transportation equipment" group, up 20 percent, reflecting a 30 percent increase in capital but only a 7 percent rise in employment. The largest decline in 1967 occurred in the tobacco industry, down 22 percent, resulting from reductions in capital accompanied by increases in employment. Capital invested equals total assets less investments in government obligations and securities of other corporations. It is stated at book value, and thus reflects the original cost of the assets and not the cost of their replacement at current prices. Capital invested is stated after deducting all reserves, such as for depreciation and other contingencies. SOURCE: National Industrial Conference Board, *Road Maps of Industry,* No. 1651.

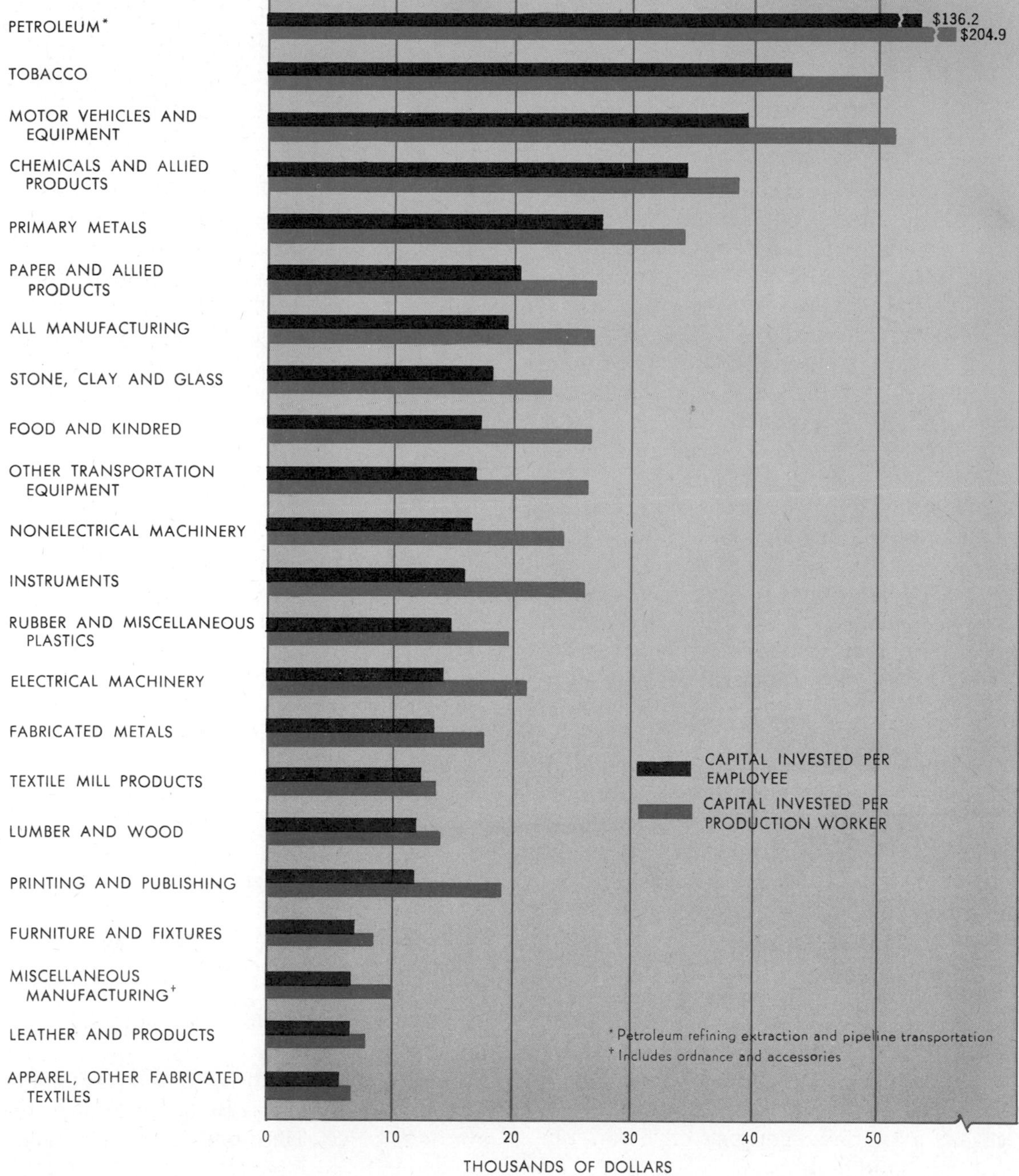
PETROLEUM*
$136.2
$204.9
TOBACCO
MOTOR VEHICLES AND EQUIPMENT
CHEMICALS AND ALLIED PRODUCTS
PRIMARY METALS
PAPER AND ALLIED PRODUCTS
ALL MANUFACTURING
STONE, CLAY AND GLASS
FOOD AND KINDRED
OTHER TRANSPORTATION EQUIPMENT
NONELECTRICAL MACHINERY
INSTRUMENTS
RUBBER AND MISCELLANEOUS PLASTICS
ELECTRICAL MACHINERY
FABRICATED METALS
TEXTILE MILL PRODUCTS
LUMBER AND WOOD
PRINTING AND PUBLISHING
FURNITURE AND FIXTURES
MISCELLANEOUS MANUFACTURING†
LEATHER AND PRODUCTS
APPAREL, OTHER FABRICATED TEXTILES
CAPITAL INVESTED PER EMPLOYEE
CAPITAL INVESTED PER PRODUCTION WORKER
* Petroleum refining extraction and pipeline transportation
† Includes ordnance and accessories
0
10
20
30
40
50
THOUSANDS OF DOLLARS

Part B
How Wages Are Determined

Wages: Reward for Labor

Wages are the prices management pays for human effort. When expressed as the price of labor per hour, per week, or for some other period of time, payment is called a "wage rate." Whether it is called a wage or a salary or a commission, the payment to labor represents a cost to the employer in return for value created. Wages also represent an income to the worker. In addition to being the most costly factor in production, payment to labor is the source of about three fourths of the nation's income. To see how labor earns wages by creating value in the market for the factors of production and then spends these wages in the market for goods and services, refer to the chart of the model in Figure 2–10 on page 33.

Differences in Wages

When you enter the market as a potential wage earner, you are interested in getting the highest price for the efforts you will perform. If you turn to the "help wanted" section of your newspaper or visit an employment agency, you can get some idea of the wage rate (price for labor for some unit of time, for example, per hour) for various jobs. As you begin to study the job market, the following questions may come to mind: Why is there so much difference in pay for different jobs? Why is it that similar jobs may pay different wages? Wouldn't everyone be better off if all jobs paid more?

Suppose you reverse your role and enter the market as a businessman seeking to hire workers. You are now concerned with costs. If you can keep the cost of production down, you can offer your products for sale at a lower price and make a larger profit. Since labor is likely to be your most expensive cost, you want to employ your workers at the lowest wage possible. You will probably ask yourself: What will determine how much I will have to pay to get the help I need? How free am I to determine what wages I will pay? Can higher wages provide labor that can create greater value?

Real Wages and Money Wages

Before we answer the question of what determines wages, we must distinguish the difference between money wages and real wages. The term *money wages* refers to the amount of dollars paid for a given amount of work. *Real wages* tell what your money will buy in the market for goods and services at a given time. It is in the latter that you as a worker are most interested. If all laborers who sought employment were working, and demanded and received a 10 percent increase in their money wages but did *not* create any additional goods and services, would they be any better off? What would happen to the few exceptions whose wages remained the same?

Wages Under the Classical Model

In Chapter 2 we learned that the laws of supply and demand determine the allocation of our resources by interacting to determine price. Here our resource is labor and our price is wages. Let us see how these tools help determine wages.

It is obvious that wages must be related to the value that labor creates. An employer cannot afford to pay his workers more than the value they create for him, for to do so would mean losing money. We must, therefore, consider labor's productivity. To do so we will assume that the cost of our other factors of production remains the same and that each worker has the same ability.

The Law of Diminishing Returns Influences Wages

Let us use for our illustration the business we started in Chapter 4, "Build-a-City." Our factory has a fixed number of machines, a fixed amount of materials for making our sets coming in each week, and a certain number of hours per week for work. As we start to add workers we find that, even though each worker may have the same ability, the value that each worker adds to the total product is not the same. At low levels of production each additional worker adds more value to the total value of the product than the preceding worker did; for example, the tenth worker might add $160 while the ninth might add only $150. However, we soon see a change. We reach a point where additional units of labor will yield decreasing value; for example, the eleventh worker might add $157 and the twelfth worker might add only $154. An increase in the quantities of one factor of production (labor, in this case) in relation to fixed quantities of other factors of production may result in an increase in total output, but eventually the additional output which results from each new addition of that factor will become less and less. This phenomenon is called the *law of diminishing returns.*

Marginal Productivity Related to Wage Rates

Because of the law of diminishing returns, an employer will hire workers up to the point where the wage received by the last worker equals the value that he creates for his employer. We call this the *marginal productivity wage theory.* Marginal productivity may be expressed as "marginal physical product" when referring to additional unit output, or as "marginal revenue product" when the additional output is stated in money value.

In our own business, if we keep a record of what each additional worker adds to the value of the total product, we can discover what each worker's marginal productivity is. Figure 6–6 shows the marginal productivity of our workers after the law of diminishing returns has

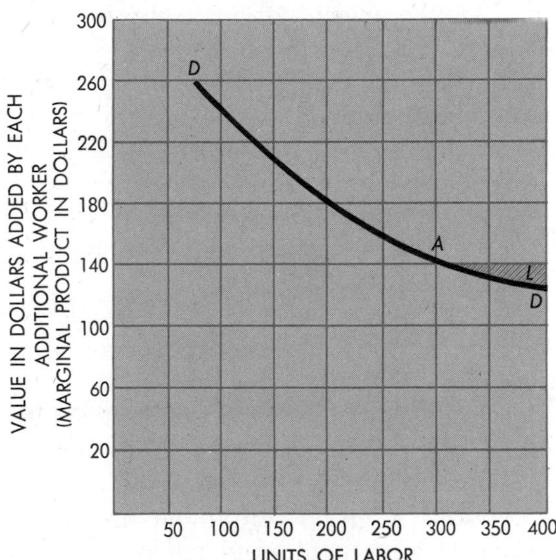

FIGURE 6–6 Marginal Productivity Theory Applied to Labor

Under pure competition wage rates are determined by marginal productivity. Demand Schedule *D* shows the marginal productivity of workers after the law of diminishing returns has set in. With 300 workers (*A*), the employer can afford to pay $140. Because each additional worker would create a lesser value than $140, the employer must cease hiring or lower wages to the level of the marginal product of the last worker hired. Area *L* is where marginal productivity is below the wage rate ($140).

set in. It is also a demand schedule for labor. Under pure competition we, as an employer, will hire additional labor as long as it will not cost us more in wages than the additional value we will receive. If we hire more than 300 workers, we will have to pay them less than $140 because they add less than $140 of value to our total product.

Maximum Wage

At this point you might ask why we, as employers, cannot pay a higher wage, since the value added by workers before the 300th worker is greater than $140. Are these workers being cheated? The answer is *no.* Since every worker in the force of 300 has equal ability and can be interchanged with every other worker, the marginal product of the last worker sets the maximum wage the employer can pay. Under pure competition, where the employer must meet the competitive market price of others, he cannot afford to lose money on any worker.

As with other aspects of the economy we have studied, the theory or model of marginal productivity sets the pattern for the way in which wages should be determined. Remember, however, that a model is an abstraction of the real world, not the real world itself. Even if we had pure competition, the value added by the last worker could be only an estimate of the employer and employee as they seek an agreement, since neither knows the exact value created by each worker. It is to the worker's interest to have that estimate set high and to the employer's to have it set low.

The Effect of Supply and Demand on Wage Rates

Let us return to the economic tools that we studied in Chapter 2 for explaining the interaction of supply and demand. They will help to explain the equilibrium point for wage rates and the number of workers employed. In Figure 6–6 we saw the marginal productivity of workers. This is our demand for labor. With a given supply of 300 workers the equilibrium point for wage rate is $140 per week. If supply remains the same (*A*), how can wages increase? In Figure 6–7 we see that by increasing demand (D_2), supply remaining the same (inelastic), we can increase wages to $160 per week. How can demand for the product, and consequently wages, be increased? Although using such methods as increasing the demand for the product through advertising and reducing foreign competition by raising tariffs will help, the most reliable way would be to increase the productivity of the worker. Our marginal productivity curve, which

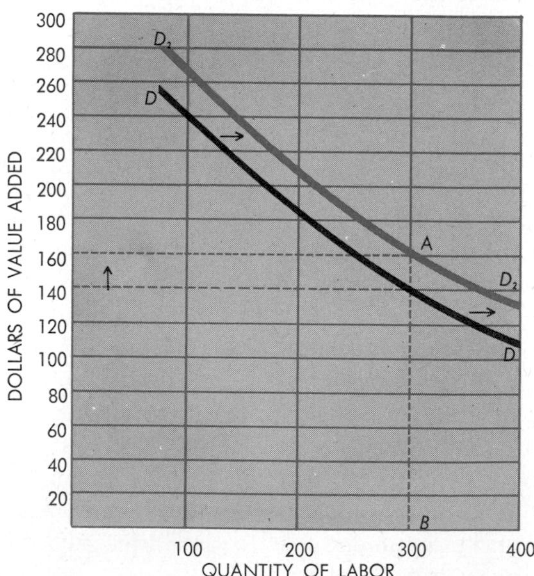

FIGURE 6–7 Marginal Productivity of Labor

By increasing demand, with supply of labor remaining the same (*A*), wages are increased. Increasing marginal productivity will bring about an increase in demand.

is our demand curve, shifts upward to show the greater productivity per worker.

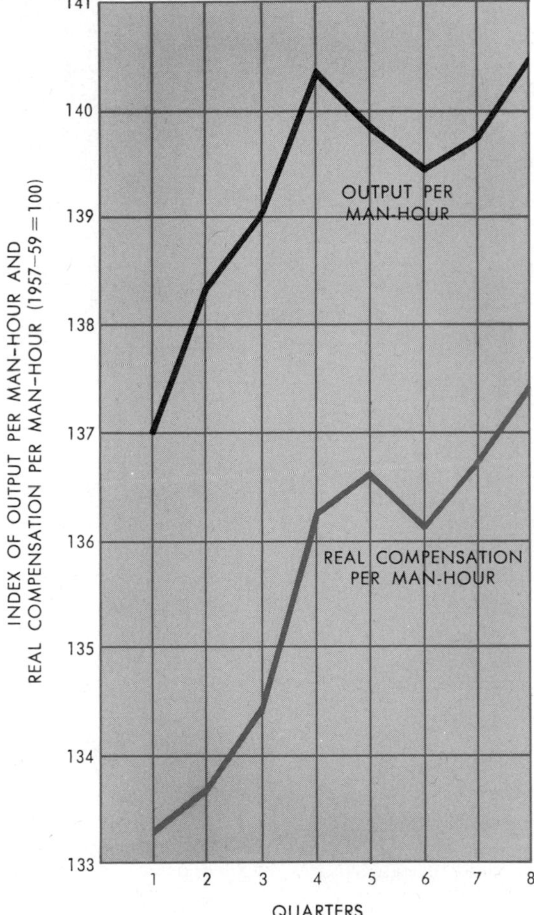

FIGURE 6–8 Output and Compensation per Man-Hour

The graph depicts trends in output and real compensation per man-hour during a recent two-year (eight-quarter) period. The period 1957–59 has been used as a base. During the first quarter, for example, output per man-hour was 137, or 37 percent higher than output during the 1957–59 period, while real compensation was about 33.3 percent higher. What is the significance of the fact that the two lines tend to follow the same pattern? SOURCE: U.S. Bureau of Labor Statistics, 1970.

Figure 6–8 shows that as output per man-hour goes up, so do wages.

Factors Affecting the Supply of Labor

The factors affecting the supply of labor are numerous and very complex. We can consider only a few of the most important influences. When we seek to hire workers for our "Build-a-City" plant, we will need many different kinds of talent. We may need skilled operators of complicated machinery, as well as electricians, plumbers, painters, bookkeepers, salesmen, foremen, and unskilled workers. When we enter the labor market, we are seeking particular kinds of labor, not labor generally. The unskilled worker without a job may want to be employed as a machine operator; however, unless he trains for this job, he does not count as part of supply in the market for machine operators.

Skill of the Worker

One of the major problems we face in our country today stems from the fact that we do not have merely a general labor market. We have many different supplies of labor. During recent periods we have had high unemployment, but at this same time we have had shortages of engineers, teachers, nurses, doctors, and many others whose skills all require long periods of training. Unemployment among unskilled workers, particularly those who drop out of school early, and among members of minority groups averages two to three times higher than the national rate of unemployment. While skilled workers can move into the unskilled labor market (obviously, few would ever want to), the unskilled worker has difficulty moving into the skilled labor market without further training or experience.

Mobility

The supply of labor is affected by the lack of mobility among many workers. Those who have pleasant associations with a particular job, frequently because of the security of a known position as compared to the risk of moving to a new situation, will tend to stay where they are, even though the wage rate might be higher in some other place. After working for a firm for several years, a worker builds up seniority, which protects him from being one of the first laid off when business declines. He may also build up funds in a pension plan and other benefits that companies offer after a certain number of years of service. This lack of mobility is even more limiting when moving involves settling in a new region. For example, the need for labor has dropped in West Virginia because the demand for coal has declined, and not enough demand for labor has come from other industries in the region. Since many workers have been unwilling to leave their homes here, the result has been a higher rate of unemployment in West Virginia than for the nation as a whole.

Minimum Wages and Supply

Since 1938 we have had laws putting a "floor" under wage rates. The *minimum wage* law passed by the national government in that year has been amended several times, the 1966 amendment setting the minimum wage at $1.60. About 74 percent of the labor force is covered by this act. Most state governments also have minimum wage laws, covering some of the workers not covered by federal statute, but in most cases the level is below the federal standard.

Figure 6–9 shows graphically what happens to the supply situation when minimum wage laws exist. Note how the increase in the minimum wage rate decreases the number of workers that employers seek to hire.

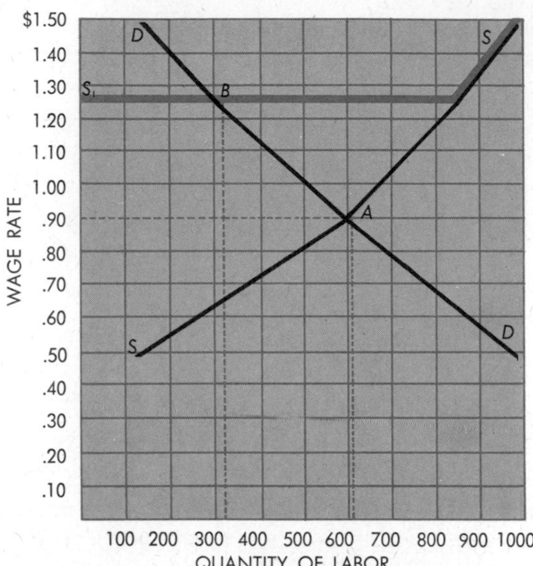

FIGURE 6–9 Effect of a Minimum Wage Law

In a free market situation, the wage rate would tend to settle at $.90 (point *A*), for here the demand and supply curves for labor intersect. Suppose that a minimum wage law is passed, requiring employers to pay $1.25 per hour regardless of labor supply conditions. The colored horizontal line at $1.25 depicts this situation. Note that the line crosses the demand curve at point *B*, a quantity of 320, indicating that employers will hire only 320 workers if they must pay the $1.25 rate. (Organized labor disputes this analysis, asserting that past increases in the minimum wage resulted in only a few isolated cases of this sort.)

Economists do not agree on the value of minimum wage laws to labor. Those who argue against these laws point out that such restrictions encourage unemployment. Many employers might want to hire additional workers, but they can do so only if these workers produce at least as much value as they receive. Those who are just entering the labor market or who have very little skill may not be worth the minimum wage rate because they would add less value to the employer's product than they would receive. Since no employer will knowingly hire a worker for more than he is worth, the minimum wage law can cause unemployment for those whose productivity is below the general level.

Those who favor the minimum wage claim that the lowest-paid wage earners have no one to bargain for them and that they are easily imposed upon by employers. Any worker who cannot create sufficient value to be paid the minimum wage rate should not be considered part of the labor force and should qualify for public assistance or training to make him more productive. Wage rates that are so very low tend to discourage employers from making their firms more efficient, thus retarding technological progress. Such rates also tend to reduce incentive among employees.

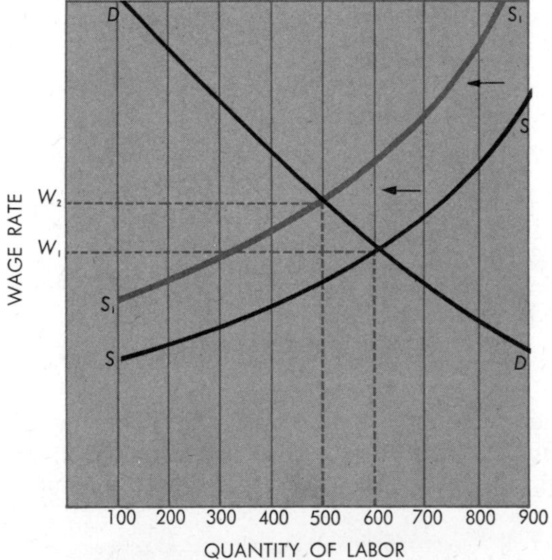

FIGURE 6–10 Effect of Union Membership Restrictions on Wage Rates

Unions that restrict their membership can increase the wage rate by shifting the supply curve to the left. What has happened to the number of people employed?

Labor Unions and the Supply of Labor

Labor unions can influence wages by controlling the supply of labor. Some unions, mainly those with highly skilled workers, restrict their membership, thus causing the supply curve to shift to the left. Other unions may be successful in organizing almost all the workers; they will try to set a wage rate higher than what it might be under purely competitive conditions. Figure 6–10 shows graphically what happens when membership is restricted.

What happens to the number of workers employed? Do you think that this shifting of the supply curve, causing a change in employment, acts as a check on how far unions go to raise wages? Explain the reasons for your answer.

Other Factors Influencing Supply

A number of laws have been passed which have had the effect of reducing the available supply of labor. While we will deal with specific labor legislation later, it is important to point out here some conditions which affect the supply of labor:

1. Prohibiting children under a certain age from working reduces the labor force.
2. Social Security payments allow older members of the labor force to retire.
3. Fixing a standard work week of 40 hours with a higher wage rate for overtime (more than 40 hours) encourages employers to hire more workers rather than have present workers put in longer hours.

Explain what happens to the supply curve for labor in each of the cases given.

Summing Up Wages Under the Classical Model

Under conditions of pure competition, where workers and employers act independently and are willing to move from market to market and have a complete knowledge of the labor market, wage rates and the number of workers employed will be determined by the interaction of demand and supply. The productivity that the last worker adds determines the maximum wage that the employer can pay.

Since the conditions of pure competition rarely exist, other factors influencing wages must be considered. Markets with a single large employer, unions, and government laws bring about changes in demand and supply, changing the equilibrium point for wage rates as well as the quantity of labor from what it might be under conditions of pure competition.

In the next chapter we will turn our attention to two of the most important influences affecting the classical model: labor unions and government. When the development of these factors has been traced, we will consider a problem significant to the future of labor.

REVIEW: THE HIGHLIGHTS OF THE CHAPTER

1. Labor is one of the four factors of production. It represents human effort used in the creation of value. This value varies with the skill and tools of the worker.
2. Labor differs from other factors of production because it can act on its own initiative and because it buys back what it helps to produce.
3. The American labor force is highly skilled, and an increasing number are engaged in white-collar jobs.
4. Wages are prices management pays for human effort. In addition to being income for the worker, wages are the most costly factor of production.
5. Money wages refer to the amount of money paid for a given amount of work. Real wages tell what the money will buy.
6. The demand schedule for labor is determined by the marginal productivity of workers.
7. Under conditions of pure competition, wage rates and the quantity of labor are determined by the interacting of supply and demand. Minimum wage laws and unions change the supply curve and, at certain levels, tend to reduce the number of workers hired.

IN CONCLUSION: SOME AIDS TO UNDERSTANDING

Terms for Review

labor
labor force
wage rate
real wages
money wages
law of diminishing returns
marginal productivity theory of wages
mobility of labor
minimum wage
demand for labor

Questions for Review

1. Labor is one of the integral parts of the productive process, yet it is sometimes called a "unique" or "peculiar" factor. What differentiates it from the other three?
2. Explain why a profile of the labor force would show that the vast majority are in the 20-to-65 age group and very few in the younger and older groups.
3. Labor has been called a commodity subject to the law of supply and demand in the marketplace. Do you agree? Why or why not?
4. To insure maximum profit, an employer will be guided, in hiring new workers and in setting wages, by the following factors: labor's productivity, its marginal productivity, and its supply and skills. Explain how each factor influences wage payments.
5. Explain why the percentage of our labor force engaged in the physical aspects of production has declined since 1900.
6. Considering the general labor market, explain the advantage a skilled worker has as compared to an unskilled worker.
7. Using the analytical tools of economics you have learned thus far, give the arguments for and against the minimum wage.
8. What factors other than minimum wages and unions influence the supply of labor?

Additional Questions and Problems

1. Draw an imaginary supply and demand graph for labor, labeling wage rates and number of workers. Show what happens when worker output per man-hour increases. Explain the changes.
2. Explain how an unskilled worker receiving $2 per hour might be overpaid whereas a toolmaker receiving $3 might be underpaid.
3. Turn to the "help wanted" section of a newspaper. List in descending order the wages paid for different jobs. Explain the reasons for the differences in wages offered.
4. "Labor benefits most when it cooperates fully with management." Explain why you agree or disagree with this statement.
5. Why does the elasticity in demand for labor affect the power of a union in influencing wages?

SELECTED READINGS

Burtt, Everett J. *Labor Markets, Unions, and Government Policies.* New York: St. Martin's Press, 1963.

Dunlop, John T. *Labor Economics.* Englewood Cliffs, N.J.: Prentice-Hall, 1965.

Galenson, Walter. *A Primer on Employment and Wages.* New York: Random House, 1966.

Heneman, Herbert G. and Dale Yoder. *Labor Economics.* 2nd ed. Cincinnati: South-Western Publishing Co., 1965.

Maher, John E. *Labor and the Economy.* Boston: Allyn and Bacon, 1965.

Perlman, Richard, ed. *Wage Determination: Market or Power Forces?* Boston: D. C. Heath and Co., 1964.

Reynolds, Lloyd G. *Labor Economics and Labor Relations.* 5th ed. Englewood Cliffs, N.J.: Prentice-Hall (Spectrum), 1970.

Labor: Its Organization and Development 7

THE AUTHORS' NOTE TO THE STUDENT

Discussions or arguments concerning labor unions are frequently filled with more emotion than fact. Often we encounter individuals who hold labor unions responsible for all of the economy's shortcomings. Some see all unions as a stereotype—undemocratic, resistant to progress, discriminatory, controlled by racketeers, and "Communist-dominated." Other extremists feel organized labor has been the only group to advance the rights not only of the working man, but of all society. They label criticism of any union as propaganda disseminated by business to discredit organized labor.

A brief look at the history of organized labor would show that neither of these extreme positions is an accurate evaluation. Those who would like to see labor unions dissolved will have to recognize that unions are probably here to stay and are an important part of the American economy. It is equally important for those who find only virtue associated with unions to recognize that abuses can creep into any organization. When that happens, government steps in with controls in an attempt to protect those who are unfairly treated. Once we have established that unions are here to stay and that some kind of government regulation is inevitable, we are in a better position to understand the American labor movement and the problems, as well as the progress, associated with it.

In this chapter we will trace the rise of the American labor movement, analyze labor-management relations in general (specifically, the weapons available to each and the methods used to resolve differences), legislation affecting labor, and the special labor problems resulting from automation.

A STUDENT'S NOTE TO THE STUDENT

I had some of the material in this chapter in my American history course, so I was able to go through it quickly. For those who never had any labor history there are quite a few terms to learn. If you were brought up to dislike unions completely (I wasn't), you may have some second thoughts.

The stimulating portions of this chapter come in the discussions of wage–price spirals and automation. The arguments for each side of these controversial problems seem reasonable, and you will find yourself vacillating from one position to the other as you read each separately.

If you have a discussion in class, you might inquire about the background of those taking pro- and anti-labor positions. Very revealing to see how strongly our backgrounds influence our decisions.

Part A
A Sketch of the Labor Movement

Causes of Union Development

The history of the labor movement can be traced back to the Industrial Revolution and the establishment of the factory system in the latter part of the eighteenth century in England. With the introduction of the factory system, the worker was placed in a new position. No longer could the worker provide his own tools and move from employer to employer or set up his own business. He became dependent on the owner of the new and expensive tools. He received wages; but, since he no longer supplied any capital, he had to forgo interest (payment for capital). Labor was the only thing the worker could offer the employer. This placed the worker in a poor bargaining position, since he had to accept whatever wage the employer offered. Having been downgraded from a relatively independent craftsman to a mere factory hand subject to the decisions of the employer, his discontent grew.

The Start of Collective Bargaining

Whether workers were getting a fair rate for their efforts, considering that productivity tended to be low, is not certain. However, we are sure that workers suffered from poverty, long hours of work, and poor working conditions. When they compared their miserable existence with that of their employer, they decided that they were not getting a fair share of the returns. Working together in a factory made it easy for them to communicate their mutual discontent to one another. If they could unite and agree on what changes they wanted, they could face their employer with strength. They could then send a representative to bargain with the employer concerning wages, hours, and conditions of work. The procedure by which a representative of workers and a representative of employers fixed the terms of employment was slow in developing. However, it marks the beginning of *collective bargaining,* which was to become the major source of union strength.

Slow Growth of Early Unionism

Although labor unions can be traced back to the 1790's in the United States, their growth was slow and their strength weak until the 1930's. Five major factors are largely responsible for this slow growth:

1. The lack of any federal policy recognizing unions as collective bargaining agents for workers
2. The hostility of the courts, which prosecuted unions under conspiracy laws
3. The strong resistance on the part of American businessmen to accepting unions
4. The individualism of the American worker
5. The lack of effective communications necessary to the success of mass movements

The effects of these factors will be seen as we trace the growth of unions.

Before the Civil War unions were primarily local craft or trade unions made up of skilled workers. These groups rarely had any affiliation with unions in other cities. With no federal legislation and with few state laws recognizing the existence of unions, the courts had to decide most disputes between labor and management. Unfortunately for the unions, the courts turned to common law. Accordingly, they held that combinations of workmen that sought to raise wages were criminal conspiracies and hence illegal. Although the decision in the case of *Commonwealth* v. *Hunt* in 1842 ended the conspiracy interpretation, the courts in general continued to discourage the growth of unions by refusing to concede their legality and by declaring illegal the methods, such as strikes, used by unions to obtain their demands.

The Knights of Labor: Early National Union

One of the first important national unions was the Knights of Labor. It was organized in 1869 by Philadelphia garment workers, under the leadership of Uriah S. Stephens, as a secret society. It tried to include farmers, small merchants, and even professional people as well as manual workers. Besides seeking to accomplish the traditional objectives of labor—higher pay, shorter hours, and better working conditions—it showed interest in extending public education, prohibiting child labor, establishing an income tax, having government ownership of the railroads, and many other causes. Because of these broad interests, it was called a reform union. After dropping its secrecy, it grew quickly, reaching a membership of 700,000 in 1886. Although its avowed method of reaching its goals was political action, its progress is usually attributed to several successful strikes and to the great energy of its most important grand master, Terence V. Powderly.

Because the Knights of Labor was composed of many different elements seeking many different objectives, its success was inevitably of short duration. Several unsuccessful strikes and a weakening of Powderly's leadership hastened the decline. Although the career of the Knights of Labor was short, its contributions cannot be dismissed. It helped to reorganize some weak existing unions and assisted in the formation of other unions. It brought the problems of labor to the attention of Congress and the President, and because of its diverse membership won support from outside the field of labor.

American Federation of Labor: A Modern Labor Union

The modern labor movement in America can be traced back more directly to the formation of the American Federation of Labor. Started in 1881 as the Federation of Organized Trades and Labor Unions, and more formally organized in 1886 in Columbus, Ohio, as the American Federation of Labor, its character and approach to labor problems differed markedly from the reform and political nature of the Knights. Reflecting the thinking of its leader, Samuel Gompers, for over a third of a century, the AF of L tried to bring trade unions together in a loose federation. Gompers' approach has been called "bread-and-butter" or "business" unionism because he steered his organization away from any idealistic policies or political entanglements and emphasized the immediate economic gains of higher pay, shorter hours, and better working conditions.

Instead of trying to embrace as many workers as possible in one big union, Gompers preferred the more conservative approach of craft organization, in which those doing the same kind of skilled work (plumbers, for instance) are organized into the same union. These craft or trade unions would then affiliate with the AF of L, retaining a great deal of autonomous power. Craft organization leaves little room for the unskilled worker. You will recall that it is far easier to control the supply of skilled workers than that of unskilled workers.

Gompers' Philosophy

Gompers ran his union as a "hardheaded businessman" would run his business. He refused to commit his union to the support of a political party, preferring to reward the friends and punish the enemies of labor at the ballot box. He wanted government to stay out of all union-management negotiations, being more fearful of what an unfriendly government might do to hamper the organized labor movement than optimistic about what good a friendly government might do. Some radical thinkers, including Marxists, crept into the union, but Gompers showed no sympathy for them or their doctrines. Perhaps the best illustration of the Gompers philosophy was expressed in his reply to an inquiry as to what labor's ultimate goals were. He replied simply, "More, more, and more."

We can sum up the following guiding principles of the AF of L under Gompers' leadership: (1) Concentrate only on direct economic benefits for the worker. (2) Have no alliances with any political groups or party. (3) Organize along craft lines, allowing freedom for the unions within the federation. (4) Keep government out of labor-management affairs.

Progress and Reverses in Union Growth, 1898–1947

The AF of L grew slowly from its birth until 1898, at which time its membership numbered 278,000, slightly more than 1 percent of the labor force. However, the six years from 1898 to 1904, sometimes referred to as the "honeymoon period of capital and labor," saw the membership jump more than six times to 1,676,000, more than 5 percent of the labor force. A second period of rapid growth took place during the period of World War I, rising from 2,000,000 in 1914 to 4,078,000 in 1920, or one out of every ten workers.

Decline in the 1920's

During the 1920's a number of important factors combined to cause a serious decline in the influence and membership of unions. In the course of this setback the AF of L was reduced to 2,532,261 members. Among the causes of decline were:

1. Vigorous antiunion activity by businessmen under the leadership of the National Association of Manufacturers
2. Lack of good public relations, resulting in loss of middle-class sympathy
3. Blame placed on unions for the rising cost of living
4. Use by management of labor spies and *strikebreakers*
5. Use by courts of injunctions, based on the principles that property rights must be protected and that law and order must be maintained at all costs
6. Use of police and militia to limit strikes

In addition, labor leaders themselves must share the blame. Their insistence on trying to organize skilled workers at a time when assembly-line production increased the demand for unskilled workers caused a large segment of the labor force to be neglected.

Years of Rapid Growth, 1933–1947

The period from 1933 until 1947 was the most fruitful in all the history of American organized labor. Membership in all organized labor groups grew from about 3,000,000 to over 15,000,000, approximately one out of every four workers. Three principal factors were responsible for this remarkable growth: (1) new federal legislation, (2) new leadership and a revitalization within unions, and (3) World War II and the expansion of industry.

From the passage of the Norris-LaGuardia Act of 1932 until the passage of the Taft-Hartley Act of 1947 the federal government encouraged union development as never before. Injunctions were limited, yellow-dog contracts were made unenforceable, and collective bargaining rights and minimum wages were made part of federal legislation. These acts reflected a growing sentiment in favor of labor; their effect was to make it easier for labor leaders to organize workers.

Craft unions are sometimes called horizontal because they include workers with the same or similar skills, no matter what industry they work in. Industrial unions may be called vertical, since all workers in an industry, no matter what their skill, are in the same union.

The CIO and Industrial Organization

After the death of Samuel Gompers (1924), William Green became the leader of the AF of L. His policies were generally considered conservative; and he, along with the majority of the leadership, continued to place greatest emphasis on *craft* (or trade) organization. Although *industrial unions*—in which all workers in an industry, regardless of their job, belong to the same union—were always permitted in the AF of L, they were given little encouragement.

However, many of the leaders of industrial unions felt that the best opportunities for further organization were in the steel and automobile industries, which were better suited for industrial organization. Under the leadership of John L. Lewis, president of the United Mine Workers, a Committee for Industrial Organization was created in 1935 to encourage the formation of industrial unions within the AF of L.

A conflict between those favoring industrial organization (sometimes referred to as "vertical organization") and those preferring craft organization (sometimes referred to as "horizontal organization") led to the formation of a new and separate union, known after 1938 as the Congress of Industrial Organizations. After several successful strikes the workers in the steel and automobile industries were organized. As the CIO gained prestige, union membership increased rapidly. When the AF of L saw the success of its rival in organizing workers in mass-production industries, it too began to press for industrial organization.

Union Strength Increases During World War II

By the beginning of World War II organized labor had over 10 million members.

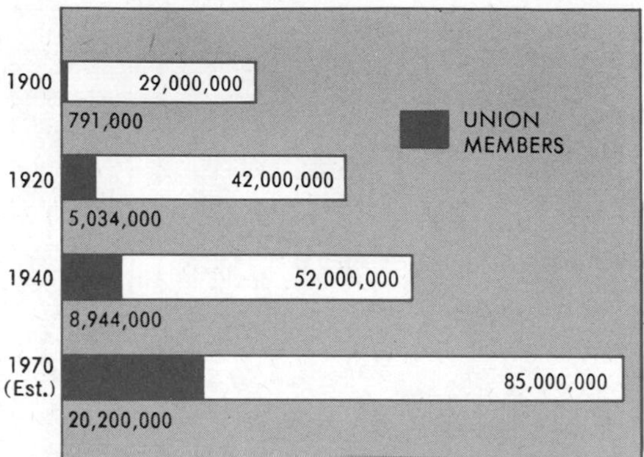

FIGURE 7–1 The U.S. Labor Force and Union Membership

This bar graph shows the growth of the labor force and of union membership. The figures for the total labor force include the unemployed as well as the employed and part-time as well as full-time workers. Note that 1970 figures are authors' estimates from available data. SOURCE: U.S. Bureau of Labor Statistics.

The CIO's share was only slightly less than that of the AF of L. With many new workers joining the industrial work force, membership jumped to approximately 15 million by the end of the war. Unions gave a no-strike pledge for the duration of the war and had, in general, an excellent production record.

Even before the war was over, however, the public's favorable image of labor had begun to change. Several strikes in 1944 and a record high number of strikes immediately following the war contributed to the change. Strikes in such key industries as meat-packing, coal, steel, and even transportation caused major inconvenience to the public. In addition, the cost of living skyrocketed and many people preferred to place the blame directly on labor rather than on the removal of price and wage controls. The pendulum, which had seemed to swing in favor of labor for a number of years, was now moving against it. Shortly, this change was reflected in legislation.

Postwar Conditions Bring Reform and Consolidation

Labor had hailed the passage of the National Labor Relations Act of 1935 (known popularly as the Wagner Act), but it resented bitterly the passage of the Labor-Management Relations Act of 1947 (known popularly as the Taft-Hartley Act). It is difficult to give an unbiased appraisal of an act that has caused such emotional controversy. Most impartial observers would agree on the following:

1. The Taft-Hartley Act reversed the trend by which government bolstered the power of unions and it applied controls over unions as well as management.
2. It tried to establish standards for the internal management and operation of unions, although it had difficulty in securing compliance.
3. It sought, with only limited success, to avoid the undesirable effects of major strikes on the economy.

While labor seems to have learned to live with what it originally called a "slave-labor act," those who expected the Taft-Hartley Act to be a cure-all soon discovered its weaknesses. Investigations by Congress which disclosed corrupt practices of some union officials, including unauthorized use of union funds and undemocratic methods of getting and maintaining control of the union, led to the passage of the Labor-Management Reporting and Disclosure Act of 1959 (popularly known as the Landrum-Griffin Act). A weakness of regulatory legislation was shown by the inability of the Railroad Labor Act (in any other industry it would have been the Taft-Hartley Act) to avert a threatened

TABLE 7–1 Major Labor Unions in the U.S.

Union	Affiliation	Membership
International Brotherhood of Teamsters, Chauffeurs, Warehousemen of America	Independent	1,755,025
International Union, United Automobile, Aerospace and Agricultural Implement Workers of America	Independent*	1,472,696
United Steelworkers of America	AFL-CIO	1,120,000
International Brotherhood of Electrical Workers	AFL-CIO	897,114
International Association of Machinists and Aerospace Workers	AFL-CIO	903,015
United Brotherhood of Carpenters and Joiners of America	AFL-CIO	800,000
Laborers' International Union of North America	AFL-CIO	553,102
Retail Clerks International Association	AFL-CIO	552,000
International Ladies' Garment Workers Union	AFL-CIO	455,164
Hotel and Restaurant Employees and Bartenders International Union	AFL-CIO	455,022
Amalgamated Clothing Workers of America	AFL-CIO	386,000

* Became independent July 1, 1968.

Although only about 25 percent of the American labor force is unionized, it should be noted that strong unions are solidly entrenched in our most important industries. Can you identify any significant segments of the labor force which are not unionized? SOURCE: U.S. Bureau of Labor Statistics.

major railroad strike in 1963. On that occasion, presidential and congressional intervention introduced compulsory arbitration on some issues.

The Great Merger

Early in the 1950's the AF of L and CIO began to talk about merging. The major influences that acted to bring the two giant unions together were:

1. The feeling that unity might provide organized labor with greater political power to stem legislative attacks
2. The fact that leadership within the unions had changed hands, eliminating some of the personal animosities that had been an obstacle to a merger
3. The slow growth in membership that set in after the close of World War II
4. The increasing interest on the part of the AF of L in using industrial organization

In 1955 the two unions were joined, resulting in a giant association representing the common interests of almost 16 million workers.

Independent Unions

Outside of the AFL-CIO, which has over 15 million members, are over 4 million workers organized in independent unions. The largest of these is the International Brotherhood of Teamsters, Chauffeurs, and Warehousemen of America, with over 1.7 million members, and the United Automobile, Aerospace and Agricultural Implement Workers of America, with almost 1.5 million. The former was expelled from the AFL-CIO in 1957 on charges of corruption; the latter left the

AFL-CIO in 1968 after being suspended for withholding dues in a dispute over Federation policies. These two giant organizations formed an Alliance for Labor Action in 1969. The ALA denied the AFL-CIO's charge that it had become a rival federation, asserting that it is simply an alliance to promote union organizing and social action. When the Chemical Workers Union became affiliated with the ALA it was ousted by the AFL-CIO, although the CWA had argued that its affiliation with ALA in no way indicated a desire to end its ties with the AFL-CIO.

Recent History

The last decade has produced little that labor can cheer about. Membership in unions has remained almost the same in spite of the increase in the labor force. Legislation has placed greater control over unions and their leaders; investigations by Senator McClellan's Labor Committee uncovered corrupt practices, and several prolonged strikes and threats of strikes have made the public and its representatives less than friendly. In addition, the number of manual workers, who are most likely to join unions, has not increased as fast as has the number of white-collar workers. The latter identify more with management and are less inclined to join unions. However, organized labor is no longer the weak "underdog" that enlists the sympathy and energies of outsiders looking for a righteous cause. It is recognized as part of the American way of life. Whether the pendulum will again swing in its favor in the future remains in doubt.

Part B
Labor-Management Relations—Focus for Conflict

Although labor and management both profit by prosperity, since a "big pie" allows everyone to have larger portions, conflicts about the distribution of the "pie" arise. Each side tries to make sure that its position and demands will prevail. To do so, both management and labor use methods they consider necessary to "win."

Weapons Used by Management

Weapons used by employers to combat unions have frequently been very effective, but some have been considered extremely harsh by labor. In addition to the methods previously described, management has also used the following devices:

Company unions were set up by management to discourage or prevent workers from joining an existing union or starting a union of their own. These unions were largely dominated by management.

Yellow-dog contracts made workers sign a contract not to join a union as a condition of employment. If they did join a union, they violated the contract and were subject not only to being discharged but to being sued as well.

Blacklists containing the names of union organizers were circulated among employers to prevent these men from getting jobs and to warn employers of what these men might try to do if hired to work for a company.

A *lockout,* an employer's strike, was also used. By closing his business, or threatening to close it, the employer could bring great pressure to bear on workers to agree to his demands.

An *injunction,* a court order restraining some person or group from particular actions, was sometimes used. Employers

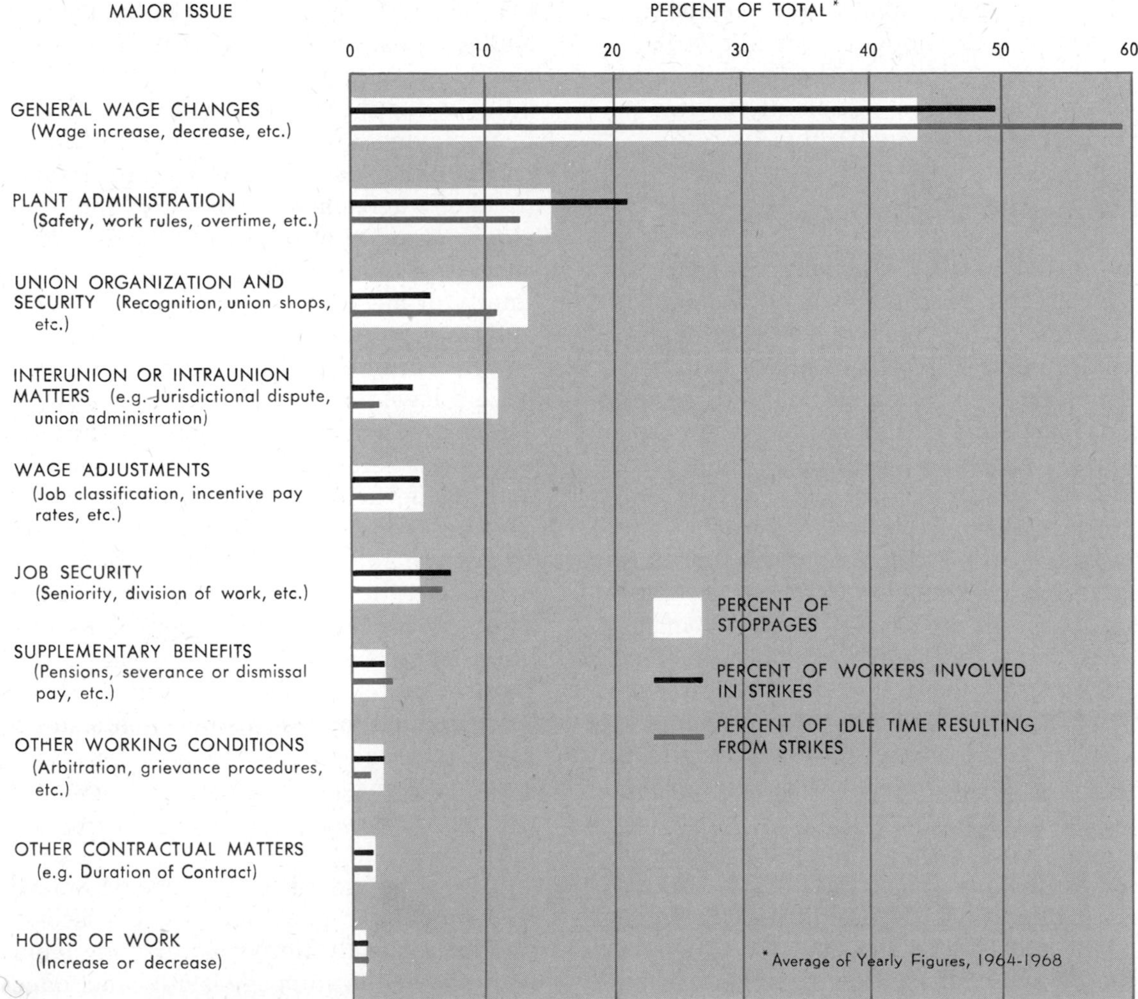

FIGURE 7–2 Important Issues in Work Stoppages

Wages have always been a principal factor in work stoppages. Because of inflation during the period covered by this graph, concern over wages became even greater than usual. In 48.4 percent of the strikes during this period, government mediation was used. A formal settlement was reached in 90.3 percent of the stoppages. SOURCES: National Industrial Conference Board, *Road Maps of Industry,* No. 1635 and U.S. Bureau of Labor Statistics.

would request judges to issue injunctions to prevent unions from striking or picketing, claiming such action threatened their property. Although the union could defend itself, judges were often less than sympathetic with the workers' cause, and frequently the issuance of a temporary injunction was enough to break a strike.

All of these devices have been declared illegal or have been sufficiently limited in use to render them ineffective.

Weapons Used by Unions

Unions also have weapons which have been used to win demands. The heart of unionism is collective bargaining, in which union officials negotiate with representatives of management to secure such benefits as higher wages, shorter hours, improved working conditions, longer vacations and sick leaves, and better retirement benefits. Because employees are many and employers few, only by uniting do members of unions feel they can compete successfully with management in bargaining. In order to achieve this equality, the union seeks to be recognized as the bargaining agent for the workers in the making of a labor contract. This is a legal agreement between labor and management covering all conditions of work and labor relations for a specific period of time. To represent the workers more effectively, the union tries to enlist all the workers in the company. It does this by one of the following means, listed in order of preference:

The *closed shop* makes it a requirement of employment that the worker be a member of the union. By limiting membership, the union can control the supply of workers. This practice is now illegal.

The *union shop* allows the employer to hire anyone, but the new worker must join the union within a specified period—usually between 30 and 60 days.

The *agency shop* requires all workers to pay dues to the union because the union acts as their agent in bargaining, but workers are not required to join the union. This arrangement reduces the tension among those who feel that a worker should have a right to join or not to join a union without being discriminated against in employment.

The union may ask the employer for a *checkoff* agreement, whereby the employer deducts from the employee's paycheck his union dues. This insures continuity of membership and protects union authority.

Two variations of the above conditions have developed within recent years. The *maintenance-of-membership shop* requires workers to continue their membership in the union for the duration of the contract under which they are working. If they are not members of the union, they do not have to join. The *preferential shop* exists when management agrees to hire union members as long as they are available, in preference to nonunion workers. In opposition to these arrangements, many employers have preferred an *open shop,* wherein management does not recognize any union as bargaining agent for its employees.

The *strike* is a work stoppage organized by labor. It is most likely to be used at the time of expiration of an existing labor contract. If the stoppage is not sanctioned by the union, it is called a *wildcat strike.* Without the power to strike, unions would be in an extremely weak bargaining position. Not only is the employer faced with the loss of income but he may lose some of his customers permanently. In addition, his fixed costs, which in some cases may be substantial, will continue.

TABLE 7–2 Work Stoppages, Selected Years, 1885–1969

Year	Strikes and lockouts	Workers involved (thousands)	Man-days idle (thousands)	Year	Strikes and lockouts	Workers involved (thousands)	Man-days idle (thousands)
1885	695	258	n.a.	1933	1,695	1,168	16,872
1890	1,897	373	n.a.	1935	2,014	1,117	15,456
1895	1,255	407	n.a.	1939	2,613	1,171	17,812
1900	1,839	568	n.a.	1943	3,752	1,981	13,501
1905	2,186	302	n.a.	1945	4,750	3,470	38,025
1915	1,593	n.a.	n.a.	1949	3,606	3,030	50,500
1917	4,450	1,227	n.a.	1952	5,117	3,540	59,100
1920	3,411	1,463	n.a.	1957	3,673	1,390	16,500
1925	1,301	428	n.a.	1960	3,333	1,320	19,100
1929	921	289	5,352	1964	3,655	1,640	22,900
1930	637	183	3,317	1969	5,700	2,481	42,869
1932	841	324	10,502				

n.a. = not available

More man-days of work are lost because of accidents, illness, and absenteeism than because of strikes. Although wages remain the single most important issue, other factors are becoming increasingly important. SOURCE: U.S. Department of Labor, Bureau of Labor Statistics, *Analysis of Work Stoppages.*

Strikes are very costly for workers as well. Though the union often compensates for loss of pay by providing strike benefits and some states give unemployment benefits, a prolonged strike will force most workers to dip into their savings or to borrow money. Even when a strike results in the workers' winning most of their demands, it may take years for the workers to make up for the lost income. This has led some to believe that a strike is never worthwhile. Others point out that the threat of a strike would be ineffective if strikes did not take place. Still others base their argument on principles, claiming the strike to be the only real weapon labor has in its struggle for its rights.

Because strikes may cause inconveniences to the public and receive a great deal of newspaper coverage, many people get a false impression of their number and severity. Less than one half of 1 percent of man-days of work have been lost because of strikes, considerably less than the amount of time lost due to accidents, illness, and absenteeism.

Picketing is an activity carried on by unions during a strike. By placing picket lines around a business, the workers hope that their presence and their signs will prevent nonunion men (scabs) from taking their jobs. They also try to persuade customers to avoid doing business with the company. In many parts of the country people have respected picket lines, and the weapon of picketing has helped unions win their strikes.

A *boycott* is a refusal by a union to patronize a business with which it is having a dispute. A *secondary boycott,* now illegal, occurs when the union also refuses to deal with anybody using the goods of the employer with whom they are at odds. The secondary boycott provisions of the Taft-Hartley Law seem to be subject to a variety of interpretations. For example, in 1960 a union picketed retail stores carrying the products of the employer with whom they were having a dispute. The

National Labor Relations Board ruled that this constituted an illegal secondary boycott.

A *union label* signifies that the product was made by union workers and according to union standards. Organized labor has tried to make consumers conscious of buying only goods with such labels.

The *slowdown* occurs when workers purposely reduce the speed at which they work. This increases the cost of production to the employer and will reduce his profits. As a form of protest it represents the direct action occasionally used by workers during the early growth of unions.

Political action has been an important method by which labor has sought to accomplish its aims. Financial contributions, together with meeting halls, posters, and sound trucks, are used to help candidates who are "friends of labor." While it is highly debatable whether the unions have any considerable control over their members when they go to the polls, few politicians, particularly from highly industrialized states, are willing to risk the antagonism of organized labor.

Part C
Governmental Influence on Union Development

Labor Legislation

One of the major factors in determining the pattern of union development has been labor legislation. As you know, laws passed by the Congress are subject to the interpretation of the courts. Until the late 1930's the courts were frequently unfriendly to labor unions.

Early Labor Laws

The Sherman Antitrust Act, aimed at business combinations, was more frequently used against labor unions in the 1890's than against business. In part to correct this situation, Congress passed the Clayton Act in 1914, exempting labor unions from prosecution under the antitrust laws. However, judicial interpretation still persisted in restricting the growth and activities of unions.

It was not until the 1930's that labor was able to feel the benefits of legislation passed in its behalf. In 1932 the Norris-LaGuardia Act made the yellow-dog contract unenforceable in federal courts and placed restrictions on the use of injunctions in labor-management disputes.

Wagner Act

The most important law passed in labor's behalf was the National Labor Relations Act, or Wagner Act, of 1935. Labor frequently refers to it as the Magna Carta of the labor movement. It recognized labor's right to bargain collectively. To implement this, it set up the National Labor Relations Board (NLRB). Among its duties the Board supervises elections, determining who will represent the workers in their bargaining with employers. The NLRB also investigates any complaints concerning violation of contracts. The Act prohibits management from interfering with attempts of unions to organize, from having any part in the administration of the union, and from practicing discrimination in the hiring or retaining of an employee because of membership in a union. Many students of the labor movement think that labor could not have achieved its present strength without the favorable provisions of the Wagner Act.

Fair Labor Standards Act

The Fair Labor Standards Act of 1938 established minimum wages and maximum hours in industries engaged in interstate commerce. It also called for overtime pay with double pay for Sundays and holidays when not part of the regular work week for the particular job.

Taft-Hartley Act

The Labor-Management Relations Act, or Taft-Hartley Act, of 1947 amended the Wagner Act. In the eyes of its supporters, the Taft-Hartley Act brought about a better balance between labor and management. Just as the Wagner Act specifies unfair practices of management and makes them unlawful, so the Taft-Hartley Act specifies unfair practices of labor. It prohibits unions from coercing workers to join, *featherbedding* (forcing employers to hire more workers than they need), calling secondary boycotts, calling a *jurisdictional strike* (one called by rival unions, each seeking authority), or failing to bargain with employers in good faith. In addition, it outlaws the closed shop and allows the government to suspend for 80 days (the "cooling-off period") a strike which may "imperil the national health or safety." Unions are required to give a 60-day notice of their intention to strike.

One of the most dramatic controversies over the Taft-Hartley Act has been over Section 14(b), which permits states to pass laws prohibiting the union shop. These "right-to-work" laws have been passed in 19 states,[1] primarily in the Deep South, the Southwest, and the farm belt, where union organization is least extensive. Labor claims that these laws seriously hamper its attempts to recruit members. Those in favor of these laws and of the right of states to pass such laws insist that union membership should never be made a condition of employment.

Landrum-Griffin Act

The Labor-Management Reporting and Disclosure Act, or Landrum-Griffin Act, of 1959 was designed to reform corrupt unions and make their practices more democratic. It regulates union elections and also restricts some undesirable people —communists and former convicts—from holding union offices. In addition it places a tight control on the reporting of union finances, and guarantees the individual worker's right to participate in all proceedings of the union. The effectiveness of this legislation is open to question. However, organized labor has accepted most of the law without vigorous protests.

An Example of Collective Bargaining: Focus on Agreement

To explain how the process of collective bargaining works, let us take a simple fictional example. Suppose that a new but growing firm has about 100 workers who have shown no desire to join a union. An established union learns of this situation and sends an organizer to the plant to speak to the employees. He tells them that wages are higher in unionized plants; that working conditions are better; that workers under union contracts enjoy greater job security, because they cannot be dis-

[1] 1970.

charged arbitrarily; that fringe benefits are better in a union shop (that is, more insurance, sick time, vacations, and the like); and that his union will in other ways promote the welfare of its members. Most of the workers are impressed, and the union petitions the NLRB to become the exclusive bargaining agent for them. A date for voting on this question is set.

Management will probably be distressed at the prospect of having to deal with a union. They undoubtedly will feel that they have been treating the workers fairly. Perhaps they will attempt to deter unionization by giving some of the things the union is promising. The organizer will scoff at this, warning the workers that "what the Lord giveth, the Lord can take away," and that these benefits can be assured only if acquired by contractual right and not subject to the employer's whim. If management has been paying the workers their full marginal revenue product, they may fear that a wage increase will force them to reduce the size of the labor force, install labor-saving machinery, or raise prices. Raising the price will bring a decline in sales if the customers can find substitutes or can get the product more cheaply from competing firms. The firm may even suffer losses and eventually be forced out of business. Even if this does not occur, management will resent union action that they see as infringing on their right to run the business as they please. The only alternative may be to join with other employers to counter the union's power.

If the workers vote to have the union represent them, the NLRB declares that union to be the sole bargaining agent. The firm must accept the situation. It will call upon its lawyers and economics consultant, and they will sit down at the bargaining table with the representatives of the union. The union, likewise, probably will have attorneys and consultants, and a labor contract will be drawn up. A typical contract will specify that the company recognizes the union as exclusive bargaining agent for the type of employees specified, ban discrimination against union members, define what constitutes a work day or work week, provide for lunch and relief periods, set forth the conditions and rates for overtime work, indicate the wage rates for the various types of jobs covered, list the holidays to be recognized as nonworking days, set the terms for vacations, and spell out seniority and security provisions. Procedures for handling grievances will be detailed, along with the conditions under which a worker may be disciplined or discharged. There may also be provisions for the health and safety of the employees, apprenticeship and training, sick leave, insurance, retirement benefits, severance pay, and leaves of absence. The union will agree not to strike, and the company will agree not to have a lockout for the duration of the contract.

No union contract, however detailed and well planned it might be, can cover every possible problem that might arise. Indeed, disputes often occur over the meaning of various parts of the contract itself. When labor and management have reached an impasse, there are several possible ways of solving the problem.

Methods of Reaching Agreement

Conciliation, mediation, and arbitration are means of settling disputes. Some use the term *conciliation* to refer to attempts at peaceful settlement by direct conference between employer and employees (or their representatives) without the assistance of outsiders. Others use the term to mean the intervention by a third party who attempts rather informally to bring the two sides together. He may suggest the terms of a settlement, but he has no power to compel. The conciliator may guide discussion, but he makes no decisions.

Mediation is often used synonymously with conciliation, as defined in the second instance above. Others consider mediation to be more formal than conciliation, often involving the use of a commission before which the two parties will appear with their attorneys. In any event, the mediator may investigate the situation and suggest solutions, but he cannot force the parties to accept. Good mediators are usually persons who are trained in labor law and economics, and in their role as "industrial diplomats" they must be strictly objective and impartial. The mediator should be someone who is respected by both parties.

If mediation fails, the disputants may agree on *voluntary arbitration.* They will agree to have a third party enter the case and, furthermore, they will agree to accept his decision. (Some union contracts spell out the conditions under which the parties will resort to arbitration. For example, it may be decided that the arbitrator's authority will be limited to interpretation of the terms of the contract.)

Compulsory arbitration exists when government directly or indirectly compels the parties to submit their differences to an impartial outsider for adjudication. Compulsory arbitration has been used in Australia, New Zealand, and France. Kansas, in 1920, set up a Court of Industrial Relations as part of a system of compulsory arbitration for certain industries. Both management and labor opposed the system, for both prefer free collective bargaining to government decree.[2] The U.S. Supreme Court in 1923 declared unconstitutional the Kansas Court's power to fix wages in industries that are not public utilities, and in 1925 held that the fixing of hours of work through compulsory arbitration by a state agency infringes upon the liberty of contract and rights of property guaranteed by the Fourteenth Amendment's due process clause. The Kansas legislature then abolished the Court. During wartime emergencies and disputes posing a threat to the public health or safety, the Federal government has sometimes taken actions which had the effect of compulsory arbitration. In 1963, for example, when the Railway Labor Act failed to settle a complex case involving work rules, a bill was passed which required arbitration of the dispute. In signing this law, however, President Kennedy specified that it was not intended to establish a precedent for compulsory arbitration. Generally, then, compulsory arbitration is rare in the United States.

Labor and management both realize that industrial peace is important for an industry and for the economy in general. Once a contract has been signed, differences that arise are usually settled by an orderly and peaceful procedure. Strikes and other labor disputes capture the headlines, but the vast majority of cases are settled quietly and peacefully. After a union becomes established in an industry,

2 "With compulsory arbitration you're over a barrel," said the late Michael Quill, President of the Transport Workers Union. (On WNBC-TV, January 7, 1961.) A natural enemy of Mr. Quill, the National Association of Manufacturers, stated, "Compulsory arbitration . . . leads inevitably to a totalitarian state." (In *NAM News*, January 4, 1947.)

management often accepts it with good grace. Contracts set forth the responsibilities as well as the rights of labor; peace is virtually assured for the duration of the agreement (three years, often), and it may be much easier to deal with one man or committee representing all the workers than with each of them as individuals.

The Classical Model and Labor Today

The classical model is no longer the exclusive guide in determining wage policy. The reasons for departing from this model are many and complex, but all the causes may be traced back to (1) the Industrial Revolution, (2) the development of organized labor, and (3) the realization that labor is not merely a factor of production to be bought in the marketplace. The number of persons employed in industries where individual workers can draw up separate contracts with their employers has been reduced considerably in all fields and to almost nothing in our mass production industries. Organized labor, while making up only about 25 percent of our labor force, has a definite influence on wage rates of unorganized workers. State and federal legislation on minimum wage rates, maximum hours, child labor laws, and conditions of work have brought about changes in the supply and demand curves as applied to labor.

New Trends in Labor Relations

Historians frequently refer to the last hundred years as the era of the "rise of the common man." More specifically, they point to the increased dignity associated with labor. Papal encyclicals, the spread of liberal ideas, and state and federal legislation have emphasized the importance of humanism in labor relations. In more recent times, economic thinking has emphasized the importance of the purchasing power of the general public. In keeping with this trend, Henry Ford recognized that the automobile industry could be a huge success only if his workers could afford to buy the products that they made. Labor has been recognized as a very significant consumer in the economy. In Chapter 13 we shall see the relation of income to consumer spending.

Industry-Wide Bargaining

If you refer to your newspaper, you can probably find that bargaining between labor and management is going on in a way that would have been difficult for economists to anticipate only a few years ago. Sitting around a bargaining table might be the representatives of the steelworkers or automobile workers on the one side and those of a great corporation such as United States Steel or General Motors on the other. The contract that they sign will probably apply not only to the workers of the corporation concerned but also to labor throughout that particular industry. Negotiating labor contracts which will set a pattern for workers in an entire industry is known as *industry-wide bargaining.*

Settlements arrived at in key industries frequently set a pattern for settlements in many other mass-production industries. New kinds of agreements often become widely accepted, too. Establishment of a 3.2 percent wage increase based on an estimate of a 3.2 percent increase in productivity per worker, an *escalator clause* which provides workers with automatic increases and decreases based on fluctuations in the cost of living, or using the principle of profits as a basis for determining wage increases, when gained in one contract, probably will be applied to other contracts. Even the wages of those not organized are eventually affected.

The Classical Model Is Still Important

Although all the evidence presented here indicates a change from the classical model, it is still doubtful that we have departed greatly from that model. The productivity of labor is, in the long run, the major factor in determining real wage rates. While unions may limit the supply of labor available, causing wages to rise, these wages can come only from increased productivity. Let us consider further the effect of a change in wage rates.

Suppose that a strong union is able to bargain for an increase in wages of 5 percent when productivity has gone up only 3 percent. Such a change will increase the cost of production per unit and force the employer to pay for it by cutting into his profits or by raising prices to the consumer. In industries where there is little competition the additional cost will probably be passed on to the consumer immediately. In competitive industries prices will rise eventually because of the additional purchasing power in the hands of the workers, who are also consumers. However, in the interim some of the weakest firms will be forced out of business. Under these conditions unemployment will probably rise and thereby cause wages to fall.

If prices rise 2 percent to pay for the additional cost, the 5 percent increase in wages will have a purchasing power of only 3 percent, the same as the increase in productivity. Some critics of labor use the illustration just given as proof that labor is responsible for what is called a *cost-push* inflation. They maintain that wage increases that are in excess of increased productivity per man-hour have raised costs and forced prices up. Defenders of labor reply that the cost for additional wages should come from excessively high profits. In the negotiation for a new contract in the automotive industry in 1964, Walter Reuther, head of the United Auto Workers, argued that the higher wages he asked for could be paid from the huge earnings which the automobile manufacturers were making and even allow for prices on cars to be lowered. Some critics of industry go a step further and say that business welcomes the opportunity to give a wage increase because such action permits raising prices not only high enough to pay for the additional cost but even higher, so that profits will be larger than ever.

Do Unions Raise Wages?

The debate on the influence of unions in raising wages will undoubtedly continue with no definite answer. Variations will be found from industry to industry. We do know that monopoly power in both industry and labor has brought about changes in the supply and demand for labor. We also know that labor as a whole cannot long receive wages in excess of the value it produces, and that probably some government regulation is necessary to make sure that no segment of the economy will disrupt the development of the American economy as a whole. Equally important, we can all agree that if we can make the "pie" (the total goods and services produced) grow faster than the mouths that will consume it, everyone can have a bigger portion. A highly skilled labor force, characterized by a high degree of productivity, has been one of our country's chief assets in giving us a high standard of living. There can be no substitute for it.

Part D
The Problem: Is Automation a Blessing or a Curse to Labor?

Labor has always been interested in a market in which the demand for labor is high and the supply small. Such a market condition will allow wages to remain high or move still higher. If, on the other hand, large numbers of people move into the labor market without a corresponding increase in the number of jobs, wage rates are threatened. Over the long run we find that employment seems to be going up steadily, with few interruptions, but that the percentage of people unemployed has not always declined in a complementary fashion. The major explanation for this seemingly odd phenomenon is that more people are joining the labor force than are leaving it. This means that we have to increase the number of jobs available just to prevent the number of unemployed from going up, to say nothing of reducing the number of jobless.

Labor and Technological Change

An additional complication that poses a threat which many consider more serious is illustrated by the cartoon showing machinery replacing human labor. This is an old problem that has always concerned labor, and it has been identified in many ways, most frequently by the term *technological unemployment.* Today we usually refer to the introduction of machines to replace human labor as *automation.*

Although there are many definitions of automation, the major element distinguishing it from the meaning given in the paragraph above is that it involves a continuous operation of production linking together the several or many different jobs to be performed, usually by some feedback system. In the 1920's and 1930's the assembly-line production technique was greatly refined and extended in this country. A product would start at one end of an assembly line and would be conveyed, frequently by a belt, past many workmen, each of whom would add to or perform some kind of operation to make the finished product. Automation differs from the described assembly-line technique in that machines control machines. Through a system of feeding back infor-

"Hey, Joe! It says our jobs are next!"

SOURCE: Ed Valtman, The Hartford *Times.*

mation, the machines on the assembly line are told when they are to perform their job on the product passing by and what that operation will be.

Automation has already been developed to a great degree in the production of petroleum, chemicals, and certain phases of steel, paper, plastics, and even automobiles. In the office and research laboratory the computer can perform many kinds of operations, store tremendous amounts of information, and, most important for our study, replace workers. Management uses automation or any other kind of mechanization when doing so will reduce costs and perform the job as well as or better than human beings will do it.

Management and Technological Change

While we are focusing our attention on the effects of automation on employment, it is important to recognize the far-reaching problems which this new development in technology presents to management and education. Investment in machinery, research, and education takes on new significance as both firms and workers struggle for positions on a more flexible economic ladder. It is true that firms with large amounts of capital can support large research staffs, but ideas that change production techniques or consumer demand can and do come from small businesses. No firm, no manager, and no worker can afford to take success for granted. Rapid technological progress in today's world may very well make present standards of production obsolete for tomorrow's market.

To understand better the effect of automation on unemployment, let us look at the problem from three different points of view. Do not assume that the "truth" is to be found in any one position. While some viewpoints may be more politically expedient, they may not be characteristic of the real world in which we live. Examine the questions that remain to be answered after reading the three viewpoints presented. Your answers to these questions may help you arrive at a conclusion of what policy, if any, we should have in trying to resolve the problems that automation may create. Make sure that you understand when you are expressing value judgments, when you are stating facts, and when you are using economic reasoning.

Automation as a Threat to Labor

Testifying before the Joint Economic Committee of Congress, two of the most prominent labor leaders in the country pointed out some of the problems which automation and other technological changes pose for labor. Certainly the most serious threat has been the replacement of human labor by machines. A few facts illustrate this change. The food and beverage industry increased its production 20 percent but decreased the number of workers in production and maintenance by 8 percent. Textile mills had a similar rise in production during this period but dropped 22 percent of their workers in production and maintenance. In basic steel, production has increased only slightly, but production and maintenance jobs declined by 52,600. Meat consumption has increased in recent years, but employment in the meat packing industry has declined by approximately 50,000 workers.

Although it is true that white-collar jobs in the chemical and electrical machinery industries have increased faster than blue-collar jobs have decreased, opportunities for those discharged have been very small. Many skilled and semiskilled workers have seen their jobs downgraded or eliminated. They have found that their skills are obsolete and that new training and experience are necessary.

The much-publicized retraining and relocation program can help, but it does not bring about a solution to the problem. A study of a well-financed retraining program set up after a plant had been closed showed that of the 431 production workers who could have benefited from the program, only 13 completed the course and only seven found jobs involving their new skills. Few workers appear anxious to take a retraining course, and many are either too old or do not have the ability to learn the kinds of skills that are in demand.

Wages will decline in jobs where technological changes reduce demand. The general wage level is likely to go down as displaced workers try to find new jobs. It is estimated that some two and a half million jobs will have to be found each year in the decade ahead to take care of those who are replaced by technological developments and new workers looking for their first job.

A world-famous mathematician who has contributed much to the development of automatic control machines predicted that if we were to have an all-out effort in producing automated equipment, we would have a depression that would be far worse than the Great Depression of the 1930's. Furthermore, human labor would be competing with machinery, which is the equivalent of slave labor. Only if we are willing to abandon our worship of progress and our willingness to allow the few to benefit at the expense of the many can our new knowledge be a blessing rather than a curse.

Automation as a Blessing to Labor

The major reason for the remarkable advance in man's standard of living is the increase in his productive capacity. Behind this increased productive capacity is the technological progress that has given man tools that perform more efficiently. The latest development in the Industrial Revolution is automation. It promises to help man achieve an even higher standard of living by producing goods more cheaply, reducing hours of work, and allowing man more leisure to develop his talents and enjoy the fruits of his labor. Nowhere is this better illustrated than in the United States, where technological progress has been the greatest and the standard of living the highest.

The fear that automation will bring widespread unemployment is unfounded. There has never been as much automation as we have today, and there have never been so many people employed. In an interview on the subject of automation a labor leader representing a lithographers' union said that his union was in favor of automation because it brought down unit costs sufficiently to allow employers to pay higher wages with a 35-hour week, 3-week vacations, 10 paid holidays, and many other benefits. Membership in his union has increased at a far faster rate than the general population. While admitting that some workers may have some difficulty for short periods of time in retraining or in relocating, these inconveniences are offset by the widespread long-range benefits reduced costs bring.

A representative of one of America's major corporations pointed out to a congressional committee that automation can provide new and increased employment opportunities by (1) lower-cost, higher-volume business, (2) the expansion of service industries, (3) the supplying of automated equipment, and (4) the developing of new products, leading to the expansion of existing firms and the creation of new enterprises.

The same arguments which carriage makers advanced when the automobile was introduced are being used by those who fear the computer and other automatic control machines. Looking back with historical perspective, we should welcome this revolution as something positive in man's effort to free himself from drudgery and provide himself with more of the things he wants.

A Moderate Position

Between the two extreme positions stated above is one that recognizes the advantages of technological progress but seeks to avoid the hardships that come to many in the transition process. In many industries management and labor have developed elaborate plans to ease the adjustment of workers who are replaced by machines. These plans include the establishment of job retraining programs financed by management, with some of the money coming from savings realized by using new machinery. Other programs include the introduction of new equipment in a slow and orderly way to prevent mass layoffs, the reduction of hours by increasing vacation periods, and the establishment of funds to be given to discharged workers for a period of time to lessen the hardships of the period of unemployment. The federal government, in its manpower and redevelopment program and its program to make "war on poverty," is helping to alleviate the burdens of those affected.

Considering an Answer

In spite of the efforts just described, a study by the Bureau of Labor Statistics indicates that over 1 million workers lost their jobs in a recent 6-year period because of technological changes. This leaves us with the following problems that you, the citizen, will have to decide.

Can we rely on the classical model to provide answers to the problem? Will the absence of any government aid, or even aid from business, make the worker more mobile in seeking a job, even if he may suffer hardships in the period between jobs?

Can labor and management work out solutions together without the aid of government? What is management's responsibility, if any, to displaced workers? What is management's responsibility to its stockholders in trying to maximize profits by cutting costs? What is management's responsibility to the consumer in passing on reduced costs in the form of lower prices?

Can management, in conjunction with labor, ease the difficulties of automating without reducing competition? Under conditions of pure competition, won't the firm which automates first and to the greatest extent, disregarding the hardships that may result to its workers, be in the best position to make the most profits?

If the government must give assistance, as it has now done, how far can it go without interfering with our free-enterprise tradition? Will government interference lessen the mobility of labor, and thereby delay the long-range solutions to the problem? Does government have a responsibility to protect workers from the hardships of technological changes over which the worker has no control?

REVIEW: THE HIGHLIGHTS OF THE CHAPTER

1. Labor unions are organized to improve the bargaining position of workers. The history of organized labor has moved like a pendulum, with progress made from 1898 to 1904, 1914 to 1920, and 1933 to 1947. The periods before, in between, and after were characterized by unfriendly courts, unfavorable legislation, and conflicts with employers.
2. The Knights of Labor, the American Federation of Labor, and the Congress of Industrial Organizations were the major labor organizations shaping American labor policy.
3. Unions are organized along both craft and industrial lines.
4. Both employers and unions have used many weapons to win their demands. Many of the most severe practices of both groups have now been outlawed.
5. The federal government gave its official endorsement to unions in the Wagner Act. The Taft-Hartley Act attempted to balance the power of unions and management.
6. Collective bargaining is the heart of unionism. Conciliation, mediation, and arbitration are methods of reaching agreement.
7. Automation is the latest technological change to threaten the employment opportunities of workers.

IN CONCLUSION: SOME AIDS TO UNDERSTANDING

Terms for Review

injunction
closed shop
collective bargaining
reform union
craft union
industrial union
company union
yellow-dog contract
blacklist
jurisdictional strike
lockout
union shop
maintenance-of-membership shop
open shop
preferential shop
boycott
conciliation
compulsory arbitration
featherbedding
"right-to-work" laws

Names to Know

Knights of Labor
Norris-LaGuardia Act
Landrum-Griffin Act
AF of L
CIO
Taft-Hartley Act
Wagner Act
National Labor Relations Board

Questions for Review

1. What changes did the Industrial Revolution bring about in regard to the position of labor?

2. What major factors impeded the growth of the labor movement in the United States?
3. Contrast the objectives of the Knights of Labor and the American Federation of Labor. Justify the labels "reform union" and "bread-and-butter union" as applied to each of them.
4. Compare the position of organized labor in the 1920's with its position in the 1930's. Explain the reasons for the difference.
5. What weapons has management used against labor, and what weapons has labor used against management? Evaluate the effectiveness of each in resolving labor-management disputes.
6. Why has organized labor sometimes referred to the Wagner Act as the "Magna Carta of the labor movement"? What were the objectives of the Taft-Hartley Act with regard to the unions?
7. "In spite of many factors interfering with the classical model's approach to wage determination, the theory it offers is still important in explaining wage rates." Explain the meaning of this statement.

Additional Questions and Problems

1. In a brief essay, justify the demands of labor for the following:
   (a) An increase in wages coupled with a demand that prices of the produced article remain the same.
   (b) A share in the profits of industry without a direct contribution to the risks.

   Now draw up the notes for a speech of rebuttal by the head of a large corporation.
2. Select two leaders in the American labor movement and explain the differences in their philosophy and their methods. Evaluate each one in terms of his effectiveness in helping to solve labor's problems.
3. Describe government's role in labor-management relations. To what extent should government intervene in labor disputes? Why?
4. What are the arguments against compulsory arbitration
   (a) by unions?
   (b) by management?

   Present the argument of the public in support of compulsory arbitration of major labor disputes.
5. Bring the following ideas into a discussion of automation:
   (a) We must create two and a half million new jobs each year to keep our labor force employed.
   (b) Fifty percent of the jobs of 1975 have not as yet been created.
   (c) We must learn to use leisure time intelligently or automation will be a curse, not a boon.
   (d) Today's education must be technical and must emphasize skills.
   (e) Automation may create a temporary unemployment problem, but in the long run it will increase the number of jobs.

SELECTED READINGS

The American Federationist. Washington, D.C.: American Federation of Labor and Congress of Industrial Organizations. (Published monthly)

Barbash, Jack. *Structure, Government and Politics of American Unions.* New York: Random House, 1966.

Bok, Derek C. and John T. Dunlop. *Labor and the American Community.* New York: Simon and Schuster, 1970.

Bowen, William G., ed. *Labor and the National Economy.* New York: W. W. Norton & Co., 1965.

Estey, Marten. *Unions: Structure, Development, and Management.* New York: Harcourt, Brace & World, 1967.

Evans, Robert. *Public Policy Toward Labor.* New York: Harper & Row, 1965.

Jacobson, Julius, ed. *The Negro and the American Labor Movement.* Garden City, N.Y.: Doubleday and Company, 1968.

Marshall, Ray. *The Negro Worker.* New York: Random House, 1967.

Pierson, Frank C. *Unions in Postwar America: An Economic Assessment.* New York: Random House, 1967.

Ulman, Lloyd, ed. *Challenges to Collective Bargaining.* Englewood Cliffs, N.J.: Prentice-Hall (Spectrum), 1967.

Weinstein, Paul A., ed. *Featherbedding and Technological Change.* Boston: D. C. Heath and Co., 1965.

Wirtz, Willard. *Labor and the Public Interest.* New York: Harper & Row, 1965.

Natural Resources, Capital, and Management: Their Uses and Rewards

8

THE AUTHORS' NOTE TO THE STUDENT

Although labor is extremely important in producing the goods and services we want, there would be no products without the other three factors: natural resources, capital, and management. We are concerned here with what contribution each of these factors makes in the production process, how business enterprise acquires the right amount of each, and what rewards are received for the part which each factor plays. Having a limited supply of all factors of production, we find that the question of how we allocate these resources to produce what the consumers want is still our central problem. As with labor, the rewards must be based on what each unit of a factor contributes to the total value of the product. We will have to return to our classical model of pure competition in order to determine resource allocation, as well as to study conditions which deviate from it.

A STUDENT'S NOTE TO THE STUDENT

Remember the theory of marginal productivity as it applied to labor in Chapter 6? Well, this chapter applies the same principle—utilizing additional units of each factor until the cost for hiring the last factor (*MC*) equals the value created by the last factor (*MRP*). The bar graph in Figure 8–2 helps. I found it interesting to apply this principle to landlords deciding whether it's worth it to fix up their slums.

Two concepts or definitions surprised me—economic rent and the economist's definition of profits. They sound alike. The inelastic supply curve for rent also bothers me. Don't we find uses for things which had no real value before a use was found for it?

The problem at the end of the chapter is really quite interesting, since I knew little about Henry George and some of the other novel ideas introduced in Part E.

Part A
Production and Distribution Characteristics of the Factors of Production

Selecting the Best Combination of Factors

We have already indicated that production involves the combining of certain amounts of four ingredients—natural resources (such as land), labor, capital, and management—to make the goods and supply the services we want. The businessman goes to the market for the factors of production knowing that he wants to produce certain kinds of goods in certain amounts and that, in order to do so, he will have to buy certain quantities of each of the factors of production. He should have some idea of the value of the products he will make when he offers them for sale in the consumer market. Actually he cannot be sure of this value, since prices may change, but he tries to make a logical estimate. He will then buy the best combination of the factors of production to produce the goods. Determining how many units of each factor to use so that his costs will be lowest and his revenue highest is the key to his success in business. It is also the answer to our basic question of allocating our limited resources to yield the greatest return in satisfaction to the consumer. This principle can be seen in the following example, Table 8–1, where changing the combinations of the units that we put into production will yield a different value for the output (same cost but more revenue).

The successful business adds factors of production so long as the marginal revenue product (the value in dollars that the last factor adds) is as large as or larger than the marginal cost (the cost in dollars for employing the last factor added).

TABLE 8–1 Input-Output Analysis of Factors of Production

	Units	
Natural Resources	6	
Labor	60	Yields 100,000
Capital	8	units of
Management	26	production
	100	

	Units	
Natural Resources	6	
Labor	58	Yields 110,000
Capital	12	units of
Management	24	production
	100	

Altering the composition of the factors of production can increase our efficiency. The problem for the businessman is to add units of each factor only so long as the cost for each unit (the marginal cost) is less than the value which that unit can add (the marginal revenue product).

We are assuming that each input unit, regardless of which factor of production is considered, costs the same. In the example we increase our output by reducing our labor and management inputs and increasing our capital inputs.

Each additional unit of production creates additional value, known as the marginal product. As long as the costs of additional units that we add (inputs) are no more than the value of the additional value created (output), we can continue to add factors to expand our production. As we noted in Chapter 4, the businessman will expand his production, requiring additional factors of production, to the point where his marginal cost is equal to his marginal revenue. Since each factor of production reaches the point of diminishing returns at a different level, we will have to decide which factors will be the most profitable to add. Using the technical information that shows the amount of output capable of being produced by specific inputs is known as the *production function.*

Dividing Return Among the Factors

Many people think of distribution as the movement of goods from the initial producer to the final consumer. The economist has a special meaning for distribution relating primarily to the problem of *For Whom. Distribution*—or, more accurately, *functional distribution*—is concerned with who, or what groups, will get what portion of the value or income created. Another way of stating this question is: How do we divide the "pie"? The size of the portion which each factor receives is the reward for the value each has contributed. Stated in an oversimplified way, the value that each factor contributes is determined by the supply and demand for each of the factors in the market.

Although we measure the value that each factor receives in dollars, we call the reward that each receives by a different name. Labor receives wages; natural resources, rent; capital, interest; and management, profits. Figure 8–1 shows the portion received by each factor in 1929 and in 1970. Remember that the "pie" that was divided in 1970 was far larger than

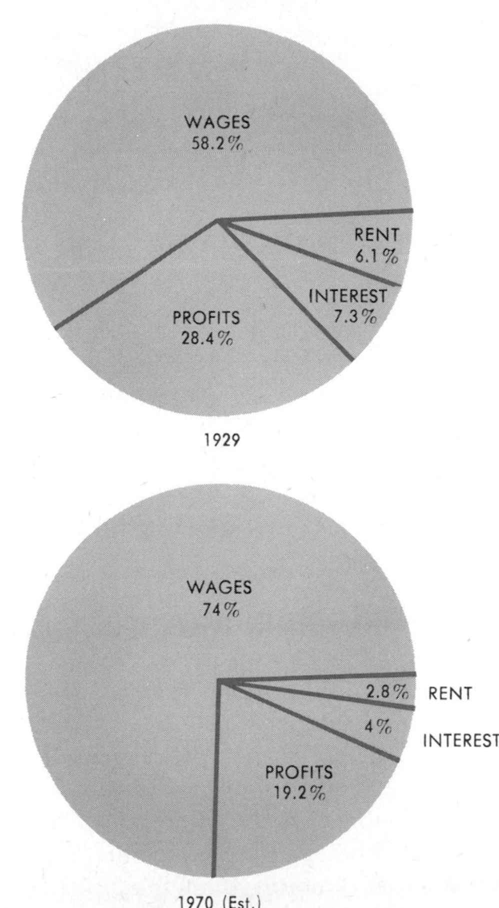

FIGURE 8–1 Distribution of National Income Among the Factors of Production

The figure for profits combines corporate profits before taxes and the income of unincorporated enterprises. Figures for 1970 are the authors' estimates based upon recent data. SOURCE: U.S. Department of Commerce.

THE MARGINALISTS AND NEOCLASSICAL ANALYSIS

The Industrial Revolution brought with it a host of social and economic problems that caused great discontent in Europe during the nineteenth century. Not satisfied with the answers provided by the classical economists, people turned to new methods, such as socialism, trade unionism, and government intervention, to find solutions.

Some economists were unwilling to accept either the popular alternatives to laissez-faire or certain aspects of classical economic thinking. These men, including W. Stanley Jevons and Alfred Marshall of England; Karl Menger, Friedrich von Wieser, and Eugen Böhm-Bawerk of Austria; John Bates Clark of the United States; Herman Heinrich Gossen of Germany; and Léon Walras of France, developed a new approach—the marginalist or neoclassical school.

Marginalism focuses on the problem of resource allocation. Given a certain quantity of the factors of production, how can these factors be used to satisfy the most needs? Like the classical economists, these men set their theories within a laissez-faire environment and oppose interference with the free market. They concentrate on microeconomics—the analysis of the single firm, the individual producer and consumer, and the formation of price for a single good. Their early theory starts with the concept of marginal utility as it relates to demand, and later spreads to cover marginal cost on the supply side. The marginalist sets forth the use of marginal productivity to account for the payment to each of the factors of production and to assist the businessman in maximizing his profits. Emphasis is on the yield from each unit added, since this return influences the decision to buy or sell more.

Marginalism is still important, although its use has been modified by more recent theories. Of these the most significant is the macroeconomic approach of Keynes.

that in 1929, thereby allowing all factors to receive more.

Marginal Productivity Applied to the Factors

In Chapter 6 we learned that the theory of marginal productivity is based on the law of diminishing returns. You will recall that as we add more workers beyond a certain point, each additional worker will add to the total value of our production a lesser amount than the preceding worker. This means that it is wise for us to keep adding workers only up to the point where the marginal revenue product (the value added by hiring one more worker) just equals marginal cost (the addition to total cost accounted for by that additional worker). If we go beyond that point, we will be paying the new worker more than the value that he adds to our total revenues. Figure 8–2 shows this graphically.

This same theory is applied to the other factors of production. Adding either land or capital will show the same pattern of decreasing yields as units are added. When the last additional unit costs more than the value created by that unit, profits are bound to be less. The producer should stop adding factors of production before this, when the marginal cost for resources and the marginal product—the added value obtained from the resources—equal each other.

To make our understanding of the theory of marginal productivity more accurate, we must differentiate between marginal physical product and marginal revenue product. The former refers to the physical units added by the last additional factor whereas the latter refers to the dollar value added. Because businessmen and owners of the factors of production are interested in making the most dollars and because of certain technical aspects that need not concern us, we will use marginal revenue product.

Importance of the Right Combination of Factors

In conditions approaching pure competition, the incentive for businessmen to seek new combinations of the factors of production to reduce costs and increase profits insures that the economy, and ultimately society, will progress. The development of new machinery costing less than the workers it replaces frees the displaced workers to seek jobs where their marginal productivity might be higher. This, of course, assumes that there are jobs for the displaced workers and that they are willing to move to another place for work. As we have seen, there is reason to question whether these assumptions about job opportunities and labor mobility are correct.

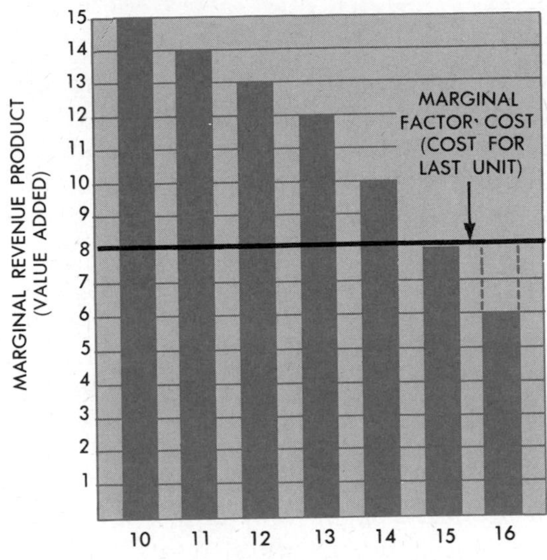

FIGURE 8–2 Most Efficient Production

It will pay the businessman to continue adding units of factors of production as long as the value created by the last unit (the marginal revenue product) is not less than the cost for hiring the last unit (the marginal factor cost). The use of the sixteenth unit in this case would result in a loss. Where should the producer stop adding units of factors of production if the cost goes up to 10?

Firms that operate under conditions of imperfect competition must also consider their costs. However, because such firms have some control over supply and thereby can keep their prices higher than they would be under pure competition, they can afford to be less efficient. The poorly managed business operating under conditions of partial monopoly is able to conceal its wasteful use of limited resources under the cover of higher prices. The consumer must pay the difference.

Part B
Natural Resources and Rent

Natural resources (land, for example) are the ingredients that nature provides for use in production. Resources are distinguished from the other factors of production primarily because their supply is fixed. Our nation must be considered very fortunate in the abundance and variety of its resources.

The Nature of Rent

When we use the term "rent," we are most likely to think of a tenant paying a certain amount of money per month for the use of property owned by a landlord. It may be a family "renting" an apartment, a businessman "renting" a store, or a salesman "renting" a car. When used in this way, *rent* means the price that is paid for the use of some durable good such as land, or buildings, or equipment, or even all three. Economists have a more exact term, *economic rent* (see p. 177), to distinguish this use from "renting" as applied above. *Land rent* is the price paid for land or other natural resources. It is the price paid for any factor of production that cannot be reproduced. It is subject to the same laws of supply and demand as are all other factors of production; but because the supply of natural resources is fixed, the supply curve is perfectly inelastic. This means that the price of rent is determined by demand. In our discussion we will use land in its common usage, recognizing that all natural resources may be treated in a similar manner.

Why Do We Pay Rent?

Some of you may wonder why rent should be paid when nature, rather than man, has provided us with our natural resources. Why should anyone receive payment for something given to all of us? The answer is to be found in returning to our basic question of allocating limited resources to meet unlimited wants. With the supply of land and other natural resources inelastic, many businessmen and consumers will seek to own or use this fixed supply for their own benefit. But who should rightfully get it? Obviously, this should be the person who needs it most. How do we tell who has the greatest need? The classical economist would answer that it should be offered to the person who is willing to pay the most. This is because we determine value in our economic system by prices. Let us illustrate this idea by using the case of our "Build-a-City" business. After considering the advantages of several possible locations, we shall examine in detail the merits of the last location for three possible customers.

The Right Location

We would like to find a location for our "Build-a-City" plant that is reasonably close to our source of supply for labor, for wood, and for inexpensive transportation to our consumer markets. The rent for land in the heart of the metropolitan area is very costly. Retail stores that depend on the gathering of thousands of consumers are all bidding to get the choice locations in the downtown area. With the supply of land so limited and the demand so great, the rent (the price for the use of the land) will be very high. Since we do not need thousands of customers to come to our plant, paying the high rent for this location would be a waste of money.

We cannot locate our plant in the residential section of the city because of zoning laws and "economic laws." It would make little sense for us to pay the cost charged to those seeking to rent or build apartments or homes in this residential area. Besides, the smoke and noise from our factory would create ill will toward our company.

Five miles outside the city on a major highway there is a piece of land for sale. It is large enough for our plant and for parking spaces for our employees. Very few residential dwellings are located there. Most of the surrounding area is now being used for farming. Public transportation for employees is available, since a bus from the city goes by the site every half hour. Our supply trucks can avoid costly delays in city traffic, and there is a railroad feeder line less than two miles away. Those competing with us for the land are farmers and land speculators who anticipate the expansion of suburbs, perhaps 10 years from now. Our productivity per acre is far greater than that of the farmer, and the land speculator cannot afford to pay money out for 10 years without any income merely in the hope that he may get a high price at some time in the future. We can afford to rent the land at a price slightly higher than either the farmer or the land speculator, because we can get the highest return from it. Our limited resources of land are thus finding their greatest value to society. Figure 8–3 shows this relationship graphically.

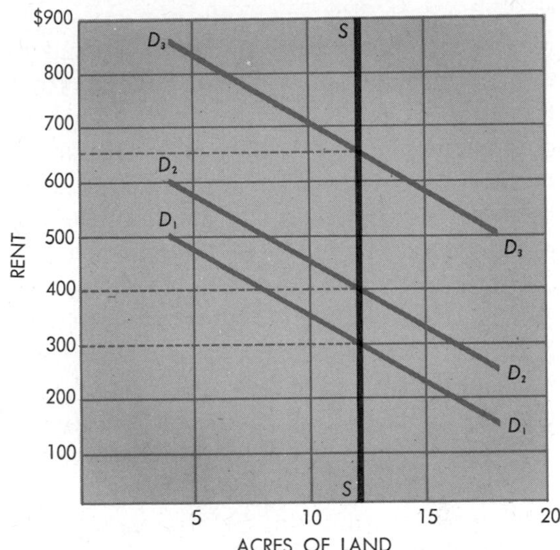

FIGURE 8–3 Price Determination of Land

Because the marginal revenue product of our business (D_3) is higher than that of the farmer (D_1) and of the speculator (D_2), we will be able to rent the land. Explain why we will not have to pay our full marginal revenue product for rent ($650) in the example shown here.

In the example we have used, the land would not reach its full marginal revenue product. This is because in bidding for the land, the land speculator, who was the second-highest bidder, believed that his potential marginal productivity was a great deal less than ours. Since he was the only other person to bid against us, we were able to secure the land for slightly more than $400. If another manufacturer had been bidding against us, we might have had to go up to our full marginal revenue product of $650.

Economic Rent

David Ricardo, one of the great classical economists (see p. 409), explained rent as the return arising from differences in the productivity of land. It can be figured as the difference between the income derived from using the land and the cost of producing that income. If the cost to a farmer for producing $5,000 worth of wheat is $4,000, including payment to himself for his labor and his initiative and enterprise, then the economic rent would be $1,000. The farmer must pay himself for his labor and the capital he uses at the same rate as if he were working and using his capital for someone else. If he used more productive land so that the yield per acre was greater and his wheat was worth $6,000 while his costs remained the same, then the economic rent would be $2,000.

Even before you began to study economics, you may have heard the terms *marginal, submarginal,* and *supramarginal* applied to land. Actually these terms have a very specific meaning in economics. *Marginal land* refers to land in which the cost of producing income from it is equal to that income. With no surplus, it is no-rent land. *Submarginal land* describes land in which the cost of producing income from it is greater than the value of the income. This is wasteful use of our resources. *Supramarginal land* is land in which the cost of producing income from the land is less than the value of that income. Land that might be submarginal at one time may become marginal or even supramarginal when the demand for the products produced from it increases, causing prices to rise and income to go up. During World War II, when the demand for food increased, land that was submarginal and hence not used previously was brought under cultivation. The higher prices for food increased the income that could be derived from this land beyond the cost of production. Several years after the war, when war-ravaged countries were able to satisfy their own food requirements, the demand for our food declined. This brought prices down and caused much of this poor land to be withdrawn from use.

Relation of Slums to Rent

One of the major problems facing urban centers today is the existence of large slum areas. These neighborhoods not only provide substandard housing, but they also are costly to society in that the environment rarely offers residents the opportunities necessary to develop their full potential. In addition, crime rates are higher and health standards lower in slums than in other areas.

The reason most frequently advanced and usually accepted for the existence of slums is that the people living there cannot afford to pay a sufficiently high rent to make it worthwhile for the owners to improve present structures or to replace existing ones with better housing. The marginal cost for inputs (improving these homes) will not yield sufficient output, or marginal revenue (higher rent). If the owners do improve or replace their substandard housing, they usually raise their rent. Low-income families are then faced with trying to find new housing that they can afford. Since the chance of making money on good low-rent housing seems slight, few businessmen are willing to make the necessary investment.

Many Americans do not believe that the classical model has provided an adequate solution to the problem of low-cost housing. As a result, the federal government, acting through city and state governments, has aided in the development of low-cost housing. Public housing, started in 1934, has produced about 800,000 dwelling units. Many other Americans have objected to this approach, since it is considered an interference with the free-

TABLE 8–2 Changes in Housing Costs, 1949–1969

	1949	1969
On-site Labor	$3,227.40 (33%)	$ 3,696.12 (18%)
Materials	$3,520.80 (36%)	$ 7,802.92 (38%)
Land	$1,075.80 (11%)	$ 4,312.14 (21%)
Overhead and profit	$1,467.00 (15%)	$ 2,669.42 (13%)
Financing	$ 489.00 (5%)	$ 2,053.40 (10%)
Average Price	$9,780.00	$20,534.00

Note the dramatic increases in land and financing costs. How do these increases relate to our discussion of land rent and competition for the use of loanable funds in this chapter? SOURCE: U.S. Bureau of Labor Statistics and NAHB Economics Department.

enterprise system. A more recent kind of aid has been the urban renewal and slum clearance program under way since 1949. Under this plan the federal government gives funds to cities for clearing land of existing substandard dwellings. Once the land is cleared, it is sold at a low price for redevelopment, including housing, by private builders. An objection to this method is that it fails to provide enough low-cost housing, being designed more often for middle-income groups.

Recent investigations of rents in slum areas in New York City have caused many to question whether rents are really low and whether landlords could not improve their dwellings without raising rents any higher.

Part C
Capital and Interest

Competition for Use of Loanable Funds

In Chapter 1 we defined capital as man-made instruments of production. We should expect interest to be the payment or reward to the owners of capital for the part their money plays in obtaining the means of production. When we think of interest, however, we are more likely to think of it as payment to those who lend money from those who borrow money.

In our economy, business, consumers, and the various levels of government all borrow money, and of course pay for its use. In borrowing, they compete with one another for the use of loanable funds.

Business Pays for the Use of Capital

When we consider the productive process from the viewpoint of management, we must first decide what to produce and then determine what natural resources and labor are needed to make these goods. If production is to be increased, it can most frequently be done by putting tools (machinery) into the hands of the worker to make him more productive. How will he be able to get these tools?

Let us first explain in a very simple way how the tools may be obtained, assuming that this is the only business in our society. Under our present system of production we produce $1,000 worth of goods per day. We now take 20 percent of our workers and shift their efforts into the manufacture of tools of production. This reduces the value of the items we are producing for consumption to $800 a day. After 10 days we have sacrificed $2,000, but we have also completed the machines that we need to produce more goods. These machines represent added capital and were obtained by the company by sacrificing present output of goods. Is it worth it? Only if the value of our production has increased sufficiently to pay back the $2,000 we have lost plus some value in addition. If additional value is achieved, it is the result of the increased capital (tools) we added to the production process. This capital, like the other factors of production, must be paid for.

In our complex society today we define interest as the price paid for the use of money or loanable funds. The businessman who wishes to increase the size of his store—adding capital—or to buy machinery for his factory (also capital) borrows money. He expects to be able to increase his business enough to pay back the principal (the amount of money borrowed) and the interest (the price for borrowing the funds) and still have money left over. The money he has borrowed has come from those who have saved some of their income instead of spending it all on consumer items. This in turn has freed workers who might have been producing consumer goods to engage in the production of capital goods. Furthermore those people who have money saved are now able to lend it for the production of capital goods and thus to receive interest as their reward for sacrificing their present desires to consume. We can now see the relationship between interest as payment for loanable funds and payment for capital.

Consumers Pay for the Use of Loanable Funds

Consumers as well as businessmen borrow money. As of late 1970, consumer credit outstanding amounted to more than $123 billion. The reasons for consumer borrowing are many, but in each case the borrower induces the lender to forgo the use of his funds by offering interest. Some loans may be looked upon as an investment, as in the case of money borrowed for a college education. Some may be used to take care of an unexpected crisis. Some loans are for the purchase of goods that are costly but that are used for many years (durable goods). Demand for loanable funds by consumers competes with the demand for loanable funds by businessmen. In each case the borrower pays interest for the use of the lender's capital.

Government Pays for the Use of Loanable Funds

The federal, state, and local governments also need to borrow money. Sometimes this money is borrowed to pay for major capital improvements, such as road construction; sometimes to meet an unforeseen emergency, such as a flood; and, in the case of the federal government, to finance a planned deficit to help overcome a depression. State and local governments often compete with others seeking to borrow, thus causing interest rates to rise. The federal government helps the smaller units of government to borrow funds by allowing the interest on their bonds to be tax-free.

Determining Interest Rates

Interest is stated as a rate of return for money borrowed, whether for business, for consumer spending, or for government use. The rate of interest specifies how many dollars the borrower has to pay for every $100 he borrows for one year. For the lender it is how many dollars he will receive for each $100 that he lends per year. A business that borrows $5,000 from a bank at 5 percent must pay back $5,250 at the end of one year. When interest is paid in advance, the borrower receiving principal minus interest, it is called *discounting.*

Stating interest as a rate rather than using absolute figures ($250 in the above example) allows the borrower to make a comparison with others borrowing different amounts. A business borrowing $10,000 for one year with $400 of interest is thus paying more dollars in interest than in our example above, but is paying a lower interest rate (4 percent).

The examples used above assume that the borrower has the use of the entire principal for the full year. If payments are made on the principal before the end of the full term of the loan (many small loans are paid monthly), the interest is higher. This is because interest is being paid on the full amount ($5,000) when some of the principal has already been repaid.

There are many reasons why interest rates may vary:

1. The difference in the risk of repayment
2. The duration (long-term loans generally command higher interest rates)
3. The cost of administering the loan (short-term loans are far more costly when figured as a percentage of the loan)
4. The ability to shop around for the best "buy"

Pure Interest

Economists frequently speak of "the" interest rates as though the factors just mentioned did not exist and every borrower paid the same rate. They are referring to "pure" interest, which is the rate paid for the use of money without the factors mentioned above being taken into consideration. The rate of interest for long-term United States government bonds is usually cited as the closest approximation of pure interest, because the factors mentioned previously are almost eliminated.

The Demand for Loanable Funds

Demand for loanable funds refers to the amount of dollars that people will borrow at different rates of interest for a given time. These demands come most often from the money requirements of businessmen, consumers, and governments. If we defined interest as the price paid for loanable funds, we could rightfully anticipate the reappearance of our familiar model of demand and supply.

Demand of Business

What determines the shape of a demand curve for loanable funds? Once again the law of diminishing returns appears, with the result that the marginal revenue product of money causes our demand curve to slope downward. The first $1,000 that we borrow to improve the looks of a store or add to the productive capacity of a factory will generally yield a bigger return than the next $1,000. The second $1,000 will usually yield a bigger return than the third $1,000, and so on. The businessman must try to determine how much above the additional cost of adding units of capital he can earn and compare it to the cost of the interest he pays. He can afford to borrow up to that point where the interest for the last amount he borrowed (his marginal cost for loanable funds) is equal to the amount he can earn above his costs on the last unit he bought with the money he borrowed (his marginal revenue product). Thus if he borrows an additional $10,000 and must pay $600 for its use for a year, it will not pay him to borrow these funds unless he can anticipate earning more than this amount from the use of this money. Here, as with wage rates and rent, we see the theory of the marginal revenue product determining the demand. Because the money is usually spent on items that last many years, the businessman is forced to estimate what the yield will be on each unit of capital he buys.

Demand of the Consumer

Most of the money borrowed by consumers will not be used in the production process. However, it will probably be used for satisfying the needs of the borrower. It will, therefore, be subject to the law of diminishing marginal utility. This will produce a demand curve quite similar to the one applicable for the businessman; that is, it is downward sloping. Demand for meeting emergencies is very inelastic; for durable consumer goods such as automobiles, more elastic; and for luxury items, most elastic.

Demand of Government

The federal government's demand curve for most loanable funds is inelastic. The reason is that most of the national government's debt came about during such emergencies as wars and depressions, when it was impractical to cover all expenditures through taxes. The demand curve of state and local governments is more elastic.

Inelastic Tendency

Because interest represents a relatively small part of the cost for capital expenditures or the buying of durable goods, demand for loanable funds is probably a good deal less sensitive to interest rates than the classical economists believed. Also, low interest rates usually have little effect in encouraging investment by firms when business conditions are declining. It is for this reason that the demand curve tends to be somewhat inelastic, particularly during depressions or recessions.

The Supply of Loanable Funds

The supply of loanable funds refers to the amount of dollars that lenders will offer at different rates of interest for a given time. The sources of loanable funds are personal savings, business savings, and lending by commercial banks.

Most savings by individuals come from those who are in the middle and upper income groups. Over half of personal savings comes from families whose income is in the highest 5 percent in the nation. These people are more likely to save because they can buy the things they need and still have money left over. Much of our saving is for a particular purpose, such as a college education, a house, or protection in case of loss of income.

Most business saving finds its way back into business to support its growth. Particularly since World War II, companies have shown a tendency to use money from profits to support expansion rather than paying out all in dividends or borrowing money on the open market. Although such businesses are not contributing to the market for loanable funds, they keep existing supplies of loanable funds at a higher level by satisfying or reducing their own needs. When not using their savings, they sometimes make these funds available to other businesses.

When commercial banks make loans available to borrowers, they are extending credit. This provides a major source of loanable funds needed by businesses as well as by consumers. These functions will be explained more fully when we discuss banking in Chapter 15.

Not all savings are available as loanable funds. Some individuals and businesses may decide that they would prefer to keep their savings in a form that would not make their money available to borrowers. Their decision as to whether to hold their money or make it available is determined by their *liquidity preference,* the desire to keep savings in the form of ready cash.

Amount of Loanable Funds

What determines the amount of loanable funds? While economists are not in complete agreement, most recognize that higher interest rates will cause some savers to transfer some of their money from a highly liquid condition (cash) to loanable funds (interest-bearing securities). Modern economic theory places greater emphasis on the relationship of savings to the general economic well-being of the nation (national income). People save more as income rises. Greater savings will provide more money for loanable funds. We can conclude that the supply curve of loanable funds slopes upward, opposite to the direction of demand

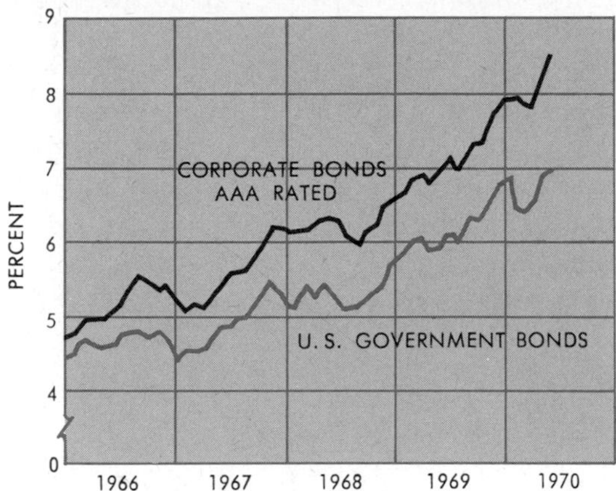

FIGURE 8–4 Long-Term Rates on Corporate and Government Bonds

Yields on bonds rose to record-high levels in 1970. Why would the rates on both corporate and government bonds tend to follow the same basic trend? Why are the rates lower on government bonds? SOURCE: International Division, Irving Trust Company of New York, *Business Conditions U.S.A.*, July 1970.

for loanable funds, and like most of the supply curves we have been discussing.

Interaction of Demand and Supply of Loanable Funds

Interest rates, like the other factors of production, are determined by the interaction of demand and supply. With a given demand for loanable funds and a given supply, interest rates will be at the point where supply and demand curves meet.

According to classical theory, interest in the free marketplace exercises a major influence in regulating the economy. In answer to the question of how to allocate our resources, loanable funds will be steered into those businesses which can afford to pay the highest interest rates. These are the same businesses which have the highest marginal revenue product and are producing the things that the consumer wants most. High consumer demand, supply remaining equal, means high prices. High prices will induce businessmen to expand their capital facilities, even if they must borrow at high interest rates. This results in increasing the production of goods consumers want. It will usually bring higher profits as well.

Another regulatory role that interest is supposed to play is that of keeping savings and investment in balance. When business conditions are poor, there will be more loanable funds available (supply) than businessmen and consumers want (demand). Interest rates will go down to a point where many businessmen will find it profitable to borrow. This will help stimulate the economy. If business conditions are rising so fast as to create a threat of inflation and a shortage of loanable funds, interest rates should rise enough to discourage marginal producers from expanding. This subject will be discussed further in Chapter 13.

How sensitive the demand and supply of loanable funds are to interest rates is a matter of controversy. Recently a flow of loanable funds to higher-paying markets outside this country was accompanied by a policy of tight money. This situation caused some economists, who had previously minimized the influence of interest as a factor in the distribution of loanable funds, to reevaluate their answers.

How Free Is the Market for Loanable Funds?

Until the 1930's the price for loanable funds was largely determined by demand and supply in a free market. While the government has become increasingly involved with the total economy, the lending market has become much less free. The government, by borrowing large sums of money—more than business and consumers during World War II—influences the interest rates set by the Federal Reserve Bank. Government support for certain kinds of loans—to housing, small business, and the farmer—and its powers of taxing and spending also affect a very large portion of the market. Because of this government influence most economists refer to the price for loanable funds as an *administered price,* subject to modification by individuals. Some economists believe that the government has gone too far in trying to control the money market. Others think that it is the duty of the government to control the money market in order to help keep the economy prosperous.

Part D
Management and Profits

What Is Profit?

Management, or enterprise, is directly responsible for initiating production. The businessman (entrepreneur) takes his cue from consumers, deciding what they want or, in the case of a new product, what he thinks they might want. If he believes that he can organize a business by assembling the other three factors of production into an efficient producing unit and selling his product so that his revenue will be greater than his cost, he will go ahead. It is the expectation of making a profit that is his incentive.

Profit means different things to different people. According to some public opinion polls, many people are not sure what it is, but they are sure it is too large and represents too much of the consumer's dollar. The worker may look at profit as an unfairly large payment to management that deprives him of a higher wage. The businessman thinks of profit as being the difference between his total revenue and total cost. Let us now see if we can develop a more exact definition of what constitutes profit.

Gross profit is the difference between what a businessman sells his product for and what it costs him. The merchant buys $100,000 worth of merchandise during the year and sells it for $135,000. His gross profit is $35,000. The percentage difference between his cost and selling price is 35 percent, and he calls this his "markup."

Net profit is what the businessman has left after he has paid his expenses—rent, wages, and interest—and has set aside money to allow for the loss due to depreciation (wearing out) of his capital. Our merchant has to subtract his payment of rent ($3,000), wages ($10,000), interest on money borrowed ($500), repairs and upkeep ($500), taxes ($500), electricity and other expenses ($500). His expenses for operating his business come to $15,000. His gross profit is $35,000 and his net profit is $20,000.

Economists have a narrower definition of what constitutes profit. They are concerned with payment to all the resources that have gone into production, whether they come from outside the business, like those listed above, or from inside the business. As we learned in Chapter 5, costs that come from the outside are called *explicit costs.* Those costs within the firm we called *implicit costs.* Economists point out that our merchant has not paid himself a wage (some prefer the term "salary") or interest on his own capital that he has invested in his business. If he worked for someone else for the same hours and with the same skill, he would be paid a going market wage for his effort. Likewise, if he took his money out of the business and placed it in securities involving similar risks, he would receive dividends. Since economists are concerned with the allocation of resources and their efficient use, they must think in terms of *alternative costs* (sometimes called *opportunity costs*)—the value that could be produced if these implicit factors were used in the production of other things. If the merchant could get a job paying him $12,000 a year and earn 5 percent, or $1,000, on his investment of $20,000 of capital, economists would insist that he subtract an additional $13,000 from his net profit. *Economic* (or *pure*) *profit* is what is left after all explicit and implicit costs for wages, rent, and interest are paid. Of course, it is possible to have a loss instead of a profit. What is the economic, or pure, profit of our merchant?

Why Should There Be Profits?

Since our merchant has been paid for his labor and for interest on his capital, why should he receive profits as well? Probably the most important justification for profits is that the expectation of profits acts as a motivating force to get people to:

1. Start businesses to produce goods and services that consumers want
2. Think up new or better products to attract customers (innovation) and assume the risks of production
3. Improve the efficiency of production, resulting in the use of fewer resources at lower cost
4. Provide funds for improvement and expansion of the firm

To see how the expectation of profits might influence business decisions, let us return to our own business venture, "Build-a-City." Why did we wish to start a business at all? We all had jobs that gave us a living wage. In addition, statistics were available to us showing that an average of 300 businesses fail throughout the nation each week. Why look for trouble? Probably we took the chance because we felt that we could be one of the small number of firms which succeed in making large profits, more than we could earn in our present jobs. It may have been the profit motive which caused us to think about a new product that consumers would want, or it may be that we thought about the new product first and then decided that the idea could be put into action, thus providing us with a profit. In either event society benefits by the motivation that profits give to producing new and better products. The economist Joseph Schumpeter (see p. 87) believed that much of society's progress could be attributed to the influence of the profit motive on new ideas in business.

With our business operating successfully, we now look for ways to improve it. We experiment with new forms and different kinds of wood, and we work to achieve more efficient production. By obtaining new machines, buying raw materials from different sources, and hiring more workers rather than paying overtime, we are able to cut our costs. These reduced costs may lead to additional profits. In a less favorable situation, where competing producers have lowered costs and taken away some of our business, we may have to find methods of reducing our costs to make any profit at all. In either event the motivation of profits has benefited us as well as society.

If our business is doing well enough so that we are thinking of expanding our productive capacity, we will have to obtain additional funds. We can borrow the money by selling bonds or going to the bank. However, if interest rates are high, we may want to finance it ourselves. Rather than taking our profits out of the business and enjoying a higher standard of living now, we use these profits to pay for expansion. Because of implicit costs we must decide whether our money, resulting from profits, will yield more by being invested in our own business or by being invested in something else. We may consider the element of reducing our risks by diversifying. This can be done by putting our profits in other kinds of enterprises. What influences will determine the course we will follow?

What Are the Sources of Economic Profit?

If we lived in a society which had pure competition and a static economy where no changes ever took place in products, efficiency, consumer preferences, and sources of supply, we would have no economic profit. With all knowledge complete, all factors would receive their marginal revenue product and the market price would leave no surplus for economic profit.

The real world we live in is not static. It is changing constantly—and in many different directions. Our economy rarely sees pure competition at work. Therefore, economic profit does exist. When it exists because of innovations or inventions or efficiency—all of which allow a firm to have a temporary advantage—profit may be looked upon as a just reward. Sometimes profit results from pure chance, such as a major change in supply or demand, or both, that makes existing inventories more valuable. Sometimes profits are made by not paying the factors of production their full marginal revenue product. These sources of economic profit stem primarily from dynamic aspects in society and cannot be easily avoided. What is more, they are usually associated with progress and will hurt the economy only rarely, and then only temporarily.

Effect of Competition on Profit

Profit, in the long run, can easily result from differing degrees of imperfect competition. Under strong competitive conditions an industry that is making high profits will attract additional firms into the field, causing prices to decline. If, however, barriers such as patents are placed in the way of new firms entering the field, profits may continue to be high. If a business concern is able to restrict supplies (shift the supply curve to the left), prices will be artificially high and yield higher profits. A study of the profits of various industries in the United States showed that those which were most competitive—textiles and clothing—had the smallest profits, whereas those that were most like monopolies and oligopolies—automobiles and electrical equipment—had the largest profits.

Patents and Copyrights

There are two special cases that we should recognize in which government action endorses monopoly and thereby interferes with a competitive market in determining price. In order to encourage inventions and new ideas, the government issues *patents* to inventors. Upon approval from the United States Patent Office, the inventors will have a monopoly on their inventions for 17 years. *Copyrights* on the publication of literary productions are issued to authors for 28 years and may be renewed. The monopoly prices allow for higher profits, but these profits are the rewards for furthering progress.

Franchises

A *franchise* is a license granted by some governmental authority to a business, giving it the exclusive monopoly to perform a particular service in a given area. A franchise is usually granted to a natural monopoly because it is in the interest of society to prevent duplication of service. Under the franchise prices are regulated by government and profit is considered a major factor in determining those prices. Public utilities are perhaps the best example of this practice. In such cases, the franchise grants an exclusive monopoly to perform a particular service. Prices are regulated, usually in relation to profit.

How Large Should Profits Be?

The debate on the size of profits seems to be a never-ending one. Although our classical model calls for no economic (pure) profits in the long run, it does allow for temporary profits. Such profits help to allocate resources where society thinks they are needed most, and the profits also motivate business to operate efficiently and provide new and better products. Actually it is the expectation of making profits that causes businessmen to take risks, to innovate, and to increase their efficiency. However, if businesses did not make profits, there would be no expectation, and thus no motivation to produce.

Since perfect competition is rare, the amount of profits is partially determined by the varying degrees of imperfect competition. Monopolistic practices may yield excessively high profits, causing consumers to pay more for the product than they would under competitive conditions. These higher prices may also protect inefficient operation and interfere with the allocation of resources. Very high profits in an industry have frequently brought governmental investigations by Congress, the Justice Department, and various regulatory agencies.

Businesses that involve great risk will have to offer opportunities for substantial rewards to provide incentive. Those businesses that are quite stable can attract firms without having to offer such high rewards. When the conditions of supply and demand that are characteristic of pure competition are too distorted by interference with a relatively free market or by special circumstances such as war, some government action is called for. A tax beyond the normal corporation profits tax, known as the *excess profits tax*, was in operation during World War II. It is an example of government action to protect the consumer.

Profits after taxes for all business corporations have tended to fluctuate rather closely with general business conditions. The variation in profit from industry to industry shows how competition can act in limiting profits.

Perhaps the only answer that we can safely give to the question of what size profits should be is: They should be as

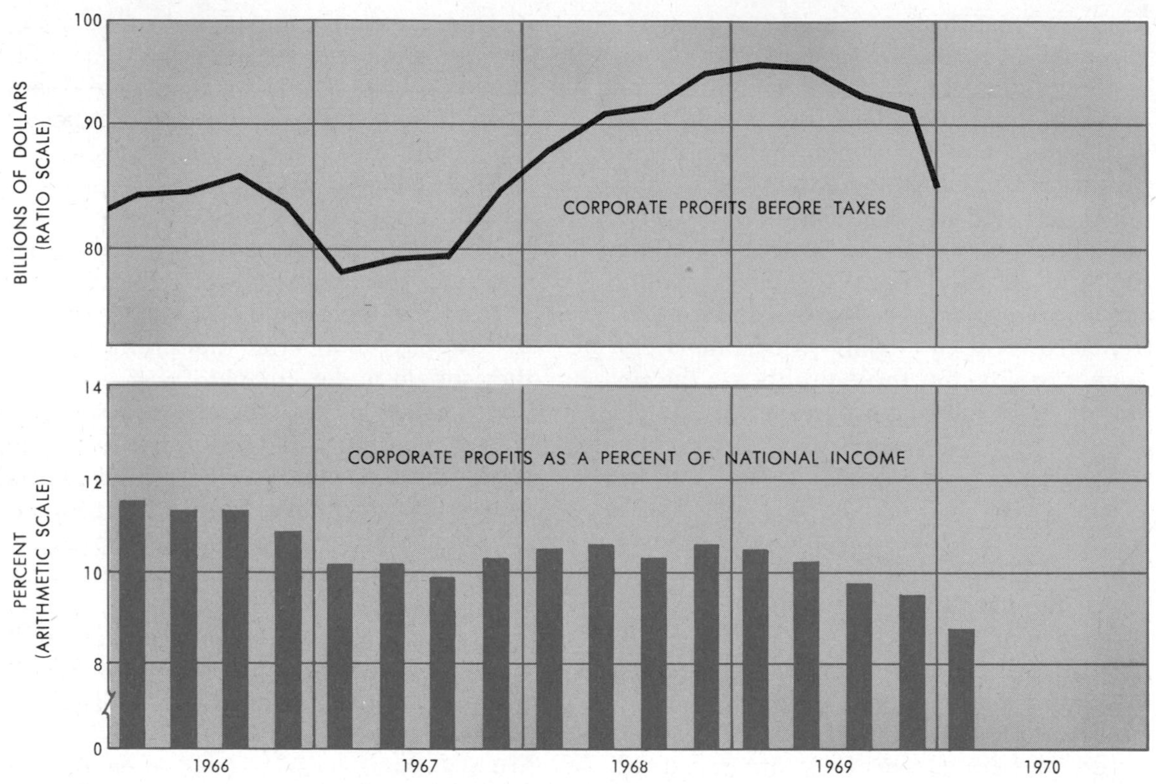

FIGURE 8–5 A Look at Corporate Profits

As the graph shows, corporate profits tend to fluctuate, both in absolute dollar terms and as a percentage of the national income. During this period, prices continued to rise. How, then, might the declines in profits be explained? SOURCE: International Division, Irving Trust Company of New York, *Business Conditions U.S.A.*, July 1970.

large as necessary to attract enough businesses to provide an adequate supply of the goods and services that consumers want at prices they are willing to pay.

Part E
The Problem: Should We Rely on the Classical Model to Distribute Income Fairly to the Factors of Production?

In Chapter 5 and again in this chapter we have shown how the various factors of production are paid. Our model calls for each factor to be used to that point where its marginal factor cost and the marginal revenue product are equal. Each businessman, when he enters the market for the factors of production, tries to follow the marginal product theory, although he may not be familiar with the technical aspects of it. He certainly will not buy an additional factor of production unless he thinks it will give him greater value than what he has to pay for it. According to the classical model, if all businesses operate in this way, the businessman will realize his greatest possible profit and society will benefit from the most efficient allocation of its limited resources.

There are many critics of this theory. Most of the opposition has focused on the concern that one factor of production might receive too large a portion of the "pie" at the expense of other factors. Some critics have suggested eliminating the use of the classical model entirely on the grounds that the assumptions it makes are no longer applicable. Others have suggested altering it in such a way that it will be more in keeping with the world that is. In our discussion of the problem, you will find samples of both kinds of reasoning, with comments and questions. You will be shown a broad spectrum of ideas. Consider all the alternatives before reaching a tentative conclusion. Keep in mind the total productive process as well as the role of functional distribution to the factors of production.

Critics Who Oppose the Model

The best-known critic of capitalism and the chief architect of scientific socialism (communism) was Karl Marx (see p. 45). We have already looked at some Marxist thinking in Chapter 3. However, his theory of the value of labor is pertinent to our present discussion of the fair distribution of income to the factors of production.

Marx's Theory of the Value of Labor

All wealth, said Marx, is the result of the labor that is put into its creation. Natural resources have no value unless man uses them. Capital is a product of man's labor. The income that landowners and investors receive is unearned because they are contributing nothing to the value of the product. What the capitalist receives in the form of rent, interest, and profit is surplus value that rightfully belongs to the worker. The worker is exploited and the capitalist is the exploiter, dividing society into two hostile groups. The capitalist accumulates more and more capital, but the worker does not have the purchasing power to buy back the goods he produces. This leads to declining demand and periodic depressions. Eventually a revolution will take place, and labor will then receive the full value for its product.

According to Marxian theory the United States, with its predominantly private-enterprise economy, should see labor receiving a progressively smaller and smaller share of the national income and landlords, investors, and management receiving an increasingly larger share. However, Figure 8–1 shows that, in fact, wages have been the only reward that has increased as a percentage of the national income. Marx further indicated that, with capital accumulating faster than it is needed, interest rates should be constantly falling. However, although this may be true in the long run, the opportunities for capital investment have usually kept pace with the supply.

If the market with its pricing mechanism does not determine answers to the allocation of resources—the *What, How,* and *For Whom*—what will? Is a central planning board, as in the case of communism, in a better position to make decisions than the market, where the consumer is the decision-maker? While it is true that the market economy of the United States may have some weaknesses, has the Soviet Union, claiming to follow the Marxian model as a guide, done any better?

Henry George and the Single Tax Movement

Another critic, although of only a portion of our model, was an American writer named Henry George. In his famous book *Progress and Poverty,* published in 1879, George advocated a plan that caused such interest that it resulted in the sale of over a million copies of his book. He even came close to winning the election for mayor in New York City.

Henry George reasoned that, although the supply of land in the world is fixed, the number of people using it increases. With the increase in its use, the value of the land increases. Thus, land on the edge of a city will increase in value as the population of the city spills over into the suburbs. The owner of the land is now able to collect a higher rent than before, even though he didn't earn it. Since he did not make the land or improve the land, what he receives in rent is unearned increment.

Henry George believed that the receipt by landlords of pure, or economic, rent was the cause of all poverty. If this rent were taxed at 100 percent, all society would share in the value which nature and the movement of population made possible. He said that the income from such a tax would be sufficient to finance all government activity and permit the abolition of all other taxes. Because of this, it was called the Single Tax Plan. The money saved by eliminating other taxes could then be used in the production process.

A most obvious shortcoming of the single tax proposal today is that rent is estimated to be less than 3 percent of the national income whereas government expenditures are over 25 percent. Another practical difficulty lies in determining how much economic rent is derived from a particular income payment. These criticisms, however, are not applicable to the justice of taxing economic rent; they apply only to the single-tax proposal and its implementation.

A more valid problem, although one still concerned with implementation, is how to make the last owner of land that has changed hands many times pay when his cost for the land reflects the "profits" made by previous owners. While the government might overcome this objection by paying the present owners with long-term bonds, the interest shown by the public and most economists is too small to expect any such action in this country. Some underdeveloped countries are considering such a proposal.

Critics Who Accept the Model with Modifications

Throughout our study of economics we have made reference to the world that "is" and the world that "ought to be." So far, the "ought-to-be" world has largely been our classical model operating under market conditions of pure competition. In Unit III we will introduce a new model (Keynesian) that is playing an increasingly important part in the American economy. However, among those who accept most of the classical model, there are those who feel that the world that "is" has so distorted the original theory that new methods should be applied to the functional distribution of income. These new methods would either revive the intent of the classical economist who sought an efficient and fair method of distribution or recognize the importance of other values in our Western heritage. Several brief examples will illustrate this point.

The Need to Conserve Natural Resources

The unique feature about natural resources in comparison with other factors of production is their relatively fixed supply. This results in an inelastic supply curve and means that demand is the cause of changes in price (rent). When the demand for natural resources increases rapidly, owners of natural resources are anxious to take advantage of the high prices.

Because the supply of resources is limited, critics question whether price alone should be allowed to determine use. If it is, farmland may be overworked to produce crops selling for high prices, with no regard for renewing the fertility of the soil. Timber may be cut without replacing cut-down trees with young seedlings. Because oil belongs to the owner of the property on which it comes to the surface, even though most of it may be under the ground of neighboring properties, wasteful drilling procedures are encouraged. Resources are often used today for immediate gain, with little thought for the needs of future generations.

Until the beginning of the twentieth century the thought prevailed that our country had an unlimited supply of natural resources. Wasteful practices were allowed because new sources of supply were constantly being discovered. Finally, men such as Theodore Roosevelt and Gifford Pinchot, Chairman of the National Conservation Commission; Frederick Haynes Newell, Chief Engineer of the Reclamation Service; and others made great efforts to have the government step in to conserve our resources so that future generations would not suffer because past and present generations were selfishly concerned only with their immediate satisfaction. While most of our conservation program has been designed to encourage individuals to practice conservation (rewards for crop rotation, for example), the government has at times been forced to abandon the policy of laissez-faire. Withdrawing from use substantial tracts of public land has won public support, although it has been criticized by some private interests as interference with our private-enterprise system and the market mechanism for the allocation of resources.

The Need to Limit Unearned Interest

We have justified the payment of interest as a reward for saving instead of consuming and as a necessary condition if the economy is to have sufficient funds to buy the capital needed for its growth. We cannot expect people to make funds available without some reward. Actually, on the whole, interest rates in this country have been quite low, due in part to the availability of loans to businessmen, farmers, veterans, and others through agencies of the government. Criticism of our present system of distribution of rewards for loanable funds is concentrated on those receiving interest from inherited wealth.

The right to hand down property—including loanable funds—is part of our entire concept of private property. Very few people in our country would question the right of anyone to bequeath to his heirs enough for them to live decently and to have the means to get a good start in life. However, many have questioned the fairness of allowing heirs to live on accumulated fortunes without earning anything themselves. To prevent what may be called "unearned interest" and the perpetuation of a "moneyed class," states have passed *inheritance taxes* (on those receiving) and the federal government has imposed *estate* and *gift taxes* (on the estate or giver). These taxes have been aimed primarily at estates above $60,000. Since there are various "loopholes" in the inheritance laws, few people have protested.

Some economic historians claim that it was through the accumulation of huge fortunes that we were able to have enough loanable funds in this country to support our economic growth. With high taxes on accumulated wealth we may dry up our sources of loanable funds and the government will have to step in to supply what is needed for our capital expansion.

Critics ask whether it is justifiable for unearned income to furnish the capital for economic growth. Since the overwhelming majority of our population does not have enough funds to furnish businessmen with capital, would we be better off if the government made decisions as to where loanable funds should go?

The Need to Limit Unearned Profits

Profits have been justified as necessary to reward management and owners for risks, efficiency, innovation, and invention. When profits are made because of monopolistic practices, they hurt society rather than benefiting it. Most economists in our country would recommend more vigorous competition to eliminate unearned profits resulting from imperfect competition. However, many have doubted whether any government policy can produce sufficient competition. To prevent profits from going above the amount they might be expected to reach under pure or near-pure competition, taxes may be imposed on the amount above a "fair" profit. This was done during World War II and again during the Korean conflict, but most people accepted it as only an emergency measure. Why cannot such an excess profits tax be used at all times? Will it diminish or destroy incentive? Will it penalize our most efficient? Does the society really benefit when it permits monopolistic practices, even if it taxes excess profits?

Considering an Answer

How free do we want our economy to be? Do the economically strong receive greater rewards than are received by the weaker factors involved in production? To what extent should rewards be based on the degree of service to society? What problems can a planned economy have in distributing its shares to the factors of production? Will the controls started on August 15, 1971 usher in a new era of planning? Will the market be destroyed as the major method of allocating resources? How may your values influence your decision?

REVIEW: THE HIGHLIGHTS OF THE CHAPTER

1. Dividing the income received from production among the factors of production is called functional distribution.
2. The interaction of supply and demand will determine the price for each factor of production.
3. Additional units of factors of production will be added up to the point where the marginal revenue product and the marginal factor cost are equal.
4. Getting the right combination of factors can improve the efficiency of production.
5. Rent is most commonly defined as the price for the use of some durable good. Land rent is the price for the use of natural resources. Economic rent is the price paid for any factor that cannot be increased or decreased in response to price changes.
6. Unlike other factors, the supply of land (and of most other natural resources) is fixed and is shown by an inelastic supply curve.
7. Although some critics question the justification of paying rent, such payment helps allocate natural resources efficiently.
8. Interest is the price paid for the use of loanable funds. This is like saying that it is payment for the use of capital because of the use that is made of this money.
9. Businessmen, consumers, and governments borrow money and pay interest.
10. Interest is stated as a rate of return. Rates vary because of risk, time, administrative costs, and competition in the market.
11. Demand for loanable funds is subject to the influence of the marginal revenue product for businessmen and diminishing marginal utility for consumers; it is inelastic for the federal government.
12. Supply of loanable funds comes primarily from individuals in the highest income group and from business itself. Higher interest rates will tend to decrease the liquidity preference of people.
13. Since 1930 the price of loanable funds has been determined less and less by the free market as government has increased its borrowing and its control over interest rates.
14. Profit means something different to the public, the businessman, and the economist. The economist, who is interested in payments to all factors of production, must consider both explicit and implicit costs before figuring economic profits—what is left over after all other factors have been paid.
15. Profit serves our economy well when it is used as incentive for management to make products wanted by the consumer, to increase business efficiency, and to stimulate progress. Economic profits are eliminated in a static economy with pure competition. Profit from imperfect competition represents inefficient use.

IN CONCLUSION: SOME AIDS TO UNDERSTANDING

Terms for Review

functional distribution
marginal cost
marginal revenue product
land rent
economic rent
submarginal land
single tax
copyright
franchise
liquidity preference
administered price
production function
loanable funds
interest
principal
discounting
gross profit
economic profit
net profit
explicit costs
implicit costs
alternative costs
patent
"fair price"
excess profits tax
surplus value

Questions for Review

1. Allocating the various factors of production and distributing rewards to them are basic problems of business enterprise.
   (a) What determines how a firm's revenues will be divided among the factors of production?
   (b) What might induce a businessman to change the way in which he combines the factors of production?
2. Explain the relationship between success in a competitive market and efficiency in combining the factors of production.
3. Explain the relationship between the demand for land and the determination of rent.
4. Using the classical view of rent, explain why payments of rent for land differ with varying degrees of productivity.
5. Interest, like rent, represents payment for use—in this case, use of loanable funds.
   (a) Explain how paying interest for the use of money can be justified.
   (b) What factors determine the rate charged?
   (c) How has the role of the federal government influenced the rates of interest?
6. Interest differs in some respects from the payments made to other factors of production.
   (a) Explain the reasons for variation in the demand for loanable funds which influence the individual consumer, the businessman, the federal and local governments.
   (b) How may changes in interest rates help regulate the economy?
   (c) When and why is the demand curve for interest inelastic?
7. Interpretations of the word "profit" differ according to the individual's point of view. Explain the meaning of the term "profit" to the businessman, the public, and the economist.
8. What is the role of profit in a free economy? What are the arguments in favor of profit? Against?

Additional Questions and Problems

1. Henry George was among those suggesting modification of the classical model of capitalism.
   (a) Explain the basic ideas of the single tax as advocated by Henry George.
   (b) What effect would the application of his theory have on land development today?
   (c) What are the major objections to his theory?
2. The meaning of "fair profit" is different to producer and consumer, and varies from one industry to another.
   (a) Study the information available on some of the cases in the drug industry and present the arguments of the producer and the government concerning prices and profits.
   (b) Study some of the requests of public utilities (railroad, telephone, electricity) for rate changes and indicate the factors used by these utilities to determine the base they use.
3. Explain the statement "Profits are the lifeblood of the American capitalist system."
4. As a major factor of production, labor is entitled to a proper reward.
   (a) To what extent is labor justified in demanding a greater share of business revenues?
   (b) What are the arguments for and against profit-sharing plans for labor?
5. Should government ever impose limits on profits? Why or why not?
6. What explains the fact that about 74 percent of national income goes into wages today, as compared with only 58.2 percent in 1929? What does this development imply for the economy?
7. Explain in detail why the addition of units of capital, land, and labor by businessmen will not necessarily bring greater returns.
8. Evaluate the Marxist theory of the value of labor. How does this theory compare with actual distribution of income in the U.S.S.R. today?

SELECTED READINGS

Bain, Joe S. *Pricing, Distribution, and Employment,* rev. ed. New York: Holt, Rinehart & Winston, 1953.

George, Henry. *Progress and Poverty.* New York: Robert S. Schalkenbach Foundation, 1954. (Originally published in 1879)

Hibbard, Benjamin H. *A History of Public Land Policy.* Milwaukee: University of Wisconsin, 1965.

Landsberg, Hans H., and Sam H. Schurr. *Energy in the United States: Sources, Uses and Policy Issues.* New York: Random House, 1968.

Leftwich, Richard H. *The Price System and Resource Allocation,* 4th ed. Hinsdale, Ill.: Drydon Press, 1970.

Marx, Karl. *Capital* (3 vols.). New York: International Publishers Co., 1967.

Marx, Karl, and Friedrich Engels. *Communist Manifesto.* New York: International Publishers Co. (Originally published in 1848.)

Stigler, George J. *Production and Distribution Theories: The Formative Period.* New York: The Macmillan Co., 1968.

Government and Its Developing Role in the Economy

9

THE AUTHORS' NOTE TO THE STUDENT

Although the classical model depends on the market, with price rather than government allocating the resources of the nation, no one would deny the increasing role of government in answering many basic economic questions. In this chapter we will consider what part the government is supposed to play in the classical model, the part that it is playing today, and the controversy concerning its future role in the economy. Attention will be paid to both regulation and production by government.

Government, like business, pays out money and is paid for its activities. How government prepares its budget, what outlays are included in that budget, and what taxes government imposes are questions which affect everyone in the nation. We will examine some of the principles used as guides in finding solutions to many of the controversial problems concerning government's role in the economy.

A STUDENT'S NOTE TO THE STUDENT

For me this was the most controversial chapter in the book—not what was said but how it affects me. As the father of two young children, I would like to see more money for better schools, socialized medicine, and lots of other government services. As a small property owner, I scream about my taxes going sky high. As a college student with a working wife, I think I would like to see all taxes shifted to business and income. As a business major, I know I'll see things differently in 10 years.

The chapter helped me analyze each of the alternatives, but my conflict of self-interest and indecisive values has left me confused.

Part A
The Nature of Government's Role in the Economy

Government's Role in the Classical Model

The classical model is frequently referred to as the private- or free-enterprise system because it places its emphasis on the decisions of the consumer and the decisions of the businessman arrived at individually without interference by the government. What is produced is determined by the consumer—registering his demand in the market—and by the businessman—seeking to make profits—catering to the consumer's wishes. According to the classical tradition the individual is in a better position to know what he wants and what is good for him than is the government. Any interference by the government would alter the free flow of goods and services as ordered by the consumer.

Quite a different condition exists when the government makes all the decisions on the allocation of resources—the *What, How,* and *For Whom.* Those advocating such a system would admit that the individual's wants might not be met, but they would hasten to point out that those who control the government are in a better position to decide what is good for the entire society.

We pointed out in Chapter 1 that no nation practices either of the previously described conditions in pure form. However, the first point of view plays a major role in the economic planning of the United States, whereas the second philosophy guides the Soviet Union in its economic programs.

Although the classical economist wants a minimum of government interference, he still recognizes the importance of maintaining an environment in which the market economy can flourish. If capitalism is to function, certain conditions must exist and be preserved.

Pillars of Capitalism

Private property, the right of the individual to exercise reasonable control over the things he owns, provides a major incentive for producing. Related to this is *freedom of contract,* allowing individuals to enter into agreements resulting in production and distribution of goods and services. *Economic freedom*—guaranteeing the individual the right to move within the economy to the job he wants, to buy or sell property as he sees fit, and to start a business if he wishes to—permits the economy to change. *Competition* assures efficiency of production and safeguards the consumer.

The four conditions just described are the pillars of the classical model and must be present if the system is to function smoothly. It is government's role in the classical model to see to it that these conditions exist, that the nation is protected internally (the police and fire departments) and externally (the armed forces), that the life, the liberty, and the property of all within its boundaries are safeguarded.

Capitalism, Government, and Our Business

Let us consider for a moment the importance of the requisites of capitalism in connection with our theoretical business, "Build-a-City." When we incorporated, we went to the state government to obtain a charter. Having a charter gave us status as a separate entity before the law. Economic freedom allowed us to enter into this business, and gave us the assurance that what we earned was ours (taxes excluded). If our property were not protected from thieves, fire, and foreign invasion, we would have little incentive to work hard, save, and build a larger plant. If we could not be sure of the enforcement of contracts, we would be gambling every time we filled a big order for a customer. Refusal on the part of the customer to meet his contractual obligations could mean our ruin. In each of these instances we depend on government not to perform the economic functions but to assure an environment where economic functions can be carried out.

Historical Role of Government in the American Economy

Although our "ought-to-be" world places great restraint on government action, a brief look at the roles government has played shows how far we have moved from the classical theory. Let us examine some of the beliefs developed and practices followed concerning the changing role of government's activity in our economy.

Government as a Help to Business

Since business is responsible for organizing our factors of production and producing our wealth, anything that government can do to aid business will help the entire economy. Alexander Hamilton in his "Report on Manufactures," supporting tariffs as a protection to industry, and Henry Clay with his American System, favoring protective tariffs and a "home market" for American products, believed that the country would benefit if business thrived. The development of protective tariffs, land grants to railroads, strong patent laws, and guarantees on certain business loans are examples of government intervention on behalf of business.

Government Intervention to Enforce Competition

The passage of antitrust laws—the Sherman and Clayton acts—was received with mixed feelings by classical economists. Some claimed that it was proper for the government to maintain competition to insure the survival of capitalism. Others argued that such laws represented needless government interference. They said that to break up trusts was to penalize the most efficient and would only reduce incentive.

Government as a Help to Weaker Economic Groups

Because business was strong and had advantages at the market for buying the factors of production, many thought that government should step in and help weaker groups. This idea resulted in the exemption of labor from the antitrust laws and in such aids to labor as minimum wage and maximum hour laws. Price supports for agricultural products are also an interference with the free-market price, but they represent a further attempt to aid weaker economic groups.

The government has played an increasing role in protecting the consumer. Most recently this role has been expanded to include protecting the environment from pollutants. This is discussed more fully in Chapters 11 and 19.

Government as a Producer in the Absence of Business Venture

Although most consumer needs are met by business, some needs have not been fulfilled. When this condition exists, it is usually because business produces to make a profit and only indirectly seeks to fill needs. Originally there was no profit to be made in producing electric power in the Tennessee Valley; under these conditions private enterprise had no incentive to risk capital that appeared to have little chance of returning a profit. The federal government, which has no need to show a profit but is obliged to consider the needs of its citizens, moved in to fill the void. In the case of atomic energy, private enterprise did not have the resources to develop so costly an industry. Utilities at the local level and Social Security at the national level are other areas in which the government is a direct producer.

Government as a Stabilizer

When the market mechanism of the classical model fails to do its job, the new economics calls for the government to supplement the forces of supply and demand. It does this by using the budget to create surpluses and deficits and through some control over the money supply. This is occasionally reinforced by "jawboning" or temporary wage-price controls. Unit III will develop these ideas in some detail.

How Deeply Should the Government Be Involved in the Economy?

One of the major controversies today concerns the degree of government involvement in the economy. Although you as students do not yet have all the necessary tools to analyze this question (we return to it in later chapters), it is important for you to give it preliminary consideration in order to understand the purposes and thinking behind the controversy.

Most Americans, accepting the free-enterprise system, would agree that government should take whatever steps are necessary to preserve the pillars of capitalism. Protecting property, insuring the enforcement of contracts, and assuring economic freedom require government involvement. Enforcing competition is far more controversial, though most citizens agree that the government must have the right to protect the consumer from monopolistic power. Sharp differences of opinion exist concerning the desirability of government regulation of the market; even greater differences exist relative to what government should produce. Many political campaigns have been, and undoubtedly will continue to be, waged over this issue. A closer look at the issue reveals that there is a broader area of agreement than disagreement among Americans, although campaign oratory sometimes might seem to indicate otherwise.

Principles Guiding Government's Role in the Economy

Both tradition and theory have provided us with the following principles, which many economists believe will help guide us in deciding how deeply the government should become involved in the economy:

1. Government should remain outside the economy so long as the people's needs are being met by private enterprise. When these needs are not met and there appears to be little chance of their being met by business, government must step in. In launching Telstar and Syncom, government went into partnership with business, doing what private enterprise alone could not do. The initial subsidization for the SST with the Boeing Corporation is another example. Controversy has long existed

THE INSTITUTIONALISTS AND REFORM

One of the outstanding contributions of the United States to economic thinking was the development of the institutionalist approach to economics. Thorstein B. Veblen (1857–1929), John R. Commons (1862–1944), and Wesley C. Mitchell (1874–1948) were the three dominant figures of this school.

Unhappy with the many social and economic ills of the early 1900's, these men were not satisfied with the laissez-faire approach of the classical and neoclassical economists. Studying the environment, they disclosed the existence of widespread poverty, depressions, growing monopoly, and government favoritism towards business. In such circumstances they were unwilling to trust society to the "magic" of economic laws that were supposed to correct all imbalances and bring about a "harmony of interests."

In place of the theorizing of the orthodox economists, the institutionalists substituted the study of the environment and its institutions as an approach to the "real" world. Finding socialism unacceptable because of its militancy and its conflict with the established order, they sought social reform through greater participation of the government in the economy. Let the government act as an umpire between competing economic groups and interfere when extreme imbalances in the distribution of income develop! Let the government provide social security, reform credit institutions, and enforce protection for the weaker economic groups!

Many of the reforms advocated by the institutionalists have become an integral part of our social and economic system. With the accomplishment of these changes, which include some of the New Deal legislation, and with some of their thinking expressed in later theories, such as the Keynesian, the institutionalists today have only a small following. Yet few could deny their important role in developing our present economic institutions.

---

concerning the adequacy of private enterprise to meet the health needs of all citizens. Despite the passage of Medicare and other bills expanding medical coverage, debate still continues on the role of government in this field. The market is much preferred as an allocator of resources, but there are times when government controls may be called for.

2. When government does furnish a service or product, it should do so through existing facilities and capacities of business. The government uses military equipment, but business builds much of this on contract with the government. There is little controversy when the government orders private enterprise to build the equipment necessary for sending a man to the moon or for supplying our armed forces. In contrast, controversy does exist over the ownership of atomic-energy power plants which supply power for communities. In this case the government has already spent a tremendous amount of money for research; in addition, facilities must be built and paid for. Controversy also extends to public facilities sold to business.
3. If government must furnish a service, it is more acceptable if it is done at the local and state levels. There is little controversy over local support of public schools, but some controversy still exists over federal aid to education.
4. Services that do not lend themselves to a market economy but are generally

agreed by citizens to be necessary for the society as a whole are handled by government. All of us recognize the need for national defense, but what price should each citizen pay for it? In this connection the fact that the state has the power of compulsion is important. Those who do not feel the need for national defense must still share in the cost. Government support of the arts is a subject of controversy because not all citizens agree that it is a necessity and because generous contributions by families and foundations have made the problem noncritical.

Differing Influences of Citizens and Consumers on the Economy

Although people are usually both citizens and consumers, the influence of these groups on the economy is not equal. A look at the differences in their influence gives us added bases for comparing the decision-making process of private and public sectors of the economy.

1. A citizen is able to influence the public sector of the economy by casting his one vote. Theoretically, each citizen's vote counts the same as every other citizen's, although it must be recognized that money can affect this voting. A consumer, by spending his dollars in certain ways, helps to determine what will be produced in the private sector. The rich man, by spending many more dollars, has a far greater influence, although this is balanced to a certain extent by the fact that there are many more people of modest means than people of wealth.
2. A citizen has little influence on the specific expenditures in the public sector, since his representatives cannot run on a platform listing how all public revenues will be spent. Special elections for specific projects, such as school bond issues, are the exception. The consumer can carefully consider each purchase, weighing the satisfaction he may receive from it against all other possibilities.
3. Citizens frequently organize themselves into political groups to increase their influence over the public economy. Only rarely have consumers organized to effect a change in the private sector.

In considering whether some aspect of the economy is better suited for the public or the private sector, the student should weigh his influence as a citizen and as a consumer. Abraham Lincoln's words might be used as a guide: "The legitimate object of government is to do for the community of people whatever they need to have done, but cannot do at all or cannot do so well for themselves in their separate individual capacities."

The Growth of Public Expenditures

One of the most striking facts about the American economy is the tremendous increase in expenditures by all levels of government in the last 40 years. Governments today are spending over 30 times as much as they did in 1930. Whereas one out of every nine dollars of our national income was spent by government then, over one out of every four dollars is spent in the public sector today.

Appraisal of Increase

Those who are in greatest sympathy with the tradition of the classical model are deeply concerned about this trend, and on occasion have used increased government spending as evidence of what they call "creeping socialism." Although there can be no denying the increase in the size and activities of the public sector, the actual data can greatly distort this increase in several ways:

1. Prices today are almost three times as high as they were in 1930, requiring the government, as well as businessmen and consumers, to pay three times as much to receive equal goods or services.
2. Our gross national product, the total value of all our production, is about four times as large today as in 1930, so that the *percentage* of our total income going into the public sector has increased very little. Compare Figure 9–1 with Figure 9–2.
3. In 1930 our country had a minimum of international military commitments, whereas today we consider ourselves the leader of the free world. Greater responsibility has resulted in a tremendous increase in government expenditures. In recent years the cost of our multibillion-dollar space program has added to the increase in government spending.

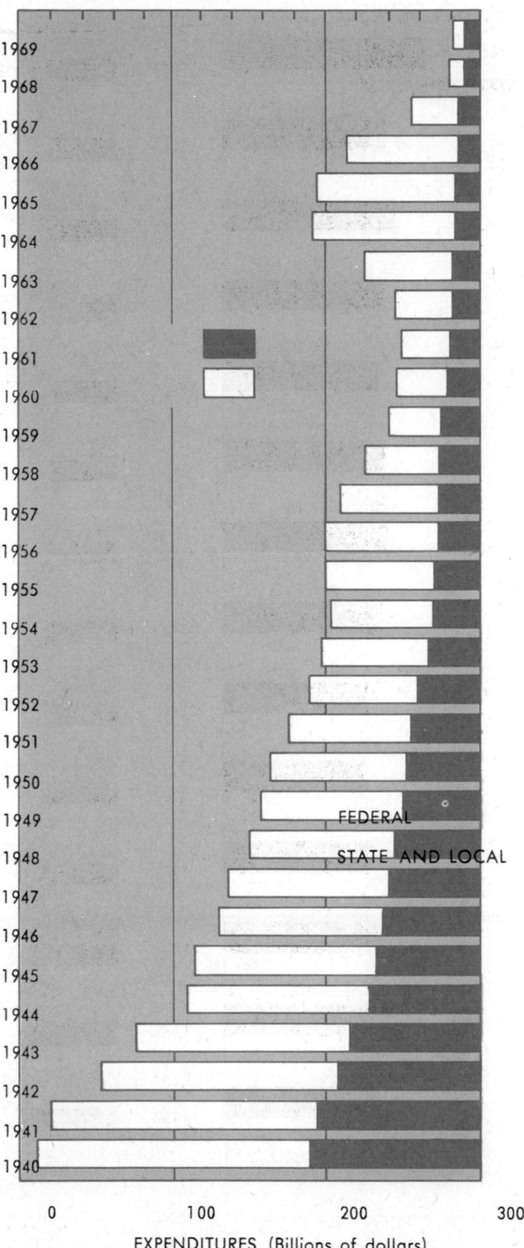

FIGURE 9–1 Growth of Public Expenditures, 1940–1969

SOURCE: Bureau of the Budget.

Since few people would deny that national defense is a legitimate function of government, inclusion of the cost of World War II and recent military expenditures along with other government expenditures cannot be used as proof of "creeping socialism."

The change in government expenditures as a percentage of gross national product may be seen in Figure 9–2. Note that, while a shift from federal to state government expenditures has taken place, the percentage of federal expenditures to GNP has remained fairly constant, about 20 percent. In 1954 federal government purchases amounted to slightly more than 10 percent while state and local purchases were about 8 percent. By 1965, just prior

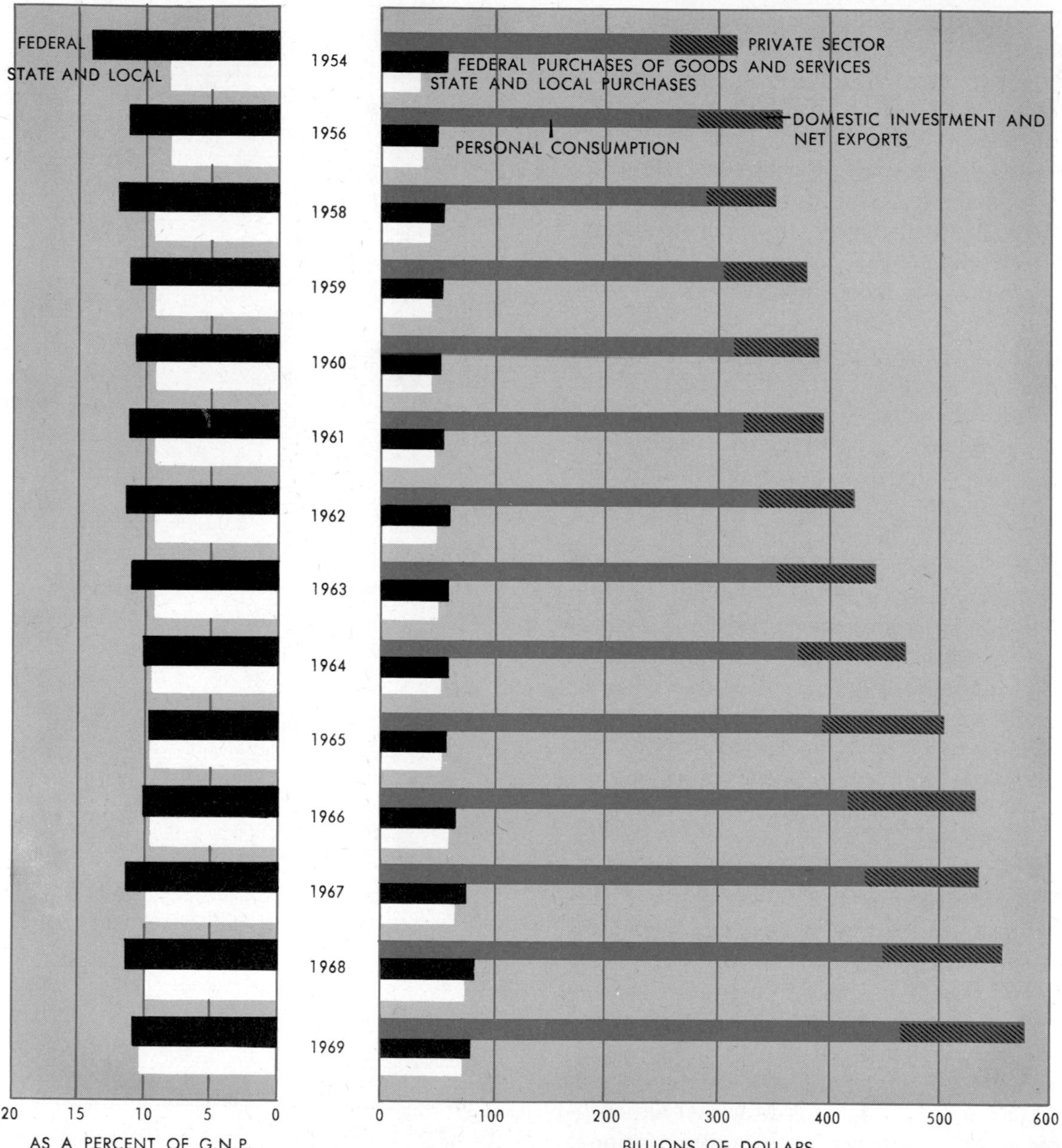

FIGURE 9–2 Gross National Product and the Government's Share

SOURCES: U.S. Department of Commerce and The Conference Board.

to the escalation of the Vietnam War, purchases were almost equally divided. As the war was stepped up, the federal government increased its percentage of expenditures. Yet American withdrawal, along with greater federal aid to states, should bring state and local expenditures above that of the federal government.

When we compare recent federal budgets with those five or more years back, we see a major change of terms to describe new attitudes and viewpoints. Instead of lumping social security, education, and health programs under the general title of *public social welfare,* the newest budgets refer to expenditures for *human and physical resources.* Emphasis is placed on meeting human needs, improving our environment, education and manpower training, and revenue sharing. These terms may reflect the renewed desire to shift funds from defense to greater fulfillment for the individual, but factors beyond the control of the U.S. may determine whether this can be accomplished. A flare-up in the Middle East or declaring a major city a disaster area after a tornado may upset the most carefully prepared plans.

Increase in Public Services

There can be little doubt that government's role in the economy has increased not merely in dollars spent but in services rendered. The public has wanted more security, more equal opportunity, more services. Specifically we have increased our guaranteed minimum family income payments against all threats, our educational opportunities, and our health services. Most of the money for these programs have come from our increased wealth, GNP. Just as more people are able to buy more and better goods and services in the private sector, so our government has been able to provide additional services from the "bigger pie" in which everyone shares.

Besides additional services by government, the growth of regulatory agencies and the existence of laws regulating the private sector have greatly increased the role of government in the economy. Antitrust legislation, labor legislation, banking legislation, and the creation of the Federal Trade Commission, the Interstate Commerce Commission, the Securities and Exchange Commission, and the Federal Communications Commission illustrate how far we have departed from one aspect of the classical model, in which government remained outside the economy even though this departure strengthens other aspects. Although historians, with their advantage of hindsight, may be able to evaluate whether we have gone too far, we are obliged as citizens to come to some tentative decisions now about the economic course on which we should steer our ship of state. And although you might wish to come to a conclusion at this time, you should probably make it a tentative one. Many other important economic concepts are yet to be considered, and you may wish to change your mind.

Part B
The Nature of Government Expenditures

Planning for Spending: The Mechanics of Preparing a Budget

Although differences exist in budget procedures at different levels of government and for different state and local governments, the mechanics of budget making usually follow a certain pattern. The procedure described suggests the desirability of a balanced budget. Exceptions to this general rule will be noted later when we come to Unit III.

Administration Initiates Budgets

The chief executive (President, governor, mayor) calls upon his administrative heads to prepare estimates of their departments' needs as much as 18 months in advance of actual expenditures. The administrative heads consult their staffs, their past budgets, and the demand for new or expanded activities within their departments. They submit an estimate of their needs, sometimes higher than they expect to receive, since they know it will be easier for them to cut down than it will be to obtain additional appropriations. The chief executive consults with his budget director and recognizes that his expenditures add up to a sum far beyond what he can expect government revenues to be. This means that, unless he reduces his budget, he will have to ask for additional taxes—not always a popular request with the electorate. Since administrative heads are responsible for the operation of their departments, the chief executive usually allows them to make the necessary adjustments. After the chief executive receives the revised estimates, he either accepts them, or, if the total request still seems too high, he, together with his budget-maker and close associates, will make the final reductions.

Legislature Approves Budgets

The budget, usually a thick document resembling the telephone directory of a large city, is submitted to the legislative branch, which must give final approval. Once

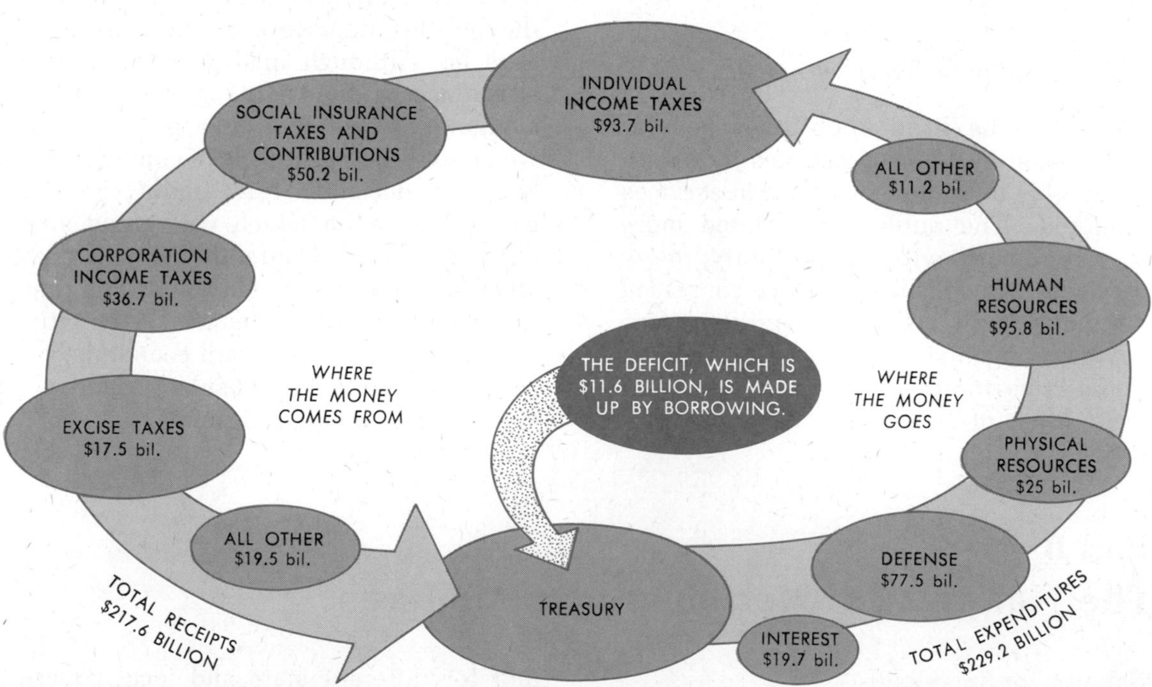

FIGURE 9–3 The Federal Budget: Four Aspects of Its Relation to the Economy

SOURCE: Bureau of the Budget.

there, the budget goes to various committees, which scrutinize sections of it. Because of the complexity of such a document, experts must be called in and hearings must be held. Some interests will be seeking special privileges; others are concerned with keeping taxes low. The House Ways and Means Committee and the Senate Finance Committee (or a joint committee) make final recommendations before submitting it to the entire legislature. At the state and local levels of government the pattern is similar. Rarely does the chief executive get all he asks for. The budget which finally emerges is usually a compromise of many forces. A similar but less complex procedure is generally followed at other levels of government.

Types of Budgets

Before this country accepted the new economics, which we will consider in Unit III, all governments used either the *administrative budget* or *cash budget.* The former is the administration's request for funds. The cash budget is more inclusive and includes additional money collected and spent by government, including such trust funds as social security. Most recently the federal government has been using the unified budget which is designed to show the total inflow and outgo of funds reflecting whether such a budget will be in deficit, surplus, or balanced.

The deficit budget is designed to stimulate the economy while the surplus budget hopefully will contribute to holding down inflation.

What Governments Spend For

As you have seen, almost all spending is carried on at the three major levels of government—federal, state, and local. Some similarities exist in the nature and procedures of spending at all levels. However, the three levels of government differ significantly in the things for which they spend their money.

Federal Expenditures

In analyzing federal expenditures one fact stands out above all others: the major portion of outlays is either for national defense or for expenses resulting from international conflicts in the past. Table 9–1 shows approximately one half of the budget going for national defense, interest on the national debt (primarily due to military expenditures), veterans' services and benefits, international affairs and finance, and space research. It would be easy to conclude from this example that federal expenditures have risen almost exclusively because of our international commitments. This is *not* so. We spend almost as much today on labor and welfare as we did for all federal expenditures for the average year in the 1950's. About the same amount of money was spent on agriculture by the federal government in 1970 as for all federal expenditures in 1935. Although changes in price levels account for some of these dramatic differences, and defense outlays continue, the fact is that government involvement in other areas of the economy has increased significantly.

State Expenditures

Total state expenditures and total local expenditures are about the same, each about one fourth of total government expenditures. From 1964 to 1970 budgets doubled, with revenues increasing faster at the state level and expenditures more at the local level. Most of this increase has been due to the expansion in highways, education, and welfare, the three accounting for more than half of all state expenditures. Public welfare, hospitals, and

TABLE 9–1 The Federal Budget

BUDGET RECEIPTS AND OUTLAYS
(in millions of dollars)

Description	1970 actual	1971 estimate	1972 estimate
Receipts by source:			
Individual income taxes	90,412	88,300	93,700
Corporation income taxes	32,829	30,100	36,700
Social insurance taxes and contributions:			
Employment taxes and contributions	39,133	42,297	50,225
Unemployment insurance	3,464	3,604	4,183
Contributions for other insurance and retirement	2,701	3,072	3,151
Excise taxes	15,705	16,800	17,500
Estate and gift taxes	3,644	3,730	5,300
Customs duties	2,430	2,490	2,700
Miscellaneous receipts	3,424	3,800	4,134
Total receipts	193,742	194,193	217,593
Outlays by function:			
National defense	80,295	76,443	77,512
International affairs and finance	3,570	3,586	4,032
Space research and technology	3,749	3,368	3,151
Agriculture and rural development	6,201	5,262	5,804
Natural resources	2,480	2,636	4,243
Commerce and transportation	9,310	11,442	10,937
Community development and housing	2,965	3,858	4,495
Education and manpower	7,289	8,300	8,808
Health	12,995	14,928	16,010
Income security	43,790	55,546	60,739
Veterans benefits and services	8,677	9,969	10,644
Interest	18,312	19,433	19,687
General government	3,336	4,381	4,970
Allowances for:			
Added amount for revenue sharing	—	—	4,019
Pay increase (excluding Department of Defense)	—	500	1,000
Contingencies	—	300	950
Undistributed intragovernmental transactions	−6,380	−7,197	−7,771
Total outlays	196,589	212,755	229,232
Budget deficit	2,845	18,562	11,639

SOURCE: Office of Management and Budget.

health are the largest remaining areas of expenditures.

Local Expenditures

Local government expenditures are concentrated primarily on those things which local residents feel most directly and over which they believe they should have the most direct control. Education accounts for nearly half of the expenditures; following far behind are highways, police and fire protection, public welfare, health and hospitals, and government control. With the cost of education increasing so rapidly, and local governments being so restricted in their taxing powers, local units have been forced to turn more and more to the states for financial aid. Now the states

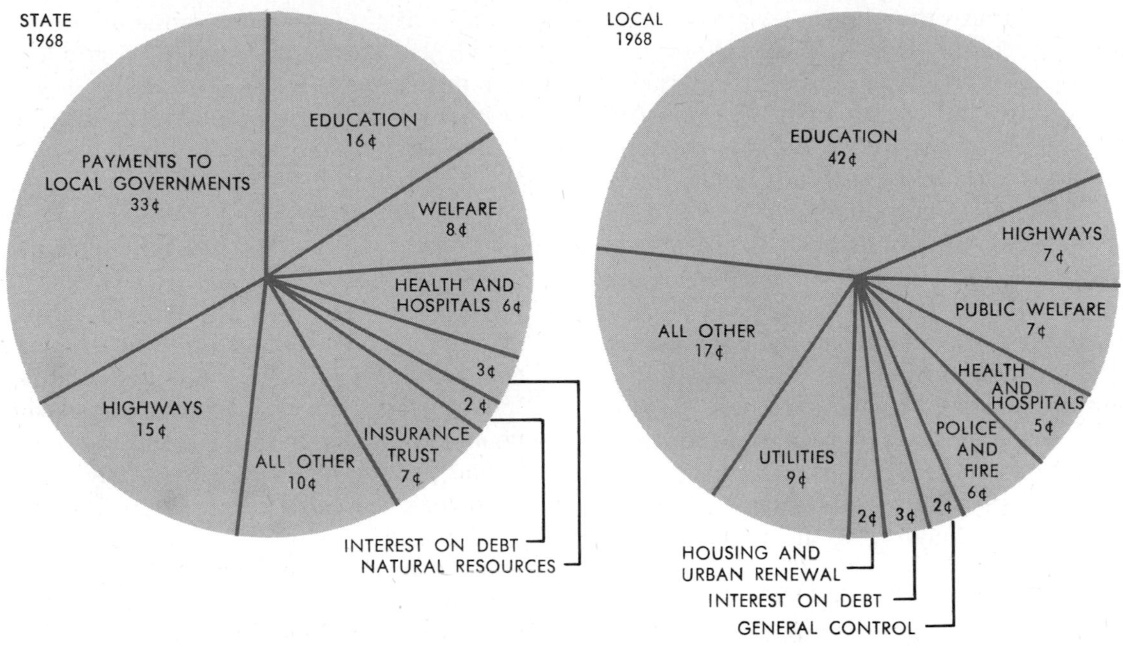

FIGURE 9–4 Combined State Expenditures and Combined Local Expenditures
SOURCE: U.S. Department of Commerce, Bureau of the Census.

and local communities are turning to the federal government for revenue sharing.

Before World War I local governments accounted for over half of all government expenditures. When the federal government moved into the field of welfare in the 1930's and increased its military expenditures in the 1940's, local government expenditures fell to about one eighth of the total. However, this trend has been reversed. Like state government expenditures, local outlays have been increasing faster than expenditures of the federal government. Most students of public finance are of the opinion that unless local units of government are given additional powers of taxation, they will have to turn more and more to the state and federal governments either for funds or for the direct furnishing of services. Figure 9–4 shows how all state and local governments spent their money in 1968.

Part C
The Nature of Government Revenues

Sources of Government Income

Governments finance their expenditures from a variety of sources, including taxes, receipts from other levels of government, earnings from government enterprises, fines, and fees. While taxes are, by far, the major source of government income, receipts from other levels of government are important. The federal government gives grants to states on a matching basis for welfare and health, and most recently to local governments for fighting poverty. State governments give funds to local governments, frequently on a per capita basis. New York state distributes 63 cents of every dollar of its revenue to local units of government in this way.

Money collected from public agencies often called "authorities," is a more important source of revenue at the local and state levels. The same is true for fees, licenses, and fines. Taxes, however, remain the single most important source of revenue, particularly at the federal level.

Why Must Governments Tax?

With all levels of government in our country spending about one fifth of our gross national product and employing about one out of every six workers (including members of the armed forces), it is quite clear that these governments represent the largest buyers in both the market for goods and services and the market for factors of production. If governments hire about 18 percent of all workers, they are taking these workers away from possible jobs they might have in the private sector. These workers are producing something (usually services) that the society, acting as citizens rather than consumers, has decided it needs. This production is considered more valuable to the nation, as determined by our elected government, than if these workers were employed in the private sector. We get the factors of production to work for government rather than private enterprise by offering sufficient dollars. Where does the government get the money to pay these dollars? The easiest and most obvious way to answer this is to refer to the sources of government revenue previously listed. However, such an answer ignores the problem of the relationship of government activity to the total economy.

Before we consider this problem further, we should observe that the federal government alone in our nation may legally print money to pay its bills. The greenbacks printed during the Civil War were money of this kind. A few changes in existing laws would allow the federal government to do the same thing today. If it did so, it could eliminate taxes and people would have more money to spend in the private sector for the many things they wish but could not previously afford. This sounds wonderful but, as you probably suspect, there is a major flaw. The weakness here comes because we are likely to think of wealth in terms of money rather than in terms of goods and services.

Returning once again to the relationship of government to the total economy, you may recall that our basic economic problem is limited resources to fill unlimited wants, forcing us to make choices. If we utilize all our factors of production most efficiently and this production adds up to 100 units, all within the private sector, there will be no resources left to produce units of production in the government sector. If we decide that we need 20 units of production that government produces, we can get it only by increasing our resources (which in this instance we cannot do) or by taking factors of production away from the private sector. By printing money to pay for its production, the government increases the dollar demand without increasing the supply of production. This results in price increases, as you may readily see by consulting Figure 2–9, the graph for supply and demand on page 32.

In contrast, the government, by taxing, takes away from people money they might spend in the private sector. This reduces the demand for units of production in the private sector, freeing the units of production that are now unemployed, and allows for a transfer of the factors of production from the private to the public sector. If payments by government and private enterprise are the same, taxes of 20 percent reduce the demand of people by 20 percent in the private sector market. Units of production in the economy can now be divided, 80 units produced by private enterprise and 20 units produced by government. By taxing, government has diverted the factors of production from the private sector to the public sector without threatening stable prices.

What Determines a Fair Tax?

Few people think of taxes as payment for certain services received by government. The major reason for not thinking in these terms is that it is difficult for us to put a price tag on the specific benefits we receive from government. Supply and demand may determine the price of consumer goods, such as clothing, and they may even suggest the proper allocation of resources between education and defense. However, they do not answer the question of how much you, as a taxpayer, should pay for such services as fire or police protection, which is another matter entirely. This in turn raises the question of what principles should be used to determine tax assessment.

Benefits Received

The oldest principle applied to the determination of a fair tax is that of *benefits received*. Differing little from purchases made in the private sector, this principle asks the taxpayer to pay the government according to the benefits he derives from government. While it is logical to tax gasoline to pay for roads used by cars, buses, or trucks, we could hardly expect people on welfare to pay the tax that will be used to support them. A much more complex problem is the determination of the benefits derived by each citizen from a collective service such as defense, or police or fire protection.

Ability to Pay

Most people in our society believe that those who have the greatest wealth or the highest income should pay the most taxes, regardless of the benefits they get from government. The reasoning behind this principle is that as a taxpayer's wealth or income increases, his ability to pay taxes increases even faster. Using the theory of diminishing marginal utility explained in Chapter 2, the payment of the last dollar of $20,000 of income will involve far less sacrifice than the parting with the last dollar of a $10,000 income. While very few people would suggest that all taxpayers should make equal sacrifices, the practical needs of raising revenue without causing an undue hardship make this principle acceptable without testifying to its absolute fairness.

Determining the fairest principle to use for a just tax is a question of values rather than of economic science, and is determined in the political process. Nevertheless, the American people have apparently accepted to a certain extent the principle of *ability to pay*, and our American tax system reflects this acceptance.

Other Factors in Evaluating Taxes

Many other factors, in addition to fairness, must be considered before levying a tax. From the government's standpoint, the total revenue that a tax yields is a primary consideration. Local and state governments must find taxes that provide a fairly predictable and steady income. The federal government needs a tax program that is flexible enough to help the economy during changes in business activity, as we will see in Chapter 12. Consideration must be given to the cost of collecting a tax, since high costs incurred in administering it, both for the taxpayer and for the government, may make it uneconomical.

Effect on Production

Another major consideration is the effect that the tax has on production. One of the most frequently used arguments against a high income tax is that it destroys the incentive of businessmen and employees to work harder and more efficiently. The favorable results for the economy from the federal income tax reduction in 1964 have given weight to this point of view. Although evidence can be found both to prove and disprove that taxes affect initiative, few economists would deny that a point can be reached at which such an effect could take place. It must, therefore, be kept in mind in the preparation of new taxes or the raising of rates.

Effect on Specific Goods

Taxes can have significant influences on the sale of specific goods or services sold. A tax on oleomargarine affects not only its sale but also that of similar products, such as butter. A cabaret tax may force the proprietor of a restaurant to eliminate entertainment. A tax on electricity may lead to increased buying of gas appliances. Using your knowledge of demand and supply curves, tell what happens to the quantity purchased when a tax forces the price up. Does it matter whether the demand is elastic or inelastic? For an illustration of the effect of an excise tax on the sale of fur coats, turn to pages 4 and 5 of the classical model insert that follows page 34.

Reflection of Values

Some taxes reflect our society's moral values. It is far easier for lawmakers to place a tax on tobacco and liquor than on almost any other commodity. It is easy to get the impression that society is saying, "If you smoke and drink, you will have to pay for your indulgence in more ways than one." Those who believe that high taxes can discourage people from buying cigarettes or liquor underestimate how inelastic the demand for these products is.

Convenience

No taxpayer finds a tax convenient to pay, but those who write our tax laws must consider the time and manner of collection that will cause the least hardship. Before World War II, when the federal income tax was relatively low, payments were generally made by income taxpayers once a year. Most families would find such an arrangement today almost catastrophic. The burden of paying taxes becomes more tolerable through the withholding of a predetermined amount from each paycheck or by making payments four times a year. Simplicity of directions for payment is also important.

Shifting the Burden

A factor which those who make our tax laws must carefully consider is, Who will bear the ultimate burden of the tax? Frequently a tax placed on one person or group can be *shifted* to someone else. A manufacturer may shift the tax placed on him to the retailer. The retailer, in turn, may shift the tax to the ultimate consumer. It is important to determine the *incidence* of the tax, that is, where it finally comes to rest and where shifting can no longer take place. Taxes can be shifted backward to the initial producer as well as forward to the consumer. The effects of shifting can be more far-reaching than merely asking the consumer to pay more. The increase in price can cause sales to decline, eventually resulting in the loss of jobs. A good tax should place the incidence where the tax-makers intended it to be.

Evaluating Ability to Pay

In seeking to evaluate a tax for fairness according to the ability-to-pay principle, economists have frequently used one particular criterion: that taxes should be judged on the relationship of the tax rate to the tax base. A *tax rate* is the percentage that is taxed. The *tax base* is the subject on which the tax is levied. If the tax rate increases as the tax base increases, the tax is *progressive.* If the tax rate remains the same, regardless of the tax base, the tax is *proportional.* If the tax rate decreases as the tax base increases, the tax is *regressive.* Figure 9–5 shows the differences graphically.

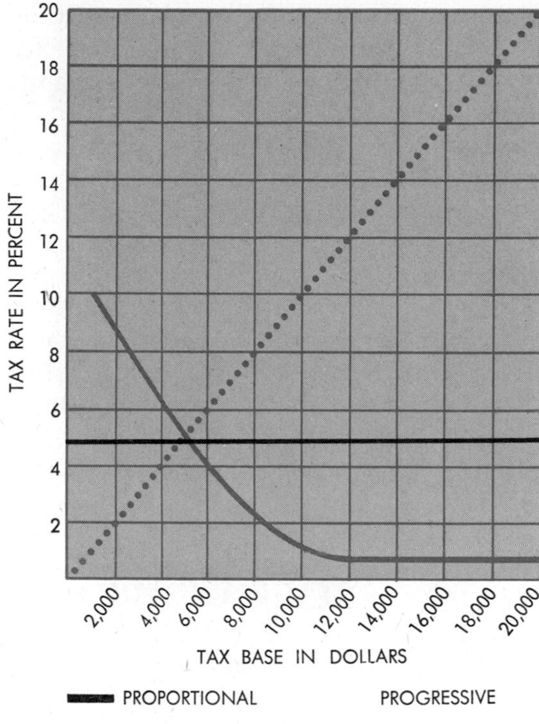

FIGURE 9–5 Evaluating the Ability-to-Pay Principle

In evaluating taxes according to the ability-to-pay principle, they may be classified as progressive, proportional, or regressive, depending upon the relationship of the tax rate to the tax base.

Using an income tax as an example, a regressive tax would be one in which the first $1,000 of income might be taxed at 10 percent, the next $1,000 of income at 8 percent, the next $1,000 at 6 percent, the next $1,000 at 4 percent, the next $1,000 at 2 percent, and 1 percent for all additional income. With this tax rate a man with a taxable income of $5,000 would pay $300, or 6 percent of his income, while a man with a taxable income of $10,000 would pay $350, or 3.5 percent of his income. A proportional tax would call for a uniform rate, say 5 percent, so that our man with the lower income would pay $250 while our wealthier man would pay $500.

A progressive income tax might call for 1 percent on the first $1,000 of taxable income, 2 percent on the next $1,000, 3 percent on the next, continuing with an increase of 1 percent in the tax rate on each additional $1,000 of income up to $90,000. In this case the first man would pay $150, or 1.5 percent, and our second taxpayer $550, or 5.5 percent.

The regressive tax places the greatest burden on lower income groups, whereas the progressive tax falls most heavily on people with higher incomes. Few taxes are enacted that are deliberately designed to be regressive. This would be bad politics and would run counter to our sense of justice. However, any tax in which every taxpayer pays the same number of dollars, regardless of his income or tax base, is very regressive. The poll tax is an example. A retail sales tax that is placed on all purchases appears to be proportional, say 3 percent, but is, in effect, regressive. This is because the lower income groups spend a greater proportion of their income (frequently all of it) than the upper income groups; the spending of those with high incomes is relatively less affected by the sales tax. Many economists believe that, in determining ability to pay, income is probably a better tax base than amount spent.

As we continue our study of taxation and government spending in Chapter 10, additional problems of evaluating taxes will appear. Each tax must be examined in the light of our total tax structure. Also to be considered are the implications of government spending in excess of income, to be discussed at length in Chapters 13 and 16 and related to spending policy.

REVIEW: THE HIGHLIGHTS OF THE CHAPTER

1. The classical model calls for a minimum of government interference in the economy so as to allow the allocation of resources to be according to consumer preferences. It is the responsibility of government to provide an environment favorable for the market economy by preserving the pillars of capitalism: private property, freedom of contract, economic freedom, and competition.
2. Government's role in the American economy has become more active as it seeks to satisfy the needs of the people. How deeply involved government should be in the economy is controversial, although tradition and theory have provided principles to guide our answers.
3. Citizens and consumers may be the same people, but their influence on the economy is different.
4. Public expenditures of the federal, state, and local governments have increased enormously in the last 30 years, although inflationary prices and military expenditures account for a substantial part of this increase. An additional factor has been our demand for more and better services, particularly in education and welfare.
5. Government budgets are prepared by chief executives and their administrative staffs, but they require legislative approval. Political considerations play a part in their preparation and passage.
6. The major source of government revenue is taxes. Government imposes taxes to move resources from the private to the public sector without jeopardizing prices.
7. Taxes may be evaluated according to the principles of benefits received or ability to pay, their revenue yield, their effect on production and the allocation of resources, their convenience to the taxpayer, and the shifting of their inci-

dence. A tax may be judged progressive, proportional, or regressive, depending on the relationship of the tax rate to the tax base.

IN CONCLUSION: SOME AIDS TO UNDERSTANDING

Terms for Review

pillars of capitalism	regulatory agency	regressive tax
administrative budget	Clay's American System	ability-to-pay principle
cash budget	benefits-received principle	tax rate
tax shifting	progressive tax	tax base
incidence of the tax	proportional tax	

Questions for Review

1. The classical model of capitalism forms the basis of the American economic system.
   (a) Describe the four basic pillars of the capitalist system.
   (b) What role must the government play to insure an environment favorable for the proper functioning of the capitalist system, even though this role is contrary to the original system?
2. Throughout our nation's history the federal government has aided business development in many ways.
   (a) Describe the various methods that the government has used to help business.
   (b) Why has government's role in the economy increased? Is this good or bad? Why?
3. As the economic strength of part of the business sector increased, the role of government in relation to business changed.
   (a) Describe the steps which were taken to insure competition.
   (b) How did the government help weaker sectors of the economy?
   (c) How did the government take over some of the functions of the business community? Why did the government take this action?
4. Write two brief paragraphs giving the arguments for and against the involvement of the government in regulating the market and in entering the field of production.
5. Every individual may have an impact on the national economy. Briefly describe the two roles in which the individual can use his influence. What is the effect of each role on the public sector and the private sector of the economy?
6. Increased government spending has a significant influence on the economy as a whole.
   (a) Evaluate the charge that increased spending by the federal government is evidence of "creeping socialism."
   (b) Indicate how the changing role of government is reflected in the increase of government spending.

7. A government can print money, borrow from people or from banks, or raise taxes to pay its bills. How might each of these measures affect the economy?
8. In levying taxes, one important consideration is the "fairness" of a particular tax or of an entire tax system.
   (a) Distinguish between a progressive and a regressive tax.
   (b) What is meant by a proportional tax?
   (c) What danger does the "soak the rich" idea present?

Additional Questions and Problems

1. In describing the role of the various factors of production, some economists suggest that the government must be included. Defend this idea by indicating the role government plays.
2. "Democratic capitalism has provided a middle road between complete laissez-faire and complete government control." Criticize and defend this statement.
3. To what extent is it possible (and desirable) to keep government from influencing the economy?
4. United States citizens have a dual role, both as voters and as consumers, in exerting their influence on our economy.
   (a) Give three examples of each role the citizen plays.
   (b) Describe two conditions in which his two roles may cause him to have opposite points of view on the same matter.
5. The trend toward increased government spending may be interpreted in a variety of ways.
   (a) Using the graphs in Figures 9–1 and 9–2, describe the reasons why both are needed to give a full and true picture of the government's increase in expenditures.
   (b) List two arguments which could be used by those who say that we are on the road to "creeping socialism" and two answers in rebuttal.
   (c) In a brief paragraph explain how added government services have increased the cost of government.
6. In the course of our nation's history, government has played an evolving role in the economy.
   (a) Make a time line of the economic development of the United States, listing the highlights of the opposing forces, aids to business, and controls over business.
   (b) How do these actions reflect the philosophy of the role of government on the economic scene?
   (c) Does the added activity of the government indicate a possible weakening of our capitalist system?

SELECTED READINGS

Allen, Frederick Lewis. *The Big Change: America Transforms Itself, 1900–1950.* New York: Harper and Row, 1952. (Also available in paperback edition: Bantam Books, N.Y., 1961.)

Bernstein, Peter L. and Robert L. Heilbroner. *A Primer on Government Spending.* New York: Random House, 1968.

Galbraith, John K. *The Affluent Society.* 2nd ed. Boston: Houghton Mifflin Co., 1969.

Heller, Walter. *New Dimensions in Political Economy.* New York: W. W. Norton, 1967.

May, R. J. *Federalism and Fiscal Adjustment.* New York: Oxford University Press, 1969.

Ott, David J. and Attiat F. Ott. *The Federal Budget.* Washington, D.C.: Brookings Institution.

Government and Public Finance 10

THE AUTHORS' NOTE TO THE STUDENT

In the preceding chapter we discovered that the major purpose of taxation is to reallocate resources from the private to the public sector. In addition, we learned some new tools for evaluating taxes. Now we are ready to apply these tools to several of our more important kinds of taxes. In this chapter we move from an academic lesson to the practical application of theory.

With the cost of government rising each year, both the private citizen and the government must choose between alternatives in taxes as well as in spending. We must once again face the related problems of scarcity and the maximizing of our satisfactions. To determine how to raise the revenue required, we must consider two additional criteria: the fairness of each tax and its probable effect on production. Once again we find that people's values influence the ways they use analytical tools to arrive at their conclusions.

An alternative to raising revenue by taxes is borrowing. Our frequent government borrowing has resulted in a huge public debt. There are few areas of economics where people are so concerned and yet understand so little. Are we in danger of going bankrupt? How can this debt harm us? Does it differ from a private debt? Should we try to pay it off? If we did, how would it affect the economy? In this chapter we examine these and other questions. Hopefully, we should arrive at some tentative solutions.

A STUDENT'S NOTE TO THE STUDENT

I read this chapter when the Congress was playing with a large planned deficit budget, the state legislature was arguing over the largest single tax increase in the state's history, and members of the local board of education were sitting on the edge of their chairs waiting to find out how much state and federal aid would be forthcoming. If you want relevance, it's in this chapter.

The only thing you might find tricky is figuring out how the sales tax and real estate tax are regressive. Just remember to switch the tax base to income rather than expenditures or the assessed value and you won't have any trouble. The section on the "consequences of a public debt" may give you a new way of looking at this subject. My parents still have a real hang-up on this subject.

The thing that bothered me most is that this land of equal opportunity is not so equal. Compare the sources of revenue from different types of taxes between state and local governments in Figure 10–1. After learning how to analyze taxes, I don't see any real fairness in carrying the tax burden.

Part A
The Federal Tax System

Tax Revenues: Progressive or Regressive?

As we have observed in Table 9–1, our federal government secures its revenue from a wide variety of sources. It is obvious that *individual* and *corporation income taxes* are the largest source of revenue. Apart from *employment taxes,* such as Social Security payments which go into the federal trust fund, over one half of all federal revenue comes from income taxes. A very small portion of our total revenue comes from estate and gift taxes and from customs collections, which were a major source of revenue in the nineteenth century. A larger share comes from federal *excise taxes,* which are sales taxes often placed on specific goods and services, such as alcohol, tobacco, gasoline, motor vehicles, jewelry, and admissions to places of entertainment. These taxes are frequently the result of the treasury's constant efforts to raise new revenue without causing too much political backlash.

Other than income taxes and estate and gift taxes, federal taxes are regressive. Taxes on commodities and services are not based on the buyer's income. Although people with higher incomes are more likely to spend the greater amount for jewelry, furs, and admissions to expensive places of entertainment, this is more than compensated for by the percentage of income spent by the people in lower income groups for such needs as gasoline, automobiles, and appliances. The latter have also been most affected by the raising of federal excise taxes. Social Security payments may seem to be proportional to income. However, since they are based on a maximum tax base ($9,000 in 1972), people earning more than this amount have that portion free from this tax. Part of the regressive feature of Social Security taxes is lessened when benefits are considered.

"First dollar I ever earned—after taxes."

SOURCE: Don Orehek, *Look* Magazine.

Taxes on the transfer of estates and on sizable gifts have been collected by the federal government since 1916. The great majority of people never need concern themselves with estate taxes, since the tax base does not start until deductions above $60,000 are reached. However, above this amount the rates are highly progressive, reflecting the strong sentiment against an aristocracy of wealth. Taxes on large gifts are used to discourage the evasion of estate taxes by transfers made before death.

Income Taxes: Major Source of Revenue

Among those who favor the ability-to-pay principle of taxation, net income of individuals or businesses is usually considered the fairest tax base. Although there is broad support for taxing net income at a progressive rate, there is considerable controversy over what to consider as net income, what deductions to allow, and to what extent corporations should be taxed. A few examples will illustrate the problem of trying to find an answer to what is fair for all and yet will provide adequate income.

What Constitutes Income?

Should food grown by a farmer to feed his own family be counted as income? Should payment in kind, such as commodities given to a lawyer by a client, be counted as income? Should fringe benefits, generous with some companies and meager with others, go untaxed? Why should a homeowner be allowed to deduct his real estate taxes from his income whereas the tenant who pays these taxes to the landlord in rent is allowed no such deduction? Is the standard $650 exemption fair for an infant as well as for an adult? Should a person such as a baseball player or an actor, who earns a high income during a short productive period of his life, be asked to pay the same rates as a person whose income is more evenly earned throughout his working life? Should income made by the sale of property that has increased in value be taxed as income earned "on the job"? Should a tax be imposed on a corporation's profit as well as on the dividends received by the stockholders? Should profits reinvested in a business be taxed in the same way distributed dividends are?

Our federal income tax laws have to provide answers to all these questions. None of the answers can satisfy all of those affected. The correct answers of today may not be satisfactory tomorrow. As you encounter these problems in preparing a tax return, injustices will probably be obvious to you. The problems facing our lawmakers in trying to meet each individual citizen's needs and standard of values are very great. Remember that our tax laws do attempt to reconcile these differences.

Preparing a Personal Income Tax Report

The tax base for income taxes is called *taxable income*. Taxable income is what remains after subtracting allowable deductions and exemptions from gross income. Most wage earners can figure their federal income tax by adding together the sum of their wages from all employers, their interest from savings, their dividends from stock in excess of a certain allowable amount, and any other unrecorded income. The total thus arrived at represents gross income. From the total they then either subtract the *standard allowable deduction*—10 percent of gross income up to a maximum amount of $1,000 (1970)—or they itemize their deductions if their total will exceed the standard deduction, and then subtract these deductions from gross income. Itemizing deductions usually pays only when expenses for some accident or illness are high; when interest payments, usually for mortgages on homes, and taxes are significant; or when some loss from theft or casualty adds up to a substantial portion of what the standard deduction would be. Contributions to charitable organizations and certain expenses related to the earning of income are also deductible. Exemptions or credits are then subtracted from this sum. An exemption is a specified amount on which the taxpayer does not pay any tax. The federal government allows $650 for the taxpayer and $650 for each dependent who receives more than half his support from the taxpayer. Double exemptions are allowed for the blind and for people over 65. Exemption rates will increase in 1972.

When all deductions and exemptions have been subtracted from the gross income, the amount remaining is the taxable income. Once that has been determined, the taxpayer turns to the appropriate tax rate schedule to determine what his tax is. It is generally better for married couples to file a joint return. Table 10–1 shows the rates for 1971 for married taxpayers filing a joint return.

Evaluating the Personal Income Tax

A brief study of the table on tax rates shows how progressive our federal income tax is. Rates start at 14 percent on the first $500 of income for individuals or $1,000 for married couples, and go to 70 percent on all income above $100,000 for individuals and $200,000 for married couples. The rates above 14 percent do not apply to the entire income. Each portion of the income is taxed at a different rate. Although a wealthy married man who has a taxable income of $200,000 has reached the 70 percent bracket, his tax on his entire taxable income amounts to slightly more than 55 percent. Before the Revenue Act of 1964 the tax rate reached 91 percent on incomes above $200,000 for individuals. How would you evaluate such a tax rate?

It is difficult to shift the incidence of the personal income tax. However, there are ways of avoiding taxes by finding "loopholes" in the laws and even by criminal evasion. *Avoidance* is a legal way to reduce tax payment, whereas *evasion* refers to illegal means. Both have the effect of reducing the government's revenue from personal income taxes. The Tax Reform Act of 1969 has closed some of the "loopholes," but few economists are satisfied that sound economic judgments rather than expedient politics were the major factors responsible for the change.

TABLE 10–1 Tax Rate Schedule for Personal Income Tax for Married Taxpayers Filing Joint Returns and Certain Widows and Orphans (taxable years beginning after December 31, 1970)

If taxable income is: The tax is:
Not over $1,000 14% of taxable income

Over	But not over		Of excess over
$1,000–	$2,000	$140, plus 15%	$1,000
$2,000–	$3,000	$290, plus 16%	$2,000
$3,000–	$4,000	$450, plus 17%	$3,000
$4,000–	$8,000	$620, plus 19%	$4,000
$8,000–	$12,000	$1,380, plus 22%	$8,000
$12,000–	$16,000	$2,260, plus 25%	$12,000
$16,000–	$20,000	$3,260, plus 28%	$16,000
$20,000–	$24,000	$4,380, plus 32%	$20,000
$24,000–	$28,000	$5,660, plus 36%	$24,000
$28,000–	$32,000	$7,100, plus 39%	$28,000
$32,000–	$36,000	$8,660, plus 42%	$32,000
$36,000–	$40,000	$10,340, plus 45%	$36,000
$40,000–	$44,000	$12,140, plus 48%	$40,000
$44,000–	$52,000	$14,060, plus 50%	$44,000
$52,000–	$64,000	$18,060, plus 53%	$52,000
$64,000–	$76,000	$24,420, plus 55%	$64,000
$76,000–	$88,000	$31,020, plus 58%	$76,000
$88,000–	$100,000	$37,980, plus 60%	$88,000
$100,000–	$120,000	$45,180, plus 62%	$100,000
$120,000–	$140,000	$57,580, plus 64%	$120,000
$140,000–	$160,000	$70,380, plus 66%	$140,000
$160,000–	$180,000	$83,580, plus 68%	$160,000
$180,000–	$200,000	$97,180, plus 69%	$180,000
$200,000		$110,980, plus 70%	$200,000

The personal income tax is designed to be progressive. Can you think of ways in which people with high incomes can avoid its progressive intent? SOURCE: U.S. Treasury Department, Internal Revenue Service.

The personal income tax supplies a large proportion of the federal government's revenue. It tends to reduce the inequality of income existing before taxes. Thus, the taxpayer who earns $6,000 before paying income tax may retain $5,500, whereas the $60,000-a-year man may be left with $42,000. Both benefit about equally from government expenditures, but the low-income taxpayer has paid 8 percent of his income in federal personal income taxes while the high-income taxpayer has paid 30 percent. The other more regressive taxes we have mentioned reduce some of this difference.

The fact that there are high rates on high incomes does not mean that people in higher income groups pay most of the taxes. The United States Treasury Department reported that in 1968, 52 percent of all federal income tax money came from taxpayers whose adjusted gross income was below $15,000, and less than 10 percent came from those with adjusted gross income above $100,000. Of course, a far higher percentage of our population is in the lowest tax bracket than in the higher ones.

Corporation Income Tax

Business corporations, like individuals, must also pay taxes on their income. In fiscal 1972 the federal government anticipates collecting $36.7 billion from corporation income taxes. This amounts to approximately 40 percent of what the federal government plans to collect in personal income taxes and more than 16 percent of the federal government's total revenues.

A corporation income tax is based on a corporation's annual income after it has paid its expenses. Dividends to stockholders are not included as expenses. Unlike the personal income tax, there are only two rates, 22 percent on earnings up to $25,000 a year and 48 percent on all other earnings. This follows the principle of ability to pay, but it is far less progressive than the personal income tax. The incidence tends to fall on the stockholders in highly competitive businesses because shifting it to the consumer will raise prices but cut down on sales. In oligopolies, where prices can be largely determined by the producers, the customers frequently must bear the burden.

Evaluating the Corporation Income Tax

The corporation income tax is often criticized as an example of double taxation. Not only must the company pay taxes on its profits, but also individual shareholders must pay personal income taxes on dividends paid by the company. The principle of ability to pay is ignored in taxing dividend income. The small stockholder has been given some relief by the provision allowing taxpayers to deduct the first $100 they receive in dividends from their personal income ($200 for married couples filing joint returns). In addition, money that is gained from the increase in the value of stock sold at least six months after its purchase is considered a capital gain. The law allows the seller of such stock to pay at a lower rate on the capital gain. However, gains from stock owned for less than six months are taxed at the rate of regular income.

Many businessmen have complained—probably with some justification—that high corporate taxes interfere with their opportunities to reinvest their profits in their business. Such interference can hinder the growth and modernization of businesses. Some industrial nations that have expanded rapidly in the last 15 years have far lower taxes on corporations than we do, and many economists believe that low corporation taxes have been a help in this business expansion. The lower tax rates on corporate income put into effect with the Revenue Act of 1964 have brought about little change in investment, but the future may see even greater changes in the corporation income tax. However, it is doubtful that the government will be willing to give up such a lucrative source of revenue.

Part B
State and Local Tax Revenues

Sources of Revenue

State and local governments, like the federal government, depend on a number of taxes for their income. Figure 10–1 shows a composite of all state and local governments' tax revenue by type. In addition to the revenue received from taxes, these governments received in 1968 about $18 billion from the federal government and

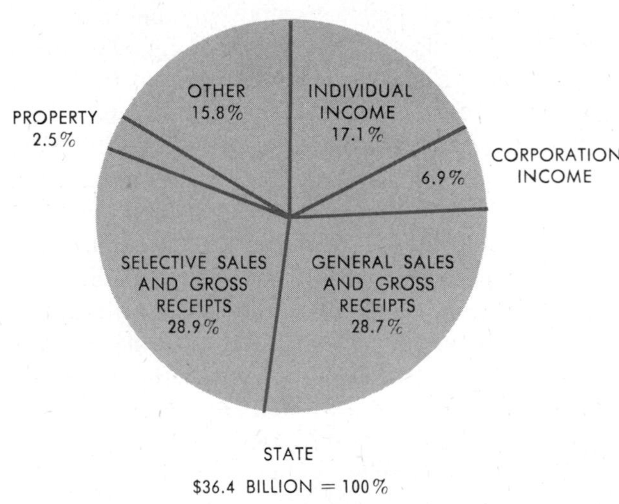

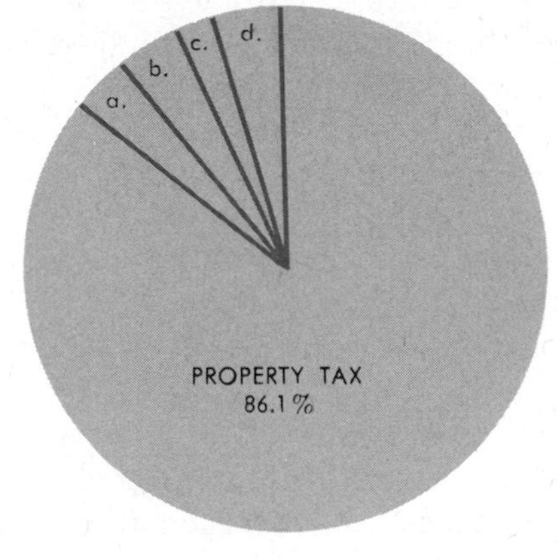

FIGURE 10–1 Sources of State and Local Government Tax Revenue, Fiscal 1968

The tax structure for states, although not as progressive as for the federal government, more closely follows the ability-to-pay principle as the individual income tax becomes a greater source of state revenue. Local governments have regressive tax structures because of their reliance on the property tax as their major source of tax revenue. The use of new kinds of taxes may make local taxes less regressive. In 1970 the Tax Foundation reported 40 cities with income taxes, almost all proportional. SOURCE: U.S. Department of Commerce, Bureau of the Census.

over $25 billion in fees and other sources. Federal grants have increased from 6 percent of total state and local expenditures in 1946 to 17 percent in 1969. Local governments now collect less than half their total revenues from taxes. The trends of the states' dependence on the federal government for aid and of the local governments' dependence on the states and the federal government have been upward each year.

State Tax Systems

The largest single source of state tax revenue is the general retail *sales tax.* Most states having such a tax impose it on all purchases, although there is a growing tendency to exempt food and medicine to ease the burden such a tax imposes on people with low incomes. Some items carry state excise taxes in addition to general sales taxes, federal excise taxes, and, on occasion, local taxes. If we remove all taxes from cigarettes the price becomes almost unrecognizable. Excise taxes are popular with legislators because they are easily hidden and less likely to antagonize voters. Collection of excises is relatively simple, involving either periodic sales reports or the sale to the manufacturer or distributor of a revenue stamp. In highly competitive industries the incidence must fall on the consumer because the producer does not have enough economic profit to absorb the additional cost. In less competitive areas the burden is either shared or shifted to the consumer, so that the tax will not cut too heavily into profits.

The general retail sales tax places the incidence directly on the consumer, but it would not be accurate to assume that the producer is unaffected. Higher prices to the consumer result in fewer sales, thereby affecting everyone. Although it is easy to collect, and the burden is seemingly light because the consumer (taxpayer) pays only a small amount at a time, the tax is very regressive and evasion is not difficult. The family with an income below $5,000 will probably spend all of it. With the exception of rent, their entire income may be subject to this tax. The family with an income of $50,000 will probably spend only part of it. That part which they do not spend is not affected by the sales tax.

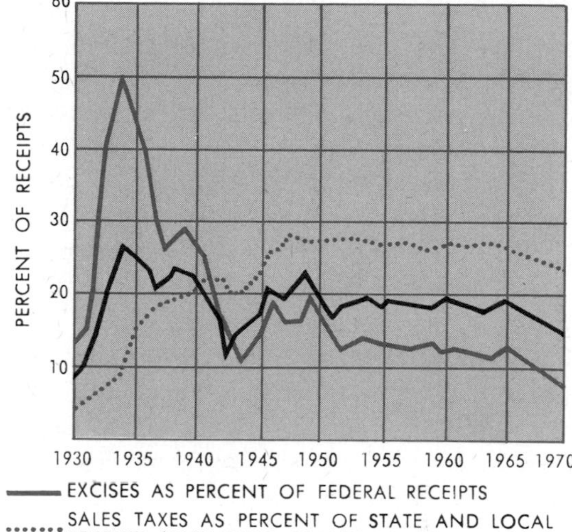

FIGURE 10–2 Excise and Sales Taxes as Percent of Government Receipts

Federal revenue from excise taxes has declined sharply as a percentage of total revenue. For state and local government this trend is less noticeable. SOURCE: U.S. Department of Commerce, Office of Business Economics.

Evaluating the Sales Tax

With three fourths of all states collecting general sales taxes and many local governments turning to it to help solve their problem of raising enough revenue, attempts have been made to lessen the regressive features of this tax. A number of states have exempted food. If medicine, fuel, and utilities are also exempted, the general sales tax becomes slightly progressive at low-income levels, proportional at middle-income levels, and regressive only at upper-income levels. Families with low incomes spend the largest portion of their income on rent and food. As income rises, a larger percentage of income is spent for other items, thereby increasing the percentage of income taxed. Actually, the percentage of incomc that can be saved in the higher income brackets increases so rapidly that the regressive features of this tax remain, even with the exemptions mentioned.

An increasing number of economists have suggested that all necessities should be exempted from excise and general retail sales taxes and that the same taxes on luxuries should be raised substantially. To follow this suggestion would allow these taxes to conform to the ability-to-pay principle. The difficulty with such a procedure lies in determining what constitutes necessities and luxuries. People with lower incomes spend a greater percentage of their income on tobacco, for instance, than do people in the upper levels of income. What is the difficulty in exempting clothing? Although there may be some items that everyone considers luxuries, such as expensive jewelry, furs, and limousines, the amount of revenue yielded by a tax on them would be too small to meet the needs of government. For a further discussion of the question of individual values related to standard of living, turn back to the problem at the end of Chapter 2.

Other State Taxes

Gasoline taxes and fees collected for drivers' licenses and automobile registration are good examples of the benefits-

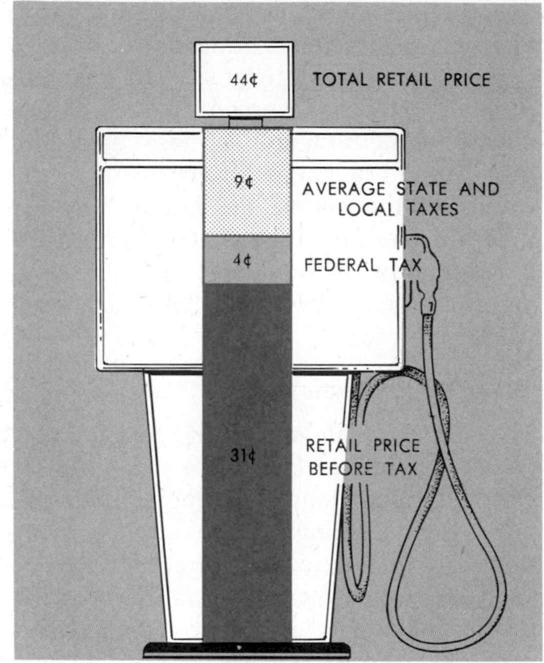

FIGURE 10–3 Taxes on Some Goods Make Up a Large Portion of the Total Cost

received principle. Some states earmark all such revenues for road construction to reassure those who use the highways that they will get what they pay for. Since drivers also benefit from other state services, it is doubtful whether putting receipts in the general revenue fund makes much of a difference in benefits received.

More than two thirds of the states have income taxes that follow the pattern set by the federal government. The rates are, however, far lower, generally running from one to 12 percent, with rates in only a few states going higher. State income taxes are far less progressive than the federal income tax but more progressive than most other state taxes.

Tax receipts from corporate income, inheritance and gift taxes, and property taxes make up the remainder of state tax revenue. The first two are progressive, while the vanishing state property tax is regressive. Inheritance taxes differ from the federal estate taxes by being placed on the receiver rather than on what is given.

Local Tax Systems

Property taxes are the oldest and, among local governments, the most widely used source of revenue. They account for 86 percent of all tax revenues raised at the local level and about half of all revenue received by local governments, including payments from state and national government sources. Property taxes are divided into two categories—real estate taxes on land, and personal property taxes on such things as securities, furniture, and cars.

One of the major reasons that property taxes have remained an important source of revenue is that it is a relatively simple matter to have them yield the revenue needed by the government. If a school district needs to raise $2 million to finance its annual operation and the property that it can tax is *assessed* at $100 million, officials set the tax rate at 2 percent of assessed valuation. If expenses go up the following year to $2.5 million, then the tax rate is merely raised to 2.5 percent.

Evaluating Property Taxes

Administration of property taxes has often been so inefficient and unfair that some people doubt that this tax should be allowed to persist. Appraising the true value of property, particularly personal property, even when it is done by experts, is very difficult, and assessors are not necessarily chosen or elected because they are experts. Not all people report all their property, and there is a strong tendency to undervalue that which is reported. The assessor cannot be expected to be an expert appraiser of all things and a detective to determine whether property is hidden, and still manage to remain on speaking terms with other members of the community. Since it is common practice to underestimate the value of property, the honest citizen is severely penalized.

Determining the value of real estate is not quite so difficult as appraising personal property, but it is doubtful that many communities achieve great accuracy in their assessments. Real estate values have climbed faster than assessments, and changes in neighborhoods have brought about changes in the value of properties. When property is sold, the value can be determined; but little real property is sold often enough to keep pace with changing values. Local governments find it easier to obtain the extra revenue they need by raising tax rates rather than risk antagonizing voters by reassessing properties in order to increase the tax base.

At one time ownership of property was a fairly good criterion of ability to pay. As our nation has become more industrialized, salaries and profits have become more important factors on which to judge a taxpayer's ability to pay. A small family

"The city cut our budget."

SOURCE: Leonard Herman, *Saturday Review*, December 26, 1970. Copyright 1970, Saturday Review Inc.

does not need as big a house as a large family. Assuming that each family has the same income and builds a house of similar quality, the bigger house of the larger family will be assessed for more, although the smaller family probably has a greater ability to pay. Cheaper property tends to be overassessed in comparison with high-priced property. Wealthier people are more likely to have influence with assessors or to threaten court action because of overassessment. Tenants usually have property taxes shifted to them as part of their rent.

Several characteristics of the property tax which have emerged from our discussion are that it is (1) regressive to a considerable degree, (2) capable of being shifted to tenants and, in the case of factories, to consumers, (3) easily evaded, and (4) almost impossible to administer efficiently. Although this tax reflects the benefit principle with regard to police and fire protection and certain other services furnished by local governments, it is frequently used to support such general services as education. Although the federal government is prohibited from using it and state governments are turning to other sources of revenue, the property tax probably will remain the major source of revenue for local governments unless recent court actions require a change.

Other Local Revenues

Sales taxes are becoming more popular with local governments, which are finding the need for more revenue but at the same time are meeting greater resistance to raising the property tax. Additional revenue is obtained by fees, permits, receipts from parking meters, and municipal businesses. A relatively new but increasingly important tax now used by several cities is a tax on wages and salaries of all persons working within the city. While this *payroll* tax ignores income from interest and profits, it does force those who work in and use the facilities of the city but live in the suburbs to share in the costs of operating the city. Who would be likely to favor such a tax?

Part C
Evaluating the American Tax System

Appraising Current Practices

A good tax system should encourage the efficient and full utilization of a nation's productive capacities without hindering the allocation of resources according to the wishes of consumers. It should yield the revenue needed to finance whatever government operations its citizens decide on without disturbing economic growth and stability. The tax burden should fall according to a principle or principles which society accepts as fair to all.

Although few would disagree in theory with using these criteria for evaluation, there is strong disagreement when our specific taxes are measured against them. There is general agreement that the ability-to-pay principle, tempered by benefits received, should determine how the tax burden should be distributed. There is less agreement as to what tax base should be used in determining ability to pay. Avoiding the use of "good" or "bad," since they involve value judgments rather than economic conclusions, let us see what generalizations we can come to about the American tax system:

1. The final incidence of many taxes at all levels of government is not where lawmakers intended.
2. Excise and business taxes ultimately do affect the allocation of resources according to the wishes of consumers. This happens because people act differently as citizens voting for services in the public sector from the way they act as consumers shopping in the private sector.
3. Business taxes affect the economic growth of some businesses, particularly small businesses, in which capital may be hard to obtain.
4. Many taxes are ill conceived and are merely politically expedient devices to raise additional revenue with a minimum of voter protest.
5. Tradition, the high yield of revenue, government needs, and inertia are responsible for the continued existence of certain taxes, even though such taxes may fail to meet most of the criteria for a good tax. One example of this statement is the property tax.
6. Federal taxes, due to the importance of the personal income tax, are mildly progressive.
7. State and local taxes, due to general retail sales and property taxes, are slightly regressive.
8. Most economists agree that taxes as a whole are mildly progressive among all families except the poorest and the wealthiest. The poorest families pay regressively whereas the wealthiest pay more progressively.
9. Federal taxes are considered to be not merely producers of revenue but also an important instrument for economic growth and stability. This use of taxes will be discussed in Unit III.
10. Many economists think that the American tax structure, while better than that of most other industrial countries, is too much of a hodgepodge resulting from considerations of political expediency, and could be improved considerably by being simplified and reorganized.

Taxes at the present time will reduce your purchases in the private sector of the economy by over 25 percent. It is doubtful that this percentage will decrease and, if the trend continues, it will likely be higher. As both a consumer and a citizen, you should be concerned about an equitable tax structure. Since our tax laws are changed frequently, you should become aware of directions in which changes might be made.

Part D
Public Borrowing and the Public Debt

Reasons for Borrowing

It might seem that the most direct way of meeting governmental financial obligations would be by taxing to the extent necessary to obtain the required revenue. However, there are times when such a procedure is not possible. When governments are unable to meet their financial obligations out of their current revenues, they can make up the difference by borrowing. This borrowing creates a public debt, the size of which is the subject of much controversy. Public borrowing and public debt are frequently compared to the borrowing and debt of businesses and families. Although these kinds of debt do have certain features in common, there are also very significant differences. Failure to recognize these differences has led to much misunderstanding of the nature and significance of our public debt.

There are four main reasons why governments borrow:

1. Short-term adjustments have to be made to correct the imbalance of revenues and expenditures. Because expenditures may be somewhat greater than expected, or tax collections slower or smaller than expected, governments make short-term loans. Expenditures tend to be spread throughout the year, whereas tax collections are frequently made only annually or semiannually. Short-term loans are easy to finance, and the interest rates on them are very low.
2. Financing major public works that will be used over many years usually requires borrowing. To wait until the government had the money would deprive people of essential services. It is sound financial policy to pay for such projects over no longer a period of time than the years during which the project will furnish services to the people. Some public projects, such as the Tennessee Valley Authority, state turnpikes, and municipal transportation systems, yield revenue from which the loans can be paid back.
3. Emergencies that cannot be anticipated cannot be expected to be paid for out of current revenues. Wars and natural disasters have added greatly to our public debt.
4. Deliberate spending in excess of current income has been done by the federal government as a means of stimulating the economy. The use of such action will be considered in Unit III.

The Size of the Public Debt

If someone had predicted 30 years ago that the gross debt of the federal government would go beyond $350 billion by the 1970's, those listening would probably have said that we would be on the verge of bankruptcy and would have runaway inflation. The truth is that, in spite of the size of the public debt, our government's credit is excellent and our economy has been expanding. This points out the difficulty in making long-range predictions.

When the term *federal debt* is used, it commonly refers to the gross debt, which includes all outstanding obligations of the federal government. Most economists consider the net debt, which includes only the federal obligations held by the public, more significant. This is because payments from one government agency to another have a relatively small effect on the economy. The figures cited in Figure 10–4 refer to the net amount, but those used elsewhere are for the gross amount.

Figure 10–4 shows the growth of the net public debt of the federal, state, and local governments and the growth of private debt. Although increased prices greatly distort the size of the increase, the rapid growth is evident. What is also obvious, but not widely recognized, is that since 1945, the end of World War II, the percentage of the net federal debt to the total debt has *decreased* significantly while the private debt has *increased* very sharply. There has also been an increase in the percentage of the debt owed by state and local governments. Those who suggest that the federal government should learn

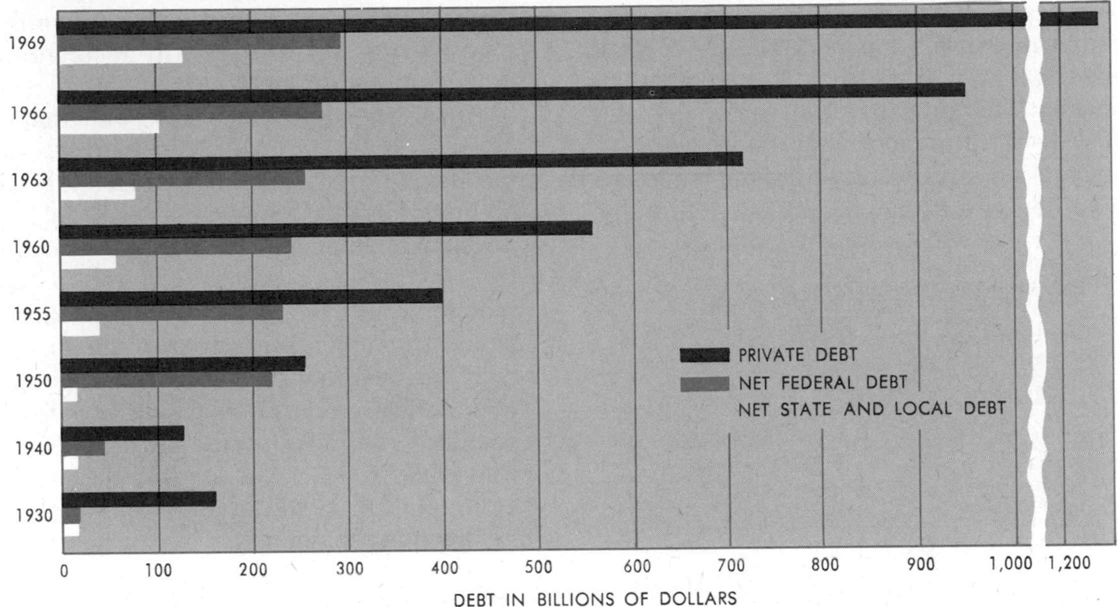

FIGURE 10–4 Growth of the Net Public and Private Debt

Although the net public debt has risen sharply, notably since World War II, private debt has risen even faster. SOURCES: Federal Reserve System, U.S. Treasury Department, and U.S. Department of Commerce.

to live within its budget as families and businesses do, are not acquainted with all the facts.

The size of any debt must be considered in relation to the size of income. A family with an income of $50,000 a year can afford to carry a debt of $5,000 better than a family with a $5,000 income can carry a $500 debt. In 1935 our gross federal debt was only $34.4 billion, and our gross national product was $72.2 billion. In 1970, our gross federal debt rose to $371 billion, but our GNP went up to an annual rate of $977 billion. The percentage of our federal debt in relation to our national income had, therefore, declined.

A similar change is demonstrated in Figure 10–5, which shows the gross federal debt as a percentage of GNP. When did the greatest increase in the debt take place? Does this correspond to the information in Figure 10–4? We can conclude that the primary cause of the present large size of the federal debt is the financing of military expenditures during World War II and the defense budget necessitated by the Cold War. Only a small portion of the debt can be attributed to government budgets purposely designed to create a debt as a means of stimulating the economy.

Ownership of the Federal Debt

Our public debt, unlike that of many other countries, is held internally. This means that the American people owe this money to themselves. Table 10–2 shows who holds the federal government securities. An internal debt is paid when the government takes some of its revenue, paid by Americans, and meets its obligations on bonds and notes held by other Americans, or, in some instances, the same

Americans. This procedure has frequently been characterized as taking money out of one pocket and putting it into another pocket. This interpretation must be qualified by pointing out that frequently the pockets do not belong to the same people. In other words, paying off an internally held debt does not mean a reduction in the total wealth, but it frequently results in a redistribution of the wealth.

An externally held debt is one that is owed to a foreign country. In this case the people of one country must take out of their pockets money that will go into the pockets of people in a different country. In this case, payment causes a real reduction in the wealth of the country paying the debt. A large part of the British debt has been held externally, and paying this debt off means a real sacrifice in the standard of living of the British people. Externally held debts are similar to private debts in terms of the real sacrifices involved in repayment.

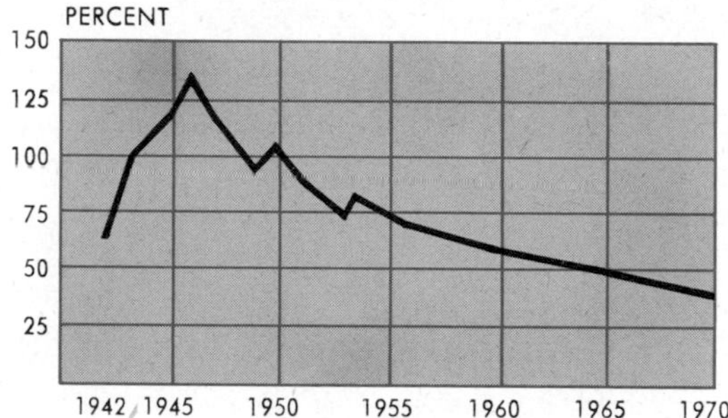

FIGURE 10–5 Public Debt as Percent of the Gross National Product

During World War II federal expenditures rose much faster than revenues, causing the public debt to skyrocket above the gross national product. The chart shows that the gross federal debt is declining in relationship to the growth of the economy (gross national product). SOURCE: U.S. Department of Commerce.

The Consequences of a Public Debt

The existence of a federal debt is always a matter for general concern. However, the average citizen is probably more concerned about the national debt than is the average economist. Let us consider some of the fears associated with our

TABLE 10–2 Ownership of United States Government Securities, November 1970

	Billions of dollars	Percent of total
United States Government Agencies and Trust Funds	94.6	24.6
Federal Reserve Banks	61.2	16.1
Commercial Banks	59.8	15.6
Mutual Savings Banks	2.7	.7
Insurance Companies	6.9	1.8
Corporations*	10.8	2.8
State and Local Governments	23.2	6.0
Individuals	82.3	21.5
Miscellaneous Purchasers†	42.1	11.0
Total	$383.6	100.0

* Other than commercial banks, mutual savings banks, and insurance companies.
† Savings and loan associations, dealers and brokers, foreign accounts, corporate pension funds, and nonprofit institutions.

SOURCE: *Federal Reserve Bulletin,* January 1971, p. A-42.

growing debt to see whether, according to the criteria of economists, they are justified.

Can We Go Bankrupt?

Many economists believe that, since the federal government has the power to tax or print money, it need never go bankrupt. The ratio of our gross national product to our debt has increased. The credit of the United States government is probably as good or better than that of any other government or institution in the world. The interest rates the government pays reflect this fact. Table 9–1 shows the amount of interest currently paid by our government.

Although some governments have gone bankrupt, their financial failure was due to declining GNP in relation to public debt. This unfavorable ratio caused a lack of confidence in the government's ability to meet its financial obligations in money that had reasonably stable purchasing power.

Will Future Generations Bear the Burden of the Present Debt?

Wars, which are chiefly responsible for the large size of the debt, imposed most of their burdens on those who were living at the time. The real economic sacrifice came when productive factors were turned to making armaments instead of making the goods and services that people of that generation would have wanted and produced had there been peace. These goods and services that might have been produced can never be realized. Why? Because the resources that would have made them were making other things, primarily armaments. Future generations bear the burden of using their productive resources to repair what has been destroyed. They are also handicapped by not inheriting the additional supply of capital goods that each generation adds to help each succeeding generation. In weighing these costs, however, we must consider whether this is too high a price to pay for the preservation of freedom.

Is the Interest on the National Debt a Burden?

Although many people are of the opinion that paying the interest on the national debt is only the transfer of money from one pocket to another, there *can* be harm to some people. To the extent that taxpayers and interest receivers are different people, so will the burdens and benefits be shifted. Those who pay high taxes tend also to receive high interest; because of this, there is doubt whether the effect of redistribution is great.

Do Government Securities Use Up Savings That Private Enterprise Needs for Expansion?

Government's problem has been to stimulate businessmen to invest, not to compete for funds. It is in part because business has not invested that government has had to stimulate the economy.

Can Increasing the Debt Be Inflationary?

If the government sought to pay its obligations by printing money, inflation would be the consequence. More money would be competing for the same amount of goods, causing prices to rise. Large-scale government borrowing at a time when all our productive resources are being used is also highly inflationary. However, government officials realize these dangers and are unlikely to take such inflationary steps. We will consider this question again in Chapter 13.

Public Debt: Some Added Considerations

Most of the answers to the questions previously raised would seem to indicate that we have little to fear from the growing public debt. Most economists believe that if the debt is closely observed and used rather than abused, it presents no great dangers. However, a policy of easy borrowing can encourage waste and stimulate inflation, especially if done at inappropriate times. It can also result in an unfavorable redistribution of income and psychologically disturb business investment. By being aware of these problems, we can be the masters of our debt rather than slaves to it, and thus derive benefits rather than harm from it.

Part E
The Problem: How Can State and Local Governments Meet Their Revenue Needs?—New York: A Case Study

On February 1, 1971 Governor Nelson Rockefeller went before the New York State Legislature and delivered his budget message. At that time it was the largest state budget in this nation's history, and it was as large as all federal outlays in 1939, $8.5 billion. Expenditures were four times larger than those the same governor submitted 10 years earlier and represented an increase of more than 22 percent over the previous year. What was more distressing was that the gap between income and expenditures was estimated at $1.4 billion of which $1.1 billion was to be met by new taxes.

Cause of Increased Expenditures

An analysis of the reasons for the financial crisis faced by New York state shows that its problems are not unique, and not necessarily more serious than those other states face. The costs for state and local governments throughout the country increased almost 400 percent in the last 20 years. Much of this increase is accounted for by inflation; some governments are victimized by its effects as much as consumers. More money is needed just to furnish the same services that were provided previously. However, more important in accounting for the large increases than inflation is the rising need for services.

More Services

The increase in living standards that the American people experienced in their private lives in the 1960's brought an expectation for increased and improved services by government.

Some of these are:

1. The increase in the birth rate after World War II brought about an increase in the quantity and quality of schools. If education was to be the institution for creating equality of opportunity and upward mobility for the disadvantaged, then family income should not be a criterion for participation, even at the college level. (See Chapter 21.)

2. The advances in medicine, including preventive medicine, must be available to everyone, not only the wealthy.
3. Social security programs with increased fringe benefits have grown in response to the public's wishes. This involves increases in the states' contributions to such programs.
4. More automobiles and more leisure time not only use up our highways faster but increase the demand for new roads.
5. Families are demanding more and better parks and public recreational areas.
6. Industrialization and urbanization make for more waste and more costly means for disposing of it. This includes sewerage and pollution control.
7. These high density areas also have witnessed sharp increases in crime and drug abuse, and the public wants the government to combat these menaces. Moreover, the public expects the government to accept responsibility for housing, mass transportation, and all the physically and mentally handicapped, even though these latter two services were largely within the private sector not many years ago.

With most local government levies placed on property taxes, which are less responsive to economic growth, state governments have been forced to increase their local assistance.

A breakdown of major budget items for fiscal 1961–62 and fiscal 1971–72 shows where the increases were made.

Cutting Expenditures

The most common outcries—certainly to be expected after a budget message calling for major increases in expenditures—are "cut out all the fat," "get rid of the frills," "learn to do with less." Few people are capable of seeing the budget as a whole. Each of us from our own vantage point sees the great needs that government fulfills for us but rarely do we have the same perspective for services that benefit

TABLE 10–3 New York State Expenditures for Fiscal 1961–62 and Fiscal 1971–72 Compared. Federal Payments Distributed Through the States Are Included.

(in thousands of dollars)

	1961–62	1971–72 Recommended Expenditures
General Government	135,592	542,083
Education	1,028,741	4,478,613
State Univ.	29,672	491,300
All other	999,069	3,987,313
Health	405,137	1,547,937
Highways and Highway Safety	570,091	1,649,014
Public Welfare	449,630	3,175,733
Services to Agriculture, Business, and Labor	164,063	292,599
Natural Resources and Recreation	59,764	355,075
Public Safety	94,432	345,194
Nonallocated General Funds	7,322	109,910

SOURCE: *State of New York Executive Budget for Fiscal Year April 1, 1971 to March 31, 1972.*

others. The governor is in a better position to see the total budget picture since he is the highest elected official who has the entire state as his constituency.

Frequently political expedience rather than any other criterion determines what will be cut and what will receive the full share. Public universities felt the political backlash of demonstrations on campus in 1969 and 1970 in their budget appropriations in 1970 and 1971. Welfare suffered in many states as the middle class reacted to political actions of the poor. Reactions made in haste may have unfortunate consequences. In our society, however, it is the citizenry who must make their voices heard and politicians who must interpret these cries and set priorities. The economist may suggest the tools for achieving goals and project the possible consequences of action, but he has no claim on determining values and priorities.

Raising the Necessary Revenues

New York state has one of the most progressive tax structures in the country. Thirty-nine percent of its state income is derived from a highly progressive income tax. Rates started at 2 percent and climbed to 14 percent with a flat deduction of $10 or $25 for single or married taxpayers, making it even more progressive. A 3 percent sales tax and fees bring in 34 percent. Both are regressive, but they are made more palatable by excluding store-purchased food, medical supplies, and services such as health services. Business pays the major portion of the remaining income.

Local government's units receive their tax revenues from the property tax and sales taxes that can range up to 3 percent. While both these taxes tend to be regressive, the 64 percent of state income redirected back to local governments came from a mildly progressive system. This revenue sharing provided directed aid to schools, colleges, and welfare and unrestricted aid on a per capita basis.

With expenditures for the next year set at well over $1 billion more than revenue, what alternatives did Governor Rockefeller have?

The Dilemma

New York state in many ways is a model to the nation in providing opportunities for all its people. Its expenditures per capita for education, health, highways, conservation, recreation, and welfare are among the highest in the country. Providing these benefits may attract the disadvantaged, offering greater hope and opportunities for upward mobility.

To pay for these services New Yorkers pay the highest combined state and local taxes in the country. In 1969 they were 61 percent higher than the mean for all states and 161 percent higher than Arkansas, which had the lowest per capita tax. Those in the upper income brackets are particularly hard hit because of the sharp progressive rates. In addition New York City has its own progressive income tax, and a payroll tax on nonresidents who work in the city. Can New York continue to raise its taxes? Figure 10–6 suggests what might happen.

Twice during the 1960's total revenue from excise taxes on cigarettes declined as tax increases encouraged smokers to smuggle cigarettes into the state. If income tax rates are increased to rates above 17 percent (including surcharges) will those in the highest tax bracket move to Connecticut or New Jersey where there are no state personal income taxes (although they are being proposed)? Will businesses move out if an additional 2 percent is levied on them? Can state taxes

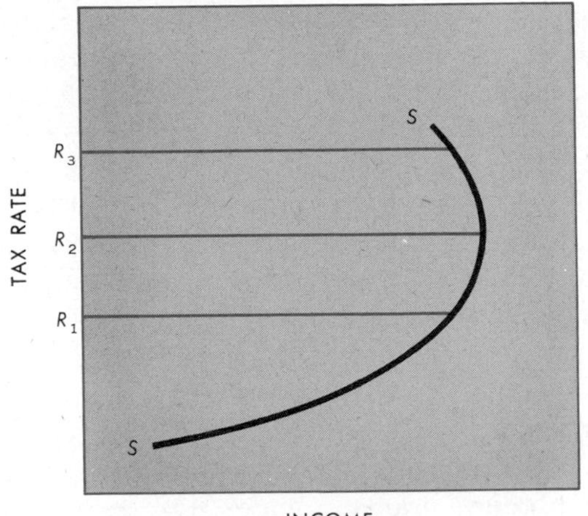

FIGURE 10–6 Possible Effect of Raising Taxes

The supply curve is elastic up to R_1. When the rate continues to increase, some people may move to states with lower taxes or be less motivated to earn extra income, resulting in **S** becoming inelastic. At R_3 the tax rate has become so oppressive that total tax revenues actually decline.

become inelastic and finally backward-bending as their rate increases? If the answer is *yes* to these questions, New York state will find itself in the most critical financial crisis in its history.

Revenue Sharing

One method to ease the crisis is revenue sharing, urged by Governor Rockefeller and recommended by President Nixon. Originally recommended by Professor Walter Heller, chairman of President Kennedy's Council of Economic Advisers, this system would grant a sum of money to state and local governments to spend as they see fit. Labeled a new federalism and appealing because it gives local control of disposition of funds, revenue sharing offers financial hope to the industrialized states which pay to the federal government far more than they receive.

Actually the federal government has been providing grants to states under various programs for many years. In fiscal 1972 the amount budgeted was $11 billion. However, all of this money was earmarked for specific functions and gave the local and state governments little choice for determining priorities. Under this "New American Revolution," the determination of how resources will be allocated will be placed close to the people where they can make their influence felt. Figure 10–7 shows the growth in federal aid to state and local governments with the category of general revenue sharing introduced for 1971–72.

For New York and all industrialized areas, revenue sharing would mean a somewhat better return on their federal tax dollar. Rural communities that have benefited from the redistribution through

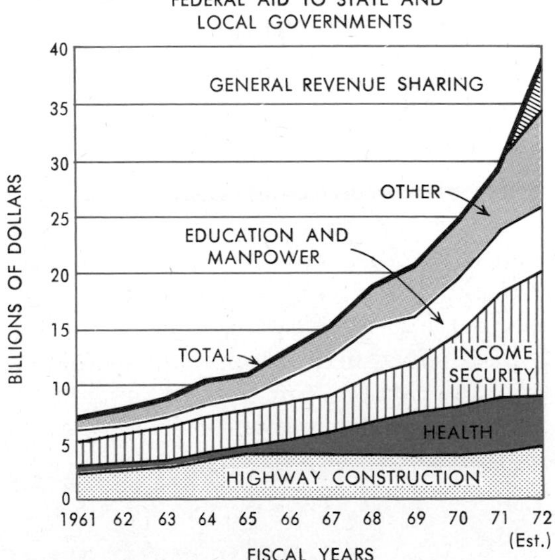

FIGURE 10–7 Suggested Revenue Sharing for President Nixon's Fiscal 1972 Budget

SOURCE: Executive Office of the President, Bureau of the Budget.

federal programs would lose some of their present advantage.

Criticism of the Plan

Opposition to revenue sharing has come from many sources with dissimilar interests. Organized labor denounced the plan because no federal standards would have to be met and discrimination at local and state levels could harm disadvantaged groups. Rural groups complained it would continue the trend of shifting resources away from them and would only aggravate the problems created by urbanization. Many groups pointed out the greater corruption and less able administrative talent at the lower levels of government. Wilbur Mills, Chairman of the Ways and Means Committee, pointed to the danger of having insufficient accountability if federal funds were allocated to the states with no strings attached. Some economists projected that in the long run the greater bill would have to be paid primarily by the richer states, even though they may have a short-term gain in the beginning.

Alternatives

Since the pressure on Congress to find some solution to help the financial crisis facing our cities and states is intense, several plans are being considered. A simple, yet highly effective, plan is for the federal government to institute a national welfare program. Since this is the fastest-growing expense in industrialized areas, it would bring immediate relief to the expenditure side of the state and city budgets. It could also set a national minimum welfare level, to discourage mobility of the poor who now move to areas where they can get more adequate family payments.

Another plan is to allow taxpayers to get credit on their federal income tax for payments made to the state and local governments. At present these taxes are only deducted from gross income, not subtracted from federal taxes. Other critics call for merely increasing the size of present federal grants.

Probable Outcome

It is likely that no single solution will be forthcoming and that the problem will not be solved in the near future. However, in deciding what course to take, the economist must ask the following questions:

1. How will each plan influence the allocation of our resources, both human and material?
2. Will the possible distortion of the market mechanism help to achieve any of our economic goals? At what cost?
3. Will the provision for short-term answers create greater long-term problems?
4. What will these plans for reallocation of resources do to incentive?

These and other questions remain to be answered.

REVIEW: THE HIGHLIGHTS OF THE CHAPTER

1. The largest portion of federal revenues comes from income taxes, both personal and corporation.
2. State revenue is obtained mainly from sales taxes, gasoline taxes, income taxes, business taxes, fees, and grants from the federal government.

3. Property taxes and state grants are the major sources of revenue for local governments.
4. Federal taxes are mildly progressive, whereas state and local taxes are mildly regressive. Much can be done to improve our tax system.
5. The public debt stems from government borrowing to make up the difference between its revenues and expenditures. The tremendous increase in the size of the debt has been a source of concern and controversy.
6. The major portion of the federal debt is the result of international conflicts.
7. The private debt has expanded faster than the public debt.
8. While a large public debt can have adverse consequences, so long as its growth is accompanied by increases in the national income and it is managed carefully, it need not cause great concern.
9. Controversy exists over whether the federal government should increase its sharing of revenue with state and local governments.

IN CONCLUSION: SOME AIDS TO UNDERSTANDING

Terms for Review

taxable income
personal property tax
taxpayer's exemption
double taxation
standard allowable deduction

sales tax
evasion
public debt
internal debt
excise tax

estate tax
federal debt
avoidance
employment tax
revenue sharing

Questions for Review

1. How does the U.S. personal income tax help to equalize our distribution of wealth? Why do some find it unfair?
2. What are some of the fiscal problems of local governments? Why do many of them need federal or state aid? Why are some of their present tax systems inadequate?
3. From your reading you undoubtedly recognize the need of the various levels of government for taxes.
   (a) What are the major sources of taxes for the federal government, state governments, and local governments?
   (b) What are the main advantages and disadvantages of each tax?
4. According to the criteria you have learned for evaluating taxes, what are the major weaknesses in the American tax system?
5. When the government is in need of additional funds, why does it often borrow money rather than print it or raise taxes?
6. What changes have taken place in the size of the net public and private debt since 1945? How do the changes in federal spending compare with changes in

the GNP over the same period? What conclusions may be drawn from this information?

7. Why are most economists not alarmed at the sharp increase in our public debt?
8. How would revenue sharing affect your state?

Additional Questions and Problems

1. Indicate the arguments you would use to a legislative committee to secure special tax privileges for athletes, performers, and authors. In your discussion it might be helpful to consider the tax laws on depletion allowances to producers of oil and gas.
2. Study the most recent federal income tax form and instruction booklet. Make a critical evaluation of the tax, explaining why you consider certain portions to be fair or unfair.
3. Evaluate the corporation income tax, the estate tax, the sales tax, and real estate taxes in terms of the benefit theory and the ability-to-pay theory.
4. Study the tax system in your state, and evaluate its fairness and its adequacy in providing revenues. By what other means does your state raise money? What improvements, if any, might be made in these methods?
5. Public and private debt have certain similarities, but they also have very basic differences.
   (a) Differentiate clearly between the borrowing done by the public sector and that done by the private sector.
   (b) Why could it be said that borrowing by the public sector cannot be judged without specific reference to the nation's GNP?
6. Develop a list of criteria for use in determining the need for public ownership. According to your criteria,
   (a) which areas should the government move out of or into?
   (b) what circumstances might cause you to alter your decisions?
7. Study the fiscal situation of your local government. What are the major needs? Are the current means of raising revenues adequate? If not, what changes might be made to improve the system?

SELECTED READINGS

Bernstein, Peter L. and Robert L. Heilbroner. *A Primer on Government Spending.* New York: Random House, 1968.

Break, George F. *Intergovernmental Fiscal Relations in the United States.* Washington, D.C.: Brookings Institution, 1967.

Eckstein, Otto. *Public Finance.* Englewood Cliffs, N.J.: Prentice-Hall, 1967.

Hamovitch, William. *The Federal Deficit: Fiscal Imprudence or Policy Weapon?* Boston: D. C. Heath and Company, 1965.

Heller, Walter. *New Dimensions in Political Economy.* New York: W. W. Norton & Co., 1967.

Levy, Michael and Juan de Torres. *Federal Revenue Sharing with the States, Problems and Promises.* Washington, D. C.: Brookings Institution, 1970.

Maxwell, James A. *Financing State and Local Governments.* Washington, D.C.: Brookings Institution, 1969.

May, R. J. *Federalism and Fiscal Adjustment.* New York: Oxford University Press, 1969.

Ott, David J. and Attiat F. Ott. *Federal Budget Policy.* Washington, D.C.: Brookings Institution, 1969.

Peckman, Joseph A. *Federal Tax Policy.* Revised Edition. New York: W. W. Norton & Co., 1971.

The Consumer and His Role in the American Economy 11

THE AUTHORS' NOTE TO THE STUDENT

The purpose of production is primarily to satisfy consumer wants. In theory, it is the consumer who provides answers to the questions of what to produce and how to allocate the resources needed for production. However, consumers' choices are limited in a number of ways—by their individual incomes, by imperfect competition, and by psychological and social pressures that influence their demands. The needs of consumers in poor countries are quite different from those in rich countries like our own.

In this chapter we will see what role the consumer is supposed to play in the classical model and what forces in our society have placed limits on his power. We will then consider whether the consumer needs protection and, if so, what kind of protection. Particular attention will be given to inequality of income, demand creation, and consumer credit.

A STUDENT'S NOTE TO THE STUDENT

This is an easy and fast-reading chapter unless you get bogged down with the Lorenz curve. While it is light on theory, many of us found the subject not only relevant but offering immediate and practical help. The most enjoyable part was not in the book but in the answers to specific questions raised in class, for example, steps in shopping for the best loan and the discussion on the value of advertising.

There were a couple of "Nader's Raiders" in class and I have to admit that they made a lot of sense. However, in spite of what they said, I still think the consumer has to bear the ultimate responsibility. I do realize how advertising can "brainwash" you and I'm no exception, but I also realize that my best kicks usually come when I'm not practical. Don't ask me to be rational all the time when I part with my very limited resources.

Part A
The Consumer and His Sovereignty

The Consumer's Role in the Classical Model

Adam Smith, the chief architect of the classical model, used the principle of *consumer sovereignty* as the foundation of his entire system. He wrote, "Consumption is the sole end and purpose of all production," and he had no sympathy with systems that favored the producers. Consumers go to the market to buy the goods and services they want. Business listens and sets production according to consumer preferences. The question of *What?* is answered by the consumer. In answering the *What?* the consumer is also influencing the allocation of resources.

Because consumers, individually and collectively, have limited resources (incomes) and unlimited wants, they will have to make choices. In making choices they seek to maximize their total satisfaction. Because each consumer knows best what will provide him with the greatest satisfaction of his wants, there should be no restraints on having him register his demands except where he may harm others. The idea that the individual, rather than the society collectively, should determine the *What* is fundamental to the classical tradition. The reasoning is that if each individual can maximize his own satisfactions, then the entire society will do the same.

Many economists believe that time and experience have made clear a flaw in this last argument, called the "fallacy of composition." They believe that what is true for the individual is *not* necessarily true for all society. Conversely, what is true for the society as a whole is not necessarily true for every individual within it.

Defining Needs

If consumers are to determine individually the *What*, they do so by deciding what their needs or wants are. The individual consumer's identification of his own needs, if done without any qualifications, can present problems. Some people have little experience and poor judgment in shopping. Money is sometimes spent on gambling, drinking, and lavish entertainment at the expense of providing necessities for oneself and family. In an affluent society like ours, wants are sometimes created as businesses seek to boost sales. Frequent style changes create quick obsolescence, and advertising influences wants that are in no way related to survival or, in many instances, to physical comfort.

Some people believe that in a society where needs go far beyond physical survival, consumers should have protection from themselves and others. Others think that consumers identify only their selfish, short-run needs and give little thought to the collective good of the society. They point to the failure to approve school bond issues at a time when purchases of luxuries are increasing.

Before doing away with consumer sovereignty, it might be wise to consider whom you will allow to decide the *What*. Undoubtedly consumers make errors, but they also learn from their mistakes. What group would you trust more?

Limitations on Consumer Sovereignty

In a mature, predominantly private-enterprise economy like our own, three factors limit the sovereignty of the consumer and the possibility of satisfying his needs completely. These factors are: (1) the distribution of personal income, (2) demand creation by business, and (3) imperfect competition. These conditions all have the effect of placing limits on the consumer. Each deserves our consideration.

The Distribution of Personal Income

A family's consumption is dependent on its income, its savings, and its credit. Of the three, income is the most important and is the major factor in determining what the other two will be. Since spending is usually adjusted to current income and expectations of future income, we need to know the characteristics of personal income to understand the consumer better.

Critics of capitalism usually concede that total wealth and total income in the United States are high. They concede that average income is high, but they say this is not a true picture of how people are actually living because the great concentration of wealth among a few distorts the average. How true is this statement?

In Chapter 20 we will take a close look at poverty, its characteristics and how to deal with it. Here we are concerned only with income distribution and how it may influence consumer spending.

Distribution of Family Income

Table 11–1 shows the changes which have taken place in the distribution of family income in selected years from 1947 to 1968. Compare the percentage of consumer units for each level of income in 1947 with that of the corresponding income level in 1968. What changes do you find in the number of units and the percentage at the various levels? The fact that vast inequalities of income remain, in spite of the trends just observed, is

TABLE 11–1 Money Income—Percent Distribution of Families, by Income Level, 1947 to 1968

		Income Level (percent distribution)										Median	
Year	Total	Under $1,000	$1,000–$1,999	$2,000–$2,999	$3,000–$3,999	$4,000–$4,999	$5,000–$5,999	$6,000–$6,999	$7,000–$9,999	$10,000–$14,999	$15,000 and over	Income	Index (1947 = 100)
All Families*													
1947	100.0	10.8	16.6	22.0	19.7	11.6	7.7	8.9	8.9	2.7	2.7	$3,031	100
1950	100.0	11.5	13.2	17.8	20.7	13.6	9.0	5.2	5.3	3.3	3.3	3,319	110
1955	100.0	7.7	9.9	11.0	14.6	15.4	12.7	9.5	12.9	4.8	1.4	4,421	146
1960	100.0	5.0	8.0	8.7	9.8	10.5	12.9	10.8	20.0	10.6	3.7	5,620	185
1965	100.0	2.9	6.0	7.2	7.7	7.9	9.3	9.5	24.2	17.7	7.6	6,957	230
1967	100.0	2.1	4.4	6.0	6.3	6.5	7.8	8.3	24.3	22.4	12.0	7,974	263
1968	100.0	1.8	3.4	5.1	6.1	6.0	6.9	7.6	23.4	25.0	14.7	8,632	285

* Families as of March of following year. Prior to 1960, excludes Alaska and Hawaii. Figures rounded to nearest tenth of a percent.

SOURCE: Department of Commerce.

evident in that more than 36.9 percent of the units had incomes under $7,000 a year, whereas almost 40 percent were over $10,000.

Lorenz Curve

One method of determining inequality of income distribution is by using the *Lorenz curve.* On the horizontal axis of Figure 11–1 we find the percentage of family units, and on the vertical axis the percentage of total personal income. If income were distributed with absolute equality, 20 percent of the family units would have 20 percent of the income, 40 percent of the family units would have 40 percent of the income, and we would eventually have a diagonal line.

However, since our lowest 20 percent of family units receive only 5.7 percent of the income, the lowest 40 percent only 18.1 percent, and so on, we find the income curve dropping below the diagonal. Figure 11–1 shows the distribution of personal income in the United States using the Lorenz curve for 1935–36 and for 1968. The fact that the distribution curve is closer to the diagonal line of perfect equality indicates the trend toward more equal distribution. Although too little evidence is available for us to draw firm conclusions, it appears that industrialized countries with more mixed economies than ours—such as Sweden, Israel, and Australia—have a more equal distribution of personal income, while greater inequality seems to prevail in less-developed countries.

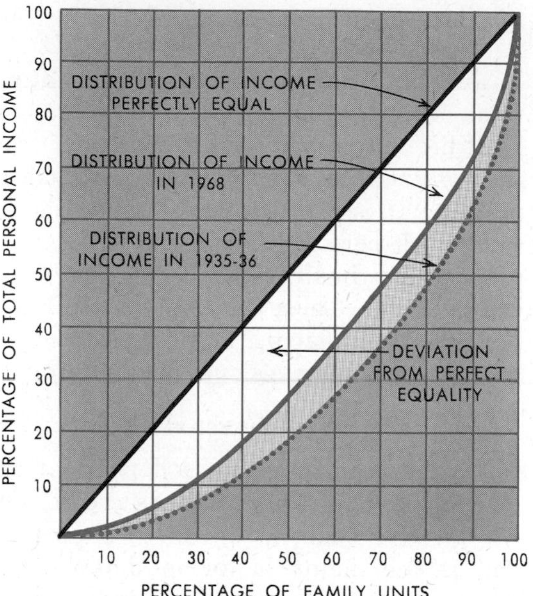

FIGURE 11–1 Lorenz Curve

The 45° line shows what perfect equality of distribution would look like. The Lorenz curve shows the degree of inequality in the distribution of personal income. SOURCE: U.S. Department of Commerce, Office of Business Economics.

Dividing Personal Income

The question of the distribution of personal income is a matter of individual values that the citizens of each country must decide for themselves. Socialists in Western Europe and in this country have advocated government ownership of basic industries and greater services by government as a means of creating a more nearly equal standard of living. However, the general rise in personal income, with even the lowest incomes more nearly adequate than in former years, has greatly reduced the appeal of the socialist argument in our country.

Income Differences and the Existence of Poverty

Even though there has been a trend toward equalization of income, inequality still exists.

There can be little doubt that this inequality has a major effect on consumer purchases in kind, quantity, and, through the viscous cycle of poverty, on income and credit for spending. Differences exist between geographic regions with the Middle Atlantic, North Central and Far Western states having significantly higher personal incomes than the South and the Mountain states. We noted earlier the substantial differences among occupations, but even within occupations there are major variations due to differences of ability and discrimination. Minority groups in particular have been hurt as they go to the marketplace to sell their factors and they are equally hurt as they buy in the production market when seeking credit or purchasing in the ghettos. Those in the lowest fifth of income received have their consumer sovereignty reduced not only by having fewer dollars but by such factors as the markets they may buy in, the credit they may need, and the information and power needed to be an effective shopper.

Impact of Inflation

The voices of the poor, complaining about merchants charging excessively high prices, were weak and almost unheard until 1969. Then, when many saw prices rising faster than earnings, a number of housewives took to the picket lines. The consumer movement, which can be traced back to the New Deal, was given another big push. This time, however, almost everyone seemed involved because almost everyone was hurt in some way.

Few economists would attribute the major cause of the inflation on any sudden change in the pricing practices of business or greater disregard for the consumers. Interest in consumer protection with accompanying legislation started growing sharply under President Kennedy when prices were relatively stable. It increased largely through the efforts of Ralph Nader and his investigation into the automobile industry. The concern and efforts of two well-known, articulate, and attractive women, Betty Furness and Bess Myerson Grant, gave the movement national coverage. The legislation and enforcement that emerged were probably more important for those with the smallest income, not only because their dollars have greater marginal utility than those of higher income groups but because they have fewer opportunities to protect themselves as consumers.

Part B
The Relation of Demand Creation to Consumer Spending

How Personal Income Is Spent

In an economy as wealthy as our own, less than half of the consumer's dollar is spent on food, clothing, and shelter. While poor countries concern themselves with producing enough to provide the bare necessities of life for their people, business in our country devotes a great deal of its energy to stimulating consumer demand for things that the consumer could get along without, and in some instances would not have thought about if no effort were made to whet his appetite. We will consider how the American consumer spends his money and what is done to increase his demand.

There may be found countless individual

variations in the ways families spend money. Each family tries to maximize its satisfactions with the income it has available. Since needs and tastes differ, budgets also differ. Speaking generally, poor families spend most of their income on food, housing, and medical care and very little on recreation. As income goes up, the expenditures for recreation, education, and household equipment increase more rapidly. Money spent for food, housing, and clothing must not be thought of as including only necessities. Eating in fine restaurants, having homes with central air conditioning, and owning clothes for formal affairs are a far cry from meeting the needs for survival. On the other hand we must be careful when we use the word "necessity." The clothing needed and purchased by a teacher is different from that of a factory worker, although their incomes may be the same. The junior executive may have a difficult time explaining to a $7,000-a-year employee that he cannot make ends meet even though he is earning $15,000 a year. However, to the executive, some things are necessities that to other people would be luxuries.

The United States Department of Commerce has analyzed the personal consumption expenditures of the American people for 1969. This analysis is shown in Figure 11–2. It should be pointed out that it is very difficult to place certain expenditures in a simplified distribution like this. The cost of food includes charges for the processing of the food so that the housewife does less of the preparation. Beverages and tobacco are included as food costs. Many appliances are included in the cost of housing. Durable goods—those things that do not need to be replaced after each use and which last for a considerable time—make up an increasing percentage of our total budgets. Because consumers can make automobiles, appliances, and other durable goods last an extra year or more, the demand for these products fluctuates considerably. Those businesses connected with the production and sale of durable goods must create demand in the mind of the consumer, if none already exists.

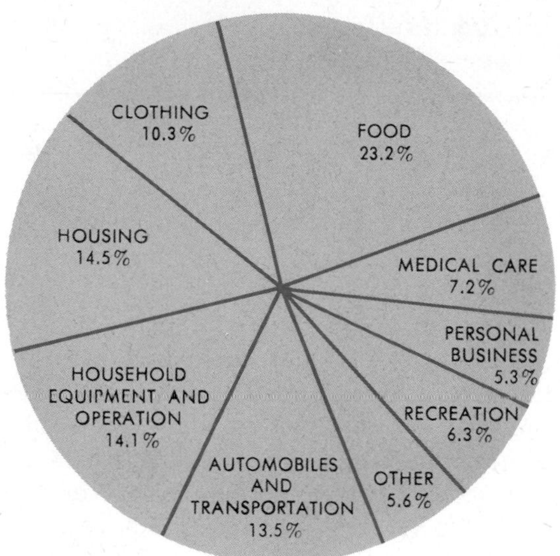

FIGURE 11–2 Personal Consumption Expenditures

As personal income increases, the percentage of income spent for food declines whereas the percentage of income spent for recreation increases. SOURCE: U.S. Department of Commerce, Office of Business Economics.

Advertising: A Key to Demand Creation

Thorstein Veblen, an economist and sociologist (see p. 201) at the University of Chicago at the beginning of the twentieth century, studied the spending habits of the American people. He observed that the rich tried to demonstrate their superiority by their extravagant purchases. He called buying expensive things for show *conspicuous consumption.* He observed that this practice occurred at all levels of income. Today we often refer to this prac-

TABLE 11–2 Personal Consumption Expenditures by Type of Product or Service

(millions of dollars)

Product or Service	1929	1939	1947	1958	1969*	1969 % of total
Food and Tobacco	21,239	20,916	56,089	82,363	131,900	23.2
Clothing, Accessories, and Jewelry	11,193	8,406	22,760	31,911	59,400	10.3
Personal Care	1,116	1,004	2,225	5,031	9,700	1.7
Housing	11,530	9,139	15,665	41,127	84,000	14.5
Household Operation	10,735	9,624	23,989	42,275	81,500	14.1
Medical Care	2,937	2,848	6,897	16,472	41,600	7.2
Personal Business	4,158	3,313	5,426	12,768	30,800	5.3
Transportation	7,612	6,365	15,172	35,634	78,000	13.5
Recreation	4,331	3,452	9,249	15,817	36,300	6.3
Private Education and Research	664	620	1,243	3,140	9,700	1.7
Religious and Welfare Activities	1,196	938	1,984	4,178	8,200	1.4
Foreign Travel and Other (net)	511	209	5	1,824	4,300	.7
Total Personal Consumption Expenditures	77,222	66,834	160,704	292,540	575,400	100.0

* Death expenses amounting to $2,100,000,000 and 0.4% of the budget are not included.

SOURCE: U.S. Department of Commerce, Office of Business Economics.

tice, especially as it affects the average family, as "keeping up with the Joneses." Read the advertisements for luxury cars and note the appeal to social status. When an advertisement says "Move up to ——," the implication is that you will enjoy more prestige. In some circles a mink coat means that the wearer "has arrived." Paintings, jewelry, and even collections of books are bought because the "best" people have these things. The assumption is that purchasing these prestige items will make you one of the "best" people.

Built-in Obsolescence

Automobile and appliance manufacturers may work hard to improve their product, but they know that style changes, along with new gadgets, will make the consumer consider his present model obsolete. This built-in obsolescence puts pressure, primarily of a social nature, on the consumer to trade in a product still in good condition for a new one. The entire structure of the market in several fields is based on "trade-ins" and "moving up." The greatest appeal of this technique is to the middle class and to a newly rich group, both characterized by social and economic mobility, to whom "status symbols" are visible evidence of their progress. People at the lowest economic level cannot afford to play this "game," while those long established at the upper economic level do not have to play it.

The Case for Advertising

Changes in hair styling and clothing, colors for decorating, and even new packaging give the "new look." The consumer is bombarded by all the media of mass communication—by $20 billion worth of advertising in 1970—over five times the amount spent in 1947. The advertising agencies, using information that psychologists have provided on the suggestibility of man, have used advertising to limit consumer sovereignty; they have thereby placed a powerful weapon in the hands of the producer. This change has somewhat altered the consumer's position from what is called for in the classical model, but this is not necessarily a disadvantage. As we will learn in Chapter 13, a mature capitalistic economy must at various times stimulate consumer demand in order to avoid a depression. This stimulus to consumer demand can come from government; it can also come from business. Advertising is business' way of stimulating consumer demand. If that demand is allowed to decline, production will fall off and so will jobs, because the income that consumers need in order to make their purchases will no longer be available.

As a means of providing information to the consumer, advertising can be looked upon both favorably and unfavorably. Proponents point out the need for advertising to acquaint the public with the existence of new products and improvements in older products. How does the businessman let the public know that he has something special to sell? If we want to sell our "Build-a-City" sets, we can send salesmen to retailers and leave to them the initiative for selling our sets. However, let us suppose that retailers are not advertising or that they hesitate to take on a new and untried product. By advertising we go directly to the consumer to inform him of our game and create a demand. Consumers can then request that retailers have "Build-a-City" sets in stock.

The Case Against Advertising

Critics of advertising point out that the great expense of advertising can be met only by large, established firms. Introducing a new product requires more money than a small producer can afford. Big advertising campaigns, aimed at *product differentiation*, lead the public to think that only the "name brands" can be trusted, since they are the only ones that have "zing" in them. This belief leads to imperfect competition, limiting consumer choices.

Other criticisms of advertising include the waste of money, since no real value is added to the product; distortion of values through television and radio; and creation of consumer demand for such things as tobacco, beer, and patent medicines. Testimony taken before a Senate investigating committee revealed that the drug industry spends more on advertising than it does on research. Critics also question the real value to the consumer of the information he is given in advertisements.

Advertising as a Part of Our Economy

Many of the criticisms of advertising are undoubtedly true for particular cases, but they need not be so for advertising in general. There is a need for the advertising industry, as for many other segments of our economy, to take stock of its code of ethics. The government has already taken steps to control certain kinds of advertisements through the Food and Drug Administration. Self-policing by business will avoid additional government controls.

In an economy where more than half of consumer purchases are for things not necessary for survival, creation of demand through advertising may be an important means of keeping business on an even level. There is little likelihood of a decline in its importance.

The Relation of Imperfect Competition to Demand Creation

Consumers' choices are limited and impeded by having markets with less than pure competition. When new firms find it difficult to introduce their products into the market either by not being allowed to enter the market or by not being able to let the consumer know about their product, progress is stifled and the consumer must take what the few large firms have to offer.

"Fair-Trade" Laws

In the 1930's a new method of pricing was introduced as a means of helping the small businessman. This practice, known as *retail price maintenance*, allowed the manufacturer to set the retail price at which his products would be sold. It prevented retailers from cutting prices on established products. During the Depression, several states passed legislation, known as "fair-trade" laws, to enforce the practice of retail price maintenance. These laws were a benefit to manufacturers, who feared that price-cutting might cheapen a product in the eyes of the consumer.

More important politically was the fact that such legislation protected the small businessman from possible price-cutting by chain stores and large department stores. Large companies could afford to sell items at a lower price because of their more efficient operation. When fair-trade laws were first passed, small business was a larger employer than it is today. Unemployment was a greater source of wasting our resources than was the poor allocation of our resources because of artificially maintained prices. Because chain stores were prohibited from price-cutting, more consumers would patronize small businesses. Increased sales kept small business active and maintained employment at a higher level.

It is hard for consumers to see anything fair in legislation that compels them to pay higher prices. On items covered by the law, prices are generally far lower in states without fair-trade laws than in those with them. There is no convincing evidence that small businesses do appreciably better in states with these laws than in states without them.

The Miller-Tydings Act in 1937 and the McGuire Act in 1952 gave the support of the federal government to fair-trade laws. Pressure by several manufacturing groups won approval for this legislation in spite of the disapproval of the federal administrative agencies most directly concerned and of labor, farm, and consumer groups. What these groups could not do is now being done by the spread of discount stores througnout the country. Some economists believe that where these stores appear, retail competition is approaching what the classical model envisioned, and the consumer is once again placed on his throne. In rural areas, mail-order businesses have increased competition and helped to reduce prices.

Part C
Consumer Credit—A Factor in Demand

Consumer Savings

Personal savings and *consumer credit* have an important effect on consumption. Since saving is the opposite of consumption, an increase in one will, for a given income, result in a decrease in the other. Consumer credit allows the consumer to expand his consumption without having to gear his buying strictly to his savings or income. In a mature economy like our own, demand creation is important. It is doubtful, though, whether demand could be expanded without consumer credit.

What Determines Savings

Consumer saving usually varies according to income. Families are able to increase the percentage of income saved as income rises. Savings for all families in our country also fluctuate with the national income, increasing as income increases. During the Depression of the thirties savings dropped so low that in 1932 and 1933 people actually spent more than their incomes, resulting in dissavings. During World War II, when incomes went up but consumer goods were in short supply, savings amounted to over 20 percent of take-home pay. Since 1951 the proportion of consumers' savings to their disposable personal income has been quite consistent, about 7 percent. Occasionally savings increase significantly. During the third quarter of 1970 the rate rose to 9 percent and probably contributed to the slowdown in the economy.

What Constitutes Savings

By savings we do not mean merely the money deposited in a savings bank, stored in a vault, or hidden under a mattress. Money paid on a life insurance policy or invested in stocks or bonds, or even mortgage payments which go beyond interest and depreciation are considered in the same category. Most families like to have a reserve of some kind. It provides a buffer for emergencies, and it gives the family additional security.

How Savings Are Held

In considering where to put savings, the consumer should consider *safety*, how quickly and easily they can be converted to cash (*liquidity*), the *rate of interest*, and how they will *fluctuate* with prices. Usually, no one form of savings can be strong in all these characteristics. Deposits in savings accounts provide safety and liquidity, but they usually yield a relatively low return and they do not give protection against sharp price rises. Stocks are not so safe, particularly if the owner does not have a long period of time to convert them into cash. However, they are more likely to yield a higher rate of return and give better protection against inflation than other forms of savings. Most consumer economists recommend diversifying savings so that changing conditions will never place the family in too difficult a position. However, each family has to determine how its own best interests will be served.

Changes in Habits of Saving

In recent years, savings have become less of an immediate factor in altering consumer decisions. This has come about because of the tremendous availability of consumer credit.[1] At one time families usually delayed purchases until they had the entire purchase price put aside. Some consumers feel that it is immoral to "buy on time" or to use credit because it is spending money that does not belong to them. It was not until the twentieth century, and primarily in the United States, that large-scale consumer credit became an acceptable and integral part of consumer behavior.

Growth of Consumer Credit

Consumer credit, not including mortgages, has increased from $5.6 billion in 1945 to

[1] The anti-inflationary policy of the Federal Reserve Board and the government in 1969–70 temporarily reversed the trend for credit expansion.

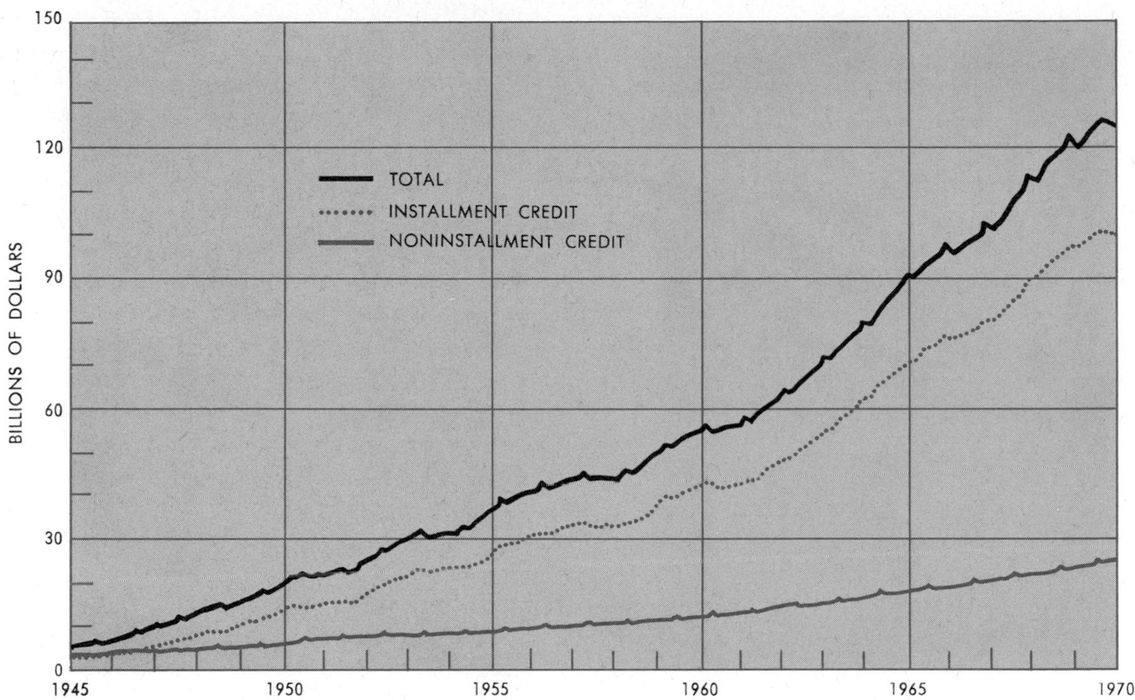

FIGURE 11–3 Short- and Intermediate-Term Consumer Credit Outstanding

SOURCE: Federal Reserve System, *Historical Chart Book.*

$123 billion in 1970. This almost twenty-twofold increase has expanded much faster than the increase in incomes. In 1945 consumer credit amounted to only 3.8 percent of disposable income, whereas in 1970 it had increased to over 17 percent. The largest portion of this increase was in *installment credit,* which differs from other consumer credit in allowing the seller to repossess the article purchased if the buyer defaults on payment. This practice involves greater risks for repayment because the article purchased loses value as it is used. More than a third of installment credit is granted for automobile purchases. Noninstallment credit is made up of charge accounts, service credit, and single-payment loans. All of these have increased from three to five times in the last 20 years. Installment credit makes up about three fourths of consumer credit. About 40 percent of installment credit is held by commercial banks, with sales finance companies, retail outlets, and other financial institutions making up the rest.

How Credit Affects the Consumer

The availability of credit has led to new patterns of consumer spending. Credit has the appearance of extending the range of choices open to the consumer. However, many people question whether use of credit always permits the consumer to exercise choice most effectively.

Advantages

One of the great difficulties encountered by most young married couples is that their needs are greatest when their incomes are lowest. When the breadwinner has his first job, furnishing an apartment, buying a car, and meeting the costs of raising young children present an overwhelming problem. A washing machine is needed more when children are young than when they grow up and leave home. Why wait and save for the washer when it can be paid for in regular installments while it is being used? Many families must purchase durable goods such as automobiles and appliances by means of installment buying or not at all.

Businessmen are as concerned about the availability of consumer credit as are consumers. They know that a drop in consumer credit can bring significant drops in consumer purchases. Credit frees the consumers from waiting until they have enough savings to allow them to make their purchases.

Some Dangers

There are serious disadvantages to credit. Buying on credit involves extra costs. Interest rates vary, but there have been enough cases reported of total interest costs being greater than the original price of the purchase to serve as a warning to those who borrow. Stores which grant credit are hard pressed to compete in price with those that demand immediate payment for merchandise.

Another danger is that credit lures people into buying things they may not need. Many people are tempted to exceed their financial means when they look only at the amount of the down payment and the size of each month's payment. "No money down and three years to pay" and "For pennies a day you can own a new ——" are catch phrases that get too many American families into debt "over their heads." Consumers can help themselves by

1. Determining what the cost of the credit will be in addition to the original cash price
2. Deciding whether their income is sufficient to carry the payments without too many other sacrifices
3. Shopping for credit as they would for other purchases
4. Reading all the print in credit contracts

Part D
Protecting the Consumer

As we sketched the design of the classical model, we learned that all the people playing a part in it—businessmen, labor, owners of other factors of production, and the consumer—were expected to act independently. Since the system is organized to provide benefits to the consumer, competition rather than cooperation between those within each group was considered essential. We have already pointed out how each of the interest groups has sought collective action to protect itself from others. While labor and management have organized to guard their special interests, the interests of the individual consumer have frequently been neglected. Consumer cooperatives, private consumer agencies, and government have all been used to provide some measure of protection for the consumer. The question remains whether the interests of the consumer are adequately protected within the limits of present practices. Before answering, we must consider

1. Why the consumer needs protection
2. What protection is now available to him
3. What people believe about the adequacy of protection

Why Does the Consumer Need Protection?

Before the big impact of the Industrial Revolution, the consumer had a relatively simple task of making choices and judging quality. Little of the merchandise offered for sale was packaged, so he could see what he was buying; and it was reasonably easy to judge the quality of the few simple items offered for sale. In some instances, if the consumer did not like what he saw, he went home and made the article himself.

Today the consumer finds himself surrounded by hordes of products, packaged in multicolored wrappings in every conceivable shape and size and all claiming to do the best job. The technical considerations necessary to determine quality are well beyond the knowledge of the average consumer. Claims and counterclaims, giveaways, coupons, packaging, and trademarks add confusion to chaos. Determining what is the best appliance, the best fabric, or even the best canned food frequently turns out to be a "hit-and-miss" choice. Making errors on quality and performance may be costly. In most instances the cost is money, performance, or satisfaction; but in some instances it might be health and safety. A poorly wired electrical appliance or a dangerous drug could produce a disaster for the consumer.

Freedom of consumer choices is frequently limited by manufacturers. We have mentioned demand creation and advertising as methods of reducing consumer sovereignty and transferring it to the producer. This tendency has gone so far that some marketing specialists have changed their attitude of giving the consumer what he wants to making the consumer want what they have to offer him. Misleading advertising, imperfect competition, buying by habit, the use of only brand names, and the unorganized position of the consumer in contrast to other groups in our economy have made the need for some kind of consumer protection vital.

What Protection Does the Consumer Now Have?

Although the original objective in the classical model was to benefit the consumer, later influences have interfered with the realizing of that aim. We have seen that some groups concerned with the factors of production, such as labor and management, organized to protect their interests. Organizing for protection became important for consumers, too, especially as created demand and "easy credit" added to the need for protection.

Consumer Cooperatives

Today consumers get protection from both private and public sources. Perhaps the most important outcome of consumers' attempts to organize themselves in order to protect their interests has been the development of *consumer cooperative* stores. Organized by consumers for the purpose of getting good merchandise at reasonable prices, the stores have spread throughout the country. The funds to start and maintain the business are supplied by the membership with a fixed interest rate or are borrowed. Merchandise is then sold at the market price but "profits" are returned to the membership according to their *purchases*. Their appeal has been primarily in rural areas, although labor unions have sometimes encouraged their development in cities.

Private Research Organizations

Two nationally famous private organizations dedicated to protecting the consumer are *Consumers' Research* and *Consumers Union*. Both organization's test and rate products in their laboratories, considering safety, quality, and price. Ratings are given to various brands on the basis of these criteria. Their publications accept no advertising, in contrast to most other periodicals. Attempts have been made to demonstrate that these organizations show favoritism, but these charges have never been proved. While budget limitations, limited samplings, and errors can creep in, these groups provide information valuable in guiding the consumer.

Business

Some retail stores and some producers of particular products set up standards and endorse these products with their name or seal of approval as having met these standards. Giant distributors of merchandise, such as Sears, Roebuck & Company and Macy's department store, have their buyers test products before they acquire merchandise that will carry their name on it. Producers of electrical equipment usually seek to have their products tested to get the seal of the Underwriters' Laboratories placed on their product, indicating that safety requirements have been met. Producers and reliable retail stores will usually stand behind the products they sell, frequently with money-back guarantees. The Better Business Bureaus and chambers of commerce help consumers by searching for frauds which cheat the public. None of these sources helps the consumer determine which products are best, but they do eliminate some dangers to consumers.

Nader's Raiders

The name Ralph Nader has recently become synonymous with consumer protection. As a young lawyer he set out largely on his own to investigate the safety of automobiles. His book *Unsafe at Any Speed* caused the government to become involved in the auto industry and stimulated a surge of interest in the consumer movement. Legislation concerning truth-in-packaging, truth-in-lending, health warnings, and the removal of unsafe products from the market were aided by the movement. Old established agencies such as the Federal Trade Commission seemed to find new interest in guarding the consumer and corporations responded by looking more closely at their products as to their safety and fulfilling their advertising claims.

Nader has caught the imagination of many young people by his unwillingness to capitalize on his notoriety. Young lawyers, economists, and others have gathered around him in this fight to aid the consumer and curb the power of the corporation. Critics have pointed out that he disregards or overlooks the research already underway by corporations, that he does not give a balanced picture in which stockholders have to be considered, and that he refuses to accept offers to work with the companies that he has taken to task. No one, however, can deny the remarkable power shown by one determined and talented person to precipitate reform.

Local and State Governments

Local, state, and federal governments provide the consumer with protection. Local governments protect water purity, sanitation of all places handling food, and safety of buildings through inspections and building codes. State and local governments check scales for accuracy, license many types of workers who perform services, and set up controls over insurance companies, banks, private educational institutions, utility rates, and credit agencies. Some states have an agency to aid consumer protection. Variations between states and units of local government in the protection offered remain so great that some federal action has been called for.

Federal Government

The federal government has passed many laws and set up many agencies designed to aid and protect consumers. The Food and Drug Administration has set up standards to protect the consumer from the introduction of harmful drugs, adulterated foods, faulty labeling, and misleading packaging. The Federal Trade Commission looks to see if unfair trade practices will hurt the consumer. The Federal Communications Commission and the Interstate Commerce Commission have some regulatory controls over rates. The Bureau of Standards and the Department of Agriculture are also concerned with protecting the consumer.

It is estimated that over 400 departments and divisions are involved in the administering of over 1,000 programs related to the consumer.

Part E
The Problem: Does the Consumer Need More Protection?

The Case for More Protection

Although a great deal of progress has been made in protecting the consumer, much remains to be done. Among the reasons for increasing consumer protection are (1) insufficient competition, (2) misleading advertising, (3) artificial demand for unnecessary or even harmful products, (4) deceit in packaging, and (5) introduction of new products not sufficiently tested to be safe beyond question.

What specific safeguards does the consumer need in order to protect his interests? When he buys on the installment plan, he should know in dollars and cents how much the interest carrying charges will be. He should know that the medicines he buys have been adequately tested; he should be able to buy drugs by their generic name rather than brand name, to be able to get them at the lowest price. His food products that are concealed in packaging or are difficult to evaluate should be graded in standardized terms. All food products, whether shipped in interstate or intrastate commerce, should be similarly graded. Heavy penalties should be imposed on all businesses shown to use not only false but also misleading advertising. Plants producing goods that could prove potentially dangerous to the consumer should be subject to regular inspection.

Although some of the above conditions are being regulated and improved under existing law, inadequate funds appropriated to the enforcing agencies have not allowed for proper enforcement. Overlapping supervisory authority has caused confusion. President Nixon has proposed creation within the Executive Department of an Office of Consumer Affairs with facilities to test products and with powers to investigate consumer complaints. Such a proposal would allow for centralizing all activities—research, education, legal recommendations, and enforcement. This may be the only way the consumer will get the protection he needs in this fast-changing and complex world.

The Case Against More Protection

The real and ultimate responsibility for protecting the consumer must rest with the consumer himself. Our political and economic systems assume that the individual in our society is rational and capable of making correct decisions. Given the opportunity for an education, the citizen-consumer is in a reasonable position to know what it is he wants and how he can express his wants. There are ample safeguards furnished by all levels of government, by businesses themselves, and by private agencies. If fraud, negligence, or harmful goods or services hurt the consumer, he has recourse to these agencies as well as to legal action. The individual, both as citizen and as consumer, has means of protecting his interests. However, just as the citizen will get the government he deserves, so the consumer will get the products he deserves.

The alternative to our present system would be a highly regimented society which would pay scant attention to the individual consumer's choices and would have little respect for his ability to determine what he wants. In the planned economy of the Soviet Union, where the *What* is largely determined by an economic planning committee, goods and services do not meet the quality of American standards. The more restrictions we place on the freedom of business to determine what and how it can produce, the less variety we will have in our choice of products.

Allowing business to share in demand creation with the consumer has advantages for everyone. In an affluent society like our own, demand creation is necessary to keep production at a high enough level to provide employment for our work force. Without it, production might very well decline to a serious degree. In addition, business invests great sums of money in the development of new products. Progress does not come exclusively from consumers. It may also be initiated by business, but it is clearly in the interest of all.

The conscientious consumer who shops carefully and makes full use of existing facilities to protect his interests is helping not only himself but the entire economy. By demanding better goods for lower prices he assures the efficient use of our limited resources as well as the introduction of new and better products. These benefits occur because honest and capable businessmen are rewarded, whereas inefficient and wasteful ones are punished. Consumers can be kings in a prosperous society, but this is possible only if they are willing to make choices and to exercise judgment.

Considering an Answer

Just as we have faced other problems, we must also be prepared to answer the question of how much freedom of choice we want. With freedom goes the responsibility of judging, and we must have knowledge if we are to exercise our choices wisely. Can the individual consumer be expected to have sufficient knowledge, in some instances of a technical nature, to make wise decisions? If government takes the first step to aid the consumer by making knowledge available, should it take a second step in advising the consumer on what decisions he should make, and a third step in taking action where the knowledge it has may be to the consumer's advantage? What responsibility has government to protect the consumer who ignores whatever knowledge is available?

In considering answers, we must recognize that a paternalistic government may provide maximum security, but possibly at the expense of individual freedom. However, the price of complete freedom may be the loss of our security. Can you find a plan which would permit a maximum of freedom without endangering our security as consumers and citizens?

REVIEW: THE HIGHLIGHTS OF THE CHAPTER

1. The classical model assumes that the objective of production is consumption. It is the consumer who determines what the production shall be as he registers his wants in the market.
2. Needs of consumers differ. In wealthy nations, a great deal of production is for goods and services not needed for survival.
3. Consumer sovereignty is limited by the distribution of personal income, the creation of demand by business, and imperfect competition.
4. A family's consumption is dependent on income, savings, and credit. The first is the most important. The Lorenz curve, used for measuring distribution of income, shows family unit incomes to be quite unequal. However, incomes tend to be more nearly equal today than they were in the 1930's.
5. Differences in income exist among regions, occupations, people of different abilities and education, and minority groups.
6. The recent inflation hurt all groups and helped stimulate consumer activity. The lowest income groups benefit most by government consumer action because they have no alternatives in the market.
7. In our economy efforts are made, largely through advertising, to create demand among consumers. Some controversy exists as to the benefits of demand creation, particularly for products which critics say are not necessities.
8. Imperfect competition, including legally sanctioned fair-trade laws, limits consumer choices and efficient use of resources.
9. Consumer savings, amounting to approximately 7 percent of disposable personal income, may be kept in a variety of ways, each having particular advantages or disadvantages in safety, liquidity, interest, and stability of value.

10. Consumer credit, which has increased rapidly in the last 20 years, allows consumers to use products while they pay for them. Credit can help consumers and business if used wisely.
11. Controversy exists as to how far the government should go in attempting to protect the consumer and to supervise business.

IN CONCLUSION: SOME AIDS TO UNDERSTANDING

Terms for Review

fair-trade laws
Lorenz curve
durable goods
personal income
installment credit
consumer cooperatives
public assistance
conspicuous consumption
built-in obsolescence
subsistence

Names to Know

Ralph Nader
Consumers Union
Thorstein Veblen
Consumers Research
Miller-Tydings Act
McGuire Act

Questions for Review

1. Evaluate the theory of consumer sovereignty associated with classical capitalism. To what extent does the consumer really guide and direct the American economy?
2. Measured against the values of political equality, the great inequalities of an economic system based on unlimited competition for profit have appeared inconsistent. What is the essential difference between equality of opportunity and equality of income?
3. How does income relate to spending for necessities, spending for nonessentials, and personal savings?
4. Explain the following statements and evaluate their truth:
   (a) Advertising is the lifeblood of producing for consumption through demand creation.
   (b) Advertising may lead to improper waste and excessive cost.
5. List the arguments for and against federal and state laws on fair-trade practices.
6. Describe the role of savings and credit in consumer spending.
7. What are the major factors the consumer should consider in determining the form of his savings?
8. How can buying on credit benefit the consumer? The seller? In what ways may credit buying harm the consumer?
9. Consumers have found it necessary to protect their interests.
   (a) Explain the reasons for the development of laws for consumer protection.
   (b) Defend the continued use of laws to protect the consumer.

(c) What steps have consumers taken to help themselves?
(d) What public and private agencies are available for help?

Additional Questions and Problems

1. Make a study of trends in consumer spending and saving. What percentage of his income is the consumer saving today? Is this percentage different from savings 5 or 10 years ago? If so, what explains the difference? Include data on consumer credit trends in your study.
2. "The ever-expanding role of government in extending fair-trade laws, curbing advertising, controlling credit, and policing by more and more government agencies presents a threat to the democratic capitalist system." Do you agree? Defend your decision.
3. Explain the meaning of the phrase *caveat emptor.* To what extent does it express correctly the philosophy of present marketing and consumption? What recent legislation has been designed to increase consumer protection?

SELECTED READINGS

Aaker, David A. and George S. Day. *Perspectives on Consumerism.* Riverside, N.J.: The Free Press, 1970.

Bell, Carolyn. *Consumer Choice in the American Economy.* New York: Random House, 1967.

Harrington, Michael. *The Other America: Poverty in the United States.* New York: The Macmillan Co., 1970. (Also available in paperback edition: Penguin Books, Baltimore)

McNeal, James U. *Dimensions of Consumer Behavior.* New York: Appleton-Century-Crofts, 1969.

Packard, Vance. *The Hidden Persuaders.* New York: David McKay Co., 1957. (Also available in paperback edition: Pocket Books, New York.)

Troelstrup, Arch W. *The Consumer In American Society: Personal and Family Finance,* 4th ed. New York: McGraw-Hill, 1970.

Waterman, Elizabeth G. *A Primer on the Economics of Consumption.* New York: Random House, 1968.

UNIT III

THE AMERICAN ECONOMY AS A WHOLE

12 Measuring the Nation's Economy

THE AUTHORS' NOTE TO THE STUDENT

This chapter is designed to introduce you to the study of modern macroeconomics, the study of the economy as a whole. Here you will learn what tools the economist uses in evaluating the basic state of the economy. Just as the physician measures the health of a patient by checking many factors, so the economist must look at many indicators to judge whether the economic machine is working properly. When the reports are in, the economist, like the physician, can diagnose and prescribe. Foremost among these tools is a new model to explain the working of our economic system.

The new model we are to examine in Unit III is known by many names—"the new economics," "the new capitalism," "the Keynesian model," and other intriguing titles. Whatever you call it, you should recognize that it is consistent with what we have described as a mixed capitalistic system. It differs from the classical model by approaching the economy from the aggregate, or national, standpoint rather than from the viewpoint of the individual firm or institution, and it modifies and adds to rather than replaces the classical tradition. It is not a different economic system in the sense that socialism or feudalism differs from capitalism. Many economists like to think of it as an extension of classical capitalism designed to meet the problems and conditions of today's world.

A STUDENT'S NOTE TO THE STUDENT

Frankly, I have very mixed feelings about this chapter. I found Part A dull, too much to memorize, but definitely necessary. I guess it's like learning to read music before you can play a piece. The reviewing of the definitions at the end of Part A is a help, and you will probably find yourself turning back to it as you read on.

I enjoyed the section dealing with business cycles and got a kick out of the "sunspot theory." (Don't knock it until you've read it.) Of course, when you are through with all these external and internal causes, you might wonder if we really know more than we did before.

The problem at the end of the chapter is really interesting. It partially makes up for the tedium in Part A. It is easy to fluctuate back and forth as you read each position. I still have strong doubts that we can keep this country humming economically without a war or military spending. When the de-escalation of the Vietnam War started, the unemployment rate went up. Maybe the next chapter will have some better answers.

Part A
National Income Accounting

The National Economy

Frequently, when businessmen and people interested in matters of business gather, conversation turns to a discussion of economic conditions. Although attention may be focused primarily on purely local conditions, broader questions will be raised concerning such topics as unemployment, prices, inventories, the stock market, steel production, and automobile and department store sales. Although such conversation may help to clarify some issues, evaluating overall economic conditions for a country as large and complex as ours is not really a simple task. One segment of our economy may be growing at a time when another segment may be declining. Some producers may be more prosperous than ever at a time when most businessmen are complaining of losses. You may be surprised to learn that a very few businesses did quite well during the Great Depression of the 1930's. Conversely, during its most prosperous times our nation has had more than two hundred business

TABLE 12–1 Major Economic Indicators

	Latest	Year ago	Change
Unemployment (issued monthly in percent of labor force)	6.0	3.9	+5.4%
Industrial Production Index (monthly, base of 1957–59 = 100)	162.6	173.6	−6.3%
Gross National Product (quarterly, in billions)	$985.5	$942.6	+4.5%
Wholesale Price Index (monthly, base of 1957–59 = 100)	117.8	114	+3.3%
Consumer Price Index (monthly, base of 1957–59 = 100)	137.4	129.8	+5.9%
Personal Income (quarterly, in billions)	$807.2	$758.1	+6.5%
Retail Sales (monthly, in millions)	$6,440	$6,229	+3.4%
Installment Debt (monthly, in billions)	$101.2	$98.2	+3%
Standard & Poor's Stock Index (weekly)	97.18	86.46	+12.4%
Raw Steel (monthly, thousands of net tons)	2,622	2,561	+2.3%
Electric Power (millions of kilowatt hours)	31,828	29,519	+7.8%
Rail Freight Traffic (billions of ton miles)	14.7	14.9	−1.4%

A variety of measurements are used in studying economic development and predicting the direction of trends. How would you assess the movement of the economy? SOURCE: *Survey of Current Business*, Department of Commerce, January, February, and March 1971.

Although the growing number and accuracy of measurements provide the economist with more workable data for forecasting, the evaluation and interpretation of such data are often the subject of controversy.

failures a week. However, businessmen know that no matter how well they may be doing at present, they will, in all probability, eventually feel the general trend of the economy. In order to make wise decisions about their own businesses, they must have some knowledge of the economy as a whole. By what means can we determine the direction of economic trends and evaluate their movement?

Keeping Our Records

In order to study economic development, many kinds of information are necessary. It is as essential for a nation to keep records of its economy for evaluation of the past and projection of future progress, as it is for a physician to keep careful records of his patients. It was not until 1929 that the United States Departments of Commerce and Labor started to keep accurate measurements of the nation's economy.

Economists know that measuring particular segments of the economy is comparatively easy. However, for detailed analysis, certain kinds of information are of special value—those concerned with the overall view. We do not want to see only the trees; we want to see the forest, too. In economics, when we examine the economy as a whole, we call the study *macroeconomics.* This approach differs from that of Unit II, where we made a detailed study of individual factors of the economy; study in that perspective is known as *microeconomics.*

Gross National Product: The Basic Measure

In reading reports of the nation's economic condition in a newspaper or magazine, you would very likely encounter the term *gross national product,* or simply GNP. It is the measure most often used to determine how well the economy is faring; it is used by government and business alike in order to determine their future policies and plans. What does GNP include? If the retail prices of all the goods and services produced during the year were added up, the figure arrived at would be the gross national product for that year.

Methods of Figuring GNP

There are three different approaches to determining gross national product. All three will yield the same answer, since each is trying to do the same thing—to measure the total value of goods and services produced in the nation during the year. The first view has already been described: GNP represents the final market price or retail value of all production. This view is easy to understand because it is exactly what GNP says it is—the value of the nation's production, or product, before subtracting anything from the total. Shortly we will be subtracting items from GNP, and the word "gross" will be replaced.

The Expenditure Approach to GNP

It is also possible to look at GNP from the point of view of goods and services bought rather than produced. This method is called the expenditures approach; it records who is buying the goods and services in the marketplace. There are four categories of buyers: (1) individuals buying as households, (2) government, (3) businesses, and (4) foreign purchasers, which we shall call "foreign investment."

About two thirds of all expenditures in the marketplace are for consumer goods and services and are made by families buying to satisfy their needs. These items include durable goods such as washing machines and cars, nondurable goods such

includes inventory

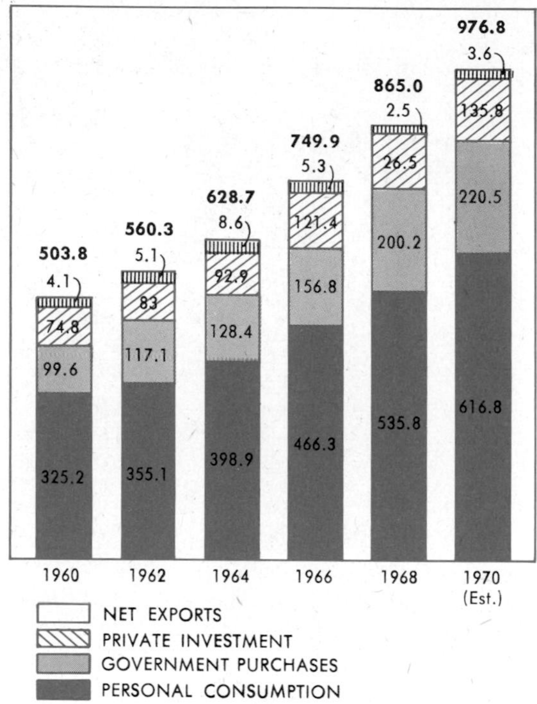

FIGURE 12–1 Gross National Product and Its Components

Of the four components of GNP, only government purchases more than doubled since 1960. Net exports actually decreased while the other components fell slightly short of the 100 percent increase. SOURCE: U.S. Department of Commerce, Office of Business Economics.

as food and gasoline, and services such as entertainment and medical expenses. Economists call these household purchases *personal consumption expenditures.*

The second largest buyer is government. This includes all levels of government and accounts for about one fifth of total expenditures. Most items of all government budgets—federal, state, and local—are included. The major exceptions are those publicly owned businesses that sell to the people—for example, the post office and some transportation systems and utilities. These are included under personal consumption expenditures.

Investment expenditures made by business account for most of the remaining purchases. Under this category are included all purchases of capital goods (such as machinery and equipment), all construction (including homes), and the differences between inventories at the beginning of the year and the end of the year. If total inventories were to decline during a particular year, it would mean that we used more goods than we produced and the difference would have to be subtracted. If inventories are higher, the additional value of goods must be added.

The final and smallest item in the expenditure approach is net foreign investment. It is calculated by adding together all the expenditures made by foreign countries in the United States and subtracting from that amount the total of all the purchases we made abroad. In 1970 this difference amounted to $3.6 billion. It is possible to arrive at a negative figure, as occurred in 1945, when net foreign investment in our country was −$0.6 billion. Because foreign investment is so much smaller than the other categories, we shall ignore it in our analysis. However, the subject will be considered further in Chapter 17.

Although the logic of the expenditure approach is clear, the question may arise of how the total value of production and the total value of expenditures can be the same when some of the product is not sold. It is true that some of the production is not sold to the ultimate consumer; but if we regard it as part of the inventory bought by other producers, then there is no difficulty in seeing that the totals of the expenditure approach and the production approach are equal.

The Income Approach to GNP

The third method of determining GNP is through analysis of income. Since the factors of production are responsible for the making of goods and services, it is possible to add up all the payments made to those involved in this production. The sum of all wages, salaries, interest, rent, and profits, plus indirect business taxes and capital consumption, must be indicated. The resulting total represents the payments, or income, side of the goods and services produced, and is most frequently referred to as *gross national income*, since it is dealing with income rather than production. However, the gross national income should be equal to the gross national product. Whether the production, the expenditure, or the income approach is used, the same total is reached —the gross value of what the nation produced for the year. Remember that product refers to the value of production, whether produced or bought, and income to the payment for that production. Figure 12–2 shows the expenditure and income approaches.

Common Errors in Computing GNP

When statisticians figure GNP, they may easily make two types of errors: (1) double counting and (2) adding transfer payments when measuring value created. Unless corrected, these mistakes give a distorted picture of economic conditions, preventing an accurate accounting and evaluation of actual production.

Double Counting

One of the problems in determining GNP, using the production method, is how to avoid double counting. You will remember that in our first definition of GNP we were careful to refer to value as the final

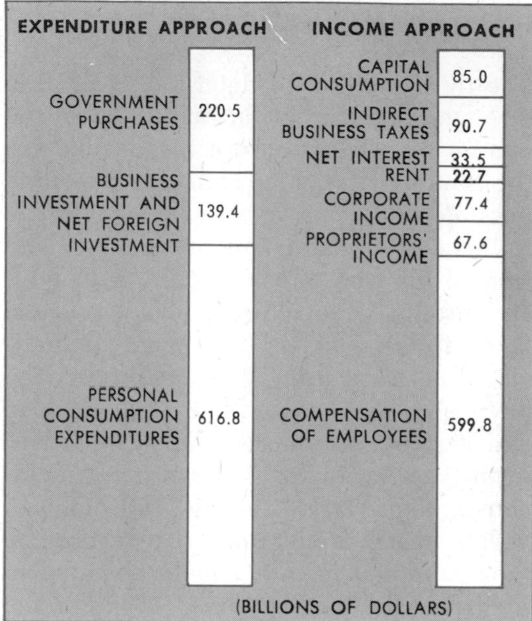

FIGURE 12–2 Two Views of the GNP, 1970

SOURCE: U.S. Department of Commerce, Office of Business Economics.

market price or retail price. An example, illustrated in Table 12–2, will make the reason for this distinction obvious.

When a farmer sells his cattle to a slaughterhouse, he receives payment for his product. The slaughterhouse sells the meat at a higher price to a wholesale distributor. The wholesale distributor sells the meat at a higher price to retail stores, which in turn sell the meat to consumers at a still higher price. Each of the above—the farmer, the slaughterer, the distributor, and the retailer—has contributed value to the final product. We must add the value that each has contributed. However, we must *not* add the total price received by each. If we do so, we will have added the farmer's contribution four times, the slaughterer's three times, and the wholesale distributor's twice. Doing so would be *double counting.* We must remember to figure only the value added in each step of production but never the total value paid by each of those involved in the various stages of production.

TABLE 12–2 An Illustration of Double Counting

	Correct Method		Double Counting
	Price Received	*Value Added*	
Farmer	$1,000	$1,000	$1,000
Slaughterer	1,200	200	1,200
Distributor	1,500	300	1,500
Retailer	2,000	500	2,000
		$2,000	$5,700

As you can see from Table 12–2, the correct value of the product added to society's wealth is $2,000, not $5,700. The value created in each stage of the production must be added only once.

GNP as a Basis for Comparison

Another kind of double counting may take place when figuring GNP on the income side. Should the money that Uncle Henry gave you for a graduation gift be added to your income when figuring GNP? If you do add it, you will be double counting. You did not create value; Uncle Henry did. Therefore, Uncle Henry will have to include in his income the gift he gave you. What you received is called a *transfer payment,* since the value was not created by you. Another type of transfer payment is the receipt of Social Security benefits. Value is created during working years, and during those years it counts as income for GNP. However, the value created to pay for Social Security is not received until payment is made during retirement. It is a transfer payment, since value created by you in the past and added to the GNP at that time is now given to you to use.

Other Weaknesses

There are other weaknesses also inherent in the determining of gross national product. Economics tends to be a rather cold, unemotional, and frequently undiscriminating discipline. When GNP is computed, we consider value only in terms of dollars and cents. In the present context only when the product or service is actually offered for sale on the market does it have value. This means that one of the most valuable contributors in our society, the housewife and mother, is not given credit for contributing to GNP. If she does the same work for someone else and is paid for it, the amount of her paycheck can be included. The same may be said of that great American institution known as "do it yourself." Steps built by someone in your family, or even by a neighbor, do not count unless some payment is made. Volunteer work done by millions of Americans is never considered as part of GNP because these people are not paid for their labor.

Another problem in the GNP approach —one that some experts consider a major weakness—is the failure to distinguish between the billions of dollars spent on luxuries and the billions of dollars spent on education, steel mills, and other goods and services associated with the strength and productivity of a nation. These critics may have a valid argument if GNP is used for comparing the military potential of nations, for example, of the United States and the Soviet Union. However, this criticism does not actually apply to the GNP as a measuring device, but rather to its use in measuring something it was never meant to measure, such as military strength. In a democratic society based predominantly on free enterprise it is the consumer who decides what goods and services he wants and, therefore, what goods and services will be produced. A system such as we have places confidence in the many rather than in the few to determine what is in their best interest.

GNP as a Basis for Comparison

Since gross national product is a measure of the real wealth of a nation—the value of all its goods and services—we may wish to consider how our country's annual GNP has grown and how it compares with that of other nations of the world. Any time that these evaluations are made, a standard measuring device must be used. Therefore, when we compare the GNP of our country at different times, we must be sure that the dollars we are measuring with are constant dollars, that is, that they purchase equal amounts of goods and services. When we compare our GNP with that of another country, we must equate its unit of currency—such as an English pound, a French franc, or an Italian lira—with our dollar. The attempt in both cases is to keep the measuring device equivalent.

Fluctuations in GNP

Tracing the growth of our nation's GNP is complicated by the fact that until 1929 the United States departments of Commerce and Labor did not keep records of the gross national product and other similar measurements. However, studies made by the National Bureau of Economic Research give a fairly accurate picture and show something of the patterns of growth of the GNP. Our annual production of wealth (GNP) increased over eight times from 1900 to 1970, and our population rose somewhat less than two and a half times during this same period. This means that the production of real wealth per person during this period increased more than three times. Figure 12–3 shows our economic growth from 1930 to 1970. Although a general upward pattern is evident, major fluctuations also appear. The decline for the 1930's indicates the seriousness of the Great Depression. Although numbers are emotionless, a brief discussion with someone who remembers the thirties, or reference to books about that period, will give you some idea of the hardship associated with those years.

With the beginning of World War II a remarkable acceleration of growth appeared. The GNP rose 75 percent from 1939 (when the war began in Europe) to 1944 (the last full year of the war). The end of the war brought about a decline, with only a moderate rise in 1948 and no increase at all in 1949. Then a sharp increase occurred because of American involvement in the Korean conflict. The drop in 1954 is consistent with the declines which occurred after our involvement in the two world wars. Apart from a decline in 1958 the rise from 1954 to the present has been consistent. The plateau in 1969 and 1970 in constant dollars is associated with the anti-inflationary policy and the withdrawal from Vietnam.

Our GNP Compared with That of Other Countries

When we compare the gross national product of the United States with that of other countries of the world, it is obvious why a famous economist referred to ours as the "affluent society." Table 12–3 shows the relative position of several selected countries in terms of GNP. Note that these statistics place the Soviet Union in second position, far behind the United States in total value of goods and services. All the other nations listed produce collectively only about two thirds of what we do. Japan's remarkable economic growth resulted in her passing West Germany to occupy third position in 1970.

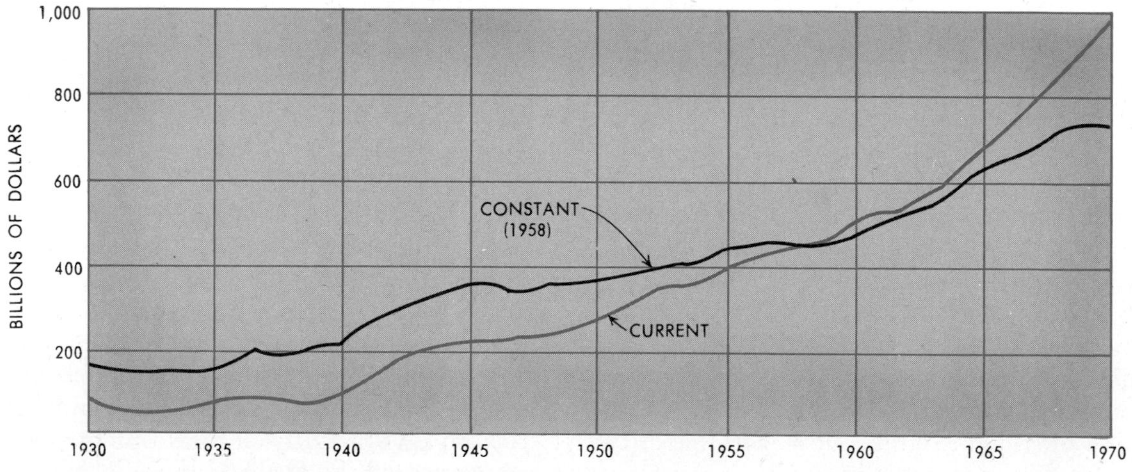

FIGURE 12–3 Comparison of GNP in Constant Dollars (1958) and Current Dollars

Why is GNP in constant dollars (1958) higher than GNP in current dollars up to 1958 and lower than in current dollars thereafter? SOURCE: U.S. Department of Commerce.

TABLE 12–3 Gross National Product for Selected Countries (billions of dollars)

Country	GNP
United States	931
U.S.S.R.	485
West Germany	161
Japan	155
France	127
Great Britain	93
Communist China	80
Italy	74
Canada	62
India	46
Greece	6
Peru	4

The figures given represent rough estimates of GNP for 1967 to 1969, with values converted to U.S. dollars. SOURCE: United Nations publications.

If the GNP of each of these countries is divided by the total population of each, the resulting amount represents *per capita output*, which provides a measure of the total value per person created in each of the countries listed. Table 12–4 gives this information. Occasionally these figures are used to interpret the relative standard of living of people in particular countries. Such conclusions are not very reliable, since they fail to take into consideration the vast inequality of wealth within a country. However, we can note that the output per American worker is more than twice that of the Soviet worker, three times that of the Japanese worker, 32 times that of the Communist Chinese worker, and 50 times that of the Indian worker. These statistics emphasize how remarkably productive our economy is.

Other Measurements

Although gross national product is the most frequently used measurement of our national economy, there are a number of other measurements closely related to GNP that are very important. As we move from GNP through four additional measurements, we should understand better the production, expenditure, and income approaches. You may find it helpful to remember that "product" emphasizes the value of what is produced, and "income" the payment to those producing.

Net National Product

One weakness of using GNP for measuring total output is that it fails to take into account the loss in value of capital goods that takes place in the course of producing the total output. Because machinery depreciates as it is used, part of the production of society must be devoted to merely replacing the value of the capital goods used up in the production process during the year. For example, a farmer has a tractor that he estimates is capable of 10 years' operation in helping to produce his crops. He recognizes that each year he

TABLE 12–4 Per Capita Output for Selected Countries (dollars)

Country	Amount
United States	$3,680
Sweden	2,665
Canada	2,087
West Germany	1,753
France	1,738
U.S.S.R.	1,678
Great Britain	1,560
Japan	1,231
Italy	1,116
Peru	241
Communist China	116
India	73

Per capita output measures the value created per person per year. These figures are rough estimates for 1967 to 1969, converted to U.S. dollars. SOURCE: United Nations publications.

must set aside a portion of the money received from the crops to pay for the value used up in his tractor in the production process. If he does not, he will be fooling himself on how much real value he has created. When the tractor breaks down completely 10 years after its first use, the farmer is confronted with the total cost of replacement.

GNP gives an exaggerated picture of output, just as the farmer received a distorted view of his income. In both instances, failure to take into consideration the fact that capital was consumed (depreciated) in the process of producing accounted for the error. This error can be corrected by finding the GNP and subtracting from it *capital consumption*, the part of the capital goods depreciated in the production process. The remainder gives a more accurate picture of the actual value of output for the year. That truer value is called *net national product* or *NNP.* It is usually about one eleventh smaller than GNP. In 1970 our GNP was $977 billion while our NNP was $891 billion, almost one eleventh less.

National Income

Although we have explained GNP from the output, the expenditure, and the income approaches, GNP and NNP traditionally show the output approach. The word "product" used in the previous measurements suggests this. *National income*, on the other hand, measures the income side and is defined as the total earned income of all the factors of production, namely, profits, interest, rent, wages, and other compensation for labor. It does not equal GNP because the factors of production are not paid two items—(1) capital consumption allowances and (2) indirect business taxes—both of which are included in GNP. Indirect taxes are such things as sales taxes, property taxes, and excises that are paid by businesses directly to the government and consequently reduce the income left to pay for the factors of production. The money put aside for capital consumption is for replacement and is not counted as income. Table 12–5 shows that over two thirds of national income goes for wages, salaries, and other forms of compensation.

Personal Income

Whereas national income shows the income earned by the factors of production, *personal income* measures the income received by individuals or households. Corporation profits are included in national income because they are earned. Out of these profits, however, corporation profit taxes must be paid to government, and some money must be put into the business for expansion. Only that part of profits distributed as dividends goes to the individual; therefore, out of corporation profits, only dividends count as personal income. The factors of production earn money for Social Security and unemployment insurance contributions; but this money goes to government (which is not a factor of production), not to individuals.

TABLE 12–5 National Income for 1970 (billions of dollars)

Compensation of Employees	600
Proprietors' Income	68
Rental Income	23
Corporate Profits and Inventory Valuation Adjustments	77
Net Interest	33
	801

SOURCE: U.S. Department of Commerce.

It is, therefore, part of national income but not part of personal income.

On the other hand, money received by individuals when they collect Social Security or unemployment compensation is not money earned, but it *is* money received. Interest received on government bonds is also considered in this category because so much of the money received from the sale of bonds went to pay for war production, which no longer furnishes a service to the economy.

Disposable Personal Income

The money that people receive as personal income may be either spent or saved. However, not all spending is completely voluntary. A significant portion of our income goes to pay personal taxes. Most workers never receive the money they pay in personal taxes, since it is withheld from their paychecks. The money that individuals are left with after they have met their obligations in regard to taxes is *disposable personal income*. Our disposable income can be divided between personal consumption expenditures and personal savings.

It is important to remember that personal saving is what is left after spending. It is quite possible to have a minus savings, or a dissaving. How can this occur?

Figure 12–4 shows how each of the five measurements of the economy discussed here is arrived at. With this information we can summarize the various measures of our national income as follows:

1. *Gross national product* (*GNP*) is the retail price of goods and services produced during a given period, usually a year.
2. *Net national product* (*NNP*) is the gross

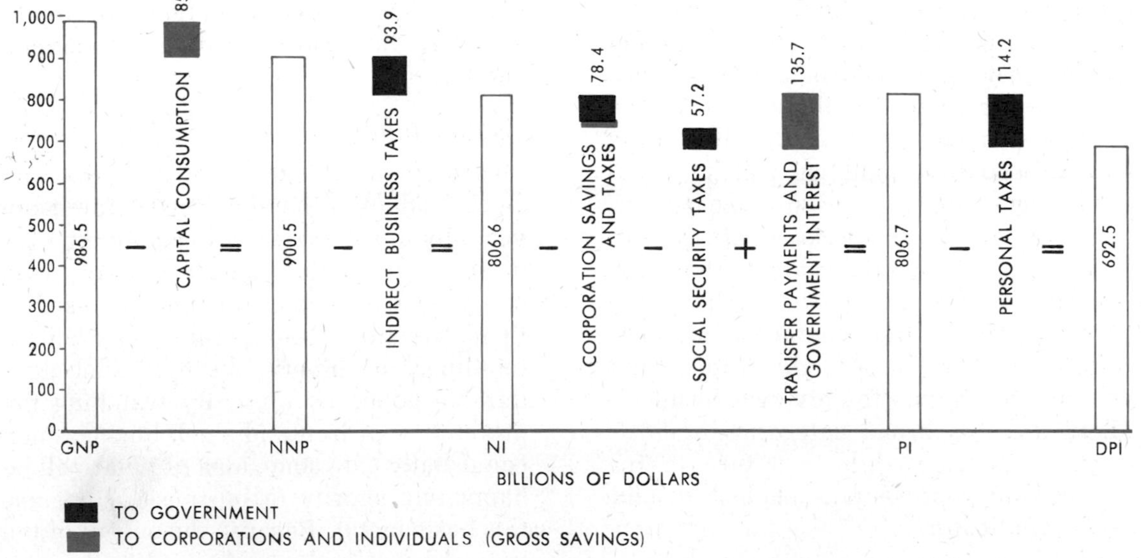

FIGURE 12–4 Measurements of the Nation's Income — Third-Quarter Rate Seasonally Adjusted, 1970

SOURCE: U.S. Department of Commerce.

national product minus the capital consumed in producing GNP.

3. *National income* (*NI*) is NNP minus indirect business taxes (not considered payment for production), or the total payments earned by factors of production.
4. *Personal Income* (*PI*) is NI minus corporation savings and taxes and Social Security payments (taxes) plus transfer payments and government interest, or it is the income received by individuals.
5. *Disposable personal income* (*DPI*) is PI minus personal taxes, or it is the addition of personal consumption expenditures and personal savings.

Part B
Measuring Business Activity

In our economic system it is business that has the primary responsibility for production. In the measurements already studied, government has occupied a very significant place, receiving income (usually from taxes) and spending money. However, even when government receives and spends, a significant portion of this is done through business. In Chapter 13 we will be concerned with the relationship between government and business in terms of the general trend of the economy. We know that business activity is vital to the nation's economy, and we will here discuss some of the ways used to measure it.

Every businessman is interested in knowing both how his particular business is faring in comparison with other businesses and what the general business climate is. On the basis of this information he can make plans for his own business. There are two broad categories of *business indicators* that he can turn to for information: representative indicators and general indicators.

Representative Indicators

Although the American economy is very complex and made up of many facets, some parts of the economy are so important that they not only give us an indication of how well that part of the economy is doing but they also show a high degree of consistency with other parts. The reason for the high correlation is usually that these *representative indicators* actually are involved in or reflect many other businesses. There are three types of representative indicators: leading, coincident, and lagging.

Leading Indicators

Measurement of our country's iron and steel production has been used for many years by businessmen to evaluate the condition and health of the economy. Iron and steel are basic metals and are used in the production of automobiles, appliances, buildings, machinery, and even such nondurable goods as toys. By watching the production of iron and steel, businessmen can usually gain some idea of what will be happening shortly in businesses that use this basic metal. Because the output of the iron and steel industry is used in the production of so many other goods and precedes the general level of business activity, it is not only a representative indicator but also a *leading indicator*.

Coincident Indicators

Freight carloadings are important because most of the goods we produce must be transported, and railroads account for a large portion of our transportation. Although railroads transport primarily heavy goods, they have been a far more reliable measurement than other forms of transportation. Unlike iron and steel production, carloadings run parallel with business activity and are called *coincident indicators.*

Lagging Indicators

A third example of a representative indicator is retail sales. A sampling of retail store sales is taken in representative cities. The sales include a wide range of the production going to the final consumers, and therefore constitute a good indication of business activity. However, the measurement for retail sales is a *lagging indicator,* following the general business trends.

Because each indicator has weaknesses, we must be careful not to trust too much to any one of them. Since the end of World War II a number of substitutes, such as aluminum and plastics, have been used to replace steel in many industries. The introduction and partial success of the compact car has reduced the amount of steel needed in the automobile industry. Increased truck and airplane transportation has cut into the railroad business. Nevertheless, as shown in Figure 12–5, these representative indicators (with the GNP in constant dollars) are for the most part reliable and reassure us of the general value of these measurements.

Look in the financial section of your Sunday newspaper to see if you can find other examples of representative indicators. Which of these do you think are leading indicators? Which are lagging? Why?

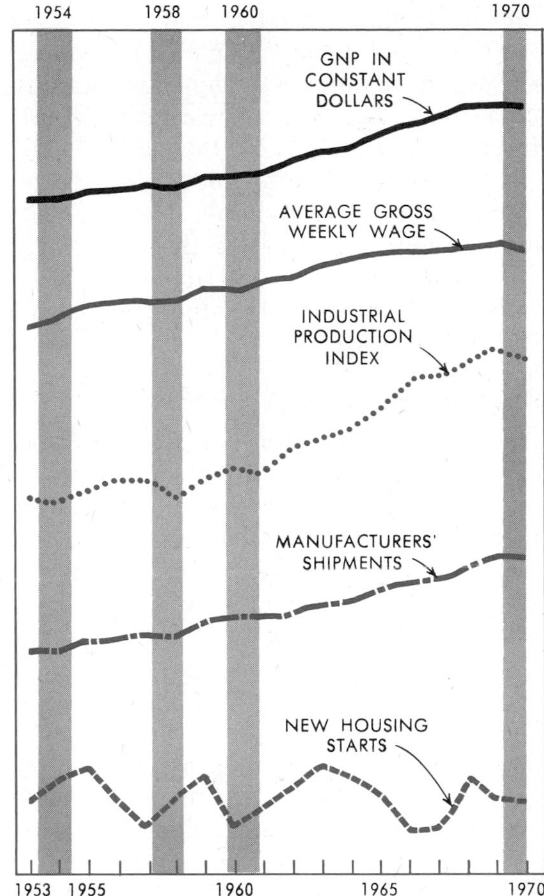

FIGURE 12–5 Business Indicators in Relation to GNP

Business indicators help economists evaluate the state of the economy. Which of the indicators shown reflects the trends of the business cycle most accurately?

General Business Indicators

Rather than rely on the measurement of one segment of the economy, even if that single indicator is representative, economists have put several different phases of our business activity together into a general, or composite, indicator. Perhaps the most widely used is that put out by the Cleveland Trust Company. It seeks to show the fluctuation of business activity back to 1790. It must rely on several different measurements for the earlier years, since data for some of our modern measurements are not available or are unsuitable. Figure 12–6 shows the changes in American business activity from 1899 until 1970, and indicates the key reasons for these changes.

Changes in Business Activity

A word of caution must be given in interpreting measurements of our nation's economy. There are three types of changes in business activity: seasonal, trend, and cyclical. In the evaluating and forecasting of business activity, the effect of these changes—particularly of business cycles—must be considered.

Seasonal Fluctuations

Some seasonal variations are caused by nature, which provides a more favorable environment for certain kinds of production, such as construction, at one time of the year than at others. Some variations are caused by man; in these, tradition often plays a part, as with gift-giving at Christmas. Economists make allowances for these differences. A chart may indicate an upturn in retail sales in January, although dollar sales were actually higher in the preceding month.

Trends

Trend changes refer to extended periods of time and indicate the long-range direction of the economy. Figure 12–6 shows more business activity in 1923 than in 1946. This does not mean that more business was done or more goods produced in 1923 than in 1946. During those 23 years our capacity to do business and to produce increased tremendously. However, our business activity in 1923 in relation to our potential in that year was greater than our business activity when compared with our potential in 1946. Figure 12–7 shows how trend is taken into consideration. Let us now turn to cyclical changes.

Business Cycles

The fluctuations that we have seen in all the measurements of our economy have been observed and studied by economists for many years. These ups and downs of the many phases of business activity deviate from what we might expect the normal increase in our economy to be; and although they do not show a perfect

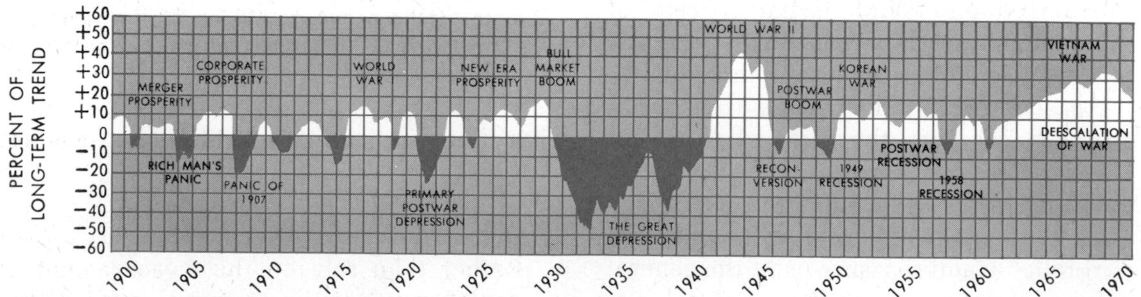

FIGURE 12–6 Fluctuations in the American Economy

The pattern of general business activity can be determined by combining several indicators into a composite. SOURCE: The Cleveland Trust Company, Cleveland, Ohio.

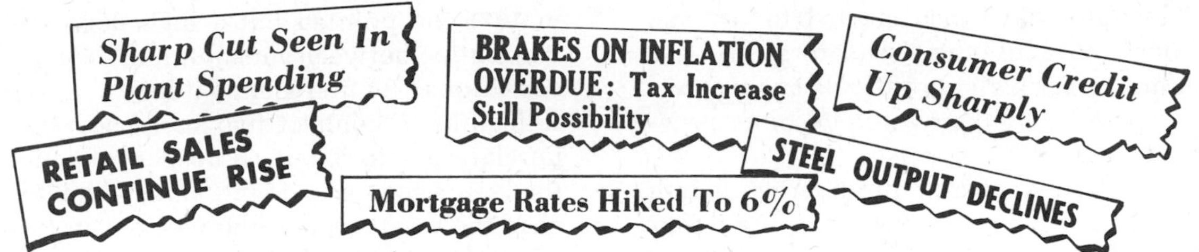

Do the changes shown in these news items add up to expansion or contraction of the economy?

rhythm, it is easy to discern a pattern. These rather regular fluctuations are called *business cycles.*

Economists have noted four phases in a business cycle. The upswing is usually referred to as *expansion or recovery,* the uppermost point as the *peak* or *prosperity,* the downswing as *contraction* or *recession,* and the low point as *depression.* The first graph in Figure 12–7 shows these four phases labeled with the terms we shall use: recovery, prosperity, recession, and depression.

Recovery is associated with increases in demand, which are reflected in production, employment, prices, and payments to the factors of production. All measurements of business activity will not rise at the same rate. Prices will tend to rise more slowly than production, and interest rates and retail sales may not increase at all in the early phase of the recovery. However, the general tendency will be upward for the great majority of indicators. When most indicators reach a high or a near-high, we are in the prosperity phase. Capital goods such as machinery will usually be on the decline by the time retail sales hit their peak, but the composite picture reflects optimism.

An examination of Figure 12–6 shows that prosperous periods do not continue indefinitely. In the recession phase some of the leading indicators—such as average hours worked, durable goods, construction, and steel—have been going down and such coincident indicators as employment, industrial production, and freight

PHASES OF THE BUSINESS CYCLE

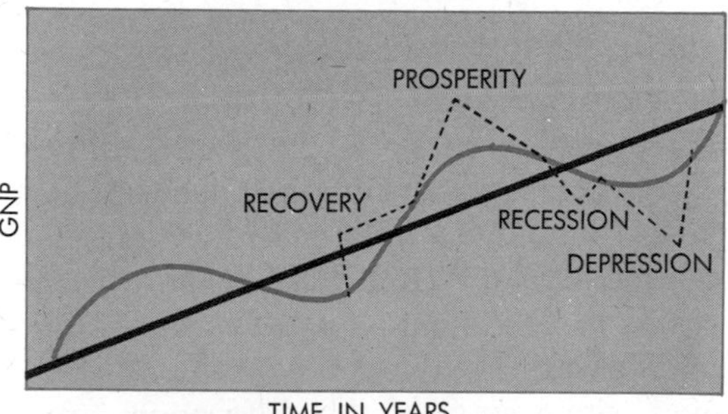

IN MEASURING BUSINESS ACTIVITY, NORMAL GROWTH RATE MUST BE TAKEN INTO CONSIDERATION. PHASES OF A SINGLE BUSINESS CYCLE ARE INDICATED.

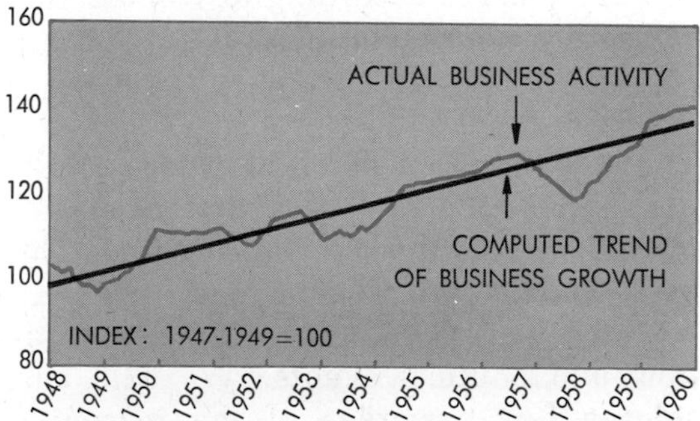

THE INDEX OF BUSINESS ACTIVITY MAY BE MEASURED AGAINST THE TREND OF BUSINESS GROWTH.

FIGURE 12–7 Measuring Business Activity

Trend is a factor that must be considered in measuring business activity. SOURCE: Morgan Guaranty Survey.

carloadings have also started to decline. When most of the indicators hit low points, a pessimistic outlook such as we associate with a depression becomes prevalent.

Studies reveal that the average length of a full cycle is slightly less than four years, that more time is spent in economic expansion than in contraction, and more time in prosperity and depression than in recession and recovery. However, the variations in the length of time and the severity of the cycles are so great that these statistics are not very useful when we try to analyze any one particular cycle.

Major Theories Regarding the Causes of Business Cycles

If we were to make a systematic study of the theories concerning the causes of business cycles, we would soon find ourselves overwhelmed. The number of theories seems to be almost as great as the number of students studying the problem. However, since most of the differences are in emphasis, we can arrange these theories in categories. The most common way to classify them is according to whether the causes are external or internal.

External Causes of Cycles

Theories based on external causes attribute fluctuations to forces that exist and operate outside the economic system. The best known are those that relate to weather, war, population growth, innovation, and political events. We will consider a few examples of the reasoning which underlies these theories.

Sunspots and Business

One of the earliest economists to develop a theory explaining business cycles was an Englishman, W. Stanley Jevons. Writing in 1875, he pointed out a high degree of correlation between sunspots and business conditions. At first glance it might appear ridiculous to connect two such seemingly unrelated factors, but on deeper reflection the logic becomes evident. Sunspots influence the weather, and the weather in turn affects agricultural production. An increase in agricultural output will bring about greater demand for farm equipment, transportation, and credit. This increase will in turn lead to a rise in business activity. Poor weather caused by sunspots will bring about a reversal in the pattern, explaining the downswing in the economy.

This theory, and other similar meteorological theories, proved to be very significant 50 years ago. Today these theories are less important because agriculture plays a smaller part in the economy of industrialized nations. Farm production, although still affected, is somewhat less dependent upon favorable weather.

Innovations

One of the most widely discussed theories—one that lends itself to a modern industrial society—is the *innovation theory*, developed principally by the late Harvard professor Joseph Schumpeter (see p. 87). According to Schumpeter new ideas and processes, whether they be new methods of doing business (supermarkets), new machines (computers), new products (television), or the opening up of new sources of raw materials (gold rush), are introduced in clusters. Although these inventions and discoveries may be made during a period of contraction of the economy, it is not until a few daring innovators put money into developing them that a wave of investments is made. This leads to an expansion of the economy, stimulating production and income. However, the wave will finally run its course, leading in time to recession and depression. During the slowdown new ideas and processes will be developed, but they will have to wait for enterprising men or firms to introduce them.

Some inventions, such as the steam engine and the automobile, have led to numerous other inventions and have resulted in tremendous investments in these areas. Other innovations have resulted only in minor investments. This is particularly true of fads, such as miniature golf and frisbies. What other innovations affecting business activity can you think of?

Internal Causes of Cycles

Theories based on internal causes relate fluctuations to factors within the economy itself. As the economy expands, forces are generated that will, at a certain level, work to bring about a contraction. Likewise, as a recession reaches the point of a depression, forces within the economy will reverse the cycle. Examples of internal causes are underconsumption, overinvestment, psychological factors, and monetary causes. We will explore the logic related to the last two of these theories.

Psychological Factors

Those who prefer the theory of psychological causation (for example, the late English economist A. C. Pigou) criticize the innovation theory, claiming that it is not basic, since new ideas are always to be found. What is more basic is the optimistic outlook of businessmen who sense an improvement in the economic climate. They become receptive to inventions that have yet to be tried. When other businessmen learn that more investments are being made, they are anxious to "get in" at the beginning of the expansion. An upswing, particularly in the more basic industries, increases employment and personal income. This, in turn, encourages consumers to go out and spend. An increase in consumer spending encourages retailers to build up their inventories before prices rise. New firms may be encouraged to enter the marketplace, further increasing investment and employment. Their entry will also lead to increased competition.

Just before the revival has reached its height and becomes a full-fledged prosperity, there will be some business leaders, cautious and pessimistic, who will begin to offset the trends, fearing that expansion has reached its limit. They will start to curtail operations, eliminating overtime work for their employees, reducing the size of their inventories, and discontinuing planned expansion. Other businessmen, hearing of these contraction activities, may become frightened. Workers may sense the uncertainty and fear a reduction in their earnings. This will affect their buying habits and will contribute to a recession.

The psychological theory, like the others examined, is criticized primarily because it is not basic; that is, it depends on other considerations. Business leaders and consumers are optimistic or pessimistic because of some other factor. President Hoover's suggestion during the depression of the early thirties that "prosperity is just around the corner" was of little value in reversing the contraction then occurring.

Monetary Theory

Another example of an internal cause is the monetary theory of the cycle, primarily developed by the English economist R. G. Hawtrey. The amount of money that banks have available for investment varies considerably. At the beginning of a revival, banks have plenty of money available and interest rates are low. The low interest rates and the ease in getting loans from the bank encourage businessmen to borrow and to expand their operations. As more and more do so, the availability of money declines and the interest rate increases. Prosperity is soon reached, but by the time it is, the banks no longer have money to lend out and interest rates are prohibitive for all but a few. Investments then decline, reducing spending and employment. Soon signs of a recession are visible. The decline will continue, finally reaching a depression. However, as the decline progresses, the supply of money that banks have available for credit starts to increase, causing interest rates to drop. Soon the easy access to low-cost loans will make investment opportunities too attractive for businessmen to pass up. Expansion will once again take place.

There is no doubt that the monetary theory explains a great deal about business fluctuations and, as we shall see in Chapter 15, proper action can do much to counter the direction of the cycle. However, there have been times when bank credit was available and interest rates were low but businessmen did not respond. Likewise, a shortage of money, with businessmen bidding interest rates up, has frequently failed to dampen enthusiasm in a period of expansion.

The Importance of Interacting Factors

Most economists believe that business cycles are caused by a number of interacting factors, and that no single formula is sufficient to explain the complex set of reactions that actually takes place. Furthermore, analysts stress the differences between one business cycle and another and usually consider the primary causes to be different for each cycle. The labels of the composite index in Figure 12–6 show the causes of the major fluctuations in the American economy in the twentieth century. Do they indicate any consistent pattern of causes for the various cycles?

The greatest fluctuations tend to occur in investment or in capital goods, which react to such external causes as wars, technological changes, and increases in population. Any additional investment due to external causes will set in motion a series of internal factors which will tend to magnify the results. Additional machinery means more jobs. More jobs will lead to bigger paychecks. Bigger paychecks increase the demand for goods and services. However, even with optimism running high the amount of capital goods will reach a saturation point and investment will begin to decline, leading to a shift in the cycle.

Although investment appears basic, it can be changed by external factors or it can be dependent on the level of income or production. Those who believe investment takes place in response to the growth of income and production, rather than the reverse, adhere to the *acceleration principle.* According to this view a high level of income is not enough to keep the economy moving upward, since the machinery in operation and the amount of merchandise in stores have been pushed to a high level, equal to what is needed. If no additional growth takes place, the only new machines and merchandise required are for the purpose of replacing those which become worn out or are sold. Therefore, an increase in the demand for automobiles will cause the automobile producer to buy new machines to manufacture the automobiles; however, once he has enough machines for this high level of automobile

TABLE 12–6 Business Fluctuation Explained by the Acceleration Principle

	Output of "Build-a-City" Sets	Machines Used in Production	New Machines Purchased		
			Replacement	Expansion	Total
1966	100,000	5	1	0	1
1967	120,000	6	1	1	2
1968	140,000	7	1	1	2
1969	160,000	8	1	1	2
1970	160,000	8	1	0	1

Merely sustaining consumer production at a high level, as shown above for 1970, is not enough to keep the producer of capital goods at the same level of production. The producer of machinery depends on a growing market at the consumer level if he is to avoid a contraction of his business. The same principle holds true for the wholesaler supplying the retailer with merchandise.

production, the only new machines he needs are to replace those that are worn out. The producer of the machinery needed to make automobiles can maintain his high level of production only when there is a growing demand for automobiles, not a sustained high demand. Table 12–6 shows how a recession can start when sales merely level off rather than taking a definite turn downward.

Anticipating Fluctuation

If businessmen are to operate successfully, they must anticipate the fluctuations of the business cycle and gear their production accordingly. To do this they frequently employ economists to determine the direction in which the economy seems to be moving. The government also employs a large staff of economists who track the business cycle and try to predict its direction. Using evidence from their studies, these specialists make recommendations in an effort to reduce the extremes of the cycle and to maintain stability in the economy.

Forecasting Cycles

Many students of economic theory, such as Joseph Schumpeter (see p. 87), have turned their attention to the problem of business cycles. Recently many economists have stressed the need to identify cyclical patterns and, if possible, to counter their severe effects.

It is important that fluctuations in business activity be predicted and corrective action prescribed. What success do economists have in forecasting business activity? There is little difficulty in predicting seasonal changes. So long as no major unexpected external cause occurs, long-range economic trends can be forecast with some accuracy. However, attempts to predict the ups and downs of the business cycle have too often been unsuccessful. Leading indicators—such as industrial stock prices, residential construction, steel production, and new orders for durable goods—have been of some help, but they have also been misleading at times. Just as jokes are made about errors in predicting the daily weather, so the economist is criticized when his carefully planned projection fails. Despite occasional mistakes, the weatherman keeps trying, and so does the economist. Each is employing new methods which will lead eventually to more accurate forecasting. We still rely heavily on the weatherman, since we know that he is right far more often than is our friend who predicts weather on the basis of the aches in his joints. In the same way business firms and government are far better off depending on the economic forecasts of the professional analyst.

In this chapter we have seen a variety of means for measuring the national economy. We have also observed the wide range of fluctuation occurring in the economy. This instability has been the major problem facing economists in the twentieth century. Recessions and depressions have meant unemployment, lower wages, reduced or vanished profits, losses and bankruptcy for business firms, smaller revenue for government, and a stifling of vitality and growth for the economy. In Chapter 13 we will examine methods of stabilizing the economy through the use of a new model of capitalism developed about 30 years ago. Before we turn our attention to solutions for the problem of economic instability, however, let us consider one aspect of it that will prove to be of particular significance to the immediate discussion.

Part C
The Problem: Is Economic Instability an Integral Part of the American Economy?

The problem defined here, unlike those previously dealt with, is not intended to be answered immediately. Rather, it is designed to help introduce you to some of the controversial thinking associated with the ideas presented in this unit. The tools needed to arrive at even a tentative conclusion will be discussed in the next four chapters, in addition to those already described here. Chapter 3, "Economic Systems Other Than Capitalism," provided some information and analysis, particularly with respect to communist criticism of capitalism and, in turn, the flaws inherent in this criticism.

Read the arguments that follow, keeping in mind that modern economic analysis and policy as developed since the mid-1930's and used since the end of World War II may provide some answers to the problem of economic instability. Whether these answers are sufficient or correct is a matter that you should consider very carefully as you continue with this unit.

A Negative Evaluation

Many economists and political leaders have looked upon our economic system—that of capitalism—with mixed feelings because of the weaknesses related to its cyclical behavior. Karl Marx, the major theoretician of scientific socialism, or communism (see p. 46), regarded capitalism as an important and essential part of the evolution of society and thought that it made significant contributions to man's attempt to find answers to the major questions of economics. He considered it far superior to the feudal system, which it replaced, in organizing society to produce the goods and services needed. By encouraging the accumulation of capital, the instruments for production could increase, thereby making greater production possible.

Marx believed, however, that the increased production would be of little benefit to the worker, whom he considered primarily responsible for production, as explained in the surplus value theory (see p. 189). The capitalist—the owner of the instruments of production—by denying the worker the full value for his production, prevented him from buying back the goods he produced. With a surplus of goods in the marketplace, competition would increase, with the stronger businesses absorbing the weaker. This narrowing of ownership would lead to a concentration of wealth among a few great capitalists, who gained their profits from unearned increment—that portion of wages that the workers rightfully earned but were not paid. An economic system thus organized would inevitably experience major business fluctuations.

Lenin, a disciple of Marx, took these ideas a step further, applying them to the world economic situation. Because workers lacked sufficient income to buy back the goods they produced, the capitalists would have to seek foreign markets for their surplus. They also needed a place to invest their capital. With an overexpansion of investment at home because of insufficient purchasing power to obtain the goods already on the market, interest rates at home would be lower than in backward nations. In order to secure these markets and investments, it would be necessary to have friendly governments or to control the governments in the foreign countries concerned. If these two methods did not work, it would become necessary to assume political control over the country. This theory is what the communists are referring to when they speak about "capitalistic imperialism."

According to Lenin, when capitalists throughout the world reach a saturation point in seeking markets and investing in backward countries, they must then turn either to wars or to wartime economies to bring an end to depressions. Huge government expenditures for armaments would stimulate production, leading to a business revival. Lenin concluded that only in an economy whose production is based purely on need rather than on profits and whose workers receive full value for their efforts can business cycles, with the misery that accompanies the depression phase, finally be eliminated.

Doubts about our economy's ability to eliminate major fluctuations in the business cycle are not confined to communists. A brief look at the actual record of business cycles—the occurrence of depressions accompanied by widespread human suffering—would cause most people to pause and wonder whether instability in business activity might not be an inherent disadvantage of our economic system. A frequent subject of controversy among responsible citizens is whether our economy could stand the effects of disarmament.

Do such doubts mean that Marx and Lenin were correct in their prophecy? Must we have war, cold or hot, in order to keep our machines humming and our workers employed? Must we choose between living in a world on the brink of a nuclear holocaust and living in a nation with millions of workers periodically unemployed and never being secure about their income? If we wish to eliminate this dilemma, must we turn to communism? None of these alternatives would be acceptable to the overwhelming majority of Americans, but there remain some irritating facts that cannot be ignored.

A brief review of any of the indicators in this chapter shows that business cycles do exist. The statistics show further that the years preceding the wars in this century were periods of depression and that wars brought recovery. After the wars primary postwar depressions set in, only to be followed by the boom of prosperity. However, without the assist brought by a war economy, the wheels of our economy slowed down and recessions started.

A closer look at the period since World War II illustrates the pattern described above. After the boom of the war and a short period of recession and reconversion to a peacetime economy, the combination of stored-up demand for civilian goods and accumulation of savings by workers ushered in a period of great prosperity. Late in 1948 the economy started to contract, leading to a recession in 1949. The next boom came with the Korean conflict, which lasted until 1953. During this time military expenditures tripled, with a corresponding expansion of production. With the end of the war came a contraction of the economy. This was short-lived, for another expansion took place and lasted four years. Recession in 1957–58 and again in 1960–61 interrupted generally good times. The recovery that followed can be attributed to our large military expenditures, our missile program, and our near-$100 billion federal budget. More recently we saw the economy strained trying to supply "guns and butter" but with the de-escalation of the Vietnam War unemployment rose above 6 percent from a low of 3.5 percent.

Although no serious depression has occurred since the 1930's and no total war since 1945, the amount of money we have spent for armaments to maintain national defense in the past several decades has certainly been a major factor in keeping a large portion of our economy working. Our defense program accounts for approximately 9 percent of our employed labor force and about the same percentage of the value of our goods and services. Certain industries and regions are almost completely dependent on defense contracts. Is the 80 billion dollars a year we spend on defense the factor that insulates us against a serious depression?

A Positive Evaluation

In 1962 a committee of economists was brought together to study the economic consequences of disarmament for the United States Arms Control and Disarmament Agency. The conclusions of the committee indicate that disarmament should almost certainly be taken by degrees and that important readjustments would have to be made to absorb the surplus capacity in defense industry if defense expenditures were reduced. However, the committee suggested that the same kind of planning we now use to take care of declining industries, such as coal, might be employed to cope with the decline in spending for the military. They suggested a plan for meeting this problem which would involve more government action, including such specific suggestions as (1) large retraining programs, (2) strengthening unemployment compensation, (3) granting more liberal benefits to workers who are released, and (4) planning for more consumer-oriented research and for diversification by shifting defense contractors to production of civilian goods. They concluded that if the government is willing to plan ahead and lead in fostering an optimistic program, there is no need for a contraction of the economy to occur as a result of disarmament.

One of the leading students of business cycles, in answer to a question about the amount of progress we have made in creating economic stability, said that although business cycles are still characteristic of our economy, their impact on individuals has been appreciably reduced in the last 25 years. The last serious depression occurred in the 1930's; by comparison the last four recessions have been extremely mild, with the longest one lasting only 13 months. Changes in the structure of the American economy and the action taken by both industry and government in response to changes in business activity have not only made our recessions shorter and less severe but they have also changed the nature of the decline. While many of the factors making up the composite picture of our business cycle continue to fluctuate considerably, personal income and consumption have been relatively stable. In addition, businessmen, knowing that the government is not going to stand idly by while unemployment mounts, no longer allow their inventories to drop quite so far. Such action on the part of business has served as a stabilizing element in maintaining production. The great progress that has been made in the last generation in reducing economic instability can be continued if coordinated action between government, business, and labor can be used with courage and vision to offset cyclical tendencies.

Although five recessions have taken place since 1948, not once did disposable personal income or consumer expenditures decline. These recessions have lasted only half as long as the average of pre–World War II recessions. The end of the conflict in Korea brought about a decline of $14.3 billion in government spending. In addition, business concerns canceled $12.9 billion in contemplated new plant equipment and inventories. Even with such reductions, the GNP declined only about $2 billion.

Karl Marx said that depressions were the result of the workers not receiving full value for their labor and consequently not being able to buy back the goods they produced. However, from 1950 to 1970 the total financial compensation to American employees of corporations rose 290 percent while corporate profits before taxes increased only about 69 percent. With consumer spending rising even during periods of minor contractions in business activity and with the poor getting richer (the number of people below the poverty level fell from 22 percent in 1959 to 12 percent in 1969), it would appear that the prophecy of Marx was less than accurate.

Considering an Answer

Now that you have read two distinct points of view, each persuasive when considered by itself, you are in a position to investigate the problem further. Although no one denies that economic fluctuations exist, there is great controversy about how serious they are to our economy and to our society. We need to examine these variations further to see if significant progress in controlling them has been made, whether a depression like that of the thirties could happen again, and whether disarmament is possible without a serious depression.

In Chapter 13 we will go on to discuss the theory of income determination, which will give you some insight into the forces that affect our level of income. The three following chapters will discuss different conditions and issues relating to the problem introduced here. After reading them, will your answer be the same as your tentative conclusion now?

REVIEW: THE HIGHLIGHTS OF THE CHAPTER

1. The study of the economy as a whole is called macroeconomics, in contrast to microeconomics, the study of individual units.
2. Gross national product (GNP) is the total retail value of all the goods and services produced during a year.
3. There are three methods used to determine gross national product: the product (or output) approach, the expenditure approach, and the income approach.
4. The product approach uses as its base the sum of goods and services produced. The expenditure approach determines GNP by totaling spending in the marketplace. The buyers are divided into four categories—individuals buying as households, government, businesses, and foreign purchasers. The income approach arrives at gross national income (GNI) and refers to total payments made to those involved in production in addition to capital consumption and indirect business taxes. The gross national income is equal to gross national production.
5. In determining GNP, the value produced for the market is counted. As a result, labor that is not rewarded by wages or payment cannot be considered part of GNP.
6. Net national product (NNP) measures the value of goods and services added to the nation and is determined by subtracting from GNP the value of the capital consumed in producing it.
7. National income (NI) measures income rather than product and is the total earned income of all the factors of production. It is NNP minus indirect business taxes.
8. Personal income (PI) is the income received by individuals before they pay their personal taxes. It is determined by subtracting Social Security payments and corporation savings and taxes from national income and adding transfer payments and government interest.
9. Disposable personal income (DPI) refers to the total value of personal consumption expenditures and personal savings. It is determined by subtracting personal taxes from personal income.
10. There are three kinds of variation in business activity: seasonal, trend, and cyclical.
11. There are four phases to a business cycle: recovery, prosperity, recession, and depression.
12. The average length of a full business cycle is slightly less than four years. More time is spent in expanding than in contracting, and more time in prosperity and depression than in recession and recovery.
13. External causes of business cycles refer to forces outside the economic system.

The ones most frequently referred to are those that relate to weather, war, population growth, innovation, and political events.

14. Internal causes of business cycles refer to factors within the economic system. These include overinvestment, psychological factors, and monetary causes.
15. Although investment (capital goods) shows the greatest fluctuation, most economists think that business cycles are caused by many interacting factors, with no simple formula sufficient to explain all reactions.
16. It is important for the health of the economy to be able to interpret trends, predict business activity, and prescribe policy in order to reduce the extremes of the business cycle.

IN CONCLUSION: SOME AIDS TO UNDERSTANDING

Terms for Review

GNP (gross national product)
NNP (net national product)
NI (national income)
PI (personal income)
DPI (disposable personal income)
Great Depression
capital consumption
external and internal theories
acceleration principle
macroeconomics
microeconomics
double counting
transfer payments
business cycle
unearned increment
representative indicators
leading indicators
coincident indicators
lagging indicators

Names to Know

W. Stanley Jevons
A. C. Pigou
Joseph Schumpeter
R. G. Hawtrey

Questions for Review

1. What is the basic difference between macro and micro approaches in the study of economics? What is the importance of each?
2. One of the tools used to compare the economic strength of nations is the GNP of each nation.
   (a) What methods may be used to arrive at GNP?
   (b) What errors may occur in computing GNP?
   (c) Why are "constant dollars" needed for a true picture of GNP?
3. What other methods and measures are available to judge the strength of the national economy?
4. How are GNP, NNP, NI, PI, and DPI determined? What is the unique feature of each? What is the use of each?
5. The state of health of the business community may be judged by various indicators. How may this evaluation be made over a long period? What dangers are there in forecasting?

6. Cyclical variations are a constant threat to economic stability.
   (a) What is meant by the business cycle?
   (b) What are its various component phases?
   (c) Describe the external and internal forces which are responsible for fluctuation in business activities.
   (d) Why is it important for the businessman to make a successful prediction of business trends?

Additional Questions and Problems

1. Obtain the latest edition of *National Economic Trends* from the Federal Reserve Bank of St. Louis, or similar material from the Federal Reserve Bank nearest you. How does this information show the relationship between monetary factors and economic trends?
2. What accounts for economists' successes in predicting business trends? What accounts for some of their errors?
3. Compare the theories of W. Stanley Jevons and Joseph Schumpeter regarding business cycles. Using specific examples to support your viewpoint, try to decide which of the two theories you consider more pertinent today.
4. What effects would a recession or depression probably have on each of the following: (a) a food processing company, (b) a firm producing machine tools, (c) a commercial bank, (d) the owner of common stocks, (e) the owner of bonds, and (f) a personal finance company?
5. Obtain the latest GNP figure, and the figure for the previous year. What adjustments would you make in the latest figure to show the *real* growth of the U.S. economy over the past year?
6. Using the *Survey of Current Business*, prepare a series of graphs showing
   (a) GNP
   (b) personal income
   (c) disposable personal income
   (d) national income

   for the years 1929, 1933, 1945, 1954, 1957, 1962, 1966, and 1970. What conclusions can be drawn from your material?
7. The occurrence of business cycles has led to criticism of the capitalistic system.
   (a) Present the basic ideas of Karl Marx in his surplus value theory.
   (b) What addition to communist theory did Lenin introduce?
   (c) How has the economic growth of the United States in the last 25 years been a refutation of these theories?
8. Business cycles have had a significant influence on our country's economic development.
   (a) Make a chart of the business cycles which have occurred in the United States from 1800 to the present.
   (b) Explain the causes of the major variations before 1933.
   (c) In your opinion should the federal government exercise more controls? Give reasons to support your answer.
   (d) What explains the long period of prosperity which typified much of the 1960's.

SELECTED READINGS

Council of Economic Advisers. *Economic Report of the President.* Washington, D.C.: U.S. Government Printing Office. (Published in February of each year.)

Hansen, Alvin H. *Fiscal Policy and Business Cycles.* New York: W. W. Norton & Co., 1941.

Silk, Leonard and Louise Curley. *A Primer on Business Forecasting.* New York: Random House, 1970.

Survey of Current Business. Published monthly. Washington, D.C.: U.S. Department of Commerce, Office of Business Economics.

U.S. Department of Commerce. *Do You Know Your Economic ABC's?* Washington, D.C.: U.S. Government Printing Office, 1963.

U.S. Department of Commerce. *Supplement to the Economic Indicators: Historical and Descriptive Background.* Washington, D.C.: U.S. Government Printing Office, 1964.

National Income Analysis—A New Model 13

THE AUTHORS' NOTE TO THE STUDENT

In the United States we have the resources and the science and technology which ensure enough production to meet our basic needs for survival, with many luxuries in addition. Unfortunately, our system has frequently operated far below its potential level of output. When workers are unemployed and resources are not utilized, our economic system is falling short of optimum performance.

Economists set up models of economic systems in the hope that these will guide us in making full and efficient use of our productive resources. Most economists set as a goal the operation of our economy at a full-employment level without inflation. In this chapter we will examine a new model that will show how the level of our national income is determined and how this income can be changed to sustain full employment without inflation. We will compare the classical model and the Keynesian model, both operating within the framework of our mixed capitalist system, to see how each is designed to achieve the goal of full employment without inflation.

A STUDENT'S NOTE TO THE STUDENT

This chapter was without a doubt the most difficult. Don't plan on one reading to get it all. After three readings and class discussion I now can say I really understand it. Before you get discouraged let me assure you that the insight you get—the different kinds of perspective—make it really worthwhile.

Let me pass on a tip that may make this chapter easier for you. First you should make sure you know the basic economic terms in Chapter 12 or at least mark the last page of Part A where they are defined so you can easily find them. Next, when you read the chapter, make constant reference to the graphs. Don't go on until you think you can understand the text through the use of the graphs. Since the basic idea of income determination is repeated three times, each in a different way, it should get clearer as you proceed. Finally, when you are done, go through the procedures developed in the colored acetate insert. It really is a *great* help.

Incidentally, when I read the newspaper this weekend I really understood what they meant about planning a budget deficit for a full-employment economy.

Part A
Full Employment Without Inflation—The Classical Answer

Identifying Our Goals

In Unit II we mentioned that economists develop theories and prepare models to show how an economic system should work in answering the major questions of allocation. We showed how, in our market economy, the price system allocates resources; we also found that some of our resources, such as labor, may not always be fully utilized. People in our country are increasingly agreed on the desirability of setting as a goal for our economy a level of production that would provide jobs for everyone who wants to work. When production is at a level below this, our economy faces a decrease in demand and a general contraction of the economy. On the other hand, if production goals are set at a level beyond what our resources can achieve, the result is inflation, not additional production. For example, employers collectively do not obtain additional labor by bidding against each other for the services of workers.

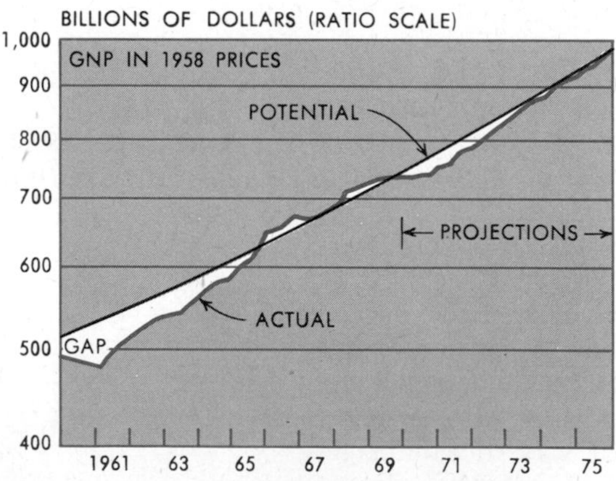

FIGURE 13–1 GNP: Potential and Actual Performance

The difference between our economy's actual level of production and its potential level is sufficient to eliminate most of our nation's poverty. SOURCE: U.S. Department of Commerce.

Most economists believe that a *full-employment economy* (one in which everyone in the working force who wants to work can find a job) without inflation is a goal for all countries. Maintaining this condition involves smoothing out the peaks and troughs of the business cycle so that stability and economic growth are consistent with the increase in resources for production. The problem may be stated in this way: How can our system yield a GNP large enough to sustain a full-employment economy without causing inflation?

GNP and Full Employment

When economists refer to a "full-employment GNP," they mean that the economy is producing enough goods and services (GNP) to employ all those in the labor force who wish to work. If some of the working force remains unemployed when the GNP is at $1.1 trillion, additional production of goods and services would be required to raise the level of employment. Increasing the GNP to $1.15 trillion might provide the jobs necessary to reduce unemployment. It is important to recognize that a small percentage of unemployment is accepted as normal. Because there are always some people in the process of moving into or out of the labor force or perhaps moving from one job to another, unemployment below 4 percent of the labor force is usually considered full employment. With almost 90 million people in the labor force, unemployment below 3.5 million would be considered full employment.

Determining GNP: The Classical Viewpoint

Although considerable agreement exists on the desirability of a full-employment economy, differences remain regarding the methods by which this condition can and should be achieved.

The classical, or laissez-faire, economist accepts the general principle that the economy should operate without interference with the laws of supply and demand and that government should be involved in the economy as little as possible. Under these conditions, flexibility of prices, wages, and interest rates will keep our economy producing at a level high enough to sustain full employment without inflation. Although there might be times when external causes would bring about production above or below a level of full employment without inflation, such deviations would be temporary. A closer look at the classical economist's position, using tools from the previous chapter on national income measurement, will help clarify how gross national product is determined.

Figure 13–2 is designed to assist in explaining how the gross national product is determined. It will be most helpful to you if you will refer to it in proceeding from

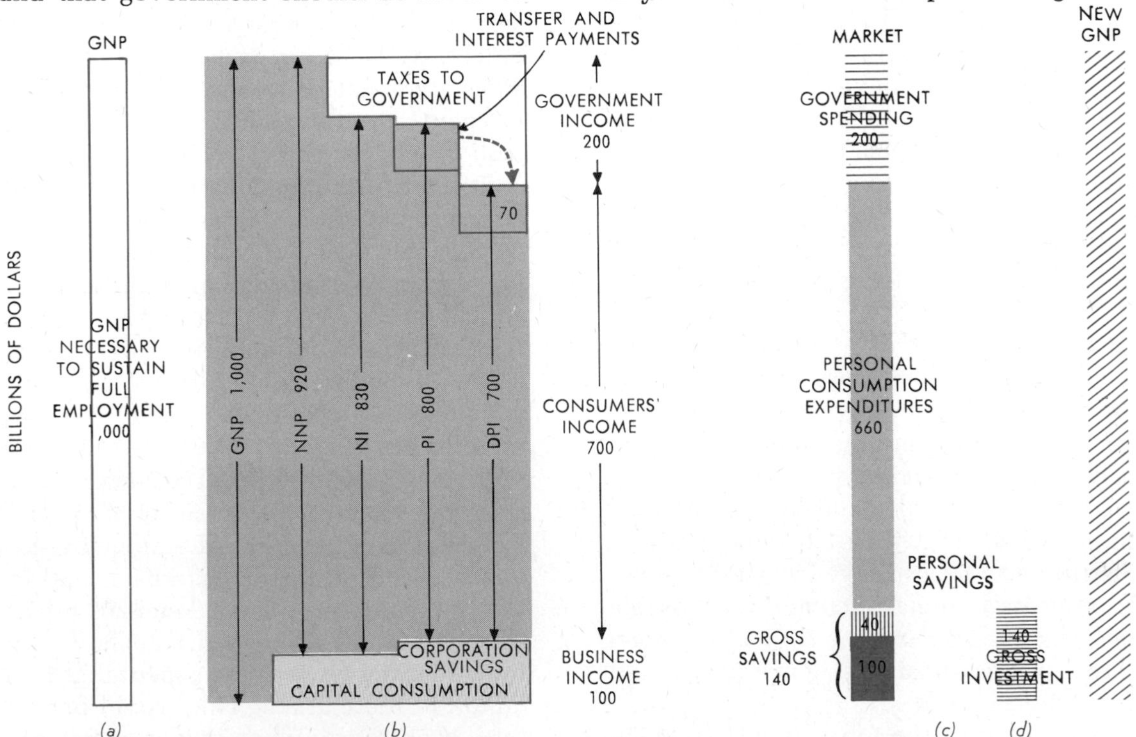

FIGURE 13–2 Determination of GNP

Gross national product will remain at the full-employment level if government spending equals government revenue and business invests all the money saved.

step to step in the explanation that follows. Figure 13–2 is divided into four parts, (*a*) to (*d*), and will be explained as we move from the left side, (*a*), to the right side, (*d*).

Full-Employment Level (a)

We have defined full employment as the amount of goods and services we would have to produce in order to employ at least 96 percent of our labor force (at or below the 4 percent unemployment rate). This amount increases each year as productive capacity grows. As the labor force becomes larger and more skilled, and as the use of equipment and other resources becomes more efficient, it will be necessary to have an ever-increasing gross national product in order to sustain full employment.

Economists can estimate the size of GNP needed to achieve a full-employment level (as in Figure 13–2) without inflation. In Figure 13–2, we use the figure $1 trillion because it is easier to work with. In reality it would be somewhat higher, depending on the growth of our productive resources and on the year being considered.

Gross National Income (GNI) (b)

You will recall that gross national income is the same figure as gross national product. The former measures the dollars received for producing whereas the latter measures the retail value of the product. In (*b*) we see how the $1 trillion of GNI is distributed. As we move from left to right, from gross national income to disposable personal income, income is divided among three groups: business, government, and consumers.

As shown at the top of the chart, $270 billion goes to government, mainly in the form of taxes. However, of this amount, $70 billion is returned to individuals in the form of transfer and interest payments. This leaves government with $200 billion. At the bottom, $100 billion is put aside by all businesses for capital consumption and by corporations for savings. Individuals retain $700 billion in disposable personal income (including the $70 billion from transfer and interest payments indicated by the arrow on the graph). The right-hand side of (*b*) is what the economy looks like before consumers go to the market to spend. Our $1 trillion gross national income is now divided into $200 billion for government, $100 billion for business, and $700 billion for consumers.

Expenditures in the Market (c)

In (*c*) we see the GNP (the product side) and the expenditures made for goods and services by those now in possession of the dollars (GNI). Keep in mind that the two sides are equal. If all the GNI ($1 trillion) is spent, all the goods and services ($1 trillion) will be sold.

To clarify the explanation, let us visualize production as taking place throughout a single year but expenditures as taking place only at the end of the year, when annual production is complete. Imagine for that occasion a giant market with the entire $1 trillion GNP for sale and with government, consumers, and business there to buy.

In (*c*) we observe that government is spending exactly the same amount as it has received (excluding the money it has taken in and returned for transfer and interest payments). It has taken $200 billion from businesses and individuals in the form of taxes and has then spent that $200 billion in the market. This would be that rare occurrence when government balanced the budget—a situation that our classical economist would doubtless approve of!

Next, consumers go to the market. Consumers have $700 billion to spend—their take-home pay (DPI). However, we see that their personal consumption expenditures amount to only $660 billion, $40 billion being placed in personal savings. If this $40 billion is not spent by someone, $40 billion worth of production will remain unsold.

Now it is businesses' turn to buy. They find it necessary to replace used equipment and inventories for the production of goods and services for the next year. When businesses go to the marketplace to buy, they do not make purchases to satisfy their needs as consumers. Instead, they buy to produce or distribute goods and services to other producers, to distributors, or to the consumer. Thus, instead of calling their purchases "consumption expenditures," we call them *investments* (that which is used to further production).

In (*b*) we can see that businessmen put aside a total of $100 billion—$84 billion for capital consumption and $16 billion in corporate savings. In (*c*) we have added to this $100 billion the $40 billion that consumers have saved to give us $140 billion, a figure that we call *gross savings.* The $140 billion in gross savings means there must be $140 billion worth of production left unsold in the market. It is crucial to know what will happen to the gross savings.

If businessmen invest the total amount of gross savings ($140 billion), they will use up the remainder of GNP. Note in (*c*) of Figure 13–2 that gross savings and gross investment are the same. That part of income that had not previously been spent (gross savings) has now been used to buy up the remaining production through investment. This means that in the example all the goods and services on the market have been purchased, since all government income has already been spent, as well as most of the income received by the various factors of production which has been spent as personal consumption expenditures. As our imaginary year ends, all the gross national income has been used to purchase all the gross national product. What do you think will be the size of next year's GNP?

The New GNP (d)

Business, which provides the bulk of the GNP, has in the past year produced and sold an output worth $1 trillion. It is not likely that businesses would try to reduce their production. Since everything produced has been sold, why should business consider producing less? Lower production would mean that the price tags for all production would add up to less than $1 trillion. It would also mean that less than $1 trillion would be paid in income (GNI).

Why wouldn't companies try to produce more than in the past year? They might try, but if they did so they would immediately encounter problems, such as a shortage of workers. (At present we are assuming that no additional workers or other productive resources are added to the working force.) You will remember that GNP has been set at a full-employment level. If businesses seek to get more workers by raising wages, these workers will have to come from some other industry. The additional production in one industry will be offset by a decline in the production in another. As businessmen compete with one another for scarce workers and resources, wages will rise. However, since total production would be no greater, we would have a demand greater than supply. Prices would rise. The new GNP would *look* bigger because the prices of goods and services would be higher, and income would be greater because workers would be getting more wages. (Other factors of production would also have larger income.) This new GNP would be higher in dollars, but it would be the same as the old GNP in goods and services. In other words, if we try to move the GNP higher when production is already at a full-employment level and when capacity to produce is not being increased, the result is inflation. The exception to this situation would be an increase in capacity to produce, made possible by using more workers and more efficient machines.

We can conclude that if the economy is operating at a full-employment level and businesses invest the same amount as that which is saved, the gross national product will continue at the same high and desirable level.

Investment and Saving

What if investment is not equal to savings? Certainly business cannot always be expected to invest the same amount as gross savings. Since saving (the opposite of spending) and investment seem to be the keys to determining the new GNP, let us see what happens when they are not equal. Figure 13–3 shows gross investment when (*a*) less than and (*b*) more than gross savings.

Savings Larger Than Investment

Let us suppose that businessmen have a gloomy outlook for the next year. Some production remains, even after both government and consumers have been in the market. Businessmen, looking at the remainder, sense that there has been less buying than they hoped for (more savings), or they think that people, having bought so much in the previous year, might cut back on their spending in the next year. Under either of these circumstances businesses will be less likely to invest very much money for next year's production. They may buy fewer machines or let inventories in their stores decline. If enough businesses do this, total investment will add up to less than total savings and there will be goods and services left in the market. Companies will then cut back their production because the supply of production is greater than the demand. They will employ fewer resources. Some workers will have to be let go, some machinery will be idle, and marginal firms will be forced out of business. As a result of these changes, the new GNP will be lower. The decline in production will cause a drop in employment—below the level of full employment. It would appear from this illustration that when savings exceed investment, a lower GNP will result. This condition is illustrated in Figure 13–3(*a*).

Investment Larger Than Savings

What would happen if businessmen invested more than the amount saved? Let us suppose that they come to the market expecting that purchases in the new year will be larger than in the past year. As they start buying the remaining production, they soon realize that there is a greater demand for production than there is supply of production. You might reasonably ask how this is possible when the income side and the production side are supposed to be the same. The answer is that the money businesses use for investment comes from savings, but not necessarily from savings confined to last year. Besides, as you will learn in Chapter 15, banks can extend the credit necessary to provide money to businesses, with the result that current investment can exceed current savings.

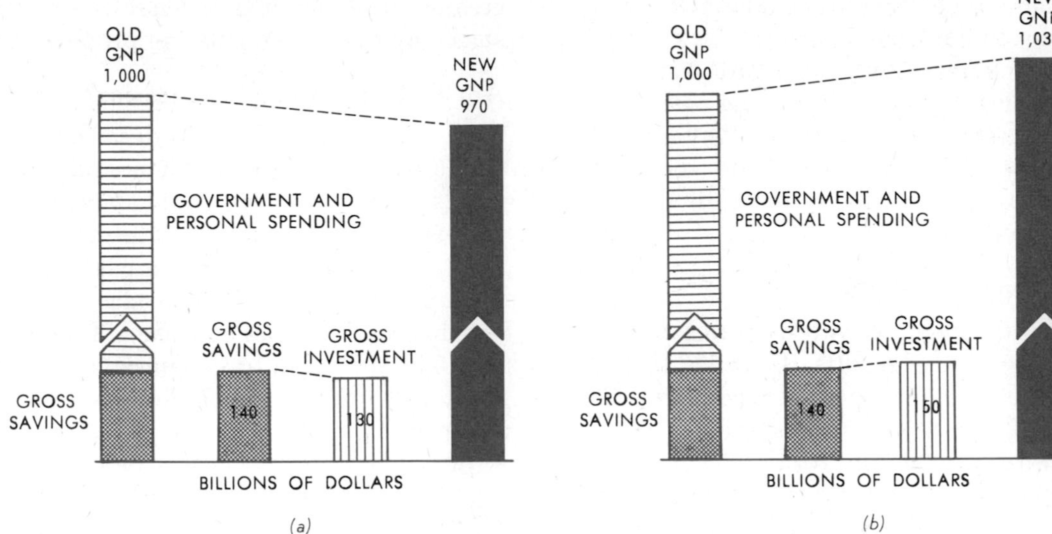

FIGURE 13–3 Relationship of Investment to Savings in Determining the New GNP

When GNP has been at full employment and gross investment is less than gross savings, the new GNP will fall. The new GNP will be less than the old GNP by some multiple of the difference between savings and investment ($140B − $130B = $10B. $1,000B − $970B = $30B. $30B ÷ $10B = 3 (the multiplier).

When GNP has been at full employment and gross investment is more than gross savings, the new GNP will rise by some multiple of the difference between them (3 × $10B = $30B greater GNP). The new GNP will be no larger in goods and services but will appear greater because of inflation.

If investment does become greater than savings, and if *aggregate demand* (the expenditures of government, consumers, and business) exceeds the aggregate supply of current production, the GNP will increase. However, since we are already operating at a full-employment level, as shown in Figure 13–2, the increase of investment over savings will lead to inflation. This occurs because the demand for production exceeds the capacity to produce. Figure 13–3(*b*) shows what happens to GNP when investment is larger than savings in a full-employment economy.

Changing Interest Rates

According to classical theory, the two conditions pictured in Figure 13–3 would be only temporary. Two factors would act to correct these situations: interest rates and wage-price flexibility. Let us see what effect these factors might have.

If businessmen invested less than savings (Figure 13–3*a*), the GNP would fall below the level of full employment. This economic decline would result in a decline in the interest rates on savings as well as lower rates for those who wished to borrow money for investment. With more money available from savings than investors wish to borrow, the laws of supply and demand would bring about a reduction in interest. The new low rates of interest would soon provide the necessary corrections in the economy. Since interest is an inducement for savings, the lower interest would produce more spending and less saving. Previously, the high interest rates may have discouraged businessmen from investing. Now lower rates for loans would encourage them to borrow in order to increase their inventory or buy new machines. With lower interest rates stimulating consumer spending and business investment, savings and investment would soon be in balance and the GNP would once again be at the full-employment level.

Wage-Price Flexibility

What if the changing interest rates did not produce all the results desired? If this were the case, the classical theorist would expect flexibility in wages and prices to do the rest of the job. With GNP still below the full-employment level the surplus labor resulting from this decline would bring about a reduction in wages. The lowering of wages would cut down the cost of production, allowing businessmen to reduce prices on their goods. These lower prices would lead to increased sales, requiring employers to hire additional workers. On the income side the factors of production would receive less in dollars (lower wages, lower profits) because prices have declined. However, costs on the product side would also amount to less because of the lower prices there. The number of dollars of GNP might be lower and the sum of the price tags might be lower, *but the all-important sum of goods and services would be at the level of a full-employment economy.* When prices and income both decline the same amount, the real GNP (that is, the goods and services produced and consumed) will not be reduced. A little time to allow wages and prices to adjust downward will bring a new dollar figure (perhaps $960 billion) for the full-employment GNP.

According to classical theory, interest rates and wage-price flexibility also exert a corrective influence when investment is greater than savings. What might the stages of this self-regulating process be?

Are There Errors in the Classical Theory?

The classical economist described the capitalistic system as a successfully self-regulating system that would always come to rest—that is, reach a state of equilibrium—at the full-employment level without inflation. According to classical theory this result occurs because of flexibility in the interest rate for savings and investment and because of flexibility in wages and prices.

In opposition to classical beliefs, how-

Before unemployment insurance, expanded government welfare, and assistance under the antipoverty program became available, the unemployed often suffered great hardship. Conditions became acute during periods of recession and depression. SOURCE: United Press International.

ever, many economists contend that events have shown that the theoretical readjustment does not always take place. Small rises and declines in the business cycle could be explained as temporary maladjustments that correct themselves; some of the larger peaks and troughs could be explained by external causes such as wars. The major economic occurrence which cannot be explained so easily is the Great Depression of the 1930's. During those years many of the economists who followed the classical tradition, as well as some of the political leaders and businessmen who accepted their theories, generally believed that "prosperity was just around the corner." They said that if we would just wait a little longer, the natural self-regulating factors that make the market economy an excellent system would correct the terrible imbalances that were producing a shrinking GNP and contributing to even greater unemployment.

Although these people were willing to wait for the corrective effort to occur, a majority of the American people apparently were not. With the growing readiness to find other solutions, the time was ripe for the introduction of a new economic model, or at least some modification of the old one. There was increasing need to explain why self-regulation was not doing the job required and to recommend action for relief.

Part B
A New Model (Government Excluded)

John Maynard Keynes and the "New Economics"

Politically, the change in our economic policy is associated with the New Deal and Franklin D. Roosevelt; in economics it is associated with an English economist, John Maynard Keynes (pronounced *kānz*). As the originator of a new model, Keynes was responsible for bringing about a major revolution in economic thinking. In the course of it many economists turned from classical theory to the "new economics," based largely on Keynes's theories. According to the new ideas, a mature capitalist economy is not always able to maintain itself at a full-employment level without the onset of inflation. Inflation occurs because the two key items for self-regulation—changing interest rates and wage-price flexibility—are not sufficiently effective in preventing it.

Does Interest Regulate Savings and Investment?

The classical economist reasons that consumers will deprive themselves of some goods and services if they have sufficient incentive. To understand the flaws in this reasoning, ask yourself these questions: Would you take your savings out of a bank and spend them if interest rates declined? Is high interest the incentive that makes you save? Although a surplus of savings is going to lower the interest rate and allow businessmen to borrow at lower rates of interest, would you, if you were in business, increase your investment when people are spending less, even if you could borrow at lower rates?

JOHN MAYNARD KEYNES AND THE "NEW ECONOMICS"

John Maynard Keynes (1883–1946), more than any other economist in the twentieth century, is responsible for modifying classical thinking among the industrial nations of the West. During the 1930's the United States and the nations of western Europe were mired in the Great Depression. As the inoperativeness of the self-correcting mechanism of classical economics became more apparent, the need for new solutions to the problem became even more acute. However, the microeconomic approach of the marginalist school provided no satisfactory answer. Many economists realized that new concepts must be introduced if capitalism was to survive.

The first significant contribution to a solution of the problem came from the Swedish economists, particularly Professor Gunnar Myrdal, using the aggregate or macroeconomic approach. Their analysis of the relationship between savings, investment, and income was very similar to the conclusion of Keynes in his monumental work, *The General Theory of Employment, Interest, and Money,* published in 1936. Keynes emphasized the correlation between national income and employment. He showed that income was determined by consumption, investment, and government spending. Consumption changes with income (as do savings), but income is mainly influenced by the amount of investment. Because investment is the least stable of the three items determining income and because it may not be adequate to maintain national income sufficient to achieve full employment, the government should intervene to promote full employment. This it is able to do through the use of appropriate monetary and fiscal policies.

Economists today recognize that Keynes's approach had certain weaknesses. It was oriented for the short run and the model was static, without significant attention to economic growth. Furthermore, he did not recognize that in the long run people's spending habits change, adapting to the higher levels of income. Nevertheless, Keynes's ideas, together with related theories of economic growth, form the basis for the "new economics," the theory most widely accepted by economists in the nations of the Western industrial world.

Now let us consider some further questions. Suppose that the economy was already at a full-employment GNP and that businesses were investing in excess of savings (an inflationary situation). With a shortage of savings, interest rates rise, thus encouraging people to save and discouraging business from investing. Would you, as a businessman, refuse to invest because of higher interest rates at a time when people are buying more and prices seem to be rising, particularly when you know that rising prices will make it easier for you, a debtor, to pay back your loan?

If your answer to each of these questions is *yes,* you have a tendency to agree with the classical theorists. Before you arrive at a final answer, however, read on and study additional information that might influence your decision. In a later chapter we will see that interest rates do play a part in encouraging and discouraging business investment, but not necessarily in the self-regulating manner identified above.

Challenges to the Classical Theory

Some of the answers which you have given to the preceding questions may conflict with the classical interpretation of the function of interest. But if interest rates are not the key in determining savings and investment, what is? Modern economists have discovered that saving and investing are seldom, if ever, carried on by the same people. In reality much of existing savings comes from families that may be motivated to put money aside for anticipated spending or for financial security. Studies reveal that savings are closely tied to the level of national income. The higher the national income, the greater the amount of savings. As for investment, the most significant factor in its determination is the amount of profit that businessmen *anticipate* making. Although interest rates can be and sometimes are factors in determining profits, businessmen will more probably react to rising or falling sales expectations. Few businesses would increase their inventories or plant equipment when the economy is contracting, even though interest rates may be low.

The theory of self-correction through wage-price flexibility is also subject to strong criticism. In this case the flaws are probably due to major differences between the classical model and the actual functioning of the economy. A downswing in the economy will undoubtedly cause some decline in wages and prices, but that downward movement is very limited. The cost of labor is actually prevented from declining significantly. This inflexibility of wages is due primarily to two factors: minimum wage laws and the power of organized labor in maintaining wage levels.

The movement of prices is equally "sticky." Many of the products we buy come from industries in which prices are administered. Other prices may also be influenced by price-fixing or by regulation by government or business. As a result recessions do not usually bring any significant decline in prices. Certainly there is not enough decline to result in any significant increase in purchasing power because of the lower prices. Therefore, instead of a downswing resulting in a lowering of wages and prices, we find fewer workers employed and prices declining so slightly that increased buying is unlikely. As a result little self-correction takes place.

Consumption, Savings, and Income

If traditional capitalism, contrary to theory, does not have a feature of self-correction, what can be done to provide a full-employment economy without inflation? As you have already learned, the GNP level is dependent on the relationship between savings and investment. Having explored the criticisms of the classical interpretation of these key factors, let us see what Keynes and other modern economists learned about them that might be useful in developing a new model for our economy—one that would remain within the broad framework of capitalism.

As we saw previously (p. 251), when we speak of savings, we are also speaking about consumption. This is true because of their complementary nature: What we do not save we spend and, of course, what we do not spend we save. Therefore, our discussion of savings is equally a discussion of consumption. We must also point out that for the present a consideration of government is omitted because we are assuming that government income and expenditure will be exactly equal. In Figure 13–2 we used the figure of $1 trillion to represent a full-employment GNP without inflation. Since government income and expenditure amounted to $200 billion, the full-employment noninflationary GNP for the private sector (including both consumers and business) would be $800 billion.

When we examine national income statistics, we find a very strong and direct relationship between consumption and GNP. As any of the five major national income measurements go up, the amount of consumption also increases. Figure 13–4 shows consumption and disposable personal income for a 42-year period. Note that consumption increased by almost the same percentage as did disposable personal income except for the years of World War II. During those years the availability of goods for private consumption was too small to be considered typ-

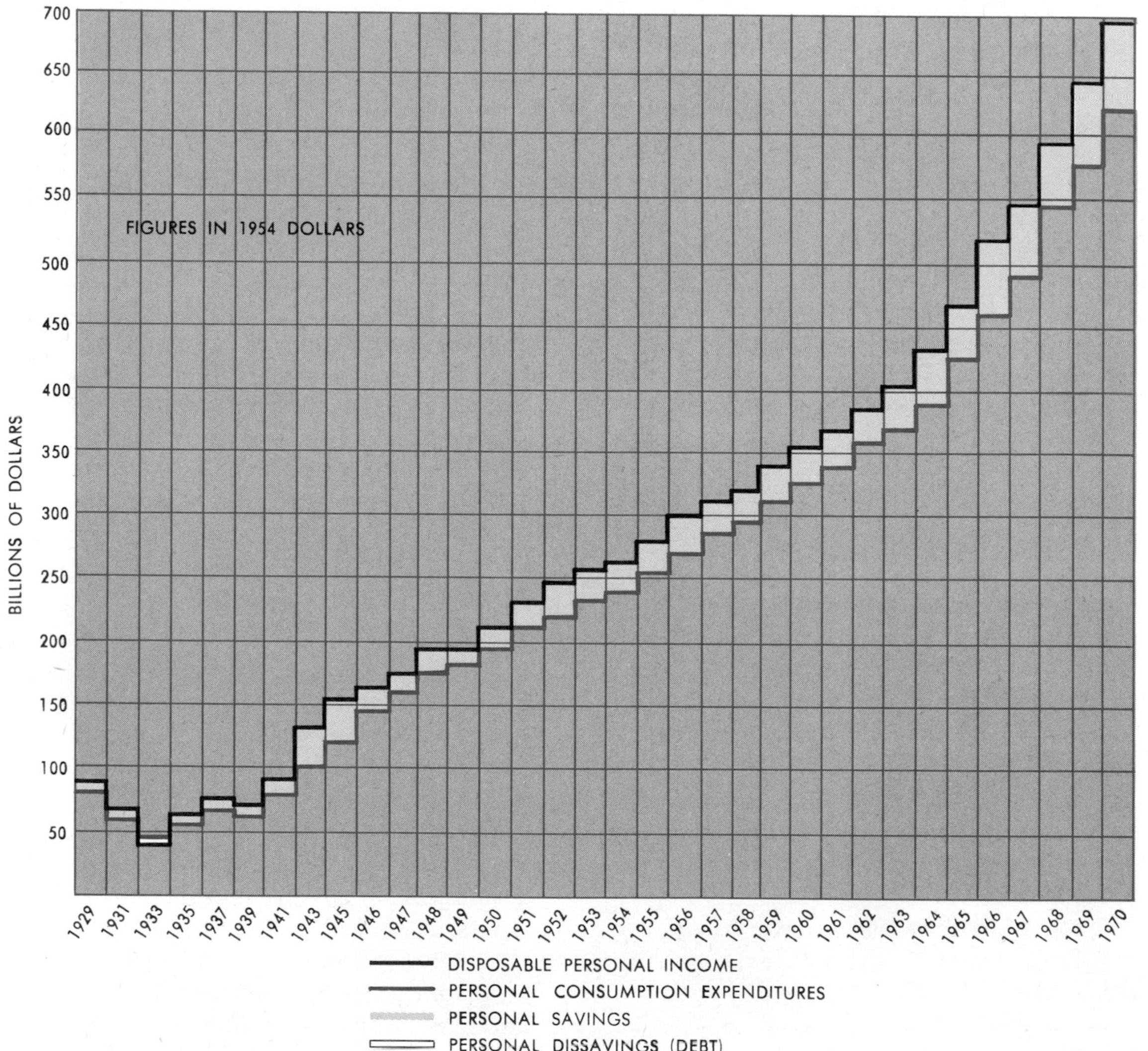

FIGURE 13–4 Disposable Personal Income Influences the Level of Consumption

As disposable personal income increases, so does consumption. Compare savings in the last 10 years with those of 1933 and the World War II years. SOURCE: U.S. Department of Commerce estimates.

ical. However, during a recent decade, consumption has been approximately 92 to 95 percent of DPI.

In 1960, DPI was $350 billion and consumption was $339 billion. Where was the $11 billion that was not spent? It must have been personal savings—that part of the DPI that was not consumed. If we measured savings for the last 10 years, we would find that, like consumption, they too have been remarkably constant.

Figure 13–4 also tells something about personal savings, shown on that graph by the light shading, for those years when DPI is greater than personal expenditures. In most years since the Depression, substantial personal savings are indicated.

Looking at the year 1933 we see something quite different. What does this change mean? If the spaces (light shading) below the black line and above the green line indicate savings, then the space (shown in white) below the green line and above the black line must indicate dissavings, or spending more than was received. How can we spend more than we earn? As we have seen (p. 251), we do it by borrowing, by using savings accumulated in earlier years, or by buying on credit.

At very low levels of income people will spend more than they earn. As income increases, consumption and income will come into balance. Soon income will surpass consumption and savings will grow. The greater the aggregate income (DPI), the greater the consumption, but also the greater the savings.

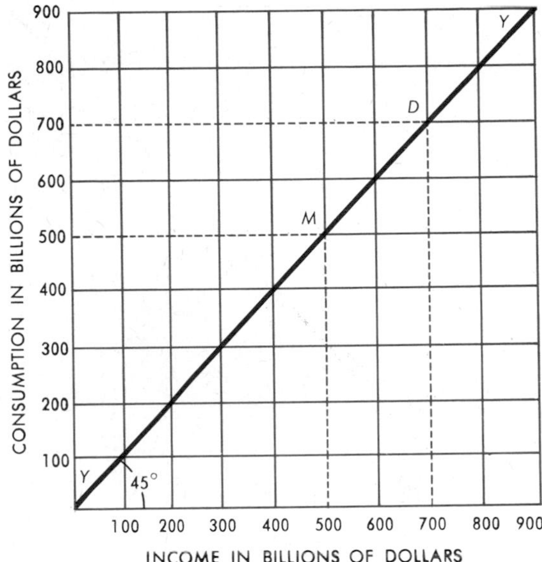

FIGURE 13–5 A New Tool: The 45° Line

Using the 45° line approach, a new tool, we can better understand the theory of income analysis. Points *M* and *D* on the line Y show consumption equal to income.

A New Economic Tool: The 45° Line

For a better understanding of the relationship between income, savings, and consumption, we should become familiar with a new economic tool, shown in Figure 13–5. On the graph the horizontal axis measures income and the vertical axis measures consumption. Line Y is a diagonal, 45°. Any point along the 45° line is equally distant from the horizontal (income) axis and the vertical (consumption) axis. Point *M* on the 45° line in Figure 13–5 shows income and consumption to be the same. It tells us that we are spending *all* our income, regardless of its size.

But do we spend all we earn? Look back at Figure 13–4. Although that graph shows consumption as increasing with income, it never shows them to be the same. Only when income was very low was consumption more than income. This means that the 45° line, Y, shows the range of incomes, but it is not an accurate picture of consumption at each level of income.

Now let us turn to Figure 13–6. Here consumption for each level of income is

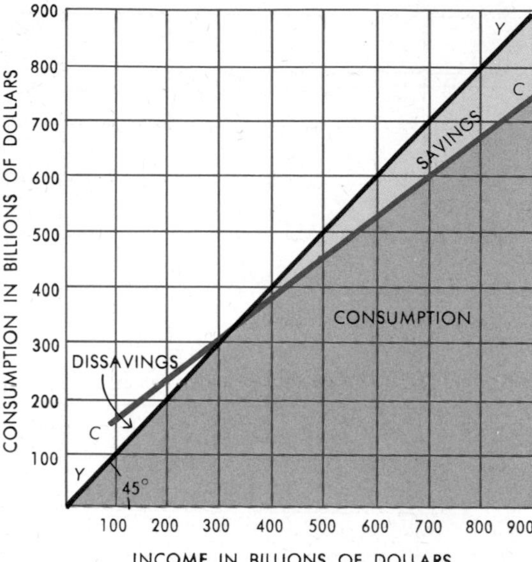

FIGURE 13–6 Schedule of Consumption and Savings

The 45° line (Y) measures levels of income. The consumption line (C) measures what spending is likely to be at different levels of income. The difference between income (Y) and consumption (C) is savings (S).

plotted. The consumption line (C) is lower than the income line (45° line, or Y). The light shaded area between consumption and income is savings. As we continue to learn about the new model, the usefulness of this new tool, national income determination, will become evident.

Propensity to Consume and Save

Although prices, consumer credit, availability of goods, and fluctuations in purchases of durable goods are all considered factors in determining consumption, most modern economists agree that income is the single most important factor. Figure 13–7 uses the 45° line to analyze income. In Figure 13–2, $1 trillion represented the GNP needed for full employment without inflation, with $800 billion of this in the private sector. With that same amount for the private sector, Figure 13–7 shows that $660 billion of gross private income will be spent by individuals in the market and $140 billion will be gross savings. Why will gross private income be spent in this way? Economists have discovered that people tend to spend and to save certain proportions at particular levels of income. This tendency to spend certain amounts at certain levels of income is called the *propensity to consume.* The tendency to save a certain amount at a certain level of income is called the *propensity to save.* With an aggregate private income of $800 billion the propensity to consume will be $660 billion and the propensity to save, $140 billion.

If we are to sustain an $800 billion gross private income with gross savings at $140 billion, how much gross investment is needed? You will recall that if the new

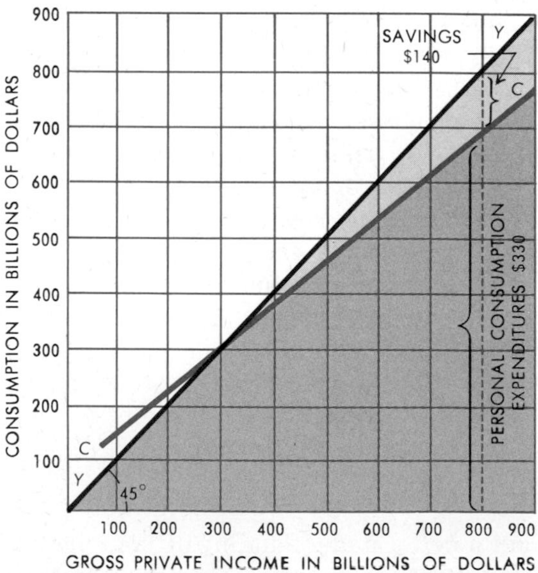

FIGURE 13–7 Schedule of Propensity to Consume

The propensity to consume and the propensity to save increase as income increases.

KEYNESIAN MODEL

This is an exercise in the functioning of the Keynesian model. Its purpose is to show you how our aggregate income is determined and how our policy decisions can bring about changes in that income.

AGGREGATE DEMAND
45°
AGGREGATE INCOME

On our graph the vertical axis measures aggregate demand (spending). The horizontal axis measures our aggregate income. A diagonal line, 45°, shows total spending of income.

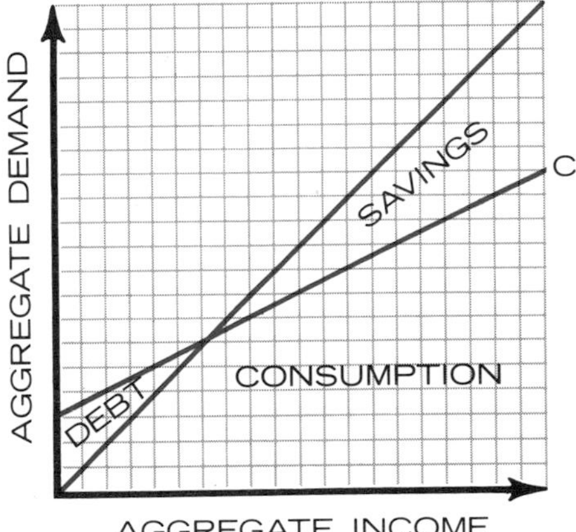

We know that consumers do not spend all their income, but will save as their income increases. Line C shows consumers spending more as their income rises. What they do not spend, they save. The area between the 45° line and the consumption line represents savings (or debt).

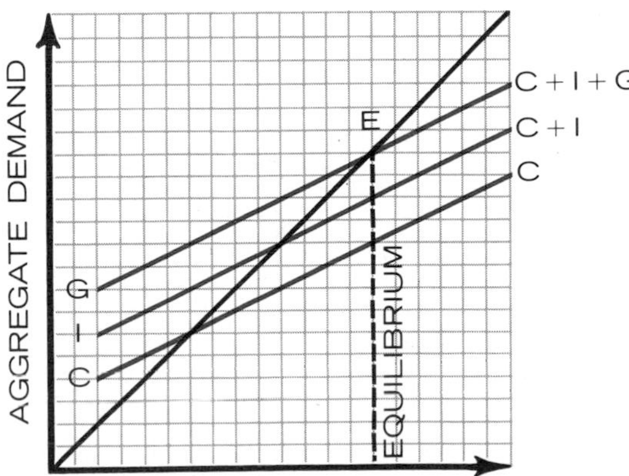

In addition to consumer spending, we have business investment (I) and government spending (G). Total spending, or aggregate demand, is shown by consumption (C), investment (I), and government spending (G). Aggregate income, or equilibrium, can be determined where the C + I + G line crosses the 45° line. This relates to the formula for income determination: $C + I + G = Y$ (income).

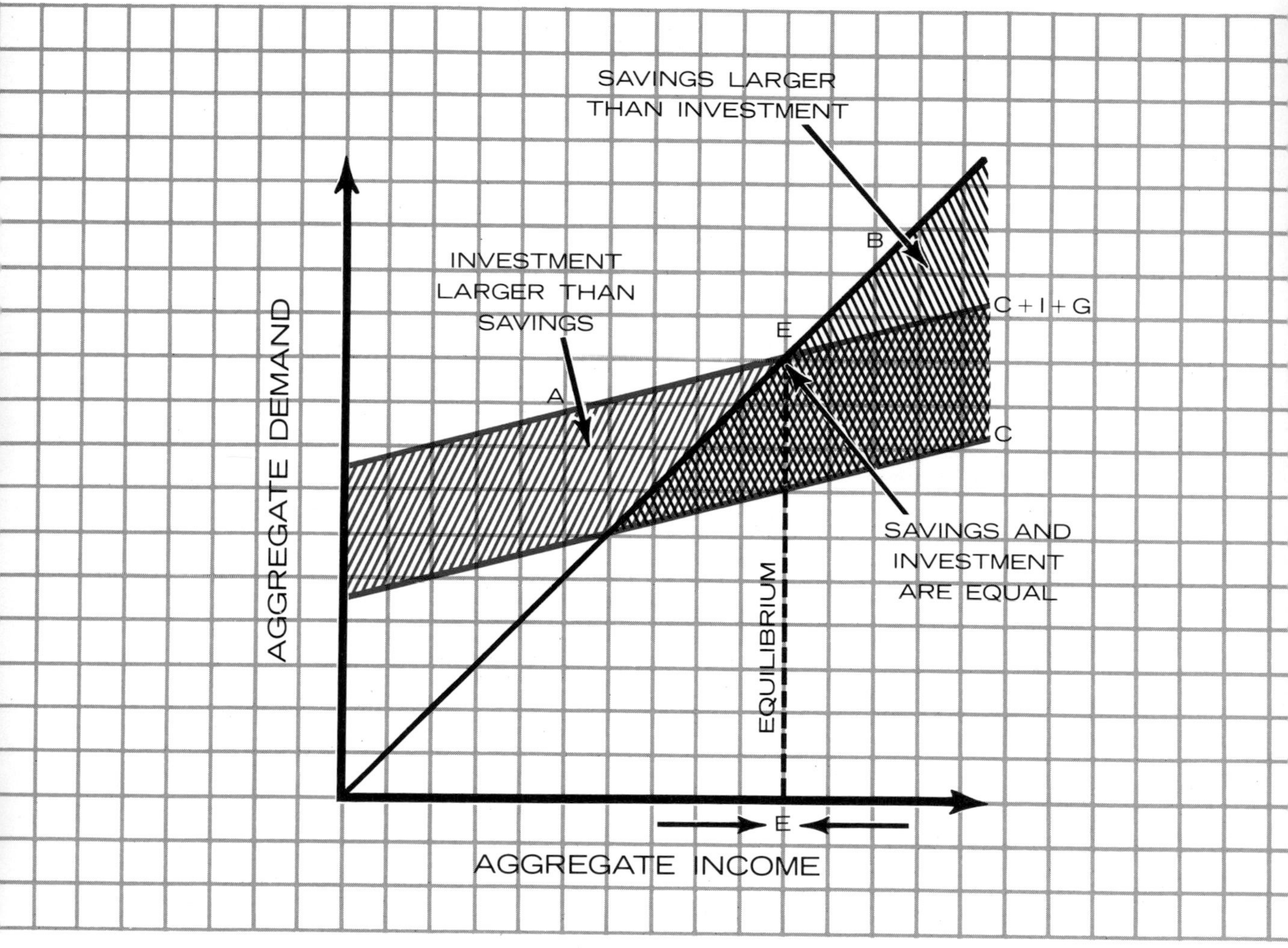

Aggregate income will be in equilibrium where investment [public (G) and private (I)] equals savings. At A, investment is larger than savings (demand greater than supply encourages expansion) and aggregate income will rise. At B, savings are larger than investment (supply is larger than demand) and aggregate income will decline. At E, investment and savings equal each other (equilibrium) and aggregate income will remain unchanged.

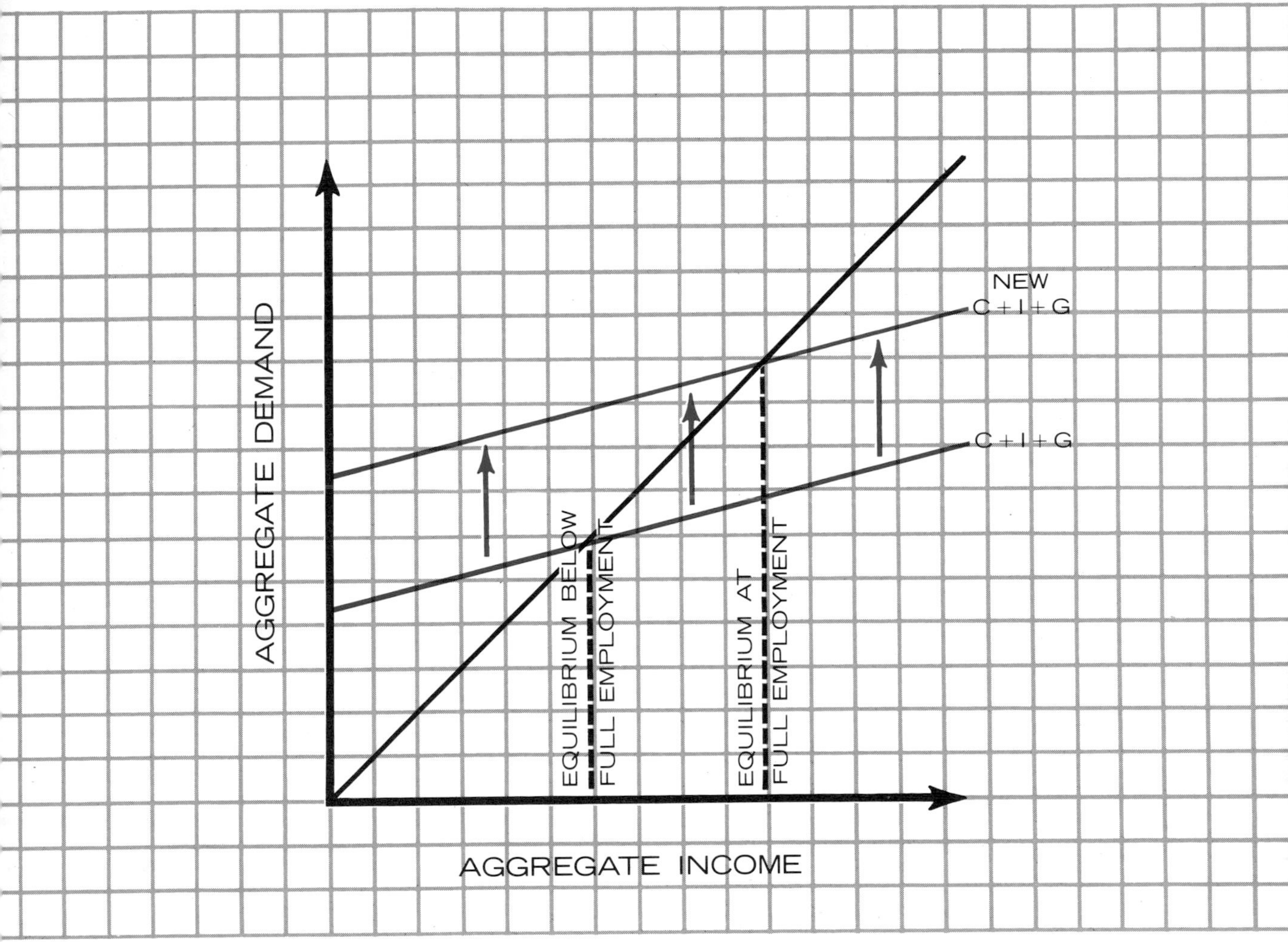

Keynesian economics, or what some call the new capitalism, calls for economic policy to bring the equilibrium point up to full employment without inflation. Graphically, this is represented by raising the original C + I + G line (total spending), which crossed the 45° line below full employment, to the new C + I + G line. The new aggregate demand is now sufficient to sustain full employment without inflation.

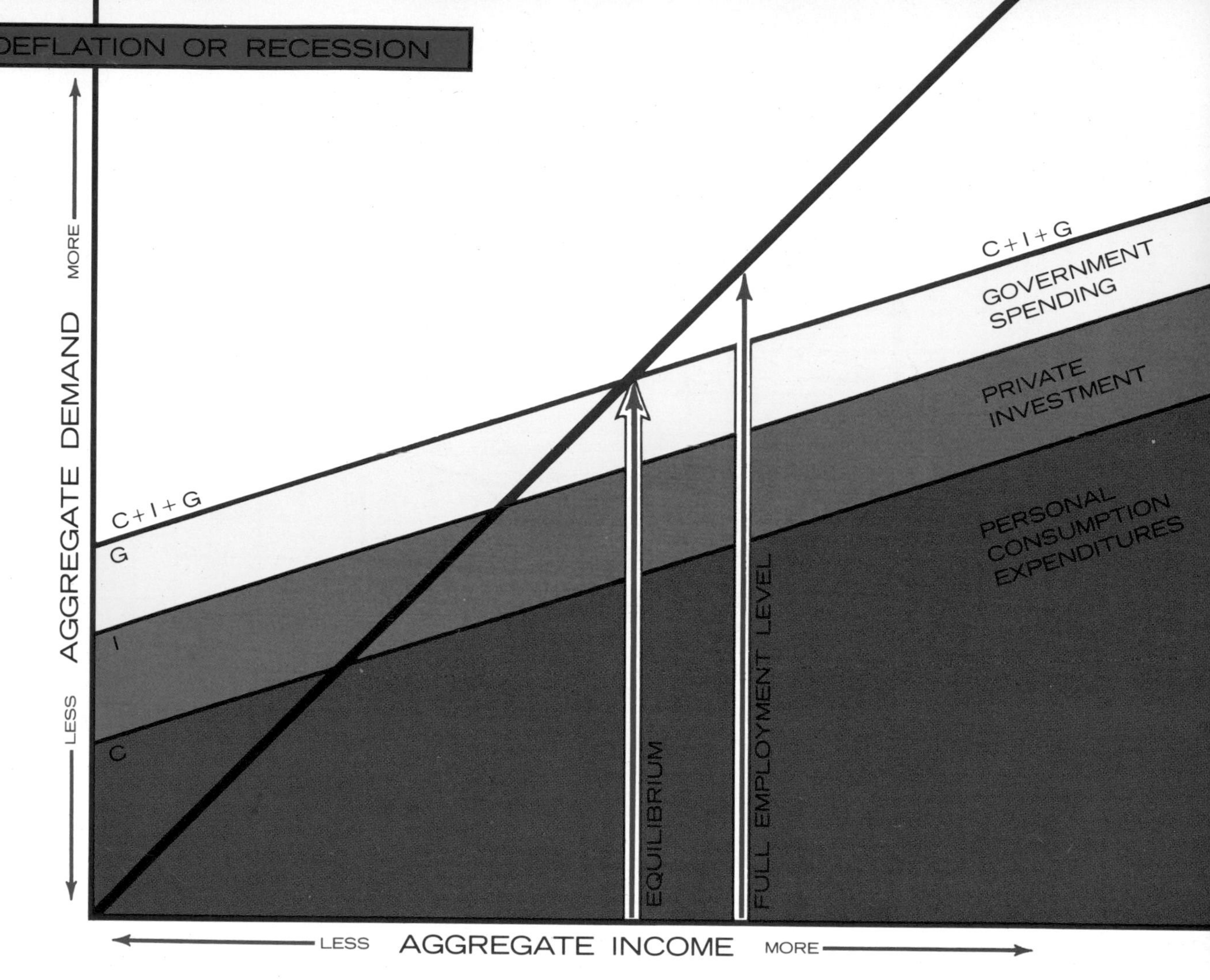

You see here a graphic representation of the economy in equilibrium below the full employment level. Personal consumption (C) ▇▇ , business investment (I) ▇▇ , and government spending (G) ▇▇ add up to total spending, or aggregate demand. The C + I + G line crosses the 45° line at equilibrium below full employment. Savings and investment are equal at this point. The economy is not making full use of its resources. It is producing below its capacity because aggregate demand is not sufficient to support full employment.

GNP or, in this case, the new gross private income is to equal the old gross private income, gross investment must equal gross savings. A gross investment of less than $140 billion will mean less production and therefore less employment and a lowering of our gross private income. A gross investment greater than $140 billion can only cause inflation, since we are already producing at full employment.

Determination of Income

Figure 13–8 shows what will happen if gross private investment is only $100 billion (*b*), $40 billion less than gross savings. Then, at the market (*c*), with $660 billion of personal consumption expenditures and $100 billion in investment, there would be $40 billion of goods and services left over (or not produced). The new gross private income will be insufficient to sustain full employment. However, instead of the gross private income dropping to $760 billion, our diagram shows it dropping to $700 billion (*e*). This is due to the *multiplier effect,* which in this case is 2½. Briefly, the multiplier effect refers to the fact that any change in spending or investment, either public or private, brings about a greater change in income. This is shown in (*d*). In our example $40 billion additional investment by business will increase income by $100 billion. Thus, the multiplier is 2½. What would happen in the example above if all things remained the same except that there was a gross investment of $120 billion? More will be said about the multiplier on page 316.

Using the 45° Line to Determine Income

Let us now consider the example previously explained in Figure 13–8, but this time let us see how it looks when we use

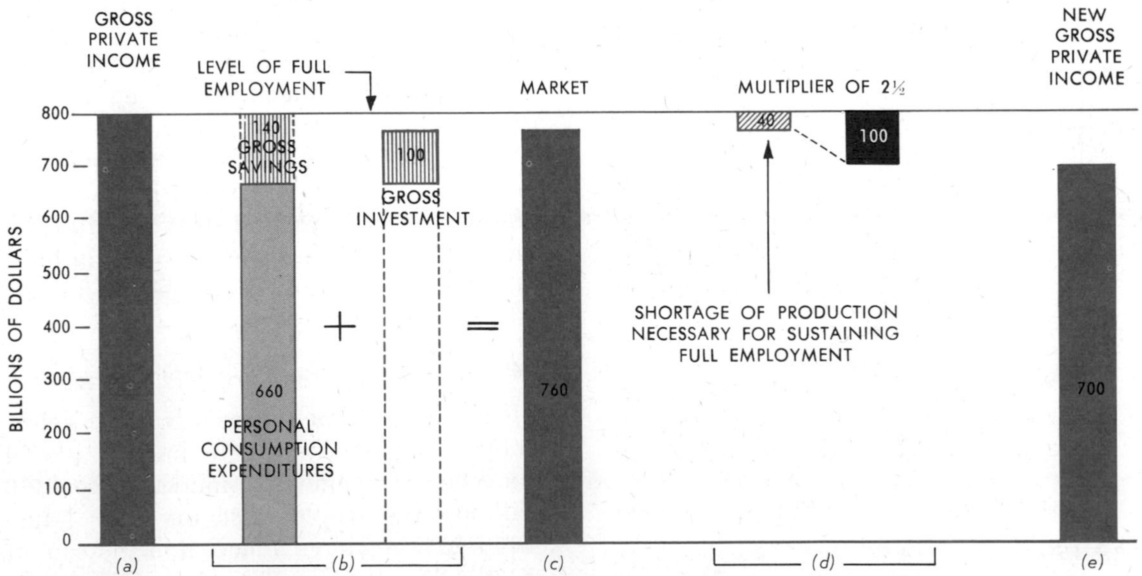

FIGURE 13–8 Determining Gross Private Income

When gross private investment is less than gross private savings ($40 billion less), the new gross private income will decline by an amount ($100 billion) greater than this difference because of the multiplier effect.

the diagram with the 45° line. This combination is shown in Figure 13–9. You will recall that the 45° line indicates income and that line *C* is the actual consumption line, or the propensity to consume (the tendency to spend certain amounts at various levels of income). Move to the right along the horizontal axis, which measures gross private income, until $800 billion is reached. The broken vertical line shows what the propensity to consume will be and what the propensity to save will be at the gross private income level of $800 billion. You can see that it is the same as that found in Figure 13–7.

When Savings Are Larger Than Investment

Let us see what happens to the gross private income when only $100 billion is invested while $140 billion is saved. The

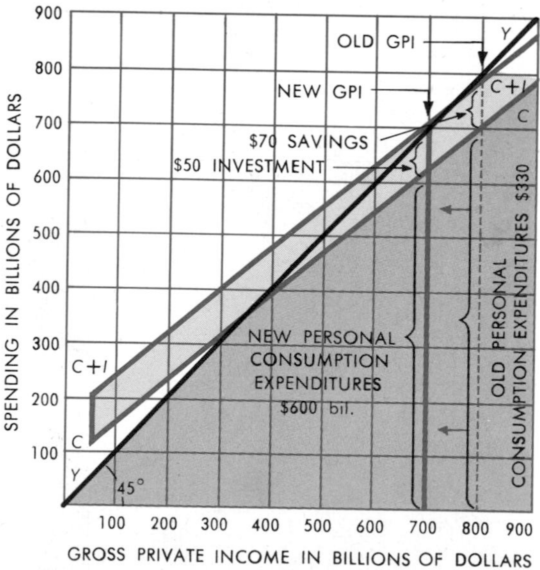

FIGURE 13–9 Determining Gross Private Income Using the 45° Line

In this graph we see the same example as in Figure 13-8, but this time we use the 45° line as a tool for analysis.

C line shows the consumer in the market. The businessman also goes to the market, so his "purchases" (investment, *I*) must be added to the personal consumption expenditures (*C*). This is done by adding $100 billion, his investment, to personal consumption expenditures, as shown in *C* + *I* (consumption plus investment). Line *C* rises because consumption increases with income. Line *C* + *I* is parallel to line *C* because investment has been fixed at $100 billion, regardless of income. We can now find the new gross private income. Locate the point where the *C* + *I* line crosses the 45° line (our income line). It is shown by the arrow labeled "New GPI" and points to $700 billion, the new gross private income.

New Income Means New Consumption

In Figure 13–9 you can see that the new GPI is lower. Personal consumption expenditures have dropped to $600 billion. This occurs because consumption is determined mainly by income. What happens to savings when income has been reduced to $700 billion? Since personal consumption expenditures are now $600 billion and since what is not spent is saved, we know that savings will drop to $100 billion. The level of spending and the level of saving have both decreased as income has fallen.

When Investment Is Larger Than Savings

Using the 45° line diagram, we can determine what gross private income would be when investment is increased to $150 billion. We would raise the *C* + *I* line $150 billion above the *C* line instead of $100 billion above. The new GPI would be at the point where the new *C* + *I* line crosses the 45° line, *Y*. What would personal consumption expenditures be? How much would savings be? Would this new gross private income be good for the economy?

By now you should recognize that if we know the nation's propensity to consume (that is, the consumption or *C* line) and we know what gross investment is, we can determine what gross private income will be. Once again we are able to see the importance of the relationship of consumption, as well as investment, to savings.

Let us leave our diagrams and statistics for a moment and consider in a very general way what these illustrations mean. A contracting economy (reducing GPI from $800 billion to $700 billion) results when retail stores do not fill up with merchandise and manufacturers do not increase production or invest sufficiently to use up the savings available. Since fewer workers are needed, income declines. When that happens, consumption also drops, and so does the ability to save. The diagrams and statistics shown here tell an unemotional story. For a more personal view of how a contracting economy may hurt people, talk with someone whose income has been lowered or who has been removed from his job because of a decline in business activity.

Fluctuating Investment and Income

We have seen the economic reactions which take place when gross private income dropped to $700 billion, $100 billion below the level needed for full employment. Now let us consider what can be done to expand income back to the $800

TABLE 13–1 Fluctuation of Investments and Personal Consumption Expenditures (billions of dollars)

	Personal Consumption Expenditures	Gross Private Domestic Investment	Gross National Product
1952	216.7	51.9	345.5
1953	230.0	52.6	364.6
1954	236.5	51.7	364.8
1955	254.4	67.4	398.0
1956	266.7	70.0	419.2
1957	281.4	67.9	441.1
1958	290.1	60.9	447.3
1959	311.2	75.3	483.7
1960	325.2	74.8	503.7
1961	335.2	71.7	520.1
1962	355.1	83.0	560.3
1963	375.0	87.1	590.5
1964	401.2	94.0	632.4
1965	432.8	108.1	684.9
1966	466.3	121.4	749.9
1967	492.1	116.6	793.9
1968	535.8	126.5	865.0
1969	577.5	139.8	931.4
1970	616.8	135.8	976.8

Gross private domestic investment fluctuated far more than personal consumption expenditures. Compare the rise and fall of investment with GNP. Lines are drawn under recession years. SOURCE: U.S. Department of Commerce, Office of Business Economics.

billion level. We cannot afford to wait for the possible readjustment that may occur (due to a drop in the wage-price level or to changing interest rates on savings and investment) to bring about the necessary expansion. What other means are available for achieving it? Might consumers be persuaded to spend more at the market? During the 1957–58 recession President Eisenhower urged the American public to buy more in an effort to stimulate business. Advertising and sales by retailers were also used extensively to increase business. Certainly an increase in consumption by the public would motivate businesses to increase investment. Greater personal consumption expenditures, *C*, plus greater investment, *I*, would certainly bring about a greater gross private income. Although it is true that both personal consumption expenditures and gross investment determine aggregate income, the variation in investment is far greater than that in consumption, as shown in Table 13–1. Note, too, that the decline in investment is accompanied by a slowdown, in the increase of the GNP as stated in current dollars.

Although not all economists agree, most of them would list the amount of business investment as a greater factor in determining aggregate income than the more stable consumption by householders. Therefore, in order to raise aggregate income to attain full employment, it is more important to get businessmen to increase their investments. In terms of the diagram with the 45° line we may say that the problem is to raise the $C + I$ line so that it will intersect the 45° line at $800 billion or whatever the full-employment level may be. Before we attempt to solve the problem of how to increase investment, let us return to the market to consider the actions of another important buyer—government.

Part C
A New Model (Government Included)

Until now we have been able to omit government from consideration because we were proceeding on the assumption that the government was balancing its budget, keeping expenditures equal to revenues. Actually, we know that this has rarely happened in recent times, particularly at the federal level. Since 1931 three fourths of our federal budgets have shown deficits, with greater expenditures than revenues. In the years since 1930, budget surpluses have occurred only 10 times. What have been the effects of the unbalanced budget on the economy?

The Unbalanced Budget

In Chapter 10 you learned that the federal government is less restricted than families, businesses, or local and state governments in keeping its budget balanced. The United States government may not only borrow money, but it can actually print money to pay its bills, as it did during the Civil War. However, such a great power, if not used wisely, might well destroy the nation's economy. The German government after World War I tried such a way out of its difficulties, with devastating inflation as the result. The Republic of China during and immediately after World War II followed the German example, with similar results. Our own government has, in general, avoided such extremes and the hardships of uncontrolled inflation resulting from the indiscriminate printing of money. The discussion that follows is concerned with the effects of an unbalanced budget as it increases the national debt.

As we have previously seen in Figure 13–2, when government goes to the marketplace, it purchases more than $200 billion worth of goods and services, slightly more than one fifth of all goods and services bought, and usually more than the total bought by businesses through gross private investment. This sizable purchase requires the employment of a large portion of our work force. In order to pay for these goods and services, the government collects revenue, chiefly in the form of taxes, from almost everyone. Paying taxes to the government limits people's spending for tangibles such as automobiles and for intangibles such as vacations. However, it does supply them with collective benefits such as schools, roads, and defense against foreign invasion. As you know, we have in our economy a long tradition of free enterprise, preferring to have individual households make independent decisions on what and how much they want of the goods and services available. However, as our society has become more complex and as people have become more interdependent, the demands and expenses of government have increased.

Growing Federal Expenditures

In Chapters 9 and 10 we observed the pattern of increased federal spending. We found that many factors contributed to this rise. Of particular importance recently have been the growing costs of national defense. When our nation became the leader of the free world, its defense costs rose sharply. We accept defense as a legitimate sphere of government activity; in addition, most of us admit that taking on the responsibility of leadership in the free world involves a greater cost for defense. However, few of us like the fact that these new obligations cut directly into our personal income, depriving us of additional goods and services.

Federal spending has increased in other areas besides defense. Demands for such benefits as better educational facilities, roads, and welfare have increased the share of government purchases from slightly more than a twelfth of the national income before World War I to about a fifth at present. Instead of making almost all our decisions at the market, we now make some of our choices regarding goods and services at the polling booths, where we vote for the party which we think will make the best decisions regarding our collective wants.

We know that government's role in the economy has increased by greater purchasing in the market and by the collecting of more revenues. Government powers also have increased through such changes as the employing (both directly and indirectly) of more workers; by greater control over business, labor unions, farmers, and professional people; and by various subsidies. Some of these controls we have already dealt with; others we will consider later. Our immediate concern is the significance to the economy of increased government expenditure and control when the government's budget is not balanced.

How does this governmental activity affect the national economy under differing employment conditions?

Determining Income with Government Included

Income Below Full Employment

Let us assume, as we did in Figure 13–2, that $1 trillion of GNP is required to achieve a full-employment economy. Let us further assume that private consumption and investment add up to $800 billion, with $200 billion still awaiting collection by the government. What would happen if government collected this $200 billion but spent only $160 billion? Figure 13–10 provides an answer. Instead of the economy's falling only $40 billion below the $1 trillion full-employment GNP level, it has declined $100 billion, due again to the multiplier effect. By spending less than was collected, the government has left goods and services unpurchased in the marketplace. As unsold stocks of their merchandise accumulate, businessmen will probably plan to reduce production below the previous year's level, since this surplus may lead to reduced prices and profits. Curtailing production will reduce the GNP below the level of full employment. Aggregate demand is $40 billion below the level of full employment without inflation. It would require an increase in consumption, investment, and/or government of $40 billion to bring aggregate demand up to a level of full employment. This insufficient amount of aggregate demand is called the *deflationary gap*.

Income Above Full Employment

In contrast with the preceding example,

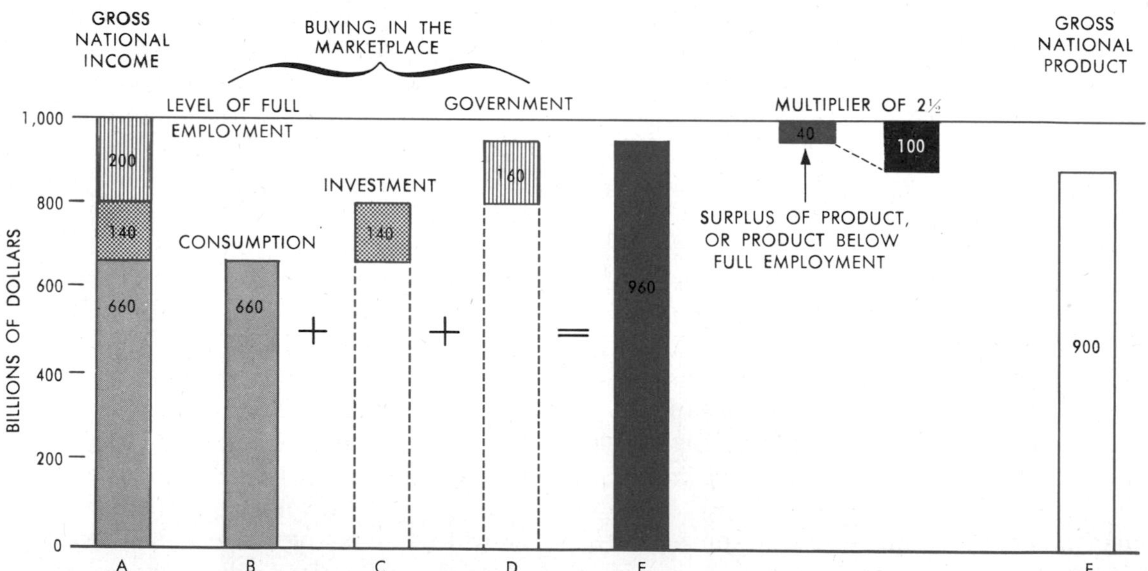

FIGURE 13–10 Income Determination When Aggregate Demand Is Too Low

If the private sector of the economy is sufficient to sustain full employment but the government collects more in revenue than it spends, the GNP will decline by a multiple of the difference between government income and government expenditures. The new aggregate income is not sufficient to maintain the economy at a level of full employment, thereby causing a deflationary gap.

let us assume that the private sector of the economy begins as in that case, but that this time government takes in $200 billion and spends $240 billion. Adding together private consumption, investment, and government spending brings the aggregate demand for goods and services to $1.04 trillion, which is above the full-employment product of $1 trillion. With the demand for goods and services above the supply and the economy already operating at the full-employment level, inflation would be the outcome. Figure 13–11 demonstrates this situation, with the multiplier compounding the effect by two and a half times. The new GNP is $1.1 trillion, $100 billion above full employment and therefore inflationary. If we reduce aggregate demand by cutting consumption, investment, and/or government expenditures by a total of $40 billion we would achieve our desired goal of full employment without inflation. Therefore, we call this excessive $40 billion of aggregate demand the *inflationary gap.*

Income Determination with the 45° Line

Let us see how the information on income determination, shown in Figures 13–10 and 13–11, looks when combined with the diagram of the 45° line.

Income Below Full Employment

Figure 13–12 shows aggregate income falling $100 billion below the full-employment income of $1 trillion, just as it did in Figure 13–10. Our aggregate income, *Y*, is determined by adding consumption, *C*, plus investment, *I*, plus government spending, *G*, together; it is found at the

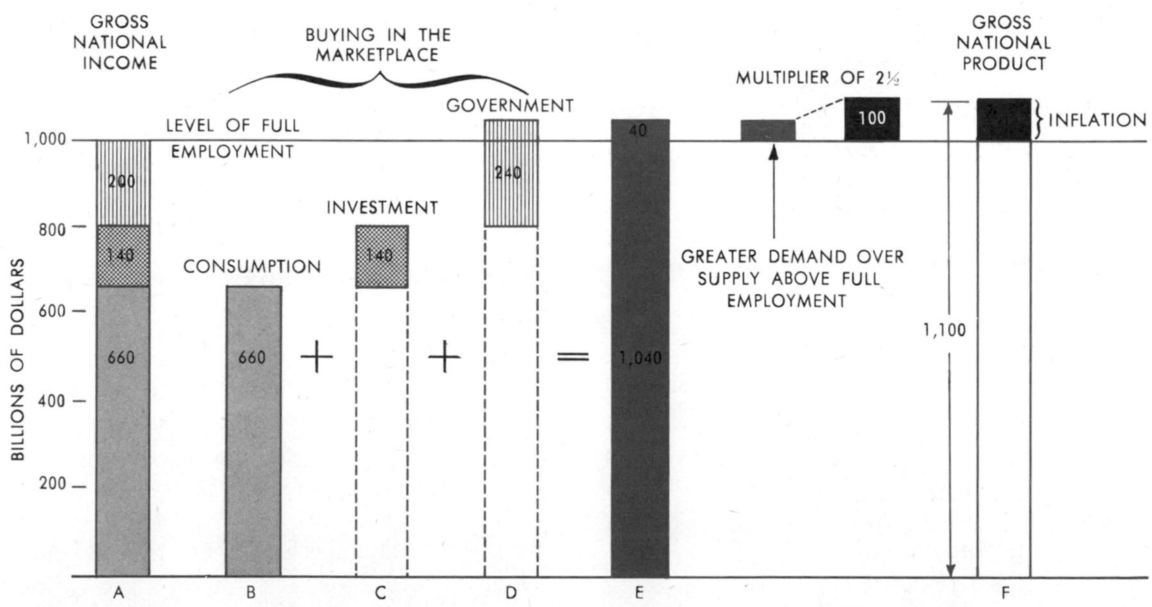

FIGURE 13–11 Income Determination When Aggregate Demand Is Too High

If the private sector of the economy is sufficient to sustain full employment but government spends more than it collects, the GNP will rise by a multiple of the difference between government income and government expenditures. The aggregate demand (total spending) is greater than the capacity of the economy to produce, resulting in an inflation.

point where the $C + I + G$ line crosses the 45° line (Y line), which is at $900 billion. Income will be below the full-employment level because $40 billion worth of goods and services have *not* been purchased by consumers, businessmen, or government or by any combination of them. Because of this surplus, businessmen in general will reduce production, realizing an income of $100 billion less (the multiplier effect) than $1 trillion, the full-employment level. An increase in $C + I + G$ of $40 billion, represented by the striped area (A) above the $C + I + G$ line, would provide the demand for goods and services needed for full employment.

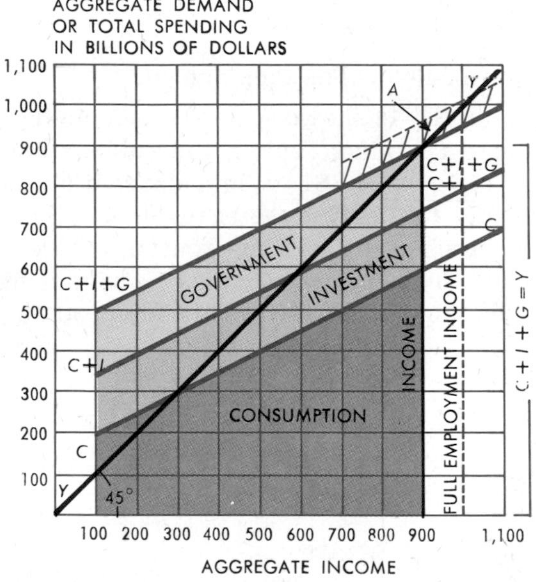

FIGURE 13–12 Income Determination Using the 45° Line—Underemployment

Aggregate income is determined at the point where aggregate demand, consumption plus investment plus government spending, intersects the 45° line. $C + I + G$ needs to be increased by $40 billion (*A*) to attain a full-employment income. *A* is the deflationary gap.

Income Above Full Employment

Figure 13–13 shows what happens when aggregate demand, the $C + I + G$, is greater than full-employment income (note Figure 13–11 also). The $C + I + G$ line crosses the Y line at $1.1 trillion, $100 billion above full-employment income. Under these circumstances the demand for goods and services is greater than can be supplied with the existing labor force. Businessmen, in their desire to fill the greater demand, bid against one another to obtain workers and other resources, causing prices to rise. Production will be at the $1 trillion level, or full employment; however, because of rising prices, the goods and services will carry a total market price of $1.1 trillion. This full-employment level is not desirable because it is inflationary. If the $C + I + G$ (the aggregate demand) can be reduced by $40 billion, supply and demand will reach an equilibrium level at full-employment income, $1 trillion. In Figure 13–13 the $C + I + G$ line must be lowered by the amount shown in the striped area (*B*), $40 billion, so that it crosses the Y line at $1 trillion, the full-employment level.

Equilibrium

By now it is clear that the relation between savings and investment is critical in the question of maintaining GNP at full employment. Let us look further at the interaction between these factors.

Think of savings as all production not bought by consumers, *C*. On our 45° line diagram it is the space between the *C* line and the 45° line. Think of investment as made up of private *I* (business) and public *G* (government). It is the space between the *C* line and the $C + I + G$ line. These areas are shown in Figure 13–14. With these revised definitions it is evident that if savings are greater than investment (government and business not buying all the production remaining after consumer purchasing), the aggregate income will fall. Savings larger than public and private investment produce a declining aggregate income ($S > I$ = declining Y). By contrast, if investment is larger than savings (government and business demand more production than that which consumers leave at the market), income will rise ($I > S$ = rising Y). Under these conditions, aggregate income will be at the point where savings and investment are exactly the same. That is the *equilibrium point,* shown in Figure 13–14 at *E*. It is also the point where our $C + I + G$ line crosses the 45° line because at that point $S = I$.

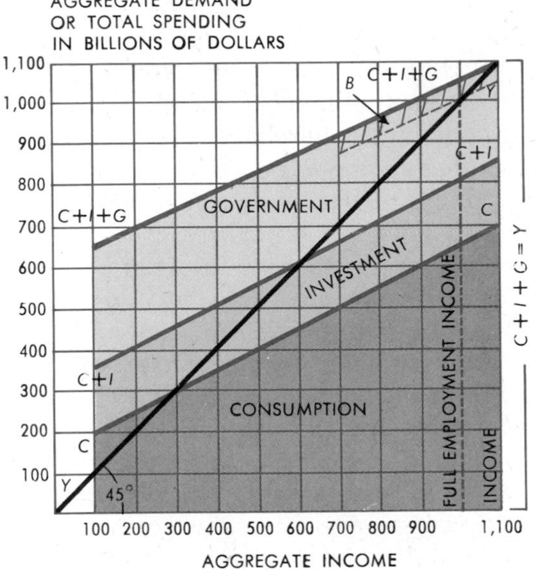

FIGURE 13–13 Income Determination Using the 45° Line—Inflation

Aggregate demand is greater than what a full-employment income can supply, thereby causing an inflation. $C + I + G$ must be reduced by $40 billion (*B*) to reduce aggregate income to the full-employment level. *B* is the inflationary gap.

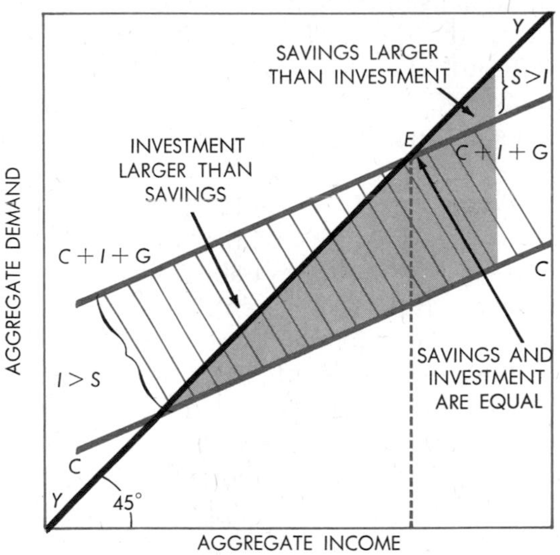

FIGURE 13–14 Determining Aggregate Income Using Savings and Investment

Aggregate income is at that point where investment (private and public) and savings (gross savings and taxes) equal each other. This is shown at point *E*, equilibrium (where the $C + I + G$ line crosses the Y line). When $I > S$, income will rise. When $S > I$, income will decline.

You will recall that a major disagreement exists between the classical economist and the Keynesian economist over the question of where equilibrium will be achieved. The classical economist maintains that if the economy is free from any restraints in the operation of the market (supply and demand operating under pure competition), equilibrium will be at the full-employment level without inflation. The new model indicates that equilibrium can be and frequently is at a point below full employment. That is so when investment is smaller than savings.

Achieving Full Employment Without Inflation

As we have noted earlier, many economists believe that one of our major goals is that of achieving a full-employment economy without inflation. Using our new tools for analysis, we would phrase it as having the $C + I + G$ line intersect the Y line at an income level high enough to support full employment but not so high as to cause inflation. It is possible to implement the goal of full employment without inflation by means of government policy. Chapter 15 will present a further consideration of the policies mentioned here.

When $C + I + G$ is too low (below $1 trillion), a policy providing for corrective measures to increase it should be put into effect if full employment is to be maintained. For example, the full-employment budget that President Nixon presented for fiscal 1972 had a planned deficit, thereby raising aggregate demand. Economists differ on priorities: whether the increases should be made by reducing personal taxes, thereby stimulating C; or cutting corporate taxes, encouraging greater I; or having additional government expenditures, whether for schools, the space program, or a new river project. There is much disagreement about which policy is best. Any of these—and many others as well—can be used to raise aggregate demand, $C + I + G$, to full-employment income.

When aggregate demand is above the full-employment income level, a policy for lowering it is needed if inflation is to be prevented. Such a measure would be the opposite of those previously used. Raising taxes, cutting government expenditures, or discouraging business investment would all help to lower the $C + I + G$ line, making it possible to achieve the goal of full employment without inflation.

The Multiplier Effect

At several places in this chapter we have noted the importance of the multiplier effect in magnifying changes. To understand better its causes and effects, we must consider it in more detail. To do this we will begin by returning to Figure 13–12. The $C + I + G$ line crosses the 45° line at $900 billion. If we add $40 billion of government purchases, the $C + I + G$ line moves upward so that it crosses the 45° line at $1 trillion, a gain of $100 billion. Additional purchases of $40 billion bring about an increase of $100 billion of aggregate income, showing graphically the multiplier effect. The same effect can be brought about by consumers' spending more or businesses' investing more, since an increase by any one purchaser or combination of purchasers in the marketplace results in raising the $C + I + G$ line and raising aggregate income by some multiple of the additional purchase.

Why the Multiplier Effect?

You are probably wondering why there is a multiplier effect. To find an answer, let us suppose that government spent an additional $40 billion more than it collected or that business increased its investment by that amount. We will assume that prices will remain constant and that we are operating our economy at a level below full employment. Thus, the injection of this new investment or government spending will not create a demand for goods and services in excess of our ability to produce them. The bulk of the $40 billion would probably be received by suppliers of goods. They would spend part of it and save part of it. The part they spent would be received by workers and other suppliers—in general by people who would in turn spend part of it and save a part. Employees receiving additional wages and businessmen receiving additional profits would take part of their money to the market to spend and would save the rest. The effect of the additional $40 billion of spending on the nation's economy as a whole would far exceed that basic figure because it would continue to be spent, though in an ever-decreasing amount. Since part of the $40 billion is spent many times, the total effect is far greater than the original amount only.

Determining the Multiplier

Since we must allow for the multiplier, we need to know in advance what the amount of it will be, if we are to make accurate predictions of change. Earlier we explained people's spending habits as a propensity to consume—the tendency to spend a certain amount of their income at a particular level of income. When income and spending increased, so did the ability to save and the amount saved. If we add $40 billion of income to the economy by way of investment or additional government spending, what portion of this amount received initially will be spent? If 60 percent, or $24 billion, is spent, we can say that three fifths of the *additional* income is the new propensity to consume. You recall that we refer to the last unit as "marginal." Since we are not speaking about what fraction of total income is spent but only the fraction of the additional unit, we refer to this three fifths as *marginal propensity to consume.* Sixteen billion dollars of the $40 billion of additional income is saved. That means that two fifths of this additional income is saved. The *marginal propensity to save* is two fifths. Marginal propensity to consume—three fifths (or $24 billion)—plus marginal propensity to save—two fifths (or $16 billion)—will equal one, or the total new income added. If you know the marginal propensity to save, you can easily figure out the marginal propensity to consume ($1 - \frac{2}{5} = \frac{3}{5}$). To find the multiplier, merely invert the marginal propensity to save, which gives $\frac{5}{2}$ (or $2^1/_2$). If you know the marginal propensity to consume,

"Reminds me of that crazy idea of Henry Ford's that you can make more selling at lower prices."

SOURCE: *Straight Herblock,* Simon & Schuster, 1964.

you can calculate the marginal propensity to save by subtracting it from 1 and then inverting to give you the multiplier ($1 - \frac{3}{5} = \frac{2}{5}$; invert to $\frac{5}{2}$, or $2^1/_2$). What would the multiplier be if the marginal propensity to consume were three fourths?

What would be the increase in aggregate income if businessmen invested $20 billion more and the marginal propensity to consume were five sixths?

Some Needed Corrections

In explaining how to determine aggregate income, we have taken some liberties by oversimplifying. This can lead to a distortion if we fail to make the proper corrections. You will recall our assumption that, though production takes place throughout the year, payment for that production and the spending of income received took place only once during the year—at the end. Our diagrams may be accurate for the past but not for determining income for the future. Although government and businesses draw up budgets for the year, and many consumers also plan their expenditures, we know that both income and expenditures are subject to an almost infinite number of changes. If consumers become excited about a product, as they did with automobiles in 1964 and 1965, they will increase their purchases. This in turn may increase investment in the middle of the year. More profits and wages increase income and the revenue that government receives from income taxes.

Economists analyze accumulated data; from this information they project plans and make forecasts. They sometimes make mistakes, since economics is not an exact science. For example, government economists overestimated income for 1971 by a considerable margin. Too many variables either cannot be controlled or are not measured with sufficient accuracy. Man tends to be fickle on the production line and in the marketplace. This does not mean that analysis, projection, and planning are a waste; we are far better off making educated guesses and trying to control conditions than gambling on the unknown. With the development of more and more measurements of the economy like those described in Chapter 12, and with data available at more frequent intervals, it is expected that economic analysis will become more exact.

The Economist and the Economy

We have now discussed some of the major tools that modern economists use in attempting to analyze the economy and to frame economic policy. The economist working for a large corporation knows that personal income will be a major factor in determining personal consumption expenditures. This is one of his major considerations when he prepares his report to management advising them on conditions affecting production goals.

Government economists are responsible for advising the executive and legislative

When private investment is not sufficient to stimulate a full-employment level of spending, government may provide the needed help. Can government supply too much stimulation to the economy?

branches on tax programs, expenditures, tariffs, and subsidies. In attempting to keep the economy operating at or near the full-employment level without inflation, they work constantly with the various measurements of aggregate income. They need estimates of personal consumption expenditures and business investment in order to determine the consequences of government spending. They seek to determine what the multiplier effect will be if the government decides on a policy of *deficit spending* (spending more than it takes in). Will such a policy bring the economy up to full employment or will it exceed the full employment mark and create an inflation? The tools we have learned to use are designed to help determine aggregate income so that sensible policies can be developed to cope with the fluctuations in the economy.

Before proceeding, let us look again at the two models described—the classical analysis and the Keynesian approach. A few economists, some businessmen, and many of the public have a greater respect for the classical approach. Some speeches in Congress are more in tune with what Adam Smith called the "invisible hand," or the market system. Since most economists do not accept either model completely and since most government planning is set up somewhere between the two approaches, the argument continues.

Part D
The Problem: Which Model?

In the beginning of our study of economics we identified the basic problem: How do we allocate our limited resources to meet our unlimited wants most efficiently? Finding an answer involves the setting up of a model or economic system that will utilize fully the resources at our disposal. The goal of all economists is to bring the four factors of production together in the right proportion at the right time to produce the right quantity of goods and services that the society has decided it wants. This must be done while achieving full employment without inflation. Anything less would be wasting our resources. There is a great deal of disagreement about how to achieve these objectives.

The following discussion presents the case for both the classical approach and the Keynesian approach. After reading these two positions, consider a typical comment made by an economist reflecting this controversy: "There are no classical economists, there are no Keynesian economists. The thinking of all economists combines elements of both theories, but for everyone, the combination is different." As you read, try to decide what place there is for each of the two positions in our total economy.

The Case for the Classical Model

The classical economist believes that the market economy can best achieve the desired goal only if the natural laws of supply and demand are allowed to operate. He would willingly admit that our economy has not yielded all it should. However, he would give as the reason for its failure our unwillingness to follow the model, not the inadequacy of the model. Our recessions, and even the Great Depression, caused the hardships they did because of interference with the mobility of the factors of production and the goods and services produced. Minimum wage laws and labor unions, administered prices and monopolistic competition, government subsidies and "confiscatory" taxes, all of which interfere with incentive and discriminate against certain industries and persons, have prevented the self-correcting mechanism of the market economy from working. Blaming the model for not achieving our economic goals is avoiding the truth, since the prescription of the model was not followed.

In order to achieve our desired goals, the classical economist thinks that we must not change the model, but rather return to a real use of the classical model. Specifically, this would involve vigorous enforcement of our antitrust laws, elimination of the union shop, and doing away with all wage and price controls. It would also require eliminating all subsidies (with the possible exception of those to new industries), reducing government involvement (by either ownership or control) in the economy, and developing a tax structure that would act as a real incentive for capital investment. It is granted that loud cries of protest would go up against such a program. However, after a short period of readjustment the economy would experience a vigorous increase as new incentives motivated the forces for production.

With wages and prices far more flexible, the goods and services that people really want would be reflected in the marketplace; that is, supply and demand would come into balance. Efficiency in production and the quality of goods and services available would all improve as competition became a more significant factor. Those whose incomes are high would work harder to increase their earnings because they would retain most of their money rather than turning much of it over to the government in the form of taxes. Those who were unemployed would have a better chance of finding work, since employers would be allowed much lower wages than at present. This would motivate them to hire more workers. Price flexibility would allow the lower wages paid during periods of moderate downturns to buy more because a slackening of demand would result in a lowering of prices. Resources would be directed where they were needed most because market prices would direct their flow. A society which is dedicated to freedom and the individual deserves the efficiency and freedom of a market economy.

The Case for the New Model

The Keynesian economist denies that a mature capitalist society can have the mobility of resources that the classical economist assumes. He also denies the possibility of the extreme flexibility of prices and wages that is needed to bring supply and demand into balance at the full-employment level. If the economy fails to respond to changes in demand and to changes in costs brought about by technological changes, and to risk capital needed to start new enterprises, it will become sluggish. When investment drops below savings, as it has frequently done, some additional spending, whether private or public, is needed to provide the stimulus necessary to the economy in order to bring it back to the full-employment level.

Since few people would accept enforced spending by the public or investment by businessmen as a solution, it would seem most logical to charge the government with the responsibility of developing policy to stimulate the economy to the desired full-employment level. Since the market has not provided the stimulus by making private spending and investment attractive enough, it is necessary that government become involved through *monetary policies* (involving interest and the availability of credit) and *fiscal policies* (budgeting by the government to create a surplus or deficit). Such additional spending will raise the $C + I + G$ high enough so that it will cross the 45° line at the full-employment level.

If the economy is overstimulated, government action to lower the $C + I + G$ line will reduce the inflationary trend. It would be inconsistent with our political principles to prevent people from spending or investing. However, government policy that would discourage inflationary action could be approved or disapproved at the polls.

Even if price, wage, and interest flexibility did provide some help in lessening unemployment, our society is largely committed to minimum wages and "fair" prices, with the result that the flexibility would be of only a limited nature. Any government that merely stands by, waiting for the natural laws of the market to act while millions of people are unemployed, would undoubtedly find itself out of office after the next election. Why should an economy—and more important, why should people—suffer when we have in our possession the economic know-how to provide a full-employment economy without inflation?

Considering an Answer

The two points of view given here represent differences not only in analysis and interpretation but also in personal values. Identify the conflict in value judgments expressed in the two positions. Which set of values do you tend to agree with? Has your opinion changed in any way in the course of our study?

Do you believe that we can change the present direction of our economy and move toward a more market-oriented society? What groups in our society would be helped most by such a change? What groups would be hurt most? Would the advantages and disadvantages deriving from the change be temporary or permanent? In what ways does the "new economics" change our traditional consumer-oriented society? Is freedom for the individual (consumer and citizen) seriously jeopardized?

In arriving at an answer, you should try to decide how the principles and reasoning presented here, as well as your new tools for analysis, apply to the basic economic problems and goals we have identified.

REVIEW: THE HIGHLIGHTS OF THE CHAPTER

1. The classical model expects a full-employment economy without inflation to be achieved merely by allowing the natural laws of supply and demand to operate and by keeping government out of the economy as much as possible.

2. According to the classical model temporary dislocations in the economy are corrected by changes in interest rates and fluctuations in wages and prices.
3. Major business fluctuations, particularly the long-lasting major depression of the 1930's, led to the acceptance of a new economic model.
4. John Maynard Keynes, an English economist, developed a new model well within the capitalistic system. He thought that insufficient attention was being paid to maintain a full-employment economy. Since interest and wage-and-price flexibility did not stimulate demand sufficiently, the government became responsible for setting policies that would accomplish this purpose.
5. The aggregate income of the nation is determined by adding personal consumption expenditures to business investment to government spending ($C + I + G =$ income).
6. According to the new model, when consumption plus investment plus government expenditures do not add up to enough production of goods and services to employ everyone in the working force who wishes to work, policies must be set up to increase spending. This can be accomplished by increasing government expenditures over government income (deficit spending), by encouraging businessmen to invest more, or by using other economic policies. Personal consumption expenditures change primarily with income and are not altered so easily.
7. When consumption plus investment plus government spending adds up to an amount that exceeds what we are capable of producing, inflation will occur. Policies to discourage personal consumption expenditures, business investment, or government spending will be needed.
8. People tend to spend particular amounts of their income at different income levels. This tendency in spending is known as the *propensity to consume.* The tendency to save certain amounts of income at certain income levels is known as the *propensity to save.*
9. The amount of *additional* income that people tend to spend is known as the *marginal propensity to consume.* The amount of *additional* income that people tend to save is known as the *marginal propensity to save.* The marginal propensity to consume and the marginal propensity to save add up to one.
10. In the planning of economic policy the multiplier effect makes it unnecessary to increase or decrease aggregate spending ($C + I + G$) by the full amount to bring that spending up or down to the level of full employment without inflation. The multiplier effect causes a greater increase in aggregate income than the amount of additional spending added or subtracted by the amount which is the reciprocal of the marginal propensity to save.
11. Most current economic policy combines elements of the classical model and the new model. Enforcement of antitrust laws and planning for a temporary budget deficit by means of a tax cut are examples of economic policies that utilize both the old and the new models.

IN CONCLUSION: SOME AIDS TO UNDERSTANDING

Terms for Review

gross national income
gross savings
full-employment economy
balanced budget
multiplier effect
$C + I + G = Y$
propensity to save
propensity to consume
45° line
deficit spending
fiscal policies
marginal propensity to consume
Keynesian model
inflationary gap
deflationary gap

Questions for Review

1. How does the classical economist answer the following questions?
   (a) How will full employment without inflation be achieved?
   (b) What accounts for our failure to achieve the level of full employment without inflation?
2. The theories of John Maynard Keynes have had a major impact on economic thinking. In what ways did he disagree with the classical economists?
3. What do the new economists consider to be the major factor in determining investment? Explain, using the 45° line diagram, why aggregate income will be at both the intersection of the $C + I + G$ line with the 45° line and the point where savings and investment (both public and private) are equal.
4. If investment is larger than savings, what will probably happen to income? Why does this take place? Under what conditions is it likely to be harmful to the economy?
5. If the full-employment level without inflation is estimated to be $1 trillion and if aggregate demand ($C + I + G$) is equal to only $970 billion, what amount of additional spending is needed? Assume the multiplier to be three.
6. Assume that the government decides to stimulate the economy by reducing taxes and/or increasing its spending. How will the marginal propensity to consume (MPC) and the multiplier enter into its consideration of how much to cut taxes and how much to spend? Which income groups will receive the most immediate benefits of these government actions?
7. If most Americans suddenly increased their savings, what would be the probable effects on the economy? When would increased savings be considered good for the economy? When would they be considered bad?
8. What factors might nullify the government's efforts to stimulate the economy during a recession or to control inflation during a period of prosperity?

Additional Questions and Problems

1. Figure 13–1 records the GNP for the United States from 1960 to 1970. Although there are fluctuations, the trend is primarily upward.
   (a) What are the major reasons for this rise?
   (b) What government policies were employed to avoid major inflationary and deflationary periods?

(c) Can there be any serious dangers associated with the continuous increase?
(d) What role does the constantly increasing federal debt play in this picture?

2. Discuss the advantages and disadvantages of stimulating the economy by means of
   (a) increased personal consumption expenditures,
   (b) increased business investment,
   (c) increased government expenditures.
3. How would a businessman, a worker, and a professional person differ in their solutions to the problem of stimulating the economy? Why?
4. Using a newspaper or popular weekly news publication, indicate news items about government policies that will affect the GNP. If you were a congressman, would you support these policies?
5. If a new industry entered a community, what effect might it have on other businesses? Do you think the citizens of the community should help finance the bringing of new industry to town? Explain the reasons for your answers.
6. Explain the differences between the multiplier effect for the entire country and for a region. Between the United States and an underdeveloped country.

SELECTED READINGS

Attiyeh, Richard, Keith Lumsden, and George Leland Bach. *Macroeconomics: A Programmed Book.* Englewood Cliffs, N.J.: Prentice-Hall, 1967.

Collery, Arnold. *National Income and Employment Analysis.* New York: John Wiley & Sons, 1966.

Hansen, Alvin. *The Postwar American Economy.* New York: W. W. Norton & Co., 1964.

Heilbroner, Robert L. and Peter L. Bernstein. *A Primer on Government Spending.* New York: Random House, 1968.

Heller, Walter. *New Dimensions in Political Economy.* New York: W. W. Norton & Co., 1967.

Johnson, Walter L., and David S. Kameschen. *Macroeconomics: Selected Readings.* Boston: Houghton Mifflin Co., 1970.

Keynes, John Maynard. *The General Theory of Employment, Interest, and Money.* New York: Harcourt, Brace & World, 1936.

Lekachman, Robert, ed. *Keynes and the Classics.* Boston: D. C. Heath and Co., 1964.

———. *The Age of Keynes.* New York: Random House, 1966.

Schultze, Charles L. *National Income Analysis.* Englewood Cliffs, N.J.: Prentice-Hall, 1964. (Also available in paperback edition from the same publisher.)

Money and Prices and Their Relation to the Economy

14

THE AUTHORS' NOTE TO THE STUDENT

The purpose of economic activity is to produce, distribute, and consume the goods and services wanted by society. In economies with specialization of production, where exchange is necessary, money plays an important role. It can be used to stimulate or discourage production, to facilitate distribution and exchange of goods and services, and to measure values. Because money is so enmeshed in people's lives, it has frequently been looked upon as an end in itself rather than as a means to accomplishing the economic purposes indicated above.

Although money is used and sought by virtually everyone, many people are uninformed or mistaken concerning its real nature and its role in serving the economy. In this chapter we will consider these aspects of money, as well as the relationship between prices and money.

A STUDENT'S NOTE TO THE STUDENT

This chapter was relatively easy in comparison to the last. The two possible stumbling blocks are computing index numbers and the quantity theory of money. Neither one presents serious problems if you follow each step systematically.

There were some things I found quite enlightening. Those of us who had no formal economics before were surprised to find that the only backing money needs is the production that it can buy. Like several others I have been a "gold worshiper" without any cause. I am at the point of believing we would be a lot better off if the government sold all its gold on the market to jewelers and dentists for whatever it would bring in. I have been advised by my instructor to wait before pressing for action on this solution until I get through with the chapter on international finance.

I still haven't made up my mind whether "jawboning" is really any good. I would think President Nixon might have tried it before completely reversing himself and jumping right into the wage–price freeze.

Part A
Money—Its Functions and Characteristics

Have you ever examined your money closely? See if you can locate a $5, $10, or $20 bill printed before 1964 and marked "Federal Reserve Note" over the portrait. In the upper left portion above the seal a statement written in fine print tells that the note is *legal tender* and that it "is redeemable in lawful money at the United States Treasury, or at any Federal Reserve bank." Does this mean that your bill is *not* lawful? At the bottom center the same note says, "Will pay to the bearer on demand X dollars." Does this mean that your X-dollar bill is *not* X dollars?

Much confusion exists about the real nature of money. Many people are under the impression that it has no value unless it is backed by gold or silver. They think that the Federal Reserve note is only a symbol for money, and that real money is the precious metal behind it. Some people look upon money as wealth, and believe that it must therefore have *intrinsic* value.

If we were to study the history of money, we would find that in different places and at different times a variety of things have been used as money. Cattle, shells, beads, tobacco leaves, and various metals—including iron, zinc, bronze, and copper—have all been used as a basis for exchange. The precious metals, particularly silver and gold, have proved most satisfactory for this purpose and have been most commonly used in modern times.

Until early 1968, the United States backed its Federal Reserve notes with 25 percent gold, but this did not mean that citizens could use gold as money or convert paper dollars to gold. This leads us to the conclusion that *it is not what money is but what it does* that is important.

The Functions of Money

Under simple economic conditions, where most goods and services were produced by the family, necessary exchanges were usually accomplished by bartering goods for goods. Hunters might exchange furs and meat for grain and ammunition. Although the variety of things that our early ancestors produced was remarkable, total production was small because they did not specialize. As specialization developed, it not only increased production but also made the barter system very nearly impossible. Although it might be possible for you to pay a doctor or a lawyer with the goods and services he wants, what would a giant corporation such as General Motors do to pay its employees? What could it accept in payment for its cars? How would it decide what stockholders should receive? Any economy with specialization of production needs a *medium of exchange.* This is the chief function of money.

Medium of Exchange

Returning once again to the basic model of our economy at work, we can see clearly how money serves as a medium of exchange. When businesses sell their goods to consumers, they receive payment in the form of money. This money is then used to pay those who created the goods and services. Since consumers are also the owners of the factors of production that created the value, they receive payment in the form of money. Money itself does not satisfy wants, but it is very convenient for helping us to exchange the many different forms of value in our society. The owner of the factors of production is exchanging for money the value he creates by using his labor, land, or capital. He prefers to receive payment in money rather than by direct payment of goods because the business that is using his services may not have the goods he wants. By giving money to the supplier of factors of production, he can go to the market for goods and services and, now acting as a consumer, buy goods and services there. In this way money becomes the single item that can be used by consumers and businesses for exchanging values.

Measure of Value

A second function of money is its use as a measure of value. How do we compare the value of a shirt with that of a seat at a concert? What is the value created by a carpenter who builds a bookcase, or by a cobbler who puts new heels on a pair of shoes? Just as we need measurements for distances, weights, and energy, so we need measurements for the value of things offered at the market. In a barter economy we can speak of a shirt as being worth a seat at a concert, but in a money economy we use a *unit of account.* In the United States the dollar is our *measure of value.* Thus, the shirt is worth $5 and the seat at the concert is worth $5. All things having value at the market may be measured with the common unit of account, the dollar. The use of such a unit aids the exchange of goods.

Store of Value

A third function of money is its use as a store of value. You may seek to accumulate your wealth, or the purchasing power that you have earned, rather than spending it immediately. Money is the form in which savings are accumulated.

Standard of Deferred Payments

The last function of money is its use as a standard of deferred payments. When you buy something but do not pay for it immediately, your payment is expressed in terms of money to be paid in the future. With the increase in installment buying this function has become increasingly important.

Characteristics of Money

For money to perform the functions indicated, it should possess a number of special characteristics that augment its use as legal tender:

1. It should be *durable* so that it will not wear out too quickly; or, failing this, it should be replaceable at a low cost.
2. It should be *portable* so that carrying it will not be burdensome.
3. It should be *divisible* so that the value of items that are fractions of the unit of account (for example, cents) can be calculated and handled easily.
4. It should be easily *recognizable* so that all will know what it is and what its value is.
5. It must be *homogeneous* so that all similar units have equal value.
6. It should have a high degree of *stability of value,* or people may hoard it, waiting for its value to increase, or spend it immediately for fear of its losing value.
7. Most important of all, it must be *acceptable.* Only when it is accepted as purchasing power in the broadest market can it truly serve as a medium of exchange.

From Commodity to Paper Money

As we have seen, commodities have often been used in simple economies as a basis for exchange. If a commodity becomes standardized as money, it will usually lose much of its commodity form and take on instead the aspect of money. When gold and silver were used as money, they became scarcer as ornaments. As economies became more complex and transactions increased, paper money representing units of gold or silver was used. This convertible paper money could be redeemed for the gold or silver that it represented. It is much easier to pay several thousand dollars in paper money than to do so with gold or silver. So long as people recognized that they could convert this paper money to gold or silver, they willingly accepted it.

Inflexibility of the Gold Supply

One of the major difficulties in using gold, silver, and other precious metals as the basis for a money system is that as an economy continues to develop and greater value is produced, the amount of money in circulation, serving as a medium of exchange, needs to increase also. However, the supply of precious metals depends more on unpredictable discoveries than on the need for it. If no new gold is discovered and if no equally acceptable money is added to the money supply, prices will probably decline. This reduction, together with the shortage of money, will have an adverse effect on business.

By reducing the amount of gold or silver that stands in back of convertible paper money or by printing money which cannot be converted, the government can expand the amount of money available to meet the economic needs of the society. By freeing the money supply from the limitations of chance gold discoveries, these methods give the government some flexibility in managing the supply in circulation.

Dangers Inherent in Commodity Money

There are, however, several dangers in allowing government to change the backing of money or to print inconvertible paper money. If government allows some money to be converted and other money not to be converted, or if it has two kinds of money (as we once did), one of which is backed by a higher-valued amount of metal, the effect known as *Gresham's law* will set in. This law states that when two types of money are in circulation and have equal stated values but are not equal in demand (the backing of one is worth more than the backing of the other), the less desirable type will drive the other out of circulation. This means that the government must either allow all money to be redeemable with the same metal or allow no money to be redeemable. In 1933 all gold and *gold certificates* were ordered to be turned over to the United States Treasury in exchange for other kinds of money, largely because some people, fearing that other kinds of money would decline in value, had begun to hoard these certificates and coins.

Another danger in a government's printing inconvertible paper money is the irresponsibility with which it may be done. *Fiat money*, which is money that circulates by order of the government, is usually resorted to in order to meet emergencies. Our greenbacks issued during the Civil War had behind them only the promise of the government to pay. If money is issued faster than the output of goods increases, prices will rise rapidly and the value of money will fall correspondingly, as we saw in Chapter 13 (see p. 311). Many economists believe that the metallic backing of money will be less significant to the economy as governments grow wiser in understanding the true role of money and as they learn to regulate the supply of it with responsibility.

Our Present Money Supply

There are many kinds of money in use in the United States today. Some, such as gold and silver bullion and gold certificates, are held by the government or Federal Reserve banks and have been used for backing other currency. Treasury notes of 1890 and national bank notes make up too small a portion of our total money to be of significance. The three major kinds of money in use may be classified as *fractional currency, paper currency,* and *bank money.*

Fractional Currency

A very useful but relatively small portion of our money supply is in the form of coins. This so-called "fractional currency"—pennies, nickels, dimes, quarters, and half-dollars—is extremely convenient for the very large number of small purchases we make. With the increasing use of vending machines and with the growing popularity of coin collecting as a hobby, a temporary shortage of coins recently developed. In a newspaper advertisement during the shortage one bank offered to pay people $1.02 for a dollar's worth of change on a particular day. The demand for "change" in that area was greater than the supply.

Coins make up about two percent of our total currency. Fractional currency is sometimes referred to as *token money* because the value of the metal it is made of is considerably less than its face value. A rise in the market value of the metal above the face value of the coins could cause some people to melt down their coins.

Paper Money

About one fifth of our money supply is made up of various kinds of paper money, sometimes known as currency. The bulk of this money is issued by the Federal Reserve banks and is known as Federal Reserve notes. Silver certificates were issued by the United States Treasury from 1878 to 1963. Legislation in 1890, largely in response to the demand of Western silver and agrarian interests, required that the Treasury buy silver bullion to back currency and coinage. Because the need for silver as a commodity has greatly increased, legislation was passed in 1963 dropping the requirement that part of our currency be in silver certificates, and $1 Federal Reserve notes were then printed for the first time. The remainder of the paper currency is made up of United States notes, national bank notes, and Treasury notes of 1890, all of which are in the process of being retired in order to create a more uniform currency.

Bank Money

Almost three fourths of our total money supply is made up of bank money, or *demand deposits.* Most people know this kind of money as deposits in commercial banks or as money in their checking accounts.

Because writing checks is convenient and so much safer than carrying large amounts of "cash," about 90 percent of all transactions are made by check. Checks are the means of transferring ownership of demand deposits. As long as checks are accepted as a medium of

TABLE 14–1 Money in Circulation in the United States, July 1970 (millions of dollars)

Currency in Circulation (total)			54,473
Federal Reserve Notes		47,730	
Treasury Currency (total)		6,743	
Fractional coins	5,664		
Silver dollars	482		
U.S. Notes	298		
In process of retirement	299		
Demand Deposits			154,700
Total Money Supply			209,173

SOURCE: *Federal Reserve Bulletin*, September 1970.

exchange, they may properly be called bank money or demand deposit money.

Near-Monies

In addition to the three kinds of actual money considered, *near-monies* are also used commonly in our economy. Families and businesses hold large amounts of liquid assets that come close to being money. The most important categories of near-money are deposits in savings banks and in savings and loan associations, savings deposits in commercial banks, and United States government bonds held by families and businesses (excluding banks and insurance companies). We cannot call these highly liquid assets money because even though they can be very easily converted to currency or demand deposits, they do not circulate as a medium of exchange. You cannot write a check on money in savings accounts (the savings bank may issue you its check) and you cannot pay for merchandise with a government bond.

Although near-monies do not circulate in the same way that currency and checks do, they are of some importance in evaluating people's spending habits and analyzing the price level.

Part B
The Relationship Between Money and Prices

Price Levels and Price Indexes

Although some disagreement exists concerning what effect the supply of money has on the economy, economists generally recognize that a change in the supply can influence business activity and the price level. The relationship between money, prices, and business activity is explained by the quantity theory of money, or the *equation of exchange* (see p. 337). Before we can understand this relationship, however, we must first consider what is meant by the price level and how it is measured.

Price Levels

If you were to look at a newspaper printed in 1933, you would be surprised at the prices prevailing at that time. You might feel envious as you read about the 5-cent bus fare, the loaf of bread or quart of milk for less than 15 cents, and the dinner at a good restaurant for $1. This kind of information about costs provides an indication of *price levels*—the average prices for things purchased during a given period of time. Price levels are extremely important because, taken together with income, they determine the standard of living.

Price levels are also important from a slightly different point of view. If prices are low, money will have greater value, since a given amount of money will buy more goods. In contrast, high prices have the effect of reducing the value of money, since the same amount of money will buy less.

Index Numbers

Price levels are usually measured by the use of index numbers. A *price index* is a device for measuring the changing value of money over a given period of time. It can also be a measurement of the average price of a number of selected commodities at a given time, such as the index designed to measure the cost of living. Since the prices of the things you buy determine the real value of your money, both definitions of index numbers are appropriate.

How Index Numbers Are Constructed

Economists make use of a number of different price indexes. Each one is designed to measure the price level of a particular market. The two most widely used are the Wholesale Price Index and the Consumer Price Index, both compiled and issued by the Bureau of Labor Statistics of the United States Department of Labor. Industrial production and farm prices are other commonly used indexes. We will use a simplified example of the Consumer Price Index to illustrate the method involved in constructing an index.

We begin by selecting a *base period*, usually three years, in which no war or major depression took place (a "normal" period). We then select a number of common goods and services frequently bought by consumers and assign a relative weight to each item. This weight is determined by economists according to the relationship of purchases among the various items. For example, more weight must be assigned to coffee than to shoes because so much more of the former is bought. Next we add up the sum of the prices times the weighted quantity for all items for each of the years selected. We then add up the sums for the three years and divide by the number of years (3) to get the average price for these items during the base period. We give that figure an index of 100.

Let us suppose that the sum of prices times a weighted quantity for selected items bought in 1957 equals $2,400, in 1958 it equals $2,500, and in 1959 it equals $2,600. The average of these amounts ($7,500 ÷ 3) equals $2,500, which becomes our index of 100 for the base period. Once the index for the base is established, the change in prices for any subsequent year can be computed in relation to the base.

Let $2,500 equal the index 100 for the base period 1957–1959. In 1971 we found that the average price times the weighted quantity for the same items priced earlier now equaled $3,500. We then use the following formula:

$$\frac{\text{1971 figure (\$3,500)}}{\text{1957–1959 figure (\$2,500)}} \times 100 = \text{CPI (140)}$$

The Consumer Price Index (CPI) of 140 indicates that it took $140 in 1971 to buy the same goods and services that one could get for only $100 in the 1957–1959 period. In other words, average prices had risen by 40 percent, and there had been a decrease in the value (purchasing power) of money.

Because the things that consumers buy change both in kind and in number, those who figure the price index must from time to time make substitutions of items selected and weights assigned. Changes must be made with great skill and care so that there will be no distortion of the measurement that gives us the price level or the cost of living index. However, we must remember that the results can be interpreted only as an approximation of actual prices or of the cost of living at a given time.

Figure 14–1 shows the changes in consumer and wholesale industrial prices from 1962 to 1970, with the period 1957–1959 selected as the base period.[1] The fact that prices were not only rising, but rising at an *increasing rate*, was a matter of great concern to most Americans. Figure 14–2 goes even further, for it indicates the loss in purchasing power through increases in federal income taxes and Social Security taxes as well as through inflation. The graph dramatically illustrates the need for additional income to maintain the same level of living. Actually, however, the average American family substantially increased its level of living. After adjusting for inflation, per capita disposable income in 1970 was about twice that of 1939.

[1] In 1971 the Bureau of Labor Statistics started using 1967 instead of 1957–1959 as the base period. This results in a smaller figure for the CPI, of course. For example, for March 1971 the CPI was 119.8 with 1967 used as the base period, whereas it would have been nearly 140 if the 1957–1959 period had been used. The purchasing power of a dollar (in the New York–northeastern New Jersey area) was 67.5 cents in terms of 1957–1959 dollars, but 80.5 cents in terms of 1967 dollars.

Why Are Stable Prices Important?

In recent chapters we have observed the relation of inflation and deflation to GNP and to other measurements of the economy as well as to the goal of full employment. Now we are prepared to consider them in a different context—in relation to money supply and prices. *Inflation* may be defined as an increase in the general price level or a decrease in the value of money. *Deflation* is a decrease in the general price level or an increase in the value of money. Economists generally agree that stable prices are desirable and that inflation or deflation has a harmful effect on the economy. There are a number of reasons that support this conclusion. Let us see how changes in price levels affect various segments of the economy.

Borrowing

One economic activity that closely follows changes in price levels is the borrowing of money. A change in the price level from the time money is borrowed to the time it is paid back means that, in effect, the original agreement is changed. The borrower will repay the lender an amount of purchasing power different from that which he originally borrowed. If the price level has risen 10 percent, the borrower is paying back dollars that will buy 10 percent less in goods and services than this same amount of dollars would have bought originally. Such a change benefits the borrower or debtor and harms the lender or creditor. Deflation also affects both debtor and creditor. How will its impact differ from that of inflation?

Fixed Incomes

Stable prices are very important to people living on fixed incomes. For them an inflation may result in a lower standard of living. A teacher who retired on a pension of $200 a month in 1958 might have expected to live out the rest of her life in modest comfort and independence. Today, being quite old, she probably requires part-time help in caring for herself and her household. This added expense and the fact that her $200 a month will now buy goods and services worth only $120 at 1958 prices may very well have reduced her to a condition of poverty.

Other kinds of fixed income are similarly affected by inflation. A life insurance policy taken out in 1940 paying the beneficiary $12,000 may have seemed adequate at that time. Today its real value is less than half the original face value. Rent and wages set in fixed dollars and covering long periods of time, as well as interest on bonds, are subject to the same loss of purchasing power when the price level moves up.

In contrast with inflation, deflation would increase the purchasing power of the incomes described here. However, the trend in recent years has not been in the direction of deflation. The years since 1940 have witnessed an almost steady increase in prices, and the purchasing power of people on fixed incomes has steadily decreased.

Investments

As you learned in Chapter 13, rising prices encourage businessmen to invest. If the investing is done when the economy is producing less than its full-employment capacity, the effect on prices will be slight because the increased dollars will result in increased production. Additional investment made when the economy is operating at or close to production capacity would accelerate the inflationary pressure, since little or no additional production can follow. Deflation, on the other hand, tends to slow down investment and thereby to increase unemployment.

The value of common stock has often risen as fast or faster than prices, thus leading many people to believe that stocks represent a good "hedge" against inflation. There is no guarantee of this, however, and during the inflation of the late 1960's stock prices declined. Deflation often brings a decline in common stock values. The value of preferred stock is often more stable.

Because the amount of interest on bonds is fixed, bonds have sometimes seemed like good investments during times of deflation. After a bond has been issued and sold, however, its market value *can* change. A bond initially sold for $1,000 might drop to $600 in the securities market. If held to maturity, the buyer will get the $1,000. If circumstances force him to sell before maturity, however, the holder may receive less than he paid for it. There are no simple guidelines for the individual who hopes to guard against inflation or deflation by putting his savings in stocks and bonds.

The Relationship Between Money and Price Level

The relationship between money and price level is of great significance in our economy. For a better understanding of how they interact, let us use as an example a simple economic situation, eliminating all costs but labor. There are 20 people in our example, and all are employed at a bakery whose only product is bread. Each day 20 loaves of bread are produced. Everyone in the economy works and receives $1 a day. At the end of the working day all are paid $1, and they go directly to

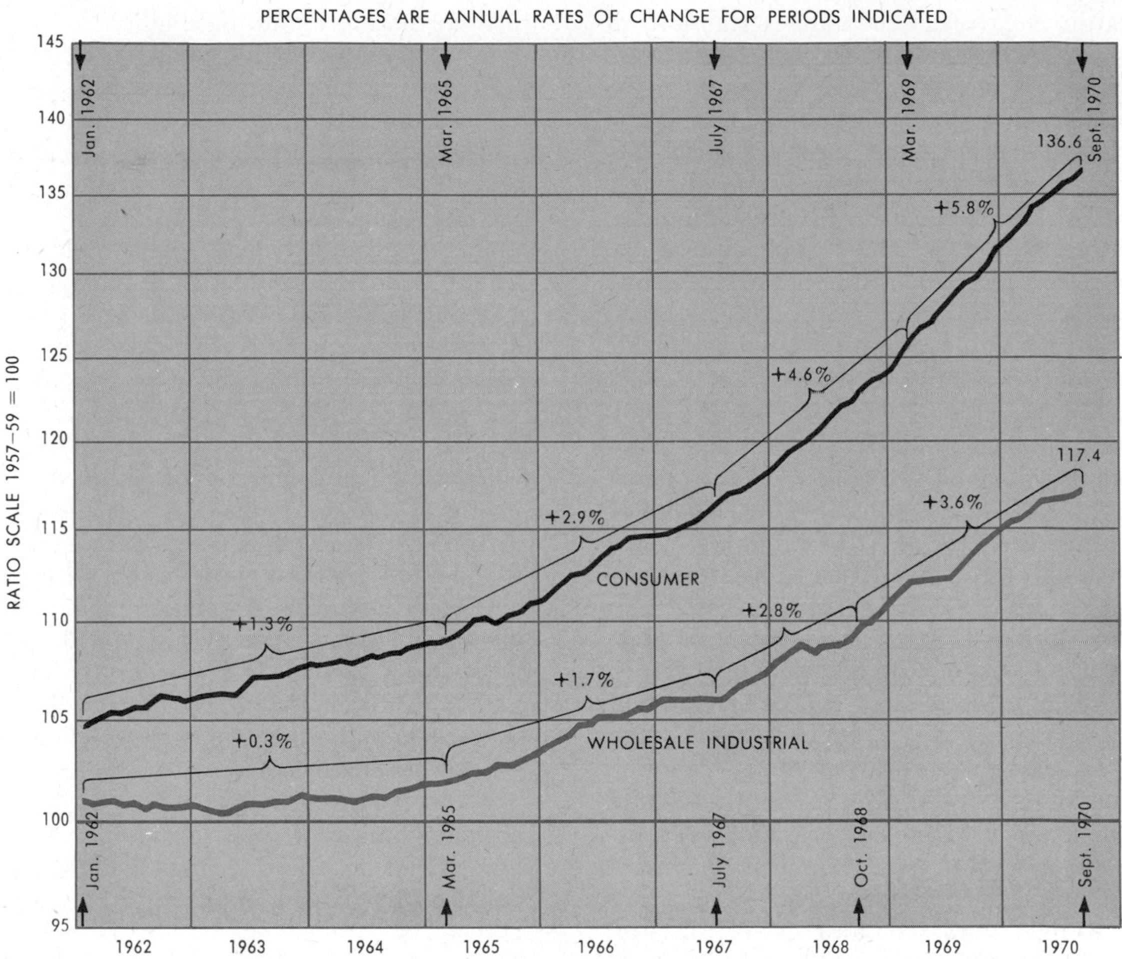

FIGURE 14–1 Consumer Price Index and Wholesale Industrial Price Index, 1962–1970

From a relatively modest rate of increase of 1.3 percent during the first part of this period, the rate of increase in consumer prices rose to an alarming 5.8 percent in late 1969 and early 1970. Although the rates for wholesale industrial prices were lower, the same accelerating trend is in evidence. SOURCES: U.S. Department of Labor and Federal Reserve Bank of St. Louis.

FIGURE 14–2 Income Needed to Match Base Period Purchasing Power: The "Two-Way Squeeze"

The "two-way squeeze" on personal income is accounted for largely by rising prices and increases in the federal income tax and Social Security taxes. Purchasing power has also been reduced by increases in state income taxes, although these were not included in the calculations for this graph. The average family (husband, wife, and two children) of 1939 had to earn less than one-half of the income of the average family of 1970 to enjoy the same purchasing power. SOURCES: National Industrial Conference Board, *Road Maps of Industry,* No. 1649, U.S. Treasury Department, U.S. Bureau of Labor Statistics, and Bureau of the Census.

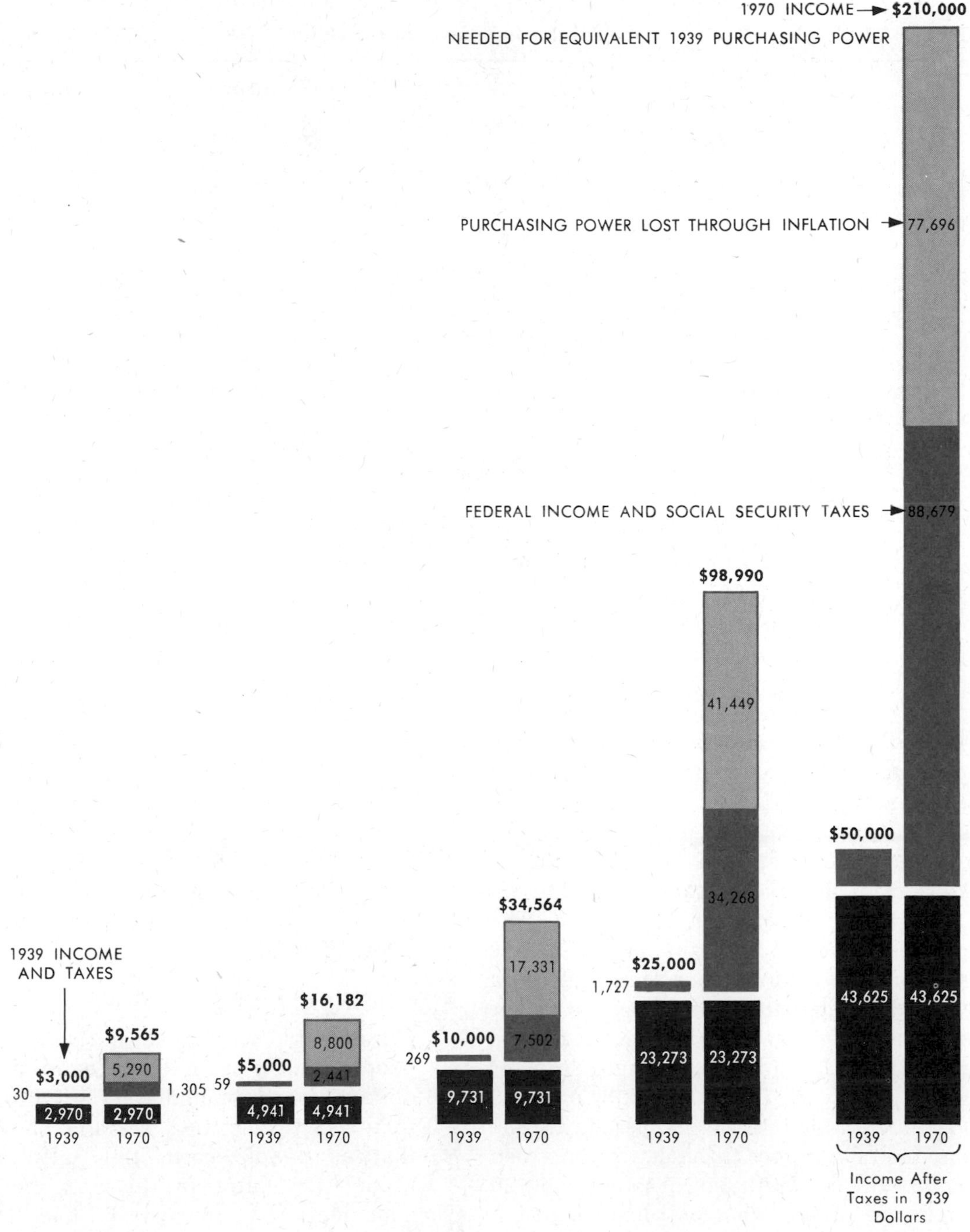
1970 INCOME → $210,000
NEEDED FOR EQUIVALENT 1939 PURCHASING POWER
PURCHASING POWER LOST THROUGH INFLATION → 77,696
FEDERAL INCOME AND SOCIAL SECURITY TAXES → 88,679
$98,990
41,449
34,268
$50,000
43,625
43,625
$34,564
17,331
7,502
$25,000
1,727
23,273
23,273
1939 INCOME
AND TAXES
$16,182
8,800
2,441
$10,000
269
9,731
9,731
$9,565
5,290
$3,000
30
2,970
2,970
1,305
$5,000
59
4,941
4,941
1939
1970
1939
1970
1939
1970
1939
1970
1939
1970
Income After
Taxes in 1939
Dollars

TABLE 14–2 Major Trends in the Purchasing Power of the Dollar

Declines	Number of Years	Percent Decline	Range of Decline	Amount of Decline	Average Decline Per Year
1808–1814	6	39	$ .87–.53	$ .34	$.057
1834–1836	2	22	1.24–.97	.27	.135
1860–1865	5	54	1.34–.62	.72	.144
1897–1920	23	70	1.75–.53	1.22	.053
1932–1958	26	64	1.26–.44	.82	.032
Rises	**Number of Years**	**Percent Rise**	**Range of Rise**	**Amount of Rise**	**Average Rise Per Year**
1814–1830	16	134	$.53–1.24	$ .71	$.044
1839–1843	4	36	.97–1.32	.35	.088
1865–1896	31	182	.62–1.75	1.13	.036
1920–1932	12	138	.53–1.26	.73	.061

SOURCE: *Banking, Journal of the American Bankers Association,* December 1964, p. 37.

the market, which has 20 loaves of bread for sale. What will the price of a loaf of bread be? If it sold for more than $1, there would be loaves of bread left over and no one to buy them. Supply would be greater than demand and the price would have to come down. If the price were less than $1, the consumers would soon bid the price up, because demand would be greater than supply. At $1 per loaf the market is cleared.

What would happen if one person of the 20 decides that the workers are being exploited and are entitled to a raise? The proprietor might perhaps agree to pay everyone $2 a day rather than undergo a work stoppage. In order to pay the higher wages he must have 20 additional dollars made available to him, giving a total of $40. However, there are still only 20 loaves of bread available per day. The day the raise comes through, workers rush to buy bread. With $40 of money and 20 loaves of bread, what will happen to the price? In a short time the increased money (demand) will drive up the price to the equilibrium level, where the market will be cleared. What would happen to the price of a loaf of bread if the proprietor reduced wages to 50 cents a day?

Let us suppose that the amount of money in the economy remained the same but that production increased to 40 loaves a day. What would happen to the price of a loaf of bread? If prices were to be stable, the money supply would have to be increased as production increased. Our example shows in a very simplified way how price level is determined by the quantity of money and the units of production offered for sale.

Velocity of Circulation

Our example may appear unrealistic, since people usually are not paid every day and do not spend immediately exactly what they earn. The fact remains, however, that as people earn, they also spend. Money circulates in the economy from consumers to producers and back to consumers several times during a year. The rapidity with which money changes hands

Price level is influenced by the effective money supply.

in this way is called the *velocity of circulation* or simply *velocity*. A \$1 bill that circulates three times, or that has a velocity of 3, has the same economic effect as \$3 that circulates once. If we produced 3,000 loaves of bread a year, the price level would react in the same way whether there was a payment of \$3,000 with a velocity of 1 or \$1,000 with a velocity of 3.

The Equation of Exchange

As we noted earlier (see p. 330), economists use an equation, called the equation of exchange, to express the relationship between money, prices, and business transactions. This equation may be written as $MV = PT$ and is explained as follows:

M is the money supply (currency + demand deposits).

V is the velocity of circulation.

P is the general price level (index number).

T is the total business transactions in the economy.

The left-hand side of the equation, MV, represents the total effective money supply or total spending for the year. The right-hand side, PT, is the total business for the year. Using our previous example, if money supply is \$1,000 and its velocity is 3, and if we produce and sell 3,000 loaves of bread, the price level can easily be determined. $MV = PT$ is easily converted to

$$P = \frac{MV}{T}, \text{ or } P = \frac{\$1{,}000 \times 3}{3{,}000} = \frac{\$3{,}000}{3{,}000} = \$1$$

If we double the money supply (M) and keep velocity (V) and transactions (T) the same, we will have doubled the price level, causing an inflation. If we double the number of transactions (T) but keep M and V constant, we will have cut the price level in half, causing a deflation. It would now appear possible to draw the conclusion that if we want the economy to grow (have a higher GNP) and yet want to maintain stable prices, we must balance an increase in actual production (T) with an increase in spending, or MV.

A case taken from actual history will demonstrate this conclusion. From your studies in American history you may recall the variable economic circumstances of the farmer in the period shortly after the Civil War until the turn of the century. During the Civil War our nation's money supply, *M,* had increased with the introduction of greenbacks. Although production increases during wars, the supply of civilian goods does not increase but may even be reduced. With money supply high and transactions in the civilian market limited, inflation results. Prices for farm products are high. Many farmers borrowed money after the Civil War for newly introduced equipment and for the development of new lands. They did so at a time when the price level was high. Although production increased rapidly after the war, the money supply did not (that is, business transactions, *T,* grew but money supply times velocity, *MV,* did not). This brought about a decline in the price level, particularly for agricultural products. As a result farmers had to pay back more in terms of purchasing power than they had borrowed.

Farmers sought a variety of answers to the problem of deflation. One solution was to increase *M* in order to generate an inflation. Higher prices would mean that fewer bushels would be needed to pay back what was owed. One early suggestion was to increase *M* by issuing more greenbacks. Later the free and unlimited coinage of silver was urged for the same reason. Although neither of these solutions was adopted, *M* did eventually increase as a result of changes such as the Sherman Silver Purchase Act (repealed three years after its passage), the discovery of gold in Alaska, and the development of the cyanide process for the more efficient extraction of gold from ore.

The cartoon suggests that big labor and big business are each reluctant to make the first move in stemming inflation. SOURCE: *New York Times,* April 10, 1966.

Changes in Velocity

Our explanation of the equation of exchange and the example of prices of farm products after the Civil War would seem to indicate that the amount of money in circulation *causes* a change in the price level. Until recently most economists believed that velocity remained almost constant. Studies have shown, however, that this is not always true, particularly over short periods of time. An increase in the amount of money may be followed by a decline in the velocity, as happened during World War II. In the period since World War II the quantity of money has grown at a slower rate than production, but velocity has increased. Still, in the long run, money velocity has been relatively stable. Although declining during the two world wars and the depression of the thirties, and increasing during the prosperous twenties, fifties, and sixties, it has nevertheless confined its fluctuations to between 2 and 4 and has been close to $3^1/_2$ during most of this period.

The equation of exchange is still regarded by economists as important in showing the relationship of money to prices and business transactions. A great deal of economic policy is concerned with the control of *M* as one way of keeping a stable price level and influencing business activity.

Effect of Changes in the Money Supply

The actual effect resulting from a change in the money supply depends to a large extent on whether the economy is operating at a full-employment level. From the end of the 1930's until 1942 there was a sharp increase in our nation's money supply, with a corresponding increase in production. During the beginning of this period over 9 million people were unemployed and a large part of plant capacity was idle. The additional money stimulated production to a full-employment level. Notice that this change took place without any significant corresponding increase in the price level (about three points). The increased amount of money was matched by an almost equal increase in goods and services, with only a moderate increase in prices. A different effect took place after the war. About one year after the war ended, the price level rose sharply, by 25 percent in three years. Although doing away with price controls was a factor, a more basic cause of the increase in prices was the accumulation of money and near-money that could be easily converted into cash and spent for goods. Since our economy was already operating at full capacity, we could not produce all the goods and services demanded by consumers and businesses. By bidding against one another they forced prices to rise.

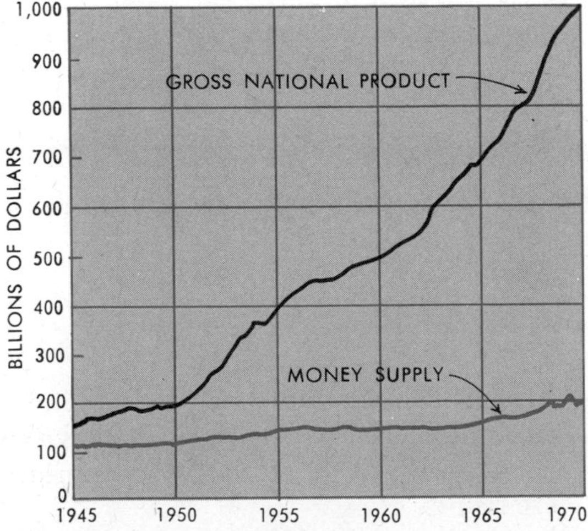

FIGURE 14–3 Money Supply and GNP

Although the money supply does not have a constant relationship to the GNP, it does fluctuate in the same direction. SOURCE: Federal Reserve System, *Historical Chart Book*.

During the 1950's and 1960's our money supply increased far more slowly than did production, as shown in Figure 14–3. The increase in velocity offset some of the effects of the slow growth of *M*. The price level increased very slowly between 1952 and 1956 and after 1959.

Demand-Pull Inflation

The classical explanation for inflation is called *demand-pull*. This label is used because it explains inflation as we have just done—too much money pursuing too few goods. Figure 14–4 illustrates four conditions in relation to price levels—two of a stable price level and one each of inflation and deflation—resulting from the relationship of money to production.

Although the demand-pull theory sounds reasonable as an explanation for much of our inflation, there are times when it seems to explain nothing. One

"JAWBONING," GUIDEPOSTS, AND ALL THAT

In their attempts to control inflation, Presidents have sometimes resorted to persuasion. This is often humorously referred to as "jawboning," implying that the administration is trying to induce labor to keep wage demands low and business to refrain from excessive price increases by avoiding formal legal action. The wage–price guideposts of the Kennedy and Johnson administrations began in 1962, when the Council of Economic Advisers suggested that they be established as "aids to public understanding" so that the public could become aware of the significance of wage and price decisions in terms of "their compatibility with the national interest. . . ."*

Going beyond this modest suggestion, the administration developed the policy of attempting to hold wage increases to no more than 3.2 percent a year, the idea being that wages should not rise faster than the average increase in productivity. In 1964 the Council of Economic Advisers defined productivity growth as "an annual average change in output per man hour during the last five years." Wage increases in excess of 3.2 percent would be regarded as inflationary.

Almost immediately, the policy became highly controversial. It was assailed by both business and labor. George Champion, Chairman of the Board of Chase Manhattan Bank, stated that "the new trend toward government-by-guidelines is one of the most insidious and dangerous on the national scene today. . . ."† George Meany, president of the AFL-CIO, said: "We just don't like the guidelines policy. . . . It destroys our collective bargaining."‡

Economists disagreed on the effectiveness of the policy. At a conference in 1966, Arthur Burns and Walter Fackler saw the guidelines as being ineffective, while Paul Samuelson and Otto Eckstein insisted that they did "influence the minds of men." A study sponsored by the Brookings Institution concluded that the guidelines did help to curb inflation, but others refuted this. A major bank argued that the 1962 to mid-1965 period was one of comparative price stability because the economy was operating within its capacity, and that when excessive growth in the money supply began (in late 1965) price–wage stability ended.

Certainly, there were individual cases in which the "jawbone" policy seemed to work. Some major industries did rescind price increases and some unions did hold down their wage demands in response to government persuasion. It should be noted, however, that persuasion was sometimes backed up by threats of action. President Kennedy had threatened to bring antitrust action against the steel industry and to reduce government

* Council of Economic Advisers, *Economic Report*, 1962.

† *Tax Review*, June 1965.

‡ *Business Week*, March 5, 1966.

such time was the period from 1956 to 1960, when the price index rose more than 10 points. During these years our economy was operating below full-employment capacity. Though it is true that *M* was increasing at a slower rate than production and some economists thought that we had more to fear from unemployment than from inflation, other economists offered a different explanation (mentioned previously in Chapter 7) for the slowdown in business activity at a time when prices were rising.

Cost-Push Inflation

These economists suggest that there is a new kind of inflation that originates on the supply, or cost, side rather than from purchases from firms which did not cooperate. President Johnson used the government's large stores of aluminum and copper to keep the prices of those items in line. Knowing that the government could reduce the market prices by selling off its own supplies, the industries agreed to roll back their prices. Many also feared direct price–wage controls and decided that "voluntary" compliance was preferable.

By 1966, nevertheless, the guidepost policy was breaking down. Wage settlements of 4 percent or more became common. In 1967, while some lip service was still paid to productivity as the standard for wage and price increases, the guidepost policy was quietly dropped. In his first press conference as President in 1969, Richard Nixon disavowed "jawboning" and the use of specific guidelines, although industrial prices were rising at an annual rate of 7.2 percent. By mid-1970, however, the President had ended his "hands-off" policy. Wage settlements were averaging 8 percent a year (excluding fringe benefit increases and the very high agreements in the construction industry), and the CPI was approaching 136. He still rejected any form of *incomes policy* (direct government efforts, ranging from informal guidelines to formal controls, to influence price and wage decisions), but he established a National Commission on Productivity to study ways of improving labor's output and thus ease the inflationary impact of higher wages. He also set up an "inflation alert" system to investigate and publicize price or wage increases that seemed excessive. Finally, in August 1971, President Nixon dramatically announced a temporary freeze on nearly all wages and prices.

At times like these, laymen may become disenchanted with the professional economist. A leading economist who had opposed the guidelines in 1966 came out in favor of some sort of incomes policy in late 1970. Two economists of equal stature offered opposite solutions to the problem. Even economists working for the Nixon administration began to disagree with one another. Does this mean that economics is useless in dealing with such a problem? Hardly! Physicians may disagree on the best treatment for a patient, while strongly agreeing on the diagnosis and the fact that some action must be taken. Likewise, with a problem such as inflation, economists may disagree on the best "cure," but will usually agree that the problem exists and that something must be done. Furthermore, unlike physicians, economists must often rely upon an uninformed public and publicity-conscious politicians to put the prescribed treatment into effect.

---

an excess of demand. The year 1956 was a good year for business, and many of the big labor unions negotiated three-year contracts containing very favorable terms. Profits were very high, and business expected that increased efficiency in production and, if necessary, some of the anticipated additional profits could absorb costs without raising prices. When a recession struck in 1958, the previously negotiated wage increases put great pressure on business to pass these increased costs on to the consumer. Economists call this kind of inflation *cost-push.*

In our economy, with its big labor unions and giant businesses, both of these groups are able to exert some pressure on the market. Although wages and prices

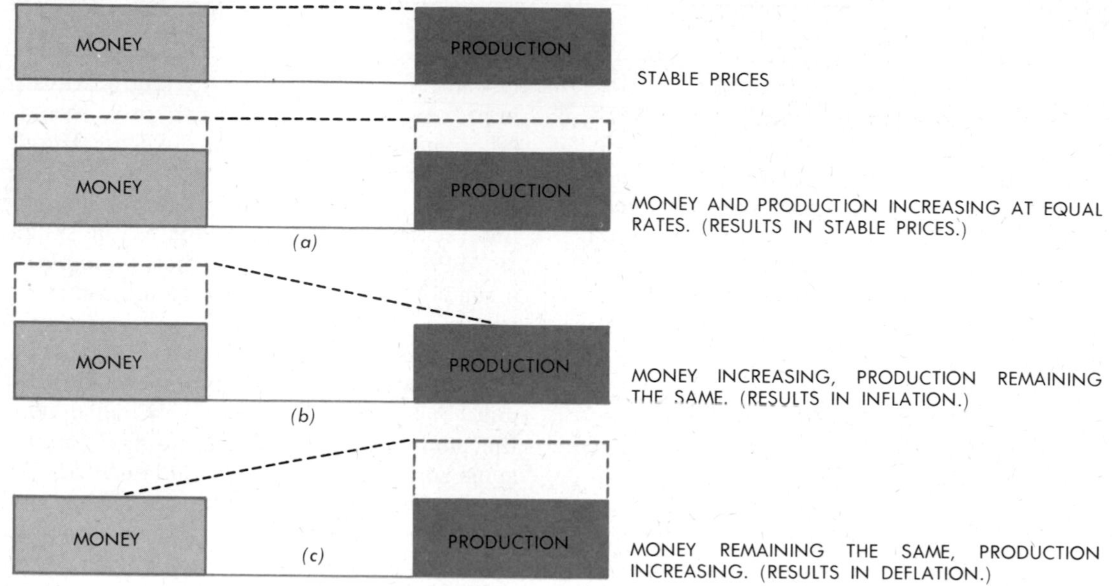

FIGURE 14–4 Money, Production, and the Price Level

The amount of money available for spending in relation to the goods and services available in the market determines whether prices will tend to be (*a*) stable, (*b*) inflationary, or (*c*) deflationary. These examples assume velocity to be constant.

seem to be flexible in their upward motion, the facts that unions can exert some control over wages and that businesses exert some control over prices have almost canceled out downward pressures. Business blames labor for what it calls the "wage-price" spiral, saying that higher wages mean higher costs, which it cannot absorb without a price increase. Labor points out the considerable power of business in controlling prices, frequently pushing prices beyond the point of paying for increased wages. These higher prices reduce the purchasing power of increased wages and cause workers to seek added gains. Management can afford to pay increases because of higher profits and increased productivity.

It is probably true that both the demand-pull and the cost-push theories of inflation have a place in explaining rising price levels. Historically, the most severe inflations have been caused by demand-pull. "Creeping inflation," or inflation that takes place slowly over a period of several years, when it occurs during periods of less than full employment can frequently be explained by cost-push. Some economists have suggested that inflationary pressures come from only certain segments of the economy rather than from total demand or overall costs. Economists have learned a great deal about inflation. With this knowledge they have been able to help in formulating policies that have been useful in preventing excessive price spirals. On the other hand, it is a mistake to think that they "know all the answers."

In our next chapter we will consider our nation's banking system, its effect on *M*, and its means of influencing business activity and the price level.

Part C
The Problem: How Dangerous Is a Creeping Inflation?

When prices rise as rapidly as they did between 1965 and 1971, economists might differ on how to cope with inflation but they will be virtually unanimous in agreeing that it is serious and that something must be done. There are other times, however, when prices increase at a more moderate rate, and the situation is described as *creeping inflation.* A view of the American economy from 1952 to 1965 shows a slow but steady rise in prices. Only twice during this time (from 1956 to 1957 and from 1957 to 1958) did the CPI jump more than two points. Controversy exists among economists as well as among businessmen and government policy makers concerning the seriousness of this sort of creeping inflation and its effects on the economy.

The focus of disagreement is the question of whether it is possible to have a desirable rate of economic growth without a creeping inflation. If a nation's population is increasing, the economy must grow simply to maintain the level of living. There are more people to share the pie, so the pie must get larger or we shall all have to settle for a smaller piece. If the level of living is to improve, then economic growth must surpass the increase in population. Some argue that a creeping inflation is necessary if the economy is to operate at or close to the full-employment level and if we are to have sufficient growth to raise our level of living. Others point to the damage inflicted by inflation, however moderate, and insist that stable prices are not incompatible with growth and full employment.

The issue is further complicated by the so-called "job-price trade-off"—a disturbing phenomenon in which price stability often appears to be accompanied by a high unemployment rate, while full employment is associated with rapidly rising price levels. Actions which will bring inflation under control sometimes seem to lead to the loss of jobs, and conditions bringing about full employment appear to push prices upward. (Full employment means that labor will be scarce. If labor is scarce, wages will rise. Wages represent a major cost of production, so rising wages lead to price increases.) Thus a hard decision must be made—shall we have price stability with high unemployment, or shall we promote full employment and bear the burden of more inflation? Is there some way to have both full employment and price stability? (See pages 449–450 for a further discussion of this problem, and for an analysis of it through the use of the Phillips Curve.)

The Case Against Creeping Inflation

Some economists believe there is no basic conflict between economic growth and stable prices. In fact, stable prices may encourage economic growth, as shown in the 1920's and more recently in 1963 and 1964. It is even possible to find prices rising when little growth is taking place. For example, from 1956 to 1958, when economic growth slowed down and the unemployment rate reached 6.8 percent (in 1958), the Consumer Price Index rose six points. There is no guarantee that the relationship between the unemployment rate and the price index as depicted in Figure 14–5 will always prevail.

Three major factors are primarily responsible for economic growth in the United States: the increasing size of the labor force, the development of a more skilled labor force, and the addition of more capital per worker. Investment in new machinery depends, at least in part, on the level of savings. Since creeping inflation discourages savings, from which the investment for new machinery comes, it acts to discourage economic growth.

Creeping inflation can, and frequently does, provide a temporary stimulus to business. Inventories are sometimes built up to guard against a rising price level, and capital equipment may be bought for the same reason. This buildup, however, can bring on a serious recession when inventories start to pile up and new machinery has been purchased at a faster rate than might be expected if prices were stable. As merchants try to sell off some of their large stocks of merchandise, they cut back on their orders to middlemen and producers. Producers have no need to order new machinery from producers of capital equipment. The recessions of 1953–1954 and 1957–1958 are frequently attributed to the desire of businessmen to reduce their inventories, which were too large in relation to the current demand.

Rising prices are a cause of hardship to many people in our society, particularly those who live on fixed or relatively fixed incomes. Older people who live on pensions and unskilled workers who may not have union protection are hurt as they see their purchasing power declining year by year. For more than 10 years after World War II the salaries of people with relatively fixed incomes declined in purchasing power as prices rose faster than salaries. This situation occurred most often where there were no strong unions to protect workers against the price rise. Even some organized workers suffer during periods of serious inflation, as evidenced by the fact that the purchasing power of factory production and maintenance workers dropped from $87.27 per week in 1969 to $86.07 in 1970 (expressed in constant 1957–1959 dollars).

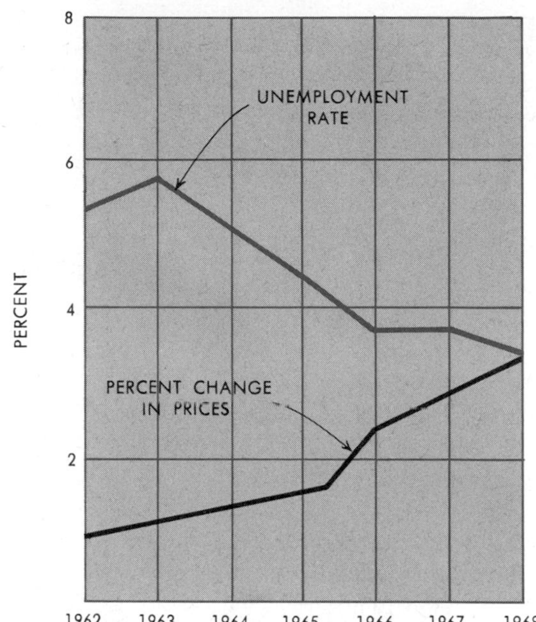

FIGURE 14–5 Relationship Between Unemployment Rate and Inflation Rate

During the period covered by the graph there was a general tendency for prices to rise as the unemployment rate dropped. What problem does this pose for public policymakers?

If wage increases could be kept in proportion to increases in output per man-hour, we could progress toward price stability without sacrificing economic growth. Labor leaders, however, are expected to obtain maximum gains for their workers. Nevertheless, those opposed to creeping inflation believe that unless some restrictions are put on the collective bargaining power of unions, there can be little hope of curbing the cost-push inflation. Any restraint on unions would be vigorously resisted. Nevertheless, the benefits derived from stable prices would far exceed any short-term gains made by those now having advantages of income or influence.

Having accepted the use of government policy to promote an economy with high-level employment, we must be equally committed to having government take whatever action is necessary for maintaining stable prices.

The Case for Creeping Inflation

As we have noted, some economists are opposed to creeping inflation, while others favor such a policy. The latter point out that the inflationary tendencies in almost all industrial countries in the 1950's and 1960's have been caused by a combination of strong aggregate demand and production costs rising faster than output per man-hour (cost-push). With strong unions demanding wage increases greater than the increase in workers' productivity, prices have had to rise also. The only way to avoid such increases is to tighten the money supply enough to increase unemployment and thereby discourage wages from rising. An unemployment rate above 5 percent of our civilian labor force can keep prices quite stable, as was shown in the period from 1960 to 1964.

Although such a policy would put an end to price increases, it also would mean that the potential growth of our economy was not being realized. Is it worthwhile for us to forgo the production of an additional 1 million workers in order to keep price increases confined to 2 percent per year instead of over 3 percent? If our economy fails to grow at its maximum rate, not only do we suffer from the burdens of an immediate unemployment problem but the future growth rate will be affected. Production (consisting in part of capital goods) lost by unemployed workers today can never be made up.

If prices increase at a steady 3 percent per year, businessmen are encouraged to keep their inventories high and to replace them quickly. Stable prices or falling prices cause businessmen to delay their investments in new merchandise or replacements, since holding off may mean buying at a lower price. Although it is true that sharp price increases may cause businessmen to overload their inventories, making the risk of a recession severe when business starts to level off or decline, the anti-recession measures taken in 1961 show that we can reduce the effect and length of these adverse trends.

Some people who fear the effects of creeping inflation suggest reducing the bargaining power of unions. Even if this solution were desirable—and a great many would say it is not—its use is very unlikely. Big unions, with their strong collective bargaining powers, are here to stay. President Johnson's appeal to union negotiators to confine wage demands to the increase in output per man-hour did not stop the United Automobile Workers from asking for and getting an increase above this amount in 1964. Some recent wage increases have been even higher.

The argument that the United States will price itself out of the world market with creeping inflation is not valid if other countries are experiencing an inflation rate greater than ours, as has often been the case. Our own competitive position may be strengthened if our price increases are more moderate than those of foreign nations, but could be threatened if runaway inflation occurs here while other countries stabilize their price levels.

The evidence points to a conflict between maximum economic growth on the one side and stable prices on the other. We may have more to fear from stifling growth and having sizable numbers of our work force unemployed than from the effects of creeping inflation. Some of the ill effects of a slowly increasing price level can be offset by such means as encouraging efficient methods of management, putting clauses in insurance and pension plans to allow for increasing price levels, establishing wage contracts that reflect the price level, and setting up investment programs that are based on purchasing power rather than on fixed dollars.

Considering an Answer

It is the economist's dream to see his country maintain full employment and rapid economic growth without any increase in the general price level. From 1963 to 1965, as the economy of the United States grew rapidly and approached the level of full employment, prices were remarkably stable and few economists worried about inflation. However, in 1966, when the economy approached full employment, wholesale prices started to rise sharply. Disagreement over policies for meeting this new situation became intense. The arguments cited in our present problem were widely used in the debate on this critical issue of economic policy.

So long as the economy is below full employment, or is "overheated" by aggregate demand in excess of the capacity to produce, little disagreement occurs. It is when the economy appears to be moving from one situation into another that controversy is most intense. At this point the values held by decision makers become as important as the tools available for arriving at answers. Is it more important to prevent a creeping inflation by sacrificing some of the welfare and full-employment proposals or to assume the risks of inflation in the hope of providing our people with more opportunities and a higher standard of living? Economic history is filled with examples of nations which suffered from uncontrolled inflations as well as nations which managed to keep prices stable but experienced a severe reduction in growth. What are the consequences to the economy if the decisions of policymakers are wrong?

REVIEW: THE HIGHLIGHTS OF THE CHAPTER

1. Many myths about money still exist in popular thinking. One of the most common is that money must have intrinsic value, as gold does, in order to function as money.
2. An economy which has specialization of production needs money as a medium of exchange.
3. Money also functions as a measure of value, a store of value, and a standard of deferred payment.
4. If money is to perform its functions well, it must be durable, portable, divisible, recognizable, homogeneous, stable in value, and (most important) acceptable to the public.

5. As an economy grows and becomes more complex, commodity money will give way to convertible paper money. Eventually, inconvertible paper money may become standard, as it has in our economy.
6. Unifying the rules on redeeming or not redeeming all money in the domestic market can avoid the effects of Gresham's law. As governments become more responsible in controlling money, the need for backing of currency becomes less important.
7. The three major kinds of money in use today are fractional currency, paper currency, and bank money or demand deposits. The last kind constitutes nearly three fourths of our money supply.
8. Near-monies are liquid assets that can be easily converted into money. Deposits in savings institutions and U.S. government bonds are important categories of near-monies.
9. Price levels are the average prices paid for goods and services for a given period. Changes in price levels can be measured by comparing the index numbers corresponding to various prices.
10. Inflation is an increase in the general price level or a decrease in the value of money. Deflation is a decrease in the general price level or an increase in the value of money.
11. Stable prices are important in protecting the debtor, the creditor, the investor, and people living on fixed incomes.
12. There is a relationship between money, the price level, and business transactions that can be expressed in the equation of exchange: $MV = PT$.
13. Although studies have shown that velocity of money varies, it has been sufficiently stable in the long run to be regarded as significant in showing the relationship of money to prices and business activity.
14. The effects of increasing or decreasing the money supply when the economy is operating at full employment will be different from the effects at a lower level of employment.
15. Demand-pull inflation occurs when too much money pursues too few goods. The excess demand results in rising prices.
16. Cost-push inflation is caused by price rises due to increasing costs. This situation can develop when wages increase faster than output per man-hour or when prices rise faster than wages, forcing workers to seek higher wages.

IN CONCLUSION: SOME AIDS TO UNDERSTANDING

Terms for Review

medium of exchange
Gresham's law
Federal Reserve notes
greenbacks
silver certificates
currency
commodity money
liquid assets
price level
inflation
velocity of circulation
intrinsic value
wage–price spiral
base period
deferred payments
Treasury notes
fractional currency
near-money
fiat money
equation of exchange
index numbers
deflation
demand-pull inflation
cost-push inflation
guideposts
creeping inflation

Questions for Review

1. Money serves many purposes in a nation's economy. List and explain the major functions of money.
2. What are the specific characteristics of money?
3. Government policies in regard to money supply and price levels make it possible to reduce the more extreme effects of inflation and deflation.
   (a) What are some actions that the government can take to influence price levels and the supply of money?
   (b) What are the potential dangers of each of these actions?
4. Recently, some leading economists have proposed that gold no longer be used as a means of payment among nations. What characteristics should a new "international currency" have?
5. Explain the effects of deflation and the effects of inflation on the following: (a) a pensioner, (b) a lender of money, (c) an owner of common stock, (d) an owner of fixed-rent property, (e) a union wage policy committee, and (f) a civil service employee.
6. Explain the statement "The business and consumer segments of our economy can plan most effectively if assured of price stability over a period of time."
7. Evaluate the following statements.
   (a) "Full employment without inflation is the underlying strength of our economy."
   (b) "Wage increases need not be inflationary."
   (c) "A mild inflation (2 to 3 percent increase in average prices per year) helps to promote economic growth and prosperity."

Additional Questions and Problems

1. Obtain the most recent available data on the United States money supply. What percentage is made up of coins, of paper currency, of bank deposits? Why do bank deposits make up the largest percentage? How does each meet the criteria of good money?

2. Why was the 25 percent gold backing removed from Federal Reserve notes in 1968? What effect, if any, did this action have on the value of the dollar? Explain. What principles of money are illustrated by this event?
3. Make a brief survey of the history of money in the United States. What forms of money have been used? What events led to the adoption of each (such as United States notes)? How successful was each as a medium of exchange?
4. Select 15 commodities and 5 services available to the consumer both in 1925 and at present.
   (a) Assign an appropriate cost to every item for each date. Make a total of the costs for each date.
   (b) Create index numbers for each item, using 1925 as a base of 100. When your lists are complete, compare the prices for each item at the different dates. What conclusions can you draw?
   (c) Explain some of the reasons for the use of the index numbers.
   (d) What weaknesses are inherent in the use of index numbers?
5. In this chapter you have been introduced to new ways of interpreting changes in our economy.
   (a) Using the chart in Figure 14–3, explain the fluctuations in GNP and money supply from 1930 to 1932 and from 1940 to 1946.
   (b) What factors of our economy made the period 1950 to 1964 one of gradual change rather than of radical upheaval?
6. Because of the delicate balance between inflation and deflation in our economy, a change in wage rates is of particular significance.
   (a) Select any of the major national labor contracts negotiated in the last two years and explain how the balance between the demands of labor and the concessions of management represents a potential inflation of the demand-pull and cost-push categories.
   (b) Assume you are the representative of the public in a labor dispute. What arguments would you use to make both union and management negotiators realize that a purely selfish approach would hurt both?

SELECTED READINGS

Bernstein, Peter L. *A Primer on Money, Banking and Gold.* New York: Random House, 1965.

Dean, Edwin, ed. *The Controversy over the Quantity Theory of Money.* Boston: D. C. Heath and Co., 1965.

Federal Reserve Bank of Atlanta. *Fundamental Facts About U. S. Money.* Atlanta: Federal Reserve Bank of Atlanta. Research Department, 1969.

Federal Reserve Bank of New York. *Money and Economic Balance.* New York: Federal Reserve Bank of New York, 1968.

Fisher, Douglas. *Money and Banking.* Homewood, Illinois: Richard D. Irwin, 1971.

Massey, J. Earl. *America's Money: The Story of Our Coins and Currency.* New York: Crowell, 1968.

Banking and the Creation of Money 15

THE AUTHORS' NOTE TO THE STUDENT

In the previous chapter we considered the importance of money to the national economy. Here we are concerned with financial institutions that deal with money and credit. Through these institutions the money that people save is made available to those who need it for investment or purchases. Like all resources, money must be carefully allocated in the right amounts, to the right places, and at the right times in order to further the production of the goods and services that consumers want.

Controlling the supply of money as a means of influencing business activity and price levels is important for the well-being of the entire economy. Our commercial banking system, largely controlled by the Federal Reserve Board, makes monetary policy decisions that influence the flow of American money. Again, we will introduce tools to help us analyze what kind of policy decisions should be made. In Chapter 13 we learned about fiscal policy, how the budget may be regulated to control aggregate demand. Here we will concentrate on how the money supply may be controlled to help achieve our economic goal of full employment without inflation. Finally, in Chapter 16 we will put monetary and fiscal policy together to show how the new economics can contribute to a healthy economy.

A STUDENT'S NOTE TO THE STUDENT

This was not an easy chapter, but it opened my eyes to a number of ideas that had previously been a mystery. I am not implying that I found all the answers. I don't think even a course exclusively in money and banking could do that. However, this entire idea of money creation is really fascinating. Our entire system seems to be based much more on accounts kept in ledgers than on the exchange of currency.

The big idea in Part A is the role of banks as financial intermediaries gathering together savings and making it available for investors. In Part B, I found Figure 15–1 a big help in visualizing how the banking process creates money. The most difficult idea for me was the open market. Let me pass on a hint. Stick to the Federal Reserve Bank buying and selling securities rather than switching in midstream to the commercial bank doing the same.

After you get through with the chapter try reading the financial section of a major paper. It is amazing how much more of it I understand. It is also amazing how far I still have to go.

Part A
Kinds of Financial Institutions

Banks and Their Functions

To many people the term "financial institution" refers to a bank, which they may think of primarily as a convenient place to deposit their valuables, particularly money, for protection against the hazards of theft and fire. Actually, there are many different kinds of businesses that may be called banks or financial institutions. Although each of these may serve a particular purpose, they all have one activity in common—collecting money from a source that does not need it immediately and channeling it to others that do have an immediate use for it. Thus, these various financial institutions serve as intermediaries in the flow of money throughout the economy. In addition to this general activity, they carry on a number of more specialized functions.

Depositories

The earliest banks were mere depositories for the safekeeping of valuables. Centuries ago many people deposited their gold in the vaults of goldsmith shops and withdrew it as needed. In order for such a bank to meet its expenses, depositors paid a fee to have their money stored. Later, as these banks issued notes payable in gold, bookkeeping and the balance sheet became important tools for keeping accurate records.

Lending

With many businesses and individuals wanting to borrow money and with funds lying idle in their vaults, banks naturally turned to the business of lending money. Depositors were told that if they would permit the banks to use their money for lending, they would not have to pay a storage fee. Under certain conditions they could even receive payment (interest) for the use of their money. The banks could afford these arrangements because they loaned the money out at a rate of interest higher than they paid to the depositors.

Money Creation

In the course of lending money, bankers discovered that the total amount of money they had on deposit fluctuated very little. Although individuals might alter the size of their accounts considerably from day to day, the total of all deposits in a particular bank remained fairly constant because withdrawals by some people were usually balanced by the deposits of others. This discovery allowed bankers to use most of the money on deposit for loans with little fear of a shortage of funds, even when some depositors wished to withdraw their money.

Using this knowledge, *commercial banks* today are in effect able to create money by using funds from *demand deposits* as the basis for additional deposits, in the form of loans extended to borrowers. This function is of great importance to individual banks and to the whole economy. Let us see how banks create money, even though we realize that our example holds true for the banking system as a whole rather than for any single commercial bank.

Assume there is a very small nation with only one bank—a monopoly bank. The bank has a total of $100,000 in cash on deposit. Its depositors have checkbooks which enable them to withdraw their money at any time simply by writing checks. Those receiving the checks, however, usually deposit them in their own accounts at this bank. Most of the cash never leaves the vault; in fact, never more than 5 percent of the cash is out of the bank at any one time. Playing it safe, the bank decides always to keep at least 10 percent of the cash on hand to meet any demand for cash that its depositors might make. In short, it has established a *reserve requirement* of 10 percent for itself. It places $10,000 in reserve (10 percent of its demand deposits) and makes the remaining $90,000 available for loans. Needing some new machinery, the Ace Construction Co. applies for a $90,000 loan. Certain that the new machinery will increase Ace's business and revenues, and that the loan will be repaid in a short time, the bank agrees. Ace gives its *promissory note* (IOU) to the bank, and the bank simply credits Ace's account with $90,000. Ace does not want the cash: it is quite content to use checks. In making this loan the bank has created credit. It has taken Ace's promissory note and converted it into money (checks serve as money). The nation's money supply has risen by $90,000. How can this be? Shouldn't there be something behind paper that is used as money? In this case it would be an error to say that there is nothing behind this new $90,000 in checkbook money, because in effect it has the assets and good reputation of Ace behind it. The bank's deposits increase to $190,000—the original $100,000 in cash plus the $90,000 in credit. Of course, the bank's reserves must now rise to $19,000, which is 10 percent of its total deposits.

Now must the bank stop this business, or can it go further? If Ace withdrew the cash, and if the recipient (the manufacturer of machinery) decided to keep the cash in its vault, indeed the bank could go no further. But this is highly unlikely. The manufacturer, Bulldozers Inc., deposits the money in its own account in the bank. All the bank must do now is deduct $19,000 from the original $100,000 (a simple bookkeeping operation), for this is the amount it has to keep in reserve against total demand deposits. Note that this leaves $81,000 ($100,000 minus $19,000) available for lending.

Assume that the entire $81,000 is loaned to Carey's Department Store which plans to add a gardening center to its existing facilities. Carey's gets a deposit of $81,000, so total demand deposits rise to $271,000. Remember that these deposits serve as money—$100,000 of which have cash behind them, while the rest are backed by the credit of Ace and Carey's. When Carey's writes a check for $81,000 to pay Dempsey Builders for constructing the new gardening center, Dempsey in turn deposits the check with the bank. The bank has lost no cash whatsoever. Its reserve of course is now $27,100, which is 10 percent of total demand deposits. Deducting this $27,100 from the original $100,000, the bank still has $72,900 available for lending.

Can this go on forever? No—eventually the bank will have made loans of $900,000. At that point its total deposits will be $1,000,000 (the original $10,000 plus $900,000 in loans). The bank must stop here, because it has to keep a 10 percent reserve. The original $100,000 in cash is now 10 percent of total deposits. With no excess reserves, the bank does not dare make further loans. But notice that the economy now has a money supply of $1,000,000. This checkbook money has $100,000 in cash and $900,000 of credit and business property behind it. The bank has created $900,000 in new money.

Fortunately, it is not necessary to go through this tedious step-by-step process to find out how much in demand deposits the commercial banking system can create. All we need to do is multiply our original $100,000 by the reciprocal of the reserve requirement. In this example the reserve requirement was 10 percent, or 1/10. The reciprocal of 1/10 is 10/1, or simply 10. By multiplying $100,000 by 10, we find that $1,000,000 in demand deposits can result from a mere $100,000 in cash. If the reserve requirement had been 20 percent (1/5), how much in demand deposits could have resulted from the same amount of cash?

Finally, the procedure outlined above was unrealistic because in reality there are thousands of commercial banks. In real life, no single bank can bring about the deposit expansion we described. If we think of the entire commercial banking system as if it were one huge bank, however, the procedure (although overly simple) works pretty much as we have indicated. Later in this chapter we shall repeat the process as it works when many banks are involved.

Other Financial Institutions and Their Functions

In addition to commercial banks, many other kinds of financial institutions exist in our economy. They are designed to meet the different requirements which people have for their savings. Each of these institutions tends to have a particular function and to serve a certain kind of depositor.

Savings Institutions

There are three major forms of savings institutions: *mutual savings banks*, *savings and loan* (or building and loan) associations, and *savings departments* in commercial banks. These institutions take the money for which people have no immediate need and place it in personal savings deposits. Although they do not often do so, savings institutions may request depositors to give a notice of intent to withdraw funds. Because of this requirement, savings accounts are called *time deposits,* in contrast to the demand deposits (checking accounts) of commercial banks, from which money may be withdrawn at the depositors' will.

Most of the savings in these institutions come from people of modest income who expect to receive interest on their money but are unwilling to take much risk. Mutual savings banks invest their deposits in real estate mortgages, government bonds, and securities that yield a return in interest higher than that paid to depositors. Savings and loan associations concentrate primarily on home mortgages. Savings banks are usually restricted by law to investments in securities that have little risk. This requirement protects those whose savings are based on modest incomes and to whom loss of these savings might be economically disastrous.

Personal Trusts

Trust companies and the trust departments of commercial banks invest the funds of people with financial security who want to provide income for their families. The money deposited in these institutions is invested in many different types of securities, usually not speculative in nature but providing an assured return. These personal trusts must not be confused with the industrial trusts mentioned in Chapter 4.

Insurance Companies

The purpose of *insurance companies* is to allow people to pool their resources in order to minimize the risk associated with accident, sickness, death, and other unpredictable circumstances. Although the money they collect must be paid out at some time, they control huge sums of money, most of which are placed in long-term investments. The largest portion is put into bonds and mortgages, although significant investments, strictly regulated, are made in real estate and stocks.

Consumer Credit Institutions

A tremendous increase in consumer credit has taken place in recent years. Consumers borrow from small finance companies, credit unions, sales finance companies, and the small-loan departments of commercial banks. Most finance companies do not obtain their loanable funds from the public. Instead they frequently turn to other financial institutions, from which they borrow at rates lower than those at which their clients can borrow. For example, Ford and General Motors have set up finance companies as an aid to their dealers in selling cars. *Credit unions* are set up on a cooperative basis and are organized for a particular group, such as civil service employees, workers in a large company, or people who live in a housing development. Members of a credit union may put their savings into the credit union and receive shares for these deposits. Each share earns interest for the contributor. Members may borrow at comparatively low rates of interest.

Other Financial Intermediaries

Large businesses frequently require money for long-term capital investment beyond the resources of most commercial banks. Such firms may decide to raise the money through the issuance of bonds or stocks. Investment banks or, less often, brokerage houses may be asked to manage the sale of these new securities.

The federal government, too, has become a major source of loans in a number of fields. Through a variety of agencies it assists farmers, home owners, small businesses, and smaller units of government. In many instances the government does not lend the money itself, but merely insures the payment of the loan to the private banker up to a certain percentage of the loan. This practice has made borrowing possible for many families and businesses to which loans might otherwise not be available.

Part B
Commercial Banks and the Creation of Money

Organizing and Operating a Bank

As we have seen, commercial banks are unique among financial institutions because of their ability to create money. Demand deposits (checking accounts) make up about three fourths of our money supply. The ability of these banks to

FEDERAL DEPOSIT INSURANCE CORPORATION

Before 1933, and particularly during the period from 1929 to 1933, bank failures were not uncommon. If a bank overextended itself in creating credit or if several of its important loans could not be repaid, depositors in the bank would frequently become panicky and begin to make large withdrawals—to make a run on the bank. Since the bank had only a fraction of its deposits backed by currency (fractional reserves as opposed to 100 percent reserves), the bank would soon be unable to meet withdrawals and most depositors would lose their money. If the bank could borrow money from another bank to pay those withdrawing money, people's confidence would return and they would probably redeposit their money. Frequently a bank merely needed time to improve its cash position by calling in some of its loans and not making additional ones. In 1933 the number of bank failures reached a peak, forcing the federal government to intervene and close the banks temporarily. To help restore the public's confidence and strengthen the banking community, Congress passed legislation setting up the Federal Deposit Insurance Corporation. This corporation, an agency of the federal government, now insures over 90 percent of all bank deposits up to $20,000 per deposit. The FDIC has built up its insurance fund by charging one twelfth of 1 percent on the total deposits of member banks.

As a result of the protection provided by the FDIC and other kinds of supervision, bank failures have been reduced to a few isolated instances, due mainly to embezzlement. Since people know that their deposits are insured, they no longer rush to withdraw their money if they become concerned about the financial condition of their bank. The delay gives the banks the necessary time to adjust their cash credit balance, and this action will serve to reduce the possibility of bankruptcy.

---

maintain and create demand deposits by means of loans and investments influences the supply of money, *M*, in our economy. Because other financial institutions do not have demand deposits and no checks may be written on their accounts, they do not exercise control over the amount of money in circulation.

In Chapter 4 we set up an imaginary business in order to explain business organization and some of its problems. Let us do the same with a commercial bank, having as our objective an understanding of the part played by these banks in our economy.

Organizing a Bank

Banking is a business in which the product offered for sale is money. As with other businesses, the incentive is to earn profits. We can best accomplish this by offering to the public what it wants and by operating as efficiently as possible. In this way we are serving ourselves and society at the same time.

We begin by calling a meeting of people who are interested in using their money to organize a commercial bank. We decide how much capital will be needed and whether we wish to function as a state or national bank. Both the state and federal governments have laws regulating banks under their authority. Having agreed that we will raise $300,000 in capital, enough for us to qualify as a commercial bank in a city of our size (40,000), we decide to petition the state banking authority to issue a charter. We become a corporation under the name The Felix Bank, and we start to sell stock in our company.

As we begin our operations, we set up a *balance sheet*—a statement showing *assets, liabilities,* and *net worth.* Assets will equal liabilities (the claims of nonowners against the firm) and net worth (the claims that the owners have against our assets). Having sold $300,000 worth of stock in our bank, we will have on hand $300,000 in cash and we will have outstanding capital stock worth $300,000. The cash is an asset of the bank. (Cash held by a bank is called *till money* or *vault cash.*) Note, however, that the stock outstanding represents claims which the stock owners have against our assets. Our balance sheet would be as follows:

Assets	
Cash	$300,000
Liabilities and Net Worth	
Capital stock	$300,000

A board of directors has been appointed, which in turn appoints a president and bank officers. A building costing $200,000 is purchased and furnished with $60,000 worth of equipment. The value of our assets has *not* changed, although those assets now have a different composition. The balance sheet will reflect this as follows:

Assets	
Cash	$40,000
Property	$260,000
Liabilities and Net Worth	
Capital stock	$300,000

The balance sheet is still in balance and always will be. People begin to deposit money in our bank, and soon we have a total of $100,000 in *demand deposits.* These are checking accounts, and the depositors can draw out part or all of their funds at any time simply by writing checks. Thus the demand deposits are claims against our bank's assets and must be added to the liabilities side of the balance sheet. The cash we received from the depositors, however, is also considered an asset which will be added to the asset side. Note the effect on the balance sheet below:

Assets	
Cash	$140,000
Property	$260,000
Liabilities and Net Worth	
Capital stock	$300,000
Demand deposits	$100,000

Assets still equal liabilities and net worth, of course. Have any other changes occurred? Checkbook money, or demand deposits, have increased. The total money supply has not, however, because the amount of currency in circulation has dropped by the same amount ($100,000), and because currency that is held by a bank is not counted as part of the nation's money supply. If the reverse occurs (that is, if someone withdraws cash from the bank) our deposit liabilities will decrease while currency in circulation will increase by the same amount. (What will this do to the balance sheet?)

Now suppose that we decide to join the Federal Reserve System. State chartered banks may join if they wish to, and if they can meet the requirements. (If we had been chartered by the United States Comptroller of the Currency as a national bank we would have been required to join.) As a member of the Federal Reserve System we must keep a *reserve deposit* in the Federal Reserve Bank. The amount we have to deposit with the Federal Reserve Bank will be a certain percentage of our demand deposits. If the *reserve requirement* is 10 percent, we shall have to keep $10,000 on deposit with the Federal Reserve Bank. If it is 20 percent, we shall have to have $20,000 in our reserve account with the "Fed." (Actually, vault cash can also be counted as part of our reserves, but banks rarely keep more than 2 percent of their deposits in cash.) If we had not joined the Federal Reserve System the laws of our state would have set a reserve requirement, and we would have been required to keep these reserves either in cash or in deposits in other banks. (The requirement varies from state to state, but the average is generally around 15 percent.)

Under Federal law, the Federal Reserve can vary the reserve requirement from 10 to 22 percent in medium-sized and large cities, and from 7 to 14 percent in small towns and rural areas. Let us assume that our bank is required to meet a 20 percent reserve requirement. (The actual figure has been somewhat smaller than this in recent years, but 20 percent will simplify our computations.) Let us also forget about vault cash. We would be foolish to keep much cash on hand, for this earns no interest, and cash withdrawals are usually matched by new cash deposits anyway. Now we must deposit $20,000 with the Federal Reserve Bank—20 percent of the $100,000 in demand deposits in our bank.

The $20,000 is the bare minimum that we must have with the Federal Reserve Bank, and we are quite certain that we shall acquire new deposits in the near future, so we might as well send even more to the Federal Reserve. Indeed, we go all the way and deposit the entire $140,000 in cash found in the balance sheet above. The new balance sheet follows:

Assets	
Cash	$0[1]
Property	$260,000
Reserve account	$140,000

Liabilities and Net Worth	
Capital stock	$300,000
Demand deposits	$100,000

We have met our legal requirement, and we have *excess reserves*. That is, we have $120,000 more than we are required to have in our reserve account. (The reserve of $120,000 is an asset for us and a liability for the Federal Reserve Bank.) This will save us the trouble of sending additonal reserves to the Fed every time our deposit liabilities are increased.

We have now reached a vital point in this discussion because the capability of commercial banks to make loans is dependent upon excess reserves. The ability of the commercial banking system to create money also depends upon reserves. In times past, reserves were regarded as a sort of safety fund to protect depositors

[1] In reality, of course, we would not deposit all of the cash. We would keep about 1-1/2 or 2 percent of our total assets in cash. Since vault cash can be counted as part of our reserves, however, it will be simpler in this discussion if we assume that all of it has been deposited with the Fed. Thus we won't have to bother adding cash and deposits in the Fed to determine our total reserves.

from possible losses. They would be drawn upon in the event that a bank was confronted with large withdrawals of cash. Under our system, however, the required reserves cannot be used to meet unexpected withdrawals of cash. If all of a bank's depositors suddenly demanded cash at the same time, its legal reserves would not suffice to cover this emergency anyway, because demand deposits may exceed required reserves. (It should be noted, however, that when depositors withdraw cash, the bank's deposit liabilities decrease. The amount of required reserves drops, thus releasing some of the bank's reserves.)

The purpose of required reserves is to give the Federal Reserve System a way of controlling the commercial banks. As we shall see, the Fed can use this power to discourage banks from extending too much credit during a period of inflation when the economy needs "cooling off," or it can use it to encourage creation of more credit when the economy needs to be stimulated. Let us also see how the Federal Reserve enters the picture in the daily business of our Felix Bank. Suppose that one of our depositors writes a check for $10,000 to pay for merchandise for his store. He sends the check to the manufacturer, who is located in another city. The manufacturer deposits the check in his account at the Liberty Bank in his city. The Liberty Bank sends the check to the Federal Reserve Bank, thus increasing its reserve account by $10,000. On the Liberty Bank's balance sheet there will be an additional $10,000 on the asset side (in its reserve account) and an additional $10,000 on its liabilities side, because the $10,000 can be withdrawn by the manufacturer upon demand. Meanwhile, the Federal Reserve Bank reduces our Felix Bank reserve account by $10,000. On our balance sheet we would decrease the asset side by $10,000 and the liabilities side by the same amount—our reserve account has decreased by $10,000, but so too have our demand deposits. The balance sheet is now as follows:

Assets	
Property	$260,000
Reserve account	$130,000
Liabilities and Net Worth	
Capital stock	$300,000
Demand deposits	$90,000

The *legal* or *required* reserve of the Felix Bank is now only $18,000, which is 20 percent of our total demand deposits. (How much do we now have in excess reserves? What is the difference between the amount of excess reserves we now have and the amount we had before? Why is the decline in excess reserves less than the decline in demand deposits?)

In addition to noting what has happened to each bank involved in this simple transaction, the reader should give careful thought to what has happened to the commercial banking system as a whole. It is extremely important to realize that, although one bank gained deposits and another lost, there has been no loss of deposits for the system as a whole. Similarly, one bank gained reserves and another lost them, but for the system as a whole there has been no loss. Even in the case of our bank, it is probable that our loss of the $10,000 would soon be balanced by a new deposit. The system is extremely dynamic. It does not stand still. Deposits now flow from bank to bank in a never-ending circle. It is when the system as a whole gains or loses deposits that the economy is affected most importantly. Next we shall see how this system creates money.

Creation of Money by the Entire Banking System

If we lend money to the limit permitted by our legal reserve, we risk having an adverse clearing balance (an overdraft) in our account with the Federal Reserve Bank. People with *derivative deposits* (deposits arising from loans we have made to our customers) usually write checks almost immediately on their deposits, far more so than those with *primary deposits* (deposits arising from cash). Thus we might find that our reserves have declined below the legal requirement, as checks drawn on our bank are presented for payment from our account with the Federal Reserve Bank.

The fear of having an adverse clearing balance limits a single bank in using its excess reserves. However, if the banking system is considered in its entirety, we can see that adverse clearing balances for some banks must be matched by favorable clearing balances of other banks. If more money is drawn on our account than we gain from checks deposited with us from other banks, we lose reserves. To understand what happens when the banking system creates money by expansion of demand deposits, let us follow an example through all the steps of the process.

Creating Money by Deposits

Mr. Smith, our imaginary customer, arrives at the First Bank with $1,000 in cash, which he deposits in his checking account. The First Bank, with demands for loans exceeding its ability to grant them, now has additional money to work with. We will assume that the Federal Reserve has set the legal reserves at 20 percent. The First Bank lends $800 to Mr. A and puts $200 in its reserve account with the Federal Reserve Bank in its district. Mr. A immediately writes a check on his derivative deposit to Mr. B. First Bank officials are not worried, since they have already anticipated that Mr. A would withdraw his money from the loan and have put the $200 aside to take care of legal reserve requirements.

Mr. B deposits Mr. A's check in his own account in the Second Bank. With $800 in a new deposit the Second Bank lends $640 to Mr. C and puts $160 (20 percent of $800) in reserves. Mr. C now pays Mr. D the amount of $640, which Mr. D deposits in his account. The Third Bank loans $512 to Mr. E and puts $128 in its reserve account. Mr. E pays the $512 to Mr. F.

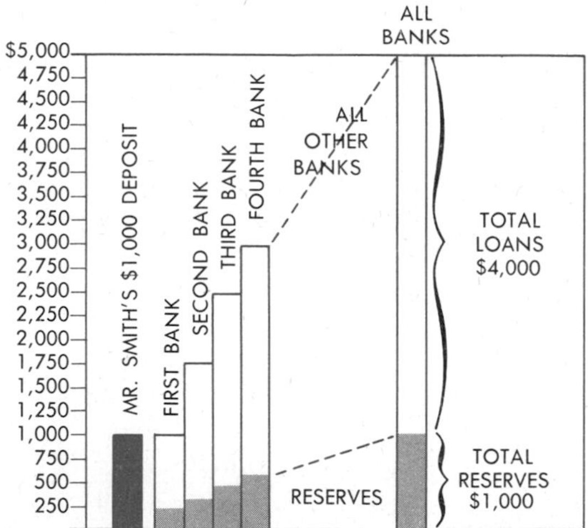

FIGURE 15–1 Expansion Process of the Banking System

Mr. Smith's new $1,000 deposit eventually serves as the support for $5,000 of deposits ($4,000 loans and $1,000 reserves) with a 20 percent reserve requirement.

TABLE 15–1 An Illustration of the Creation of Money by Deposits

Banks	Deposits	Reserves	Loans
First	$1,000.00	$ 200.00	$ 800.00
Second	800.00	160.00	640.00
Third	640.00	128.00	512.00
Fourth	512.00	102.40	409.60
All Other Banks Together	2,048.00	409.60	1,638.40
Total	$5,000.00	$1,000.00	$4,000.00

Mr. F deposits Mr. E's check in his account. With the new deposit of $512 the Fourth Bank loans $409.60 and protects its 20 percent legal reserve requirement by putting $102.40 in its reserve account.

This expansion process continues on through the banking system until all of Mr. Smith's $1,000 of currency ends up in the reserves of the banks involved. Through the banking system's process of granting loans, Mr. Smith's $1,000 has been expanded to $5,000 of deposits.

We can see in Table 15–1 that, with a 20 percent legal reserve requirement, one dollar of reserves can support five dollars of deposits or four dollars of loans. Reserve dollars are frequently called "high-powered" dollars because adding or subtracting reserve dollars has the ultimate effect of increasing or decreasing deposits by many times the reserve dollars themselves.

By now you may wonder why the First Bank could not take Mr. Smith's $1,000 deposit and add it to its reserve account. In this way the First Bank could expand its loans to $5,000. This would be acceptable if those who borrowed the money left all of it in their accounts or if the First Bank were the only bank in existence. However, people who borrow money use it; when their checks are deposited in other banks, the First Bank would not have the reserves or cash to make payment to the other bank.

You may also wonder how the First Bank (and subsequently every other bank) is able to meet its reserve requirements when the Federal Reserve Bank subtracts from its reserve account the $800 drawn on it when Mr. B deposits his check in the Second Bank. Remember that the First Bank has put only $200 of the original $1,000 in its reserve. The answer is that the First Bank, like other banks, will tend to have check clearances against its reserves offset by check clearance added to its reserve account. Because of this the $200 put in the First Bank's reserve account is enough to meet the reserve requirement.

It is important to understand that the individual banks *cannot* expand their deposits five times: each bank that lends money no longer has use of the funds. The bank's balance sheet would show that its loans and investments would be no larger than four times its reserves or four fifths of its deposits. *It is the banking system as a whole that expands our money supply, M,* through the use of demand deposits, as shown by the total in Table 15–1.

Part C
The Federal Reserve System

With the exception of the First Bank of the United States (1791) and the Second Bank of the United States (1816), our federal government concerned itself less with banking operations than did the governments of other industrial nations during the nineteenth century. This period of inactivity ended in 1913, when Congress passed the Federal Reserve Act. This legislation, later expanded, created the Federal Reserve System to serve as the central banking institution of the United States, providing currency, regulating the total amount of money in the economy according to need, and furnishing other financial services needed by both public and private sectors of the economy. Our Federal Reserve System differs from the centralized banking systems of most other industrialized nations by being a relatively new institution, by being more decentralized, and by not being government-owned. Our nation's monetary policy is in the hands of a small group of appointed specialists who are responsible for serving the interests of the general public rather than the stockholders of any single bank or group of banks and who must at times act on behalf of the government.

Organization of the Federal Reserve System

By the Federal Reserve Act our country is divided into 12 districts, each with a Federal Reserve bank located in one of the major cities in the district. Ten of the districts have at least one additional branch bank. The boundaries of each district, the location of the Federal Reserve banks, and the location of the branch banks are shown on the map. Also see Figure 15–2.

Federal Reserve Banks

Each Federal Reserve bank is owned by its member banks, which are required to buy stock in it. Member banks receive dividends, but it must be emphasized that the Federal Reserve banks do not operate for profit. Each bank has a board of nine directors, six chosen by the member banks and three appointed by the Board of Governors. Only three of the nine members may be bankers; thus the board of directors is designed to operate in the public's interest. Although the policy of each Federal Reserve bank must conform to the general policy set by the Board of Governors, many decisions are made in the best interests of the district, including what rate of interest should be charged to member banks. These decisions, however, must have the approval of the Board of Governors.

Board of Governors

The final responsibility for the functioning and policy making of the Federal Reserve System is with the seven-man Board of Governors, which oversees the entire system. Members of this Board are appointed by the President and are confirmed by the Senate for 14-year terms. These terms are arranged so that a new appointment is made every two years, a provision which minimizes the influence of pressure groups. Originally organized to coordinate the functions of the Federal Reserve banks, the Board has gradually increased its influence on the entire system.

The Federal Reserve System

The Federal Reserve System is the federal government's chief means for implementing banking and monetary policies. Shown in addition are the Treasury Department's mints, assay offices, and Bureau of Engraving and Printing. SOURCE: Federal Reserve System, *Federal Reserve Bulletin.*

Federal Open Market Committee

One of the most important functions of the Federal Reserve System is the purchase and sale of government securities. These activities are carried on by the twelve-member Federal Open Market Committee. Seven of its members are the members of the Board of Governors, and the other five are presidents of Federal Reserve banks, always including the president of the Federal Reserve Bank of New York.

This committee meets frequently to determine policy on open-market operations, which influence our money supply. It gives specific instructions to its agent, the Federal Reserve Bank of New York, regarding the purchases and sales of government securities.

Federal Advisory Council

Each Federal Reserve bank annually selects from its district a prominent commercial banker to serve on the Federal Advisory Council. This Council, which meets in Washington at least four times a year, is designed to present the views of bankers to the Board of Governors. Its powers are purely advisory.

Member and Nonmember Banks

About 5,900 of the almost 13,700 commercial banks in the United States are members of the Federal Reserve System. All national banks must be members, and some state banks are also. These member banks hold about 85 percent of all demand deposits and include all the large banks. They are required to comply with the

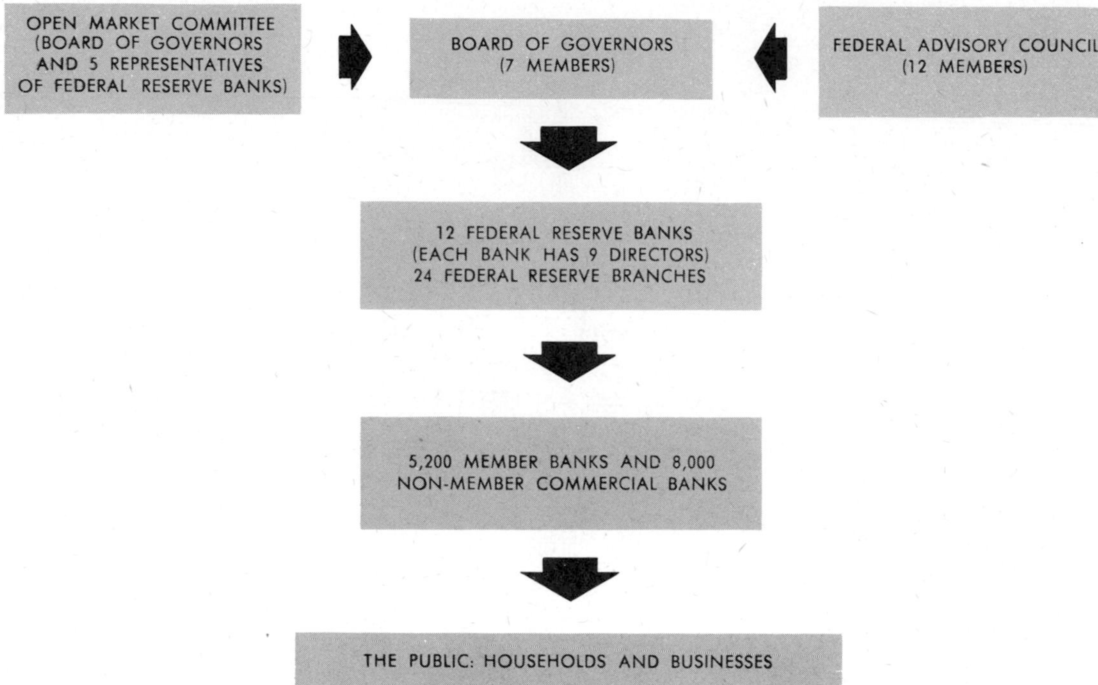

FIGURE 15–2 Organization of the Federal Reserve System
SOURCE: Federal Reserve System, Board of Governors.

numerous regulations of the Federal Reserve System, including periodic examinations by the Federal Reserve bank inspectors. The Federal Reserve System also exerts a strong influence over nonmember banks, which have working agreements with member banks and use certain services of the Federal Reserve System.

Services of the Federal Reserve

The Federal Reserve System provides a wide range of services to banks throughout the country. Through these services its influence extends from the highest levels of government down to the local community. We will examine the activities of the Federal Reserve before going on to analyze its role in determining and carrying out particular policies.

Holding Reserves of Member Banks

As you have seen, the Federal Reserve Bank in each district holds on deposit the legal reserves of its member banks. Cash in the member banks' vaults may also be counted toward these reserves. Any amount held on deposit above the legal reserves (that is, excess reserves, described previously) may be drawn upon by the member banks. Member banks try to keep a balance between having sufficient reserves to avoid falling below legal reserve requirements and having too large excess reserves which earn no interest. Banks frequently borrow from one another to maintain this delicate balance.

Providing Currency for Circulation

Currency in our country comes either

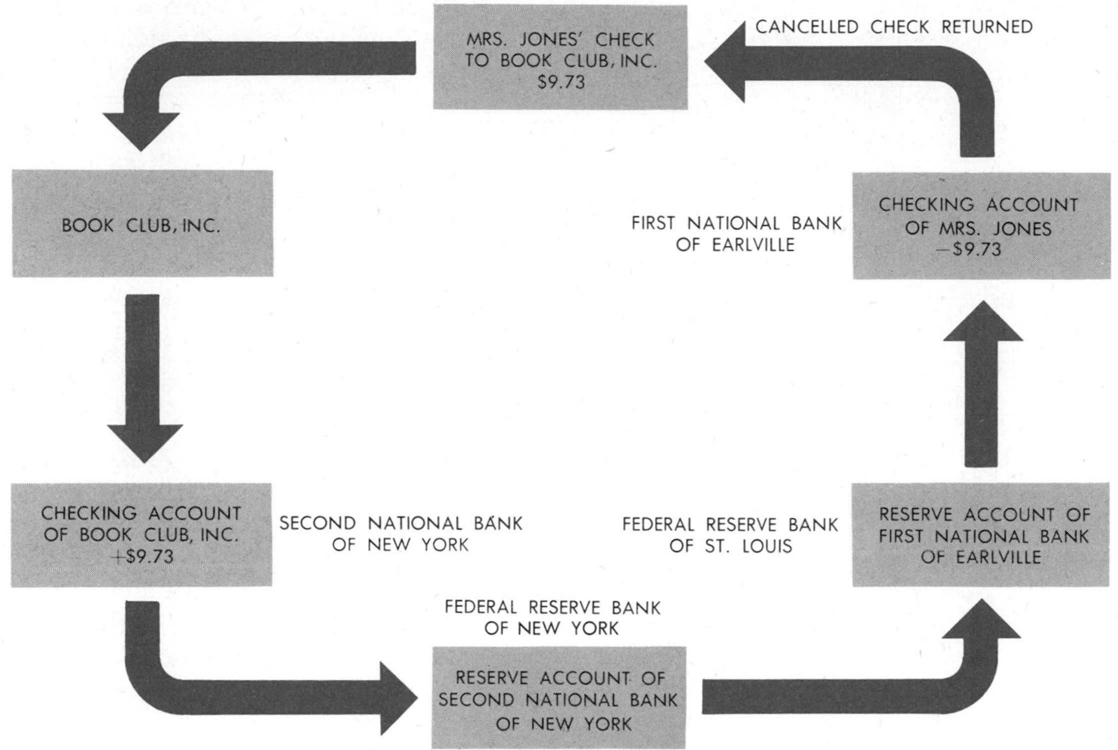

FIGURE 15–3 The Route of a Check

One of the services furnished to banks by the Federal Reserve System is the clearing of checks.

from the United States Treasury or from the Federal Reserve banks. As we saw in Chapter 14, Federal Reserve notes make up 85 percent of our currency. The Federal Reserve banks issue this currency to member banks as they need it by the simple means of subtracting it from their reserve accounts. Although there is always a need for new currency to replace that which wears out, public demand for currency increases sharply at certain times of the year, such as the Christmas season. The Federal Reserve banks keep a large supply of currency on hand so that member banks can draw on their accounts as the new money is needed.

During February, when business activity normally declines and there is less need for currency, the member banks frequently find themselves with too much cash available. They simply redeposit the surplus of currency with the Federal Reserve bank, just as their customers have done with them. This cash is then credited to their reserve accounts.

Providing a Clearing House for Checks

With more business being handled by check than by cash transactions, the process of clearing checks is almost staggering in its complexity. Figure 15–3 shows the steps involved from the time a check is written in payment for merchandise until the time it is subtracted from the checking account of the buyer.

Many large cities have *clearing houses* where representatives of each of the commercial banks can meet to settle their accounts with other banks in the city. However, checks from out of the city are turned over to the Federal Reserve Bank for collection and crediting to reserve accounts of member banks. This also includes checks of nonmember banks that may use the check-clearing services of the Federal Reserve.

Serving As Fiscal Agent for the Federal Government

Because the United States Treasury has no bank of its own, the Federal Reserve serves as its fiscal agent. This activity involves keeping most of the government's accounts. Receipts from taxes, the sale of securities, and other collections as well as payment for salaries, the redeeming of securities, and other expenses are handled through the Federal Reserve System.

Supervising of Member Banks

The authorities of the Federal Reserve banks exercise wide supervision over member banks by such means as detailed reports on the management, investments, loans, and other activities of the banks. Periodic inspections, together with those made by the Federal Deposit Insurance Corporation and by the comptroller of the currency for national banks or inspectors for state banks, help to protect the public, improve banking practices, and maintain the standards of nonmember banks.

The Role of the Federal Reserve in Controlling the Supply of Money

In preceding chapters we have seen that the nation's economy is subject to fluctuations and that such fluctuations are accompanied by changes in the price level. We found that there is a relationship between the supply of money, *M*, the price level, *P*, and business activity, *T*. As our nation's central bank, the Federal Reserve System exercises considerable influence over the size of *M*. Through its control over discount rates, open-market operations, and the reserve ratio it can help to provide a full-employment noninflationary economy. Let us see how it can use these three major tools to attain this objective.

Discount Rate

We know that the Federal Reserve banks provide a banking system for private commercial banks. Banks use this system in two main ways—for depositing funds and for borrowing. When businessmen face a shortage of funds, they go to commercial banks to borrow. When these member banks are short of reserves, they may borrow from the Federal Reserve bank. They can do this by using the promissory notes from their own customers as collateral.

The rate of interest that the Federal Reserve bank charges member banks for loans is called the *discount rate*. The Reserve bank can raise or lower that rate with the approval of the Board of Governors. Raising the discount rate to member banks will in turn cause them to raise interest rates to their own customers. Lowering the discount rate will allow member banks to offer lower interest rates to their customers.

Discount rates of member banks are set at levels similar to those on secondary reserves, such as short-term United States securities. Banks will usually sell these securities to increase their reserves before borrowing from the Federal Reserve banks. Although discount rates have a strong influence on all interest rates, they are relatively less effective when banks have large excess reserves or a great many liquid assets. See the trend of discount rates, Figure 15–4.

Open-Market Operations

The Federal Reserve System, acting as the fiscal agent for the federal government as well as the chief instrument for controlling the supply of money, buys and sells short-term government securities through *open-market operations.* These purchases and sales are made through dealers who represent investors interested primarily in Treasury bills (three- to six-month loans). Commercial banks often hold such securities as secondary assets and frequently buy and sell them to adjust their own reserve positions.

When the Federal Open Market Committee orders the Federal Reserve Bank of New York, as the agent for the System, to sell securities, this action has the effect of reducing the reserves of commercial banks, thereby reducing their ability to lend money. Let us see how this result takes place.

The Federal Reserve Bank contacts a dealer in Treasury bills and sells him $1 million worth of these securities. He buys these bills for Company A, which has surplus cash that it does not plan to use for three months. Company A wants to earn interest on this surplus money rather than let it lie idle. To pay the dealer, Company A draws checks on the several banks with which it has accounts. This withdrawal reduces the excess reserves of these banks and consequently their ability to grant additional loans. Deposits and reserves have both been reduced. Since each reserve dollar supports

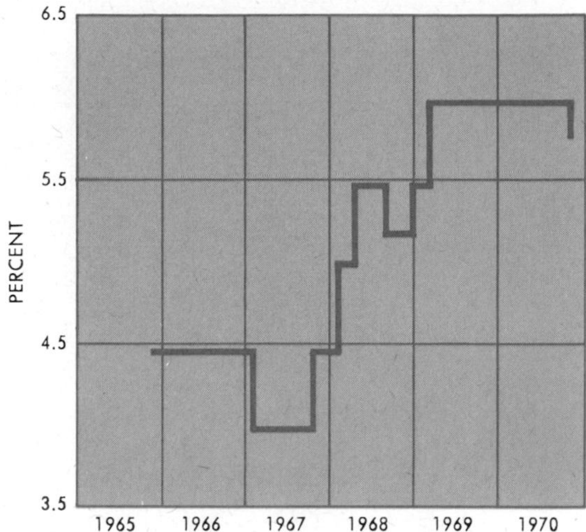

FIGURE 15–4 Discount Rates for a Five-Year Period

The Federal Reserve usually raises the discount rate when monetary policy calls for economic restraint and lowers the rate when the goal is to stimulate the economy. SOURCE: Federal Reserve System, Board of Governors.

several times as many deposit dollars, banks will be forced to restrict their credit expansion by several times the amount of the loss in reserves. When a bank buys Treasury bills, its reserves are reduced. Because its excess reserves are used up even faster, credit expansion is restricted to an even greater degree.

Suppose that the situation is reversed and that the Reserve Bank is ordered to buy securities. Company B has Treasury bills which it wishes to sell. When its dealer sells these bills to the Federal Reserve Bank, Company B receives payment through a check drawn on the Federal Reserve Bank. Company B then deposits this check in its accounts at several banks. These banks then forward their checks to the Reserve Bank for credit to their reserve accounts. Deposits and reserves

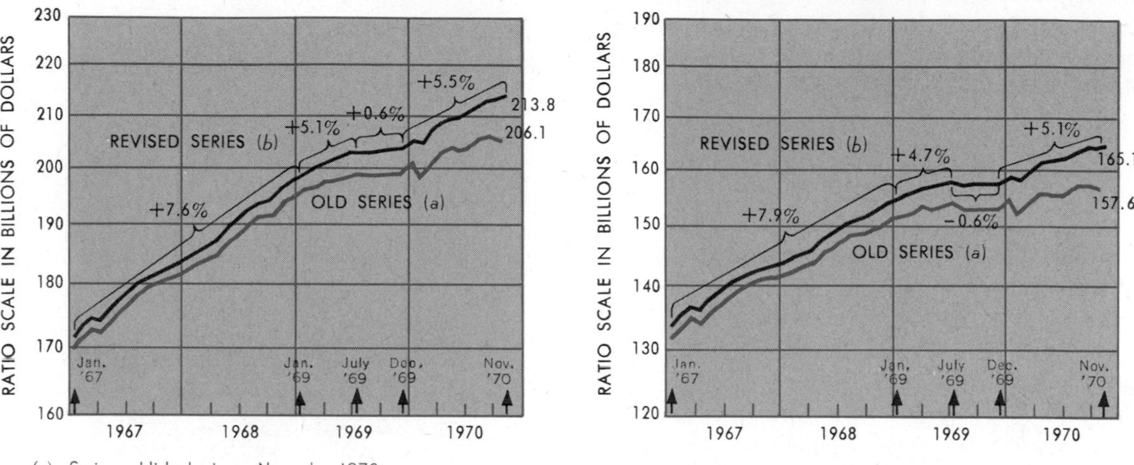

(a) Series published prior to November 1970.

(b) The revised series reflects annual revisions of seasonal factors and benchmark adjustments, as well as major adjustments for an underestimation of the old series arising from international transactions.

Percentages are annual rates of change for periods indicated.

Latest data plotted: November

FIGURE 15–5 Changes in the Nation's Money Stock

Economic growth and the growth in the money stock tend to go hand in hand. Note that the period when the growth in demand deposits leveled off and dipped slightly was a period of general economic slowdown. Demand deposits make up the major part of our money stock. In what way does this graph illustrate the importance of the Federal Reserve and the commercial banking system? SOURCE: Federal Reserve Bank of St. Louis.

have been increased equally, and since one reserve dollar can support several deposit dollars, the banks now have excess reserves to use for loans. Each dollar added to the reserves allows commercial banks to loan several dollars, creating new demand deposits.

In order to stimulate purchases and sales of securities, interest rates may have to be changed. If there are too few buyers, the interest these securities pay may have to be increased. This change will in turn affect the interest rates in all other markets.

Open-market operations are the *most important* tool of the Federal Reserve System for expanding and contracting the money supply. Unlike the other tools, this one is used on a day-to-day basis.

Reserve Requirements

As we have pointed out previously, the Board of Governors of the Federal Reserve has the power to raise or lower the reserve requirements of member banks within certain limits. For central reserve cities (New York and Chicago) and other reserve cities the minimum reserve requirement for demand deposits of member banks is 10 percent; the maximum is 22 percent. For all other banks (known as country banks) the reserve requirements for demand deposits may range from 7 to 14 percent. The reserve requirements for time deposits may vary between 3 and 10 percent.

Changing the reserve requirements is the single *most powerful* tool of the Federal Reserve for expanding and contracting the supply of money; as such, it is used sparingly. If the legal reserve requirement is 10 percent, it means that $1 of reserves can support $10 of demand deposits. A 20 percent reserve reduces the number of dollars of demand deposits a reserve dollar will support to a ratio of 1:5. Banks which have plenty of excess reserves can readily adjust as the ratio is raised. Those member banks whose reserves are low will be forced to borrow or sell securities, or do both, to meet the new requirements. If this action is taken when the discount rate is high and when the Reserve banks are not interested in purchasing securities in the open market (providing a source of cash to banks), the member banks may face an economic crisis. These banks will have to curtail their lending operations; this effect is, of course, exactly what the Federal Reserve intends to achieve when it raises the reserve requirements. Reducing reserve requirements creates additional excess reserves, allowing member banks to make additional loans. This should result in increasing the money supply.

Other Controls Used by the Federal Reserve

In addition to its three major methods of controlling credit, the Federal Reserve has several minor methods which it exercises from time to time. The major methods are aimed at the control of the entire supply of money, whereas the minor methods are aimed at particular markets.

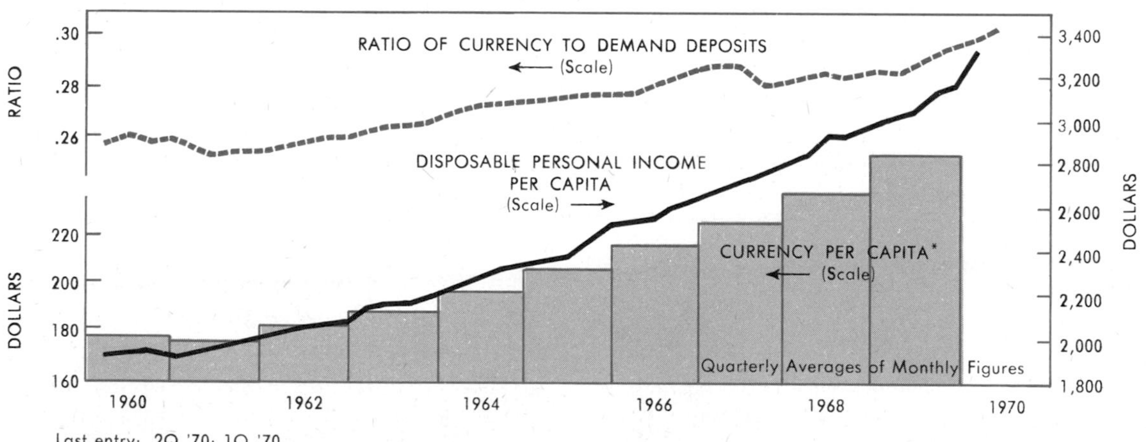

FIGURE 15–6 Personal Income and the Demand for Currency

As disposable personal income per capita has increased, currency per capita has increased also. The rise in the ratio of currency to demand deposits indicates a willingness on the part of the public to hold more currency. One possible explanation is that consumer purchases of services increased from 38 percent of total purchases in 1959 to 42 percent in 1969. Payment for recreation (up 83 percent), beauty treatments, tonsorial services, and the like (up 85 percent) are usually made in cash. The use of vending machines requiring coins has increased greatly. Another possible factor is that people may be holding more cash to evade income tax payments. Can you think of others? If this trend continues and more people choose to hold cash rather than bank deposits, how might this affect the commercial banking system and the nation's money supply? SOURCE: Federal Reserve System, Board of Governors.

FRIEDMAN AND MONETARISM

Although most American economists are of the Keynesian school and believe that fiscal policy (such as changes in taxes and government spending) are important factors affecting business activity, there is increasing interest in and growing support for the *monetarist theories* of Professor Milton Friedman of the University of Chicago. (The monetarist position is sometimes called the *Chicago School.*) According to Dr. Friedman, the main determinant of employment, prices, and the level of output is the rate at which the Federal Reserve changes the nation's money supply.

The monetarist thesis is that: (1) the actions of the Fed dominate the movement of the monetary base; (2) movements of the monetary base dominate movements of the money supply over the course of the business cycle; and (3) accelerations or decelerations of the money supply are followed by accelerations or decelerations in economic activity. (The money supply is usually defined as currency in circulation plus demand deposits. Friedman would add time deposits in commercial banks to this definition.) Severe inflations and depressions have been caused primarily by the failure to provide a stable monetary framework, according to Professor Friedman.

Arguing that open-market operations alone would be a sufficient tool for monetary policy, Friedman has proposed that the Fed abandon its practice of changing the discount rate and reserve requirements. It would simply increase the stock of money at a fixed rate (between three and five percent a year), without regard to the business cycle. This would help to prevent large and rapid price fluctuations and ensure long-run stability in the dollar's purchasing power. If the economy begins to slump, the automatic increase in the money supply will help to keep it moving; if inflation sets in, the fact that the increase in the money supply is to be kept to a modest rate will help to restrain the rising prices. It would no longer be necessary to tinker with taxes and government spending or attempt to "fine tune" the economy, and government interference with the free market would be held to a minimum.

A leading opponent of Friedman is Paul Samuelson, who holds that both fiscal and monetary policy are vital.

Margin Requirements

When people buy stock through their broker, they may pay a part of the purchase price and borrow the rest, using the stock as collateral. The percentage of the total price that must be paid at the time of purchase is called the *margin*. The Board of Governors of the Federal Reserve has the power to determine what the margin will be. When the margin requirement is set at 50 percent, the buyer must pay for half the amount of his stock purchase and may borrow the remainder. If the Board decides that there is danger of inflation due to excessive speculation on the exchanges, it may raise the margin requirement. Such a case occurred in 1958, when margin requirements were raised to 90 percent. In 1962 the margin was dropped to 50 percent. Why might these changes have been made?

Moral Persuasion

The officers of the Federal Reserve banks have frequently tried to persuade bankers to follow policy recommendations by such means as face-to-face talks, letters, and releases to the press. The purpose of this *moral persuasion* is to induce member banks to be selective in increasing or decreasing credit when it appears that granting credit for certain types of loans might be harmful, although credit for other loans might not be. This technique for regulating credit has had only moderate success, and almost no success when banking has been very competitive.

Temporary Powers

During periods when inflationary pressures seemed particularly strong, as during World War II and the Korean conflict, Congress has given the Federal Reserve additional powers over credit in selective fields. Because durable goods, such as automobiles and appliances, were in extremely short supply during the war years, the Board of Governors was able to regulate the down payment and limit the period for payment on such purchases. By increasing down payments and reducing the time for payment, demand for these goods was reduced and the inflationary pressures lessened. As supply of these goods caught up with demand, the regulations were allowed to lapse. A similar regulation in the early 1950's accomplished the same purpose for real estate. In 1971 Congress granted temporary powers to the President rather than to the Federal Reserve in order to fight inflation.

The Federal Reserve and the Use of Monetary Policy

The most important purpose of the Federal Reserve System is to control the supply of money that the nation needs in order to maintain an expanding economy with stable prices. Through the functions of the Federal Reserve, *monetary policies* can be adjusted to allow for the expansion or contraction of demand deposits according to the needs of the economy. Thus, an inflation may be met by (1) increasing the discount rate, (2) the Federal Reserve's selling securities in the open market, and (3) raising the reserve requirements on demand deposits. When particular parts of the economy are severely affected, selective controls may be used. A deflation in the economy would call for the opposite type of monetary policy. The major controls over the supply of money involve regulation of the excess reserves of its member banks by the Federal Reserve.

The monetary policies of the Federal Reserve System are a help in controlling business cycles and in promoting the objective of a full-employment economy without inflation. In Chapter 16 we will consider the use of both monetary policy and fiscal policy as instruments for maintaining a healthy economy.

Part D
The Problem: How Effective Is Monetary Policy in Achieving Our Economic Goals?

In 1961 the Commission on Money and Credit, an independent research and policy group supported by several private foundations, issued a report on our nation's financial institutions. As you might expect, there was no agreement on how well our government's monetary policy works. Nevertheless a consensus was reached on some issues. The report also produced some suggestions for improving our system and some new thinking about what monetary policy can and cannot do.

In presenting some of the arguments for and against the effectiveness of monetary policies we are not looking for "exact answers," since we do not have absolute standards for evaluating these policies. We realize that what may be the best answer in one case may not be in another. What we do hope to achieve by looking at both points of view is a better understanding of our entire monetary policy and its strengths and weaknesses.

Several qualifications must be made before presenting the two positions. We have ignored the role of monetary policy on the international scene, particularly in regard to the problem of balance of payments. There is frequently a conflict between what is good monetary policy domestically and what is good monetary policy internationally. We are also leaving the effect of *fiscal policy* (the use of government's taxing, spending, and borrowing powers to influence business activity and the economy as a whole) for consideration in Chapter 16. Since monetary and fiscal policy are very closely related, it is difficult to distinguish the effects of each one separately. If you will keep in mind that our objective here is limited to evaluating monetary policy, these limitations should not interfere with our partial analysis. You will find the arguments related to ideas discussed earlier in this unit.

Monetary Policy Is Effective

Many economists agree that economic policy should be aimed at a full-employment economy without inflation and with a rate of growth that will provide an increasing standard of living for all. Since money plays an active role in influencing price levels and business activity, monetary policy contributes substantially to the achievement of these goals through control over the supply of money.

Monetary policy is a highly effective way of stabilizing prices. By carefully watching and evaluating business conditions and price trends, the Federal Reserve can restrain inflationary and deflationary tendencies before they pose too serious a problem. Although the supply of money will change through the action of individuals—spending, saving, and borrowing—these actions in turn are greatly influenced by limits placed on the availability of money and the interest rates.

When the economy seems to be expanding too fast and too many dollars are pursuing too few goods, the Federal Reserve can limit the growth of M by raising the reserve requirements. The result of such action is that demand for loanable funds will be greater than supply, thereby increasing interest rates and forcing some prospective borrowers to postpone their plans for investing or buying. As the amount of demand deposits created through loans is reduced, inflationary pressures can be relieved.

If the economy appears to be entering a recession, more money can be made available by the Federal Reserve's purchase of securities in the open market or reduction of reserve requirements. This increase in the supply of money will result in lower interest rates, thus encouraging the marginal borrower to carry out plans for investment or purchase. By encouraging the creation of additional demand deposits through the availability of money for loans and through the reduction of interest rates, monetary policy can help to reverse the deflationary tendency that may have developed.

If we remember the equation of exchange ($MV = PT$) and assume little change in velocity (V), we can see how changing the supply of money can affect both the price level and business transactions. Only if T increases at the same rate as M will P remain unchanged.

Such policies as making money available to businessmen and reducing interest rates will not in themselves make businessmen borrow. Nevertheless an "easy money" policy creates an environment that encourages expansion. The lowering of the discount rate during the recessions of 1954, 1958, and 1960 was intended to counteract the slowing down of business activity. In contrast with this action, a policy of "tight money" was used during the upswings from 1955 to 1957 and in 1959 to moderate the tendency of business to expand too rapidly. Using monetary policy to dampen business booms and to offset declines by stimulating business expansion helps us to achieve the economic objectives of full employment without inflation and adequate economic growth.

Finally, monetary policy has an advantage over fiscal policy in that it is much more flexible. When the Board of Governors of the Federal Reserve discovers a trend in the economy, it can act quickly to meet the changing conditions. It does not have to wait for long Congressional debates, as happens in applying fiscal policy. Monetary policy can be altered quickly according to changing requirements and can be a significant factor in creating economic stability.

Monetary Policy Is Not Effective

Some economists believe that the monetary policies in current use by our government will not achieve the goals of our economy because they place too many restrictions on business. In our economy total demand is made up of consumers, government, and business. It is this aggregate demand that will determine the level of income of our nation. Of these three groups it is business at which monetary policy is primarily directed. Consumer spending and savings, except for real estate, are determined mainly by income and are little affected by interest rates. This is particularly true of installment buying. Government spending is likewise only rarely curtailed because of changing interest rates; moreover, such curtailments have occurred only in the case of state and local governments. Therefore, we can conclude that monetary policy is effective only in controlling business investment.

The "easy money" policy used to offset a recession is weak because businessmen do not borrow merely because money is available and interest rates are low. They borrow when they believe that they can earn money as a result of business expansion. During a recession, when even existing facilities of a business are not being fully used, it is unrealistic to think that the businessman will add new facilities. The period of the Great Depression pointed out this weakness in monetary policy.

A "tight money" policy can be more effective in combating an inflation than an "easy money" policy can be in dealing with a recession because it can actually "dry up" excess reserves. However, a tight-money policy also has serious weaknesses: (1) the use of internal financing by large firms in noncompetitive enterprises, (2) the conflict of interest between the Federal Reserve and the Treasury, and (3) the inability to influence a cost-push inflation.

1. Since World War II, big businesses that are not in price-competitive industries have built up large surpluses of cash by not distributing the bulk of their profits in dividends. They have been able to finance much of their modernization and expansion programs out of these funds without having to turn to the banks. In this way interest rates or the availability of excess reserves has almost no influence on curtailing their plans. Even when they do have to borrow, monopolistic firms can pass the higher interest charges on to their customers. Small businesses in competitive industries are hard hit by tight money, and such a policy discriminates against them.
2. Although the Federal Reserve is interested primarily in controlling the supply of money and will therefore effect an increase in interest rates to deal with an inflation, the United States Treasury, which uses the Federal Reserve as its fiscal agent, is interested in borrowing money at a low rate of interest. Although this conflict of interest is not always serious, it was during World War II and in the years immediately following. It could become a serious problem again at some future time.
3. Monetary policy is designed to curb a demand-pull inflation by restraining spending. Because a cost-push inflation arises from the supply side, reducing the excess reserves can actually aggravate the condition. This was illustrated in 1958, which was a year of recession as well as one in which the Consumer Price Index climbed 2.7 points. "Tight money" discouraged investment and economic expansion at a time when unemployment was growing. Some economists would argue that the recession of 1970 was similar to that in 1958 and for almost the same reasons. Monetary policy is not able to cope with such circumstances or to bring about the changes needed.

Considering an Answer

The debate on the effectiveness of monetary policy still goes on among both students and experts in economics. It is unlikely that it will ever be resolved, but in the process of searching for answers we learn more about the kinds of policies which should be used to realize our economic goals.

At this point you, the student, might well ask, "If the experts disagree, how can I expect to provide an answer?" Actually, since experts disagree over most important controversies, the final decision must be made by others—the citizens—through their support of programs and policies. Such indications of broad popular support will generally influence government action and policy.

Consider, for example, the importance of a demand-pull inflation and the problem it continues to pose for the economy. Does making money more easily available and at lower interest rates encourage investment? Does monetary policy play favorites and, if so, is this bad for the economy as a whole? These are a few of the questions that you should consider in arriving at an answer.

REVIEW: THE HIGHLIGHTS OF THE CHAPTER

1. There are many kinds of financial institutions. All are concerned with collecting money from sources that do not need it immediately and channeling it to those that do.
2. Savings institutions, personal trust companies, insurance companies, consumer credit agencies, investment banks, and commercial banks all serve a particular purpose in channeling funds. The government's influence over the process of lending has become increasingly important.
3. Banks serve as depositories for valuables and as agencies for lending money. Commercial banks create money through loans.
4. The creation of demand deposits by commercial banks is the most important source of money in our economy. Some of their money must be kept in reserve to meet the reserve requirements of the Federal Reserve for its members. Although banks invest some of their money in short-term securities—mainly United States Treasury bills—at low interest rates, they usually lend most of their money to businesses and individuals. Loans to individuals provide banks with the highest interest rates.
5. The Federal Deposit Insurance Corporation was created in 1933 to insure depositors against loss of their money in case of bank failures.
6. Although a single bank is limited in its ability to create demand deposits, the banking system as a whole can lend several times its reserves, the amount depending on the reserve requirements. A 20 percent reserve requirement (1:5) will allow demand deposits to expand to five times the size of bank reserves.
7. The Federal Reserve System acts as the central bank for the United States. It is decentralized into 12 districts, each with a Federal Reserve bank (located in a major city) and its own board of directors. The entire system is coordinated by the seven-man Board of Governors.
8. The chief function of the Federal Reserve is to regulate the supply of money according to the needs of the economy.
9. The major tools for controlling the volume of money are:
   (a) Discount rate—the rate of interest member banks must pay when they borrow from the Federal Reserve bank.
   (b) Open-market operations—the purchase and sale of securities, primarily short-term government notes, by the Federal Reserve bank.
   (c) Reserve requirements—the amount of money member banks must keep in reserve in relation to their demand deposits.
10. The Federal Reserve has also been given selective controls over specific markets, such as the purchase of stocks on margin.
11. Monetary policy is the adjustment of the money supply to help in achieving our economic goals of full employment, stable prices, and economic growth.
12. Inflationary tendencies may be offset by reducing the supply of money through such measures as raising the discount rate, selling securities in the open market, and/or raising the reserve ratio. Recession may be offset by actions opposite to these.
13. There is considerable controversy over the effectiveness of monetary policy in helping to achieve our economic goals.

IN CONCLUSION: SOME AIDS TO UNDERSTANDING

Terms for Review

savings bank
credit union
collateral
secondary reserves
legal reserve
discount rate
margin requirement
personal trusts
commercial bank
time deposit
reserve ratio
balance sheet
derivative deposits
member bank
reserve requirement
clearing house
monetary policy
monetarism
fiscal policy
tight-money policy
easy-money policy

Names to know

Federal Reserve System
Board of Governors
Advisory Council
FDIC
Open Market Committee
Milton Friedman

Questions for Review

1. What is meant by the statement "The banking system performs the role of intermediary in regulating the flow of money"?
2. A major share of the banking in our country is carried on by commercial banks and savings banks.
   (a) What differences exist between these two kinds of banks?
   (b) How does each strengthen the economy of a community?
3. Many economists feel that a system of controls over commercial banks is necessary, even if every single bank is wisely, efficiently, and honestly managed. Why is this so?
4. Why could a district Federal Reserve bank be called the "bankers' bank"?
5. Explain why banks are required to hold reserves.
6. How does the commercial banking *system* expand the nation's money supply? What is the role of the *individual* bank?
7. The Federal Reserve has a strong influence on our money supply.
   (a) Why are open-market operations called the most important tool of the Federal Reserve System?
   (b) Why are reserve requirements called the most powerful tool of the Federal Reserve System?
   (c) What are the weaknesses of the discount rate as a means of controlling our money supply?
8. Explain why the establishment of the FDIC has created confidence in our banking system among depositors.
9. In what ways does the Federal Reserve System act as the fiscal agent of the United States?

Additional Questions and Problems

1. Find in a local newspaper, or obtain from the bank at which you do business, a

copy of its balance sheet. Evaluate its financial condition, using specific references to liquidity, reserves, loans, types of securities, and reserve ratio. In what ways does this bank benefit the community?

2. Some feel that the Federal Reserve has too much control of the nation's money and credit, and that it is too independent of the Administration. Give arguments on both sides of this issue.
3. Why is the Federal Reserve Bank of New York more important than any other Federal Reserve bank? Give at least three reasons.
4. Trace the development of banking in the United States. Relate this development to general economic trends, explaining how one affected the other.
5. Using graphs, charts, or tables, show how a change in the reserve requirement from 10 to 20 percent would affect an individual commercial bank, and how it would affect the commercial banking system. Use imaginary deposit figures. Explain the possible effects on the economy as a whole.
6. How were checks cleared in the United States before the Federal Reserve System was established? How are checks cleared now? In what ways has the change affected our economy?

SELECTED READINGS

American Bankers Association, Banking Education Committee. *The Story of American Banking.* New York: American Bankers Association, 1963.

Bernstein, Peter L. *A Primer on Money, Banking and Gold.* New York: Random House, 1965.

Carson, Deane, ed. *Money and Finance—Readings in Theory, Policy & Institutions.* New York: John Wiley & Sons, 1966.

Cochran, John A. *Money, Banking and the Economy.* New York: The Macmillan Company, 1967.

Dean, Edwin, ed. *The Controversy over the Quantity Theory of Money.* Boston: D. C. Heath and Co., 1965.

Duesenberry, James S. *Money and Credit: Impact and Control.* 2nd ed. Englewood Cliffs, N.J.: Prentice-Hall, 1967.

Dunkman, William E. *Money, Credit, and Banking.* New York: Random House, 1969.

Federal Reserve System, Board of Governors. *The Federal Reserve System: Purposes and Functions.* Washington, D.C.: Board of Governors of the Federal Reserve System, 1963.

Fisher, Douglas. *Money and Banking.* Homewood, Illinois: Richard D. Irwin, 1971.

Hamovitch, William. *Monetary Policy: The Argument From Keynes' Treatise to Friedman.* Boston: D. C. Heath and Co., 1966.

Massey, J. Earl. *America's Money: The Story of Our Coins and Currency.* New York: Crowell, 1968.

Mayer, Thomas. *Elements of Monetary Policy.* New York: Random House, 1968.

Nadler, Paul. *Commercial Banking in the Economy.* New York: Random House, 1968.

Robertson, D. H. *Money.* Chicago: University of Chicago Press, 1959.

Formulating Modern Economic Policy 16

THE AUTHORS' NOTE TO THE STUDENT

In Units I and II we became acquainted with the classical approach to economics. We learned what many of the tools of this system are, how they work in the marketplace, and how they answer the basic questions of economics. In Unit III we have been introduced to a new model, the Keynesian. We have learned to use tools for both fiscal and monetary analysis so that we can not only understand our economy better, but also try to formulate policy to serve our economic goals. In the present chapter we will see how fiscal and monetary tools can be used together in an effort to achieve full employment, keep a sufficient rate of economic growth, maintain price stability, and minimize cyclical fluctuations. One of the tasks of the modern economist is to assist in the formulation of policies that will help to achieve these goals.

In previous chapters we have stressed the differences between the old and the new models. Few economists today are exclusively classical or exclusively Keynesian in their approach. They recognize the importance of a free-enterprise system and the key role of the market in allocating our resources. However, they believe that the automatic adjustment mechanism that supply and demand is supposed to make will not always promote our economic objectives. In these instances monetary and fiscal tools may be utilized to give the economy the assistance necessary. Modern economic policy is a synthesis of the old and the new models.

A STUDENT'S NOTE TO THE STUDENT

When I started to read this chapter, it was like reading a review of everything we covered up to this point. Discretionary and automatic stabilizers are introduced, and Part D has some new and interesting ideas. However, the real value for me was the chance to "put it all together." All the separate pieces and even the big "chunks" suddenly fell into place. I think I finally see what our instructor means by the phrase "economic perspective." I also think I know what he means by "trade-off." If you can't have it all, you're probably going to have to sacrifice a little bit of one thing to get a little more of something else.

I'm still not satisfied that these economists know enough. They seem to be really stumbling in this recession–inflation combination. Every one of them seems to have a different answer on what to do. I'm glad it's their problem to solve, although I can't say I enjoy the effect.

Part A
Our Nation's Economic Goals

Full Employment

Before the crisis of the 1930's, economists paid little attention to the problem of unemployment. Until that time economic theory had assumed that unemployment was self-correcting and that any tampering with the automatic mechanism of the free market would do more harm than good. J. B. Say (see p. 14), a French economist who was an advocate of the laissez-faire school, formulated an economic theory stating that equilibrium would be achieved at the full-employment level because supply would create its own demand. His reasoning was seldom questioned. Any rise of unemployment was looked upon as only a temporary condition. Past experience tended to support this theory, so there was little reason to question it. The turning point in the attitude toward unemployment came during the Great Depression of the 1930's, when unemployment rose from about 3 percent in 1929 to more than 24 percent in 1933.

The 1930's: Unemployment and the Keynesian Theory

Although progress was made in reducing unemployment by means of the New Deal measures of President Franklin D. Roosevelt, the problem of mass unemployment was a major concern until the start of a wartime economy following our entry into World War II. As economists began to lose confidence in the self-correcting mechanism of the market, they began to seek new solutions to the problem of unemployment. In 1936 John Maynard Keynes published his theory on employment. His ideas, which became the basis for the new model that we examined in Chapter 13, attracted attention immediately. Encouraged by the new ideas, economists began a reevaluation of our entire economic system that eventually led to major modifications and to the development of new policies.

Excerpt of an open letter from John Maynard Keynes to President Franklin D. Roosevelt, published in the New York *Times* on December 31, 1933:

As the prime mover in the first stage of the technique of recovery, I lay overwhelming emphasis on the increase of national purchasing power resulting from governmental expenditure which is financed by loans and is not merely a transfer through taxation of existing income. Nothing else counts in comparison to this. . . .

As early as 1933 the famous English economist recommended to President Roosevelt increasing government spending to stimulate the economy.

The Employment Act of 1946

When World War II ended, the hopes of the American people for the future were high. Once again the economy was operating at a full-employment level. With the memory of the economic hardships of the thirties still deeply implanted in their minds, the majority of the people were not willing to trust a policy of laissez-faire exclusively to determine the performance of the economy. Sharing this point of view, Congress passed the Employment Act of 1946, which stated in part:

The Congress declares that it is the continuing policy and responsibility of the Federal Government to use all practicable means consistent with its needs and obligations and other essential considerations of national policy, with the assistance and cooperation of industry, agriculture, labor, and State and local governments, to coordinate and utilize all its plans, functions, and resources for the purpose of creating and maintaining, in a manner calculated to foster and promote free competitive enterprise and the general welfare, conditions under which there will be afforded useful employment opportunities, including self-employment, for those able, willing, and seeking work, and to promote the maximum employment, production, and purchasing power.

Although the Act does not go so far as to commit the federal government to a full-employment economy, it does charge the government with the responsibility of taking steps to create an environment that will promote maximum employment. In addition, it provides for the Council of Economic Advisers, which is directly responsible to the President. The Council prepares an annual report on the health of the nation's economy and suggests methods to improve it. Presidents Kennedy and Johnson relied heavily on their chairman of the Council, Dr. Walter Heller, and adopted the first planned tax cut designed to create a deficit budget in order to achieve full employment. More recently President Nixon, previously identified as a moderate, announced his "full-employment budget" and declared himself a Keynesian. The United States has come a long way from its laissez-faire tradition.

Showing Full Employment with Our Models

If our economy operates at less than full employment, it is failing to make use of all our resources. We will be without the production that the unemployed are capable of producing. If as many as one eighth of our people live at the poverty level when we have resources that are not being used, such a situation represents a weakness in economic policy.

In Chapter 13 we saw full employment represented in models using a vertical bar graph and the 45° line. Since we shall be using these models in this chapter, let us review them briefly, using the two models in Figure 16–1 as our basic examples.

Economic Growth

We have seen in Tables 12–3 and 12–4 how the value of our nation's goods and services has grown and how high it is compared with that of other nations in both total and per capita wealth. A measure of this value increase can be seen in our growth rate—the percentage increase in our GNP in constant dollars from one year to the next. It had been about 3 percent per year from 1870 to World War II. Since World War II it has increased to about 5 percent; however, the growth has been uneven. Although no nation of the world comes close to challenging our primacy in overall wealth and though we increase the absolute value of our production more than other nations, our recent *economic growth rate* has not been as rapid as that of several other countries, notably West Germany, Japan, and—in most years of the last two decades—the U.S.S.R. Whether the Soviet Union will ever overtake the United States in total wealth is questionable, but its economic rise has tremendous international consequences.

The Importance of Economic Growth

Figure 16–1 repeats, using a higher GNP, the simplified analysis of national income of Figure 13–2, with a full-employment economy in a stationary condition. Yet, in reality, the situation is more complex.

Since our population is growing every year, output of goods and services must be increased just to keep per capita income at the same level. If we wish to improve our standard of living, we must increase production faster than population. India is an example of a nation whose output is increasing, but no more rapidly than population. This situation has resulted in a lack of improvement in the standard of living of India's people.

With our labor force growing larger every year, economic growth can be accomplished by putting the additional human resources to work. If we combine our first two objectives, full employment and economic growth, it means that our full-employment GNP must grow each year. Although a $1 trillion GNP might put a labor force of 85 million to work, a larger GNP will be required to have full employment with 88 million. When we add to this the increased output per worker resulting from new inventions, from increased skill of workers, and from more capital invested per worker, our full-employment GNP must rise even faster. Figure 16–2 shows our models in an expanding economy based on full employment and economic growth.

Our knowledge of economic growth and the forces that determine it is far from complete. We know that it depends on a variety of factors, including the capital goods we put into the hands of workers, the skill and education of workers, technological advances, and the quality and quantity of our natural and human resources. We will discuss this subject further in Chapter 18.

Price Stability

We have already noted in Chapter 14 the many problems that an unstable price level can pose to the nation as a whole as well as to segments within the economy. Although the Employment Act of 1946 does not mention price stability as a goal,

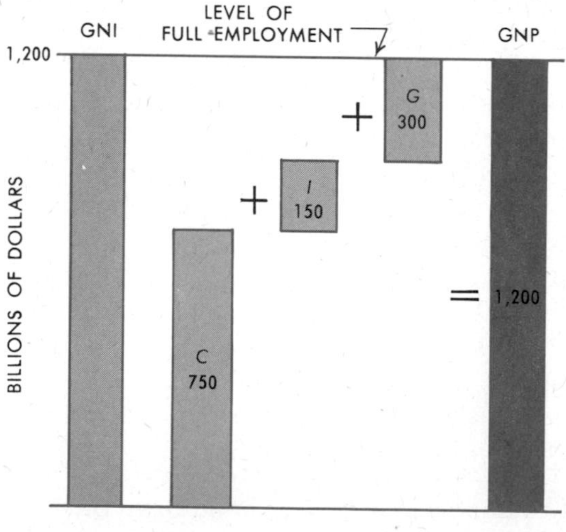

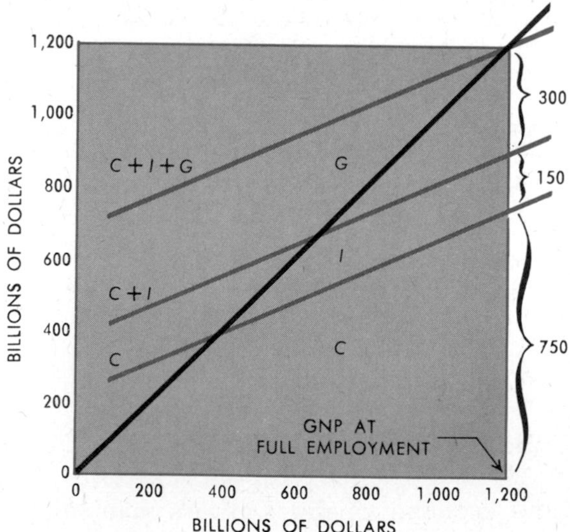

FIGURE 16–1 Models of Full Employment

These models show full employment at $1,200 billion. Personal consumption expenditures (C) + business investment (I) + government expenditures (G) = aggregate income (gross national product).

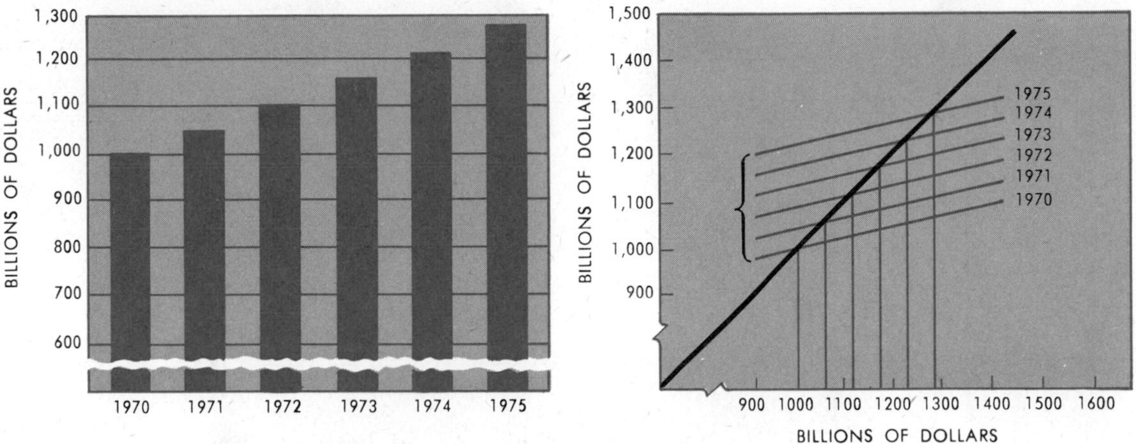

FIGURE 16–2 Models of Full Employment in a Growing Economy

Full-employment models must take into consideration the growing potential of a dynamic economy. The increases in our labor force, in our capital, and in our knowledge provide the potential for economic growth for the nation. The increase in our capacity to produce means an increasing GNP, which in turn helps to achieve a full-employment level. Projections here are made using constant dollars (1970) and assuming a 5 percent growth rate.

the attention paid to prices by the President's Council of Economic Advisers and by the Joint Economic Committee (which advises Congress on economic matters), together with the concern shown for it by every President since World War II, establishes it as an important economic goal.

In Figure 16–3 the model is used to show how the economy can maintain stable prices should it attain full employment with adequate economic growth. Under these circumstances, controlling the money supply so that it stimulates production to the full-employment level without causing an inflation becomes the goal of monetary policy.

Economic Stability

If we can achieve full employment with adequate growth and at the same time maintain price stability, there will be no extreme fluctuations in the performance of the economy. The extreme peaks and troughs shown in our business cycles; particularly the contrasts between the 1930's and 1940's, should be eliminated and replaced by slight undulations caused by the somewhat uneven investment opportunities, technological advances, and slight variations in the number of people joining and leaving the working force. Figure 16–4 shows how the business cycle as illustrated in Chapter 12 would be modified if we were able to achieve economic stability.

Other Goals

In addition to the broad overall objectives that we have noted involving macroeconomics, we identified in relation to microeconomics in Unit II a number of goals that many people consider equally important. One of the most important of these goals is the most efficient use of limited resources by business to produce the goods society wants (low prices and high-quality products for the consumer). A highly competitive market protects the

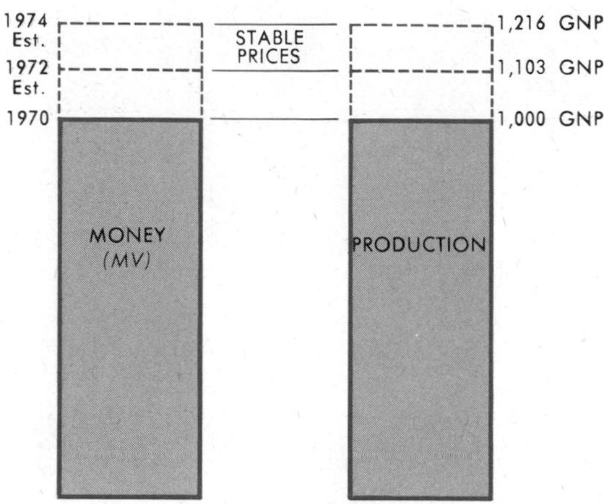

FIGURE 16–3 Growth, Money Supply, and Price Stability

GNP is at full employment without inflation for 1970 ($1 trillion). With a growth rate of 5 percent our supply of money will have to increase in order to avoid deflation. If it increases faster than production, we are likely to have inflation.

consumer and rewards the efficient producer, assuring a dynamic economy.

Another important goal is the fair distribution of income. Just as it is important to have the national economy—the "pie"—grow bigger, it is also important that whatever the size of the "pie," it be divided in a way that the society approves.

Many people would include as an objective a highly decentralized market. Others might emphasize the protection of weaker economic groups, such as small business and the farmer. Maximizing the

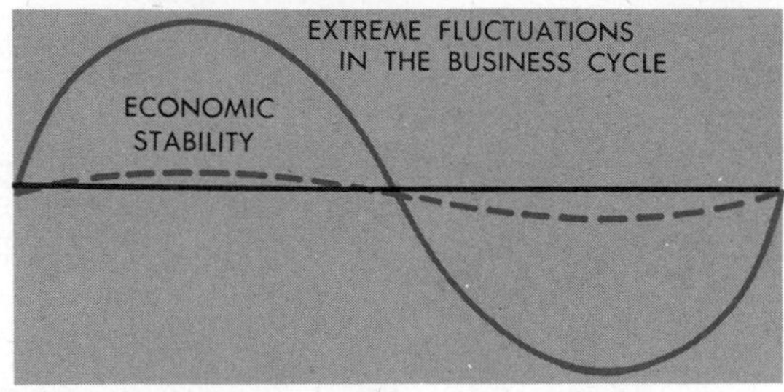

FIGURE 16–4 Dampening the Business Cycle

By achieving full employment, adequate economic growth, and stable prices we avoid extreme fluctuations in the business cycle.

freedom of both consumer and producer would be placed high on many lists. Providing equal economic opportunities for everyone has become an important goal for many people, particularly as the civil rights movement has gained strength. In Chapter 17 we will discuss free trade among nations, which many economists, including Adam Smith, have urged.

The goals of economics are decided not by the economist but by the society as a whole. Inasmuch as economic goals involve value judgments and different goals may have conflicting values, it is the responsibility of the citizens and the government in a democratic nation to determine what goals to pursue and what priority these objectives should have. When citizens, through their elected representatives, decide what goals to pursue, the economist can suggest the tools to use in order to achieve these objectives.

Part B
The New Model's Approach to Economic Policy

Having examined the broad objectives of our economy and having observed some of the tools that are used to carry out fiscal and monetary policy, we are now ready to put these tools to work to achieve our economic objectives. Specifically, we want to know how we can utilize the tools developed by modern economics in order to formulate a fiscal and monetary policy that will provide full employment, satisfactory economic growth, and price stability without major fluctuation in the business cycle. At times in this survey reference to the Keynesian model insert may be helpful.

Discretionary and Automatic Stabilizers

The tools that we have identified with monetary and fiscal policy are used to stabilize the economy; that is, they are designed to reverse the direction of the business cycle when the economy appears to be expanding or contracting too rapidly. Thus, modern macroeconomic policy is used to reduce the severity of the fluctuations in the business cycle by *countercyclical* (reversing the direction of the cycle) action. The tools by which this is accomplished are known as *stabilizers.*

Discretionary Stabilizers

Any economic tool utilized for countercyclical action on the decision of designated officials is known as a *discretionary stabilizer.* When several tools are used to compensate for the economic fluctuations and are brought into action by some governmental authority or authorities, the program proposed is called *discretionary policy.* At present all our monetary tools, such as the discount rate and open-market operations, are discretionary because action must be initiated by the Board of Governors or the Open Market Committee. A tax cut is an example of fiscal policy that is discretionary.

Automatic Stabilizers

Discretionary policy, if it is to work efficiently, is dependent on accurate forecasting. Predicting a drop in business activity and taking appropriate countercyclical action can be harmful if the forecast turns out to be wrong. Consider what would happen in a home without modern heating controls if, after a warm spell was predicted and all the fires were banked, a severe cold spell suddenly arrived instead. In economics, to guard against the difficulties of forecasting, automatic stabilizers are used. *Automatic stabilizers* are tools which work against the cycle of their own accord without any action being required by a public official, just as the thermostat of the modern heating unit in our home will automatically maintain the temperature inside at the required level, regardless of changes in the temperature outside. One example of an automatic stabilizer is the federal income tax. When income rises, not only does the payment in dollars to the government go up but the proportion of payment to income rises also. When income declines, tax payments are reduced in proportion even faster. This result occurs because the progressive feature of the income tax arranges personal incomes according to level, or bracket, each of which has its own tax rate. An upswing in business would cause people to pay higher taxes and curb some of their purchasing power. A downswing would result in smaller tax payments, leaving people with proportionately more money to spend. In a similar manner unemployment insurance acts as an automatic stabilizer.

Fiscal Policies and Their Effects

Modern fiscal policy calls for the use of public spending and public taxation to help achieve the economic goals of full employment, economic growth, price stability, and little cyclical fluctuation. Countercyclical action calls for inflations to be dealt with by the preparation of budgets that will produce a government surplus, whereas recession would be treated by means of budgetary deficits. Government, as the largest single revenue receiver and spender in the nation, is thus in a strategic position to raise or lower aggregate demand in the economy. It can do this either by altering tax rates or by changing its spending program, or by a combination of both methods. Figure 16–5 uses several models to show our economy in an inflationary boom. Let us see what fiscal policy can do to reverse the cyclical trend.

Using Taxes as a Tool

When the government taxes the people, it decreases their disposable personal income and thereby also reduces personal consumption expenditures (*C*). By increasing taxes the government can reduce *C* even further. By decreasing taxes, it can increase *C*.

In Figure 16–5 we see that the aggregate demand—consumption plus investment plus government spending ($C + I + G$)—is greater than what the economy can produce, resulting in an inflation. Modern fiscal policy calls for reducing aggregate demand to eliminate the inflationary forces. By increasing taxes and making sure that there is no corresponding increase in investment or government spending, aggregate demand can be decreased. On our models this is shown by reducing *C* and keeping *I* and *G* the same, so that $C + I + G$ is equal to full employment without inflation.

Discretionary Tax Policy

When the government economists sense a strong inflationary trend, they may suggest that legislation be passed to increase taxes. Excise taxes may be raised on a large number of goods and services, or they may be specifically directed at those goods and services which are likely to be most in demand but short in supply. The personal income tax can be increased generally or selectively. If inflationary forces are very strong, as they were during World War II, the rate increases might be placed on the lowest income group, since those people tend to spend all their income. People in the upper income groups save a substantial portion of their income; raising taxes for them would probably reduce their savings more than their expenditures. A recession calls for policies opposite to those just described in order to increase *C*. We must realize that in either situation good economics may have to give way to good politics in selecting a course of action.

Taxes can also be altered to change the size of business investment. Rarely (primarily during a war period) would attempts be made to discourage investment, since an increase in *I* usually results in increasing the productive capacity of the economy as well as the demand side. Stimulating *I* can be done by allowing businesses to deduct their new investments from their gross profits (depreciation allowance) faster than previously. A reduction in the corporation income tax will also stimulate *I*.

Taxes as Stabilizers

Probably our most important automatic tax stabilizers are our progressive personal income tax and our corporation income tax. We have already seen that an increase in the national income would bring a proportionately larger increase in tax receipts without any action on the part of Congress or the President. This would have the effect of slowing down the increase in *C* and, consequently, decreasing aggregate demand. Similarly, a reduction

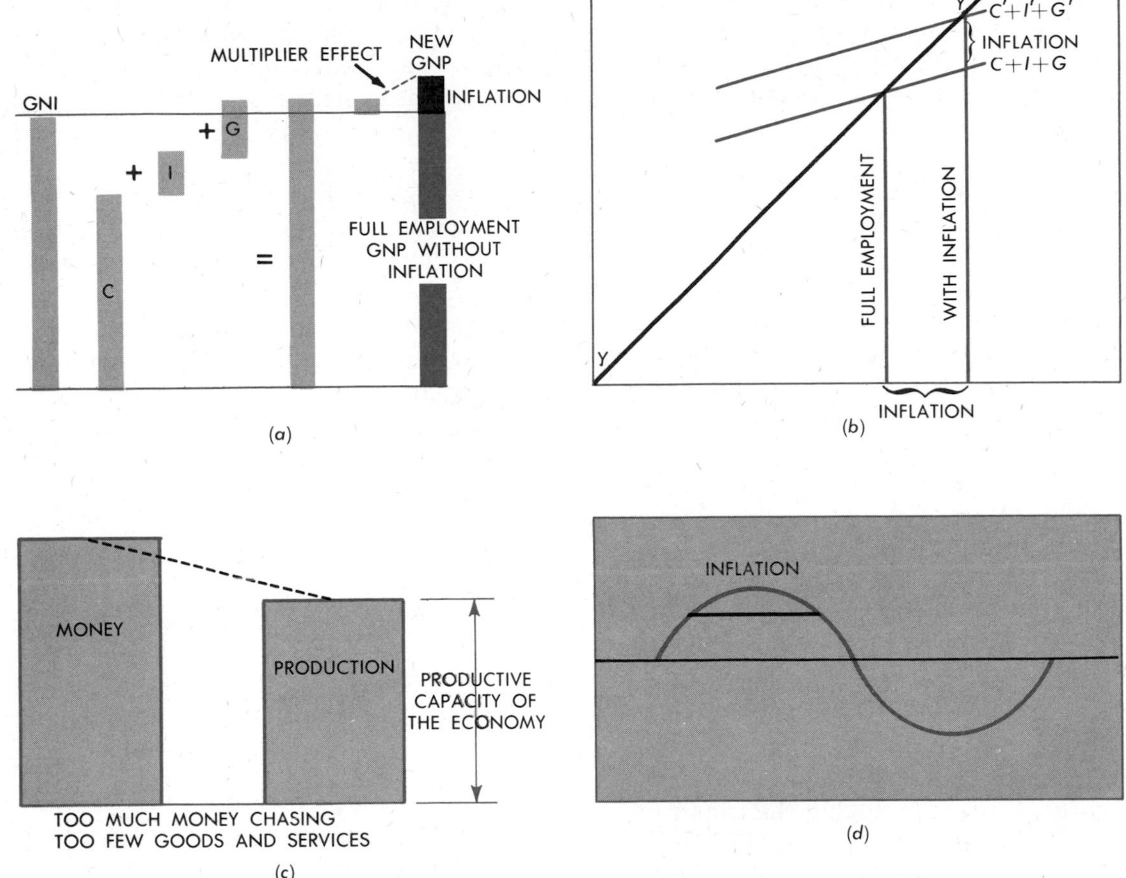

FIGURE 16–5 The Economy in Inflation

Several views of the economy in an inflation are shown here. In (*a*) and (*b*) the models for income analysis ($C + I + G = Y$) show an aggregate demand greater than the full-employment capacity of the economy. In (*c*) too much money is chasing too few goods and services. In (*d*) the business cycle is shown at an inflationary peak.

in national income would bring about a proportionate reduction in tax receipts, with a smaller reduction in disposable personal income.

Some of our other tax programs also have a stabilizing effect. For example, during periods of low unemployment the taxes that support our unemployment compensation program flow into the reserve fund much faster than money is paid out. If the business cycle should reverse itself and unemployment increase, payments would be made faster than money would flow into the fund, thus providing a countercyclical effect. The same results occur in the case of Social Security payments.

Government Spending

Unless the taxing tool is used in conjunction with government spending, fiscal policy cannot be planned effectively. Raising

C by means of a tax cut can be offset by a reduction in government spending, *G*. Likewise, reducing *C* by a tax increase can reduce aggregate demand in the private sector. However, a corresponding increase in government spending will increase the public sector and neutralize the effect. Although the illustrations cited will bring about a change in the allocation of resources between the public and private sectors, it is only through the creation of budgetary deficits and surpluses that we actually change the aggregate demand. Assuming that government revenue remains constant or nearly constant, let us see how government spending changes aggregate demand and modifies the business cycle.

Government Purchases

In Chapter 9 we learned that a very significant portion of government expenditure is used for the purchase of goods and services. Defense spending, support for our space program, and a variety of public works projects involving the construction of highways, dams, and public parks are extremely important for meeting specific needs. They also are important in accounting for a significant portion of aggregate demand.

Just as it is traditional to expect a government to prepare a budget listing the things it wishes to furnish its citizens, it is also characteristic of those who advocate the new economics to think of government expenditures as a tool to regulate the aggregate demand in order to achieve full employment without inflation. During an inflation, modern fiscal policy might try to reduce the *G*. Under such circumstances only the most important government projects would be approved, and an attempt would be made to cut all unnecessary spending out of the budget. A recession would call for increasing *G*. Those projects that were delayed under an inflationary condition would now be started. Older projects already under way might be expanded. The purpose of the additional expenditures is not merely to secure additional goods and services for the nation but also to increase the *G* element with the intention of stimulating the economy.

Government spending (*G*) is somewhat slower in affecting the aggregate demand than changes in taxes because time is required for starting projects. Once they are under way, it is difficult to stop them, even if the economy has moved out of recession and toward an inflation. They do have an advantage over a tax cut, however, because they guarantee that the funds will be spent at least once. This tends to increase the multiplier effect. They also provide for direct employment and usually help the durable goods industries, which are often hardest hit by recessions.

Transfer Payments

In addition to the automatic stabilizers financed by specific taxes for certain transfer payments, such as Social Security and unemployment insurance, the government frequently provides money out of general tax funds for direct payments to groups that are hardest hit by a recession. Money is given to states to permit them, whenever their jobless rate remains high for an extended period, to increase the length of time during which unemployment compensation is paid. By the parity system farmers receive payment from the government if they have huge crop surpluses (see p. 535). Giving grants and loans to students provides opportunities for increasing the skills of the working force as well as reducing the number of

"Annual income Twenty pounds, annual expenditure Nineteen Nineteen six, result happiness. Annual income Twenty pounds, annual expenditure Twenty pounds ought and six, result misery."
—Mr. Micawber's advice to David Copperfield

Mr. Micawber's advice may still be appropriate for the family, but many would doubt its applicability to government. What is good sense for the family may not be good for the economy as a whole because savings, when not invested, can be a drag on the economy. If private enterprise does not invest these funds, then government may develop policy that will put them to work. What policy is best for any particular time may be highly controversial.

potentially unemployed workers that join the labor force each year.

Evaluation of Fiscal Policy

There are many citizens in our country who believe that the federal budget should be balanced annually. They think that it is just as important for the nation to live within its income as it is for the family, and they believe that to do otherwise, as in deficit spending, is immoral.

The Unbalanced Budget

However, many other people think that such an attitude is at variance with modern economic theory. In fact, most contemporary economists believe that under certain conditions a balanced federal budget may work directly against the economic interests of the country. During a recession a declining national income reduces government revenues. If the budget is to be balanced, government expenditures must be sharply curtailed and taxes may have to be raised. Both actions would result in a decline in aggregate demand (*C* and *G* would fall), hastening the decline. An inflationary boom would result in increased revenue, allowing the government to increase its expenditures when resources are already being used to capacity. Higher revenues and increased spending would intensify the fluctations in the business cycle.

Countercyclical Budgets

Preparing federal budgets with a view to countering the movement of the business cycle has gained a great deal of support among economists since the end of World War II. The prolonged period of the upswing and the sharp increase in our economic growth rate following the tax cut of 1964 won over many people whose previous main concern was balancing the budget. The argument used to support passage of this tax cut was partially aimed at critics of this type of fiscal policy. Its adherents pointed out that only by increasing the tax base could we really hope to balance the budget. Reducing taxes would increase the national income sufficiently so that the drop in the tax rate would be more than offset by the bigger incomes that would be taxed. Most economists agree that the tax cut accomplished what it was designed to do. The economic upswing was prolonged, the economic growth rate was bettered, government revenues were increased, and prices were kept reasonably stable. The unemployment rate was reduced to 3.7 percent by early 1966. With increased government spending for the Vietnam conflict, the problem concerning tax policy was reversed. The question then became: "Should we increase taxes to reduce aggregate demand in order to avoid an inflation?"

Problems in Fiscal Policy

To achieve a desired effect, correct timing of fiscal policy is extremely important. Applying our tools too soon may convert a newly begun upswing into a recession. Applying our tools very late, which is more likely to happen, reduces some of the effectiveness of the policy and may cause an inflation.

It is very difficult to take the appropriate action at precisely the right time. In Chapter 12 we saw how difficult it is to predict the course of business activity. Since the various parts of our economy do not move in the same direction simultaneously, determining the best leading indicator (see p. 276) is extremely difficult.

Political considerations play a major part in slowing down the initiation of appropriate fiscal policy. If taxes are to be raised, what taxes should be selected for change? A congressman must consider which of his constituents will raise the greatest objection, as well as which tax will be best for his constituents and for the economy. If an increase in expenditures is called for, which state or congressional district will be most favored with appropriations? Historically, Congress has tended to act very slowly in response to economic changes; when it has finally acted, the action has frequently been too late or too little to be really effective. The Joint Economic Committee, in an evaluation of the use of discretionary fiscal policy in 1960, pointed out our reluctance to increase taxes to curb inflation and our unwillingness to increase government expenditures during a recession. Recently, a greater willingness to utilize these policies has become apparent. President Nixon's 1972 budget had a deficit planned in order to achieve a full-employment economy. Some economists argued whether such a budget might trigger another sharp inflationary spiral, but most of them realized the need for increasing aggregate demand to reduce unemployment.

Fiscal activities of state and local governments tend to reinforce the trend of the business cycle. When the cycle moves upward, their incomes increase and so do their expenditures. Falling incomes reduce their revenues and they respond by cutting their budgets. Raising taxes during recessions and lowering them during inflation is quite common and only serves to aggravate the unfavorable condition. Constitutional and statutory requirements sometimes require governments to act in this way, although a more common reason for this action may be the widespread belief that an annually balanced budget is desirable.

Appropriations for defense constitute, directly and indirectly, about half of our federal budget. Unfortunately for the economy our defense requirements do not run countercyclical to our business activity. With our national security having first priority on considerations of spending, efforts to avoid economic fluctuations may be hampered.

Inflationary forces of the cost-push type result from the efforts of pressure groups trying, rightly or wrongly, to improve their relative economic position. Such forces are largely immune from the stibilizers we have mentioned. Pressures from the President, such as "jawboning," or from public opinion have provided some restraint in the past, but we have no assurance that this informal method will be successful in the future. Having the Council of Economic Advisers announce what the increased productivity for the previous year has been and using this change as a guide for wage negotiations may lessen the effect of the cost-push type of inflation—if their advice is followed, that is.

Monetary Policies and Their Effects

Modern economic policy calls for the use of monetary policy as well as fiscal policy to achieve our economic goals. Through control of the supply of money and of interest rates, the aggregate demand can be influenced to move upward or downward to create greater economic stability. In Figure 16–5, (*a*) and (*b*), the $C + I + G$ must be reduced, and in (*c*) the supply of money contracted. Monetary policy works primarily in investment (I), and our discussion will be concerned mainly with policy that influences the size of I.

In chapter 15 we saw that the Federal Reserve could increase or decrease the supply of money (M) by its open-market operations and by changing discount rates and reserve requirements. In Chapter 8 we saw that interest rates are determined by the supply and demand for loanable funds. By the combined use of these tools, monetary policy can be used to influence the size of I.

Reducing Investment

If the economy appears to be entering on an inflationary spiral, the Board of Governors of the Federal Reserve will decide to take appropriate action. They will call together the Open Market Committee and give instructions to the Federal Reserve Bank in New York to sell government securities in order to reduce the excess reserves of the member banks. This action will limit the money that member banks have for the granting of loans. The Board may also decide to raise the discount rate to discourage member banks from borrowing from the Federal Reserve Banks. They probably will delay changing the reserve requirements, hoping that the course of action already outlined will be enough to tighten credit and stop the increase in prices. Their action shows that monetary policy is discretionary rather than automatic, since they had to initiate action.

Chairman Burns

SOURCE: Julio Fernández, *Time*, May 7, 1970.

As the supply of M is reduced, the supply curve shifts to the left, increasing the interest rate. The increasing of the discount rate will also raise interest rates. Since businessmen will borrow only when they think they can earn more money on what they have borrowed than what they must pay in interest, those with a low marginal productivity for loanable funds (who expect to make little on what they borrow) will postpone borrowing. Figure 16–6 shows how higher interest will reduce I.

To combat a recession, an opposite course of action would be employed. The discount rate might be lowered, the Federal Reserve Bank might buy securities, and the reserve requirements might be lowered. The increased supply of M would lower interest rates, and investments would as a result increase from (*a*) to (*b*) in the model shown in Figure 16–6.

The example that we have used here pictures investment as being generally responsive to interest rates. Most of the "new" economists do not accept this principle for low interest rates when the economy is functioning in low gear. Their objections to this theory were presented in Chapter 13 (see p. 301).

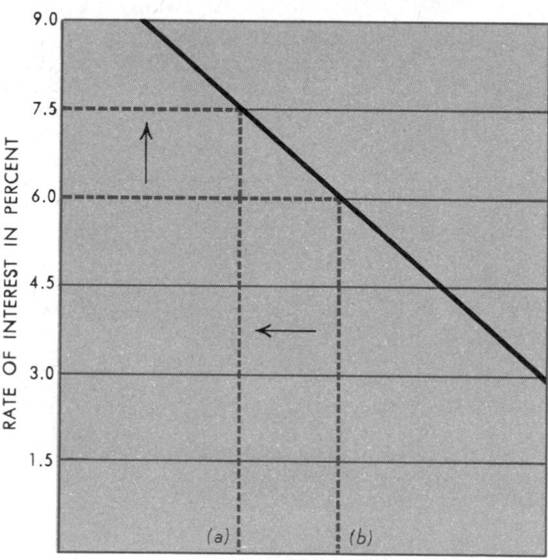

FIGURE 16–6 Controlling Business Fluctuations Through Changing Interest Rates

Increasing the interest rate (↑) reduces investment (←) from (*b*) to (*a*), lowering aggregate demand and reducing inflationary tendencies. Lowering interest rates can be used to increase investment and fight recessions, although this practice is considered more controversial than the practice of increasing interest rates.

Evaluation of Monetary Policy

We have already evaluated monetary policy in Chapter 15, but a review of our findings in the larger context of the pres-

"Damndest Seesaw I've Ever Seen."

SOURCE: Hugh Haynie, Louisville *Courier-Journal*, and L. A. *Times* Syndicate, Nov. 22, 1970.

ent chapter may be helpful. Monetary policy is more effective in controlling booms than recessions for the reason that demand-pull inflations can be curbed by restricting the supply of loanable funds. In a recession the supply of *M* may be increased and interest rates lowered, but there is no way of forcing businessmen to make investments. The old cliché, "You can lead a horse to water but you can't make him drink," describes this problem in monetary policy when the economy is contracting.

Monetary policy is far more flexible than discretionary fiscal policy and can be changed more quickly, although there is usually a time lag before the new credit policy takes effect. People who look with the most favor on monetary policy as an instrument for control point out that it is neutral in that it does not discriminate against any particular borrower. Critics disagree with this argument. They point out that the large, well-established corporations supply the funds for their own financing by using their undistributed profits, whereas small and expanding companies that must finance expansion by bank loans are hardest hit when credit controls are tightened.

Another argument criticizing the use of policies affecting the long-term growth rate of the economy is that by the tightening of credit, investment in capital goods may be discouraged. Increasing capital goods should increase the productive capacity of the economy. Although it may be temporarily desirable to reduce inflationary pressures by reducing *M*, we may also be slowing down the long-range growth potential of the other side, production. Such an effect would be undesirable.

SOURCE: Tom Darcy, *Newsday*.

Part C
The Classical Approach to Economic Policy

In our economy many forces interact to help in stabilizing economic conditions. For example, individual businesses can by their own action do much to compensate for fluctuations in the business cycle. The classical approach, through the automatic stabilization provided by the laws of supply and demand, is geared to reducing the harmful consequences of economic fluctuation. This result is best achieved, however, in a free competitive market.

When the economy is expanding and demand is greater than supply, a number of changes are set in motion. Prices will rise, thereby acting as a curb on demand. Wages will rise, discouraging employers from hiring additional labor. Loanable funds will become scarce, causing interest rates to rise and discourage additional borrowing. In those parts of the economy where demand is greatest and supply least, profits are likely to be high and to attract new capital. The expectation of profit may also lead to the transfer of capital from less profitable ventures to more profitable ones. These reactions to an expansion of the economy may eventually curb the business boom. As the economy contracts, prices will fall, increasing demand; wages will fall, encouraging employers to hire; and interest rates will fall, stimulating investment. These reactions would eventually have the effect of expanding the economy again.

In the competitive market the individual firm reacts within the framework just described. In the expanding market the businessman is less worried about price competition, since his company may already be operating at the fullest possible capacity. The buyer who is uncertain about making a purchase is discouraged by high prices and may delay action, hoping for prices to decline. The high interest rates being paid on his savings reward him for postponing his purchase. The businessman wants to expand operations, but wages are too high and the workers available are relatively less productive. Since high interest rates prohibit him from buying new equipment, he will probably decide to wait.

In a recession the businessman must be very conscious of price competition. He can hold a sale of merchandise in order to stimulate business. He can hire good workers at low wages because the supply of workers in relation to demand has increased. Maintenance, repair, or even replacement of equipment and fixtures may now be taken care of with a low-interest loan. These and other actions taken by the individual firm can help to stimulate the economy.

Problems of the Classical Approach

As you have seen several times previously, the classical approach assumes the existence of pure competition or a close approximation to that condition. Prices and wages must be flexible in order to move resources to the places where they are needed most. Many economists believe that the lack of pure competition prevents the market mechanism from doing the job anticipated by the classical economic theorist. Prices and wages are flexible primarily in an upward direction, and tend to move downward very slowly or not at all.

Some economists think that economic stability can best be achieved by a return to the framework of the classical model. Measures such as vigorous enforcement of antitrust laws and a reduction in the bargaining power of labor unions will allow us to achieve all our economic objectives with a minimum of government interference. However, such a return to earlier conditions would be very difficult to carry out at this period in our history, particularly in view of the possible political consequences.

A Synthesis of Economic Theories

Few economists today are either strictly classical or strictly Keynesian in their approach. They are aware of the fallacy of composition—the false notion that what is true for the individual is also necessarily true for society. Both microeconomics, with its emphasis on the efficiency of the firm, and macroeconomics, with its emphasis on the economy as a whole, are taken into consideration in determining economic policy. The automatic mechanism existing in a market economy is extremely important in the allocation of our resources, in answering the *What, How,* and *For Whom.* Many economists believe, however, that a policy of laissez-faire will not satisfy our economic objectives adequately, and that its assumptions about a free market cannot always be accepted. It is at this point that they turn to the Keynesian approach for assistance. They believe that the government, with powers far exceeding those of any individual or firm, can and should use the necessary fiscal and monetary tools in order to guide the economy toward its chosen objectives.

We now have an economy based on mixed enterprise, with the greatest emphasis on the private sector. It is as consumers and producers that we make most of our economic decisions; however, we also make decisions, although indirectly, as citizens. Most of the property of our country is owned privately, but our demands for schools, roads, national defense, and many services make government's role in our economy extremely important. Thus, the economic system we have today is in practice a synthesis of the old and new models. Modern economic policy has not eliminated the classical tools; it has merely combined and modified them to fit into our changing world so that we can best achieve full employment, adequate economic growth, and price stability without the harmful effects of major cyclical fluctuations.

Part D
Some Controversial Policy Suggestions

We will now proceed to consider four suggestions concerning economic policy. These policies are well known and are frequently discussed by economists, politicians, businessmen, labor leaders, and the well-informed public. One of the four has not yet been tried; the other three are in very early stages and may still be considered experimental. Each suggestion is designed to achieve at least one of our economic goals—but often at the expense of another goal.

In evaluating these policies, you will wish to consider what effect each one will have on the economy in regard to the attainment of the economic goals we have discussed. When you have weighed the relative benefits and disadvantages in fulfilling one goal at the possible expense of others, explain why you favor or reject the proposal and identify the values that guided you in making your decision.

Automatic Stabilizers

Some economists have dreamed of the day when there would be available built-in stabilizers sufficiently sensitive to respond directly to changes in business activity and successful enough to maintain smooth functioning of the economy so that we might merely sit and observe the operation. Of course, there might be an occasional need for half a turn of the economic wrench here and a full turn of the political screwdriver there, but for the most part the automatic stabilizers would do the job. Such an idea differs little from that of the classical economists, except that in this instance man would have to create the machinery and put it into action. We shall survey some recent proposals for carrying out at least a part of this suggestion.

Automatic Tax Rate Changes in Corporation and Personal Income Taxes

Although the present income taxes are already important automatic stabilizers in our economy, they are admittedly not effective enough to do away with discretionary policy in regard to tax changes. Legislation which would change the tax rate automatically without further legislation by Congress could act as a strong economic stabilizer of the economy. Every six months the GNP, the Consumer Price Index, the Industrial Production Index, and the unemployment rate would be compared with the same figures in the previous six-month report. If the combination of these measurements (combined to give a composite index number) indicated that the economy was moving ahead too rapidly for our productive capacity and that inflation seemed imminent, the tax rate could automatically increase by 2 percent (or a variable percentage depending on how sharp the economic expansion is). A decline in the composite index number, indicating a recession, would automatically reduce the tax rate.

The automatic changing of the tax rate with the change in the direction of the economy would minimize the occurrence of economic fluctuations. It would eliminate the time lag that does occur when Congress must debate proposals separately. It would also be neutral in its geographic effects so that each representative in Congress would not have to fear discrimination against his area. As the plan became refined, automatic rate changes might be reduced to three-month intervals, and greater rate changes might automatically be set for higher income groups in order to increase investment when economic growth seemed the slowest, or to give greater rate changes to the lowest income groups when the unemployment rate was growing fastest and there was a need to increase C.

Weaknesses in Automatic Tax Rate Changes

Criticism of such a plan would be most intense in Congress. Using a system based on automatic rate changes would mean surrendering one of Congress' most important powers. It is highly doubtful, even if the plan were good in all other respects, that our legislature would approve.

Taxing is only one half of fiscal policy. A change in government revenues influences our national income only in relation to our government expenditures. Such a policy would greatly restrict the flexibility of the government's spending program, and meeting specific needs might become a consideration secondary to economic stabilization in making government policy.

Guaranteed Annual Wage as an Automatic Stabilizer

Industries which are subject to major seasonal fluctuations find great variations in their payrolls and the number of workers they employ in a given year. Unions have recognized that workers in such industries have little security; moreover, the unions are under a severe handicap in budgeting their expenditures. Although unemployment insurance provides some stabilization of income, a vast difference remains between bringing home $150 in a pay envelope and receiving $70 in unemployment compensation. Salaried executives receive annual incomes that usually continue whether the business conditions are bad or good. Annual salaries provide stability of income to the individual and help in stabilizing the income of the community. If some kind of *guaranteed annual wage* (GAW) were provided for workers in enough industries, it could act as an automatic stabilizer for the nation.

In the mid-1950's the automobile manufacturers, the steel companies, and several other large companies signed contracts with unions offering modified guaranteed annual wages. The most widely used plan provided for workers with some company seniority to receive supplementary unemployment benefits from the company during periods of seasonal unemployment. The temporarily unemployed worker might have a $65 unemployment check from the state supplemented by an additional $40 (usually up to 65 percent of his regular pay) from the company. Although such a plan does not provide a guaranteed annual wage, it is a step in that direction. It not only eases the hardship of unemployment for the individual worker, but it also eases the reduction in consumption that would hurt those who depend on the worker's expenditures.

The guaranteed annual wage, and even the modified supplementary unemployment benefit plan, force the producer to schedule his output on a yearly basis and thus result in real economies in the use of capital. The money to support these plans is put into funds which can be drawn on when needed. Such funds tend to reduce the effects of the business cycle by being built up during periods of expansion and reduced during periods of contraction.

Weaknesses in the Guaranteed Annual Wage Plan

Many industries do not lend themselves to plans such as the guaranteed annual wage or supplementary benefits. In addition, the plans may increase fixed costs unduly and discourage investment. New industries and those that are declining would be particularly hard pressed to commit themselves to such costs. Such plans also reduce the mobility of labor, thereby preventing business from adapting to changes in consumer preferences. They also make expanding industries think twice about hiring additional labor because of the long-term commitments that follow. In addition, a portion of the money in the fund is restricted in its use. Since the employer would rather see steady growth than periodic fluctuations, the only change that such a plan could bring is to pass on to the consumer the added costs that may be incurred in its operation.

Qualitative Measures

Some economists have pointed out that fiscal and monetary policy might be used to push up aggregate demand to a GNP level that would support full employment without actually achieving full employment. Our economy today needs not just *any* labor; it needs *skilled* labor to meet our increasingly automated economy. The unemployed today are primarily of two groups: (1) those who are unskilled and lack either the physical, mental, or emotional requirements to find and hold jobs and (2) workers living in specific regions that have chronically high unemployment rates. Unless we direct our spending to help these two groups, our aggregate demand will have to move well into the inflationary area to reach full employment. The added dollars may increase the demand for more goods and services, but if businesses do not have workers available who have the skills to produce the goods and services, inflation, not full employment, will result. Let us see what programs exist for helping the people in these two groups.

Area Redevelopment

After many years of effort, legislation has now been passed allowing the federal government to assist areas with high chronic rates of unemployment in meeting their problem. "Distressed areas," those whose unemployment rate is considerably above the national average and has been so for at least a year, become eligible to receive loans and grants to be used for attracting new industry, for retraining workers for new skills, and for making improvements in public buildings.

The general economy of West Virginia and Pennsylvania has been severely affected by the decline in the coal industry. Unemployment rates have been high, and displaced coal miners have been slow to move out of the area to seek other employment. Attracting new industry through tax inducements and plant subsidies, and retraining programs to give the coal miners new skills, can reduce unemployment considerably without the necessity of applying inflationary pressures to the rest of the country through generally increasing aggregate spending.

So far the program has had only moderate success, but the amount of money that has been appropriated has been so meager in comparison to the needs that no fair evaluation can be made. Utilizing area redevelopment as a major program to achieve full employment without causing inflationary pressure will require a far greater financial commitment than has been made so far.

Weaknesses in the Redevelopment Plan

Critics of this program point out that state and local governments are the logical governments to administer these activities. They reason, too, that the area which benefits should be the area to pay for it. In addition, such programs reduce the tendency of labor to move where it is needed most. Inducing industries to come into these areas with the aid of government funds gives these areas a competitive advantage. Some industries might even move from an area which has natural advantages for efficient operation merely to take advantage of the government subsidy. This would be an inefficient use of our resources.

Training the Unemployable

A very large percentage of our unemployed have little chance for employment, no matter how high the aggregate demand is, because they have no marketable skill. As one part of the government's war on poverty, the Office of Economic Opportunity was set up to develop, approve, and administer job-training centers. At these centers trainees receive vocational training in such areas as office work, equipment maintenance, cooking, sales, metal work, and health services. They also receive general education because so many are school dropouts and are seriously limited in basic skills such as reading. Hundreds of Job Corps centers have been set up throughout the country, operated by businesses and educational institutions. At some of these centers trainees live on a selected site and receive room and board plus a monthly allowance. Other Job Corps projects use the neighborhood approach and try to furnish trainees with part-time jobs while they are in training. The Manpower Development Training Act has been the basis for trying many other approaches.

As with area redevelopment the funds appropriated have been meager. If these programs are to be really successful, the country must commit itself to the expenditure of billions of dollars, as we have done in subsidizing the farmer and in committing ourselves to the space program.

Weaknesses in Training Programs

Critics of these retraining programs have pointed out that such projects increase the public sector of the economy at the expense of the private sector. Even though private enterprise is involved in the training program, the money to finance such programs and approval of them must come from the federal government, and that inevitably means government control. Increasing the offerings of present school programs can accomplish the same thing at less cost and with no increase in government control. The free market, not only for the businessman's purchase of his labor needs, is still the best method of directing people to the positions that they want and that our society needs.

Post-Keynesian Thinking: An Added Consideration

Many economists have suggested that we are now living in a post-Keynesian world. The classical tradition emphasized efficiency and the Keynesian tradition stressed stability. Today, however, concern is focused primarily on maintaining continued economic growth, greater equality of opportunity, and a satisfactory standard of living for even those in the lowest economic group. Achieving these objectives depends to some extent on the use of ideas from both traditions as well as new creative thought. Let us see how such a synthesis is possible.

These economists point out that the quantitative approach, which income determination ($C + I + G = Y$) emphasizes, has not done the job of achieving a full-employment economy, although it has certainly helped. The fact that one eighth of our nation still lives in poverty has motivated the federal government to employ the qualitative approach as well as the quantitative approach. The war on poverty includes a wide array of programs aimed at raising the economic position of those who have received few benefits from our affluent society. The new federal programs to help finance education and research—two of the most important ingredients for economic growth—are reflections of this new thinking. Most unemployment today is *structural;* that is, it is caused by such factors as the lack of skills, the change in consumer preferences, and the immobility of labor. Investment in human resources (education) and in pure research and technology appears to be the direction of the future.

The recession-inflation combination that started in 1969 seemed to defy President Nixon's economic game plans. Dr. Paul McCracken, the former chairman of Nixon's Council of Economic Advisers, pleaded for more time to allow the monetary and fiscal policies suggested to work and argued against instituting an incomes policy. When the unemployment rate continued to hover around 6 percent and the cost of living continued to rise above 4 percent, President Nixon turned to other advisers and instituted his wage-price freeze. How do you explain the failure of his original game plan? Do you think his "90-day first phase" plan was successful? What do you suggest we do now?

REVIEW: THE HIGHLIGHTS OF THE CHAPTER

1. Our economic goals include full employment, adequate economic growth, price stability, and a minimum of economic fluctuation. By the Employment Act of 1946 the federal government accepted far more responsibility for establishing a favorable economic climate to make possible the achievement of our economic goals than the classical economist might have wished.
2. Other economic goals include efficient use of resources, fair distribution of income, freedom for the consumer and producer, equal opportunities for all, and freer trade.
3. The tools of fiscal and monetary policy can be used to help achieve our economic goals. They are designed to raise or lower aggregate demand to produce a countercyclical action.
4. Automatic stabilizers, such as the personal income tax and unemployment insurance, lessen the effects of the business cycle without the need for direct action by any agency of government.
5. Discretionary policy requires deliberate action. Government spending and altering taxes to produce budgetary surpluses and deficits are examples of discretionary fiscal policy.
6. Altering taxes works more quickly in compensating for the expansion and contraction of the economy, but government spending is more likely to result in a greater multiplier effect.
7. Monetary policy is more flexible than fiscal policy. By altering the supply of *M* and changing interest rates, investment may be changed. Monetary policy is more effective in fighting an inflation than a recession.
8. The classical model depends upon the automatic mechanism of a free market economy to achieve our economic goals. The lack of wage and price flexibility and the low mobility of our resources limit the market's effectiveness.
9. Since World War II, recessions have been shorter, less frequent, and less severe. Periods of expansion have been longer and less sharp.
10. Most economists today are neither exclusively classical nor exclusively Keynesian in their approach. They recognize the need for using elements of both approaches.
11. Controversial policy suggestions are introduced, discussed, and evaluated to see if they can be of help in achieving our objectives. The achievement of one goal may mean the sacrifice of another.
12. Post-Keynesian thinking emphasizes economic growth, greater equality, and qualitative methods for dealing with structural unemployment.

IN CONCLUSION: SOME AIDS TO UNDERSTANDING

Terms for Review

structural unemployment
economic growth
automatic mechanism
automatic stabilizers
area redevelopment
price stability
countercyclical policy
growth rate
unbalanced budget
guaranteed annual wage

Names to Know

Council of Economic Advisers
Employment Act of 1946
Dr. Walter Heller
Office of Economic Opportunity
Job Corps
Dr. Paul McCracken

Questions for Review

1. The ideas of Keynes led to the adoption of new economic policies for our nation.
   (a) Explain the reasons for the Employment Act of 1946.
   (b) Why may this law be considered a major change in the theory underlying our nation's economic system?
2. Considering that we are the wealthiest nation in the world, why is our continued economic growth important?
3. Economists tend to agree on our broad economic goals, although they may differ on the means of achieving them.
   (a) What are the major economic goals of the United States?
   (b) How are our economic goals determined?
4. Several tools are available for influencing the pattern of business cycles.
   (a) Explain the difference between automatic and discretionary stabilizers.
   (b) Give several examples to illustrate each stabilizer.
   (c) What are the dangers in using hasty discretionary action to bring about countercyclical activity?
5. Explain why an annually balanced budget is at variance with modern economic theory.
6. How may political considerations interfere with appropriate fiscal policy?
7. Explain the following statements:
   (a) "Monetary policy is more flexible than fiscal policy."
   (b) "Monetary policy is more effective against inflation than against recession."
8. Why is it appropriate to call the present economic policies of our government a "synthesis"? Use examples to illustrate.
9. What are the weaknesses associated with using the guaranteed annual wage as an automatic stabilizer?
10. Explain what is meant by a "qualitative approach" in contrast to a "quantitative approach." What advantages and disadvantages are there in each approach?

Additional Questions and Problems

1. Actions and policies of the federal government are basic in effecting economic changes.
   (a) Contrast the policies of the Roosevelt–Truman years with those of the Eisenhower administration.
   (b) Compare the policies of the Kennedy–Johnson years with those of the two previous administrations. Did the Nixon administration's policies differ substantially from those of his Democratic predecessors?
   (c) Make a chronological list of the agencies of the federal government that have been created since 1962 to help in stabilizing our economy. What does each agency do?
2. As a project in research, look up the statistics in GNP, employment, unemployment, and national tax structures for 1963, and then find the same figures for last year.
   (a) Prepare a table comparing the two sets of figures.
   (b) Explain the effect on the national economy of the tax-reduction legislation passed by the 88th Congress.
   (c) Why is it that many of the same economists who favored the tax reduction in 1964 urged a tax increase in 1968? What position did they take during the "mini-recession" of 1970?
3. Explain the statement "Political leaders on the state and local levels will often vote for measures contrary to what might be good economic policy on the national level."
4. Both the classical economists and the "new economists" believe in economic growth and a "fair" distribution of income. How do they differ in the means of achieving these goals? Where do they agree? In what ways does our economy today reflect classical theory? In what ways does it reflect the "new economics"?
5. Some assert that the United States has become (or is becoming) a welfare state. Critics charge that this impairs the natural functioning of the free enterprise system. Supporters claim that government welfare policies help to strengthen our economic system. Give the arguments on both sides and evaluate each.

SELECTED READINGS

Council of Economic Advisers. *Economic Report of the President.* Washington, D.C.: U.S. Government Printing Office—annual.

Gilpatrick, Eleanor G. *Structural Unemployment and Aggregate Demand.* Baltimore: The Johns Hopkins Press, 1966.

Hamovitch, William, ed. *The Federal Deficit: Fiscal Imprudence or Policy Weapon?* Boston: D. C. Heath and Co., 1965.

———. *Monetary Policy: The Argument from Keynes's Treatise to Friedman.* Boston: D. C. Heath and Co., 1966.

Heilbroner, Robert L. and Peter L. Bernstein. *A Primer on Government Spending.* New York: Random House, 1968.

Heller, Walter. *New Dimensions in Political Economy*. New York: W. W. Norton & Co., 1967.

Lewis, Wilfred, Jr. *Federal Fiscal Policy in the Postwar Recessions*. Washington, D.C.: The Brookings Institution, 1962.

Ulmer, Melville. *The Welfare State, U.S.A.* Boston: Houghton Mifflin Co., 1969.

UNIT IV

INTERNATIONAL ECONOMICS

International Trade and Finance 17

THE AUTHORS' NOTE TO THE STUDENT

In the first three units our main study has been the American economic system and its basic theories and practices. We have paid little attention to the economy of our country in relation to the world scene. In this chapter we shall consider the importance of international trade and the mechanics of international finance.

The subject of free trade is debated by economists just as the question of a freely operating market is. There is apparent logic in specialization and the law of comparative advantage; at the same time international trade has often been hampered by special interest groups that have used tariffs and other restraints for selfish motives.

An added factor in determining the extent of international trade is the method that nations use in paying one another. International finance is itself complex; in addition, its patterns often reflect political motives. International monetary policy can be a help to the movement of trade; however, it can also be used to hinder trade.

In recognition of the importance of trade and finance to world economic development, institutions such as the International Monetary Fund and GATT (General Agreement on Tariffs and Trade) have been designed and developed to encourage world trade. The degree of their success in solving age-old problems will have significance for the standard of living of most of the people of the world. Regional institutions have also been developed. We shall see the growth of one of these, the European Economic Community (the Common Market), and consider whether it poses a threat to our own economy and to our participation in world trade.

A STUDENT'S NOTE TO THE STUDENT

The thing which struck me most in this chapter was that it completely destroyed my preconceived ideas about protecting American labor from "cheap foreign competition." I still have doubts about how I would feel if I worked in the garment industry, but I am more convinced that encouraging trade is good for the nation in the long run.

The law of comparative advantage is not too difficult, but the part on international finance had me reading and rereading. Try explaining it to someone else to see if you really understand it.

Part A
Why Should a Nation Trade?

The Basis for Trade

The classical point of view toward trade is set forth by the English economist David Ricardo in his book *On the Principles of Political Economy and Taxation*:

> Under a system of perfectly free commerce, each country naturally devotes its capital and labour to such employments as are most beneficial to each. This pursuit of individual advantage is admirably connected with the universal good of the whole. By stimulating industry, by rewarding ingenuity, and by using most efficaciously the peculiar powers bestowed by nature, it distributes labour most effectively and most economically; while, by increasing the general mass of productions, it diffuses general benefit, and binds together by one common tie of interest and intercourse, the universal society of nations throughout the civilized world. It is this principle which determines that wine shall be made in France and Portugal, that corn shall be grown in America and Poland, and that hardware and other goods shall be manufactured in England.

Ricardo's ideas formed the basis for a new concept of trade for Britain and, later, for many other nations. Many of Ricardo's arguments in favor of *free trade* continue to be valid, although political and economic conditions have changed greatly since his time. Let us consider some of the ideas and influences that contributed to other theories of trade.

Advantages and Problems of Specialization

In Chapter 1 we saw that as society has grown more complex, man as a producer has had to become more specialized, exchanging the goods and services produced in order to satisfy more wants. And, as we also discovered, specialization increases production. Geographic regions of our country may specialize by taking advantage of their particular climatic conditions or their skilled labor supply or their natural resources. In the same way nations of the world have an unequal distribution of economic factors with varying conditions and advantages. These inequalities become the basis for specialization.

Along with its obvious advantages, specialization brings problems. Nations realize that too great dependence on foreign trade can be a weakness. Many industrial nations have believed that, to be strong, they must try to be self-sufficient and meet their own needs as fully as possible. However, self-sufficiency for a nation is usually relative. In analyzing the economic potential of nations, we find that some nations are far closer to self-sufficiency than others. Even the United States and the Soviet Union, with their vast territory and abundant resources, are not completely self-sufficient. They must supplement their own products and resources; moreover they can obtain many things more cheaply by importing them rather than by attempting to produce them domestically. At the beginning of the decade of the 1970's, the United States was exporting over $55 billion worth of goods and services, and importing over $53 billion worth. These amounts do not reveal the true importance of our foreign trade. For example, they do not indicate how important

DAVID RICARDO AND HIS CONTRIBUTIONS

David Ricardo (1772–1823) was, with Adam Smith and Thomas R. Malthus, one of the three great English economists who started the classical school. As an individual he defied the stereotype of the theoretician who is unable to understand or cope with the real world. Trained by his father as a stockbroker but disinherited because of family disapproval of his marriage, he amassed a considerable fortune through investments before reaching the age of thirty. The leisure thus acquired gave him time to follow intellectual pursuits—first science and then economics—after reading Smith's *The Wealth of Nations.* He wrote books on a variety of economic subjects. For a time, he served as a member of Parliament, where he was influential in reshaping Britain's policies regarding trade.

Smith and Ricardo were both deductive thinkers, framing possible answers to explain economic behavior and using logic to support their theories. However, they differed in that Smith emphasized problems of production whereas Ricardo concentrated on those of distribution. Smith was the optimist, with his hopeful analysis of economic growth and possible betterment of man's living conditions. Ricardo, in contrast, helped to earn for economics the label "gloomy science," which has since clung to this discipline. He reasoned that, because the amount of land is fixed, the constant increase in world population will make man's survival more and more precarious.

Ricardo is primarily known for his labor theory of value, his theory of rent, and the law of comparative advantage in trade. He viewed the exchange value of a commodity in terms of the labor time involved in making it. Later Marx used this theory in developing his own rationale. In explaining rent, Ricardo applied the law of diminishing returns, but did not give sufficient credit to improved technology as a means of greatly increasing the yields from land. His theory of comparative advantage, often referred to as comparative cost, was ideally suited to the new policy of free trade.

many of our imports are to the rest of our economy, nor do they reflect the importance of our exports to the economies of other nations.

Importance of Foreign Trade to the United States

To supplement its own natural resources, our country imports most of its uranium, rubber, manganese, nickel, tungsten, and cobalt—all very vital to our industrial machine and to national defense. Most of our supply of these resources comes from foreign countries. More iron ore and copper are being obtained abroad as our own supplies grow smaller or more costly to mine. As a reflection of our rising standard of living, we also import many quality manufactured items that foreign nations specialize in, such as perfume, lace, china, cameras, and pieces of art. Another category of imports is foods which our country cannot produce. Almost all of our coffee, tea, and tropical fruits are brought from abroad.

Although our nation might try to become self-sufficient in some of these imports, to do so would create new problems:

1. It would become necessary to find substitutes for some products we now want and enjoy.
2. More money would have to be spent to produce things that could be imported at less cost.

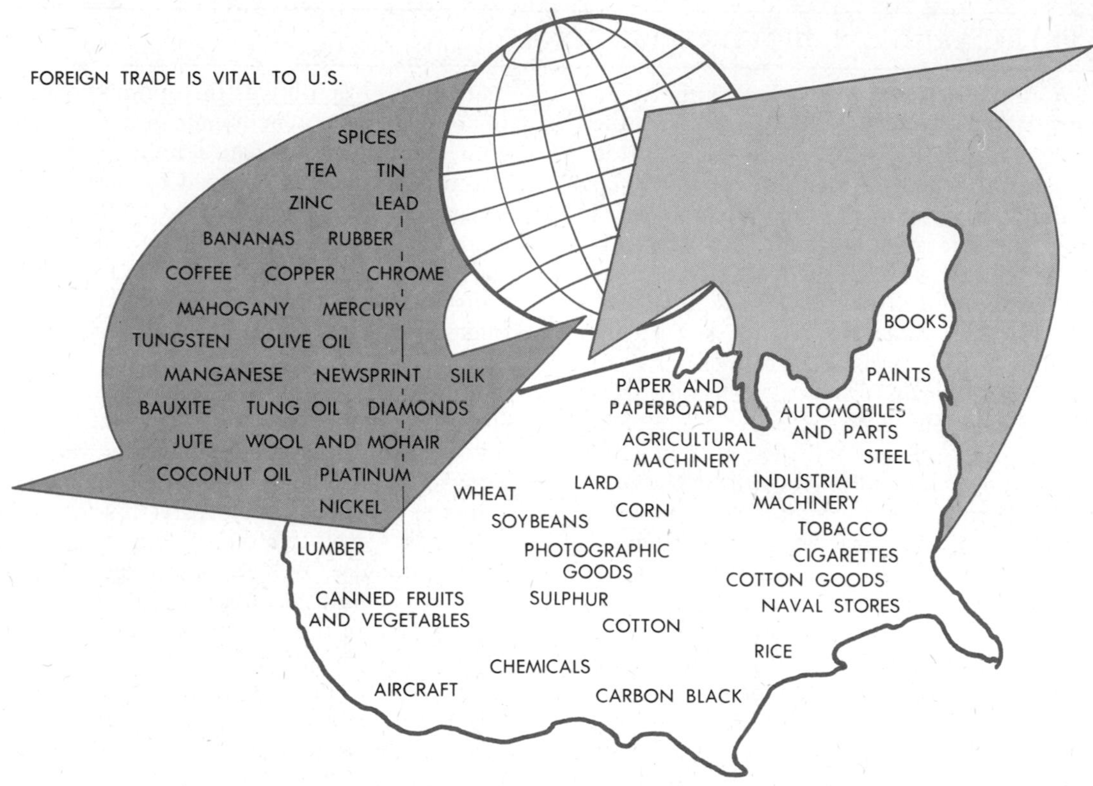

FIGURE 17–1 Foreign Trade Is Vital to the United States

Many of the items we import are necessary to maintain our high standard of living. SOURCE: "ABC's of Foreign Trade," *U.S. Trade Policy in Brief*, Department of State Publication 7713, 1964.

3. The economy of other countries which depend on our trade would be hurt. In time our exports to those nations would be correspondingly reduced.

The Law of Comparative Advantage

When one nation is able to produce a product or service more cheaply than another, that nation has an *absolute advantage*. Most people readily accept the idea that we should buy tea from Ceylon instead of trying to produce it ourselves, because our climate and resources are not suitable for tea production. Ceylon can produce it more efficiently and cheaply, and thus has an absolute advantage. On the other hand, our abundant capital, technology, skilled labor, and minerals give us an absolute advantage in auto production. If we attempted to produce our own tea we would have to draw productive resources away from other industries in which we are relatively efficient. Because the cost of producing tea would be high, its price would soar. Other goods would become more expensive as well because, by taking productive resources away from industries where they were being used efficiently, we would probably reduce the supply. Obviously it is better to buy tea from Ceylon, and let Ceylon buy cars from us. Both nations would benefit from the exchange.

The principle of absolute advantage is so simple and self-evident that few would dispute it. It is a different matter, however, with the *law of comparative advantage.* According to this principle, we can benefit from trade even if we produce everything more cheaply than any other country.

Let us illustrate this first with a simple example. Assume that an editor for a publishing firm also happens to be an excellent typist. He has an absolute advantage over his secretary in both editing and typing. Why, then, does he not do both jobs himself? Say that his output as an editor is worth $10 per hour to his firm, and his output as a typist would be $4 per hour. Clearly it is better for him to concentrate all of his efforts on editorial work and let his secretary do the typing. The secretary is not capable of doing editorial work at all, but does have some typing skill even though it is not as great as that of the editor.

Now apply this concept to foreign trade. Assume that the United States produces both computers and clocks more cheaply than Switzerland. We produce the computers four times as cheaply, and we produce the clocks twice as cheaply. We have an *absolute advantage* in both, but the Swiss have a *comparative advantage* in clocks. If we shift productive resources from clocks to computers, our output of computers will rise. Meanwhile, the Swiss should shift resources from computers to clocks. Since each country will be concentrating upon what it does best, total output will rise. Terms of trade will develop between us so that we produce enough computers for both nations, and the Swiss produce enough clocks. Total production of both items will rise because each nation is specializing in what it does most efficiently, unit costs of production will probably drop, and consumers in both countries will get more and better goods at lower cost. Of course the real-life situation is more complex, but this is the principle upon which all trade is based.

Reasons for Interfering with Free Trade

If we consider free trade only in terms of the theoretical economic arguments involved, there can be little objection to it. However, we must recognize that in reality absolute free trade seldom exists, and that those who oppose it are not without their reasons. Let us examine the arguments for and against free trade, recognizing that neither position is generally followed completely. We have for the most part followed moderate positions somewhere between the two extremes.

Mercantilism

From the sixteenth century to the eighteenth a popular viewpoint held by many economists, statesmen, and merchants was that a nation should direct its policy in such a way that it would accumulate gold and silver in its treasury. Those who held this idea considered these precious metals to be the principal form of wealth. They sought to accomplish their goals by strict regulation of trade so that the total value of the exports of the nation would be greater than the total value of its imports. The difference in value between the shipments made by each of the nations would in turn be compensated by payment in gold by the nation that showed the deficit. Mercantilism, as this system of thought was called, tried to gain a "favorable balance of trade" by following policies that would encourage exports and discourage imports. Much of the reasoning behind mercantilism stemmed from the falsely held belief that a nation, like a business, must sell more than it buys in order to prosper. This viewpoint served as a guide for the British in governing their American colonies.

The classical economists pointed out several obvious fallacies in mercantilist theory. Besides the advantages of specialization, the simple fact remains that nations must import in order to export. Precious metals cannot always flow in one directon. Also, when a nation keeps exporting its products and importing gold, the prices of its goods and services are going to rise and it may price itself out of the international market. In the sixteenth century mercantilist Spain found that many of the benefits of importing huge quantities of gold were dissipated by the inflation that followed. We know too that real wealth is the goods and services that people want, not money *per se*.

Although some of the old mercantilist theories can still be heard, most of the current objections to free trade are based on political, military, and economic considerations which differ from the earlier rationale. Those who wish to restrict international trade are known as *protectionists.* They generally favor high tariffs and other restrictions on goods imported into the country so that domestic products will not have to compete with foreign goods in their own markets.

National Defense

Protectionists often argue in favor of national self-sufficiency for reasons of defense, since wars can cut off goods that are essential to a nation's survival. Therefore, even though it might be more costly to produce synthetics, such as rubber, at home, the importance of protecting the nation must come first. Protecting home industries involved in the nation's defense by restricting the importation of such goods must take priority over economic efficiency and cost.

Critics of this position argue that such a policy encourages extreme nationalism, which is one of the causes of wars. If nations were more interdependent, not only would they understand each other better but they would be less capable of making war.

Infant Industries

Another argument advanced by protectionists is that the growth of a nation's industry must be encouraged. An industry in its early growth is at an economic disadvantage when competing with a well-established industry. For example, manufacturing was much more highly developed in England than in our country when we became independent. Our new industries could not compete with those of England. By giving these industries protection, we helped them to get started. Our country might never have become the industrial giant that it is today had we not given such protection.

Protection actually benefits not only the industry itself but also the consumer. The sacrifices that the consumer makes in the form of paying higher prices are more than offset by the additional productivity of the country, the new jobs created, and the gradual lowering of prices as competition attracts more businesses into the field and efficiency increases.

The objection to this theory is that it is not only the infant industry that asks for protection. On the contrary, Congress is besieged by the lobbies of well-established industries. Because such industries have failed to become efficient, they look for extra protection from foreign competition. At what point should developing industries no longer need protection?

Protecting the Wages of Labor

It is frequently pointed out by labor, and agreed to by management, that the high standard of living of the American worker requires management to pay high wages. By contrast, foreign firms pay far lower wages, keeping the cost of production down and allowing these firms to sell at prices below those charged by American firms. A large number of American workers might be thrown out of work because they cannot compete with poorly paid foreign labor.

Such an argument would be valid if the output per man-hour were the same in our country as it is in other countries. However, under these circumstances it is doubtful that we would be engaged in such production at all. The reason we have been able to have a favorable balance of trade for so many years is that our costs have not been higher than those of comparable foreign goods. During a recent year, American coal miners received eight times as much per hour as Japanese miners, but they produced 14 times as much. Thus, the labor cost per unit of output was actually lower in the United States. Other costs must be considered as well. In some cases where the foreign labor cost per unit is indeed lower, the other costs (such as for capital and raw materials) are higher than they are in the United States. When all costs are taken into account, if the foreign country can still produce a comparable product more cheaply, most economists would argue that the United States should either take steps to increase efficiency in that industry or abandon it altogether.

Protecting the Jobs of Labor

As we learned from the problem concerning automation in Chapter 7, any threat to employment is a serious matter to both labor and business. In spite of the high average productivity of American business and labor, the threat of foreign competition is ever present. Although in a competitive market the closing of inefficient plants may become necessary, doing so creates a difficult situation not only for the owners and workers of the firm affected but also for the community in which the business is located. Representatives from areas that are particularly hard hit by foreign competition band together frequently to lobby in Congress for the protection of the American worker. It is difficult to explain to those so affected that other industries are thriving and that other workers have jobs because foreign nations have been able to increase their imports of our products by earning dollars through their sales to us. Many economists point out that it is wiser and better for all concerned to help communities hurt by foreign imports by means of retraining programs and the locating of more efficient industry in their areas than by fighting the foreign competition.

Barriers to Trade

In the course of establishing policies to guide their economic development, nations have often turned to practices which interfere with the free flow of international trade. Protectionists have used the methods described here to accomplish their purposes, whereas people advocating free trade have tried to remove or modify the practices of protectionism.

Tariffs

The device most commonly used to restrict imports is the *tariff*. A tariff is a tax placed on goods that move into or out of a country. Such a tax is sometimes called a *duty*. Most countries, including the United States, place duties only on imports. Duties are *specific* when the sum to be paid for each commodity is a specified amount; they are *ad valorem* when the amount to be paid varies with the value of the product. An ad valorem tariff of 25 percent on cameras would mean that a $25 duty is paid on a $100 camera and a $50 duty on a $200 camera. *Revenue tariffs*, usually placed on items not produced extensively in a country, are designed for the income they yield; *protective tariffs* are designed for the protection of home industries. The higher rates of the protective tariff usually have the effect of reducing revenues because they may restrict the importation of goods.

Quota Restrictions

An *import quota* establishes the maximum amount of a particular item that can be brought into a country during a given period. It is usually even more restrictive than a tariff. One nation might willingly accept a high tariff in order to sell goods to another, but a quota set by the latter nation would place an absolute limit on the import of restricted items, regardless of the duty.

Other Hindrances

In addition to tariffs and quotas, other less direct devices have been developed to discourage trade. Controls may be placed on foreign exchange (foreign money or negotiable claims expressed in foreign money) so that an importer is denied permission to purchase it if the government wishes to prevent the entry of the product that the importer intended to buy. Uncertainty about how an imported item is to be classified and, consequently, what duty will be placed on it, can also inhibit trade. Some items may be labeled as unhealthful when the real reason for the exclusion might be that a domestic firm is seeking protection. If a government wishes to discourage trade, it can find a variety of ways for doing so.

The Development of United States Trade Policies

Recognizing the need for income, the first Congress to meet under the new Constitution passed a modest revenue tariff on July 4, 1789. Essentially an agricultural nation, we hoped to exchange our products and raw materials for Europe's manufactured goods. Soon the protectionist sentiment of Alexander Hamilton found many adherents of the ideas expressed in his "Report on Manufactures." Later Henry Clay, in his American System, continued the idea of encouraging American industry by tariffs, while providing a market for agricultural products.

Although the nation depended heavily on the revenue it received from the tariff, protectionist rates tended to increase. An exception to this trend was the interlude of lower rates, from 1833 to the Civil War, during which time the agrarian South and West dominated Congress. The rate increases resumed again once the Civil War started, and continued until 1934, when the Trade Agreements Act was passed. Some attempts were made to lower the tariff during Cleveland's administration, and a degree of success was achieved in the lower rates of the Underwood Tariff Act during Wilson's first term. However, these attempts were in turn canceled out by even larger increases in the rates of the tariffs that followed. The climax was reached with the passage of the Hawley-Smoot Tariff Act in 1930, establishing the highest tariff rate in our history—52.8 percent on the value of all goods imported.

Difficulties in Lowering the Tariff

You might wonder at this point why Congress passed such high tariffs although it realized that such an economic policy might do more harm than good to the country as a whole. The answer is to be found in the way tariffs are made. Some Congresses have started out with the intention of lowering rates and yet have passed a tariff with duties even higher than those in effect when they started. How can such an about-face occur?

There are a number of ways to resolve this contradiction. Individually, a congressman may be interested in a general lowering of the tariff—except, perhaps, for the industries in his own district. In order to get the protection he seeks for those industries, he must agree to support the protection of industries in which other congressmen are interested. The result may be Congressional "logrolling" and a higher tariff, which may actually be contrary to the interest of the general public. Another source of pressure for protective legislation is the lobbies maintained in Washington by groups with special economic interests.

A New Approach: Tariff Negotiation

Faced with a serious depression and declining foreign trade, President Franklin D. Roosevelt decided to try a new technique for lowering the tariff. Instead of asking Congress for a new tariff law, he asked it for authority to alter duty rates, up to 50 percent of existing rates. This power would allow the administration to negotiate trade agreements within a broadly defined area, and to enter into trade agreements with other nations without submitting these agreements for Senate approval. Each agreement made would be applicable not only to the country it was made with but to others also ("most-favored nation" clause).

Congress responded by passing the Trade Agreements Act of 1934, which gave the administration authority to negotiate reciprocal trade agreements. But Congress did not surrender to the President all its power to regulate tariffs. It sharply limited the duration of the law so that the President had to come to Congress regularly to ask for its renewal. Several times there was a strong movement against renewal. After World War II, amendments were passed which greatly restricted the President's power to negotiate tariff agreements.

Peril Point and Escape Clause

Two of the amendments have been the escape clause and the peril point provisions. The *escape clause* required the Tariff Commission to "take into consideration a downward trend of production, employment, prices, profits, or wages in the domestic industry concerned, or a decline in sales, an increase in imports, either actual or relative to domestic production, a higher or growing inventory, or a decline in the proportion of the domestic market supplied by domestic producers" when appraising a complaint of injury. Note that an American firm could ask for higher tariffs even when its sales were increasing, as long as imports were increasing faster. While the escape clause offered relief after an injury had occurred, the *peril point* was meant to forestall injury from foreign competition. The President was directed to list the products on which he planned to make tariff concessions at meetings of the

General Agreement on Tariffs and Trade. The Tariff Commission could then decide what duties would be needed to prevent injury to the United States industry. While the President could still reduce a tariff below this peril point, he was required to explain his reasons to Congress in a special message. These actions damaged our relations with friendly nations, caused some to question our sincerity in tariff negotiations, and induced some foreigners to withold concessions from us.

The Trade Expansion Act

With realization growing that our nation had more to gain than to lose by the expansion of world trade, President Kennedy secured bipartisan legislation which took an approach somewhat different from that of President Roosevelt. The Trade Expansion Act of 1962 gave the President the power to raise and lower duties by at least 50 percent; in addition it allowed rates to be reduced by as much as 100 percent on duties of less than 6 percent, on articles whose export from our nation and the European Economic Community makes up 80 percent or more of free world exports, and on tropical farm and forest products.

The President was also authorized to negotiate for entire categories of products, such as textiles, and to bargain with the Common Market nations as a single unit. To soften the effect on industries hard hit by tariff reductions, the Act provided for retraining programs and resettlement allowances for workers displaced through foreign competition.

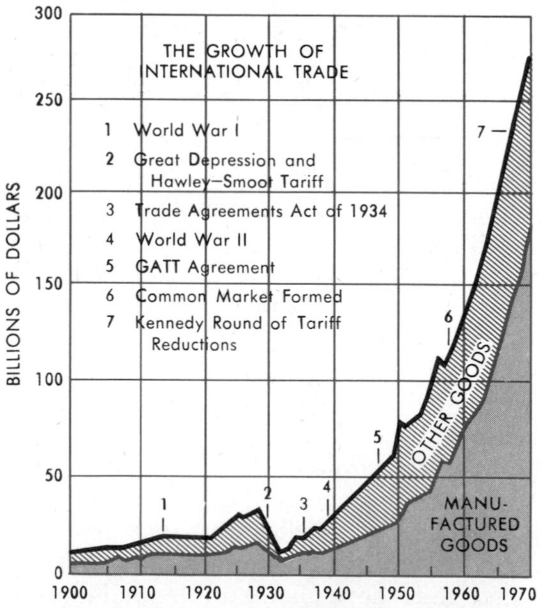

FIGURE 17–2 The Growth of Trade from 1900

This graph shows the long-term growth in world trade and major events that have had an impact on the world economic situation. SOURCE: United Nations.

Evaluation of Recent Tariff Policy

The results of our nation's policy to increase its foreign trade have been mixed. Overall, rates have been reduced considerably from what they were under the Hawley–Smoot tariff of 1930. Today more than 85 percent of all our tariff rates are under 26 percent, and more than 50 percent of our imports (by dollar value) have rates of 5 percent or less. Those who favor free trade (or freer trade) have much to be cheerful about.

In spite of the progress in rate reduction, many restrictions in the law remain for protectionists to use. A number of commodities still have very high duties, in some instances amounting to over 40 percent of the value of the imported product.

In the years since World War II the trends in international commerce have seemed to favor an expansion of trade and the use of fewer restrictions. The United States can take a major portion of the credit for setting this trend. The reciprocal trade agreements and President Kennedy's Trade Expansion Act both contributed to a new atmosphere in foreign trade.

Recognition was growing, in our own country and abroad, of the ideas that almost all nations have a vested interest in trade and that trade agreements bring mutual benefits. A threat to the concept of free trade emerged in 1971, however, when President Nixon placed a temporary 10 percent surcharge on imports. Although this was intended to compensate for "unfair" exchange rates, some economists feared that foreign nations would retaliate with similar action instead of revaluing their currencies upward in relation to the dollar. Instead of helping to improve the U.S. balance of payments, this surcharge might touch off a destructive trade war.

Part B
International Cooperation to Expand Trade

Many social scientists have long held that one of the basic causes of war—if not *the* basic cause—is the selfish, unlimited pursuit of economic gain by nations acting independently of one another. The struggle between "haves" and "have-nots" is not confined within the borders of a country; it frequently expresses itself between competing countries. If nations would recognize that the best assurance for their own economic well-being is helping to increase the size of the world's "pie," some of the tensions between nations might be significantly reduced.

World War II marked a turning point for many nations in the development of trade policies. From the horror and ravages of World War II there emerged a determination never to allow such destruction to happen again. Motivated by this spirit, the United States and some European countries took giant steps to make the entire world (and failing this, the free world) more of a united economic community.

The United States Takes the Initiative

One of the innovations of the Trade Agreements Act of 1934 was the use of tariff negotiations as an instrument of government political policy in international affairs. Shortly, the close relation of economic interests and political concerns was to be further emphasized. Even before the United States entered World War II, many Americans recognized the stake that we had in a world that was subject to aggression. Congress, therefore, modified our strict neutrality laws to allow an arrangement known as *lend-lease.* This trade agreement provided to Great Britain and her allies supplies desperately needed to carry on the war, and it left details of payment for a later date.

When we entered the war we increased our aid, so that by the end of the war we had handed over $50 billion to our allies. These countries, in turn, supplied us with $7.8 billion worth of goods during the same period. Most of the $42.2 billion balance was canceled after the war because we recognized that we had been fighting a common enemy and that repayment by these war-torn countries would impose on them tremendous sacrifices that might undermine what the aid had been able to accomplish.

Aid and Loan Programs After the War

When the war ended, the only major nation in the world whose production facilities were intact was the United States.

For the rest of the world, shortages of consumer goods presented a problem of immediate survival. Almost as pressing a problem was the lack of capital equipment, which threatened to make it difficult for the war-torn nations to solve their problems of scarcity and reconstruction for many years.

The American people rose to the occasion by showing a degree of altruism toward the rest of the world that no other nation has matched in peacetime. From 1945 to 1950, when our own domestic economy was in a period of scarcity (our aggregate demand was greater than our productive capacity), we gave to the world over $28 billion in grants and long-term loans. Most of the immediate needs we met through our contributions to the United Nations Relief and Rehabilitation Administration (UNRRA). That total reached more than $11 billion, of which the major share went to western Europe.

Early in 1948 we appropriated money under the European Recovery Program to help Europe help itself. The idea was initiated by our Secretary of State, George Marshall, and was popularly referred to as the Marshall Plan. ERP became known as the Organization for European Economic Cooperation (OEEC), and later the Organization for Economic Cooperation and Development (OECD). Much of the thinking behind the plan was to prevent the spread of communism because of the appeal communism has for people living in great economic uncertainty. However, there was also the recognition that a strong, economically healthy Europe could eventually become important for our own progress through increased trade.

Many billions of dollars of aid and loans have been granted under other programs. (See Figure 17–3.) Military expenditures under our alliance system have strengthened the defenses of the free world and have frequently provided dollars to bolster the economies of the recipient nations. Our aid for economic development for underdeveloped areas has shown how conscious we are of the importance of solving world economic problems to the mutual benefit of our own and other nations. One program that has cost little but has accomplished much in increasing living standards abroad is the "Point Four" program suggested by President Truman in 1949. It, like the more recent Peace Corps, offers technical know-how to countries whose workers lack such skills.

Today we can see how farsighted our aid policy was. Through rehabilitation and development of their productive capacities most European nations are wealthier now than they have ever been. Their prosperity and goodwill constitute a bulwark against the advance of communism. In addition we now export far more than we did before World War II.

Although U.S. government aid to foreign countries since 1945 has totaled well over $100 billion, there have been other sources of assistance as well. France, Germany, Japan, the United Kingdom and other developed nations have given substantial amounts of aid during the past decade. As U.S. development loans declined during the 1960's, commitments of the World Bank rose. American businesses have been investing billions of dollars abroad. (See Figure 17–4.)

General Agreement on Tariffs and Trade

Following the close of hostilities after World War II the United States took the initiative in expanding international trade. In 1947 we, along with 22 other nations, signed the General Agreement on Tariffs and Trade. Under the Agreement, representatives of member nations meet at

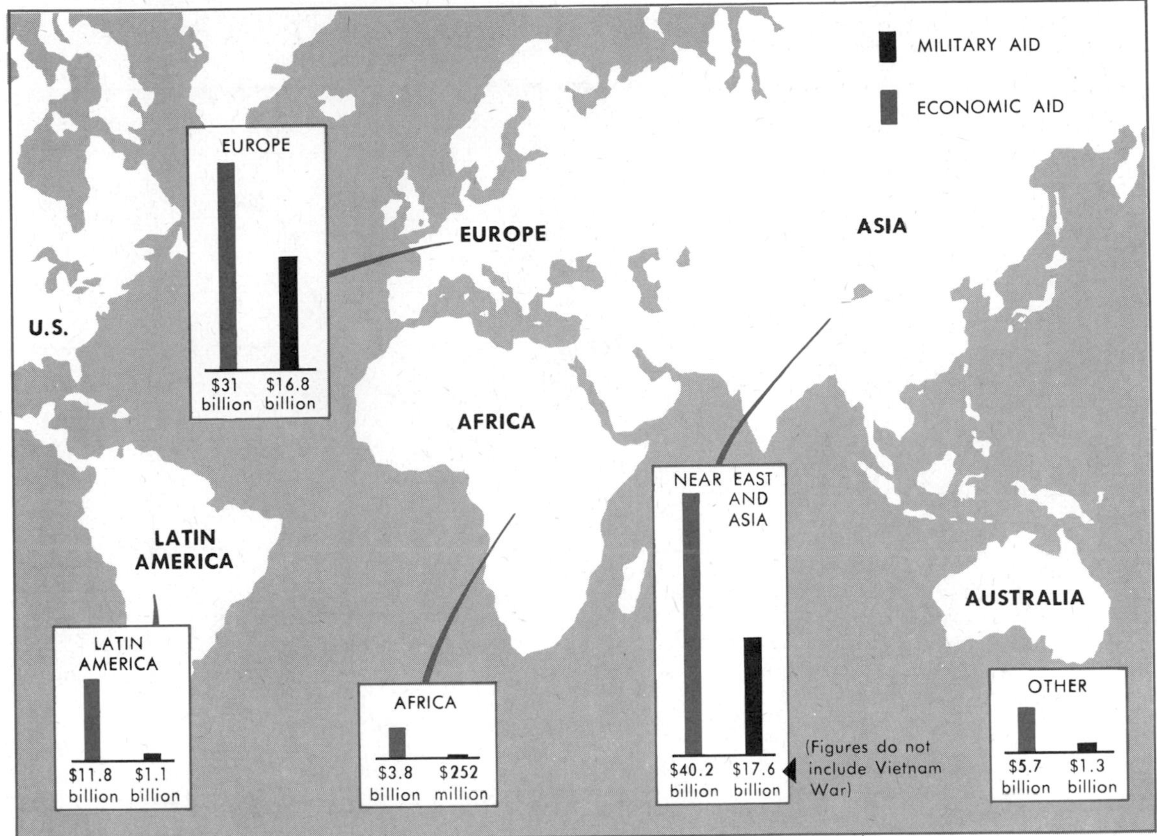

FIGURE 17–3 United States Foreign Aid, 1945–1969

Between 1945 and 1951 over 60 percent of U.S. aid went to western Europe. Between 1952 and 1957, less than half of U.S. aid went to western Europe, while the percentage going to Africa, the Far East, the Near East, and South Asia increased. After 1958, western Europe received less than 10 percent while the other areas listed received well over 70 percent. SOURCE: *Civic Leader*, Vol. 47, No. 28, May 5, 1969.

regular intervals to review mutual tariff policies and to set duties on certain goods. The Agreement has provided a useful framework for discussing multilateral trade agreements.

GATT, as the agreement has come to be called, is based on the ideas of (1) reducing tariffs through negotiations, (2) eliminating import quotas, and (3) applying the most-favored nation treatment so that there will be no discrimination against any nation. By the 1970's, there were 82 countries adhering to the General Agreement on Tariffs and Trade, and about 80 percent of world trade was being carried on under GATT rules. The major Western nations had joined GATT, along with many underdeveloped countries and some communist nations. The advantage of GATT is that trade agreements are negotiated collectively by the countries affected, and not simply on a bilateral basis. There is less chance that two nations will make agreements very favorable to one

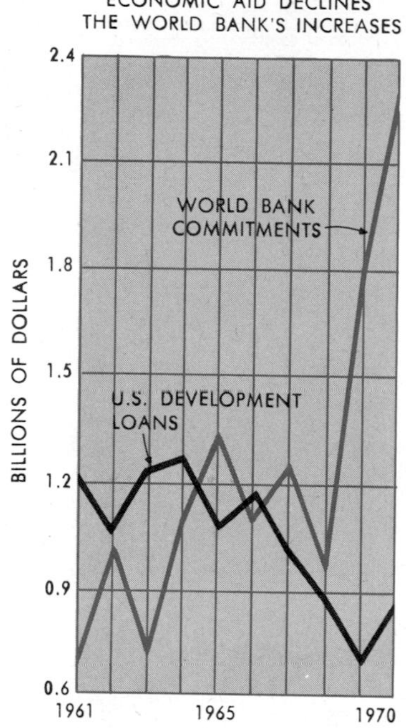

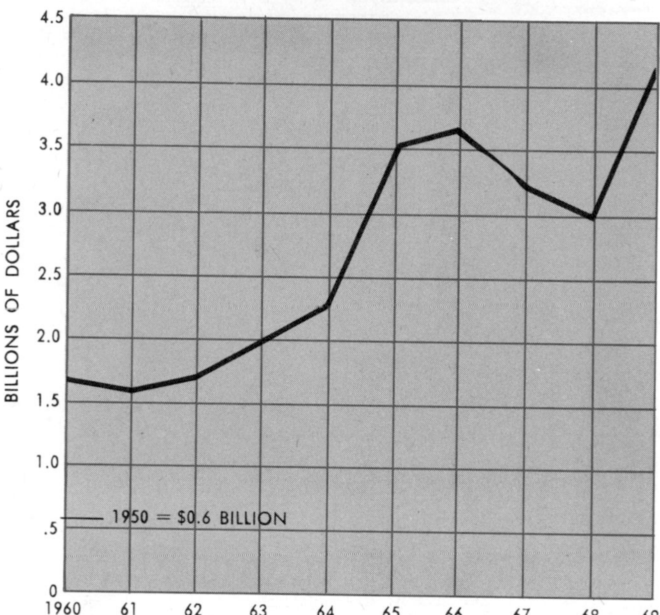

FIGURE 17–4 World Bank Commitments and Capital Outflow from the United States

U.S. foreign aid outlays have been declining. In 1968 our aid totaled $3,467 million. The total dropped to $3,151 million in 1969, and is expected to decline to $3,033 million in 1971. Although the decline in U.S. aid has been offset in part by aid, loans, and investments from other sources, many economists believe that the poorer nations are receiving too little help from the rich countries. (Over half of all capital spending abroad by U.S. companies in 1970 went to Canada and Europe—areas already rich and highly developed. Most of the planned spending for 1971 and 1972 will also go to Canada and Europe.) SOURCES: (left) New York *Times*, September 13, 1970; (right) *Economic Report of the President*, February 1970.

another but harmful to other contracting parties. The Trade Expansion Act of 1962 was designed to overcome disadvantages of the old bilateral approach and to supplement the policy for negotiations under GATT.

Starting in 1963 the world's major trading nations met in Geneva for what has come to be called the Kennedy Round of tariff talks. Each submitted a list of its "sensitive" products that it wished excluded from negotiations. The remaining products constituted a substantial portion of what is included in world trade. When the Kennedy Round talks ended in 1967, substantial tariff cuts had been agreed to on many goods. In the broadest tariff-cutting agreement in history, the negotiators cut tariffs on nonagricultural products by an average of 36 to 39 percent. Nontariff barriers, such as import quotas, were not affected, however. In 1970 in its annual report, GATT expressed fear that protectionists were becoming more influential than at any time since the 1930's. So GATT asked for a

"Tariff talks."

SOURCE: Ed Valtman, The Hartford *Times.*

new effort to reduce tariffs even further and to maintain the momentum of trade liberalization.

Protectionist sentiment continues to be strong among many groups in this country as well as in other major trading nations. Lower tariffs on agricultural products have been particularly difficult to negotiate, although the agreement by Common Market countries on an external tariff in this area is considered a "breakthrough." In the decades since World War II, progress has been made in furthering our international trade and reducing barriers to trade. But some observers think that it has been minor in comparison with what remains to be done.

Developments in Europe

In the aftermath of World War II the nations of western Europe also decided to reappraise their economic circumstances and trade policies. They realized that if they were ever to improve their economic position, they would have to forget their past jealousies and move toward some form of economic integration. The threat of Soviet expansion on one side and the encouragement by the United States on the other brought about a spirit of cooperation among previously feuding powers that even idealists had not dared hope for. The progress of these nations under the European Recovery Program strengthened their resolve for new directions of development, based on mutual benefit. What has emerged is a testimonial to the advantages of nations working together in contrast to the narrow policies of self-sufficiency pursued before the war.

First Agreements

The first significant agreement on economic integration to emerge in Europe was the economic union in 1947 of Belgium, the Netherlands, and Luxembourg called *Benelux.* Common tariff schedules for imports from other countries were set, tariffs between the three nations were reduced significantly, and plans were made for full economic integration for the future. The advantages of such an arrangement were soon evident to other powers.

In 1950, under the leadership of the French economist Jean Monnet, sometimes referred to as "Mr. Europe," France, West Germany, and Italy joined the Benelux nations and agreed to unify their coal and steel business in the European Coal and Steel Community. The success of this venture and the resolving of anticipated difficulties encouraged the six nations to move toward even greater integration.

The European Common Market

The next important step in economic integration came with the signing of the

Treaty of Rome in 1957, which launched the beginning of the European Economic Community (the Common Market, or "Inner Six"). The nations of the Coal and Steel Community agreed to eliminate all tariff and other trade barriers between them and to erect a common tariff for outside nations over a period of twelve to fifteen years. Furthermore, they agreed to coordinate other economic policies such as the free flow of capital and labor within the market and a common antitrust policy in order to encourage competition. These agreements were strongly supported by United States foreign policy.

The trade program began on January 1, 1958, with a 10 percent tariff reduction and a 20 percent increase in the import quotas on nonagricultural products for the six members within the Common Market.

Integration moved ahead so rapidly that the complete elimination of all internal industrial tariffs and the adoption of a common external tariff were achieved in July of 1968, 18 months ahead of the original schedule. As Figure 17–5 shows, trade among the member nations rose as tariffs declined. The great prosperity and economic growth rate of the EEC nations has been impressive, and it has become the second largest free-trade area in the world.

The Common Market has not always had a smooth path, however. In 1965 there were fears that the EEC might break up, as France (under De Gaulle) differed with other members over important policies. There have been differences over such key issues as admitting Great Britain to the EEC, forming a common defense against nuclear attack, how to organize a firmer political union, and relationships with underdeveloped nations. France and Germany changed the value of their currencies independently of the EEC's framework. Differences in tax systems and nontariff barriers still create problems. A

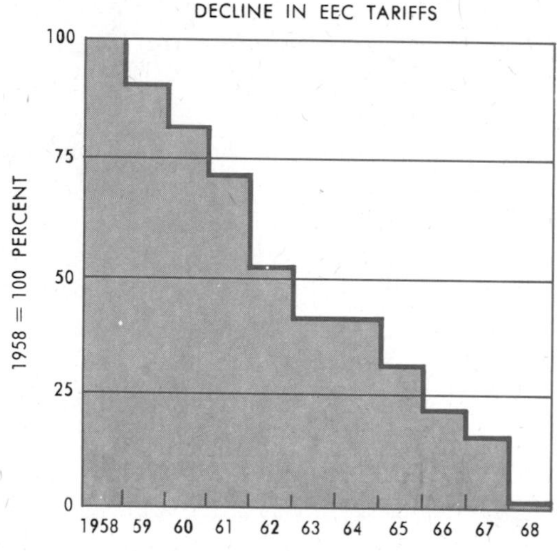

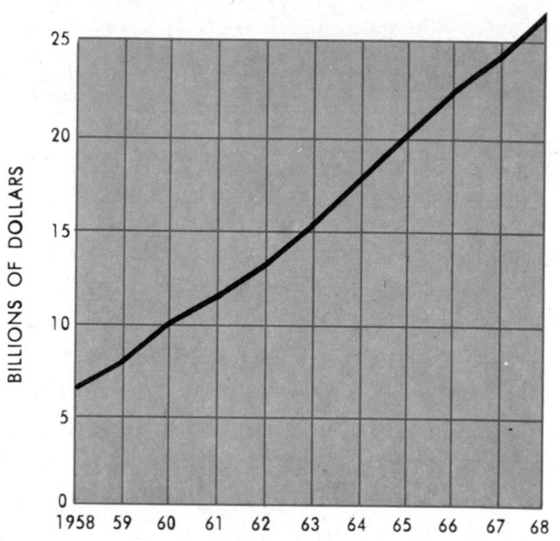

FIGURE 17–5 History of Tariffs and Trade Within the Common Market

From the beginning of the Common Market to 1968, when all tariffs on industrial goods were removed to member nations, trade rose by over 400 percent. SOURCE: Common Market.

TABLE 17–1 Growth of Trade in the Common Market (in billions of dollars)

	1958	1969	Increase 1958–1969 Amount	Percent
Trade among members				
Exports	$6.9	$36.5	$29.6	431
Imports	6.8	36.3	29.5	435
Trade with nonmembers				
Exports	15.9	39.2	23.3	147
Imports	16.2	39.2	23.1	143
Of which:				
Exports to U.S.	1.7	6.0	4.3	258
Agricultural	*0.2*	*0.4*	*0.2*	*78*
All other	*1.5*	*5.4*	*4.0*	*271*
Imports from U.S.	2.8	7.3	4.5	161
Agricultural	*0.8*	*1.3*	*0.4*	*54*
All other	*2.0*	*5.6*	*3.6*	*174*

Note: Data derived from statistics published by the European Economic Community with the exception of those showing composition of U.S. exports and imports, which are derived from U.S. Department of Commerce publications. Because of this difference in sources, the sums of the components of U.S. trade do not match the figures shown for the aggregates. SOURCE: First National City Bank of New York, *Monthly Economic Letter*, August 1970.

common system of price supports for agriculture was adopted, but this led to rapidly growing farm surpluses.

Nevertheless, the EEC has high hopes for the future. In 1970 a system of short-term support for members' currencies was established. By 1975, the European Parliament is expected to have strong budgetary power. Policies on indirect taxation and inflation control are to be harmonized, and joint management of international monetary reserves is anticipated. Full harmonization of domestic economic and financial policies is hoped for by 1980, with common positions regarding monetary relations with other countries and even a common currency. It is planned that the central banks of the member nations will become members of a European Federal Reserve System with a central board. The goodwill that engendered the Common Market also led to the creation of the European Atomic Energy Community (Euratom) for peaceful development and use of atomic energy, the Court of Justice, the Council of Ministers, the European Parliament, and the Coal and Steel Community (1952). If the United Kingdom, Denmark, Ireland, and Norway join the EEC, it will have a population greater than that of the United States, a GNP of slightly over half the U.S. GNP, and aggregate imports and exports valued at over twice the foreign trade of the United States. The United States would be well advised to maintain positive economic and political relationships with the Common Market.

European Free Trade Association

One unfortunate aspect of the Common Market is that its existence poses problems and a possible economic threat to other European nations that are not members. Great Britain did not originally want to become part of the Common Market because of her long-standing preferential trade and monetary arrangements with the Commonwealth nations. Britain imports large quantities of food and raw materials and puts very low tariff duties on these products in exchange for low rates on the products that she exports to the Commonwealth nations. If Britain were to join the Common Market with its common external tariff, she might have to forfeit the Commonwealth benefits. Until 1961 she did not consider this sacrifice worthwhile.

In 1960 another economic unit appeared in Europe when Britain joined with six other European nations—Austria, Denmark, Norway, Portugal, Sweden, and Switzerland—to form the European Free Trade Association (EFTA, or "Outer Seven"). These nations became a unit apart from the Common Market. They agreed to lower their own tariff barriers to Association members, but they made no agreements to set up a common external tariff or to integrate their economies in other ways. Although the EFTA nations have made progress in lowering their tariffs and increasing their trade, they have not had as high a rate of economic growth as the Common Market nations have had. In addition, the growth of internal trade within the Common Mar-

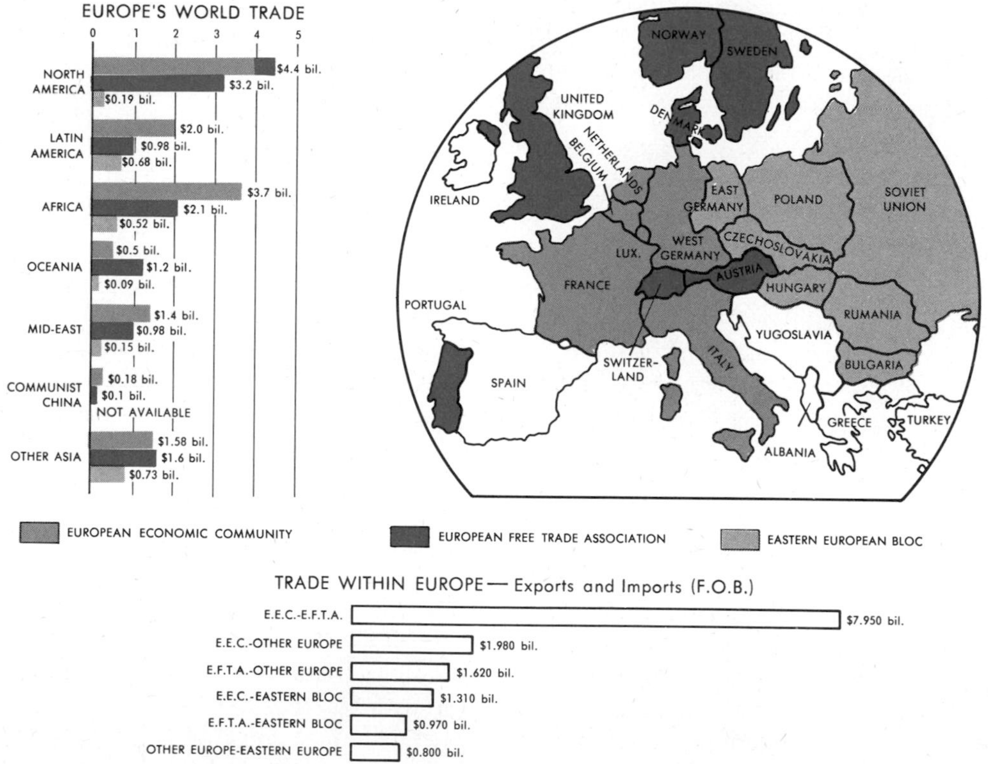

European Trade Blocs

The movement of the nations of Europe into regional trading blocs has led to a decline in tariff barriers, an easement in payment problems, and, as a consequence, the expansion of trade within each of the blocs. SOURCE: New York *Times*, January 21, 1966.

ket has been so great that there is concern that nations lying outside the Market may have their exports to Market nations displaced.

In 1961 Britain reached the decision that the Common Market offered her greater opportunities for economic development and trade expansion than she had under her existing arrangements, and she applied for membership. Other EFTA nations followed suit. In 1970 Britain, Denmark and Norway were negotiating with the Common Market for membership. It was unclear how their acceptance into the Market might affect other EFTA members.

Latin American Free Trade Association

Latin American nations watched with interest the economic changes taking place in Europe after the war. The success of the EEC led seven nations—Argentina, Brazil, Chile, Mexico, Paraguay, Peru, and Uruguay—to sign a treaty creating the Latin American Free Trade Association in 1961. By 1967 all South American countries, with the exception of Bolivia and Guyana (but including Mexico), had joined. Although tariffs have been cut or abolished on over 8,000 items and trade within the Association has increased considerably, the fact that benefits have not been equal for all participating countries has hampered negotiations.

Progress within the Latin American Association has been slow for other reasons, too. The resources and conditions for growth there are scarcely comparable to those of western Europe. Nevertheless, opportunities for economic expansion and increased trade do exist. Here, as in Europe, our nation's economic policy supported the new development. In 1961 the "Alliance for Progress" was signed between the United States and Latin American nations. Created to encourage economic development, the Alliance encouraged investment and technical assistance to promote development of industry, transportation, and trade. Some economic improvement in this underdeveloped area is already apparent. However, continuing efforts, together with political stability, are essential.

Other Regional Trade Associations

Regional associations are also appearing among underdeveloped nations in Africa and Asia. These groups vary greatly in resources and potential for trade and economic development. How successful these associations can be without a *customs union,* a common external tariff similar to that of the Common Market, is open to question.

The communist nations have also developed associations for trade, although these differ from others because of government ownership and economic control within each country. In part, these associations are a mechanism for self-defense; these nations have resented the expansion of trade in other areas of the world, especially in the Common Market. They also think that they could improve their own trading position with the West if no regional agreements such as EEC and EFTA existed.

A Democratic Alliance

United States policy since World War II has been aimed at building a stronger free world. It is designed to protect our country and its allies against the possibilities of communist aggression and to encourage sound economic growth and closer ties among these nations. Our greatest efforts were centered on western Europe, and the results have been dramatic. Now that the economies of those nations have been reestablished, we are directing more of our efforts toward meeting the needs of the underdeveloped nations. In the course of both these undertakings we have widened our own market and increased our own trade.

There is some apprehension that in assisting other nations we have created a potential threat to our own economic well-being. Will the Common Market prove to be a competitor so strong that it will cut into our trade, hurt our workers, and interfere with our economic objectives? On the other hand, is it possible for us to join together with EEC and other regional trade associations in the formation of a giant trade area, an economic association of democratic nations that could realize the potential benefits that should be obtainable through international trade? We will discuss this problem after we learn about another major barrier to trade, international payments.

Part C
International Finance—The Mechanics of Trade

Since the founding of our company that produces "Build-a-City" sets, the business has grown rapidly. Through expansion and skillful management we have been able to meet the domestic demand for our product. A recent survey of overseas markets has convinced us that demand for our product exists there also. Consequently, we have expanded production, with the intention of selling "Build-a-City" sets abroad.

It does not take us long to discover that exporting brings new problems to our business. Among these one of the most difficult is arranging foreign payment for our merchandise. In exporting our "Build-a-City" sets, we naturally want to be paid in our own currency—dollars. But how can other countries with different monetary systems pay us in dollars?

Companies which do business abroad receive payment in their own currency. French exporters would expect to be paid in French francs, English exporters in British pounds, and Japanese exporters in yen. This means that the French importer who is buying our merchandise must find some means of obtaining dollars in order to pay us. If he cannot obtain dollars, he cannot buy our sets, and our sales overseas will be reduced. In turn, trade between the United States and France will be reduced. International payment barriers between nations, like tariffs, can thwart trade. Let us see what methods and institutions have been developed to aid in selling goods in the world market.

How Foreign Transactions Are Financed

Importers and exporters in most countries need to obtain foreign currency to carry on their business. Suppose that in 1970 you wanted to import French perfume. You had to obtain some form of payment that would satisfy the French firm. Let's say that the cost of the perfume was 100,000 francs. Naturally you did not have any francs, so you went to a large bank in your city that handles foreign exchange. The bank informed you that a French franc was worth about $.18 in U.S. money. You paid the bank $18,000 (100,000 times .18) plus a small commission and obtained a special check called a *bill of exchange,* which you then sent to the French firm. This check is a claim on foreign currency (*foreign exchange*). It may be exchanged for other currency. The French firm took it to a bank in Paris and received its payment of 100,000 francs. The French bank could then present that check to a branch of the U.S. bank in France to receive its payment. If you had sold goods to a French importer, the procedure would have been reversed.

Exchange Rate under the Gold Standard

For many years gold served, at least indirectly, as the major means of international payment. The countries of western Europe, the United States, and many other trading nations were on the *gold standard.* Their monetary unit—for example, the dollar, the franc, the pound—was convertible to gold of a certain fineness. If the dollar was convertible to five times as much gold as the franc and both governments were willing to convert their currency to gold on request, the *exchange rate* was 5 to 1 (five francs to one dollar). This resembles the exchange of fractional currency to the dollar, such as twenty nickels for one dollar. Such a system is called the *gold-par rate of exchange.*

Fluctuations of the Exchange Rate

Currency, like all scarce goods, is subject to the action of supply and demand. When a nation offers attractive goods for sale at reasonable prices, other nations will want to purchase these goods. As a result the demand for that nation's currency will be great; if it were to circulate in a free exchange market for currency, its value would go up in relation to currencies that were not in such great demand. Under the gold-par rate of exchange, the value of currencies did not fluctuate much. If the demand for dollars were to go up in relation to francs, the French would merely convert their francs to gold and pay Americans in gold. There would, of course, be a shipping charge for sending the gold to this country; and it was this shipping charge, known as gold points, that determined how much the exchange rates could fluctuate. Because exchange rates were quite stable under the gold standard, international traders knew what foreign currencies would be worth. Stable conditions of exchange helped facilitate trade between nations.

Devaluation of Currency

In the 1930's, as worldwide depression set off a chain reaction of declining demand, many nations tried to stimulate their international trade by devaluation of their currency. To *devaluate currency* is to change the rate of exchange by reducing its value in relation to the value of other currencies. When nations are on the gold standard, they accomplish this by lowering the gold content (value of their monetary unit in gold) of their currency.

When France devalued the franc from $.20 to $.18 in 1969, it meant that each U.S. dollar could buy approximately 5.6 francs instead of only five. In the case of the perfume transaction described earlier, before the devaluation it would have cost you $20,000 to obtain 100,000 francs worth of goods. Thanks to the devaluation, you were able to get the same amount of perfume for only $18,000. One common effect of a devaluation, then, is that it makes it possible for foreigners to buy more of the goods of the country that has devalued its currency. By the same token, the French would be able to buy fewer American goods. In 1968, a Frenchman wanting to buy American goods priced at $10,000 would be able to get them for about 50,000 francs, for the *rate of exchange* was five francs for one dollar. After the devaluation in 1969, however, he would have to pay nearly 5.6 francs for each dollar, or about 56,000 francs.

The effect of devaluation on trade depends upon several factors. If France devalues its currency while other nations do not, then France can expect to sell more goods to foreigners, while Frenchmen will buy fewer goods from abroad. But if the other nations devalue their currencies at the same time and by the same percentage, France will gain nothing. All nations will be in the same relative position as before. The effect of a devaluation can also be offset by changes in the prices of goods. If the price of French perfume had increased by about 12 percent at the time of the devaluation, the devaluation would not have enabled you to get the perfume cheaper, and the trade advantage that France hoped to gain by the devaluation would have been wiped out. It is not likely that prices would rise immediately following a devaluation, but eventually they probably would climb. If the devaluation results in more goods being sold abroad, the price at home might rise because of shortages created by the rise in exports. The law of supply would then work to raise the domestic price and thus cancel out some of the effects of the devaluation.

Reserve Currencies

In recent times the devaluation of the dollar or the British pound has had special meaning. Because the United States agreed to buy or sell gold from other countries at $35 an ounce, our dollar was literally as good as gold. Britain, although not guaranteeing the conversion of the pound to gold, agreed to convert pounds to dollars. This, in effect, backed the pound with gold. Because these currencies could be converted to gold directly or indirectly (until President Nixon "temporarily" suspended the convertibility of the dollar into gold in 1971) and because they were so widely used in trade, many nations used the dollar and the pound as reserve currencies to back their own. As a result, a devaluation of either the pound or the dollar would affect not only these currencies but others which had dollar or pound backing.

Great Britain went off the gold standard in 1931 because prices in her economy were declining as a result of the depression. In order to keep up with other countries in her exports, her prices would have to continue to fall in order to compete on the international market. Adhering to the gold standard would require depressing prices at home as well as abroad, and this would aggravate the depression. If, however, Britain devalued her currency, she could try to keep her domestic prices up, but at the same time lower the prices of things she exported. The lower prices on her exports would result in other countries' buying more British pounds with their gold or currency.

This change in policy, however, helped the British very little because other countries soon followed her example. Preoccupied with their own national economic problems and following a policy of economic nationalism, most nations abandoned the gold standard. They were no longer willing to adhere to the fixed exchange rates that the system required, nor were they willing to buy or sell gold at a fixed price and in unlimited quantities.

Exchange Rates

After World War II, the "adjustable peg" system of exchange rates developed. Members of the International Monetary Fund (see pp. 434–435) agreed to define their monetary units in dollars or gold.

Each member established a par rate of exchange between its own currency and the currencies of others. To keep their currencies at (or near) par, nations set up stabilization funds which would hold supplies of foreign and domestic currencies. Thus, if an increase in the demand for a particular currency threatened to raise the price on the world market above the par rate, the fund could add to the supply and keep the rate stable. If the supply became too large, causing the rate to fall, the fund could buy up some of the surplus to stabilize the rate. It was hoped that these actions, along with the efforts of the IMF, would prevent competitive currency devaluations.

Governments take action to support their currencies. For example, in late 1964, after a long period during which the value of British imports exceeded that of exports, the pound sterling was sinking because of the decline in the demand for it. The British government started buying pounds with her dollar reserves in the world money markets to reduce the supply and hold the price close to the official rate of $2.80. Fearing that a devaluation of the pound would create havoc in the international economic situation, the United States and other major nations rallied to the support of the British with massive loans. In the fall of 1967, however, the British devalued the pound to $2.40. Since this was a relatively small devaluation (less than 15 percent), the other major trading nations did not attempt to protect their own positions by following the British example. (Seventeen smaller nations did devalue their currencies within five days of the British action, however.) Although some complaints were heard, the major nations were willing to let Britain devalue in the hope that it would help her solve her economic problems. An opposite situation occurred in Germany in late 1969. Because that nation enjoyed large trade surpluses, others demanded an upward revaluation of the mark. In October of 1969, Germany complied by increasing the mark's parity by 9.3 percent. An American wanting to buy German goods would have to pay about 27.3¢ for each mark instead of only 25¢ as before. Although this meant that German goods would become more expensive to foreigners, fears that Germany would suffer a recession did not materialize—at least not in the first year following revaluation.

There were fears of a world monetary crisis in May 1971, when many people holding U.S. dollars began to think that the dollar was overvalued in relation to the German mark. Dollars poured into Germany, as speculators hoped that the mark would be revalued upward. After a 20-hour meeting, the finance ministers of the Common Market countries agreed to let West Germany "float" the mark. That is, instead of requiring Germany to maintain a fixed exchange rate with the dollar, the mark would be allowed to rise in value if the demand for it increased, or drop if the demand declined. Three smaller countries—Austria, Switzerland, and the Netherlands—had to react because of their important trade relations with Germany. The Netherlands released the guilder from the fixed exchange rate and allowed it to float, Switzerland raised the value of the franc by 7 percent, and Austria raised the value of the schilling by 5 percent. American tourists abroad suddenly found that they received less when they cashed in their American travelers' checks for foreign currencies. (In Britain, for example, tourists had to pay about $2.50 for a British pound instead of only $2.40 as before.) Then, in August of 1971, as the U.S. balance of trade headed for its first deficit since 1893 and as potential foreign claims

TABLE 17–2 U.S. Balance of Payments, 1970* (in billions of dollars)

Transactions	Balance of Payments Accounts		
	Receipts	*Payments*	*Balance*
I. *Goods and Services*	63.0	59.3	+3.7
1. Mdse. Trade (goods)	42.0	39.9	+2.2
2. Services	21.0	19.4	+1.6
a. Military	1.5	4.8	−3.4
b. Investment Income	9.6	5.1	+4.5
c. Travel	2.3	3.9	−1.6
d. Other	7.5	5.6	+1.9
II. *Private Capital*	3.8	6.4	−2.6
1. Long term	3.1	5.3	−2.2
a. Direct Investment	.9	4.0	−3.1
b. Portfolio Investment	2.2	.9	+1.3
c. Bank and Other Loans (Net)	.0	.4	− .4
2. Short term	.7	1.1	− .4
III. *Government*	1.8	5.4	−3.6
1. Loans	1.3	3.3	−2.0
2. Special Liabilities†	.5		+ .5
3. Grants and Transfers		2.1	−2.1
IV. *Other*			
1. Private Transfers		.9	− .9
2. Allocation of Special Drawing Rights (SDR)	.9		+ .9
3. Errors and Omissions		1.3	−1.3
4. Changes in U.S. Reserve Assets	3.4	.9	+2.5
a. Gold (outflow is receipt)	.8		+ .8
b. Special Drawing Rights (SDR)		.9	− .9
c. Convertible Currencies	2.2		+2.2
d. I M F Gold Tranche	.4		+ .4
5. Changes in U.S. Liquid Liabilities	7.8	6.4	+1.4
a. Foreign Official Holders	7.6		+7.6
b. Foreign Private Holders		6.4	−6.4
c. International Organizations Other than I M F	.2		+ .2
Total	80.6	80.6	.0

* Preliminary
† Certain nonliquid liabilities to foreign official agencies

Note: Figures may not add up because of rounding off. SOURCE: Department of Commerce, Office of Business Economics.

on American gold passed $55 billion (while our gold stock had dropped to about $10 billion), President Nixon dramatically suspended gold payments and, in effect, ended the system of fixed exchange rates—at least for the time being. The dollar was now being allowed to float, and many currencies rose in value as compared with the dollar. Leading nations began holding conferences on the international monetary and trade situation, and economists nervously hoped that a new and better system would emerge.

The Balance of Payments

When nations have financial dealings with one another, it is very unlikely that the total value of goods purchased by one nation will equal precisely the total value purchased by the other. The nation that has made the greater purchases must make up the difference in payment. To determine whether a nation must pay or be paid by other nations, a statement, called a *balance of payments,* listing all transactions that a nation and its people have with all other nations, is prepared each year. On one side of the balance sheet are listed receipts (credits) and on the other side payments (debits). The total of receipts always balances with the total payments because the difference is always made up by the flow of money and credits into or out of a country.

What the Balance of Payments Includes

Table 17–2 shows a simplified picture of the United States' balance of payments. The largest single item on both the receipts and payments sides is the exchange of goods. Such goods are called visible items, since they represent tangible merchandise. Comparison shows that we exported more than we imported by a considerable margin, and, if this were the only item on our balance sheet, we could expect dollars and gold to flow into our country. In terms of goods alone, we have had and continue to have what many economists call a *favorable balance of trade.* Actually, because of our heavy spending of other kinds abroad, the flow is in the other direction—a condition called an *unfavorable balance.*

The word "favorable" is used because of the assumption that it is to our advantage to sell more than we buy. Many people, like the mercantilists of old, think of wealth in terms of gold instead of goods and services. If the gold were to remain idle, this so-called favorable balance of trade would lower our standard of living because we would have fewer goods and services. You recall that production, not money, is the true measure of a standard of living.

Other items on the balance sheet in addition to goods exchanged are, for the most part, invisible items, representing payment for intangibles. Payments of this kind which we must make to others include services to Americans abroad, investments by foreigners in our country that earn income for them, loans to foreign businesses and governments, and our military expenditures abroad. These payments may be made in dollars or gold (the dollars that foreigners earn may be exchanged for gold). Payments are made to us from other nations for services to foreigners, travel by foreigners in the United States, income that Americans receive from their investments abroad, investments and loans to our country, and military transfers under our aid program. These items earn for us foreign currency or gold with which to make our payments to others.

Changes in the United States' Balance of Payments

For many years after World War I the United States was a *creditor nation;* that is, foreign nations owed us more than we owed them. As our gold reserves and foreign currency holdings grew, we often had to lend money to nations with *dollar shortages* to enable them to go on trading with us. After World War II our various aid programs allowed foreign nations to continue to buy from us, and until 1949 we continued to have a surplus in our balance of payments. Our gold stocks in that year reached a peak, $24 billion, about two thirds of the estimated world total of gold.

From 1950 to 1970, with rare exceptions, the United States has had a deficit in its balance of payments, in spite of a

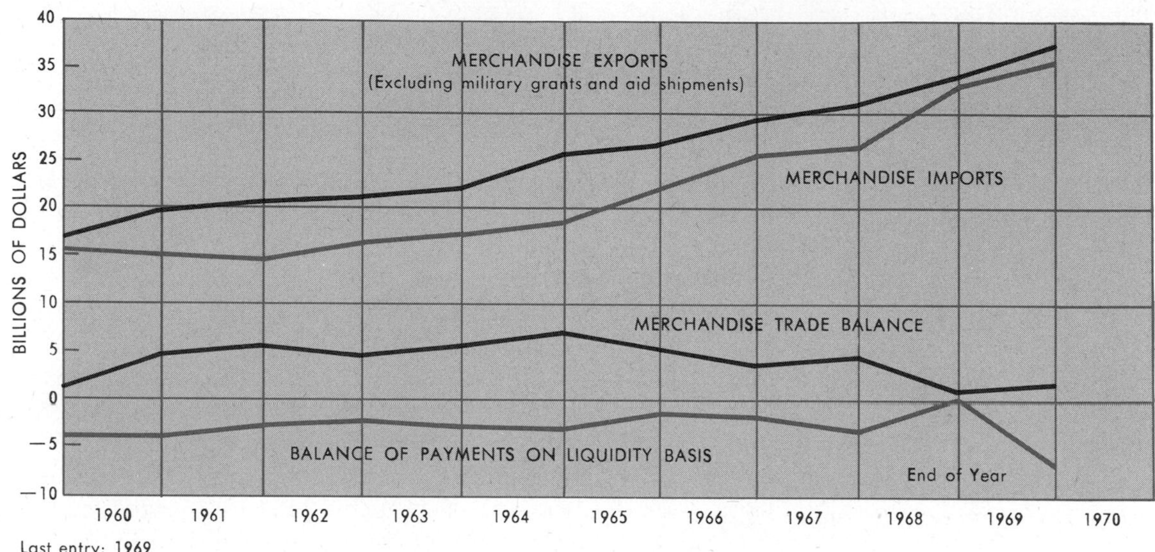

FIGURE 17–6 U.S. Exports and Imports of Merchandise, the Balance of Trade, and the Balance of Payments

Although the U.S. exported more than it imported during the period shown above, the "favorable" balance of trade became narrower toward the end of the decade. Explain the negative balance of payments during a time when the U.S. had a "favorable" merchandise trade balance. SOURCES: U.S. Department of Commerce and Federal Reserve Bank of Cleveland.

favorable balance of trade. (See Figure 17–6 for the situation during the decade of the 1960's.) Our nation's foreign aid program of economic and military assistance, together with most of the invisible items listed on the balance sheet, have more than used up the credits gained from the greater value of our exports over our imports. The resulting deficit in payments has compelled us to use our reserves of foreign currency and gold to pay our obligations abroad. By the end of 1970 the U.S. gold reserve had dropped below $12 billion, less than 30 percent of the world's estimated supply.

Of even greater consequence than the loss of our gold is that a very large portion of our deficit in balance of payments was made by giving foreign nations our short-term IOU's. If they should "cash these in" (demand payment in gold), our gold reserves would fall much lower than they have up to the present time. Indeed, in 1970 total dollar claims (redeemable in U.S. gold) held by foreign governments greatly exceeded the total value of our gold. Becoming a *debtor nation* has made us change many of our policies on trade and finance.

What does the deficit in our balance of payments mean? We were not seriously concerned about our deficit in payments until 1958, when foreign claims on our gold became almost equal to our gold holdings. We had previously built up such huge gold reserves that the possible problem of a deficit in our balance of payments never occurred to us. Today these foreign claims are even greater. If all these claims were to be made at the same time, we would not have had sufficient gold to make payment.

There was little chance that all our creditors would make a claim on our gold holdings. So long as other nations want to buy our goods in sufficient amounts there is little danger. However, American economic policy must now take our balance of payments into consideration.

Overcoming Our Deficit

A number of steps have been taken to ease the payments deficit. Military expenditure in Europe was decreased and our allies were asked to assume more of the burden of defense. U.S. military personnel abroad were urged to buy American goods whenever possible. Attempts were made to encourage more foreigners to visit the U.S. and to discourage Americans from traveling abroad. Interest rates here were raised in the hope that American investors would keep their money at home instead of seeking higher returns elsewhere. A tax was placed on purchases of foreign securities by Americans. As Figure 17–6 shows, however, these actions have been offset by the fact that the gap between our exports and imports has been getting narrower.

Because international trade is by far the most important item in the balance of international payments, it is essential that, until invisible items can be balanced, we earn a substantial trade surplus. In order to do this we must be sure that our products for sale abroad are high in quality and low in price. Moreover, inflation can no longer be considered merely a domestic problem. If prices of our products rise, foreign nations will look to other countries for less expensive goods. Making sure that our output per man-hour increases and our prices remain stable is an important way to insure the growth of our trade.

International Financial Institutions

Before World War II, two important financial institutions were organized in order to facilitate international trade and payments. The Bank for International Settlement, primarily a European institution, made it possible for the leaders of central banks to work together in arranging temporary loans to stabilize currencies and in considering other problems of importance to international finance. The Export–Import Bank, an agency of the United States government, was set up in 1934. Borrowing funds from the Treasury Department, it makes loans to help finance trade between our country and other nations. It has also stimulated private loans by guaranteeing their repayment.

Other international financial agencies were organized in the postwar years. Even before the war ended, representatives of 44 nations met at Bretton Woods, New Hampshire, and signed an agreement that created the International Bank for Reconstruction and Development, known as the World Bank, and the International Monetary Fund. The purposes of these institutions were to (1) help restore the war-ravaged nations, (2) aid underdeveloped nations, (3) assist in stabilizing exchange rates, and (4) facilitate trade by allowing nations to borrow currencies needed to pay for imports.

World Bank

By 1970 the World Bank had over 100 members, a subscribed capital of over $23 billion (over $2 billion of which was paid in), and was lending more than $2 billion. The Bank normally finances the foreign exchange portion of the costs of projects that, in its judgment, will contribute substantially to the productivity of the borrowing country. Loans go only to member governments, their agencies, or private firms carrying their member government's guarantee. The borrower must prove ability to service the loan and show that other sources of financing could not be obtained. The most common projects financed by the Bank are highways, railroads, and dams for irrigation or electric power.

The Bank has been a financial success and has earned huge profits. In fact, the Bank's conservative policies have been criticized for failing to aid poorer nations most in need of help but unable to meet the Bank's high standards. To supplement the Bank's activities, the International Finance Corporation (IFC) was set up in 1955. The IFC will make nonguaranteed loans to private enterprise in developing countries when private capital is not sufficiently available on reasonable terms. The IFC can also provide risk capital by buying stock in corporations and may invest in development banks that reloan to other institutions. When it was found that many poor nations needing housing, schools, hospitals, and the like, were unable to service conventional loans without seriously straining their balance of payments situations, the International Development Association (IDA) was created in 1960. The IDA grants "soft loans," loans made for a broader range of purposes and on more generous terms than World Bank loans. Loans are usually granted by the IDA on an interest-free basis (but with three fourths of 1 percent annual service charge) for a maturity period of 50 years. The IDA's resources are not great, however, and the gap in wealth between rich and poor nations continues to get wider.

International Monetary Fund

The International Monetary Fund serves a different purpose. It provides the largest source of international credit for short-term borrowing to facilitate trade. As with the Bank the borrowing nation must show how it expects to pay back its obligations. By 1970, 111 nations had contributed gold, pounds, dollars, and other national currencies to the International Monetary Fund in accordance with a quota agreement assigned on the basis of ability to pay. Many countries have borrowed from the IMF, including the United States.

The short-term credit available from the Fund is an aid in balancing payments between nations. If Italy were short of dollars, for instance, she could go to the Fund and buy the dollars she needs with her own currency. When her balance-of-payments position improved she would buy back the Italian lira with dollars or gold.

The Fund has served an additional useful function by obliging its members to make no change in the exchange rates of their currency that is greater than 10 percent of its original par value (value of a currency expressed in ounces of gold or dollars). Ordinarily, a 10 percent depreciation in the par value of its currency can help a nation overcome a deficit in its balance of payments. The lower prices of its export goods to foreign nations stimulate its international sales. If this adjustment does not help, the Fund may permit additional depreciation of the nation's currency.

During its first 10 years, the IMF's operation was somewhat of a disappointment. Its resources were not sufficient to meet the needs of postwar readjustments. Some nations disregarded their obligations concerning depreciation of their currencies. After the mid-1950's, however, the Fund gained prestige as a stabilizing factor in world monetary exchange. Nevertheless, there have been serious problems. During 1958–1968, for example, world trade more than doubled, but monetary reserves grew by only about 25 percent. Between 1965 and 1970, the gold reserves of central banks and governments declined. Consequently, the IMF members decided to create a new reserve asset called *Special Drawing Rights* or SDR's. The ability to create SDR's is like the ability to create more money when needed. The SDR's will be used in international monetary affairs much as gold was used; indeed they are sometimes called *paper gold.* With the acceptance of SDR's by the major trading nations, the world monetary system has been provided with a means of bringing about an orderly growth of reserves. The SDR's are being allocated among IMF members in proportion to their existing quotas in the Fund. Early in 1970, $3.5 billion in SDR's were created for the IMF members, the largest share going to the U.S. As Figure 17–7 shows, SDR's should play an increasingly important role in the future. They should take some of the pressure off the U.S. dollar, which the world has been using as a reserve currency and as a trading and financing currency. Gold may lose some of its importance, as the SDR's become the main growth element in world reserves. Most economists are pleased with this development, but it is also felt that greater flexibility must occur in exchange rates. That is, instead of attempting to keep the value of one's currency fixed rigidly, its value should be allowed to rise or fall gradually to avoid the kinds of crises that led to devaluations of the franc and the pound.

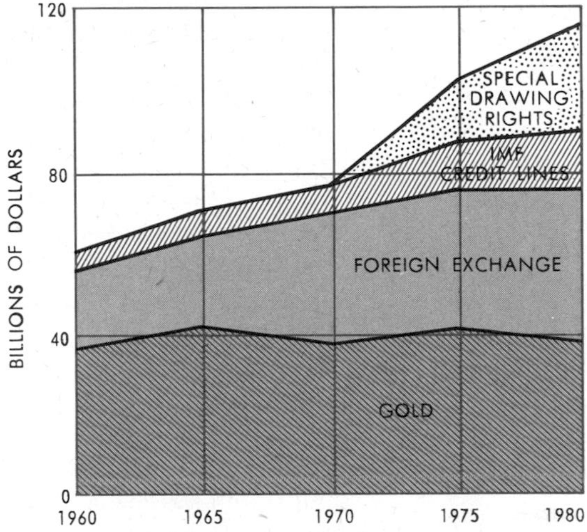

FIGURE 17–7 Changes in World Monetary Reserves

The graph shows the growth in world reserves from 1960 to 1969 and the expected growth from 1970 to 1980. Gold did not grow enough to meet the needs of a soaring world trade. The Foreign Exchange segment has been made up mostly of U.S. dollars. The creation of SDR's adds an entirely new dimension. SOURCES: International Monetary Fund for dates and *Business Week*, December 6, 1969, for estimates.

REVIEW: THE HIGHLIGHTS OF THE CHAPTER

1. Foreign trade is important because no nation is completely self-sufficient. Specialization in output by different countries offers the same advantages as it does within a single country. Most nations must rely to some extent on foreign trade for materials and products which they lack entirely or cannot produce profitably.

2. The law of comparative advantage shows how total production is maximized when each nation specializes in making those things in which it has the greatest relative advantage over other nations.
3. Among the reasons given by protectionists for interfering with the free flow of trade are need for a "favorable balance of trade," requirements of national defense, protection of infant industries, and protection of labor's wages and jobs.
4. The major barriers to trade are tariffs and quotas, although other devices are also used.
5. United States tariffs were protectionist in nature, with but few exceptions, until the passage of the reciprocal Trade Agreements Act of 1934. Shifting power to the President to negotiate trade agreements has allowed us to lower our tariffs more easily, although Congress retains power to allow exceptions. The Trade Expansion Act of 1962 gave the President additional power to negotiate trade agreements.
6. After World War II the United States took the initiative in helping to rebuild war-torn economies. It provided immediate relief with supplies of consumer goods as well as aid for long-range economic development. Technical knowledge and help to underdeveloped nations were supplied through "Point Four" grants and the Peace Corps.
7. European nations have responded well to the initiative of the United States by moving toward economic integration. This integration has led to the development of the Common Market (EEC) and the European Free Trade Association (EFTA). Other regional associations have been set up in Latin America, Africa, and Asia, but none has developed as fast and as completely and with such dramatic results as the Common Market.
8. International trade requires the exchange of currencies in the settlement of accounts. An importer must make payment to an exporter in the latter's national currency. If the importer's country lacks such currency, or does not have the means to buy it, trade may be hampered.
9. The rate of exchange is the value that one currency has compared to other currencies. For many years, when nations were on the gold standard, the rate of exchange was stable. Devaluation and the abandonment of the gold standard created great fluctuations in the exchange rate.
10. After World War II, exchange rates were stabilized in several ways, including the gold-exchange standard, the buying and selling of currencies by nations to keep their exchange rate in the money market close to their official exchange rate, and agreements under provisions of the International Monetary Fund not to make valuation changes greater than 10 percent.
11. A balance of payments is a statement listing all transactions that a nation and its people have with all other nations during a year. When payments are greater than receipts, a nation has a deficit, which results in a flow of gold out of the country. In 1950 the United States moved from a surplus to a deficit in its balance of payments. This continuing deficit became serious enough to necessitate changes in our economic policy in 1958 and 1971.
12. Several international financial institutions exist to aid nations in economic

development and foreign trade. Two of the most important agencies are the World Bank and the International Monetary Fund.

13. Controversy exists as to whether the Common Market represents a threat as a strong competitor to the United States' economy and trade or whether the growth of EEC may be the beginning of a more prosperous era for both the United States and the western European community of nations.

IN CONCLUSION: SOME AIDS TO UNDERSTANDING

Terms for Review

mercantilism
infant industries
ad valorem duty
peril point
lend-lease
Point Four
Inner Six
Alliance for Progress
exchange rate
currency devaluation
balance of payments
law of comparative advantage
favorable balance of trade
free trade
tariff
quota restriction
most-favored nation
escape clause
Outer Seven
foreign exchange
gold standard
SDR's

Names to Know

Benelux
EEC
Common Market
EFTA
David Ricardo
International Monetary Fund
GATT
Export-Import Bank
World Bank
Trade Agreements Act
IFC
IDA
Euratom

Questions for Review

1. The quotation "No man is an island" may well be applied to nations and their trade. Explain how this idea might be applied specifically to the imports and exports of the United States.
2. Foreign trade is a significant factor in the American economy.
   (a) Why can it be said that the standard of living in the United States is partially dependent on foreign trade?
   (b) Evaluate the statement "Although foreign trade represents only about 7 percent of our total economic activity, its impact is felt in every section of the United States."
3. Explain the following apparently contradictory ideas:
   (a) Nations should concentrate on producing those things which they can produce most cheaply.
   (b) It is often advisable to import some things that can be produced at home in order to help the total economy.
4. What are the arguments for and against tariffs and other trade barriers? Evaluate each argument.

5. Differences of opinion exist regarding the effect of tariffs on trade.
   (a) Make a list of possible barriers to the smooth flow of international trade and explain how each works to hinder trade.
   (b) How might freer trade affect the United States economy?
6. Defend or refute each statement:
   (a) The huge sums spent after World War II by the United States in foreign aid were necessary for Europe's salvation and our nation's own economic health.
   (b) The cost of foreign aid might well be a small investment for a large return in friendship and world peace.
   (c) American efforts at building European economic cooperation may, in the long run, result in a serious curtailment of United States trade.
   (d) Multilateral trade agreements, such as those made through GATT, are preferable to bilateral agreements.
   (e) The success of United States economic aid to Europe helped to prevent the spread of Communist influence.
   (f) Economic cooperation between the United States and Latin America has fallen short of expectations.
7. Discuss the following statements, presenting the facts involved and evaluating the general truth of each assertion.
   (a) Exports and imports are only the visible items in the balance of payments.
   (b) The invisible items may be just as important as the visible to a favorable balance of trade.
   (c) The United States has been forced to reexamine its economic policies because of a continuing deficit and gold outflow.
8. Explain:
   (a) How both the World Bank and the International Monetary Fund operate
   (b) What the major differences are between the two agencies
   (c) How these agencies contribute to world economic stability

Additional Questions and Problems

1. What major industries in the United States rely heavily on foreign trade? Find out approximately how many jobs depend on foreign trade. How is the average American affected by foreign trade?
2. Prepare a list of arguments to support each of these positions:
   (a) Favoring the policies of classical mercantilism
   (b) Favoring completely free trade
3. Compare the Alexander Hamilton–Henry Clay ideas on tariff policy with the Franklin D. Roosevelt–Cordell Hull policy in the following categories:
   (a) The United States' economic conditions
   (b) Influence on the American scene
   (c) Influence on the international scene
   (d) Resulting economic growth and change
4. Jean Monnet is considered the major architect of the EEC.
   (a) Write a brief summary of Monnet's work in the establishment of European economic cooperation.

(b) Evaluate this effort as a prelude to the establishment of a United States of Europe.

5. Trace the historical development of United States tariff and trade policies. For example, see F. W. Taussig, *The Tariff History of the United States* (New York: Capricorn Books, 1964). Relate each major law or event to general economic and political conditions of the day.
6. Make a study of the devaluation of the British pound in November of 1967, using newspapers and magazines of that period. What led to the problem? What factors involving the domestic British economy were relevant? What international factors were relevant? How were other nations affected by the devaluation? To what extent did devaluation help Britain to deal with her economic problems?
7. Make a study of the gold crisis of March 1968, using newspapers and magazines of that period. What were the long-run and short-run causes of the crisis? What actions were taken to deal with it? How well have they worked? What principles of economics are illustrated by this situation?
8. Make a study of the monetary crisis of May 1971, in which the German mark and Dutch guilder were allowed to "float." What caused the crisis? What were the immediate results? Why did some call this a "revolt against the dollar"? Why did some say that this was a "tactical victory" for the U.S.? Why did it make Europeans angry with the U.S.? How did this forewarn the action taken by President Nixon in August of the same year?

SELECTED READINGS

Balassa, Bela, ed. *Changing Patterns in Foreign Trade and Payments.* Rev. ed. New York: W. W. Norton & Co., 1970.

Baldwin, Robert E. *Nontariff Distortions of International Trade.* Washington, D.C.: The Brookings Institution, 1970.

Freeman, A. Myrick. *International Trade: An Introduction to Method and Theory.* New York: Harper & Row, 1971.

Ingram, James C. *International Economic Problems.* 2nd ed. New York: John Wiley & Sons, 1970.

Krause, Lawrence B. *European Economic Integration and the United States.* Washington, D.C.: The Brookings Institution, 1968.

Machlup, Fritz. *Remaking the International Monetary System: The Rio Agreement and Beyond.* Baltimore: Johns Hopkins Press, 1970.

Mikesell, Raymond. *The Economics of Foreign Aid.* Chicago: Aldine Publishing Company, 1968.

Preeg, Ernest H. *General Agreement on Tariffs and Trade.* Washington, D.C.: The Brookings Institution, 1970.

Snider, Delbert A. *International Monetary Relations.* New York: Random House, 1966.

Wells, Sidney J. *International Economics.* New York: Atherton Press, 1969.

Young, David. *International Economics.* Scranton: International Textbook Co., 1970.

Economic Development 18

THE AUTHORS' NOTE TO THE STUDENT

It is generally agreed that economic growth is desirable, although there are differences of opinion regarding the proper rate of growth and the means to promote it. In particular, government's role in promoting growth is a matter of considerable controversy. Most Americans want a better life in the future, if not for themselves, at least for their children and grandchildren. Practically everyone agrees that we should try to eliminate poverty and want in America, although again not everyone agrees on how we should accomplish this. These issues are only a few aspects of our concern with economic growth.

Economic growth and development are discussed in several parts of this book. Emphasis is placed on measurement and the factors that determine growth, especially the American experience.

A STUDENT'S NOTE TO THE STUDENT

There seem to be so many different things to remember in this chapter: the deflator, Okun's law, the Phillips curve, etc. It all fits in and it helps explain some of the "missing parts," but this "composition" didn't come to me until the second reading.

If I were to tackle this chapter again, I think I would read it over quickly the first time to get the broad picture. I would then return to the sections that need concentrated effort, like Okun's law, and learn these well. Finally, I would read to fit all the pieces together. It really isn't that hard, but it takes some time.

As a history major I found Part B on economic growth in this country very helpful. Frankly, I'm a little cynical about economic forecasting.

Part A
Fundamentals of Economic Growth

Raising the Level of Living

Nearly all people would like to live better than they do now. Most people want more goods and services than they now enjoy. It is sometimes argued that an increase in material wealth does not necessarily imply an increase in human happiness. Until someone finds a way of measuring the relationship between wealth and happiness, however, the economist will continue to assume that there is a high positive correlation between the ownership of more goods and services and human satisfaction. Certainly, no one has proven that a *decrease* in a household's stock of material goods makes people happier.

If our economy did not grow, one individual or household could achieve a higher level of living only by reducing the level of living of someone else. That is, wealth would have to be transferred from one household (or one sector of the economy) to another. One person could become richer only by making someone else poorer. Some economists feel that a certain amount of redistribution might be desirable. Pointing to the *law of diminishing marginal utility*, they argue that an extra dollar of income means a great deal of satisfaction to a man now getting $50 a week, but would mean very little to a man receiving $1,000 a week. The richer man would hardly miss a dollar if it were taxed away from him and given to the poorer man. Total human satisfaction could be increased, then, if some of the income of the rich were taken away and given to the poor. Our progressive income tax system is based upon this principle, for the upper income groups are taxed at a higher rate than the lower income groups.

Nevertheless, even the very rich often resent government actions which reduce their incomes. In a growing economy, everyone can enjoy a higher level of living without a major redistribution of wealth. The poor can be brought up to a higher level of living, and the rich can get richer. One group need not impose upon the other. Internal conflicts become less of a threat when an entire population enjoys a relatively comfortable level of living. Political and social unrest are all too common in countries or areas where serious poverty exists.

Growth Strengthens a Nation

Until such time as all nations and people become saints, national strength will be necessary for survival. There has been great controversy in recent years over the size and use of America's military establishment. Without taking a stand on this matter, it seems reasonable to assert that the United States is compelled to maintain a substantial military force relative to other nations. Potential enemies have grown stronger, and a growing economy makes it possible for the U.S. to support a more powerful army, navy, and air force. If our own economy grows economically, we can support a stronger military establishment with no hardship. If our economy does not grow, we could strengthen the military only by taking productive resources away from the civilian sector of the economy. One reason for the success of the Allies in World War II was the fact that America had great ability to expand its economy to meet wartime demands.

Growth Helps the World Economy

Today there are few economic problems which can be confined within national borders. The world's nations have become increasingly interdependent economically. Although America is more nearly self-sufficient than most other countries, we still rely upon others for many needs and wants, and others rely heavily upon us. If the American economy has serious problems, other nations will be affected. For one dramatic example of this, recall the *gold crisis* of 1968. Many foreigners felt that the United States dollar was losing its value in relation to gold and possibly in relation to some other currencies. The United States had not acted firmly enough to control its balance of payments problem and the problem of inflation to suit many foreigners who held United States dollars. They began to exchange these dollars for gold, causing the United States to lose gold rapidly and threatening the entire world monetary structure.

The United States dollar has been serving as a form of international currency. A lack of confidence in American ability to cope with such problems as inflation and balance of payments deficits raised questions about America's role as a world leader. This was not so much a problem of growth because the American economy had been growing at a rapid rate. We had not proven to the satisfaction of the rest of the world, however, that we could control that growth in such a way as to prevent inflation and balance of payments problems. A lagging growth rate would also have worldwide effects. Many nations depend heavily upon trade with the United States. A lagging economy could be reflected in less trade with other nations, thus damaging their economies as well.

Most of the new nations are desperately in need of aid from the developed nations. As we pointed out in Chapter 17, our aid to the war-torn countries of Europe after World War II was very successful in bringing about their economic rehabilitation. This has been to our own advantage, for by helping to strengthen their economies we created more markets for American goods, we enjoy many of the products now being produced by those countries, and we helped to erect barriers against the spread of communism. Similar achievements might result from aid to the underdeveloped or "emerging" nations. If we can help them to take their place in the world as economically and politically viable nations, we can reap benefits for ourselves as well. Violence and radicalism often feed upon human misery, and this can perhaps be avoided if our assistance helps those economies to grow. As the people of the new nations improve their level of living, they become better able to purchase American goods and to provide us with materials which we need. If our economy grows, we will be better able to aid the poorer nations without depriving our own people of their high standard of living.

A serious problem faced by many new nations is that of insufficient capital. In fact, they are often faced by the well-known *vicious circle* which is diagrammed in Figure 18–1. Per capita income is usually very low in the underdeveloped countries. Because they earn very little money, most people can save very little. Nearly everything they earn is used immediately for food, clothing, and other consumer goods. For capital investment to occur, there must be savings. That is, someone must be willing and able to defer consumption so that money can be put into factories, machines, and tools. With too little money for capital investment, there will be low productivity per man-hour. Low productivity per man-hour results in low per capita incomes, and the vicious circle is complete. Many economists believe that only through aid from the richer nations can the "have-nots" break this vicious circle, and that the most effective use of aid is to build up the poor nation's capital base. This will enable it to improve real per capita income by modernizing its economy. Again, rapid economic growth on the part of the richer nations makes it possible for them to assist the poor countries without lowering their own standards of living.

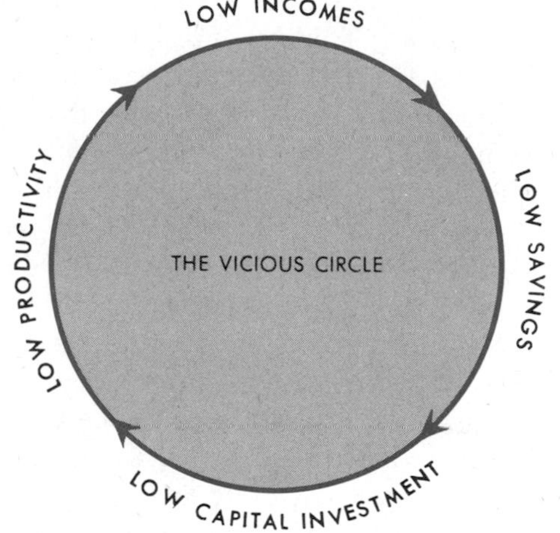

FIGURE 18–1 The Vicious Circle

Low incomes, typical in new nations, result in low savings, which in turn result in low capital investment. Low capital investment means that man-hour productivity is low because of the lack of modern tools and equipment. Low productivity means low incomes. How can the new nations break out of this circle? What does it imply for their national economic policies? What does it imply for the richer nations?

Measuring Economic Growth

Nearly every topic discussed in this book has some bearing on economic growth and development. In Chapter 12 we set forth some of the instruments or "yardsticks" which can be used in measuring economic growth—the GNP, NNP, NI, PI, and DPI. In Chapter 13 we analyzed national income and considered the problem of creating full employment without causing inflation, and we expanded upon this further in Chapter 16. It should be re-emphasized, however, that one does not necessarily get a true picture of the economy's growth simply by looking at the "raw" GNP figures, or the other aggregative measures. Only when we see that the *real per capita income* is rising can we say that our economy is growing. If we choose the GNP as our yardstick, we must adjust the GNP for changes in the price level and for changes in population.

By dividing the GNP (or any of the other measures) by the population, we get the *per capita* figure. We must also alter the GNP to account for changes in prices. Remember that the GNP is usually expressed in "current dollars"—prices of goods and services for the current year. It should be obvious that this can be misleading. If the GNP figure has increased by 5 percent during the past year, but average prices have increased by 6 percent, has there been real economic growth? Obviously not. We cannot say that there has been real growth unless the percentage change in GNP is greater than the percentage change in average prices. Now, if the population has increased by 10 percent while the GNP in constant dollars has increased by only 5, it is clear that population growth has outrun the increase in the production of goods and services. The level of living of the average person would decline, for more people would be compelled to share the limited supply of goods and services.

A figure known as the *GNP deflator* is used to measure average change in prices of everything that goes into the gross national product. It is the most comprehensive measure of price change that we have. Suppose that the GNP deflator for a certain year is 2 percent, and that GNP (expressed in current dollars) grows by 6 percent. The growth in *real* GNP would thus be 4 percent. In other words, only 4 percent of the increase in the GNP figure represented increases in the output of goods and services; the remaining 2 percent was accounted for by higher prices. By deflating the GNP, we express it in "constant dollars." The GNP deflator, which is provided by the Office of Business Economics of the United States Department of Commerce, adds together many price indexes. (See Chapter 14, pp. 330–332 for an explanation of price indexes.) The ordinary GNP figure is based upon current prices ("current dollars"). Then, each item which is reported (including consumer goods, capital expenditures by business, and items purchased by government) is divided by a separate price index (a deflator) to correct for changing price levels. Price indexes compiled by many government agencies are used by the Commerce Department. Recently, 1958 has been used as the *base year* (the year used for basis of comparison). In the spring of 1971 the base period for the Consumer Price Index was changed from 1957–1959 to 1967, but 1958 was still being used as the base period for the General Price Index as used in the national income accounts. The General Price Index is better than the Consumer Price Index for adjusting the GNP for inflation, because it takes account of all prices, not just the prices of consumer goods and services.

Deflating the GNP is a simple matter, as long as the deflator is known. For example, between 1958 and 1964 the GNP as expressed in current dollars rose from \$447.3 billion to \$628.7 billion. The deflator, meanwhile, rose from 100 to 108.9. To find the 1964 GNP in terms of "constant dollars" (dollars of 1958 purchasing power), divide \$628.7 billion by 108.9 and multiply the result by 100. The adjusted GNP is \$577.3 billion. This gives a truer picture, for the current-dollar figures suggest that GNP grew by about 40 percent between 1958 and 1964, while the real GNP growth was actually less than 30 percent. In Figure 18–2 note that the 1970 GNP in current dollars was \$985.2 billion. Expressed in 1958 dollars, however, it was only \$727.5 billion. It is the real increase in goods and services, not simply their value in terms of current dollars, that shows growth. In summary, then, to determine whether the nation today is enjoying more real wealth than it had in some past year, one must adjust the GNP for price changes and then divide by the population. This gives the *real per capita GNP.* If it is greater than the real per capita GNP of the previous period, the economy has grown.

Growth and the Goal of Full Employment

In the Employment Act of 1946, the United States Congress declared "that it is the continuing policy and responsibility of the Federal Government . . . to promote maximum employment, production, and purchasing power." Full employment, growth, price stability, and preservation of economic freedom were established

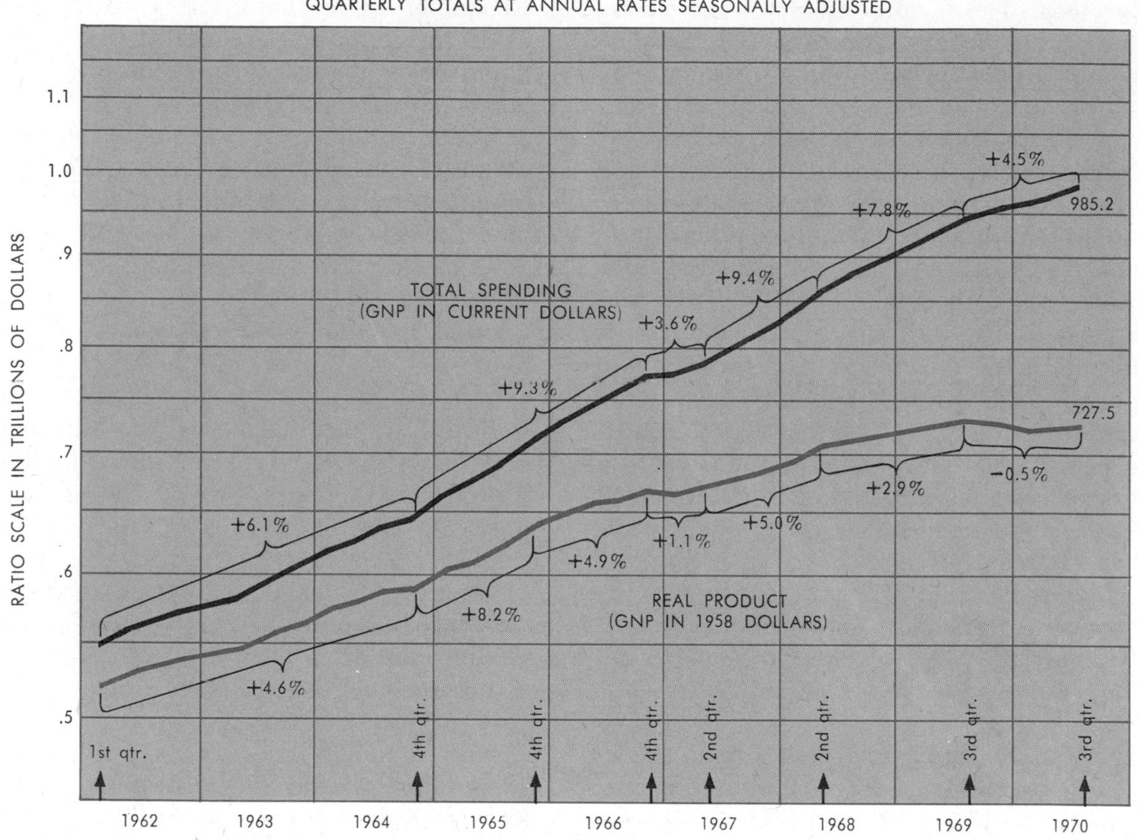

FIGURE 18–2 Deflating the GNP

The upper line represents the GNP expressed in current dollars. The lower line shows the *real GNP*—the GNP has been adjusted to account for changing prices. The percentages are annual rates of change between periods indicated. They are presented to aid in comparing most recent developments with past "trends." Latest data plotted: 3rd quarter. SOURCE: U.S. Department of Commerce; prepared by Federal Reserve Bank of St. Louis, *National Economic Trends*, October 22, 1970.

as American economic goals, either expressly or by implication. The goal of affording "useful employment opportunities . . . for those able, willing, and seeking to work" was not simply a matter of justice for individuals. When unemployment exists in a nation, growth is impeded because the nation is not utilizing all of its productive resources. The unemployed worker is the one who suffers the greatest immediate hardship, but society as a whole shares the loss. Goods or services which the unemployed worker might be producing are not being produced, so the total wealth of the nation is less than it could be. These goals are not easily achieved, however, and some of them tend to conflict. In this section we shall draw upon two useful analytical tools of economics to show the relationship between growth and unemployment. These relatively new economic concepts are Okun's Law and the Phillips Curve.

Okun's Law

Refer back to Chapter 13, Figure 13–1, and note that the actual GNP for the period shown in the graph fell short of the GNP that could have been achieved. Simply to provide jobs for new workers entering the labor force each year, the economy must show substantial growth. When productive resources are unemployed, the economy produces less than it could. Although our GNP has grown over time, the process has been extremely uneven. During the Great Depression, the GNP declined in absolute terms. During the relatively moderate recessions following World War II, the GNP rose in absolute magnitude—but at a below-normal rate. Let us examine the figures. Substantially full employment existed in 1929, and the GNP was $203.6 billion (in terms of 1958 prices). Then came the Great Depression, and the GNP (again in 1958 prices) fell to $141.5 in 1933. In 1959, the GNP was $475.9 billion. It rose to $487.8 billion in 1960. This growth was not sufficient, however, to absorb all new workers entering the labor force and all the new capital equipment. The growth rate was too slow to prevent unemployment of both men and capital goods. Indeed, the unemployment rate increased from 5.5 percent in 1959 to 5.6 percent in 1960. The American economy was not realizing its full potential.

If government wants to bring the GNP up to full potential, it must have a fairly good idea of how much additional spending is needed. This is true whether the government decides to achieve full employment by increasing its own spending, by reducing taxes, by lowering interest rates, or by some combination of these actions. If the increase in government spending falls short, or if a tax cut should fail to work as desired, the problems of unemployment and lagging growth will remain. If the government increases its spending too sharply or cuts taxes too drastically, total spending will rise beyond the ability of the economy to increase total output proportionately. The result will be inflation. (See Chapter 13, Figures 13–11 and 13–13 for graphic analyses.)

The first task, then, is to find the amount by which our economy is falling short of its full-employment potential. The "potential" to which we refer is the GNP which would prevail if all of our productive resources were fully employed. (Full employment is said to exist when the unemployment rate is no higher than 4 percent). *Okun's Law* (developed by Professor Arthur Okun, former chairman of the President's Council of Economic Advisers) expresses the relationship between the rate of unemployment and the desired change in the GNP. The formula is as follows:

$$\text{GNP gap} = 3 \times (U - .04) \times \text{actual GNP}.$$

"GNP gap" refers to the difference between the potential GNP and the actual GNP. The letter "U" refers to the actual rate of unemployment. The subtraction of .04 is to account for the fact that we usually define full employment as occurring when no more than 4 percent of the labor force is unemployed. The numeral *three* is included because statistics seem to show that a change of 3 percentage points in GNP is necessary to bring about a change of 1 percentage point in the rate of unemployment. For instance, suppose that we have a 7 percent rate of unemployment. To bring this down to the desired 4 percent level, we must reduce unemployment by 3 percent. Since the GNP must rise by 3 percent in order to reduce unemployment by 1 percent, we shall need a 9 percent increase, in this case (3 × .03). Now, if the actual GNP is $800 billion, we simply multiply that figure by .09 to find out how much must be added to bring the unemployment rate down to 4 percent. In this case, then, $72 billion must be added ($800 billion × .09). The GNP gap is $72 billion, and our potential GNP is $872 billion.

Assuming the accuracy of our data and the validity of Okun's Law, we have now provided the government with extremely valuable information. It must not be concluded, however, that the government should increase its own spending by $72 billion to solve the problem. As we pointed out in Chapter 13, the *multiplier effect* must be taken into account. A dollar that is spent by one person (or by business or government) becomes a dollar in income for someone else. If the recipient of that dollar spends it, it becomes a dollar in income for a third party. The third party may spend it by purchasing goods or services from a fourth party, and so on. In short, the dollar must be added several times in order to determine its effect on total national income. If it changes hands four times before the round of spending comes to a halt, the effect is just the same as if *four* dollars had been injected into the economy—each being spent only once. Thus, if government should increase its spending by $72 billion, the GNP would rise by a much greater amount. If each new dollar of spending by the government resulted in three dollars worth of *additional* spending, the GNP would rise by *four* dollars for every new dollar of government spending. The multiplier, in this case, would be four. The GNP would not increase simply by the $72 billion, it would increase by $288 billion (4 × $72 billion). (Refer to Chapter 13 to see how the multiplier is determined.) Clearly, then, the task of stimulating growth through additional government spending or through cutting taxes is a ticklish one. Indeed, if government action causes total spending to rise faster than the ability of the economy to produce more goods and services, the problem of inflation will appear.

When a GNP gap exists, there is usually disagreement over the action that should be taken. Some favor direct government spending to stimulate the economy; others favor a tax reduction. The multiplier, if known, gives an indication of how much additional spending is needed to bring about a specific increase in GNP. If we know that the multiplier is four, and if an additional $72 billion is needed to close the GNP gap, then the government should increase its spending by $18 billion. (Divide 4 into 72 billion. Multiplier of 4 × $18 billion = $72 billion.) If the government-spending approach is used, we can at least be sure that production will rise by $18 billion when government increases its spending by this amount. If the multiplier figure is accurate, the GNP gap will be closed by exactly the right amount.

If we rely upon a tax reduction, however, there is less certainty. At least this is the argument given by those favoring government spending. If we were to cut taxes by $18 billion, it is very probable that people would not spend all of the additional disposable income (the "marginal income") they received as a result of lower taxes. Some would be saved. If the *marginal propensity to save* were 25 percent, then only 75 percent of the $18 billion would be spent. The production of consumer goods would rise by only $13.5 billion because $4.5 billion of the tax reduction would be saved by the people. It is probably safe to conclude, therefore, that equal changes in government spending and in taxes will have different effects on the GNP. The picture is complicated further by the fact that when Congress changes the tax laws it does not specify how much is to be collected. Tax rates are set for various income brackets. Furthermore, as GNP changes, the amount collected in taxes changes. A rising GNP means that many people are moving into higher tax brackets and paying higher rates. Since the multiplier is based upon the spending and saving propensities of the people, and since these propensities tend to change as personal incomes change, the multiplier figure can vary as a result of changing tax rates. This means, then, that if changes in taxes are to be used to stimulate the economy, the government must do more than simply determine the tax reduction needed to close the GNP gap. It must also try to determine how the multiplier will be affected by changes in tax rates.

Supporters of tax reduction as a stimulus often argue that it is more in keeping with our free enterprise philosophy. Many feel that government should keep its spending to a minimum and should avoid interfering with the economy as much as possible. If the economy needs to be stimulated, they say, let the people do the job through additional spending. It is also argued that the effect of a tax cut is more immediate because workers' take-home pay is increased and will probably be spent quickly, while government may take considerable time to start the additional spending. Whichever side one chooses in this controversy is often a matter of economic philosophy. If we are in search of greater certainty, however, it seems that the effects of government spending are more predictable. Nearly everyone agrees that our economy must grow, but there is wide disagreement on how much and by what means. Next we examine the danger inherent in stimulating the economy and in attempting to bring about full employment.

The Phillips Curve

One of the annoying things about economics is that the solution to one problem often brings with it a new problem. For example, it is generally agreed that government policymakers were successful in ending the nagging problem of unemployment that typified the early 1960's. By mid-1967, the unemployment rate had dropped to 3.9 percent, but economists were then fearing inflation. One leading conservative economist asserted that unhealthy increases in prices would occur whenever the unemployment rate dropped below 5 percent, while many labor unions, civil rights leaders, and liberals were urging that action be taken to reduce the rate to 3 percent. The President's Council of Economic Advisers sometimes changed its goals. In 1962, when the rate was nearly 6 percent, the Council set 4 percent as an "interim" goal. In 1966, they decided that 3.5 percent was a reasonable rate. But the threat of inflation in 1966 brought another change, and in 1967 the CEA warned that the unemployment rate could not go below 3.7 percent without bringing about an "unacceptable" rate of price increases.

The problem is that the conditions which ensure high employment often lead to rising prices; and the conditions which guarantee price stability are very often associated with a disturbingly high rate of unemployment. The *Phillips curve* (developed by Professor A. W. Phillips of the London School of Economics) attempts to show the relationship between unemployment rates and price changes. Examine Figure 18–3.

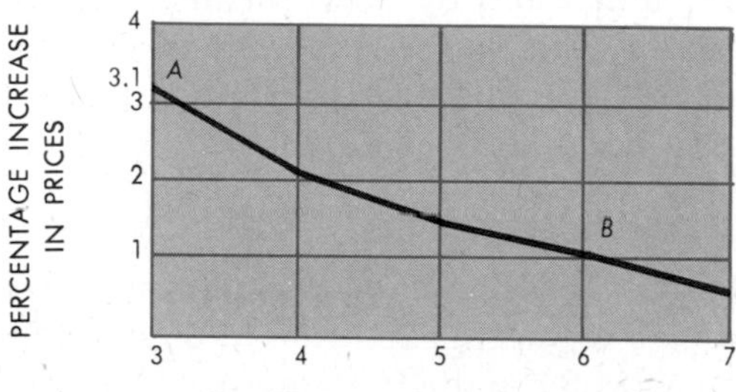

FIGURE 18–3 The Phillips Curve

Based upon the situation between 1953 and 1964, the Phillips curve shows that a 3 percent rate of unemployment would result in a 3.1 percent increase in average prices per year. A 6 percent rate of unemployment would result in only a 1 percent rise in average prices. If the curve were perfectly horizontal at zero, what would this mean?

Unemployment rates are shown on the horizontal axis. Percentage changes in prices (as measured by the GNP deflator) are shown on the vertical axis. The curve has been drawn on the basis of information provided by the U. S. Commerce Department's Office of Business Economics. The data are based upon economic experience in the United States from 1953 to 1964. Note point *A* on the curve. This indicates that an unemployment rate of 3 percent would be associated with a 3.1 percent increase in average prices per year. Point *B* shows that prices will rise by only 1 percent a year if 6 percent of the labor force is unemployed. (Professor Phillips studied the British economy from 1861 to 1957 in developing his curve for Britain's economy, and concluded that inflation would occur when unemployment fell below 5 percent. He found that wages tended to rise sharply whenever the unemployment rate was less than 5 percent.)

Some economists feel that the Phillips curve does not provide an accurate picture of the situation in the United States. The curve in Figure 18–3 might be accurate in terms of the 1953–1964 period, but it does not necessarily follow that it can be used to forecast price trends today. The curve is based upon conditions during a period of fairly high profits and moderate growth. When the economy surged ahead more rapidly in 1966, the curve failed to give an accurate picture of the relationship between unemployment rates and price increases. The curve must be used with caution, then, for conditions are subject to change. In 1953, prices were stable although unemployment was down to a 3 percent rate. By 1957, on the other hand, a 4.5 percent rate of unemployment was needed to ensure price stability. The Phillips curve can give us an approximate picture of the relationship between price increases and unemployment rates, and government policymakers can get a rough idea of how far they can increase aggregate demand (at least in the short run) without creating a serious inflation. This relationship is sometimes called the *job–price trade-off,* implying that in order to increase employment we must sacrifice price stability, or that we must accept a higher rate of unemployment if we want stable prices.

The Essentials for Growth

If economic growth is to occur, certain essential ingredients must be present. There are elements which must be present before a nation's economic growth can begin, there are problems involving the factors of production, and there must be efficient utilization of productive resources. These are considered below.

Political Stability

An inefficient or unstable government, political unrest, or a poor governmental structure often retards growth. There are nations which have great natural wealth and even a good supply of the skilled technicians necessary for the efficient exploitations of these resources, but which are stagnating economically because of political problems. In fact, a "flight of capital" often occurs when political unrest plagues a nation or an area, as those with investment funds send their money to other countries where political stability exists. Businessmen will not invest readily in an area where the weakness or inefficiency of the government renders it unable to protect property and to ensure a reasonable amount of tranquility.

Economic Unification

A highly diversified economy can be good, as long as a nation is using its resources efficiently. A nation may produce a great variety of goods and services and enjoy rapid growth. The economy should be unified, however, in the sense that there are few barriers to trade and exchange. Goods should be free to flow from one part of the country to another; good roads and other transportation facilities must exist to unite all parts of the land; there must be a stable system of money and exchange so that payments can be made anywhere quickly and easily; and the factors of production should be able to transfer from areas of surplus to areas where shortages exist. New nations which have failed to establish uniform standards of exchange, which are torn by tribal disputes, or which lack good transportation and communication facilities are suffering from retarded rates of economic growth. In the United States, on the other hand, the Constitution adopted in 1789 wiped out the restrictions that states had been imposing on each other's commerce and trade, thus creating a great "common market" in America.

The Spirit of Enterprise

The modern industrial nations are populated by people who have a desire for material advancement, who are willing to assume the risks involved in starting new business ventures, who are not afraid to experiment with new techniques, and who willingly depart from traditional practices which might hamper economic growth. In the underdeveloped countries, on the other hand, one often finds people who are satisfied with things as they are, who consider any change as being a threat to cherished traditions, and who lack the intense drive "to get ahead." Historically, Japan illustrates both types. Until the middle of the nineteenth century, Japan was mired in ancient traditions and isolationism which prevented progress. Then suddenly, the Japanese decided to adopt modern modes of technology and in an amazingly short period of time became a leading industrial, commercial, and military power.

Natural Resources

Nature fixes the supply of many resources which are necessary for growth. Some nations have an abundance of natural resources, while others are practically barren. The climate and the condition of the soil will limit agricultural development. Some natural resources, such as certain minerals, are nonrenewable. Once they have been exhausted they cannot be replaced. The United States is rich in natural resources, although there are serious shortages of some necessary minerals. (It is said that Americans could not have telephone service without some 50 different materials which must be imported from foreign countries.) No nation is so blessed by nature that it can afford reckless waste of its resources.

Technology

Natural resources alone do not ensure growth or a high level of living. Indeed, there are nations today with an abundance of natural wealth but with very low per capita incomes. This is largely a result of the fact that those nations lack the know-how which is a prerequisite to intelligent use of their resources, have poor transportation facilities, lack the commercial setup needed for marketing their resources, or have too few capital goods. Yields per acre are low in areas of rich soil, because the farmers lack the modern equipment and knowledge that would result in bountiful harvests. Improvements in technology can bring increases in productivity by making existing resources (such as labor) more efficient. While it is important for a nation to increase the quantities of labor, capital, and natural resources, if possible, improvements in quality are equally essential. For example, between 1909 and 1929 increases in the quantities of capital and labor accounted for most of the rise in the real per capita GNP in America. Since 1929, however, the rise in GNP has been more rapid than the increase in the amount of capital and labor can adequately explain. During the 1909–1929 period there was a 10 percent rise in output for every 6.5 percent increase in capital and labor. During the later period, there has been a 10 percent rise in output for every 4.2 percent increase in those productive resources. This is explained by improvements in quality—more technical knowledge and better education.

Human Resources

A nation's productive capacity is affected by the quantity and quality of its population. Obviously, the size of the labor force depends in part upon the size of the population. It is possible to have too few or too many people for efficient utilization of resources. During America's early years, there were too few people (about 5 million concentrated along the Eastern seaboard) for the efficient exploitation of our great natural wealth. Specialization cannot develop when the population is too small because families will have to do too many things for themselves. When most households had to raise their own food, manufacture their own tools, build their own houses, and the like, they could not become specialists in any one task. As population increased, it became possible for people to specialize in one thing and then to exchange their surplus production for the things produced by other specialists. Greater efficiency and productivity were the results.

Of course, overpopulation can also be a problem. (See Malthus, p. 453.) As we have seen, if population increases faster than the nation's real GNP, the real per capita GNP will decline. Because of the law of diminishing returns, increases in the labor force while the other factors of production remain stable can result in lower marginal productivity. Increases in the American population have not had the tragic results predicted by Malthus because these increases have usually been accompanied by great increases in our stock of capital goods, by the discovery and exploitation of more natural resources, and by improvements in technology and education. Because America is blessed

PARSON MALTHUS AND HIS THEORY OF POPULATION

Thomas Robert Malthus (1766–1834), professor of history and political economy, parish minister, and close friend of David Ricardo, is most noted for his book *An Essay on the Principle of Population*. Disagreeing with his father and with the utopian ideas that man could be perfected and was moving in that direction, Malthus predicted a dismal future for mankind.

Starting with Benjamin Franklin's observation that population in the New World tends to double approximately every 25 years, Malthus framed a theory of population. He said that there is a tendency for population to increase in a geometric progression (1, 2, 4, 8, 16, 32) whereas food supply tends to increase in an arithmetic progression (1, 2, 3, 4, 5, 6). This theory represents an application of the law of diminishing returns to the subject of population. The implications for man's future are clear. With a limited amount of land and an ever-increasing population, mankind is doomed to live in eternal misery. Increasing the output of food would be of little lasting benefit because it would eventually result in a higher birth rate.

In the past, war and pestilence and famine held the population in check. However, with improvements in health and living conditions, these means could no longer be sufficient or acceptable. Ricardo recommended moral restraint as a primary solution, as well as late marriages, discontinuing aid to the poor, and keeping wages at a low level. Harsh though these remedies seemed, they were essential to keep population within limits for which food could be available.

Malthus did not foresee either the tremendous increase in productivity that would be brought about by the Industrial Revolution or the eventual reduction that would take place in the birth rate in highly industrialized countries. Nevertheless, when the present situation of rapid population expansion and slow rate of economic growth among the emerging nations is considered, many wonder whether Malthus' conclusions may not be correct and his theory of population still relevant.

---

with so much natural wealth and other productive resources, the law of diminishing returns (as the labor supply has increased) has not had the same effect as in other nations. Note, for example, India's population in relation to her land base and the United States population in relation to our land base. Our capacity to produce food has outrun the rise in population, enabling us actually to produce more than we need and to shift resources from agriculture to other pursuits. The *optimum population* is the population size at which a nation's real per capita income (or real per capita output) is highest. Figure 18–4 illustrates this.

First, examine the lower curve. In this imaginary situation we see that the nation's per capita output rises as its population grows until it reaches 200 million persons (point *A* on the curve). This is because greater specialization becomes possible as the population grows in relation to the other productive resources. At 200 million persons, per capita real output (and income) is $1,000. As the population continues to increase, however, the per capita output declines. The law of diminishing returns is making itself felt, for capital and natural resources are being overly utilized and each worker has fewer capital goods and materials with which to work. Population is growing faster than the nation's capacity to produce, so the average person must accept a smaller piece of the national pie.

The upper curve indicates the effects of an increase in the nation's supply of

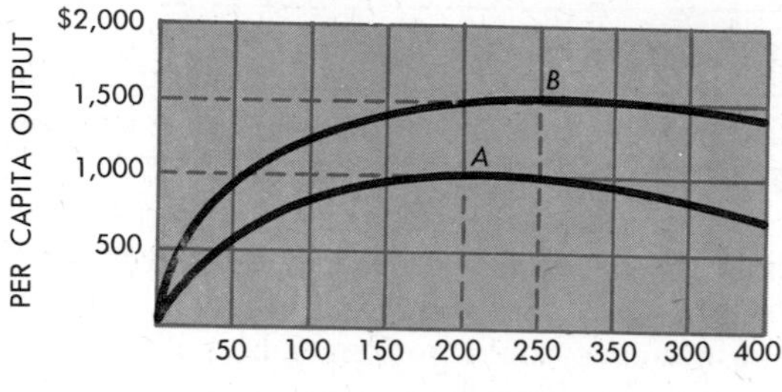

FIGURE 18–4 Optimum Population Curves

The lower curve depicts a nation with an optimum population of 200 million. At that level, the per capita output is at its highest possible point—$1,000. When improvements in technology, additions to the nation's stock of capital goods, or new sources of raw material shift the curve upward, the nation's optimum population will be 250 million, and the per capita income will be $1,500. What is the nation's real GNP in each of these hypothetical cases?

natural resources, of capital goods, or of improved technology. The optimum is now 250 million people (point *B* on the curve), and the nation can support more people at a higher level of living. Per capita output at the optimum population level is now $1,500. It should be noted, however, that in reality it is difficult to say what a nation's optimum population is, because relevant conditions are always changing.

The *quality of the population* is as important as its size. Most modern industrial nations have a high-quality population. Workers are well trained and educated, they are in good health, they usually submit to "industrial discipline" (getting to work on time, for instance), and they regard labor as respectable. In many of the underdeveloped lands, on the other hand, illiteracy, lack of training, poor health, high percentages of very old or very young people, and the viewing of labor as "lower caste" are all too common. The *labor population* of a nation is determined by deducting from the total population figure the numbers of children, old people, the disabled, those living entirely on property incomes, those who do not wish to work, and others who are not employable. The labor population produces everything for the *consumer population,* which is the entire population.

As some industries decline while others rise, and as education changes, the composition of the labor force changes. For example, the farm population in 1915 was 32.4 percent of the total United States population; by 1970 only about 5 percent were living on farms. American manpower devoted to agriculture, fishing, and forestry has declined from over 50 percent in 1880 to less than 10 percent today. The percentage of workers engaged in public service, the professions, transportation, finance, trade, and public utilities has risen meanwhile. The relative size of age groups has changed also. Those between 18 and 65 are considered to be of *working age.* The *dependent age groups* are those too old or too young to work. In 1950 there were 64.4 people below 18 or over 65 for every 100 persons of working age, giving us a *dependency ratio* of 64.4. In 1964, the dependency ratio was 85, meaning that for every 100 persons of working age there were 85 who were either too young or too old to work. By 1968, the dependent age groups made up over 45 percent of the total population. In the early 1960's, the dependent age groups accounted for the largest gains in the American population. (It is expected, however, that the population in the working age group will grow much more rapidly in the 1970's and 1980's.) On the other hand, gains in technology and education can make it possible for the existing labor force (about 40 percent of the total population) to support more people. In 1950 the median years of school completed by persons (aged 25 years and older) in the civilian labor force was 9.9. By 1969 this had risen to 12.3 years, and by 1985 it is expected to be 12.6 years. Also, there have been steady increases in output per man-hour.

Capital Formation

The importance of capital has been stressed earlier in this chapter. The efforts of workers would result in low man-hour productivity if those workers were equipped with nothing more than their bare hands. Capital goods, which include everything from such a simple tool as a hammer to highly complex machinery and plants, greatly increase the productivity of labor. One of the reasons why the productivity of American workers is usually so much greater than that of foreign workers is that Americans have better machinery, tools, and equipment with which to work. By 1970, the amount of capital invested per production worker in American manufacturing exceeded $24,000—as compared with a little over $5,000 in 1939. Of course, there are vast differences among industries. In the apparel industry, about $6,000 was being invested per production worker in 1970, while in petroleum the figure was over $170,000.

There has been a tremendous increase in America's stock of capital goods. The percentage of GNP accounted for by gross capital formation (GCF) is the *gross capital formation* rate. Thus, if our GNP is $800 billion, and if $80 billion of that total is spent on capital formation, the GCF is 10 percent. Between the end of the Civil War and World War I, about 25 percent of the real GNP was devoted to private domestic investment. During the depths of the Great Depression (1932), less than 4 percent of GNP was devoted to private domestic investment. Since World War II, approximately 15 percent of real GNP has been devoted to capital formation. (Of course, some capital items are publicly produced. These include public schools, roads, airports, and the like. Capital items produced by government are referred to as *social capital.*) In 1970, America's total stock of capital goods was six times that of 1900.

We should take into account, however, the fact that some of the new capital goods are used to replace old, obsolete, or worn-out capital items. Thus, we must deduct depreciation from the gross capital formation figure to get *net capital formation.* For instance, if $60 billion were spent on capital formation, but $20 billion of this simply replaced capital items that had worn out or become obsolete, the net capital formation would be only $40 billion. Indeed, it is possible for the net capital formation rate (NCF) to be zero or even to be negative. In some of the underdeveloped countries, capital is being used up faster than it is being replaced. Thus, the NCF would be negative. This has even happened in the United States. During the worst years of the Great Depression and during World War II, gross private domestic investment was not as large as the depreciation occurring. We had a *gross* capital formation rate of 3.3 percent in 1932, but the *net* figure was a *minus* 25 percent.

In recent years, the highest capital formation rates have usually been found in communist nations, where as much as 30 percent of GNP may be devoted to capital formation. In modern free enterprise countries, the GCF has been between 15 and 25 percent. In underdeveloped countries, rates between 5 and 15 percent are common, but NCF is often much lower.

Production Possibilities Frontier

At any particular time, there is a limit to the amount of goods and services that a nation can produce with its existing resources. This may be referred to as its *production possibilities frontier.* If a nation is fully and efficiently using its existing resources, it is producing on the production possibilities frontier. A decision must be made, however, as to the type of things produced. If we are fully and efficiently using our resources, and we decide that we need more military hardware, we can increase our stock of military goods only by decreasing our production of something else. Capital, labor, and materials will be shifted away from some other item (such as passenger cars) to the production of tanks, planes, guns, etc. In order to get more military goods, we must sacrifice nonmilitary goods. The *real cost* of the new military hardware will be the nonmilitary goods which we sacrifice. If we decide to promote economic growth by increasing our stock of capital goods, we must sacrifice consumer goods in order to do so. The production possibilities curve is a convenient device for illustrating this point.

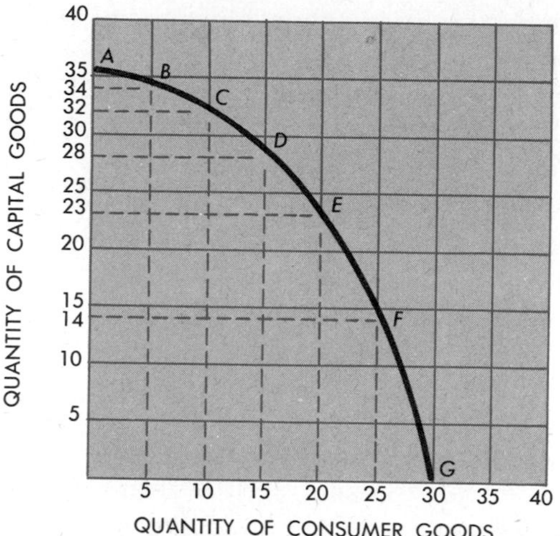

FIGURE 18–5 Production Possibilities Curve

We have divided the nation's output into two types of goods—capital goods and consumer goods. In this imaginary situation, the curve shows how many units of each type can be produced if the nation is fully and efficiently utilizing its resources. At point *A* we can produce 35 units of capital goods but no consumer goods. At point *G* we can produce 30 units of consumer goods but no capital goods. At point *F* we can have 14 units of capital goods and 25 units of consumer goods. How does this curve illustrate the law of increasing costs?

Figure 18–5 illustrates an imaginary production possibilities frontier. Capital goods are shown on the vertical axis; consumer goods on the horizontal. If the nation were producing at point *A* on the production possibilities curve, it would turn out 35 units of capital goods, but no consumer goods at all. This would hardly be desirable, for the people would have machines, tools, factories, etc., but no shoes, food, and other items that provide immediate consumer satisfaction. If the nation produced at point *G,* it would turn out 30 units of consumer goods, but no capital goods at all.[1] Society would enjoy a great deal of food, clothing, cosmetics, and other consumer goods, but it would

[1] At this point the inquisitive student might be raising a few questions. What are "units" of capital goods and "units" of consumer goods? The "units" can be anything we find convenient for our purpose. We could have said "capital goods in billions of dollars" and "consumer goods in billions of dollars." Since we have divided all the nation's output (by definition) into consumer goods and capital goods, the sum of the two actually produced would be the nation's GNP. Where does government enter the picture, in view of the fact that we talked about $C + I + G$ in Chapter 13? We have arbitrarily decided to include all public goods in one category or the other. Thus, social capital (government spending for roads, schools, etc.) has been included in the category "capital goods."

regret this in the future. Existing capital goods would be wearing out, and eventually there would be a decline in the output of consumer goods because the capital items needed to produce them would be disappearing. Since both extremes are undesirable, then, where should a nation produce on its production possibilities curve? There is no simple answer. Each society must make a choice, and ideally it should try to strike the right balance between capital and consumer goods. If, in this case, the nation chooses point *F* on the curve, it would produce 14 units of capital goods and 25 units of consumer goods. About 36 percent of its total output would be devoted to capital formation.

In choosing to sacrifice consumer goods to produce more capital items (or vice versa), society must consider the *law of increasing costs*. To see how this works, we can construct a table based upon the curve in Figure 18–5 showing the various production possibilities. Table 18–1 shows the alternatives open to society, by indicating how many units of consumer goods the nation can have if it produces a certain number of units of capital goods. It also shows how much of one item we must sacrifice in order to get more of the other. At each step, check the table against the curve in Figure 18–5.

When we moved from point *A* to point *B*, we sacrificed one unit of capital goods and gained five units of consumer goods. When we moved from *B* to *C*, we sacrificed two units of capital goods to gain five units of consumer goods. Moving from *C* to *D*, we give up four units of capital goods to get five more units of consumer goods. At each succeeding step, the sacrifice of capital goods becomes greater. Finally, we have to sacrifice 14 units of capital goods to get five more units of consumer goods. Why does this occur? It occurs because productive resources are not always perfectly adaptable to alternative uses. At first, as we shifted some of our resources from the production of capital goods to the production of consumer goods, we experienced a large gain in the latter. We took resources that were not well suited to capital goods production and began using them more efficiently to turn out consumer goods. After a time, however, we started to shift resources away from the production of capital goods which were really not well suited for the production of consumer goods. Thus, the real cost of producing more consumer items rose, for we had to sacrifice larger and larger numbers of capital goods.[2] (The curve is sometimes called a *transformation curve* because, in effect, we are transforming capital goods into consumer goods when we take resources away from the production of the former to increase our output of the latter.)

Up to this point we have assumed that the nation is using its productive resources fully and efficiently. Of course this is not always true in real life. If there is unemployment, or if technical inefficiency exists, the nation will not be producing at some point on the curve. It will be producing somewhere *inside* the curve.

The solid black curve in Figure 18–6 shows us what the nation *could* be producing if it were using all resources efficiently. The point marked *U* shows us where it is actually producing. In this

[2] Suppose that the law of increasing costs did *not* apply, and that constant costs were experienced instead. This would mean that each sacrifice of capital goods would yield an equal increase in consumer goods. The curve would no longer be concave in relation to the origin. Use a ruler to draw a straight line from 30 on the vertical axis to 30 on the horizontal. Set up a production possibilities table based upon your new "curve" to prove this point. (What would the curve look like if *decreasing* costs were experienced?)

TABLE 18–1 Production Possibilities Schedule

Possibilities	Capital Goods	Consumer Goods	Sacrifice of Capital Goods	Gain of Consumer Goods
A	35	0	0	0
B	34	5	1	5
C	32	10	2	5
D	28	15	4	5
E	23	20	5	5
F	14	25	9	5
G	0	30	14	5

case, it is producing 10 units of capital goods and 10 of consumer goods. If the nation could achieve full employment and/or could use its resources with maximum efficiency it could produce much more of either or both items. Note the arrow marked X. This indicates that the nation could continue to produce 10 units of capital goods and could increase its output of consumer goods from 10 to about 23. Note arrow Z. This shows that the nation could continue to produce 10 units of consumer goods and raise the output of capital goods to about 27. There are, of course, many other possible combinations. Arrow Y suggests that the nation could have 20 units of capital goods and about 17 units of consumer goods. In any event, unemployment, underemployment, and inefficiency result in a denial to the public of goods and services they could be enjoying. (If we were to draw a production possibilities curve for the United States showing the situation in 1933, would we be producing at a point *on* or *inside* the curve?)

It is impossible to say exactly which point on the curve is best for a nation, because conditions are always changing. However, every nation should attempt to achieve a good balance between capital and consumer goods. Suppose a nation chooses to devote its productive capacity very largely to consumer goods, at the expense of capital formation. Its consumers might be affluent for a while, but

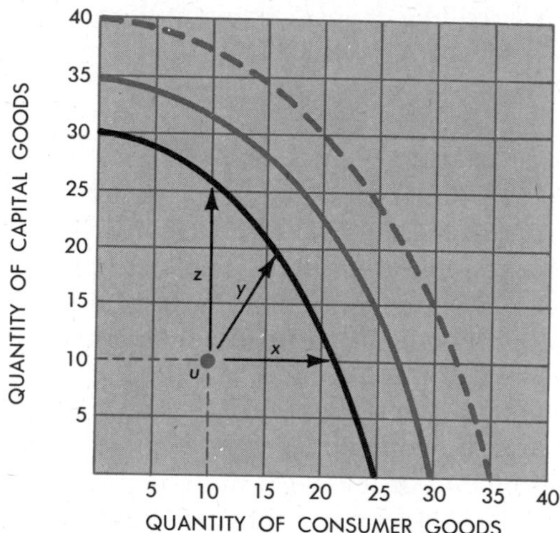

FIGURE 18–6 Unemployment and Changing Production Possibilities

The point marked *U* inside the solid curve illustrates unemployment, when the nation is producing fewer goods and services than it can. If the nation moves toward full employment, it can have more capital goods, more consumer goods, or more of both. The colored curve shows that the nation has increased its productive capacity—its production possibilities frontier has moved outward. The dotted curve shows an even greater increase in productive potential. What would a point outside (to the right of) all of these curves suggest?

economic growth can be retarded. As a nation grows economically, its production possibilities curve shifts outward. New workers entering the labor force, new sources of raw materials, and new capital equipment increase the nation's productive capacity. The solid blue curve in Figure 18–6 illustrates the outward shift. Again, note that the nation can produce more capital goods without sacrificing any consumer goods, or more consumer goods without sacrificing any capital goods, or it can produce more of both items. The nation might also fail to produce at some point on the new curve, meaning that unemployment, underemployment, or inefficiency exists.

Finally, notice the broken-line blue curve. Let's assume that two imaginary nations start with the same production possibilities curve—the inner solid-line black curve. During a period of five years, Nation A's curve moves outward as represented by the solid blue curve. Nation B's curve, during the same period, moves outward as represented by the broken-line colored curve. What accounts for the difference between the two new curves? Nation B chose to devote more of its output to capital formation and less to consumer goods production than did Nation A. While the people of Nation A were enjoying their TV sets, cosmetics, fine clothing, etc., the people of Nation B were doing without some of those things in order to build up their capital—factories, machines, tools, and the like. In the future, the people of B may be better off because they will have the capital equipment with which to produce more goods and services. They were willing to sacrifice current consumption for a better life in the future. Their rate of economic growth may surpass that of Nation A. During a recent period, the growth rate of the U.S.S.R. was about 6 percent, while that of the United States was only 3 percent. The Soviet Union had been devoting a larger proportion of its output to capital formation than had the United States. How can the curves in Figure 18–6 be used to illustrate these facts? Assuming that both nations were producing at points *on* their production possibilities curves, which nation would be producing at the higher point? How does this sort of analysis help to explain differences in standards of living between the U.S.S.R. and the United States?

One final note about the production possibilities curve. We have used it to illustrate the "trade-off" between capital goods and consumer goods and to stress the importance of capital formation for economic growth. The curve has several other uses. Whenever we can divide a nation's output into two categories, the curve becomes a useful tool for analysis. For example, we could put "military goods" on the vertical axis and "nonmilitary goods" on the horizontal. (In 1968, some economists were criticizing President Johnson for saying that we could have both more military and more civilian goods. With full employment prevailing in 1968, many felt that we could increase our military goods only by sacrificing consumer goods. A higher tax on personal incomes was one means employed for bringing about this shift in production.) We could put "public goods" (government) on one axis, and "private goods" on another, thus showing that in a full-employment economy the government could increase its share of the GNP only by reducing the share of the private sector. The curve could be used to show agricultural as compared with nonagricultural production. Can you think of any other possible uses for this analytical device?

Government Encouragement

The extent to which government should use its power to influence economic growth is a matter of great controversy. Some oppose government interference; others feel that government should take concerted action to stimulate or hasten economic development. Economic growth became an objective of the federal government during the administration of President Kennedy. Nearly everyone was concerned about the fact that the Soviet economy had been growing more rapidly than ours, and President Kennedy stated his intention of increasing real GNP by 4.5 percent a year during the decade of the 1960's. Although our government lacks complete control over the economy, it can help to promote full employment, reallocate productive resources, redistribute income, conserve natural resources, and change the composition of the nation's output.

Even during our early history, government had some effect on economic development. There were corporations jointly owned by government and private individuals, such as the first and second United States Banks. The railroads were given government subsidies, and government lands were given away or sold at low prices. We have already seen how monetary and fiscal policies can influence spending for investment. If government action creates full employment without inflation, it helps the economy move from a point inside the production possibilities curve to a point on the curve. Where government is authoritarian, as in the U.S.S.R., the state may directly decide how much of the GNP is to be devoted to capital for-

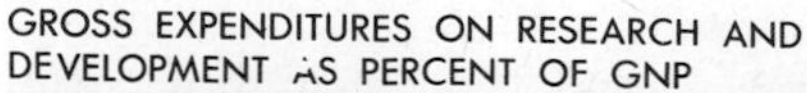

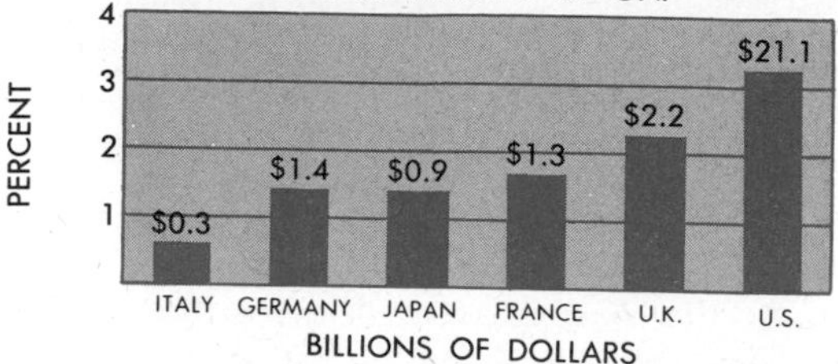

GROSS EXPENDITURES ON RESEARCH AND DEVELOPMENT PER CAPITA

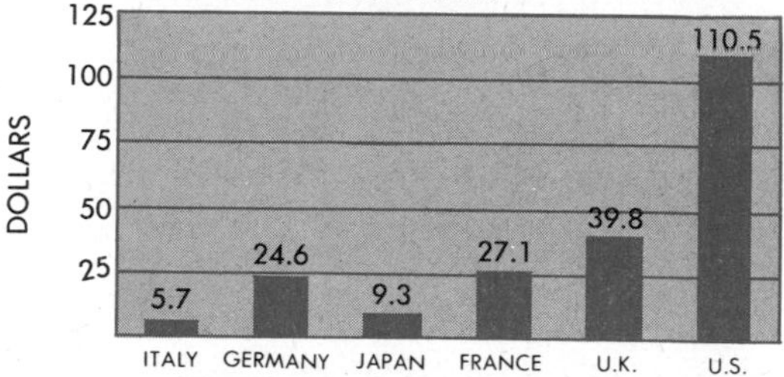

SCIENTIFIC MANPOWER EMPLOYED IN R & D PER 10,000 POPULATION

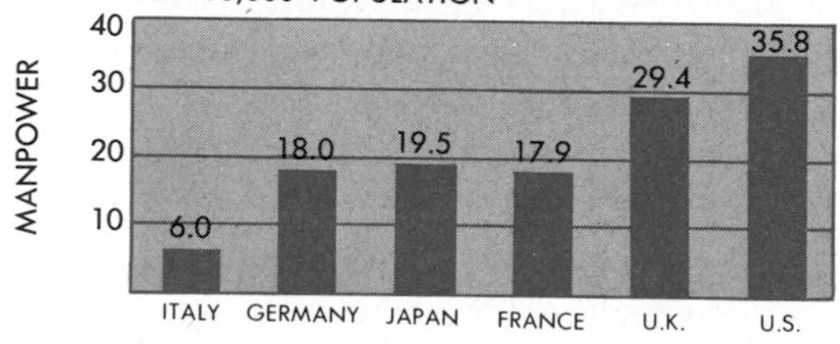

1963 1964 1963 1963 1964–65 1963–64

FIGURE 18–7 R & D Level and Structure in Selected Countries

The term R & D, as defined by the Organization for Economic Cooperation and Development, "covers all work undertaken for the advancement of scientific knowledge, undertaken with or without a specific practical aim in view (applied and basic research) and the use of the results of basic and applied research directed to the introduction of new products and processes or the improvement of existing ones." Scientific manpower refers to the total full-time equivalent of scientists, engineers and technicians engaged in R & D activities. SOURCE: National Industrial Conference Board, *Road Maps of Industry*, No. 1585, January 1, 1968.

mation and how much to consumer goods. Soviet citizens had no choice, especially under Stalin. They were forced, sometimes by brutal and oppressive means, to sacrifice current consumption so that the U.S.S.R. might develop a greater industrial base.

In democratic societies, government action can be less direct. If the policy is to encourage capital formation, this might be achieved by increasing taxes on consumer goods and on personal incomes, while giving tax concessions to business to stimulate more investment. Government can also help by providing the necessary educational facilities, highways, ports, airports, and other "social capital" items. It can subsidize basic research. (*Basic research* is often supported by government because it may have no immediate commercial use. *Applied research* attempts to find practical uses for the general principles and new knowledge discovered through basic research.) Federal spending on research and development rose from about \$3.2 billion in the fiscal year 1954 to approximately \$16.7 billion in 1967. It was slightly lower than this in 1971, however. Altogether, about \$28.5 billion was being spent in the United States for research and development by 1971, with government funds paying for over 50 percent of it. (The actual research may be done by private industries or universities which receive federal funds for this purpose. About 70 percent of government-financed research and development work is done by private industry.) As Figure 18–7 shows, the United States has been devoting a greater percentage of its GNP to research and development than other leading industrialized nations of the free world. Figure 18–8 shows the 1971 outlays for research and development.

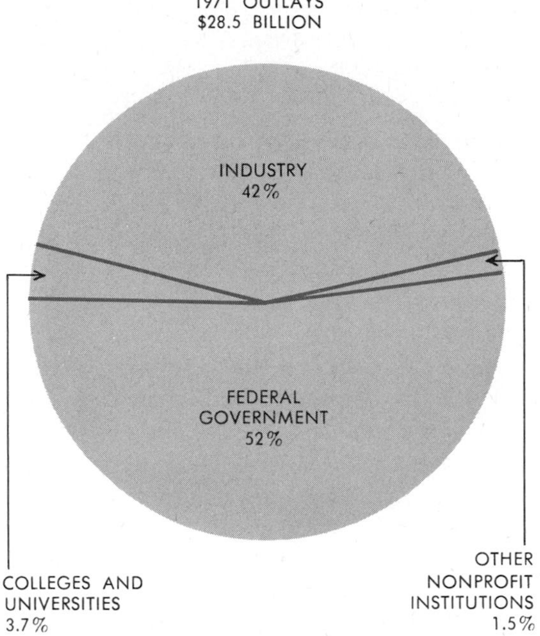

FIGURE 18–8 Outlays for Research and Development, 1971

Although most of the money for R & D comes from the federal government, industry actually performs 72 percent of the research. The federal government performs 13 percent, colleges and universities 12 percent, and other nonprofit institutions the remainder. The government's planned R & D outlays for 1971 were slightly below those of 1967, and the percentage of all R & D accounted for by government dropped from over 60 percent to about 52 percent. SOURCES: *Chemical and Engineering News* and the New York *Times*, January 4, 1971.

Government also makes *investment in human capital*—that is, it attempts to improve the quality of the population by promoting education and better health. These are areas which do not attract sufficient private investment because they do not make high profits. For example, in 1965 public educational construction (in constant 1957–1959 dollars) was valued at about \$3,064 million, as compared with only \$636 million for private educational construction. Few private schools make a profit, and yet the need for more highly educated people is becoming very pressing. By promoting health and education, government can help move the production possibilities curve to the right. By 1967, public investment in human capital made up 6.1 percent of GNP, as contrasted with less than 3 percent in 1929. (About three fourths of this is provided by state and local governments. Governments finance over 75 percent of educational expenditures in the United States. From 1950 to 1965, government provided no more than 25 percent of the financing of medical care, but became more important as a source of funds for medical expenditures in 1971.)

Finally, government can encourage growth by providing an atmosphere of freedom and security. Knowing that their property is being protected, that law and order prevails, that profits will not be confiscated by unreasonably high taxes, and that they are free to assume risks and run their businesses as they see fit, many businessmen will be convinced that investment may bring good returns in the future. Of course, government may step in to promote competition when there are threats from monopolies or from irresponsible unions.

Part B
Economic Growth in America—A Brief History

In analyzing a nation's economic progress, many economists have found it helpful to think of this as a sequential development. An important work in describing how economic development takes place was written by an economic historian and State Department advisor, W. W. Rostow. In his book *The Stages of Economic Growth: A Non-Communist Manifesto,*[3] the author describes five stages of economic growth, which follow an evolutionary pattern of development.

Stage I: The Traditional Society

Rostow's first stage is the *traditional society,* in which technology is primitive; the thinking of the people is governed more by custom, tradition, and superstition than by a scientific outlook; and the masses of the people are ignorant. America seems to have skipped this stage. As Adam Smith put it in his famous book *The Wealth of Nations* (published in 1776), "There are no colonies of which progress has been more rapid than that of the English in North America."

Stage II: Preconditions for "Takeoff"—1607–1842

America starts with Rostow's second stage, *preconditions for "takeoff."* The colonists came from European countries which had already broken away from their traditions, had experienced a rebirth of learning, and had acquired many of the characteristics which are conducive to growth. We lack accurate statistics for those early decades, but it is possible that there was a rise in per capita income. The population rose from about 2,500 in 1620 to nearly 4,000,000 in 1790; and although

[3] Walt W. Rostow, *The Stages of Economic Growth: A Non-Communist Manifesto* (New York: Cambridge University Press), 1960.

the average American of 1790 might not have lived at a much higher level than the early colonists, he certainly did not live at a lower level. About 90 percent of the people were engaged in agriculture or related activities. Agricultural efficiency did not increase much during the colonial period, so it is reasonable to assume that per capita income did not grow a great deal as a result of gains in agricultural productivity. On the other hand, the shipping industry was an important source of income, and there were very definite gains in efficiency in this sector of the economy.

The colonists had the ideas and the attitudes that were conducive to economic development. They were adventuresome, willing to take risks, and desirous of producing goods and services for which there was a demand. After a few understandable mistakes, they concentrated their efforts on producing things which they could produce more efficiently. The value of their exports to England rose fivefold from 1700 to the beginning of the Revolution. Americans probably enjoyed a level of living equal to, or higher than, that of people in England. The colonies became a major power in shipping and in shipbuilding. Government in the colonies was relatively stable, although some feel that the lack of strong central government for America was a negative factor. Others assert that growth was encouraged by the fact that several colonies existed and that each was quite free to adapt to environmental conditions as it saw fit.

A formal education was not considered necessary by many of the frontier settlers, but as early as 1647 Massachusetts passed a law requiring a grammar school in every town of 100 families. By 1769, nine colleges had been founded in the colonies, including Harvard (1636), William and Mary (1693), Yale (1701), and Princeton (1746). As the Revolution approached, America could boast a brilliant, articulate, and highly educated leadership.

The growth of water transportation encouraged specialization. Thus the South began to concentrate upon rice, indigo, and tobacco; the Middle Atlantic region on flour, grain, livestock, cornmeal, pork, and beef; and northern New Englanders on fishing, shipping, and shipbuilding. Merchants became rich, and accumulated savings which could be used for investment. Capital was also attracted from abroad, and farmers contributed to America's real capital formation by improving their land and erecting new buildings.

Negative factors during this period were shortages of labor and capital, a small population scattered over a large land base, British colonial policies which discouraged free trade and the development of manufacturing,[4] and the shattering effects of the Revolutionary War. After achieving independence, the United States found itself deeply in debt, faced with difficulties in obtaining commercial concessions from foreign countries, threatened by rebellion, and saddled with a weak central government.

The new Constitution adopted in 1789 paved the way for political stability and economic growth. The new government could levy taxes, deal with the Revolutionary War debts, coin money, assume full responsibility for foreign affairs (including tariff and trade matters), control interstate commerce, protect property, enforce contracts, and in other ways

[4] The extent to which British policy damaged the colonial economy is a matter of some dispute among economic historians. For an interesting discussion of this, see Douglass C. North, *Growth and Welfare in the American Past* (Englewood Cliffs, N.J.: Prentice-Hall, 1966), Chapter 3. North also criticizes Rostow's theories, particularly as they apply to the United States. See North, *op. cit.*, pp. 86–89.

establish stable conditions which would encourage business investment and economic development. The assumption of state debts incurred to aid the Revolution, and the decision to pay the foreign debt, established the credit of the federal government. Bonds issued to pay the debts were circulated as a medium of credit and helped to form a base of credit for the country. The first Bank of the United States, established in 1791, strengthened the country's banking system by performing some of the functions of a central bank, acted as a fiscal agent for the government, provided a safe paper currency, and helped improve the nation's capital market.

Eli Whitney's invention of the cotton gin in 1793 made cotton-growing a profitable enterprise, and cotton exports increased rapidly. In the same year war broke out between England and France, adversely affecting the shipping and trade of Europe. This gave the United States an advantage in carrying much of the trade of the world. The value of our exports rose from about $20 million in 1790 to nearly $110 million by 1807. The rise in re-exports (goods imported and then exported) was equally dramatic. During the 1793–1807 period, the United States enjoyed full employment, enlarged the domestic market, increased its productivity, and experienced a growth in urbanization. This prosperity came to a halt, however, when President Jefferson placed an embargo on shipping in an attempt to keep us out of the European war. In 1812 we went to war anyway.

Because of the embargo, and the war, business investment shifted from shipping to manufacturing, and over 80 new cotton mills were built within a two-year period. These new industries were hit hard by British competition after the War of 1812 ended, however. Some economic historians feel that we were not yet ready for these manufacturing industries, that they were artificially protected by the war and the embargo, and that we would have been using our resources more efficiently if we had adhered to shipping. Industrialization progressed during the 1830's and 1840's, however, and the latest available research suggests that productivity and per capita income were rising. (The new figures are not conclusive, however.) Greater specialization developed after the War of 1812, as the various regions concentrated upon those products for which they were well suited. The use of steamboats on American rivers and the building of canals and roads made possible more trade among regions. The Northeast stressed manufacturing, shipping, commerce, and insurance; the South was noted for cotton; and the West produced foodstuffs. The United States doubled its land area during this period through the Louisiana Purchase and other territorial acquisitions.

Stage III: The "Takeoff"—1843–1859

If Rostow's analysis is correct, the year 1843 marks the beginning of America's "takeoff." A serious depression came to an end, industrial expansion accelerated, and industry spread to areas outside the Northeast; the production of machinery as well as finished goods became important (ranking seventh in terms of value added by 1860), steam engines came into use in factories, and railroad-building began in earnest. In 1843 there were 4,185 miles of railroads in the United States. Ten years later there were 15,360 miles; and by 1860 the figure was 30,626. In 1840, we had more than 60,000 miles of surfaced roads, as compared with about 25,000 miles in 1830. In the period under consideration (1843 to 1859) the value of manufacturing output increased by about 270 percent, and the value of agricultural output more than doubled. There was about a 300 percent increase in the value of construction and in the output of our mines. Education had an important part in our economic development, and by 1850 the ratio of students to total population was greater (about 20.4) in the United States than in any other western nation except Denmark (21.73).

The effects of the railroads have probably been overestimated by economic historians, but they were very important nevertheless. The railroads reduced transportation costs (although their rates were often higher than water rates), helped make it possible for manufacturing to spread, increased the availability of our natural resources, had an effect on farm output and settlement in the West, and further stimulated trade among regions. The federal government gave over 130 million acres of land to the railroads, and another 48 million were given by the states. (State government also supported canal-building, providing over 70 percent of the funds invested in canals.)

Again, the United States grew in area by acquiring Texas (1845), Oregon (1846), California (1848), and more land in the Southwest (1853). Government actions encouraged land settlement. Laws passed in 1785 and 1796 had set 640 acres as the minimum amount of public land that could be purchased, but later acts decreased the minimum to 320 in 1800, 160 in 1804, 80 in 1820, and 40 in 1832. Large amounts of land were given to war veterans. The Preemption Act of 1841 specified that "squatters" would have first rights to buy the land upon which they had settled without title. Previously, they might be evicted. Under the Graduation Act of 1854, if land was not sold at the government's minimum price it could be sold at a lower price. The California gold rush of 1849–1850, the discovery of copper in Michigan's Keweenaw Peninsula in the 1840's, and other "mineral rushes" also attracted settlers. Thus, the vast increase in population did not result in the law of diminishing returns because the available supply of natural resources and capital was also growing. (The number of people per square mile of land was actually lower in 1850 than it had been in 1840.)

Between 1840 and 1850 the iron industry made rapid progress because of the large-scale use of steam power, replacement of the open forge by a closed furnace, and the substitution of coal for charcoal. Steam power freed the textile mills from limitations imposed by waterpower. The use of standardized parts and quantity production became more common, and a greater variety of machine-shop products (plows, harvesters, reapers, threshing machines, stoves, sewing machines, etc.) was being manufactured. The telegraph (developed by Morse in 1832) was put into operation in 1844. A revolving disc harrow, a binder, and a chilled plow were developed for farm use. During the last decade of this period (1849 to 1859) over 17,000 new factories were established, and the value added by manufacturing nearly doubled. (*Value added* refers to the value of products minus the cost of materials, supplies, fuel, and purchased energy.) The percentage of the labor force engaged in nonagricultural occupations rose from 31.4 in 1840 to 41.1 in 1860.

Foreigners, as well as Americans, were eager to invest in American enterprises. Many foreigners shipped gold to American banks, thus enabling them to obtain

American bank notes which could be used for investment here. In the years 1843 and 1847, in particular, gold came into the United States in large amounts. (Imports of gold exceeded exports by over $16 million in 1843 and by over $20 million in 1847.) Since American banks issued notes in excess of their gold holdings, the inflow of gold helped to increase the nation's money supply. On the other hand, the speculative nature of the foreigners' interest here often caused them to withdraw their gold quickly and thus helped cause a contraction of bank notes and a fall in prices. Gold from California and Nevada, of course, added to the money supply. (The amount of gold coined in 1850 was over three times that of 1849—nearly $32 million worth in 1850 as compared with about $9 million worth in 1849.)

In summarizing Stage III, we can say that there was a distinct rise in the nation's per capita output; probably between 30 and 50 percent. (There is some doubt, it will be remembered, whether or not per capita output grew during the previous phase.) The discovery of gold, great additions to the nation's land area, the growth of manufacturing and transportation, improved technology, and an increase in the labor supply are factors instrumental in this development.

Stage IV: The Drive to Maturity—1860–1900

During the period which Rostow called "The Drive to Maturity," a high rate of capital formation continues. The economy is already moving toward industrialization. New inventions appear, and older ones are improved and used more intensively. A rapid rise in per capita output occurs. The period from 1860 to 1900 is thought by some to represent America's drive to maturity. Although well aware of the criticisms of Rostow's stages, and realizing the somewhat arbitrary nature of the selection of these precise dates, your authors find them as convenient as any others for our brief analysis and description of America's growth.

The Civil War exacted a terrible cost in men (over 600,000 killed and nearly 400,000 wounded) and in material resources. Many parts of the South were devastated. The South's cotton output dropped from 5,387,000 bales in 1859 to 299,000 in 1864. There was little physical damage in the North, but productive resources that might have been used for economic expansion were shifted to war purposes. (How might this be illustrated on a production possibilities curve?)

The productive capacity of the West and the North grew, despite the war. In the 1860's, the new methods of converting pig iron into steel which had been developed by Kelly in 1851 and Bessemer in 1856 were adopted. Inventions during this stage included the electrically-powered streetcar, celluloid, dynamos, the telephone, Edison's incandescent bulb, the phonograph, the automobile, the linotype machine, an electric welding machine, a pneumatic hammer, radio, motion pictures, and the Diesel engine. The United States became a predominantly industrial economy. The percentage of the labor force engaged in agriculture dropped from about 59 in 1860 to only 38 in 1900. Steel production rose from less than 20,000 to over 10 million long tons between 1867 and 1900.

Railroad mileage grew from less than 31,000 in 1860 to 193,000 in 1900. An oil boom followed Drake's successful drilling for petroleum near Titusville, Pennsylvania, in 1859; and petroleum soon replaced whale oil. Drilling became nationwide after 1884. Textile production grew in the South, and the shoe and ready-made clothing industries expanded.

The westward movement continued. Under the Homestead Act of 1862, settlers could obtain 160 acres of land as long as they lived on it and made improvements. A married settler could get 320 acres. During periods of rising demand and rising prices of agricultural products, the movement to new land accelerated. Railroad construction raised land values and reduced transportation costs. Western farmers could now produce for Eastern markets. McCormick's reaper and Case's thresher reduced the time required to harvest an acre of wheat from 33 hours to one hour.

Farmers complained of high interest rates on money they borrowed, charged that the middleman, the railroads, and grain elevator owners were monopolists who reaped all of the farm profits, and asserted that their real incomes were declining. Recent research suggests that the farmers in general were not as badly off as they claimed. In 1890, less than 40 percent of the farms in the North Central region were mortgaged, and the highest figure in any state was 60 percent. Railroad rates fell more than the price level in general, benefiting the farmer. Statistics for several farm states show that the farmer's share of the price received for grains was rising over the last two or three decades of the nineteenth century. Between 1865 and 1890, prices of farm goods did not fall as much as prices in general—at least that seems to have been the trend, despite sharp ups and downs. Some historians assert that the farmer's real income was probably rising. (Of course, there were many individual instances in which farmers suffered as charged.)

The farmer was troubled, however, by price fluctuations and by the erratic pattern of farm incomes. Farm income was probably rising (or at least steady) except for the decade of the 1870's, when it fell. In any event, agricultural output rose because more high-quality land was going into production and efficiency was increasing. (Cropland rose from 163 million acres in 1860 to 319 million in 1900. The use of commercial fertilizer soared from 164,000 short tons to 2,730,000 during the same period.)

Immigrants poured into the country during this stage, the figure exceeding 450,000 in some years. Most of the immigrants were in the working-age group, and many already trained in some useful occupation. Improvements in sanitation and health added to the average life span of the native American. Increases in farm productivity made it possible for one farmer to feed more people, so younger members of farm families often moved to the cities. Nearly 40 percent of the population in 1900 lived in urban areas, as compared with less than 20 percent in 1860. The drive for a better-educated population intensified during this stage, with the growing cities leading the way in demands for improved schools. Free universal education became common, and the Morrill Act of 1862 provided federal land grants to states for the support of colleges of agriculture and the mechanical arts. Nearly every state had an agricultural college by 1900 (only three had them in 1860). Engineers and scientists, as well as farmers, were trained by these schools.

Greater efficiency in the raising of capital was developed after the Civil War.

The number of banks (excluding mutual savings banks and unincorporated banks) rose from 1,502 in 1860 to 8,738 in 1900. The National Banking System, established in 1864, ended some of the chaos that had typified our money and banking. Greater safety was provided for depositors and noteholders, and a uniform currency was adopted. The number of bank failures was reduced, but the currency was not as elastic and there was less mobility of capital funds. Nevertheless, the short-term capital market became more efficient, and the amount of money in circulation rose markedly (from about $442 million in 1860 to over $2,366 million in 1900). Foreign investment in the United States was rising during this phase, except for a dip in the late 1870's. (Foreign investment in 1900 was about seven times that of 1860.)

Perhaps this stage is best summarized by a few facts about manufacturing. In 1860, cotton textiles (a relatively simple industry) was the first-ranking manufacturing industry by value added. In 1900, foundry and machine-shop products stood in first place. Employment in manufacturing had increased by about 400 percent. The value of output in manufacturing had risen from $0.82 billion in 1859 to $5.04 billion in 1899. The total value of output in agriculture, mining, manufacturing, and construction had gone from $2.57 billion to $10.20 billion. Whereas in 1870 the United Kingdom accounted for 31.8 percent of the world's manufacturing output and the United States for 23.3 percent, by the end of that decade the United States had passed Britain for world leadership. By 1900, the United States accounted for 30.1 percent, as compared with the United Kingdom's 19.5. The estimated real per capita GNP had risen from an average of $165 (in 1957 prices) during the 1869–1873 period to $231 during the 1897–1907 period, a gain of about 40 percent.

Stage V: The Age of High Mass Consumption—1901 to the Present

Since 1900 the United States has been moving upward economically, except for such setbacks as the Great Depression of the 1930's. The United States became the leading industrial nation of the world, producing over 42 percent of the world's manufacturing output by 1929. (Germany was in second place, with 11.6 percent, the United Kingdom having dropped to third with 9.4 percent.) The nonagricultural labor force rose steadily, while the agricultural labor force rose only slightly until 1910, then began to decline. The population became predominantly urban around 1920. The total population grew from about 76 million in 1900 to nearly 123 million in 1930. Petroleum production was well under 100 million barrels in 1900, but had soared to over a billion barrels by 1929. The production of electrical energy had a similarly spectacular rise. About 8,000 motor vehicles had been registered in 1900, but by 1929 the figure had reached a staggering total of over 26 million.

The tremendous expansion in manufacturing output was influenced by technological innovations, but this does not completely explain high growth rate. The same changes in manufacturing technology had also occurred in such European countries as Germany, France, and Great Britain, but our development went on at a greater rate. A general increase in efficiency has to be taken into account. Highly skilled craftsmen and scientists continually improved the methods of using capital equipment. Some economists stress the high quality of the American labor force—a quality explained in large measure by education (*investment in human capital*).

The American businessman is also given credit for providing drive, daring, and organizational ability that gave our economy this upward push. Energetic and highly efficient financial institutions, such as investment banks, helped to channel funds to business for capital formation. The establishment of the Federal Reserve in 1914 provided a badly-needed central banking system. There were serious labor problems in the early part of this stage, and working conditions were often extremely bad; but recent research indicates that real wages rose between 1900 and 1914. There was a sharp but short recession after World War I, after which we experienced another surge of growth, increases in real wages, and rising incomes. The 1920's were noted for growth in industries producing durable goods (the automobile, the refrigerator, and the radio, for example) for consumers. The farm sector of the economy did not share in the general prosperity of the 1920's, however.

In 1929 came the great stock market crash, after which the United States plunged into the terrible depression of the 1930's. There had been a brief postwar recession in 1920–1921, followed by a return to prosperity in many sectors of industry. The developing automobile industry, roadbuilding, and urban construction are often cited as the foundations of the prosperity of the 1920's. There were underlying weaknesses, however, in coal mining, shipbuilding, textiles, leather, railroad equipment, and agriculture. From the crash of 1929 to 1933, about four fifths of the value of corporate stock vanished. These years saw over 9,000 bank suspensions, a drop in investment from over $16 billion to less than $2 billion, the GNP declining from $103.1 billion to $55.6 billion, 25 percent of the labor force unemployed (over 13 million in 1933), and the index of industrial production plunging from 103 to 56 (with 1935–1939 equaling 100). Losses exceeded profits during part of this period, and capital was being used up faster than it was being replaced (that is, the net capital formation rate was negative). Exports dropped from over $5 billion worth in 1929 to less than $2 billion in 1932. The value of imports experienced a similar decline.

It is easy now, in the light of modern economic theory and knowledge, to look back and say what could have been done to prevent or at least to mitigate the depression. The Federal Reserve did little to offset the decline, and even worsened it in 1931 by raising the rediscount rate. President Hoover's efforts were greater than many historians have given him credit for, but they were too feeble to cope with a problem of such magnitude. Franklin Roosevelt took office during the depths of the depression, and on the very day that he took the oath of office he began a vigorous drive to revive the economy. Dozens of laws were rushed through Congress, designed to provide relief for the distressed, bring about recovery, and institute reforms which might prevent future depressions.

The United States went off the gold standard and devalued the dollar in order to raise prices (the wholesale price index, based upon 1926 prices, had dropped from 95.3 in 1929 to 64.8 in 1932). *Deficit financing* (then called "pump priming") was tried, as the federal government decided to spend more than it received from tax revenues. Government spending was not large enough to bring about a rapid recovery, however. Under the National Industrial Recovery Act (later declared unconstitutional), industries were permitted to make collusive agreements that might otherwise be considered violations of the antitrust laws. It was hoped that this would encourage business to increase production. The Agricultural Adjustment Act (also found to be unconstitutional) tried to raise farm incomes by limiting production. Organized labor received protection and encouragement under the Wagner Act, a social security system was established (including unemployment insurance), the securities markets were brought under government regulation, the Federal Reserve's powers were increased, and bank deposits were insured under the new Federal Deposit Insurance Corporation. The Tennessee Valley Authority (TVA) and other public works projects were built.

Roosevelt's New Deal did not bring about a complete or rapid recovery, although the situation seemed to be improving between 1933 and 1937. In 1937, a sharp setback occurred. Some give the New Deal the lion's share of the credit for the eventual recovery; others stress the coming of World War II. Full employment was again achieved during the war. Industrial production rose to a point nearly two and one-half times that of the 1935–1939 period, and the GNP of 1945 was over twice that of 1940.

In evaluating the New Deal it must be remembered that neither Roosevelt nor his advisors had much understanding of Keynes and his theory of income determination. Reforms were instituted mainly on the suggestions of the institutionalists (see Chapter 9, p. 201) and were initiated out of compassion for the poor. Much more information is needed for a thorough evaluation of the New Deal, but certainly the role of government in the economy increased markedly, and it is now quite widely accepted that government should intervene to end or to prevent a recession, to bring about full employment, and to stimulate growth. Some of the federal government's moves during the 1930's were less expansionary. If we look at all levels of government during the 1930's, we find that between 1933 and 1939 (with the exception of 1936) they were *not* spending more than they were taking in. The combined effect, then, was not expansionary. Income became more equally distributed (see the Lorenz Curve, p. 246), possibly because of the progressive income tax rates, which became very high during World War II.

Every major war had been followed by a depression, and it was feared that history would repeat itself after World War II. Government was now committed to maintaining full employment, however, and with a greater share of total economic activity in its grasp, the government was able to use its powers more effectively. There have been recessions, but no full-scale depressions since World War II. High unemployment rates have existed at times, but this has not always been associated with a general decline in business activity. Modern American industry needs highly trained labor, and those without skills have found it difficult to find jobs even in periods of prosperity. Certain industries have declined, affecting whole areas. (Coal mining in Appalachia is a well-known example.)

Many have been concerned about our rate of growth. Between 1953 and 1960, our GNP (in constant 1958 dollars) grew at an annual rate of 2.4 percent, as compared with 5 percent for the 1948–1953 period. The rate improved in the 1960's, averaging 4.7 percent annually between

1960 and 1966. (Putting these three periods together—1948–1966—we get a rate of 3.9 percent.) In per capita terms, the figures are somewhat lower—0.7 percent for the 1953–1960 period; 3.2 percent for 1948–1953; 3.3 percent for 1960–1966; and 2.2 percent for the longer 1948–1966 span. The high rate of the late 1940's and early 1950's was above our long-term historical growth rate; the slow growth of the 1950's was below it. The real GNP has grown at the rate of 3.3 percent since 1890, a rate which will double the GNP every 21 years. What troubled many people is the fact that our rate was lower during the 1950's than that of Japan and several European nations, although our per capita GNP was well above all others.

The noted economist Edward F. Denison studied the Western European nations to determine why their growth rate exceeded that of the United States in the 1950's. He concluded that the most important reason was the shift in those countries from low-productivity occupations to more modern endeavors. (In particular, workers shifted from agriculture to industry in large numbers.) Better managerial techniques and "the advance of knowledge" were also important factors. Small-scale enterprises operated by families gave way to big business. Per capita consumption rose, especially for consumer durable goods (such as cars, radios, TV sets). This meant larger markets, which made possible the adoption of large-scale production techniques. Europeans did not have to develop these techniques on their own; they could simply adopt those already being used in America.

Despite the Great Depression, the slow growth of the 1950's, and other setbacks, America's growth has been impressive. There was an elevenfold increase in our real GNP between 1890 and 1960. Additions to our stock of capital and our labor force account for over half of the increase between 1909 and 1929. After 1929, technological innovations and education played a more prominent role. A better-educated labor force, the shift from agriculture to industry, improvements in the use of large-scale production, rapid advances in technological knowledge, and greater labor efficiency help to account for the rise in productivity over the past four decades. (Output per man-hour increased at the rate of 1.6 percent a year during the earlier period; at 2.7 percent after 1929.) As for the fear that others might surpass us, some economists feel that this is unfounded. Japan had the amazing growth rate of 10.9 percent during the 1950's, but dropped to below 10 percent between 1960 and 1965 while our growth rate improved. By 1971, Japan's productive power was growing at a rate more than double that of either the U.S. or U.S.S.R. She had become the third greatest industrial power in the world, and her per capita output was about equal that of the Soviet Union. Nevertheless, Japan's GNP was only about 20 percent of the U.S. GNP; she is poor in the natural resources needed for industry while the United States is rich in raw materials; she has begun to assume greater obligations for foreign aid and for research and development; and nations that had been welcoming Japanese goods now threaten to erect tariffs and other barriers. Furthermore, Japanese industrialists are becoming concerned about a labor shortage, while citizens are complaining about the damage that rapid industrial development has done to the environment.

Our real GNP may actually be greater than the recent figures suggest. As we have become richer, the consumption of services has become relatively more important; and productivity increases in services are hard to measure. Improvements in the quality of goods are not always shown in the GNP figure. In any event, our GNP is double that of the U.S.S.R., and with 6 percent of the world's population we still produce about 33 percent of the world's goods.

Part C
Forecasting Growth

In this section we shall give a brief projection of growth in the United States to 1980. We do this not because we have great confidence that the predictions will be accurate, but because the student should have some idea of how such predictions are made. We have selected our data from many sources, but we shall concentrate on a recent study published by the U.S. Bureau of Labor Statistics, *The U. S. Economy in 1980*.

By 1980 the GNP may reach $1.4 trillion (in 1968 dollars). This implies that the rate of growth will be 4.3 percent a year. The labor force should total 100 million workers, about one fifth more than the 1968 figure. Excluding farm workers and government employees, the average workweek probably will decline to 37.8 hours. Nonfarm productivity is expected to increase by 2.9 percent a year, while farm productivity may grow by 5.7 percent annually. The value of personal consumption in 1980 is expected to be nearly $900 billion, and services and durable goods will account for a higher proportion than they do now. Government spending will be about $290 billion (this includes all levels of government), but as a percentage of total spending in the United States this may represent a slight decline from the current figure. Business investment could total $222 billion, and this would be a greater percentage of GNP than at present. There is a possibility that net exports will increase fivefold by the end of this decade. Expenditures for new housing are expected to double, hitting $53 billion by 1980. The nation's population will probably exceed 235 million.

Bases of the Predictions

Research done by many agencies was used in making the above projections. Among these were the U.S. Department of Labor, the U.S. Department of Commerce, the President's Council of Economic Advisers (CEA), the Joint Economic Committee, and the Bureau of the Budget. Some other institutions working in this area are the Twentieth Century Fund, the Conference Board, the National Planning Association, the Stanford Research Institute, the Committee for Economic Development, the Economics Department of the McGraw-Hill Publishing Company, and the Wharton Economic Forecasting Associates of the University of Pennsylvania. All make valuable contributions to economic forecasting, although their predictions sometimes differ. In 1970, for example, Wharton predicted that the 1971 GNP would be $1,046 billion, while the Department of Research of IBM projected $1,059 billions. (Both were making current dollar predictions.)

Many assumptions underlie economic forecasts. Among the assumptions made in establishing the predictions given above were that there would be an improvement in the international situation, a reduction in defense expenditures, no radical change in the current institutional framework of the American economy, and lower fertility rates than in the recent past. It was also assumed that technological, social, economic, and scientific progress will continue, that monetary and fiscal policies will bring about a good balance between relative price stability and low unemployment rates without reducing long-term growth rates, and that there will be cooperation among all levels of government (with the U.S. Congress giving more funds to state and local governments) in coping with domestic problems.

Because the Vietnam War created unusual demands upon the economy, the projections for GNP, productivity, working hours, industrial employment, and industry demand were based from 1965 rather than from 1966 when the war was "escalated." The labor force projection was based upon predictions made by the Bureau of the Census. Note that the working-age population can be predicted quite accurately because everyone who will be of working age during the 1970's has already been born, and that immigration and death rates are usually fairly steady. The "educated guess" about the decline in the average workweek was based upon an expected increase in part-time employment (because of the rapid growth in the retail trade and service industries where part-time work is common). The productivity projections for farmers take into account improvements in fertilizers, machinery, and farming techniques. It is very difficult to measure the real output of government, so productivity in that sector was assumed to be constant, while the expectation of nonfarm productivity gains in the private sector assumes that the long-term rate will prevail through the 1970's. Data on increases in the number of new families, changes in consumer habits, and long-term historical trends were examined to arrive at the estimate for personal consumption expenditures in 1980. In projecting government spending, greater attention to social welfare programs, education, community development, pollution control, housing, highway construction, public health, conservation, and parks was anticipated, while outlays for the armed forces and defense establishments were seen as declining. The rise in business investment was seen as coming from a 100 percent increase (or more) in inventories, a large gain in office building construction, rising expenditures for equipment, and a rise (although less important than the other elements) in new plants. The increase in housing expenditures was estimated on the basis of a growing recognition of the need for better housing in ghettos, the growing numbers of young adults who will be seeking their own apartments, and the large number of older persons who will want to live in retirement developments.

Using Projections

Economic projections can be of use to many people. Educational institutions should have some idea of what professions will be in need of trained workers in the future so that they can plan to provide the essential training. School guidance counselors ought to know what sorts of jobs will be available in order to be able to offer good advice to students. Both industry and government will depend upon

TABLE 18–2 Predictions of GNP for 1975

Source of Prediction	Expected GNP in Billions of 1965 Dollars
Joint Economic Committee	$1,090
Twentieth Century Fund	1,025
Conference Board	1,020
National Planning Association	988
Stanford Research Institute	913
Committee for Economic Development	909

projections in planning their policies for recruiting personnel, setting pay scales, establishing training programs, and expanding their research efforts. City, state, and regional planners will look to the projections for guidelines. For example, if the projections show that there will be a population increase of a certain percentage in a given area, the public housing authority will have an idea of how many new dwelling units will be needed.

Although projections do have great value, they must be used with care because much uncertainty still exists. See Table 18–2, for example, and note the differences in GNP projections. Remember that many assumptions underlie projections, that these assumptions are made by human beings, and that humans can make mistakes. In projecting the population, for example, the Bureau of the Census makes assumptions relating to births, deaths, and immigration. Such things as a new cure for a major disease or a change in immigration quotas could upset the projections. Assumptions are made regarding the average number of children that each woman is expected to have, but fertility rates have varied from year to year. Which year or years would be best to use as a base? Sometimes several projections will be made, based on varying assumptions. Again using the Bureau of the Census for an example, we note that they have made population projections for the year 1985 ranging from 241,731,000 to 274,748,000 people. Which of the GNP predictions in Table 18–2 would you accept? Perhaps instead of accepting the precise figure given by any single source, it would be safer to speak in terms of a range of possibilities.

REVIEW: THE HIGHLIGHTS OF THE CHAPTER

1. Economic growth is important if a nation wants to raise the level of living, maintain its military strength, and play an important role in the world economy.
2. To measure economic growth, we must determine the real per capita income. That is, the nominal GNP (the GNP in "current" dollars) must be adjusted for price changes and must be divided by the population. To deflate the GNP, we simply divide the current GNP figure by the latest GNP deflator and multiply the result by 100.
3. The goal of full employment may conflict with the goal of price stability. Okun's Law can be used to show the relationship between the unemployment

rate and the desired growth in GNP. Additional spending by government can close the GNP gap, or a tax reduction can be used to stimulate more spending by the people. The latter would probably be less certain.

4. As we approach full employment, average prices usually rise. The Phillips curve is a device for depicting the relationship between the unemployment rate and changes in average prices.
5. The ingredients of economic growth include political stability, economic unification, a spirit of enterprise, a good supply of natural resources, a highly developed technology, a population of the right size and quality, and an adequate rate of capital formation.
6. When a nation is utilizing its productive resources to the fullest, it can increase its output of one thing only by sacrificing others. Thus, in a full employment economy, we can have more capital goods only by sacrificing some of our consumer goods. This can be illustrated by the use of a production possibilities curve (also called a transformation curve).
7. Government can encourage growth by providing schools, roads, port facilities and other "social capital" items; using fiscal and monetary policies to control inflation and bring about full employment; supporting research and development; investing in human capital; and maintaining an atmosphere of freedom and security.
8. During our colonial period, we developed an efficient shipping industry, greatly increased the value of exports, achieved a high level of living, became important in shipbuilding, began regional specialization, and accumulated investment capital. The Constitution adopted in 1789 strengthened the central government and made it possible for us to establish conditions more conducive to economic development.
9. The invention of the cotton gin made cotton-growing a profitable enterprise, and the war between England and France gave the United States an advantage in the world's shipping trade. Jefferson's embargo ended this period of prosperity, and our war with England caused a shift in investment from shipping to manufacturing. Productivity and per capita income probably rose during the 1830's and 1840's, internal transportation facilities improved, and greater regional specialization developed.
10. Between 1843 and 1859 roads and railroads were built, manufacturing output rose greatly, the United States grew in land area, steam power came into large-scale use, and a number of important inventions were developed. Gold was discovered in California, and foreigners were eager to invest in American enterprises.
11. Between 1860 and 1900, there was a high rate of capital formation, per capita output rose, the nation became more highly industrialized, the westward movement continued (and the frontier disappeared), immigrants poured into the country, the banking system was improved, and the U.S. became the world leader in manufacturing output.
12. Since 1900 the United States has grown at a substantial rate, although the Great Depression and other setbacks occurred. The population became predominantly urban in 1920, manufacturing output expanded tremendously, highly efficient financial institutions emerged, and the banking system was

strengthened by the Federal Reserve. Government's role in the economy increased sharply during and after the Great Depression. Our growth rate was slow in the 1950's, but picked up in the 1960's. The decade of the 1960's saw the longest period of uninterrupted prosperity in U.S. history.

13. The U.S. economy will probably grow at a healthy rate in the next 15 years, thanks to increases in man-hours of work, higher labor productivity, large increases in capital investment, expenditures for research and development, and consumer spending. The population will have a better education, and the dependency ratio should decline.
14. Economic forecasts can be wrong because of such things as war, international economic problems, and errors in predicting the rate of growth. Forecasters differ widely on the actual rate of growth and the GNP that will be achieved in the future, but most agree that the American economy will expand substantially during the next 10 or 15 years.

IN CONCLUSION: SOME AIDS TO UNDERSTANDING

Terms for Review

vicious circle
real per capita income
deflating the GNP
constant dollars
money income
real income
Okun's Law
GNP gap
multiplier
marginal income
marginal propensity to save
capital formation
gross capital formation rate
social capital
net capital formation rate
production possibilities frontier
real cost
law of increasing costs
transformation curve
investment in human capital
traditional society
the "takeoff"
National Industrial Recovery Act
Agricultural Adjustment Act
basic research
applied research
human capital
Phillips Curve
job–price trade-off
flight of capital
optimum population
labor population
consumer population
dependent age groups
dependency ratio
Preemption Act of 1841
Graduation Act of 1854
value added
the "drive to maturity"
Homestead Act of 1862
Morrill Act of 1862
deficit financing
Thomas Robert Malthus
Adam Smith
Walt W. Rostow
A. W. Phillips
Eli Whitney

Questions for Review

1. What are the major reasons why the United States economy must grow?
2. Explain the "vicious circle." How does it illustrate the importance of capital investment? What does it imply for American foreign aid policy?
3. What is meant by "deflating the GNP"? Why is this important? How does the GNP deflator work?

4. Two tools that are useful in explaining problems of growth are Okun's Law and the Phillips Curve. Explain how they are used. What are their possible weaknesses?
5. What are the essentials for economic growth? To what extent does the United States possess these elements?
6. How does the population affect growth, both in terms of quantity and quality?
7. What is the difference between gross capital formation and net capital formation? Which is better to use as an indicator of growth? Why?
8. Explain the production possibilities curve and its various uses. How can it illustrate the law of increasing costs? Why is it sometimes called a transformation curve? What does it mean if we are producing inside the curve?
9. What are the various means by which government can shift the production possibilities curve to the right?
10. Contrast the factors mainly responsible for growth in the phases identified. How do they differ?
11. What facts do economists take into consideration when attempting to predict the long-run rate of growth?

Additional Questions and Problems

1. Find out what the latest GNP figure is. Using the GNP deflator, "deflate" the GNP and express it in constant dollars. Do the same with your personal income (using the CPI in this case).
2. After doing problem no. 1 above, find the real per capita GNP and compare it with the real per capita GNP of last year. What is the rate of real growth?
3. Explain each part of the formula:
   $\text{GNP gap} = 3 \times (U - .04) \times \text{actual GNP}$.
4. Gather as many figures as you can on the unemployment rate and on percentage changes in prices for the past four or five years. What relationship, if any, seems to exist between the two sets of data?
5. Study an underdeveloped country which interests you. To what extent does it possess the essentials for growth? What does it lack? What might be done to speed up its growth?
6. Explain why two countries may adopt the same technological innovations but experience different growth rates. What does this imply for the United States today?

SELECTED READINGS

Anderson, C. Arnold and Mary Jean Bowman. *Education and Economic Development.* Chicago: Aldine Publishing Company, 1965.

Bangs, Robert B. *Financing Economic Development: Fiscal Policy for Emerging Countries.* Chicago: University of Chicago Press, 1968.

Denison, Edward F. *The Sources of Economic Growth in the United States and the Alternatives Before Us.* New York: Committee for Economic Development, 1962.

———. *Why Growth Rates Differ: Postwar Experience in Nine Western Countries.* Washington, D.C.: The Brookings Institution, 1967.

Gill, Richard T. *Economic Development, Past and Present.* 2nd ed. Englewood Cliffs, N.J.: Prentice-Hall, 1967.

Hacker, Louis M. *The Course of American Economic Growth and Development.* New York: John Wiley & Sons, 1970.

Kunkel, John H. *Society and Economic Growth.* New York: Oxford University Press, 1970.

Meier, Gerald M. *Leading Issues in Development Economics.* New York: Oxford University Press, 1970.

Mincer, Jacob, ed. *Economic Forecasts and Expectations: Analysis of Forecasting Behavior and Performance.* New York: National Bureau of Economic Research, 1969.

North, Douglass C. *Growth and Welfare in the American Past: A New Economic History.* Englewood Cliffs, N.J.: Prentice-Hall, 1966.

Phelps, Edmund S., ed. *The Goal of Economic Growth.* Rev. ed. New York: W. W. Norton & Company, 1969.

Randall, Laura, ed. *Economic Development: Evolution or Revolution?* Boston: D. C. Heath and Company, 1964.

Rostow, Walt W. *The Stages of Economic Growth: A Non-Communist Manifesto.* New York: Cambridge University Press, 1960.

Stekler, Herman O. *Economic Forecasting.* New York: Praeger, 1970.

Tangri, Shanti S. and H. Peter Gray, eds. *Capital Accumulation and Economic Development.* Boston: D. C. Heath and Company, 1967.

Wan, Henry H. *Economic Growth.* New York: Harcourt Brace Jovanovich, 1971.

UNIT V

CONTEMPORARY PROBLEMS OF THE AMERICAN ECONOMY

The Economics of Pollution 19

THE AUTHORS' NOTE TO THE STUDENT

A United States senator recently referred to America's waterways as "a vast floating garbage can." Our metropolitan areas are thick with sulphur dioxide and carbon monoxide and have been described as aerial swamps. Mercury has been reported in the waterways of 33 of the 50 states. The problems in this country are duplicated in Japan, Italy, Greece, the Soviet Union, and Sweden. Reports show serious illness and even death caused by pollution from raw sewerage, poisonous industrial wastes, and emissions from the internal combustion engine.

The problem is one that has bothered conservationists for decades. It is now being felt in sufficient intensity to concern the public. The economist has also turned his attention to the causes, costs, and possible cures for pollution. We will try to provide some insight into the dimension of the problem and the directions we may take to cope with it.

A STUDENT'S NOTE TO THE STUDENT

If you get through reading this chapter without being shaken up, it must be because you've read about the problem before. The facts seem to pour out and jar you out of complacency. I'm convinced—and so are many of those I spoke to—that if *we* don't do something *personally*, it isn't going to get done. You have nothing to lose but yourself.

The concepts of the social cost and internal or external costs (that is, who pays) provide another way of looking at things. Our views of higher GNP's and materialism may have to be traded off for survival. When I finished this, I felt like lashing out at corporations and the older generation. Make them pay! It's kind of a silly attitude because we all have to pay.

Part A
Assessing Pollution Damage

It is extremely difficult to ascertain in money terms the damage caused by pollution. According to J. H. Dales, pollution costs are the sum of public expenditures to avoid pollution damage, private expenditures to avoid such damage, and the *welfare damage* of pollution.[1] By *welfare damage,* Dales means the money equivalent of pollution damage that is not prevented. It is with welfare damage that we shall first concern ourselves.

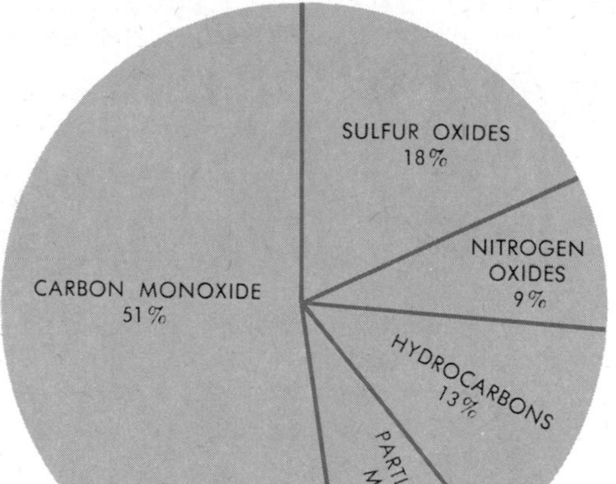

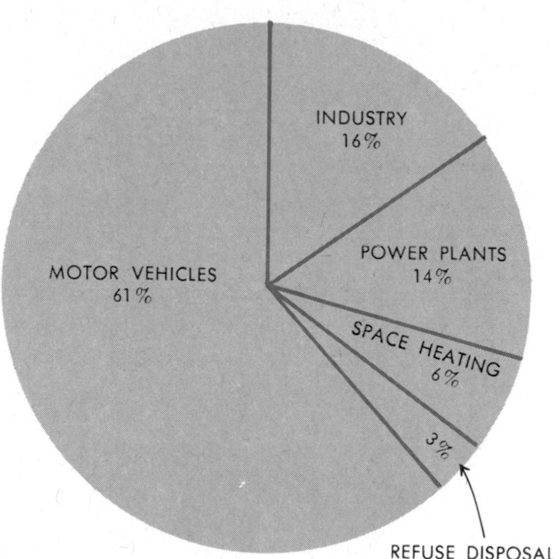

FIGURE 19–1 Air Pollution in the United States (Percentage by Weight)

SOURCE: National Air Pollution Control Administration.

Air Pollution Damage

Because of air pollution, houses must be painted more often, clothes must be laundered more frequently (incidentally contributing to water pollution), and crops are damaged. In parts of New York, New Jersey, Florida, California, Oregon, and Washington, air pollution is now costing farmers more in crop damage than the combined effects of wind, cold, and ice. An expert from the University of California estimates that air pollution damage in California is costing over $100 million a year, while an agricultural authority in New Jersey asserts that the farmers of his state are losing more because of air pollution than from bad weather, insects, or other pests. Farming in some parts of the United States has been halted by pollution from autos and factories. For example, farming has been largely eliminated in the Niagara Falls region of upstate New York because of the increase in the number of chemical factories there. (Naturally, the estimated costs of losing these

[1] J. H. Dales, *Pollution, Property and Prices* (Toronto: University of Toronto, 1968).

farms and their output must be weighed against the gains enjoyed by the presence of the chemical firms.) Figure 19–1 shows the major air pollutants and their sources.

The New York State Health Department estimates that air pollution costs New York state residents about $65 per year on the average, but at the same time admits that the full effects of air pollution are not known. That state's Health Commissioner says that heavy contamination of the air can be decreasing the average New Yorker's longevity by 20 percent. Heart and respiratory diseases are aggravated by small changes in day-to-day pollution, thus hastening the deaths of many city residents. Obviously, the damages in terms of human health are hard to measure in dollar terms. The public tends to become concerned when dramatic episodes occur sporadically.

Hundreds have died during thermal inversions. A *thermal inversion* occurs when a layer of warm air forms over an area, trapping the cooler air beneath it. Smoke and other pollutants that would normally move up and disperse over a wide area are trapped below, forming a thick haze or "smog." Table 19–1 gives the death toll from several thermal inversions.

"Finish your soup, dear, before it gets dirty."

SOURCE: Alden Erikson, *Look* Magazine, June 13, 1967.

TABLE 19–1 Death Toll from Thermal Inversions*

Date	Place	Deaths
1930	Meuse Valley, Belgium	63
1948	Donora, Pennsylvania	26
1952	London, England	4,000
1953	New York, New York	200
1956	London, England	1,000
1962	London, England	300
1963	New York, New York	400
1966	New York, New York	80

* Deaths occurring daily in urban areas as a result of continuing air pollution are not included—only those deaths "in excess of normal." The deaths are for human beings only. In the Donora episode, 800 animals were also killed by the polluted air.

Recent estimates of the damage caused by air pollution in the United States have ranged from about $8 billion to over $20 billion a year. Some authorities refuse to give a specific figure.[2] It is often considered important to place a dollar figure on the damage done by pollution so that the public can be given an indication of the benefit to be derived from correcting it. A taxpayer would be less likely to complain about an additional dollar on his tax bill if he were aware of the fact that the dollar would be used to eliminate a pollutant that is doing $1.50 worth of damage to his property or health.

Water Pollution Damage

It is sometimes easy to determine the cost of water pollution damage in specific instances or in particular areas. Profits in

[2] In discussing damage done by air and water pollution, Allen Kneese, Robert Ayres, and Ralph D'Arge simply say that the costs are "in the tens of billions of dollars annually." See their book *Economics and the Environment* (Washington, D.C.: The Johns Hopkins Press for Resources for the Future, 1970.)

Connecticut's clam industry have dropped from about $48 million in the 1920's to about $1½ million today. (The $48 million was actually about $20 million in the prices of the 1920's. We have inflated the 1920 figure to equate 1920 dollars with today's dollars.) This is largely because of pollution and the destruction of marshes. The estimated value of an estuarine acre off the coast of Maine ranges from $16,781 to $33,563, based upon the potential harvest of shellfish and bait worms. This gives us at least a rough idea of the damage by pollution of the estuaries coming from chemical factories, petroleum refineries, pulp mills, and pesticide factories concentrated in the coastal states. Nearly 570,000 acres have been destroyed as fish and wildlife habitats. California has lost 67 percent of her estuarine habitat, while half of Connecticut's tidal marshes have been obliterated. An inventory of damages resulting from mine drainage in the Ohio basin in one year revealed the following:

$1,143,000 damage to steamboats and barges
$407,000 damage to industrial water supplies
$364,000 damage to domestic water supplies
$76,000 damage to power plants
$76,000 damage to river and harbor structures
$5,000 damage to floating equipment (U.S. Engineers)

These and other figures on water pollution damage fail to take into account such factors as the destruction of the natural beauty of a waterway and the loss of its recreational value.

Solid Waste and Noise Pollution

Other evidences of pollution are unsightly junk yards, rubbish littering the side of a road, and waste materials found in parks or other public and private places. Abandoned automobiles alone constitute a major problem in some areas. In 1960 2,500 abandoned cars in New York City had to be towed away by the authorities; by 1970 the number had reached 72,961 per year. If we estimate the disposal cost at $50 per car, the New York taxpayer is spending $3,648,050 for this alone. The city of Philadelphia is spending about $2 million a year to clean up litter *over and above* its regular garbage and refuse collection costs, while Washington, D.C., is spending about $1½ million. The reader is reminded here of the *opportunity cost principle,* which suggests that the *real cost* would include the educational facilities, health clinics, roads, or other goods and services which the citizens could be enjoying for the money spent on the clean up.

More difficult still is the problem of measuring the damage of noise pollution. The market value of a house in a neighborhood adjacent to an airport will be less than that of a similar house in a similar neighborhood in a quiet area. This difference can be measured very precisely, but there is no way of measuring the damage done by the fact that one's sleep is disturbed or that one's nerves become frayed by the noise of the aircraft.

Pollution as a Social Cost

Pollution is generally considered to be a *social cost*—a cost borne by the people as a whole rather than by the producer or consumer whose economic activities brought it about. In large measure, pollution may also be called an *external cost*. If a firm pours wastes into a stream instead of disposing of them in a manner that does no harm to the public, the cost of the waste disposal has been shifted to society as a whole and thus becomes a social or external cost borne by those who suffer from the pollution. Of course, if a firm installs facilities for the harmless disposal of its wastes, the costs of these facilities would be considered *internal costs* and would be included with the other costs of production. Unit costs might indeed rise, and the firm might pass the additional costs on to its customers. Some of the added cost could be borne by the shareholders, in that their dividends might be decreased. In any event, the producers and the consumers of the product would be carrying the burden of waste disposal rather than the public at large. Although more and more industries are attempting to cut down on the pollution of the air and water, the costs of pollution and waste disposal are still largely social costs.

Social costs are said to be outside the price system. This helps to explain the difficulty encountered in measuring pollution costs. Waste material that a firm dumps into a river is not bought and sold in the marketplace. If it were, it would be an easy matter to measure it in terms of dollars and cents. The value would be included in the Gross National Product. As economist Kenneth Boulding puts it, "When somebody pollutes something and somebody else cleans it up, the cleanup is added to the national product and the pollution is not subtracted. . . ."[3] The plant's accountant does not assign a cost to the wastes that his firm is pouring into the stream. Of course, there may be some charges for the use of sewer systems, the cost of putting filters on furnaces, payments for collection of trash, and other charges related to the waste material.

[3] Kenneth E. Boulding, "Fun and Games with the Gross National Product—The Role of Misleading Indicators in Social Policy," in Harold W. Helfrich, Jr., ed., *The Environmental Crisis* (New Haven: Yale University Press, 1970), p. 161.

Wastes create a cost for someone, and any part of this cost which is not borne by the manufacturer is an external or social cost. Social cost can be either direct or indirect. The man who has to repaint his house every year because of smoke emanating from a nearby factory is directly bearing part of the cost of air pollution. Some will be borne by society collectively, as in the case of a tax increase to build sewage treatment plants. This would be considered indirect.

The problem of accurately measuring the cost of pollution damage will not be solved easily. We can produce figures on the cost of cleaning up a polluted lake, the price of a new sewage treatment plant, and even crop damage resulting from air pollution. We can estimate the additional cost of building maintenance necessitated by smoke and harmful gases in the air. The costs of illness and death related to pollution are not so easily ascertained, however. Lung ailments rise in areas of heavy air pollution, but it is hard to say how much of the cost of treating them can be attributed to air pollution as opposed to other causative factors. And, as yet, we have devised no way to place a money value on the effect that pollution has on our esthetic values. A once-beautiful stream now clogged with filth has become an eyesore, but we do not know how to measure the esthetic deterioration that has occurred. At present we do not even know whether certain of the chemicals going into our waterways are harmful, and experts disagree on the potential damage of thermal pollution (pollution caused by the discharge of heated water into waterways). An essential first step will be to develop universally accepted standards that can be used as yardsticks, and a great deal of research will be needed.

Part B
Some Causes of Pollution

Many of the major causes of pollution have been implied above. Industry usually gets the lion's share of the blame, but farmers, individuals, and even government itself contributes to the problem. Some see pollution as a natural consequence of our economic growth and development. As Boulding puts it, "The ultimate physical product of economic life is garbage. The system takes ores and fossil fuels . . . out of the earth, chews them up in the process of production, and eventually spews them out into sewers and garbage dumps."[4] It is no coincidence that the waste produced in the United States is growing at about the same yearly rate as the increase in the GNP. Few economists propose that economic growth be halted as a means of controlling pollution. Instead, they tend to concentrate on some of the following specific causes.

Population Growth and Concentration

As the population increases, more waste can be expected to accumulate, our natural resources will be exploited at an increasing rate, and there will be increasing demands for the production which in itself contributes toward the problem. Unrestricted population growth and the rapid expansion of technology and industry are cited by many as the major overall causative factors in our environmental crisis. By 1970, Americans were pouring 2 million gallons of sewage into the nation's waterways every second. From the end of World War I to the middle of this century, the United States used up more of most metals and mineral fuels than had previously been consumed by all the people of the world throughout all of human history! Even if the population remained static, however, the problem would still be serious.

We must look beyond the simple fact of overall population growth to realize its effects on the environment. More people mean an increasing demand for more production—production which is bound to increase waste and pollution. It should be noted, however, that the urban portion of the population is growing rapidly. In 1950, 97 million people lived in urban areas in the United States. By 1970 urban population had reached 159 million, and by 1980 it is expected to rise to 197 million. In rural areas where there is a small population, waste and pollution are often tolerable because they can be spread over the countryside.

Waste materials can be safely discarded in a stream when the stream has enough

[4] *Ibid.*, p. 162.

oxygen to sustain its underwater life. Bacteria in the stream attack the wastes, the bacteria are consumed by higher organisms, and the water becomes pure by the time it reaches the next town. Sewage in a stream will pose no threat to health if it is allowed to flow far enough, because it will be purified by dilution, green plants, the sun's rays, and oxygen. But as cities and towns have grown to the point where three fourths of the people live on 1 percent of the land, urban areas are closer together and downstream towns must use water that has been polluted by those upstream. The water does not flow far enough for nature to purify it.

Population congestion also aggravates air pollution. An increase in the number of automobiles produced and sold is usually seen as a good sign for the economy. But it also means that more fumes will enter the air as the cars are used. (In the process of producing more cars, waste accumulation, and water and air pollution will rise.) More smoke will enter the air from home heating systems. Studies have shown that death rates from lung cancer (per 100,000 of population) are twice as high in large cities (population over one million) as in rural areas. As more people attempt to use a public good, such as water or air, the quality of that good in terms of the service that it renders to each individual will deteriorate. Water, air, and public land (such as public beaches or parks) are limited in supply—in technical terms, the supply curve is inelastic. For a time, more users can be accommodated with little or no deterioration in quality. Each has a "threshold," however. When the threshold has been reached, *interference effects* become obvious and the individual derives less satisfaction from use of the public good. Deterioration in quality then increases disproportionately.[5] (See Figure 19–1.)

Industry

While technological advances have helped make our economy grow and have helped us enjoy a higher level of living, they have also contributed toward pollution. Industrial production rose by over 700 percent in the first half of this century, and huge amounts of water are used by industry. Table 19–2 indicates the amounts of water used in the manufacture of certain products.

Of course, industries can often use the same water over and over. This constant reuse will destroy the quality of the water, however, unless it is purified before being returned to the source. (Some industries do purify the water they have used, often returning it to the stream cleaner than it was before.)

Total water use in the United States has risen from 40 billion gallons a day in 1900 to over 411 billion gallons a day in 1970. By 1980 it is expected to reach 494 billion gallons a day. Since 1900 there has been a 900 percent increase in the amount used by public water utilities, nearly 800 percent in water used for irrigation, over 300 percent in rural domestic use (in spite of the fact that the farm population has dropped drastically), nearly 2,700 percent in the use of steam electric utilities, and over 800 percent in industrial and miscellaneous uses. (The latter three refer to self-supplied uses.)

Some of the effects of the increasing utilization of our water supplies are tragic. In 1968, for example, nearly 15

[5] For a highly technical analysis of this problem, see Jerome Rothenberg, "The Economics of Congestion and Pollution: An Integrated View," *American Economic Review*, May 1970, pp. 114–121.

TABLE 19–2 Water Use by Various Industries in the U.S.

Product	Amount of Water Used to Manufacture
1 ton of synthetic rubber	660,000 gallons
1 ton of viscose rayon	200,000 gallons
1 ton of wool	140,000 gallons
1 ton of steel	65,000 gallons*
1 ton of sulphate paper	64,000 gallons
1 ton of smokeless powder	50,000 gallons
1 ton of newspaper pulp	40,000 gallons
1 ton of aluminum	30,000 gallons*
1 automobile	15,000 gallons
1 gallon of alcohol	236 gallons

* In some cases the amounts are considerably less. One steel company in California, for example, reuses water so that it can make a ton of steel with only 1,100 gallons of water. A ton of aluminum can be made with as little as 1,200 gallons of water.

million fish were killed as a result of pollution, as compared with less than 9 million in 1966. Industrial operations accounted for the death of over 6 million fish in 1968, and agricultural operations for 375,000. Sewage systems killed over 6 million. In 1970 commercial fishing was stopped in several places because of dangerous levels of mercury coming from industrial wastes. Figure 19–2 shows U.S. areas in which mercury is a problem. Vermont decreed that no fish caught in its waters could be sold, while other states posted signs warning people that it was all right to fish for pleasure, but not to eat the fish they caught. In 1971 the Food and Drug Administration warned the public not to eat swordfish because of the high levels of mercury discovered in some swordfish catches.

The rapidly growing chemical industry is producing an estimated 500 new compounds annually, and by 1971 there were about 12,000 different toxic chemical compounds in use in American industry. The highly publicized "death" of Lake Erie was brought about in large measure by the fact that 7 million pounds of chemicals were being dumped into it daily, robbing the lake of its life-supporting oxygen. Other industries dump wood bark, chips, sawdust, oil, blood, manure, and mineral wastes into our water. Acid drainage from coal mines helped to make the waterways of the Ohio Valley what authorities referred to as a cesspool, an open sewer, and "a vast floating garbage can." The Cuyahoga River has been so clogged with oil and sludge that it has actually been a fire hazard! An estimated 70 percent of industrial thermal pollution is caused by the steam-generated electrical power industry. Steam electric utilities consumed 5 billion gallons of water a day in 1900. By 1970 their use exceeded 132 billion gallons a day, and is expected to reach nearly 162 billion gallons by 1980. With a growing population and more industry, more electric power plants are appearing all the time, and more are needed. Some authorities are alarmed at this trend, asserting that thermal pollution is destroying fish and plant life in our waterways. As Figure 19–1 showed, however, industry is also an extremely important factor in air pollution.

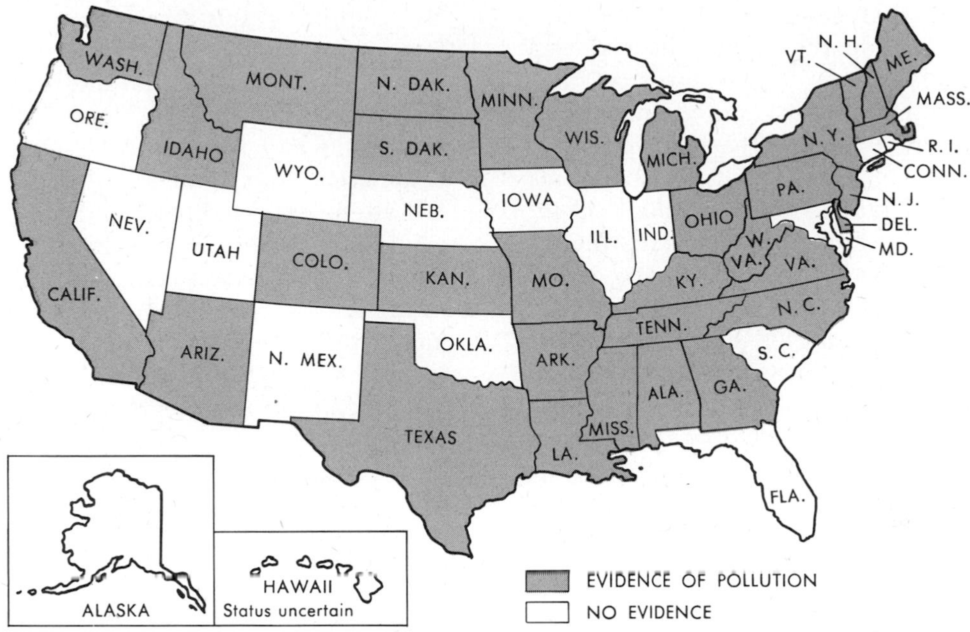

FIGURE 19–2 Where Mercury Pollution Is a Problem in the United States

Thirty-three of the 50 states report waterways that have been hurt by mercury pollution. SOURCE: Nev York *Times*, September 11, 1970.

Agriculture

Into our waters go the drainage from dairy barns, pigpens, manure heaps, poisonous insecticides, and fertilizers. Furthermore, through poor conservation, farmers, ranchers, and lumbermen have helped to create pollution problems. The United States once had 522 million acres of farm land. At least 50 million acres have been ruined, and another 50 million are nearly gone. Most of the vital topsoil has been lost on another 100 million acres. When America was first settled our topsoil averaged nine inches in depth—it is now down to six. When we consider that it takes nature from 500 to 1000 years to create one inch of topsoil, we can see the seriousness of this problem. As Americans moved west and rapidly populated the continent they inflicted damage on ou soil, forests, and grasslands. For example, cotton would be planted in Georgia because cotton was profitable. This crop quickly uses up the fertility of the soil, however. Instead of planting another crop that might help to restore the soil, the cotton planter would simply pack up and move westward to begin again in Mississippi.

Meanwhile, "cut-and-run" timber companies would destroy the forests of one area as rapidly as possible, then move on to the next state. Entire forests were stripped bare, young trees that might have reseeded the area were destroyed, and cattle and sheep were allowed to graze on the cutover land, thus destroying any new growth that appeared. Poor farming techniques and the destruction of forests and grasslands helped to create the conditions that led to the terrible dust storms which swept away the topsoil from millions of acres of farm land and destroyed crops in many other areas as well. The great dust storms dumped dirt on cities hundreds of miles from the Middle West and helped to pollute rivers and streams. (A single storm on May 11, 1934, carried away 300 million tons of topsoil; another in April 1954 destroyed 11 million acres.) Insufficient plant cover, heavy cultivation, and intensive grazing were basic causes.

Failing to realize the full value of grass, pioneer farmers plowed up nearly 250 million acres of grassland and helped to create the conditions that made dust storms, water pollution, and floods possible. Originally, the United States had 820 million acres of commercial timberland, but this has been reduced to a little less than 500 million. Small lumber firms find it costly to replant trees and engage in other conservation practices that may lower or even wipe out their profit margins. It takes from 30 to 50 years for a newly planted tree to reach commercially useful size, and the "little guy" simply cannot wait that long. Since water can be conserved by maintaining forests over a large portion of our watersheds, the destruction of forests has had the effect of aggravating our water problem. A *watershed* is the area from which water is drained by the rivers of a region. If a watershed's coverage of vegetation is destroyed, the land cannot absorb enough water. As much as four feet of water can be absorbed and stored in eight feet of forest soil which is littered with twigs and leaves. A good watershed is like a huge blotter, which minimizes erosion and keeps the water from running down slopes too rapidly, carrying away valuable topsoil, polluting the streams, and causing flooding.

As private developers (and even some government agencies) have converted farm land and forest areas to industrial, commercial, and housing sites, they have too often destroyed trees and other greenery.[6] To a certain extent, trees and other plants help control air pollution. The green leaves attract and hold pollutant-laden dust particles which are subsequently washed into the soil, where they may eventually disintegrate into basic soil elements. Many farmers are unable to afford the costs of good conservation practices, with the result that the social costs of poor conservation have been enormous. Note, for example, the tremendous amounts of the taxpayers' money that have been used for such things as the Soil Bank and reforestation projects.

Consumers and Households

Few individuals realize the extent to which they contribute to the waste and pollution of our waters. Each person may be using as much as 100 to 200 gallons per day. Table 19–3 shows estimated typical household water uses.

More than 20 million Americans rely upon private septic tanks for sewage disposal. The postwar rush to the suburbs, where new homes were built beyond existing sewer lines and water mains, accounts for this. In a rural area a septic tank poses no problem as long as it is in the proper kind of soil and water table, with ample underground space separating it from drinking water supplies and streams. However, septic tanks in sub-

[6] This is occurring at the rate of about 1 million acres a year.

TABLE 19–3 Water Use by the Typical American Household

Purpose	Estimated Amount
One Bath	30 to 40 gallons
One Shower	10 to 20 gallons
One washing-machine cycle	20 to 30 gallons
One washing of dishes	10 gallons
One toilet flush	3 to 5 gallons
One dripping faucet	4 gallons a day
Leak in toilet bowl	35 gallons a day
Sprinkling lawn (8,000 sq. ft.)	30,000 gallons per year

urban regions cannot be relied upon to cope with the tremendous amount of water wastes poured into them. They cannot efficiently contain and dissolve the new synthetic phosphate detergents. (In 1971, New York's Suffolk County, where 95 percent of the people have septic tanks, outlawed the sale of detergents.)

The consumer also contributes to air pollution through such things as failure to maintain properly home heating systems, burning leaves and rubbish, and extensive use of the automobile. (Again refer to Figure 19–1 and note the contribution of the motor vehicle to air pollution.) The individual who is careless in discarding trash, the home gardener who employs poisonous insecticides and herbicides, and the housewife who insists upon detergents instead of soap and plastic instead of biodegradable containers all contribute to the environmental problem.

Other Causative Factors

Ironically, government itself often contributes to the problem of pollution. In a congested city, sewage treatment plants and incinerators for waste disposal may partially solve one aspect of the problem, while at the same time these facilities often help to pollute the air. The federal government has had problems with the disposal of atomic wastes and poisonous gases.

In addition to the steady and somewhat predictable pollution caused by industries, farms, and municipal sewage disposal, we are also faced with sporadic and accidental incidents. These may be highly dramatic, as in the case of the oil tanker *Torrey Canyon* which was stranded off the southwest coast of England or the eruption of an offshore oil well off Santa Barbara, California, in 1969; or they may be little known, such as the problem caused when a plant technician opened the wrong valve on a piping system and poured 6,000 gallons of poisonous aniline into the Kanawha River. These unpublicized accidents are very numerous. There were 550 such incidents in the Ohio Valley alone during a recent three-year period.

Thus the causes of pollution are many and varied. Some are economic in nature, arising out of the productive process and related to the conditions of the market system that encourages ever-increasing output of goods and services. Some are related to daily living, as the waste from millions of human beings enters our water supply in the form of toilet flushings, bathwater, dishwater, and laundry washings. The finger of blame can be pointed in many directions.

Part C
Controlling Pollution

Before we can take steps to control pollution, we must know what is causing it, how much pollution is costing society, what feasible steps can be taken to control it, and how much it will cost to control it. Unfortunately, we do not have easy answers to any of these questions. As late as July 1970 a federal official stated that he was unaware that mercury was being dumped in waterways. He had assumed that, because of the high value of this poisonous element, it was being reclaimed. Further studies will be needed to determine exactly how much mercury residue in fish constitutes a danger to human health, the extent to which thermal pollution is dangerous to marine life, which of the new chemicals constitute hazards, and so on.

Often, not only the amount but the nature of the pollutants entering our waterways undergoes change. Each pollutant has to be factored out separately and tested to determine its effects on the water. As yet there is no efficient way to monitor phosphate concentrations in sewage water, and these can change rapidly during the course of a day. (Phosphates are the oxidized form of phosphorus present in household detergents, and their presence in sewage water varies, depending upon the time of day that the average housewife is doing her washing.) If they cannot be measured rapidly, it is difficult to determine what quantity of chemicals to add to the water to eliminate them. One authority fears that it is even possible to pollute the water by adding excessive chemicals to "unpollute" it. The nitrogen in sewage can be eliminated by letting it flow through large cooling towers. When exposed to air, it is eliminated in the form of ammonia gas—thus a water pollutant becomes converted into an air pollutant!

One thing is certain. The cost of dealing with pollution will be enormous. It is estimated that it will take $100 million per year for 50 years to clean up San Francisco Bay. The restoration of Lake Michigan will cost $10 billion. Government at all levels has been increasing spending to control pollution, but pollution is often rising at a more rapid rate. Pollution in Long Island Sound doubled during the decade of the 1960's, for example. Between 1966 and 1968, the amount of contaminates entering the air increased by 9 million tons. Between 1965 and 1970, 58 state-aided munipical sewage projects were completed in New York state at a cost of $19 million, but no improvement resulted. In February 1970 President Nixon announced a $10 billion program to build sewage treatment plants over a five-year period. This represents a significant increase over previous expenditures for pollution control, but some environmental experts point out that it is less than $10 per capita per year, and they fear that the funds will be used to build outmoded treatment plants.

Internalizing Pollution Costs

Some people propose that the costs of pollution be internalized. That is, the cost would be borne by the one doing the polluting. At first glance this seems to be a fair and simple solution, but let us consider some of the possible implications.

The automobile is said to be a major factor in air pollution, and federal projections show that unless controls are instituted, air pollution by automobiles will continue to increase. (See Figure 19–3.)

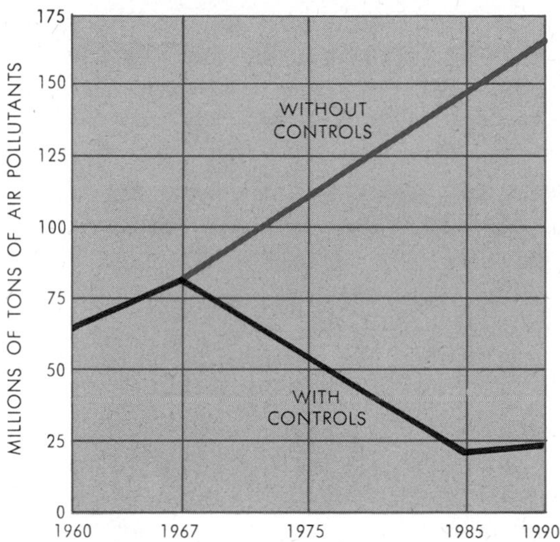

FIGURE 19–3 Air Pollution by Automobiles

Although controls can reduce pollution caused by motor vehicles, pollutants are expected to rise again after 1985 because of projected increases in the number of cars. SOURCE: New York *Times,* July 11, 1970.

The United Automobile Workers union has gone so far as to urge Federal action that would, in effect, banish the internal combustion engine from automobiles by 1975. The UAW, along with several conservation groups, also urged that pollution-control devices be installed and that the manufacturers keep them in repair without cost to the auto owner. This would include installation in used cars as well as new. Few economists would oppose the idea of pollution control devices in cars, but most would seriously doubt that this can be done "at no cost." The question is—who pays the cost?

American industry has been increasing its anti-pollution efforts. In 1970, industry planned to spend $2.3 billion in environmental control, an increase of 37 percent over 1969. One firm alone, a large automobile manufacturer, increased its emission research from $51.2 million in 1969 to $70.2 million in 1970. Oil companies, too, are spending huge amounts to develop gasoline with a lower lead content. The costs of these efforts will be passed on to the consumer, at least in part. A leading emission control engineer estimates that the type of exhaust system needed to meet federal standards for 1975 may raise auto prices by $200 or $300. The price of nonleaded gasoline is expected to be from one to five cents more per gallon than leaded premium grades. Recently a power company in Illinois was granted a 4.5 percent rate increase because of its planned expenditures for pollution controls.

Some industries are in a better position than others to pass these costs on to the consumers. Much depends upon elasticity of demand. (See Chapter 2, page 23 for a discussion of elasticity.) If demand is relatively inelastic, as is the case in many of the necessities of life, price can be increased without a correspondingly great decline in sales. If demand is relatively elastic, the percentage drop in sales will exceed the percentage increase in price, meaning lower total revenues for the firm. Some firms might be forced to curtail operations (this has already happened in some cases) or even to close down altogether.

Some Possible Allocation Effects of Pollution Control

Pollution control, then, can bring about a reallocation of resources. Suppose, for example, that substantial increases in the prices of motor vehicles and gasoline bring about a sharp decline in sales. Auto workers might be out of jobs, many gasoline stations might go bankrupt, the sales of auto accessories and tires might drop, and so on. Many people whose livelihoods directly or indirectly depend on the automobile would suffer, at least temporarily, until they shift to new occupations. Thus some of the cost of controlling pollution would press heavily upon them. Those who had ceased to be motor vehicle owners would shift to public transportation, increasing the demand in that sector. In view of the fact that many public transportation facilities, such as commuter railroads, are already obsolete and inadequate, there would be urgent need for new investment here. Undoubtedly a substantial amount of the cost would ultimately fall on the taxpayer. So, once again, the cost would be borne by the general public. Of course fares might also rise. Since demand for the services provided by public transportation facilities is often inelastic, the consumer would also feel the pinch. (When New York City subway fares were increased by 50 percent in 1970, the number of riders dropped by only about 5 percent—a highly inelastic situation.) If the pressure on public facilities brings a fare increase, a disproportionate share of the burden will be assumed by the low-income consumer. The effects would be *regressive*. The working man who earns $100 a week and who must ride the commuter train and finds his transportation cost rising by $1 per week, is paying an extra 1 percent of his pay a week. The $500-a-week executive riding the same train is paying only one fifth of 1 percent extra.

These are but a few of the possible allocation effects. Many more could be considered (an entire book could be devoted to them), such as the possibility that greater overall efficiency might ultimately occur if more people would ride commuter trains instead of driving their cars on our congested highways. Here we are simply trying to point out the importance of careful economic analyses before deceptively simple solutions are adopted.

"Trade-Offs" and Pollution Control

A number of "trade-offs" must be considered. In the hypothetical example of automobile and gasoline costs given above, we are dealing with a situation in which we would have to trade jobs in the automotive and related industries for less air pollution. An actual case is that of the home construction industry. Several states are taking drastic steps to force communities to build or improve sewage treatment facilities. Although there is a dire need for more housing, in some areas construction has slowed down or even halted because of the costly sewage disposal requirements. Costs of homes have risen by as much as 30 percent.

Chesapeake Bay presents another illustration. The population of the Baltimore area is soaring, and industrial development and shipping are vital to the area's economic growth. These factors are increasing the problem of pollution, however. The Army Corps of Engineers is dredging Baltimore harbor and the Chesapeake and Delaware Canal. This will aid shipping and commerce, but it will also aggravate the pollution problem. Already, the discharge of human waste from the 6,000 ships entering and leaving Baltimore each year is equal to the sewage of a city of 25,000 people. Unless the people of the area are willing to accept such things as a zero population growth and a slowdown in industrial development, they must increase expenditures on pollution control.

The trade-off effect often involves two industries. On Long Island, for example, there were 41 duck farms which had been accused of polluting the shellfish beds of the bay, resulting in a loss to the shellfish industry of $2.5 million a year. If the duck farms install waste treatment facilities and pass the cost on to the consumer, the consumer will be trading off ducks (the price of duck would rise) in order to enjoy more clams. These and many other trade-offs should be taken into account by consumers and citizens before they decide what public anti-pollution policies to support.

Negative Incentives and Recycling

Several ways have been suggested to make the polluter bear the costs. One of these is the proposal that effluent or emission fees be imposed on the creators of pollution. This scheme represents an attempt to rely largely on the market system. The fees would serve as *negative incentives,* inducing polluters to keep such things as harmful smokestack emissions below specified levels. Those who discharge noxious fumes into the air or sewage into the water would pay a fee based upon the emission of smoke per hour or the amount of sewage effluent. The polluter would be induced to keep emissions as low as possible and perhaps even to try to find ways of filtering the emissions to recapture usable chemicals. The sludge collected as a result of the sewage treatment process could be used as fertilizer. Dried blood can provide nitrogen for the soil, and steamed bone meal, finely ground, is a source of phosphorus. These are waste materials from packing plants, and, since the amount of oxygen required to decompose these wastes is ten times greater than that needed for ordinary sewage, the value of recovering these products instead of dumping them in our waterways is apparent. Distillery wastes can be dried and used for cattle fodder; vanillin and alcohol can be made from sulphite wastes; and molasses can be made from citrus peelings. Thus, by *recycling* or reclaiming waste products, at least some of the costs of pollution control might be defrayed. Those in favor of effluent fees assert that such fees would provide the incentive to find uses for waste products and to develop more efficient methods of reducing pollution. Opponents fear that large firms would simply see them as "licenses to contaminate" while small firms might have to shut down (thus reducing competition and possibly encouraging monopoly or oligopoly in the industry) because of added costs.

Taxes to Control Pollution

Some people feel that government should use its taxing power to control pollution. For example, President Nixon in 1970 proposed a levy of 2.3 cents per gallon on leaded gasoline, while Senator William Proxmire (Democrat of Wisconsin) proposed a 1-cent-per-pound "disposal tax" on all goods except consumables that will require disposal within 10 years of origin. Under Proxmire's plan, manufacturers would receive a credit against the disposal fee if they reuse such items as returnable soft-drink bottles. Senator Gaylord Nelson (Democrat of Wisconsin) suggests a tax on packaging that would be about equal to the cost of disposing of it. Vermont has placed an effluent tax on industrial pollution. One economist proposes an excise tax on automobiles high enough to pay the cost of getting rid of junked cars. (He acknowledges that this would probably be a "mild deterrent" to the use of autos, and implies that this would be a good thing.) Others point out that these schemes would place the burden on the consumer, resulting in a shift of the market toward low-pollution commodities which might be inferior to those the consumer actually prefers.

Direct Government Controls

Direct governmental controls and regulations are favored by many. In 1970 Illinois enacted a law that is perhaps the most comprehensive in the nation. A single Environmental Protection Agency was established to consolidate the pollution control authority of several state boards and commissions, and a State Pollution Control Board was set up to develop pollution standards and hear cases brought by the enforcing agency. Polluting companies can be required to post a performance bond to ensure compliance with orders for improvements, and the Environmental Protection Agency can even seal up a firm's equipment during pollution emergencies.

Rigorous action by one state can mean little, however, if other states fail to adopt similar plans. Waterways, air currents, and winds do not stop at state lines. Thus, the citizens of one state may often bear the cost of pollution emanating from another state. Unified control by the federal government might seem to be the logical answer, but fear and distrust of federal authority is endemic in the United States. As one Chamber of Commerce representative once put it, "We should not have to run to Washington every time we want to flush the toilet."[7] One way around this is to form regional compacts in which several states cooperate. A good example is the Ohio River Valley Water Sanitation Compact (ORSANCO), entered into by the states of Indiana, West Virginia, Ohio, New York, Illinois, Kentucky, Pennsylvania, and Virginia in 1948.[8] The formation of these compacts is not an easy matter, however. ORSANCO was approved by Congress in 1936, but 12 years elapsed before the participating states actually entered into the compact. The citizens of some states were reluctant to accept a tax burden to build sewage treatment facilities for the benefit of their neighbors; the fear of a regional authority was only slightly less than the fear of federal authority; other priorities became paramount during World War II; and many questions arose on how the Compact's budget would be prorated among the participating states. Once these difficulties were ironed out, however, ORSANCO scored some dramatic achievements. Originally, less than 1 percent of the 2,800,000 people living along the banks of the Ohio had treatment facilities; now, over 99 percent are served by sewage treatment plants.

Actually, federal action to control pollution is not a new concept. In 1899 Congress passed the Refuse Act, permitting private citizens to bring to the attention of federal attorneys information about the discharge of refuse into navigable waters. The law provided fines from $500 to $2,500 a day and 30-day jail sentences, and stipulated that the citizen who reports the polluter may receive half the fines collected.

Other early laws were the Public Health Service Act of 1912, which authorized re-

[7] *Hearings* of Committee on Rivers and Harbors, House of Representatives, 79th Cong., 1st Sess., November 1945, p. 183.

[8] For an excellent history of this Compact, see Edward J. Cleary, *The Orsanco Story: Water Quality Management in the Ohio Valley Under an Interstate Compact* (Washington: The Johns Hopkins Press for Resources for the Future, 1967).

search on water pollution, and the Oil Pollution Act of 1924, which attempted to control oil discharges in coastal waters only. The modern history of federal action began with Public Law 845 in 1948. This law stated that national policy was "to recognize, preserve and protect the primary responsibilities and rights of the states in preventing and controlling water pollution," but offered technical aid and grants of money. Interstate compacts were encouraged. Subsequent legislation (including Public Law 660 in 1956, the amendments of 1961, the Water Quality Act of 1965, and the Clean Waters Restoration Act of 1966) broadened the base of federal involvement, strengthened enforcement provisions, authorized more funds for sewage treatment plants and research, established quality standards for interstate waters, and made it unlawful to discharge oil into the territorial waters of the United States.

The federal goverment did not begin to act against air pollution until the passage of the Air Pollution Act of 1955, which authorized expenditures for research and aid to state and local governments. Under the Clean Air Act of 1963 and its 1965 amendments, more funds for grants and research were provided, the federal government was empowered to take action to abate interstate air pollution, and the Secretary of Health, Education and Welfare was authorized to set standards controlling emissions from new motor vehicles. The Air Quality Act of 1967 (amended in 1970) established air quality regions and enabled the Secretary of HEW to approve quality standards adopted in those regions. More money was provided for research on controlling pollution from the combustion of coal, oil, and gasoline.

The year 1970 saw a marked increase in interest in the pollution problem. Federal officials called upon the auto industry to eliminate nearly all hydrocarbon and carbon monoxide emissions by 1975. Public Law 91-224 tightened controls over pollution of waters by oil and sewage from vessels and discharges from mines, and established controls over thermal pollution from atomic power plants. The federal government moved against states as well as private companies accused of polluting waterways.

Many states also stepped up their activities. Michigan, for example, passed a law allowing citizens to file suit against anyone (including the state itself) who might be contaminating the air, water, or land resources. The costs, however, were seen to be staggering. New York estimated that it would take $4.2 billion to eliminate industrial and municipal waste from the state's waterways. In the private sector, some banks began to sell "earth bonds" paying from 5 to 5¾ percent interest to raise money to lend at low interest rates to environment-conscious companies. Several oil companies intensified work on developing low-lead or nonleaded fuel. Other firms are at work on such things as a safe DDT (an insecticide accused of being a major polluter), and incinerators that will dispose of solid waste without causing pollution.

Summary and Conclusion

While all of these efforts are encouraging, it is clear that much more will be needed. A major problem will be that of convincing the public that everyone will have to bear some of the costs, directly or indirectly. Cost/benefit analyses should be helpful, insofar as such analyses are possible. If the public can be shown that for every dollar spent on pollution control there will be more than a dollar's worth of benefits, stronger support will be forthcoming. This may not always be possible, however, because of the fact that many of the costs of pollution (such as physical discomfort caused by smog, shorter life span resulting from polluted air, and esthetic deterioration) cannot be expressed in money terms. Thus, even if the benefits as measured in dollars and cents appear to be less than the money costs of curing pollution, the steps to effect a cure must be taken anyway.

Currently the public appears to be concerned about pollution but to have an unsophisticated notion of the sacrifices that will have to be made to cope with it. A recent Gallup poll found that 51 percent of the adults sampled were "deeply concerned" about pollution, and that 75 percent of these would be willing to "pay something" to improve the situation. Over half of those who were willing to pay something, however, meant $10 or less. If every man, woman, and child in the United States contributed $10, the total sum would be less than half the amount needed to clean up New York state's waterways alone! In spite of some excellent work being done in the private sector, industry will not generally dip into profits for pollution abatement unless forced to do so. The firm that increases its costs by installing pollution control devices may lose ground to its competitors who do not do likewise. A firm will not recycle or reuse wastes unless the revenues derived therefrom at least equal the costs of recovering and reusing the wastes. Costly research and experimentation will be needed to determine whether or not recycling pays off. One paper mill has found that it costs $100 a day to operate a purification facility, and that it recovers $500 a day in reusable chemicals as a result. Another study reveals that the typical junked automobile can produce $56 worth of marketable metal products at a processing cost of $51. In these cases, the benefits clearly outweigh the costs. But this will not always be true. One large oil company got back only 10 cents for every dollar expended on attempts to recover such things as sulphur and sulphuric acid. Richard D. Vaughan, Director of the U. S. Bureau of Solid Waste Management and himself a proponent of recycling, points out that waste management now costs the nation $4.5 billion annually, and that it will require an increase of 18.5 percent in expenditures over a period of 10 years to do an effective job of coping with waste. One nonprofit conservation organization estimates that the costs of pollution tend to outweigh prevention costs by 16 to 1, however.

In any event, the costs will have to be shared by everyone. If industry is forced by law to install pollution control facilities, the cost will appear in the price of the product or service, and the consumer will pay. The public cannot expect to continue to increase its use of electricity, for example, without creating a need for more power plants. Power plants will add to pollution unless forced to use more expensive fuels and procedures, and the cost of these will be added to the consumer's electric bill. If industry is given a tax deduction for pollution-control expenses, the cost is being passed indirectly to the general taxpaying public. To estimate the burden in this case, we would have to examine the tax system. For example, suppose that the federal government allows business firms to deduct the cost of all pollution-control devices and activities from their federal taxes. The government needs a certain amount of income, and a major source of this is the personal income tax, which is progressive. (See Chapter 9, Part C, and Chapter 10, Part A, for a discussion of taxation.)

To the extent that those paying the personal income tax must make up for the revenues lost because of the pollution-control deductions, the burden will be somewhat progressive—that is, those with higher incomes will generally pay a greater percentage of their incomes than those at the lower levels. Suppose, on the other hand, that a state whose taxes are *regressive* grants tax deductions for pollution control. Now the lost revenues must be made up by the general taxpayer, and the lower level person pays a greater percentage of his income. Thus, in a consideration of who will pay for pollution control, we must also seek to determine how fairly the burden will be distributed. Economic analysis alone will not solve the problem, but an application of such concepts as opportunity cost, "trade-offs," and cost/benefit analysis will help to shed light on the situation and perhaps will result in more intelligent proposals for the best solution.

REVIEW: THE HIGHLIGHTS OF THE CHAPTER

1. Air and water pollution is becoming a worldwide problem, causing damage to wildlife, plants, physical property, and human health.
2. Pollution costs are the sum of public and private expenditures to avoid pollution damage plus "welfare damage."
3. The full effects and costs of pollution are difficult to measure.
4. Estimated costs of air pollution in the U.S. have ranged from $8 billion to $20 billion a year.
5. Pollution is generally considered to be a social cost—a cost borne by the people as a whole.
6. Economic growth, industrialization, population increases, and urbanization are explanations for increasing pollution.
7. Private industry, government, farmers, and individuals all contribute to pollution.
8. The costs of pollution control must be weighed against the benefits to be derived therefrom.
9. Poor conservation of trees, grass, and soil have helped cause pollution.
10. The "cures" for some forms of pollution help to cause other kinds of pollution.
11. Pollution control measures can help bring about a reallocation of resources.
12. "Negative incentives" such as effluent or emission fees represent one possible means of controlling pollution; recycling or reclaiming waste products is another.
13. Taxes on leaded gasoline might help control air pollution, while disposal fees could encourage industry to reuse items which are now simply discarded.
14. Local and state action is often ineffective because problems cross political lines.
15. Although the federal government passed a pollution control law over 70 years ago, only recently has it moved vigorously to deal with this problem.

IN CONCLUSION: SOME AIDS TO UNDERSTANDING

Terms for Review

welfare damage
social cost
external cost
internal cost
direct cost
indirect cost
interference effects
watershed
thermal pollution
"trade-offs"
effluent fees
negative incentives
recycling
disposal tax
ORSANCO
Refuse Act

Questions for Review

1. What are some of the major evidences of pollution damage?
2. Explain the difference between internal and external costs.
3. Why is the cost of pollution so difficult to measure?
4. Explain the difference between direct and indirect costs of pollution.
5. How do economic development, industrial growth, urbanization, and population increases help cause pollution?
6. List some of the specific causes of pollution and explain the effects of each.
7. Explain how poor conservation in general has helped to cause pollution.
8. Is it possible to internalize the costs of pollution? If so, how? If not, why not?
9. In what ways might attempts to control pollution bring about a reallocation of resources? How might various groups be affected? What does elasticity have to do with this?
10. What are some of the possible "trade-offs" relating to pollution control?
11. Explain the use of "negative incentives" to control pollution.
12. What is meant by recycling?
13. How can government use its tax powers to help control pollution?
14. Discuss the strengths and weaknesses of local and state efforts to control pollution.
15. What are the problems involved in trying to spread the costs of pollution control so that everyone bears a "fair" share?

Additional Questions and Problems

1. Make a study of mercury pollution, which received widespread attention in newspapers and magazines in 1970–1971. How does this problem exemplify some of the concepts discussed in this chapter?
2. What are the major pollution problems of your own city, state, or area? Examine the causes, the costs of pollution damage, and the proposals for dealing with the problems. Evaluate each proposal in terms of the economic principles set forth in this chapter.
3. Examine government's role in conservation and pollution control in your area. Evaluate government actions in terms of effectiveness and in terms of possible allocation effects.

4. Trace the history of the U.S. government's efforts to deal with pollution, and evaluate those efforts in terms of the problems that exist.

SELECTED READINGS

Battan, Louis J. *The Unclean Sky: A Meteorologist Looks at Air Pollution.* New York: Doubleday Anchor, 1966.

Davies, J. Clarence. *The Politics of Pollution.* New York: Pegasus, 1970.

DeBell, Garrett, ed. *The Environment Handbook.* New York: Ballantine Books, 1970.

Esposito, John C. and Larry J. Silverman. *Vanishing Air: The Ralph Nader Study Group Report on Air Pollution.* New York: Grossman, 1970.

Forbes, R. J. *The Conquest of Nature: Technology and its Consequences.* New York: Praeger, 1968.

Fortune Editors. *The Environment: A National Mission for the Seventies.* New York: Harper & Row, 1970.

Goldman, Marshall I., ed. *Controlling Pollution: The Economics of a Cleaner America.* Englewood Cliffs, N.J.: Prentice-Hall, 1967.

Helfrich, Herold W., Jr., ed. *The Environmental Crisis.* New Haven: Yale University Press, 1970.

Herfindahl, Orris C. and Allen V. Kneese. *Quality of the Environment: An Economic Approach to Some Problems in Using Land, Water, and Air.* Baltimore: Johns Hopkins Press, 1967.

Jarrett, Henry, ed. *Environmental Quality in a Growing Economy.* Baltimore: Johns Hopkins Press, 1966.

Moss, Frank E. *The Water Crisis.* New York: Praeger, 1967.

Task Force on Environmental Health. *A Strategy for a Livable Environment.* Washington, D.C.: Government Printing Office, 1967.

United States Government. *The Cost of Clean Water and Its Economic Impact.* Washington, D.C.: Government Printing Office, 1969. (Three volumes.)

Wolozin, Harold, ed. *The Economics of Air Pollution.* New York: W. W. Norton & Company, 1968.

20 Poverty amid Affluence

THE AUTHORS' NOTE TO THE STUDENT

In the 1950's an increasing number of economists began to question whether poverty in this country was still a problem. Many journalists have popularized the title of John Galbraith's book, *The Affluent Society.* A battery of statistics seemed to confirm this optimism until one author showed us the other side of the coin. Michael Harrington in his book *The Other America* offered a new view of poverty, one that had been invisible to most Americans.

A casual stroll through a central city or a quick reading of any news-magazine points out our inconsistencies. We are both rich and poor. We have reduced the number of poor and increased the number on welfare. We have increased our proposed solutions and seem more frustrated than ever in finding workable answers.

In this chapter we will examine who are the poor, what are the causes for their poverty, and what are some of the proposed solutions. We will then take a careful look at discrimination and what role it plays in our economy. In the final part we will examine the military–industrial complex to see whether it is in some way responsible for our problems of poverty by the directing of resources to satisfy one set of priorities over another. Will the "trade-off" better satisfy our individual and national goals? Can such a question be resolved?

A STUDENT'S NOTE TO THE STUDENT

This chapter has to be the most controversial in the book. I think most of us started reading with preconceived ideas and while most of us probably learned new facts and solutions, I suspect we merely reinforced our existing prejudices.

There were a number of interesting questions that came to mind when I read this, and many others were raised in class. As you go through this chapter ask yourself these questions. Is poverty a condition or a state of mind? What does one economic class owe to another? How valid is the notion that high progressive taxes will kill incentive and defeat the purpose of reallocating resources? What happens when we redirect our resources away from defense and find the Pentagon was right in their warnings? Can we absorb the people laid off in defense industries by hiring them elsewhere?

Don't expect to find all your answers here. You won't. I did find some new questions to ask and new ways of looking at things.

Part A
Poverty and Its Causes

What Is Poverty?

After a meeting of community leaders, called to organize a collective effort to fight poverty, a county supervisor approached a representative from the U.S. Department of Agriculture and asked the reason for all the concern. He had been living in his county for 20 years, knew every mile of it, and there just was no poverty to be found. There could be no doubt that he knew his constituents better than outsiders—that is, how they lived and their levels of discontent. Why stir up discontent when folks are happy with the way things are? At a well-publicized meeting of his constituents in which the poor were asked to participate, the very low attendance testified to the accuracy of the supervisor's evaluation of the image his people had of themselves.

A statistical check showed the per capita income in that county to be 59th out of 62 counties in the state, 38 percent below the average per capita income. In spite of this apparent low standard of living, only 1.6 percent of its population received public assistance in contrast to 6.7 percent for the state. Was the county supervisor right when he denied that there was poverty in his county? The federal government recently defined poverty as any urban family of four having an annual income below $3,720. Since few countries in the world have average family incomes to equal this figure, are we realistic when we define poverty?

Poverty is relative, largely determined by the mode of living of the community in which one lives and the level of expectations that people have set for themselves. The typical welfare recipient might have a car, a television set, and a refrigerator (all purchased secondhand)—which might seem strange to most foreigners. Welfare recipients frequently appear better dressed than many college students from the middle and upper classes. They may even be suffering from malnutrition while being overweight from consuming too many calories. How do we explain these apparent contradictions?

While most of America's poor are well-off when compared to the poor of 50 years ago or the poor in Latin America, their income may be less than half of the current median family income. The fact that the poorest 20 percent of families in this country receive 5 percent of our total income while the richest fifth have 46 percent is reason for concern. While some diversity may reflect differences in ability and ambition, many people believe the diversity is extreme and reflects inequalities in opportunity. Undoubtedly very few Americans seek absolute equality of income as their goal. Consequently we can expect to have some parts of the population poorer than others. Nevertheless, most Americans would probably agree that the degree of inequality in income severely restricts equality of opportunity in education, employment, and basic services such as health care and judicial counsel. By providing greater equality of opportunity we lessen the gap in income between the upper and lower income groups.

Defining the Poor

As we have seen, it is difficult to find a definition of poverty that everybody will

TABLE 20–1 Poverty Index Figure for Nonfarm Families

Number in Family	Line of Poverty
1	$1,920
2	2,460
3	2,940
4	3,720
5	4,440
6	4,980
7 or more	6,120

SOURCE: Social Security Administration.

agree with. For the sake of convenience and because it is widely used, we will accept the *poverty index figure* for nonfarm families in 1970 used by the Social Security Administration. It is a sliding scale based on family size. For farm families the figure is about 30 percent less.

This index has been criticized for many reasons, including its failure to take account of accumulated family assets, which might be considerable, and major differences in regional cost of living and individual family needs. Nevertheless it provides a starting point.

Who Are the Poor?

In drawing a profile of the poor it is very easy to distort reality, even when using facts. It is true that there are more than twice as many whites in the poverty category as blacks, but it is equally true that only 10 percent of the white population is poor while almost one third of the black population is in this category. (See Figure 20–1.) Even more surprising is that over half of the poor are in families in which the head of the household has worked during the year and in more than half of these the employed person worked for 50 or more weeks of the year. A closer examination of the facts reveals many of these families are headed by a mother who is unskilled and forced to provide for her family. Others found in this category are those in poor health, marginal in ability, or old.

We do know that in 1970 one out of every eight Americans was living in poverty and that the rate may be expected to fluctuate with the general level of business conditions. Strong economic growth will help reduce unemployment and move people out of the poverty level. During the 1960's the number of people officially listed as poor was reduced by over 14 million, according to the Office of Economic Opportunities. Nevertheless, the number of "unemployables" and those whose handicaps do not permit their earnings to rise above the poverty level will be sufficient to make poverty a continuing, major problem. Nearly 40 percent of the poor live in households without a wage earner. Most are either elderly, mothers without a husband and their dependent children, or the handicapped.

As mentioned before, standards for poverty in rural areas are 30 percent below those for people living in cities, yet one out of every five farmers lives below even this poverty level. Migration to the city has reduced the number of rural poor, but it may be a factor in increasing the poverty problem of the city. Government programs have done little more than make life somewhat more tolerable for these people.

Children under age 18 constitute the largest poverty group. They make up 40 percent of the poor while constituting 15 percent of all children under 18. The most tragic aspect of this group is the handicap that they have as they move into the labor force. Frequently these children have low motivation, poor education, and other characteristics of a poverty culture that may lead to a vicious

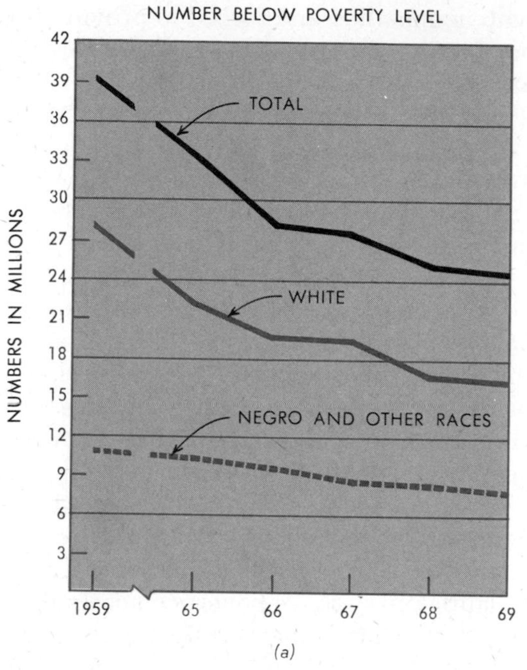

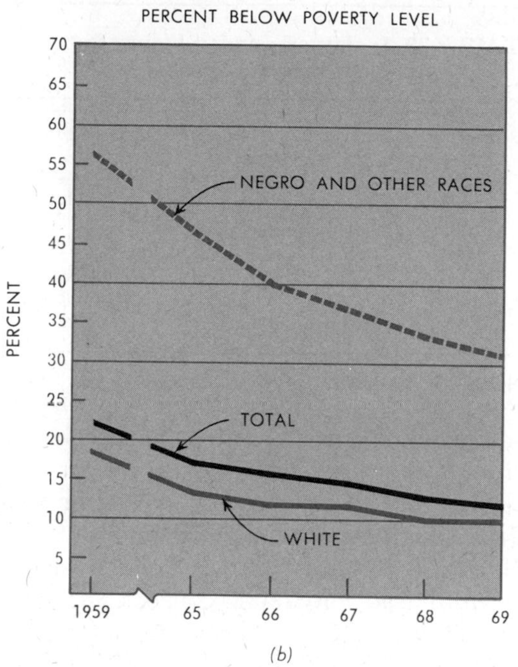

FIGURE 20–1 Who Are Below the Poverty Level?

There are more poor whites than blacks (a) in absolute numbers, but the percentage of blacks below the poverty line (b) is over three times as large as that of whites. The downward trend is encouraging. SOURCE: Bureau of the Census.

cycle of poverty. The chance for escaping from the ghetto is slim when no adult is present for most of the day, when older children are saddled with unwanted responsibilities (such as taking care of younger sisters and brothers), when income arrives in the form of a welfare check, when government employees such as social workers or policemen are seen as a threat, and when school is a source of frustration and embarrassment. If the adolescent observes firsthand the ease of obtaining income quickly through illegal methods, while most employment means long hours, low pay, little chance of advancement, and little job security, why bother to try? Society may furnish facilities intended to improve the upward mobility of the poor, but the environment may be so confining and deadening to the individual that no real motivation ever develops.

What Are the Causes of Poverty?

Business fluctuations contribute to increasing or decreasing the number of persons living at the poverty level, but most of these so affected must be considered the marginally poor. More permanent causes for poverty are: (1) inadequate education, (2) physical and mental handicaps, (3) inertia, and (4) inequality of opportunity. Usually several of these causes interact in such a way that it is difficult to identify which is the major one. Nevertheless, an examination of each cause is needed if we are to develop a plan for dealing with this problem.

Inadequate Education

In a recent study the U.S. Bureau of the Census showed the direct relationship between education and income. Starting with an income level for male earners of $1,500 to $1,999 and completing their analysis with those earning $25,000 and more, there was an increase in the median number of school years completed for each of the 12 income brackets listed. In the lowest bracket 8.4 school years were completed; for the $7,000 to $7,999 bracket, average school years rose to 12.3; for $10,000 to $14,999, 12.8 school years were completed; and for those in the highest income bracket 16.3 years of school was the average. Those who never get to high school earn about one third the income of those who complete college. High school graduates earn about 60 percent of what the college graduate does. Less education also means fewer kinds of job opportunities and higher unemployment rates.

Those with little education pay penalties in the size of their income. Moreover, studies have revealed that these same people have poor buying habits. They spend their small incomes less efficiently because they know less about comparative shopping, frequently borrow and understand little about high interest rates, and have less knowledge of alternatives for satisfying their needs.

Physical and Mental Handicaps

There can be little doubt that the percentage of physically and mentally handicapped is higher among those in the poverty category than in the population at large. Since physical stamina, alertness, emotional stability, and intelligence are all important assets for success in the job market, those who are deficient in these characteristics have difficulty competing.

The U.S. National Health Survey found the number of restricted activity days per person to be twice as high for their lowest income group as for their highest income group. The same pattern was found for days spent in a hospital. The U.S. Department of Health, Education, and Welfare found that the poor start out with poor health and have less opportunity to "purchase" better health. Those 65 or older comprise more than one sixth of the poor. About 30 percent of families whose head of the household is 65 or older are living in poverty. Age is obviously a physical handicap.

There is a statistically significant link between poverty and those admitted to hospitals for mental disorders, although there is no acceptable theory as to why. Perhaps more significant is the fact that 14 percent of the population have intelligence quotients below 85. Not many in this intelligence bracket can be expected to earn the median income, and many are handicapped in learning skills that can pay them enough to rise above the poverty level. Should those whose physical and mental handicaps affect their ability to earn a decent income be forced to have a lower standard of living?

Inertia

Two serious causes for poverty that may be grouped together under the heading of inertia are poverty culture and labor immobility. In both cases an extra push is required to bring about positive change.

Those born into a family having a poverty culture are more likely to remain in it than the larger number born outside it are of falling into it. Children raised in homes of the disadvantaged, frequently with working mothers, have been found to have serious handicaps in learning by the time they are ready to enter school. Schools in the ghetto are usually less equipped to provide a good education than are schools in middle-class neighborhoods. The relationship between education, job mobility, and income is frequently fuzzy in the minds of the poor. Recognition is frequently given for anti-establishment values, or there is overcompensation by inappropriate spending, for example, by purchasing big cars. The home is frequently the source of tension rather than comfort. Drugs and alcohol become a means of escape and a way of life. Society may provide institutions for help, but the poverty culture may be so deeply ingrained by adolescence that such institutions may be beyond the grasp of these young people.

Another form of inertia that causes as well as perpetuates poverty is the immobility of many of the poor. The shutting down of a local factory in an area without compensating employment opportunities or the decline of an entire industry may cause many to fall into the poverty level. According to our classical model these workers should move to regions and industries where expansion is taking place. In some instances new skills might have to be developed or a decline in job level accepted, but this is the cost of a dynamic economy. Unfortunately many of the poor have little knowledge of the opportunities elsewhere, no desire to dislodge their existing ties in the community, or too much invested in a home to move.

Inequality of Opportunity

While all the above may be classified as inequality of opportunity, our major concern here is whether this inequality is related to minority groups. In 1970 the median income of Negro families was not quite two thirds that of whites, and per capita income was only slightly more than half. Unemployment rates for nonwhites were slightly more than double those for whites from 1967 to 1969. Some may suggest that the difference between the median incomes of blacks and whites can be explained by differences in their educational attainments. Table 20–2 shows that blacks earned from 67 to 74 percent of what whites earned with equal educational attainment. Thus a black with four years of high school had a median income of $5,801 while his white counterpart earned $8,154. For those with some college, the black's median income was $7,481 in contrast to $10,149 for the white.

Almost all studies show significant im-

TABLE 20–2 Median Income of Men 25 to 54 Years Old, by Educational Attainment

	Median Income 1968		Negro Income as a Percent of White
	Negro	White	
Elementary:			
Total	$3,900	$5,844	67
Less than 8 years	3,558	5,131	69
8 years	4,499	6,452	70
High school:			
Total	5,580	7,852	71
1 to 3 years	5,255	7,229	73
4 years	5,801	8,154	71
College:			
1 or more years	7,481	10,149	74

SOURCE: U.S. Department of Commerce.

provements in the economic status of minority groups. In addition there are a sufficient number of instances, particularly among professionals and in management, where comparably trained blacks receive more than whites. Colleges and corporate management responded to the charges of racism by rushing into the market and bidding up the salaries for qualified blacks. Many trade unions reacted only under severe pressure. In all instances, attempts were made to get the most "visibility" out of the blacks hired, and many blacks still level the charge of "tokenism" at these employers.

If major improvements have been made in combating economic discrimination, why has there been the revolt against poverty, particularly by blacks? The importance of this and other questions related to discrimination demand special attention. We will return to them in Part C of this chapter.

The Market and the Economy

In each of the causes identified above there is a mixture of economic, social, and political factors. It should be clear at this point that poverty cannot be viewed as an exclusively economic problem. Nevertheless we should consider it within the framework of a market economy.

We have learned that the market mechanism plays a key role in the allocation of our resources. The product market distributes goods and services by the interaction of demand and supply, but demand is largely determined by income received in the factor market. The fairness in which that income is allocated is the subject of heated controversy not only among economists, but among all of us. Incentive and efficiency are the usual reasons advanced for allowing demand and supply to interact without interference. We have learned, however, that interference with the market mechanism is commonplace by business, labor, and government. Is the market the unbiased distributor? If it is, will that guarantee the distribution that society wants? If not, should we change it?

We already know that government has played a continuous and increasing role in altering the market, with subsidies to business in the form of tax allowances and shelters, price supports to the farmer, minimum wages for the worker, and welfare payments for the poor. In each instance a reallocation has taken place that would have been different if the government had not stepped in.

We have also seen combinations of businesses and workingmen band together to influence the market mechanism. The consequences are not merely confined to an inefficient use of resources but also the extension of the inequalities of income distribution.

In Part B we will consider some of the proposed solutions to poverty. In each case there is some alteration of the market. You should consider what society is striving for and what the cost will be in trying to achieve our goals. Some economic principles to keep in mind are: (1) each worker, whether he works or not, can increase or decrease the GNP by his marginal product; (2) the marginal product of a worker depends on his innate as well as his developed abilities; (3) most individuals do not keep their marginal product but pay some of it to the public sector; (4) payment to the public sector should reflect the ability to pay based on diminishing marginal utility; and (5) society may wish to trade off efficiency for other values.

Part B
Proposed Solutions

Getting at the Causes

Since there are many reasons for poverty, it is doubtful that a single satisfactory solution will be found. Solutions must be related to causes. Consequently we will consider (1) eliminating recessions and encouraging economic growth, (2) public programs to improve education and upgrade job skills, (3) rehabilitating the physically and mentally handicapped, (4) government aid to depressed areas, (5) eliminating job discrimination, (6) supplementing the income of the working poor, and (7) providing income for the unemployable.

Eliminating Recessions

We noted in our study of business cycles that recessions are accompanied by rising unemployment, smaller profits, increasing business failures, and a shorter workweek with little overtime pay. As the decline sets in, those immediately above the poverty line become part of the category classified as poor. As the economy begins its revival and moves upward towards prosperity, persons move up and out of the poverty category. Thus the understanding and application of Keynesian countercyclical policy, along with long-term economic growth, has been a very important step in reducing the number of poor. Since Franklin Roosevelt's cry in 1937 for a program to aid the one third of a nation that lived in poverty, we have reduced the fraction to one eighth. Economists have made significant strides in understanding how to tinker with aggregate demand, but our experiences in 1969–1971 tell us that we still have much more to learn.

If we master the use of automatic and discretionary stabilizers so that our economy is operating at its full potential, we will have taken a major step in confining the effects of poverty. It will assure the maximum-sized GNP from which any reallocation may draw on, as well as making producers out of those who are submarginal workers in a below-full-employment economy.

Education and Job Training

The U.S. Office of Education has reported in a number of ways the increasing educational attainment of the American people. In 1929 only 29 percent of those in the age bracket for graduation from high school were high school graduates. Forty years later the percentage had climbed to 77 percent. Total per-pupil expenditures increased during this same period 336 percent in *constant* dollars. The median school years completed by those over 18 years old increased from 10.9 years in 1952 to 12.3 years in 1969.

More recently there has been a recognition of the major differences that exist in the quality of education provided in ghetto schools as contrasted with schools in middle-class urban and suburban neighborhoods. Compensatory programs have been developed so that reading specialists, additional guidance counselors, and extra equipment have helped to close the gap. Public higher education has expanded at an unprecedented rate with several states moving toward open enrollment. New York state has provided special programs to improve basic skills of underachievers so that an open admissions program does not become a revolving door.

Since 1963 the government has committed itself to providing both young and old with skills so those outside the labor force may become part of it and those with outdated or little sought after skills might upgrade them. Starting with the Manpower Development and Training Act in 1963 and expanding the program to include the Neighborhood Youth Corps, New Careers, the Job Corps, etc., the programs have expanded from 59,200 enrollees and a federal obligation of $56 million to 860,000 enrollees and $755 million in 1968.

Off-the-job training frequently fails because the newly-trained worker finds no vacancy for his skill. On-the-job training is somewhat better in furnishing permanent employment, particularly in the development of paraprofessionals such as teacher aides.

Rehabilitation of the total individual is frequently needed rather than mere job training. The 1960's may be looked upon as a period of experimentation, furnishing some hope for those who needed it.

Rehabilitation

Government involvement in health programs, both physical and mental, has increased each year in both cost and type of program. Free clinics, as well as complete or partial subsidizing of hospital care provided by local and state governments, has been accepted for many years. Federal involvement became important after World War II when over 12 million veterans became eligible for some benefits. Medicare became part of the Social Security program when medical costs soared and it was recognized that the elderly could easily have their savings wiped out through illness or accident, putting even more of them into the poverty class. Medicaid was developed to help the poor, using the matching-funds technique for payment. Social Security also provides funds for the blind and disabled. The increasing number of public hospitals, particularly mental institutions and outpatient centers, provided additional services at little or no cost to patients.

The principle of providing equal opportunities for all, which led to the development of public education up to the level that the individual could profit from, is now being applied to health. The cost for treatment of illness is probably no more than one fifth the cost of lost production resulting from the illness, and recognition of this fact has brought about an extension of our public commitment. Recent inclusion in school budgets of items for breakfast as well as lunch reflects the desire to get at the causes for illness.

Government Aid to Depressed Areas

Most Americans have heard of our foreign aid program to aid the "have-not" countries. An analysis of our own country shows that it may be divided into "have" and "have-not" states, and even wealthy states include regions which are depressed.

Many economists would view this condition as nothing to be alarmed about since a healthy dynamic society would have expanding and contracting markets. As they see it, declining areas merely reflect changes in consumer demand, technology, or other factors, and the market will automatically adjust by the movement of labor and capital to areas showing economic expansion. These economists' great concern would be the external interference with the market mechanism.

The "new economics" is not satisfied with the market as it operates and present-day government policy reflects the desire to take public compensatory action. An analysis of federal programs involving funds to the states shows that 17 states pay out more than they receive, thereby helping to subsidize 32 states. One state breaks even. Depressed regions have been aided by the infusion of funds largely through the Economic Development Administration of the U.S. Department of Commerce and its regional commissions in Appalachia, New England, Coastal Plains, Ozarks, Four Corners, and Upper Great Lakes. Supplementary federal grants have been pumped into these areas to support education, housing, urban renewal, and the domestic "peace corps"—VISTA (now part of ACTION)—when the unemployment rate rose significantly above the national average.

It is difficult to evaluate this approach because there is no way of knowing whether labor would be more mobile without it or whether that labor's productivity would be any greater if utilized elsewhere. So far the amount of money used has not provided any reversals in the economic trends in the regions affected. Collectively these programs have served to make life somewhat more tolerable for the poor.

Eliminating Job Discrimination

Fair employment practices commissions have existed in a number of states for many years. They attempt to prevent any kind of discrimination based on race, religion, age, or sex. The federal government became involved through the Civil Rights Act of 1964 which prohibited discrimination by employers and unions, and set up an Equal Opportunity Commission. Legislating against discrimination may be viewed as a first step; enforcement as a more difficult next step.

There are many encouraging signs. The inclusion of the statement "Equal Opportunity Employer" in classified ads has become common in many parts of the country. The increase in the percentage of black families having an income above $10,000 a year rose from 8.5 percent in 1960 to better than 20 percent by 1970. Increases of over 100 percent from 1957 to 1967 have occurred in the number of nonwhites in the professions, managerial class, and in retail trades. Progress cannot be denied. Nevertheless a comparison of the rate of unemployment, median income for comparable training, and the following observation by the late Whitney Young, Jr. of the National Urban League, all show the long road ahead:

> We can still usually tell what floor we are on in a corporation by the whiteness of it. In the basement, it might be all black; on the first floor it's sort of polka dot, but as you go up it gets white, and soon you get near the top and except for that guard or the receptionist out front you don't see many blacks.[1]

Supplementary Income

We pointed out earlier that approximately half the poor are employed at least part-time. If one of our major goals is to reduce the number of people living in poverty, we can achieve this result best by concentrating our efforts on upgrading the skills of the working poor, as shown above, and/or by supplementing the income they receive from their jobs. To many economists, supplementing the income of the working

[1] Quoted in an article by Richard Clark, "Working in a White Man's World," *Time,* April 6, 1970, p. 93.

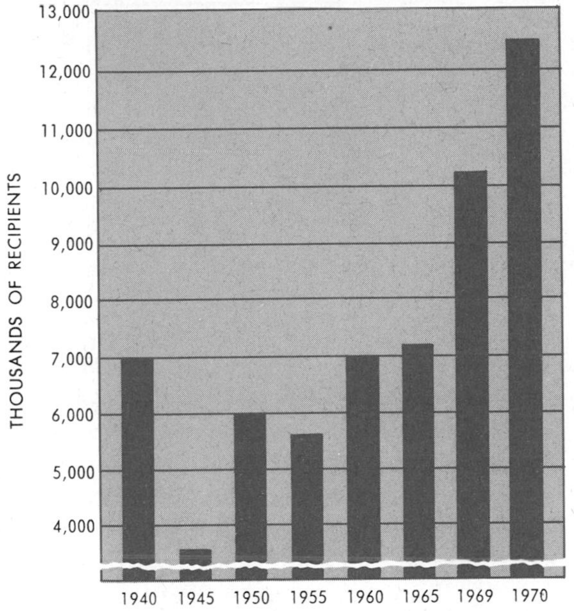

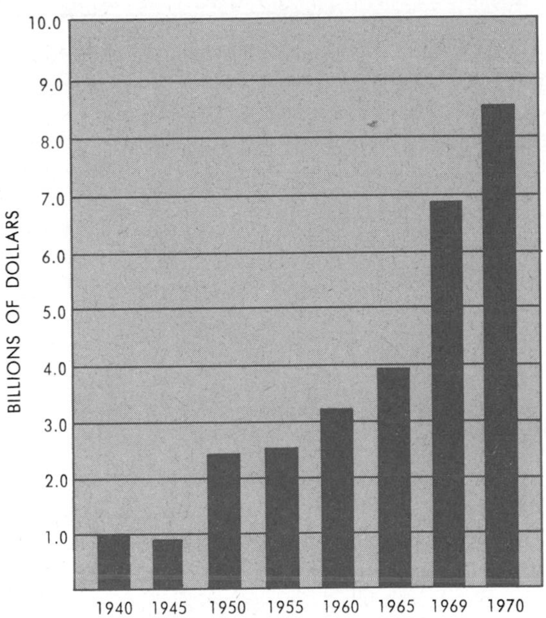

FIGURE 20–2 Public Assistance: Recipients **Public Assistance: Total Money Payments**

The sharp increase in number and total payments made to welfare recipients indicates the serious weaknesses in our present programs and possibly in our economic structure. SOURCE: U.S. Department of Health, Education, and Welfare.

poor, conceived in such a way as to provide incentives to work, should have the highest priority in the war on poverty.

Many existing welfare rules are designed to encourage the father to desert his family in order for them to be eligible to collect Aid to Families with Dependent Children (AFDC). Other rules discourage the mother from working part-time by reducing her welfare income to such a degree that, after paying her job-related expenses, she is left with less total income than if she had not worked. Recent amendments to the Social Security Act have allowed AFDC mothers to exclude a portion of their income earned, so that welfare payments are only fractionally reduced.

Two new proposals, the Family Assistance Plan (FAP) and the negative income tax, were considered by the federal government in 1970, and it is almost certain that the 1970's will see elements of both adopted and modified as experience shows the strengths and weaknesses of each.

President Nixon's *Family Assistance Plan* is designed to replace the public assistance programs in the 1935 Social Security Act as amended. It has three major features: (1) direct federal payments to all needy families with children including the working poor and families with unemployed fathers, (2) establishment of a minimum income for all needy families, and (3) federal administration of eligibility requirements, payment procedures, and work or training registration requirements.

Table 20–3 shows the payment schedule for a family of four.

Eligibility criteria for FAP payments are: (1) the presence of a child under 18,

TABLE 20–3 Proposed FAP Payment Schedule for Family of Four

Earnings	Nonexempt earnings	"Tax" at 50%	Net Payment	Net Income
$ 0	$ 0	$ 0	$1,600	$1,600
720	0	0	1,600	2,320
1,000	280	140	1,460	2,460
1,500	780	390	1,210	2,710
2,000	1,280	640	960	2,960
2,500	1,780	890	710	3,210
3,000	2,280	1,140	460	3,460
3,500	2,780	1,390	210	3,710
3,920	3,200	1,600	——	3,920

or 21 if regularly attending school, in the household; (2) a family's resources other than its home, household goods, personal effects, and property essential to its means of self-support must not exceed $1,500; and (3) nonexempt income must not exceed twice the basic family benefit to which a family may be entitled—or, to put this another way, total income must not exceed the applicable break-even level.

The kinds of income exempt are food stamps, private charity, training incentives, student income and scholarships, home-produced goods that are consumed, and the first $720 of family income plus 50 percent of the balance.

The *negative income tax* is very similar to the Family Assistance Plan but it guarantees an income to every individual and family rather than just to families with children and adults on public assistance. In addition it does not provide for any excludable income, it provides payments as a matter of right rather than proven need, and it does not require recipients to register for work or training. It is for this

TABLE 20–4 Negative Income Tax Payment Schedule for a Family of Four

Earnings	Negative Income	Negative Income Tax (25%)	Subsidy*	Total Income
$ 0	$4,000	$1,000	$3,000	$3,000
500	3,500	875	2,625	3,125
1,000	3,000	750	2,250	3,250
2,000	2,000	500	1,500	3,500
3,000	1,000	250	750	3,750
4,000	–0–	–0–	–0–	4,000
	Positive Income	Positive Income Tax		
5,000	5,000	154*	–0–	4,846

* Based on $1,000 of taxable income at 15.4 percent.

last reason that Congress, which is sensitive to the work ethic, preferred to consider the Family Assistance Plan first.

The basic idea of a negative income tax is to use the same procedures, now used to collect tax revenue from people with incomes above a certain minimum level, to provide financial assistance to people with incomes below that level.

Table 20–4 shows a possible payment schedule under the negative income tax for a family of four. This illustration provides for a minimum income of $3,000, but the amount of the subsidy (and total income) can be altered by adjusting the negative income tax rate and/or what figure one may consider negative income.

A family of four is entitled to tax exemptions of $4,000. According to the Tax Reform Act of 1969, the dependency allowance would be $3,000 (4 × $750) and the minimum standard deduction for taxes, contributions, medical expense, interest expense, and so on, is $1,000. A family of four that has an income of less than $4,000 has a negative income and would be entitled to an income subsidy. The subsidy would be some proportion of the negative income; in this example, 75 percent is used. The "break-even" point is where the family neither receives a negative income nor pays a positive income tax.

Professor Milton Friedman, a conservative economist who prefers to reduce government's involvement in the economy, and Professor James Tobin, a liberal economist and member of President Kennedy's Council for Economic Advisers, have endorsed this plan. Can you explain why?

Providing for the Unemployable

Several of the plans listed above provide for income in money or in kind for those unable to work. The concept of a guaranteed annual income, a floor which no individual or family should drop below, has been considered seriously for the last

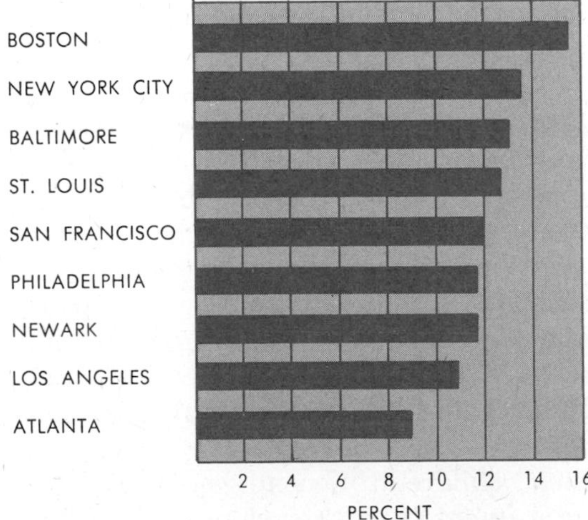

FIGURE 20–3 Percentage of People Receiving Welfare in Selected Cities

In several of our largest cities over 1 in 10 of the people are on welfare. SOURCE: Department of Health, Education, and Welfare.

David and Goliath?

SOURCE: King Features Syndicate copyright.

10 years. With this country's total affluence, why should anyone be below a subsistence living standard? The majority of Americans would probably accept this concept for those who are sufficiently handicapped that useful employment is out of the question. They would be less anxious to accept the responsibility of "subsidizing" the marginally handicapped, who are difficult to identify, and the culturally handicapped. The habit of classifying work and income together is such an integral part of our tradition that it is all too easy to accept the assumption that those on welfare are lazy. Some people in our society are questioning our basic values and wondering where responsibility should be placed for an individual's failure to be a member of the labor force. If the answer is that both the individual and the society share the responsibility, perhaps both have to make sacrifices.

Part C
The Economics of Discrimination

In Part A we identified the poor and the causes for poverty. In Part B we considered the solutions. We noted that certain minority groups are more intensely plagued by poverty than the rest of society and we pointed out the discrimination against them. Why should we have a separate section of this chapter devoted exclusively to this group and, considering the tremendous strides made in the last 10 years, why is this group complaining?

While we will be focusing most of our attention on blacks here, other minority groups, particularly Puerto-Rican Americans, Mexican-Americans, and the American Indians, have many of the same problems. Many in each group are developing a high degree of ethnic consciousness with emphasis on the problems they face in a predominantly white society. However, it would be wrong to assume that there are not unique problems faced by each.

Blacks Singled Out

The United States has had a long history of poor immigrants coming to this country, working hard, and integrating themselves into the American mainstream. Almost no government programs existed to help these groups. They made it on their own. Today there are numerous programs designed to help the poor become more quickly integrated. Are blacks different from the Irish, the Italians, the Jews, or the Poles?

The Europeans arriving in New York City, looking forward to a new life, soon found themselves belonging to two worlds: the ghetto which they occupied from sundown to sunup which provided them with familiar surroundings and security, and the integrated world where one made a living from sunup to sundown. They heard of and saw evidence to support the upward mobility of those who worked, succeeded, and educated their children. Second-generation children found an open society, or nearly so, and usually left the ghetto. Enough immigrants fulfilled the dream of America being the land of opportunity to reinforce the motivation for others to try.

Few blacks came to this country by

choice. When they got here it was a closed society, a caste system rather than class system. For them there was no development of cultural identity and no visible sign of upward mobility; moreover, daily incidents humiliated them. Legislation which held out hope never came near to fulfilling the promises. Frustration in implementing school integration, equal employment opportunities, voting rights, and open housing made many blacks cynical.

There can be little doubt that the 1960's provided measurable progress, but to many black leaders there is a sense of urgency. No longer are they willing "to wait their turn." Their turn is conspicuously overdue.

Major upheavals almost never come where there is no hope, no improvement. The seeming restlessness of the blacks is most intense now because there is evidence of improvement. With it has come a more rapidly rising set of expectations. The gap between the black's expectations and the improvement in his well-being has increased and caused the outpouring of discontent.

Benefits to the Economy

The singling out of the blacks would not only help Negroes as a group, but would benefit the American people as a whole. This is the reasoning of the Council of Economic Advisers in their 1968 report to the President.

> If Negroes received the same average pay as whites having the same education, the personal income of blacks and of the nation would be $12.8 billion higher. If Negroes also had the same educational attainments as white workers and earned the same pay and experienced the same unemployment as whites, their personal income—and that of the nation—would be $20.6 billion higher. The entire economy would benefit from better education of Negro workers and an end to job discrimination. Industry would earn additional profits. The total Gross National Product would rise by an estimated $23 billion, or an extra 3.7 percent.

Therefore, according to this report, the economic cost of discrimination is high not only to blacks, but to all Americans. By singling out blacks and attempting to better their economic standing, we would be helping many Americans, regardless of race, to achieve a more decent and prosperous standard of living. Some may disagree with these findings, but the problem of black preferential treatment must be dealt with in all phases of economic life.

Disunity Among Blacks

In the past, the unity of the black community usually cut across class lines. Most Negroes, regardless of their economic and social status, were subject to the same discrimination in public places, from Ralph Bunche to an unskilled black laborer. This provided a common bond among blacks of all social classes. But today many middle-class blacks have benefited from the Negro revolution. The census shows that young northern black couples with children earned only 75 percent as much as their white counterparts in 1960, while in 1970 they earned the same as their white counterparts:

> One well-known Negro leader pointed out that American industry has stimulated middle-class progress by upgrading the educated Negro—a fact which is simultaneously appreciated, scorned, and exaggerated by unemployed blacks. The resentment felt by this new underclass of blacks is likely to show itself in frustration behavior—such as riots—

and in other forms of hostility, not only toward whites who "have it" but also toward blacks who have "made it."[2]

During the same time span the number of black families with a mother as head of the household jumped 50 percent. The majority of these families are poor and with high rates of crime and delinquency. The differences in the upward mobility and even the opportunities for such mobility provide a different perspective for both blacks and whites. Many black leaders point out that this disunity weakens the cause of blacks and they must rally together in a common cause for betterment of the race in order to be effective. Other leaders feel the united approach interferes with integration, the only real solution.

Changing Employment Patterns

Both the U.S. Department of Commerce and the Rand Corporation in separate studies predict a decline in employment in the 25 largest metropolitan areas and a major shift in new employment to the suburbs. With nonwhites concentrating in central cities their unemployment rate is projected to rise to five times that of the labor force as a whole.

While government programs are designed to ease unemployment in the black community the major source of employment in this country is private enterprise. Government has helped by offering tax incentives to employers for developing their operations in primarily black communities. However, employers have complained about being unable to find qualified blacks. This is generally due to their use of traditional hiring practices and their lack of understanding of the Negro community and black labor markets. On the other side black communities have not always been efficient in making job information available or in advising the unemployed on how to search for a job.

Unions and Blacks

A recent study of membership in labor unions showed blacks to be less than 1.5 percent of construction workers, 6.4 percent of retail clerks, and 30.5 percent of laborers. There is an inverse correlation between higher-paying jobs and the percentage of black membership. Investigations have shown past practices of discrimination, some slight improvement as pressure has been applied to modifying the apprenticeship system, and some instances of a shortage of blacks willing to apply for or stay with the apprenticeship program.

The labor picture looks brightest for blacks in industrial unions rather than in the more elite craft unions. One sixth of those employed by the three major automobile companies were black. While few of the top jobs are held by blacks there is evidence of increasing upward mobility.

Some experts see the trade union movement as the best means of reducing racial competition because of the common interests of the workers. If so, some unions will have to change their image in the eyes of the blacks.

Black Capitalism

If the American economy is identified with private enterprise, then blacks have to feel left out of it. Of the approximately 11.5 million businesses in the United States less than .5 percent (45,000) are owned by blacks. Of these, not one is included

[2] Bayard Rustin, "The Lessons of the Long Hot Summer," *Contemporary Report*, New York, 1967, p. 6.

among the 500 largest corporations, only two are listed on a major stock exchange, and the overwhelming majority are an assortment of barber shops, restaurants, grocery stores, hotels, and other family enterprises valued from $5,000 to $50,000. Newark, New Jersey has about 400,000 people, and more than half of them black. Yet only 10 percent of the city's licensed businesses belong to blacks.

Many economists agree that black capitalism is necessary if blacks are to become an integral part of the economy. Disagreement is greater on how far this idea should be pushed. Some are afraid that extending this idea too far can lead to black separatism while others think of this as a desired result.

Probably the two major problems faced by blacks are the difficulty in obtaining capital and the shortage of managerial skills. The government can and has helped in both, although the results have been less than encouraging. The Small Business Administration has provided direct loans and the government has given backing to encourage direct borrowing. Training programs in business skills have been offered, but the blacks' interest in them has been somewhat less than hoped for. White businessmen have worked with blacks in a number of cities to help launch new businesses. Friction between the two groups has developed at times because whites do not usually know the black community and assume that its behavior patterns are no different than whites'. In addition, there is sensitivity as to how far whites can go without becoming dominant.

Black Separatism

If the economic problem of discrimination asks "How can minorities become part of the American economy, contributing and receiving their full share?" then a subsidiary question that economists must ask involves opportunity costs: "Where should we apply our limited resources to obtain the maximum results?"

Some social scientists and black leaders believe that the most effective strategy is to invest in the black ghetto. They argue that integration does not work and can frequently make a bad situation worse. When blacks move out of the ghetto they are forced to compete for housing, business property, and jobs. In each case their color and limited resources are handicaps. If money and energy were poured directly into the ghetto to provide low-income housing, support for business loans, job training centers, and continuing and remedial educational programs, the ghetto would become a dynamic economic community.

Those in support of "ghetto dispersal" claim that nothing less than a complete change in the total structure of the metropolis will solve the problem. This plan involves providing blacks with the tools to break out of the ghetto, setting up job training centers linked to industry's needs, employment placement for positions outside the ghetto, and an improved transit system for greater mobility. Low-income housing, rent subsidies, and reorganization of our welfare system, which can stifle mobility, will help break down the misunderstandings and insecurities that whites and blacks frequently feel toward each other. Just as immigrants broke out of the ghetto by integration during the workday, blacks can follow the same path.

It is doubtful that total integration is possible in the 1970's, and the need for improving the economic life of the black cannot wait. It would seem important to put our resources to use both in "gilding the ghetto" and in encouraging ghetto dispersal by increasing the opportunities outside it. These approaches need not be contradictory; they can be complementary.

Part D
The Military-Industrial Complex

In this last section of this chapter we will examine a major target of critics of our present system of priorities—the military–industrial complex. Briefly these critics fear that the United States has built a Gargantuan monster with an insatiable appetite for resources that prevents us from solving our most important problems and contributes to creating new problems. If we could control this structure and reduce our outlays to realistic needs, we would free billions of dollars to be used in solving our domestic problems, primarily poverty. We will first examine the arguments used by these critics and then consider whether a reordering of priorities might bring about the suggested improvements.

It is not realistic to dismiss these critics as "radicals," "malcontents," "kooks," "communists," or "the new left." President Eisenhower said in his farewell address to the American people on January 17, 1961, "We must guard against unwarranted influence by the military–industrial complex." Senator William Proxmire of the Subcommittee on Economy of Government has pointed to the growing community of interests between the Pentagon and defense industries that can work against the public's best interest. Still growing is the list of notables to the left and right of center (but all within the mainstream of American political thought) who warn the American people about the excessive spending and uncontrollable power of this complex. The close fight in the Senate in 1970 over the appropriations to support the Anti-Ballistic Missile Program (ABM), the reactions to the exposé of the F-111B and the C-5A, and the fact that military appropriations bills are now more carefully scrutinized, show our growing concern with our present order of priorities.

Some Dimensions

The U.S. Arms Control and Disarmament Agency estimates that since 1900 the world has spent more than $4 trillion on wars and military preparedness and that this figure will double within 10 to 20 years, depending on whether expenditures continue at the present level or increase at the rate shown in the 1970's. Military expenditures by the U.S. Department of Defense in 1970 amounted to $76.6 billion, and since 1945 we have spent as much money for military purposes as the total value of all business and residential structures in the U.S.—$1.1 trillion.

For this expenditure the United States has an awesome arsenal of weapons. We have sufficient nuclear warheads and the delivery capability to overkill the Soviet Union more than 1,000 times, and an inventory of conventional and not-so-conventional weapons with destructive power many times greater than that assembled by all nations involved in World War II. Despite these awesome dimensions in dollars and power the Pentagon claims that during the Vietnam War, it has had to reduce its expenditures for research, development, and new weapons to a dangerous level. As the Southeast Asian war grinds down, reducing costs, the military claim they need these savings to catch up for the neglect in buying and developing new weapons, particularly strategic weapons, in case the arms limitation talks fail.

Procurement

Each year the Pentagon signs tens of thousands of contracts with prime contractors to maintain our war machine. In 1970 almost $50 billion was spent, mostly in defense-oriented industry. More than half of this amount went to the 100 largest suppliers. The pattern was similar but on a smaller scale for the Atomic Energy Commission (AEC) and the National Aeronautics and Space Administration (NASA).

These defense contracts have involved the military with some of the largest industrial corporations in the world. Some of these, such as Lockheed Aircraft and General Dynamics, do almost all their business with the government. Their dependence on each other can present a threat to the best interests of the public. In the case of General Electric, General Motors, or Textron, defense contracts are sufficiently large over a long enough period to establish for these companies a supportive policy for defense appropriations. Profits can be made through supplying the defense needs of the United States. Is this Adam Smith's "harmony of interests"?

In addition to a concentration of military spending among a relatively few, some geographic areas are far more favored than others. The late L. Mendel Rivers, Chairman of the House Armed Services Committee, managed to favor his home district of Charleston, South Carolina with defense appropriations. Located there are: The Charleston Naval Shipyard, a naval weapons station, a Polaris submarine base, an air force base, a marine corps air station, an army supply depot, two naval hospitals, and Parris Island Marine Corps Recruit Depot. Adjacent to his district is an AEC nuclear weapons plant run by DuPont. Since 1965, the year that Congressman Rivers became chairman of his committee, the following defense contractors moved to his district: Avco, McDonnell Douglas, General Electric, Lockheed and J. P. Stevens.

Inefficiency

Government purchases are usually made by advertising, accepting sealed written bids, and awarding the contract to the lowest or next-to-lowest bidder. The Armed Services Procurement Act allowed for so many exceptions that bids could be ignored and the Pentagon could make its decisions without binding rules. There is little doubt that the need for secrecy, speed, and flexibility are important where national defense is the case. However, the performance of a number of industries that have been involved in major defense contracts shows poor quality, the passing on of unexpected costs, the questionable performance of the final products, and a serious disregard for costs. Investigations of several important weapons projects showed that what was produced did not meet the specifications originally given and, in the case of the

F-111B, resulted in substantial outlays by the government without receiving what was requested.

It has been estimated that defense industries use more than $13 billion of government-owned property in their production, allowing them the equivalent of obtaining interest-free loans. There is some disagreement on how profitable these industries are, but without a truly competitive market, inefficiency can largely go undetected. Finally, the government does not want to see these industries fail, and, as in the case of Lockheed with its great loss on the C-5A, it can provide a loan and/or a direct payment to keep a major supplier operative.

It is quite common for people in government to move into the private sector, performing duties that they have skills and experience in. (Sometimes the transfer is from the industry to government.) The early retirement plans in the military make this desirable and common. This interchange can be beneficial, particularly where the skills required are highly specialized and there is a shortage of experienced personnel. An investigation of the military moving into high positions in defense industries is understandable, but such a transfer can result in purchases not completely in the public interest. The number of personnel involved in the interchange has resulted in an investigation in which Senator Proxmire cautioned of the danger of this "growing community of interest" that could be detrimental to the public good.

Regional Dependency

Several regions in our country are economically dependent on defense contracts and/or AEC or NASA contracts. The year 1970 marked a change in priorities with decisions to shift resources away from areospace and defense. As a result, the Boston, Los Angeles, and Seattle areas were hit hard with declining business activity and high rates of unemployment. What was unusual was the kind of unemployment—highly-trained specialized personnel, many with advanced degrees. The regional multiplier effect soon caused the more traditional type of unemployment.

The dependency of these regions on defense contracts for their economic well-being puts tremendous pressure on their congressional representatives to support military appropriations. Not all congressmen respond to regional pressures, but such regions would do well to have more diversified industry. Our government could make decisions on the allocation of resources with less political pressure if there were less of this dependency effect.

In Defense of Our Military Expenditures

The critics of military defense spending have conveniently overlooked a number of significant changes that have altered our priorities and could threaten our security. Figure 20–4 shows that military as a percentage of GNP has actually declined from a high of 9.5 percent in 1968 to about 8 percent in 1970. This decline becomes even more pronounced when we realize that there was a decline in dollars spent during this time despite the fact that inflation would account for an additional $8 billion reduction in real dollars. Defense Secretary Laird has pointed out that costly delays in purchasing new sophisticated weapons and cutting expenditures for research and develoment—particularly in missile defense, delivery systems, and nuclear weapons—have placed us in a weaker military position. Evidence of the development of new Soviet hardware, both offensive and defensive, may have altered our relative position of strength since we have been placing substantial portions of our resources in Indochina.

Caspar W. Weinberger, Deputy Director of President Nixon's Office of Management and Budget points out that at the peak of the Korean War 13.5 percent of our GNP went for defense expenditures and in 1962, before our involvement in Vietnam, we spent almost 9 percent. (See Figure 20–4.) The General Accounting Office reported that the Pentagon has shelved 130 projects for the development of new weapons with a price tag of $140 billion. If the United States is to fulfill its treaty obligations with many nations around the world and maintain its own strength it must maintain technical superiority in its weapons, and armed forces. It is only by this strength, Weinberger claims, that our diplomacy can be effective. If the Strategic Arms Limitations Talks (SALT) with the Soviet Union are successful, major cuts in spending could be made.

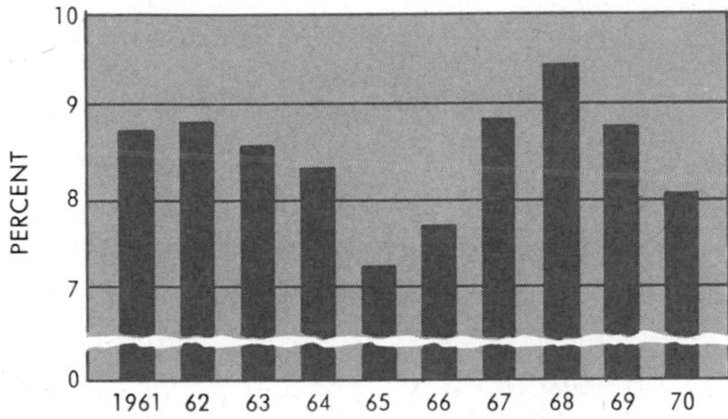

FIGURE 20–4 Percentage of GNP for Military Expenditures

Since 1968 military expenditures as a percentage of GNP have declined significantly. Whether our national security has been affected and, if so, for what benefits, is difficult to determine. SOURCE: U.S. Department of Defense.

Military Service as a Stepping Stone

Historically the peacetime army or other branch of service has served the role of employer for many young men who could not find a place for themselves within the civilian economy. Since World War II, however, attitudes have changed (as have employment opportunities) and few people have been looking at the military life as a career seriously, except those enrolled in our military colleges. Two recent developments may have brought another reversal in this attitude: (1) the experience of soldiers from disadvantaged environments finding greater opportunities for limited recognition and mobility, and (2) the significant increases in pay, reflecting the desire to encourage enlistments.

Until the draft law was changed in 1970, discrimination against those not attending college was notable. In effect this was discrimination against the poor. However, many of these young men found that they had greater opportunities in service than they had in the ghetto or living in rural poverty. In some instances they were given instruction in skills that were transferable to civilian employment. Advancement into the ranks of noncommissioned officers had few barriers for blacks, although only 2.1 percent of commissioned officers were blacks. For those discharged soldiers who found the civilian economy hostile, the re-enlistment and longevity pay served to attract them back into service.

Serious consideration is being given to the development of a voluntary army. To do so will require sufficient wage scales to attract and keep men. While it is doubtful that any economist would advance this proposal as the solution to the problem of poverty, it is playing a growing role in providing income, performing a necessary service that this country needs, and offering job training for an important group of people. Without the armed forces as an alternative employer, the social costs resulting from the young unemployed could be a greater strain on our resources.

What Benefits in a Trade-Off?

From 1968 to 1970 there has been no significant change in dollars spent for military defense. During this same period, expenditures for welfare, education, health care, and housing have increased by approximately 20 percent. Expenditures for human resources including all levels of government far outweigh expenditures for defense. In spite of this reordering of priorities we have made few positive gains in helping the hard-core poor (see Figure 20–2). While we do not know what the cost for neglecting our weapons development might be, the tragedy could come in finding out.

Conclusions

There can be little doubt that the American people showed some rearrangement in their priorities in 1970. The gradual disengagement in Vietnam, the challenging of the Anti-Ballistic Missile Program and Supersonic Transport (SST) in Congress, and the cuts made in military spending, all give evidence of a change in mood. To those who support this trend, their elation may be short because no final decisions have been made. The budget for 1972 calls for an increase in spending, which could continue throughout the 1970's. Only their continued vigilance can make this turn of events significant. Those who fear the consequences of this possible change might look for stronger arguments to support their case, since a resistance has grown up to a "Pax Americana" position. Disengagement appears to be a popular idea. The only path that appears to offer a chance for success is to establish a direct connection between our own nation's security and the state of our military defense. Most Americans would be willing to make sacrifices if they were convinced their nation is truly in danger from outside forces.

It is doubtful that a switch from military expenditures to the poverty problem could solve the problems of the poor, since the redirection of some money resources must be accompanied by the other resources necessary to solve problems. If we took 30 percent of our defense money and gave it to the poor, we still would be faced with the cultural aspects of poverty, the dislocation of those working in defense industries who might become eligible for economic aid, and national insecurity. We need to attack poverty by dealing with its causes. Manpower in defense might be retrained to work on social problems including poverty, traditional approaches to education need to be changed to reach the poor, and nonwhites need compensatory opportunities to be brought into the mainstream of our economy. The painful process will be, as always, that the solving of one group's problems will involve sacrifices for others. Survival as a dynamic society may be threatened if we do not find answers.

REVIEW: THE HIGHLIGHTS OF THE CHAPTER

1. Poverty has many meanings since it is cultural, relative, and subjective. In the United States it is differently defined for rural and urban areas, and it changes with time.
2. For practical purposes the Social Security Administration defines poverty by the number in the family and for farm and nonfarm. For a nonfarm family of four in 1970 the poverty line was $3,720.
3. A profile of the poor shows that a disproportionately high percentage are made up of blacks, children from families headed by a mother, and the elderly. There are many working poor whose earnings are below the poverty line.
4. Business fluctuations increase or decrease the number living at the level of poverty by affecting the marginally poor.
5. Major causes for poverty are inadequate education, physical and mental handicaps, inertia, and the inequality of opportunity.
6. Proposed solutions include eliminating recessions, increasing economic growth, improving education, upgrading job skills, rehabilitation of the physically and mentally handicapped, government aid to depressed areas, eliminating job discrimination, and income supplements and income for the unemployables.
7. The decade of the 1960's saw the percentage of those below the poverty line fall from 22 percent to 12 percent. It also was a time when welfare rolls swelled from 7 million to 12.5 million, with expenditures increasing even faster.
8. Two major plans for supplementing income are the Family Assistance Plan and the negative income tax.
9. Studies show that several minority groups have been discriminated against within the American economy. Most notable are the blacks, the Puerto Ricans, the Mexicans, and the American Indian.
10. Unlike other immigrant groups, blacks did not come to this country by choice. Their opportunities within the American economy have been seriously interfered with.
11. Discrimination hurts the entire economy, not merely the blacks. Eliminating it might cause the GNP to increase over 3 percent.
12. Disagreement exists on how discrimination should be dealt with. Both blacks and whites argue about separatism vs. integration, militancy and compensatory programs in contrast to upgrading job skills, education, and greater law enforcement. Controversy also exists in evaluating discrimination in unions and in black capitalism.
13. Many who are concerned with the problems of poverty point to the resources being allocated for defense. They warn that the alliance between the military and the defense industries poses a danger to the public's needs, and they suggest a reordering of priorities to solve our domestic needs.
14. Defenders of our military point out that a switch has already taken place with significant declines in military expenditures as a percentage of our GNP. Such cutbacks have already jeopardized the striking power of our weapons systems and have threatened our diplomacy and security.

15. It is still a major question whether the benefits received by switching defense dollars to the war on poverty will accomplish what its advocates promise without harming our national security significantly.

IN CONCLUSION: SOME AIDS TO UNDERSTANDING

Terms for Review

working poor	Family Assistance Plan	black capitalism
poverty index	military–industrial complex	ghetto dispersal
poverty culture	negative income tax	black separatism
supplementary income	unemployable	

Names to Know

Fair Employment Practices Commission	Equal Opportunity Employer	FAP
	AFDC	ABM

Questions for Review

1. Poverty means different things to different people. Comment on the following:
   (a) Poverty is relative in time, place, and expectation.
   (b) Poverty is a culture.
   (c) Poverty is a statistic.
2. The poverty index figure has been criticized in several ways.
   (a) Do you think the Social Security Administration which set the index has provided a realistic scale?
   (b) Is it fair to set the farm index 30 percent below the nonfarm index?
   (c) What factors does the scale overlook?
3. Throughout your study of economics, policies have been presented for achieving the national goals of full employment without inflation. Why will the achievement of that goal not solve the poverty problem?
4. Poverty is caused by a number of factors. Show the relationship of it to:
   (a) education
   (b) culture
   (c) mobility
   (d) health
5. Compare President Nixon's Family Assistance Plan with the negative income tax. Which of the two would:
   (a) have the broader coverage
   (b) benefit the working poor most
   (c) be the easier to administer
   (d) help a childless family

6. Would you favor calling Part C of this chapter "black economics"? Explain your reasons.
7. Why is it unfair to compare blacks with immigrants? Can you provide counter-arguments to show where comparisons might be justified.
8. What are the reasons advanced for black separatism? For ghetto "dispersal"? Where does "black capitalism" fit?
9. What are the dangers that critics of the military–industrial complex have pointed out? What defense has the Pentagon offered?
10. How might your attitude about military expenditures change with a change in career and region?
11. How can you justify the authors' inclusion of a section on the military–industrial complex in a chapter on poverty?

Additional Questions and Problems

1. Investigate one of the antipoverty programs such as VISTA, the Neighborhood Youth Corps, or the Job Corps. Set up a system of evaluation. Do you think it produced results that justified the expenditures made?
2. There are significant philosophical differences between the system of welfare used in the 1960's, the Family Assistance Plan, and the negative income tax. What are they? What is your position and why?
3. Trade or craft unions have frequently been accused of discriminating against certain minority groups. Study these charges, the evidence you collect, and present your own conclusion.
4. Investigate "black capitalism." What factors have helped or hindered its development? Should efforts to expand it be continued?
5. What safeguards would you propose to avoid the charges of alleged conspiracy against the public good for military procurement? Should defense industries be nationalized?
6. In what way might a professional army help the poor?

SELECTED READINGS

Committee for Economic Development. *Training and Jobs for the Urban Poor.* New York: Committee for Economic Development, 1970.

Galbraith, John Kenneth. *The Affluent Society.* Boston: Houghton Mifflin Company, 1958.

Harrington, Michael. *The Other America: Poverty in America.* Baltimore: Penguin Books, 1962.

Melman, Seymour. *Pentagon Capitalism: The Political Economy of War.* New York: McGraw-Hill Book Company, 1970.

President's Commission on Income Maintenance Programs. *Technical Studies.* Washington, D.C.: U.S. Government Printing Office, 1970.

Public Affairs Office Defense Supply Agency. *An Introduction to the Defense Supply Agency.* Washington, D.C.: U.S. Government Printing Office, 1968.

Sheppard, Harold L., ed. *Poverty and Wealth in America.* Chicago: Quadrangle Books, 1970 (A New York *Times* book).

Tabb, William K. *The Political Economy of the Black Ghetto.* New York: W. W. Norton & Company, 1970.

Theobald, Robert. *The Guaranteed Income.* Garden City, N.Y.: Doubleday & Company, 1967.

Problems Faced by Other Segments of Our Economy 21

THE AUTHORS' NOTE TO THE STUDENT

In this last chapter we concentrate on the special problems faced by four important segments within our economy—farmers, small businessmen, the aged, and suburbanites. We then move to the problem of education that affects all of us. Finally we will try our hand at forecasting what is ahead, recognizing full well that it is a dangerous game but an action that must be taken if our society is to plan ahead.

In each of these cases (with the exception of our projection for the 1970's) we will follow the same general procedure. Once we have identified the problem, we will consider its causes, its development, and its present status. Finally we will examine the proposed solutions and try to draw some conclusions of our own.

Keep in mind that these problems do not have a single "right" answer. You should look upon your solutions as tentative because, as conditions change, as your understanding grows, and as your values and ideas are modified, you may wish to change your opinions. By this continuing search, you, the student and citizen, are acquiring the skills and knowledge necessary to arrive at the solutions which are best for you and the society you live in.

A STUDENT'S NOTE TO THE STUDENT

Reading this chapter was a good way to end the course. The reason? It justified learning some of the dull theory, and it related to problems that in some way are relevant to most everyone.

In some ways I felt frustrated. I guess I took this course to find out specific answers to questions that have bugged me for a long time. Instead I have found too many logical positions and yet none that satisfy me. I think the term "trade-off" (if you want more of one thing it is at the cost of something else) is beginning to sink in. In fact, that idea may be what economics is all about.

Part A
The Farmer

Defining the Problem

When we speak of a problem in the social sciences, we are referring to an unresolved controversy that can be defined and analyzed. We know that within the wide scope of such questions lesser related issues may also exist. One serious problem in our economy is that of "agriculture," or "the farmer." Usually when people speak of "the farm problem," they are referring to the relatively low income of the farmer in comparison with the income of other groups in the economy. Some people confuse the problem with its causes; they identify the problem as the relatively low prices which farmers receive for the products they sell in contrast to the high prices farmers pay for the products they buy.

In approaching the problem we face the question of what our farm policy should be. By keeping a wide perspective, we are recognizing that another large segment of our economy may not be sharing sufficiently in the nation's affluence and that changes in policy can improve the situation.

A Century of Change

In the last 100 years American agriculture has, like industry, gone through major changes. Among the important differences are the number of people employed and the amount of food produced. Just before the Civil War about one half of our labor force was engaged in agriculture, with each farmer producing enough to feed approximately five people. Today about 4 percent of our labor force works in agriculture, and each farmer feeds 50 people. These changes have come about as a result of a technological revolution —the agricultural counterpart of the Industrial Revolution—that has increased worker output at an amazing rate. The use of machinery, improved methods, hybrid seeds, special fertilizers, and better insecticides has made it possible for fewer and fewer farmers to supply more and more food. See Figure 21–1.

These innovations have brought significant changes in the character of farming. One indication of change is the fact that farming "as a way of life" is disappearing and is being replaced by farming as a business. To be successful the modern farmer must deal with problems similar to those of the businessman. He needs large amounts of capital to invest in improvement. Like the single proprietor he

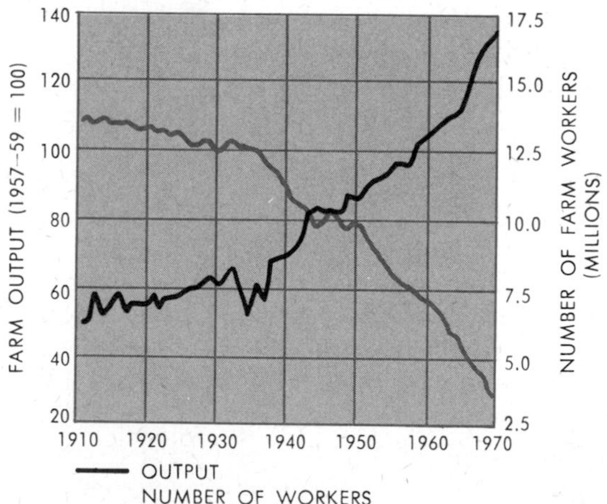

FIGURE 21–1 Relation of Farm Output to Number of Workers

The remarkable rise in farm output has been accompanied by an equally dramatic decline in the number of farm workers. SOURCE: U.S. Department of Agriculture.

must have knowledge of all aspects of the total operation, and be prepared to compete successfully.

Another important measure of change is the size of the farm unit. A steady reduction in the total number of small farms is in marked contrast to a corresponding increase in large operating units. Today fewer than 10 percent of the nation's farms account for over one half of the total sales of farm products. By contrast, two thirds of U.S. farms produce about 10 percent of our agricultural output. Although the importance of agriculture in the economy has declined relative to industry, it remains the largest single producer.

In the twentieth century, one aspect of farming has not changed. Economists recognize that farm income tends to fluctuate far more widely than industrial income does. For example, during the two world wars prices rose faster for farm products than for industrial goods, and the farmer's income increased accordingly. These short periods of prosperity were more than offset by tumbling prices and income after the wars, particularly during the years of the Great Depression in the thirties. Overall, the income of farmers has lagged far behind that of other groups.

Causes of the Farm Problem

We have seen that farming, like other parts of the economy, has undergone vast changes in the past century. But these changes do not in themselves constitute a special problem warranting favored treatment. We must go on to consider whether other factors operate to make the farmer's problems different from those of other producers. Is there anything unique in his situation that should single him out for special consideration?

Of all the sectors of our economy farming comes closest to meeting the conditions necessary for pure competition. If we disregard the role the government has played, we find in agriculture all the criteria identified in Chapter 2 as necessary to have the market mechanism work. If this is so, why has government intervention become necessary?

Inelastic Demand for Farm Products

Perhaps the single most important factor behind the farm problem is the inelastic demand for agricultural products in general, and for the major farm products in particular. Although our increasing population and larger incomes create a need for more food, the demand for food rises more slowly than the demand for industrial products. After all, no matter how great our income, we can eat only so much! In addition, rising incomes bring about a change in demand for certain foods. Poor nations must feed their people with grains, such as rice and wheat, whereas richer nations use more meat. In the former, large segments of the population may be permanently undernourished; in the latter, people may be more concerned with reducing their calorie consumption than with increasing it.

Let us see how the American wheat farmer is affected by our increased national wealth. For a graphic analysis of this problem, let us turn back to page 4 of the classical model of supply and demand, following page 34. Note that the demand schedules are inelastic, more vertical than horizontal. This situation exists because the American people can afford to buy food products made from wheat with very little reduction in other purchases as the price rises. On the other hand, if the price declines, they will not increase their other purchases by large amounts.

According to the supply and demand graph, supply (*S*) intersects demand (*D*) so that the quantity exchanged is 1.4 billion bushels and the price is $2.12 per bushel. The wheat farmers will receive $2.968 billion. When we turn the transparent page, we see that the new supply and demand curves would intersect where Q^1 (quantity exchanged) is 1.6 billion bushels and P^1 (price) is $1.50 per bushel. The wheat farmers, producing more wheat than before, receive only $2.400 billion, or $.568 billion less than they did before. We might conclude that wheat farmers collectively make the greatest gain from growing less wheat rather than more.

At first glance it appears that the solution to the wheat farmers' problem is simple—let them all grow less wheat! Unfortunately, this solution is an example of the fallacy of composition. The same paradox found in thrift and savings exists also for the farmer—what is good for the individual is not necessarily good for the entire group. If you were a wheat farmer, even the largest wheat producer in the nation, you would know that the amount of wheat you grew was not large enough to influence the price of wheat. Under these circumstances the more wheat you grow individually, the greater your income will be. Let the other farmers cut down!

Added Costs—The "Middleman"

You may frequently have heard complaints about the increased cost of food. If food prices are apparently so high, why do farmers complain about the low prices they get for their products?

As producers, farmers receive only a small part of the final retail price of food products. Much of this price is made up of charges for services such as processing and distributing. Those who work in this intermediate area, between producer and consumer, are known collectively as the *middleman*. Their costs have risen steadily, and new costs, such as for special packaging or processing, may have been added, resulting in even higher retail prices. The price for a package of cereal is many times greater than the value of the grain that has gone into it. In terms of the final retail price the farmer's share may be relatively small. See, for example, how the price of bread is shared, in Figure 21–2.

Too Many Farmers

In agriculture, like industry, significant increases in worker productivity have taken place. Because of this and also

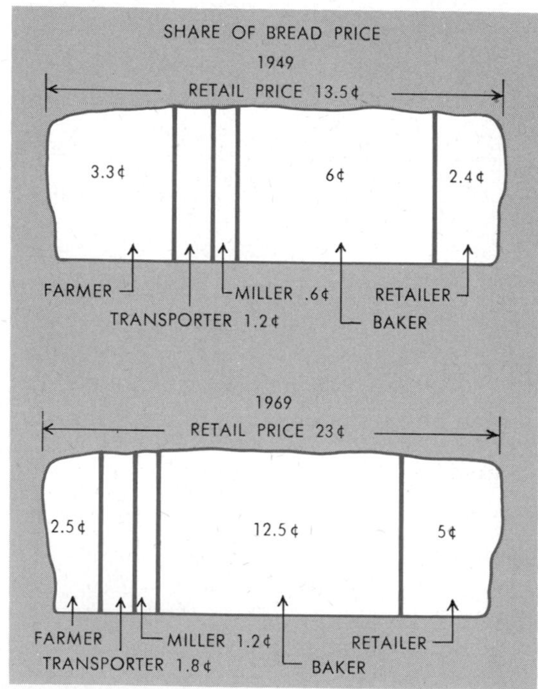

FIGURE 21–2 Who Share in the Price of Bread?

The cost of processing food has increased while the share that the farmer receives for food products has declined. SOURCE: *Food Costs—Farm Prices,* June 20, 1970, House of Representatives, Committee on Agriculture.

because of the relatively slow increase in the demand for food products, fewer and fewer farmers are needed to produce an adequate supply. Usually readjustments occur according to the classical model. The surplus of producers causes income to drop and directs the marginal farmer into other areas of the economy that yield a better return (remember the law of diminishing returns?). However, although it is true that the total number of farms and of farmers has declined, it has not done so at a fast enough rate.

There are several reasons for this slow rate of change. We have seen that, for many Americans, farming is a way of life. The farmer is his own boss. He can bring up his children away from what he may consider to be the "evils of the city." The air he breathes and the food he eats, the space he has and the kind of work he does, bring rewards beyond merely earning a living. In spite of the hard work and financial limitations, the farmer is, by his own standards, leading the best kind of life.

The fact that there are more farmers than are needed creates a problem, further complicated by the fact that the birthrate in rural areas is higher than that in cities. Although the mobility of young people in rural communities is high and many farmers are being absorbed into urban centers, there are still too many farmers in terms of our needs.

Prices and Competition

The prices of agricultural products reflect the fact that farming is highly competitive. Were it not for government intervention, these prices would be determined in the free market. In contrast, the prices of products which the farmer buys are, for the most part, not subject to the same kind of competition. (See Figure 21–3.) Many of the things he purchases come from industries with administered prices, where price decreases rarely occur. This difference in competition puts the farmer at a disadvantage in comparison with other producers in the economy.

When some people complain that agricultural products get special treatment, the farmer is quick to point out that many of our industries are able to keep their prices high because of tariff protection. He also accuses labor of causing higher prices because of the control that unions have over the supply of labor. Why should he be subject to a high degree of competition when others are not?

Special Risks of Farming

Few sections of our economy are as much at the mercy of the weather as farming is. A severe storm or drought can seriously damage, or even wipe out, a farmer's crop. Insurance protection against certain disasters is available, but the cost of adequate protection is prohibitive. In any event, efforts to offset risks add to the cost of production and reduce possible profit.

The Beginning of Federal Aid

The history of federal aid to the farmer goes back over one hundred years and embraces a wide variety of projects. The Morrill Act of 1862 provided for the establishment of land-grant colleges primarily designed for the education of the rural population and for promoting education in agriculture and the mechanical arts. In the 1920's more specialized assistance was made available. Government credit agencies were established to grant the farmer low-interest loans. A Federal Farm Board was created by President Hoover to encourage crop limitation and the formation of cooperatives on a voluntary basis. A half-billion dollars was supplied to help stabilize prices. The

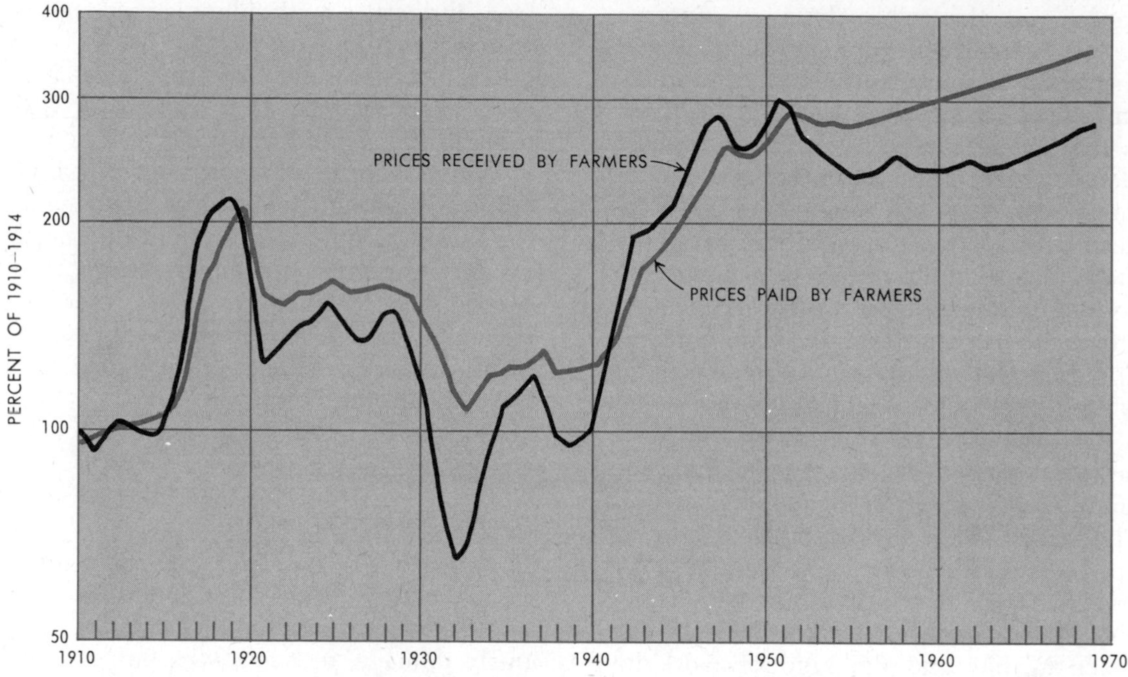

FIGURE 21–3 Prices Received and Paid by Farmers

Prices received by farmers exceeded prices paid by farmers, when measured as a percent of 1910–1914 prices, only during the two world wars. The critical world food shortage in the middle of the 1960's had improved the farmer's position, but it was only a temporary relief. SOURCE: U.S. Department of Agriculture, Economic Research Service.

Rural Electrification Administration was created in the 1930's to help bring the benefits of electric power to sparsely populated areas where supply by privately owned ultilities would have been uneconomical. The Agricultural Extension Service was created to do research and provide information on improving farming techniques. Crop insurance at a price below the cost to the government was started in 1938 to protect the farmer against losses caused by weather and insects.

In recent years the government has helped the farmer by means of the sale and distribution of food both at home and abroad. School lunch programs, food stamps, and donations of food for foreign disaster areas have helped to relieve surpluses. Farmers whose products are sold abroad have received help from *subsidies,* by which the government makes up the difference betwen the higher domestic price and the lower foreign market price. Efforts to lower tariffs on agricultural products in order to increase world trade have also been a help.

In spite of the number of such aid programs and their implementation from public funds, it is recognized that they have had only limited value. They have not provided basic, long-term solutions to the farm problem. Other approaches, however, have provided more effective help. These solutions have had two primary purposes: (1) raising the price received by the farmer relative to what he must pay for goods and (2) raising the farmer's income. It is usually assumed that incomes will rise if prices are increased.

Later Programs for Farm Aid

The depression crisis of the 1930's led to new and broader measures to help the farmer. Most of these were designed to raise prices and to improve the farmers' income, although a few included other values as well. Each program has been initiated by federal legislation and has been modified by successive administrations.

Parity and Price Supports

The key idea behind most of the major solutions offered to solve the farm problem from the New Deal to the present is *parity.* Parity is an attempt to provide a basis for economic equality for the farmer in relation to other groups in the economy. Specifically, it is designed to keep the purchasing power of a unit of farm production (a bushel of wheat, for example) equal to the purchasing power of the units of production that the farmer buys.

Under the New Deal, parity was based on prices for the period from 1909 to 1914, considered to be "normal" years for the farmer's economic position in relation to that of other economic groups. If the price index of the goods the farmer bought during those years averaged 100 and the average price of a bushel of wheat during this same period was $2, the attempt would be made to keep approximately the same relationship in prices. If, in 1929, the price index of the products the farmer bought was 150, what price would the farmer receive for his bushel of wheat if he were to maintain the same purchasing power for his unit of production?

Let us set up an equation to express the price relationships involved here. The price per bushel of wheat during the base period (a) divided by the price index for products which farmers buy during the base period (b) equals the (parity) price per bushel of wheat in the current period (c) divided by the price index for products which farmers buy in the current period (d):

$$\frac{a}{b} = \frac{c}{d}$$

In our example $\frac{\$2}{100} = \frac{X}{150}$ or $3 per bushel of wheat. The $3 per bushel would give the wheat farmer the same purchasing power for the product he sells as the real cost of the things he buys.

Now that we have seen how parity prices are arrived at, let us see how, in actual practice, payment of the parity price is made to the farmer. Farm prices above the free market price are maintained largely through the operation of the Commodity Credit Corporation, a federal agency. If the support price is $2 a bushel and the market price is $1.80, the farmer puts his crop into storage and receives a government loan amounting to $2 per bushel. If supply drops sufficiently to raise the market price above $2, he takes his crop out of storage, sells it, and repays the loan. If the price fails to go to $2, he merely keeps the $2 per bushel that the government has lent to him and the government must take the loss. More than $3.5 billion was extended for price supports by the Commodity Credit Corporation in 1970. This amount is smaller than in some previous years.

With few exceptions, farmers have accepted the parity formula as fair. Many other people, however, think that this system tends to favor the farmer at the expense of other groups in the economy. Critics of the parity price system point out that the period from 1909 to 1914 was an unusually good time for farmers in comparison with other producers. They also emphasize that output per worker and output per acre have increased very rapidly in agriculture; as a result, abiding by parity gives higher prices to farmers than to other producers in the economy. In addition, this program has not only cost the consumer more money in higher prices, but as a taxpayer he has to pay the high costs for storage.

Many changes have already been made to modify the original parity system. Some legislation has called up rigid price supports for specific crops, such as wheat, corn, cotton, tobacco and rice. Other laws have established flexible price supports which allow the Secretary of Agriculture to alter the parity price as he sees fit. Congress has never permitted parity to be 100 percent; the parity price range has generally fluctuated between 70 and 90 percent. (On April 30, 1971 it slid to 69 percent.) The base period for which parity is computed has been changed to more recent dates in some instances.

Further changes in the parity system may be expected. Because our legislatures have had a disproportionately large rural representation, farm legislation has been based mainly on the parity formula. However, the character of future legislatures is changing, since the Supreme Court decisions in *Baker* v. *Carr* (1962) and succeeding cases have established the need for redistricting to maintain the principle of "one man, one vote." As rural influence is reduced, the parity principle may not continue to be the basic formula for farm legislation in the future.

Acreage Control and Soil Conservation

Recognizing that low farm prices for farm products are the result of inelastic demand and too great a supply, the government has based some programs on efforts to restrict the supply. Under the New Deal a program was begun which tried to do this through *acreage control,* limiting the number of acres to be planted. The farmer was paid according to the number of acres withdrawn from cultivation as well as for the use of certain soil-conservation measures.

If yield per acre had remained constant, this plan might have been effective in reducing surplus. However, a reduction of supply did not occur. Farmers withdrew their poorest acres from cultivation, used more fertilizer and the best hybrid seeds, and produced even more than before.

In recent years other programs, similar in nature, have been used, and have proved only slightly more effective in reducing surpluses. The *soil bank* program of 1956 paid farmers to withdraw land from the cultivation of cash crops and to substitute the planting of timber or cover crops. It was based on the ideas of restricting output, giving the farmer an income subsidy, and conserving soil.

In general, the programs for limiting production through restricting the use of land have not been very successful. No significant reduction in the supply of farm products has been accomplished.

Price Differential Plan

Successive Democratic and Republican administrations have proposed plans to maintain guaranteed price supports to the farmer but at the same time to allow the consumer to pay the free market price. If crops were sold below the support price in the market, as would probably happen, the farmer would be paid *directly* the difference between the market price and the support price. In this way storage costs could be reduced and the consumer could benefit by lower prices. Whether the direct subsidy to the farmer to make up the difference between the two prices would cost the taxpayer as much as the savings made by consumers and by reduced storage charges is difficult to determine. Public opinion has never given strong support to this plan.

Increasing Demand

Many programs have been proposed and a great deal of money has been spent to create new uses and develop new markets for our surplus crops. Except for increased sales abroad, both private enterprise and government have failed to find new ways to alter demand significantly.

Dumping on Foreign Markets

The suggestion—seemingly simple and obviously humanitarian—has been made that we sell our surpluses abroad, particularly to friendly nations, at very low prices. The loss might be considerable for a year or two, but this practice might win us friends, serve as a weapon in our diplomacy, and eliminate our surpluses.

It would indeed be nice if the problem were that simple. However, such a policy would antagonize those nations which need to sell agricultural products in order to import other goods. Argentina and Canada would be seriously harmed in the sale of their wheat, as Egypt would be in the sale of cotton. In addition, the practice of *dumping* (selling at prices well below normal market prices) can be met by retaliation, which could hurt our own trade.

Retraining Programs for Farmers

We have seen that one cause of the farm problem is the fact that there are too many farmers. In reality, most of our farm programs have been designed to help the marginal farmer, who has difficulty subsisting under even the most favorable conditions. A major criticism of the programs based on price supports and income subsidization is that a large portion of the money spent on them goes to successful farmers who do not need such help. Many younger people from marginal farms would welcome the chance to move elsewhere if they had some other way to earn a living. Farming is the only occupation that many of these people know, and they feel uncertain about entering new fields.

The retraining programs recently set up include opportunities for farmers as well as for unskilled urban workers. It is still too early to evaluate the success of these programs. However, indications are that the mobility of the farmer into other areas of the economy is too low to regard this as a major solution, especially for those farmers already over 35 years of age.

Should We Return to a Free Market?

People who resent what they consider favored treatment for the farmer point out that the expenditure of many billions of dollars on agricultural programs has added to the existing prosperity of large-scale farmers but has done little to help provide the owners of small farms with more than a subsistence living. They suggest that we return to a free market for farm products; in time the marginal farmer will be eliminated and surpluses will be reduced. Such a change would be no more than we ask of the small businessman.

If we have any confidence in the market mechanism as an efficient means of allocating our economic resources, we should allow it to operate in agriculture. That segment of our economy is obviously overexpanded. So long as the American people subsidize farm products so heavily, the mobility of the farmer out of agriculture will remain low.

Under the price support system, payments of more than $250,000 in a single year have been made to one farmer for not producing crops. This is a clear example of inefficient resource allocation. We should shift to other areas of the economy a part of the money now spent on agriculture. Although justification can be made for helping people whose incomes are very low, the question remains whether farmers in general should be singled out for special treatment. Recently a limitation of $55,000 per crop was placed on the support system, but the real effect of this has been minor.

The arguments favoring a free market for farm products are answered by pointing out that the market conditions of agriculture are unique. Other segments of the economy, such as industry and labor, create their own protective devices. Administrative prices set by industry and wages negotiated by labor unions accomplish the same purpose as price supports—prices which are higher than would usually exist in a free market. Government provides industry with subsidies through tariff protection, and it subsidizes labor through minimum wages. Unemployment insurance protects most workers in a way not anticipated by the classical economist. Since farming fits the model of perfect competition more closely than do other areas of the economy, it needs government help to achieve what other segments have taken for themselves.

Looking Ahead

By now you are able to appreciate the complexity of the farm problem. It is compounded by questions of economics, ethics, and politics. To solve it will require not merely technical knowledge but a consideration of values.

In reality, the very nature of the farm problem may be changing, and future solutions must allow for new conditions, such as a decrease in surpluses. In 1964 the size of our surpluses in all grains began to decline, due to heavy shipments abroad. In 1966 some economists, worried that our supplies of certain agricultural products were too low in spite of record harvests, recommended reversing our crop-limitation program. In 1971 we produced the largest crop in our history, and were once again plagued with a surplus.

What should our farm policy be? Are any of the proposed solutions described in this chapter satisfactory? Should we combine several of them? What new conditions must be anticipated? If a solution is found, will it be adopted? These are the questions you must ask yourself as a responsible citizen. As a consumer, a producer (possibly a farmer), and as a citizen you will be very much affected by the decisions to be made concerning our farm program.

Part B
The Small Businessman

Defining the Problem

In the late 1950's Ben Chase was employed as a butcher in a grocery chain store. He knew his trade well, worked hard, saved whatever he could, and dreamed of starting a business of his own. His wife, Gertrude, also had a job and added her savings to her husband's. In 1960 they heard of a small slaughtering and meat-packing establishment that was for sale in a rural area. With their own savings, a loan from a relative, and a loan from a bank, they bought their own business.

Ben and Gertrude worked hard, sometimes more than 65 hours a week. They were good managers, and they knew how to deal with the farmers and the meat distributors. Their business grew. They had made enough contacts with farmers to insure a continuing supply, and they had no difficulty in selling everything they could produce. Now semiretired, they own a business worth a million dollars. They have lived the American dream.

A Different Story

When George Morris returned from military service in 1967, he got a job in a men's clothing store. He worked for two years learning many aspects of the business. At the end of that time he made the decision to go into business for himself. For $15,000 he bought a rundown store in a rather poor business location. His own savings and a loan from his parents supplied $10,000 of the cost; he borrowed the additional $5,000 from a bank.

George knew that the price was low in part because much of the merchandise was out of style. However, he believed that as he sold these goods (he had no capital to buy new merchandise and he had not established a credit rating yet) he would be able to replace them with the stylish clothing that people wanted. He hoped that by marking down the prices on what he had, he could soon clear out his old stock. He also counted on patronage from his many friends.

Two months after George opened his store, a new men's clothing store, part of a chain, opened three blocks away. Now the stock of suits that had but a short time ago been in style could not be sold for even a third of their original cost. George did not take in even enough money to pay his rent and his note at the bank. Most of his merchandise was valueless. By the end of one year George Morris was bankrupt, his store just another among the statistics of business failures.

Every year thousands of people like those in our hypothetical cases try to attain success in business. What they fail to realize, or choose to ignore, is that the average life expectancy of a business is less than seven years, that about 40 percent of all retail businesses last less than two years, and that many of those that do survive pay their owners less than they could earn by working for someone else. If we define small businesses as those firms employing fewer than 50 persons and with annual sales of less than $1 million, then 98 percent of all businesses are small. Yet the importance of small business in the nation's economy, together with the uncertainty of operations of many small firms, raises the question whether small business will continue to play an important role in our economy.

Changes in Business

Until the Civil War almost all business in our country was small by any definition. Big business appeared first in manufacturing, where high fixed costs made large-scale operations the only efficient method of producing. In transportation, too, the large initial investment and high fixed costs made large-scale operations more feasible.

Increase in Size

One of the clearest examples of change is found in the field of merchandising. Since colonial days the country store, or general store, owned by a proprietor or by several partners, has been a symbol of business enterprise. By 1900, however, the pattern of ownership began to change as the department store and chain store appeared. Chain stores could buy in huge quantities and save on per-unit costs; if sales lagged in one store, merchandise could easily be transferred to another. Mail-order houses also cut into the trade of the general store. Soon automobiles made it possible for people to shop outside their own neighborhood. Advertising in mass media gave large stores the advantage of a big market. Today these businesses and, more recently, discount houses, pose a seemingly overwhelming threat to small business.

By 1970 about 40 percent of all employees covered by Social Security were employed by huge businesses constituting only 1 percent of the total number of all businesses. On the other hand, only 6 percent of the workers are employed by the smallest business firms that make up 60 percent of the nation's employers.

Problems of Small Business

The Senate Select Committee on Small Business reported that although the nation was prospering, small business was not getting its full share. Firms with fewer than 250 employees did half the nation's business. Yet recent studies show small business gaining additional sales at a lesser rate and their profits growing at half the rate of big business.

We have seen that small businesses like George Morris's carry a high risk of failure. Between 1945 and 1959 the average number of business failures per year was 4,000, involving liabilities of $169 million per year. In the period from 1960 to 1969, the most prosperous period in our nation's history, the average number of business failures annually had increased to 15,000, with over $1 billion liabilities per year. With a major recession, we may expect the rate of failures to increase appreciably.

Advantages of Small Business

If those of you who look to small business as the opportunity for the fulfillment of the American dream are discouraged by the statistics given here, there are other figures that tell a different story. There are over 5 million small businesses in this country. More businesses are born each year than die, and their number is increasing at a faster rate than our population.

If small businesses can continue to grow in number and size, they must have some benefits to offset the many handicaps. Small companies do have an advantage in certain kinds of business. Their scale of operations is particularly well suited to the making and retailing of highly specialized products, of articles that are subject to frequent and drastic style changes, and of items requiring craftsmanship as opposed to standardization. Professional and service establishments—such as barbershops, specialty stores, and shops producing special equipment or parts involving much hand labor—are also usually best organized as small firms. The supplying of components to big business by subcontractors is an established practice that is growing each year. New products are as likely to come from small firms as from large ones, particularly in cases where demand is uncertain and where no specialized machinery has been developed.

Although there may be more George Morrises than Ben Chases, the fact remains that the small businesses which both men represent constitute an extremely important and vital part of our economy. Small firms are more mobile and can move in and out of business in response to fluctuations in the demand for their goods and services, with less effect on the economy. They can change their production or sales more easily, and they can perform functions in the economy that big business cannot and does not want to do. For these reasons small business not only needs to remain, but will remain.

Pros and Cons of Starting a Business

The fact that the number of our business establishments is increasing indicates that, to many people, business constitutes opportunity. Though some, as we have seen, fail, others go on to become prosperous concerns. Some go on to become large companies with almost unlimited opportunities and rewards.

Benefits

In reality, hope for material gain is only one of the reasons why people go into business. Among other objectives and considerations are the following:

1. People think that self-employment will permit a greater degree of personal independence and freedom of action than is possible in large organizations.
2. They will have a greater opportunity to try out their own ideas, since the bureaucratic aspects of big business often make such ventures difficult or impossible within the framework of a larger organization.
3. They think that they can make the American dream come true. There are enough cases of success to make it a possibility, even if the risk is great.
4. The owner looks forward to reaping all the benefits from his own labors. He will not have to share with others what he himself has created and developed under a single proprietorship.
5. There is greater community recognition in being in business for oneself. This is true so long as one is successful.

Disadvantages

Along with the potential benefits of going into business, there are certain definite disadvantages:

1. When one works for someone else, paychecks are regular, hours are usually shorter, and there is no financial risk of losing one's savings or of being unable to repay borrowed money.
2. The responsibilities of owning a business are considerable. Decisions have to be made frequently, and upon their outcome may rest the fate of the business.
3. The owner of a single proprietorship holds ultimate responsibility for all the problems of the business.
4. The regulations and restrictions made by all levels of government concerning business are usually irksome and sometimes costly.
5. Fringe benefits are frequently broader for employees than for employers.
6. Working for a very large business can sometimes offer greater income security than working for oneself.
7. There is an opportunity for advancement and reward in large business.

Why Do Businesses Fail?

A number of studies have been made of why businesses in general, and small businesses in particular, fail. A very small number of failures, less than 10 percent, were caused by such factors as poor health, fraud, disaster, neglect, and marital difficulties. The studies showed two main causes—poor management and insufficient capital—to be the most important.

Too many people go into business without sufficient training and knowledge to cope with the many demands of business. To the eager young man trying to make his mark in the world on his own, or to the retired couple who want to earn a few extra dollars to supplement a pension, it may seem simple to open up a filling station or a grocery store. Using these facilities as customers is quite a different matter from running them as successful business ventures.

Another important cause of failure is lack of capital. The typical small businessman starts out using all his own savings and borrowing as much as he can; he still probably has too little money to carry him through the first critical year, when sales are likely to be small. Banks are not eager to lend money to new and unproven firms. When they do, interest rates are likely to be high. Suppliers are seldom willing to advance much merchandise or raw materials until good credit ratings are built. With little capital, few new firms are able to take advantage of discounting their bills, a method of deducting a small percentage from the bill if paid within a specified period of time. They may not have the money or the credit to take advantage of bargains that they find. A business with sufficient capital, one that is more frequently found among big corporations, has inherent advantages.

Lack of capital is frequently found to be responsible for other failures. When a downturn in the economy occurs and the pressure to continue operating increases, the big business with adequate capital available can more easily subsist until conditions improve. Inadequate capital can lead to poor accounting records because satisfactory employees cannot be hired. The absence of ready, accurate information on sales or inventory can lead to inefficient operation.

Other Causes of Failure

Additional causes for failure include:

1. Too low a volume of business to cover fixed costs.
2. Overexpansion and overbuying during a business boom.
3. A general inability to control inventory.
4. Poor location, including competition from big business.
5. Lack of specialized knowledge. The small businessman is seldom an expert in all phases of business operation. He has to perform so many different functions that he can seldom become the master of any of them. He may often wish that he had never gone into business "on his own."

The Need for Small Business

Although we have at present a greater number of "births" than "deaths" in business, the large number of failures and the hardships and small return for time and effort may someday reverse this trend. Is small business important enough to our economy to justify aiding it?

Besides the figures cited previously on the contribution small business makes to increasing the size of our national output, there are many additional reasons for answering this question with a resounding *yes:*

1. Small business is the proving ground for ideas and resources, particularly human resources. Some businesses are started because their owners have new ideas of marketing, new methods of producing more efficiently, and new products to offer the consumer. Man-

agers of small firms get experience and become managers of large firms.

2. Small business increases competition and keeps big business "on its toes." Although there are few drastic changes from one year to the next in the list of the 500 largest businesses in the country, the changes that do occur point up the fact that small business can grow to threaten the position of giants that may be less progressive.
3. Small business is more flexible and can adjust to changes more quickly. This allows it to perform certain services and to make certain products more efficiently than big business can. Specialized demands cannot always be met by big business. This is particularly true where demands are subject to erratic changes, as in women's clothing; highly specialized and limited markets, like specialized bodies for certain kinds of motor vehicles; and markets, such as gravel, that must be local in nature because of excessive transportation costs.
4. The economy needs the mobility of small firms within a particular market as well as between different markets. As the demand for goods and services changes, the need for more or fewer business firms and for special kinds of business operations also changes.
5. Finally, we associate small business and its opportunities with our system of democracy. It provides the chance for economic mobility in relation to social position, allowing people to move from one group to another. Small businesses also provide a significant number of leaders in community life. Look at the leadership of service clubs, parent-teachers' associations, and charity groups and you will find many men from small companies.

What Can Be Done to Help Small Business?

The evidence we have seen indicates an affirmative answer to our question "Does small business still have an important role to play in our economy?" It has also shown, however, that small businesses have many difficulties in surviving, and that many do not operate as efficiently as they might. Therefore, they may waste our limited resources.

We have seen that the two chief problems of small business, accounting for most of their failures, are managerial incompetence and insufficient capital. In both instances, the government has taken steps to provide assistance.

Small Business Administration

Although there are many agencies—private, local, and state—which help business, the largest and most important agency devoted exclusively to small business is the Small Business Administration. This agency, established by Congress in 1953, carries on the following activities:

1. It makes available to small businessmen information on management. Pamphlets on such subjects as factory construction, production techniques, and marketing are published periodically as aids to small manufacturers. For people in marketing there is material on sales training, location appraisal, personnel management, profit planning, and similar technical subjects.
2. It helps to provide access to capital and credit at reasonable rates. In addition to making its own loans, the SBA supervises small-business investment companies, which have been set up

under special legislation for the purpose of furnishing capital to small business.

3. It helps obtain for small business a fair share of government contracts.
4. It provides loans to small businesses that have suffered from disaster such as fire, floods, and storms.

Other Government Aid

The federal government gives added help to small business by setting lower rates in the corporation income tax for profits up to $25,000. Unincorporated businesses—and most small businesses are unincorporated—do not pay a corporation income tax. State and local governments often give small businesses an advantage in taxing, although this is frequently offset by special inducements made by communities to encourage big business to move into their location.

Local and state governments, and even geographic regions, have organized development and credit corporations to help business. State departments of commerce offer numerous services to businessmen. State universities frequently set up bureaus and research facilities which they make available to business.

Self-Help

Chambers of commerce, retail merchants' associations, and various other trade organizations offer many services to businessmen. Less publicized but just as important are the cooperatives that have been organized by small businessmen to give them the buying power of large companies. The National Retail Grocers Association is made up of regional cooperatives. Money put in by independent grocers is used to buy a warehouse and trucks, and to employ workers who will buy, store, and distribute merchandise to the individual stores. By banding together on their purchases, they have much the same buying power as huge chain stores do. This eliminates at least one advantage of big business over small firms.

Conclusion

Small business plays a very important role in our economy; but as in the case of the farmer the question remains whether it is receiving a fair share of the "pie." Much of small business is marginal business and, as such, seems to get only what is left over. Part of the problem of small business stems from the economics of size, but equally important are problems that can be solved through better management techniques. Some help has come from government and some from the efforts of businessmen themselves. There is evidence to indicate that additional help may be needed.

Part C
The Aged

Defining the Problem

Another group for our special consideration is the elderly people of our nation. The conditions which affect them become of increasing concern as a growing percentage of our population is included in this category. The problem is further intensified by social changes (in family structure) and by economic changes (in enforced retirement and possibly limited income).

In a free agricultural society the position of older people is usually secure. As owner of the family farm, the head of the household—most frequently the father—retires from work when he feels ready and passes the operation of the farm on to his children. The children realize that they will inherit the source of the family income; because of this they help to care for the farm and for their parents. The children are dependent on inheriting the farm, and the place of their elders is almost guaranteed. The farmhouse is frequently large enough to accommodate the entire family; if it is not, the children can build another house on the farm.

In an industrial urban society the place of the aged may be a precarious one. Because of the greater mobility of children, families tend to be more fragmented. Most housing is designed for two generations rather than three. More and more the state has assumed the responsibilities for the aged which were traditionally undertaken by the family. Because the family is no longer so cohesive a group, social problems of recognition, recreation, and companionship become more difficult of solution.

In an agrarian society the old are able to continue performing some productive economic functions. In an urban industrial society discrimination against older people starts at about 45 years of age and continues, so that 65 has become a mandatory retirement age in many businesses. In 1970 about one person out of five in the age group over 65 was working or looking for work. Those who were working were frequently in lower paying jobs with lower prestige.

The income of people over 65 is far below the national average and they make up a disproportionately large percentage of those included under poverty. One reason is the limitation placed on earnings of people receiving Social Security payments. Another is that prices seem to go up faster than Social Security payments, although this problem is likely to be solved by applying an escalator clause. While poverty among all Americans is decreasing, poverty among the aged is increasing. Another fact that points to the seriousness of the problem is that the average age of our population is increasing. In 1900 those over 65 made up only 4 percent of the population. Today they account for nearly 10 percent, or about 20 million people.

Medical science in the United States has increased our life expectancy from 47 years in 1900 to over 70 years in 1971. Should we allow the latter portion of these added years to be filled with poverty and despair for so many people? Do we have the resources to furnish a measure of economic security and to provide facilities for brightening the lives of the elderly? We can now pose the question of what should be done to create a more secure and happy life for the aged.

The Effects of Social Security

Before the passage of the Social Security Act of 1935 the prevailing attitude was that each individual was responsible for providing for his own retirement. If this was not done, the question was asked, "Why should society have to take over the burden?" There was little recognition that an urban industrial society made people more interdependent and less able to control their own circumstances. This thinking, which might have been satisfactory when we were a nation of farm families, was carried over to a different kind of society.

In the absence of other provisions the poor and the aged were dependent on private charities and the meager provisions made by state and local governments. The Great Depression of the 1930's brought the problem into sharp focus and stimulated the passage of our major Social Security program, under the supervision of the federal government.

Philosophy Behind Social Security

The importance of the Social Security Act of 1935 does not lie in its details. Its importance is to be found in its philosophy, which transfers responsibility for the aged from the individual and the family to the society. Individualism and the market economy were, in a limited sense, replaced by collective responsibility. Those who opposed this change were heard to cry "Socialism!" Each successive amendment for increasing benefits has been greeted in the same way.

Whether people choose to call the Social Security program socialistic or not is less important than the facts that

1. a public need existed that was not being met, and our Social Security program provided an answer
2. the financial basis on which the program is being run demands that payments be made by the individuals who will receive benefits
3. the United States was far behind such other industrial nations as Germany, France, and England in providing a security program for its people

After more than 35 years of operation our Social Security program is an integral part of the American economic system. The question is no longer whether to have Social Security or not; it is rather how far its coverage should be extended.

How Social Security Works

The major operational principle behind Social Security is forced insurance. The individual must make payments to the government so that he may be protected when he can no longer provide for himself. The principle is the same as that used by private insurance companies. At present, protection includes a pension for old age, payments to survivors of breadwinners, unemployment insurance, and medical, hospital, and nursing-home care for the aged.

Since its inception the law has been broadened to include the vast majority of people in the labor force. For employees, payments are made by equal contributions from the employer and employee, except for unemployment insurance. The self-employed pay one and a half times what employees pay. Both the rates and the tax base have gone up during the years that Social Security has been in effect. The rates are scheduled to climb still higher in order to keep the program self-sustaining.

The program of unemployment insurance is set up by the states within an approved framework designated by the federal government. Employers pay the entire tax and the federal government provides matching grants to states and pays part of the administrative costs.

The Medicare program passed by Congress in 1965 has been a blessing to many older citizens who lack the means to take care of their own health needs. Recently the program has been expanded.

Today application for a Social Security number is often one of the first steps taken by the student-citizen on becoming an active producing member of the economy. Since the coverage under Social Security laws changes frequently, it is advisable for a worker to contact his local Social Security office and obtain the latest information on rates, benefits, and procedures.

Solutions to Help the Aged

The problems of the aged are many, and although it is true that our Social Security system has been a great help, serious problems remain. Many solutions have been offered, and some have been tried on a limited scale to help improve conditions for our older citizens.

Private Pension Plans

In 1964 the average payment made to an individual collecting a retirement pension from Social Security was less than $85 a month. Recognizing that payments from Social Security were inadequate to provide a decent standard of living for the aged, unions have, since World War II, included pension plans for retired workers in contract negotiations. These pension systems have grown at an accelerated rate, so that today the assets of private funds are greater than those of public funds. It is too early to evaluate fully how extensively the benefits from these and other private pensions will reduce the economic distress of participants on retirement. There is no doubt, however, that such added retirement income will be of great help.

Changing Social Security

There have been many criticisms of the way our Social Security laws operate. The two complaints heard most frequently concern the regressive nature of the Social Security tax and the failure to regulate payments on a cost-of-living basis. The tax is regressive because, given a fixed tax base ($9,000 in 1972) people with incomes over that amount pay a smaller percentage of their total income into the Social Security fund. If the Social Security tax were levied on a person's entire income, it would be proportional. The extra revenue derived could permit additional benefits. Critics of this suggested change point out that benefits already tend to favor those who have contributed less, and that the present plan tends to redistribute somewhat in favor of the lowest income group.

There is no doubt that an increase in the cost of living reduces the real income of benefits received. The proposal that payments be made according to the cost of living would provide guaranteed purchasing power. Opponents counter by pointing to the repeated increases that Congress has given and probably will continue to give. Any increases in existing benefits mean that present workers are subsidizing workers already retired. Deciding whether benefits should be increased is a problem of values to be solved by you as citizens, not by economists.

Preventing Discrimination in Employment

Several states have passed laws prohibiting discrimination against older workers. However, legitimate differences in physical ability between older and younger workers limit the effectiveness of these laws. Somewhat more effective have been the special counseling and placement services set up by states to help older people find positions for which more mature workers are suited. A few private agencies have established businesses employing only older workers. They are hired at prevailing wages, and prices on the products must be competitive. It is too soon to evaluate their success, although latest reports reveal no great changes.

Housing

Nearly two thirds of the people 65 and over own their own homes. This figure looks less encouraging when the condition of these homes and the problems of maintaining them are investigated. Many are in a state of disrepair, with the owners physically or financially unable to make improvements. Increases in property taxes have caused great hardship to the aged, since they usually live on fixed incomes. When younger people complain about the opposition of the elderly to school bond issues, they sometimes fail to recognize the hardship that older people face in paying the higher property taxes. Fixing property taxes at the amount in effect when people reach 65, or allowing some exemption for the aged as is done in the federal income tax (double exemption for those 65 and over), would help older people in planning for their retirement years.

Congress has passed special housing legislation making it easier for builders to invest in the construction of "communities for the elderly" and in other housing projects. Unfortunately, these projects are often too costly for those who are most in need.

Leisure Time

One of the most difficult adjustments that people have to make on retirement is filling the hours that were previously occupied with work. An additional problem is the feeling of depression that many older people have because they no longer consider themselves useful members of society. To meet these problems many communities have set up "golden age" and "senior citizen" clubs that offer opportunities for many kinds of activities, as well as opportunities for making social contacts. Both public and private agencies have set up programs, including adult education and recreation classes. Unfortunately, many of the elderly do not have the opportunity, the desire, or the knowledge of available facilities to take full advantage of them.

Conclusion

Like farmers and small businessmen, the aged have been faced with problems that seem a long way from solution. As a group they have not found the prosperity that would provide them with the means to make their retirement more than bearable.

Involved in finding answers to these problems is the basic question "How shall we allocate our resources?" Whether current producers (our present working force) should help support our past working force (those retired) is in part a question of social ethics. Economists point out that Social Security acts as an automatic stabilizer in compensating for the business cycle, and that it also helps in a very modest way to redistribute income.

Whether the individual should assume most of the responsibility of providing for his old age or whether there should be collective responsibility is a question of values. Economic analysis can help us to infer what the consequences of each course of action may be. The fact that you are born into a society with established values does not mean that you cannot or should not try to change them.

As one who is likely to be or is part of the working force you will probably have to accept the idea that the society has assumed some responsibility for certain segments of the population, including the aged. However, you should, as a responsible citizen, decide whether you favor increasing or decreasing the collective responsibility. Do you want people of each generation to pay their own way individually or collectively in providing for their old age, or should our working force help to subsidize the older members of society when the resources they have set aside are inadequate to care for their needs? Do you want more benefits guaranteed when you retire? Do you want to control these benefits yourself or do you want Social Security to provide them? You may not always get your way, because as a citizen you agree to abide by the decisions that your democratically operated government makes. However, as a citizen you should realize that you not only have a right, but also have an obligation, to help in the process of making these decisions.

Part D
Urban Economic Problems

Defining the Problem

Today, economists and other social scientists in increasing numbers are turning their attention to the problems of urban areas. In 1800 only 5.6 percent of the United States population lived in urban areas. By 1920 over half of the population was urbanized, and today the percentage is about 70. By 1975, it is expected that about 73 percent of all Americans will reside in cities and suburbs. By the year 2000, 85 percent of the population will probably be found in urban areas.

What Is an Urban Place?

An *urban place* is one in which there are 2,500 inhabitants or more. All other areas are classified as *rural*. Not all of the rural inhabitants, however, are engaged in agriculture: persons residing in rural areas but not engaged in agriculture are classed as the *rural nonfarm population*. Since World War II, the growth of population has been relatively slow in the central cities, but rapid in the suburbs. For example, in 1960 about 48 percent of those living in metropolitan areas lived outside the central cities; by 1970, however, 55 percent were living in the suburbs. During the 1960's only four of the nation's largest cities showed population gains. A central city and its suburbs within commuting distance make up a *metropolitan area*.

As yet, there is no firm agreement on how to define *metropolitan area*. In 1949, the U.S. Bureau of Census used the term *standard metropolitan area* to describe "a county or group of contiguous counties which contains at least one city of 50,000 inhabitants or more." The counties must be "essentially metropolitan in character and socially and economically integrated with the central city."[1] This term was replaced in 1960 by *standard metropolitan statistical area* (SMSA), a term which dropped the requirement that there be a city of at least 50,000. Instead, an SMSA county may contain two cities side by side (twin cities) with a combined population

[1] U.S. Bureau of the Census, *Census of Population: 1950*, Vol. I: *Number of Inhabitants*, 1952, p. iii.

of 50,000. These cities must be regarded as a single community economically and socially, and the smaller one must have at least 15,000 inhabitants. An SMSA may have two cities of 50,000 or more people each and may still be regarded as part of the same metropolitan area. A metropolitan area with several central cities is sometimes called a *polynuclear structure.*

A county in an SMSA is considered metropolitan if it meets several criteria: for example, in a metropolitan SMSA county at least 75 percent of the labor force is engaged in nonagricultural work, and at least 50 percent of the population lives in areas with a population density of 150 per square mile. A county is considered to be integrated with the county of a central city if 15 percent of its workers are employed in that county. Over 200 SMSA's have been identified in the United States. Still, there are many problems of classification. In New England, the administration uses cities and towns instead of counties in order to determine SMSA's.

There are the two major population centers of the United States, and the term *standard consolidated area* (SCA) is often used in referring to them. The New York-Northeastern New Jersey standard consolidated area is made up of four SMSA's, for a total of 17 counties. The Chicago-Northwestern Indiana SCA is made up of two SMSA's. Still, the definitions are not firm. The Regional Plan Association, which now defines the New York region as 22 counties in three states, may in the future extend this figure to 31 counties. Jean Gottman, an authority on metropolitan growth, concentrates on an area from northeastern Virginia to southern New Hampshire and west to the Appalachian Mountains. He calls this vast urbanized region *megalopolis.* Some observers believe that by the year 2000 there will be at least three megalopolitan areas in the United States. The current northeastern megalopolis will spread to western New York state; another will stretch between San Francisco and San Diego; and the third will extend from Chicago to Pittsburgh.

Despite these differences in definition, one thing should be clear. It is generally agreed that when analyzing urban problems we cannot confine ourselves to a single city, that most urban areas are suffering from the same sorts of illnesses, and that we must attack these problems on an area-wide basis.

Multiple Problems

Cities are plagued by many problems, but in the brief space permitted we can identify only the most difficult ones and present the solutions tried by a few cities. Of course, each problem touched on here deserves further study. The questions raised by this discussion may help steer the interested student on the right track in using the analytical approach.

Haphazard Growth

Some of our cities and towns were carefully and wisely planned, but many have grown in a haphazard fashion. Towns usually grew up along natural or man-made highways and waterways, such as harbors, branches of rivers, or intersections of roads. Some of today's busiest streets were once cowpaths; these winding, narrow unplanned arteries play havoc with modern traffic. Even where street patterns were carefully planned, the planners could not always anticipate the coming of the automobile and the need for off-street parking, the great increase in population, and the growth of urban commerce. Because there were no effective zoning laws in earlier times, industrial plants can be found in residential areas or near schools. Such conditions can have negative effects upon a city's economy, but the immediate cost of correcting them is prohibitive. Of course, from the long-run point of view, the real cost of *not* correcting them will be very serious. Is the classical market mechanism for the allocation of resources responsible for this problem? Should the classical mechanism be modified, and, if so, how? What disadvantages might develop under new policies?

Congestion

Crowding human beings and motor vehicles into small geographic areas can have serious economic consequences. New York City has about 70 percent of the people living in the New York SMSA, as compared with 57 percent for Chicago, 46 percent for Philadelphia, and only 41 percent for Los Angeles. (New York City's percentage would drop to about 30, however, if we used the SCA—standard consolidated area—instead of the SMSA). New York county has a population density of 77,000 persons per square mile, while Putnam County (part of the same region) has only 133. High population density often results in high crime rates, overcrowded housing,[2] serious traffic problems, and high disease rates.[3]

All cities, and even many small towns, are plagued by traffic congestion. By 1963, 91 percent of all travelers in the United States were using motor vehicles instead of trains or other means of transportation. Because many people insist upon using private automobiles on city streets, even though public transportation facilities are faster and cheaper, the density of registered automobiles is as high as 3,000 per square mile in some cities. Over 3 million people enter the business district of New York City daily, and of these nearly a million come by private automobiles. Yet studies have shown that railroads can carry 22 times as many people over the same distance during the same period of time as can private autos. Clearly, commuter trains would be more efficient, but public policy has often favored highways over railroads. It is not unusual to find a city devoting nearly a third of its land area to streets—land which might be used for industrial establishments or residential construction. New York City's streets, for example, take up more of its land than its residential, commercial, and industrial areas combined. Traffic congestion adds to the cost of doing business. A garment manufacturer in New York found that it took 10 men a total of 12 hours to unload a truck in the congested business district, while it took two men only three hours in a suburban area. Congestion is one of the major reasons why manufacturers have been leaving central cities. Would any of the solutions to the problem of haphazard growth help solve the problem of congestion?

Loss of Industries

Many central cities are losing industries to the suburbs or to other areas of the nation. During the 1960's New York City

[2] A dwelling is said to be overcrowded if it houses more than one person per room, on the average. A *PPR Ratio* (persons per room) is obtained by dividing the number of persons living in the dwelling by the number of rooms. If the PPR ratio is greater than one, it is overcrowded.

[3] Recently, the tuberculosis rate in a heavily populated area of New York City was found to be over five times that in lightly populated areas.

lost 124,000 manufacturing jobs, for example. The city accounted for only one out of every four new jobs added in the New York metropolitan area during that period.

Wherever businesses leave central cities, the causes (sometimes called *centrifugal forces*) are similar.

1. The *spatial force,* stemming from the intense competition for space within cities, is often said to be the major reason for the outflow of business. While modern industrial processes frequently demand plants which are spread out, the available buildings in cities extend upward. Compared with the suburbs, there are few vacant spaces inside cities. Commercial pursuits, industry, and transportation (exclusive of public streets) take up only a small percentage of the total land area of many metropolitan regions. For instance, these activities occupy about 16 percent of the land in the Los Angeles metropolitan region and only about 10 percent in the New York and Pittsburgh metropolitan areas. Lack of suitable space, then, is pushing many firms out of the cities.
2. The *situational force* refers to unsatisfactory use of the available space and facilities in cities. Available buildings might be located too far from transportation facilities, sources of supply, or markets. Heavy congestion in the area where a firm is located can greatly increase its production costs. Inadequate commuter services in the city can make it difficult for workers to get to their places of employment. Often, more convenient arrangements can be found in the suburbs.
3. *Antiquated facilities* which are no longer suitable for modern manufacturing methods can send business to the suburbs. It may be cheaper to build a new plant outside the city than to modernize existing structures within the city.
4. *Higher labor costs* in cities are often cited by businessmen who depart. According to the National Bureau of Economic Research, there is a direct relationship between the size of a city and the average hourly wage of industrial workers. For example, by 1970 the wage index in New York City had reached about 197 (using 1953 as the base year), while in Providence, Rhode Island, it was only about 164. Class A accounting clerks in Trenton, New Jersey, were receiving $118.50 per week, while those in New York were being paid $138. Carpenters employed in industrial plants in Greenville, S. C., (population 61,242) worked for $2.52 per hour, while those in Houston, Texas (population 1,213,064) enjoyed wages of $4.05.

   It must be realized, however, that these differences in wages may be attributed partly to differences in the productivity of the workers: capital is generally more abundant relative to labor in large cities than in small towns. Business has also expressed dissatisfaction with the quality of unskilled labor in cities. In any event, the prospect of lower wages might motivate some businessmen to leave large cities.
5. *The high taxes and high land values* which are typical in central cities can send business to the other areas. A few years ago, the mayor of a southern town wrote to northern industrialists, offering them very low carrying charges, tax exemptions for up to 99 years, sites and buildings, and wages considerably below those in northern

states. Lack of strong unions also attracted businesses to the South. Some of the "runaways" who accepted such offers were disappointed, however, and now the land values and taxes in small towns are getting closer to those in the cities.

6. *The general deterioration* affecting many cities is sometimes given as a reason for leaving. This includes rising crime rates, the growth of slums, the exodus of middle-income people, obsolete public facilities (such as ports, roads, and commuter trains), and even "anti-business" attitudes on the part of some city officials.

Of course, in some cities the loss of manufacturing is balanced by gains in other fields. Buildings no longer suitable for manufacturing can sometimes be turned into offices. There will be temporary dislocations, however, because workers who were employed in industry are not always equipped to get other jobs. And the fact still remains that there are more jobs being created in the suburbs than in the cities. In a recent five-year period, for example, the number of jobs in the suburbs grew by 30 percent, whereas the number of jobs in a dozen leading metropolitan areas grew by only 12 percent.

In order to assess the real significance of employment trends in a city, one must always place the data in a broad context. The United States Department of Commerce has developed the *regional share concept* for this purpose. An estimate of the number of jobs a region has gained or lost relative to other areas shows its relative attractiveness. For example, Phoenix, Arizona, would have gained 20,570 jobs in the 1950's if its industries had grown at the same rate as the nation as a whole. Actually, it gained 127,244 jobs. The difference between the two figures—106,674—is the *regional share* for Phoenix. In this case, the region did much better than the national average. Scranton, Pennsylvania, on the other hand, lost 8,594 jobs. It would have *gained* 9,754 if its industries had grown at the national average. Thus, Scranton's regional share was *negative* 18,348. Most of the large losses were in the Northeast; most of the large gains were in the South, Southwest, and West.

What steps might a city take to prevent the loss of industry? Would these measures aggravate other problems? What role should the state and national governments play, if any? What noneconomic factors might influence the loss of industry?

The Changing Population

In many of the central cities, the composition of the population is changing. The middle-income groups are moving to the suburbs, while the poor are moving into the central cities. Between 1960 and 1965, Cleveland lost 90,000 people to the suburbs, most of whom were in the middle-income group, and gained 25,000 poor. In a one-year period, the percentage of households in New York City earning $10,000 or more per year dropped from 29.5 to 26.6. Meanwhile, the percentage of households earning less than $2,000 rose from 15 to 16.8. As a result, New York dropped from rank 22 to rank 45 in terms of effective buying power per household. Looking at the long-term trend, we find that in 1950 New York City accounted for over 56 percent of New York state's personal income in 1950, but less than 48 percent in 1965, and that per capita incomes are now as much as $1,500 higher in some of the suburban counties than in the central city.

Changes in the composition of a city's population have profound effects upon its economy. People moving *out* of the city are usually those who are capable of paying taxes. They are generally people who have relatively high levels of education and technical skills, and thus great earning power to contribute to a region's economy. They require fewer public services and assistance than the poor who are moving in. The poor persons flocking *to* the central cities are often without the training, skills, or formal education needed to obtain the jobs available in the cities. In the poor neighborhoods of central cities, unemployment rates for nonwhite adults averaged 6.6 percent in mid-1970, while the rate for nonwhite teen-agers was a staggering 34.2 percent. The *subemployment rates* are much higher.[4] For example, when the unemployment rate in San Antonio's poverty areas was 8.1 percent, the subemployment rate was 47.4 percent.

Most poor people inhabiting central cities have need for more and greater services in education, health care, housing, and aid to dependent children but are unable to pay the costs. This places the burden on the middle-income or high-income residents, the very people leaving the cities. The influx of the poor and the rising taxes in the cities are reasons often cited for the outflow of the more affluent groups. The cities, then, face a financial problem, as the cost of public services continues to rise while the tax base continues to fall. Because the productivity of industrial workers has increased greatly, they command higher wages than the policeman, the teacher, the fireman, the social worker, the public administrator, and other producers of services, who are producing little more than they did 30 or 40 years ago. There is a greater need for them, however, and they too must receive higher wages if their services are to be retained. If cities attempt to solve the problem by raising taxes on existing industries, these industries often threaten to move out also. Many of the mayors of central cities are pleading for federal aid, on the ground that the problems with which they are forced to deal are essentially national. For example, they maintain that it is not the fault of the cities that impoverished and unskilled rural people are moving in.

[4] The official unemployment rate generally considers only those who are out of work but actively seeking jobs. The subemployment rate is more meaningful in understanding the problems in the cities, for it includes all those counted in the official unemployment rate, plus those who have given up looking for work, those with part-time jobs, and those with full-time jobs who make too little to rise above the poverty level.

Too Many Governments

Water which has been polluted by one city or town often flows through another city, town, county, or state. Air currents carry poisonous fumes across political boundaries. Traffic, workers, goods, services, and money capital flow from one political jurisdiction into another. Added to these problems is the prediction previously stated that by the year 2000 there will be at least three areas in the United States which can be classified as "megalopolis," centered around such major cities as New York, Chicago, and Los Angeles. In any event, the problem of "too many governments" will become worse unless the situation is changed.

On the average, there are 87 separate governments in each of the metropolitan areas. The U.S. Department of Commerce defines a government as "an organized entity having governmental attributes and sufficient discretion in the management of its own affairs to distinguish it as separate from the administrative structure of any other governmental units."[5] If we omit school districts (which are often counted as governments), California has nearly 2,000 governments, New York state has over 2,000, and Illinois has over 4,000. One county in the New York metropolitan area (Nassau) has 64 villages, three towns, two cities, and nearly 300 special districts. Altogether, there are nearly 1,500 governments in the New York region. It is inconceivable that such regional problems as air pollution, water supply, traffic congestion, crime, and industrial development can be handled efficiently when governmental responsibility is so fragmented.

Area-wide problems are aggravated by the lack of one central regional authority. For example, the new Bay Area Rapid Transit District, a 75-mile complex linking three counties and several cities in California, is designed to serve 1.4 million people. The project was started in 1962, when it was realized that the area's urban transportation problems could not be solved by more freeways. (New freeways or expressways sometimes aggravate congestion by inducing more people to use cars instead of commuter trains or buses.) Delays resulted when participating communities demanded modifications in the original plans. Meanwhile, inflation has increased the cost, so that the system will need at least $144 million more than originally anticipated. Even within one governmental jurisdiction, there are similar problems. Many urban governments have changed little, if at all, since colonial days. Governmental structures which were adequate in the "horse and buggy days," or which developed in a haphazard fashion, cannot cope with the overwhelming problems of today's cities. For instance, in one major city, a person attempting to establish a parking lot must deal with 21 different government agencies.

[5] Bureau of the Census, *Governments in the United States* (Washington, D.C.: Government Printing Office, 1953), p. 6.

Many city officials feel that they are being forced to carry burdens which are actually regional or national. State legislatures are often under strong rural influence, if not downright domination, and many rural representatives are unaware of city problems. It is not unusual to find that city residents pay over half of a state's taxes, but receive less than half of money spent by the state. People living in the suburbs usually use the central city's services, or rely upon the city for their jobs or their businesses, but are rarely willing to help the city cope with its economic problems. While the population of central cities is either declining or becoming less affluent, the general expenditures of the cities must rise. For example, per capita expenditures in Washington, D.C., rose by about 185 percent in a recent 10-year period. New York City's welfare costs alone increased tenfold in a decade, while its total population remained about the same.

Return to Chapter 10 and review the problems that local and state governments have in raising sufficient revenue. Should these smaller units of government have increased taxing powers, or should they receive more revenues from the national government on a per capita basis? Why?

Possible Solutions

Some cities have made commendable progress in solving certain of their problems. Los Angeles has built hundreds of miles of aqueducts to provide an adequate water supply. Cooperation between Pittsburgh business leaders and city officials on air-pollution control has helped bring a revival of that city's economy. With the help of federal urban renewal funds, about a third of New Haven, Connecticut, is being rebuilt. San Francisco is converting some of its decaying waterfront facilities into shops and restaurants. The Port of New York Authority, established in 1931 by New York and New Jersey, has built bridges, tunnels, airports, and terminals. It operates a commuter railroad and is building a huge world trade center. With the exception of the railroad, each of these facilities pays its own way. (The Port Authority has no power to tax; it can raise money only by charging fees for the use of its facilities and by selling bonds.) But even with its cumulative investment of about $2 billion and its staff of 8,000, the Port Authority can deal with only a small fraction of the area's problems.

Perhaps the first priority for metropolitan areas is to end the fragmentation of political authority and establish some sort of area-wide governmental structure. This will not be easy, however, when a metropolitan area spreads out over state borders, as well as city and county lines. When critical problems threaten an area, cooperation often seems more feasible. For example, the states of Delaware, New Jersey, New York, and Pennsylvania established the Delaware River Compact in 1961 for cooperative development and use of the Delaware River's resources. The agreement included plans for a commission to control water supply, pollution, flood protection, watershed management, recreation, and hydroelectric power. Although all of the participating states have been threatened by serious water shortages and pollution, the compact was achieved only after 30 years of maneuvering. Since most governments jealously guard their sovereignty, it is likely that area-wide administrative structures will be established only for specific functions and problems.

The federal government must take the initiative in dealing with many urban problems, and in promoting regional cooperation. (The federal government was a party to the Delaware River Compact, but Congress must approve all projects involving federal expenditures.) Some feel that the federal government should handle all welfare problems. This would perhaps help eliminate the vast differences in welfare programs throughout the country, and prevent one area from "exporting" its welfare problems to another. Such schemes as the Model Cities program, administered by the U.S. Department of Housing and Urban Development, can help eliminate urban slums. Although some private bankers and construction firms are attempting to promote more building in urban slums, they are being deterred by the probabilities of high risk and low returns. Thus government funds will be needed if we are to provide adequate housing for millions of slum dwellers.

To stem the outflow of industry, some states and cities are providing loans and mortgage insurance, giving advice to small businessmen, developing sites and constructing plants to be leased to private firms, and even training jobless workers for the types of positions which are available. Obviously, more of this type of activity is needed.

A federal Department of Transportation was established in 1966. Its purpose, said President Johnson, is "to untangle, to coordinate, and to build the national transportation system for America that America is deserving of." This department is charged with the responsibility for developing plans for urban mass transit programs, doing research on transportation problems, and administering demonstration programs to see if faster trains can revive passenger service between major cities. It might also help to provide objective advice and guidance to regions where the institution of unified transportation policies is prevented by the number of governmental units involved.

Regional planning is essential if the haphazard growth of the past is to be avoided in the future. For example, it is useless for one town to enforce rigid zoning codes which keep out "nuisance factories" while an adjacent community permits industries to move in. A regional plan does not try to specify the use of every square foot of space, but it does take into account such factors as changing population, industrial development, transportation needs, recreation and open space, and residential construction. Such a plan can help to insure a region of adequate industrial growth, for example, while protecting its residents from the encroachment of noisy, smoke-producing factories. Again, the success of regional planning will depend upon the cooperation of the many industries and communities involved.

Finally, all citizens must realize that urban problems will affect the entire nation. It will not be possible in the future to escape from these problems by moving to other areas—there may be no "other areas." The federal government was planning to devote 1.9 percent of its total expenditures in 1971 to housing and community development, as compared with 2.7 percent for agriculture—and yet only 5 percent of America's population is rural, while nearly 70 percent is urban. In recognition of the magnitude of these problems, the president of the University of California proposed in 1968 that all of his state's colleges and universities unite in a program to deal with the "moral, economic, . . . racial, [and] economic crisis" gripping our cities. Some major universities are establishing centers for urban studies to bring together economists, sociologists, political scientists, architects, and others whose cooperation and skills are needed to solve urban economic problems. The problems of urban areas are becoming monumental, and they will have to be faced not only by professional social scientists, but also by an enlightened citizenry.

Part E
Education—Investment in the Future

Changing Demands in Education

In 1900 about one out of ten children of high school age was enrolled in high school and one out of twenty-five of college age was enrolled in college. Today nine out of ten are enrolled in high school and better than one out of three is in college. In 1900 total expenditures for public schools below the college level were $215 million for a school-age population of 21 million. In the 1969–1970 academic year these expenditures were $40.6 billion for 46 million children below the college level. As a nation, we spend more money on schools than on any other single enterprise except defense. Education can claim the honor of being the fastest growing major industry, with increases in annual expenditures running above 10 percent for the last few years.

Population Change

There are four major reasons to account for the increasing expenditures in education. First, the national birthrate (number of births per 1,000 population) rose dramatically from 17.9 in 1940 to 23.6 in 1950. In the decade from 1950 to 1960 it was more than 23.3, but has declined somewhat since then. The effect of this increase on the number of pupils enrolled in public and private schools combined can be seen in Figure 21–4. The rapid gain in both elementary and secondary enrollment for the first decade is projected at a somewhat lower level for the second. However, the rate of college enrollment is expected to remain steady.

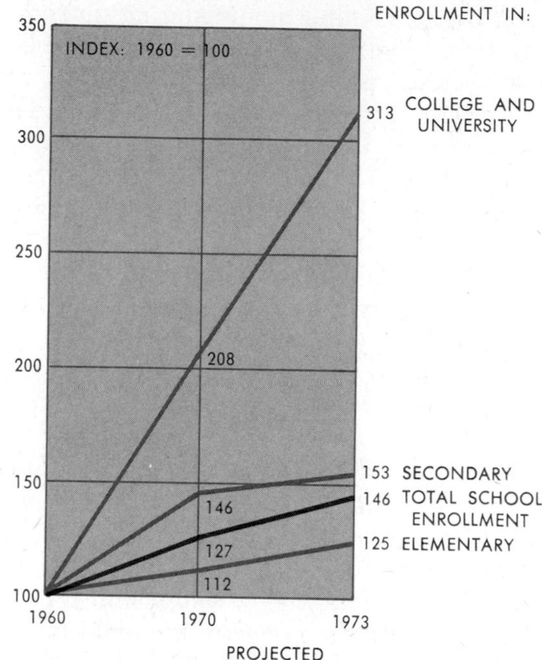

FIGURE 21–4 School Enrollment

The rapid increase in our population during the postwar years has had a tremendous impact on our educational system during the last decade, and the end is not yet in sight. SOURCES: U.S. Department of Health, Education, and Welfare and Office of Education.

More Years of Education

A second cause of increased expenditure is that the average number of years of schooling has increased even more dramatically than the increase in population. The number of students who graduated from high school in June 1955, was 1.2 million. In June of 1969 it rose to 2.8 million, an increase of almost 133 percent. In 1952 the median school years completed by the total labor force was 10.9. By 1970 it rose to 12.5. During this same time span the percentage of those in the labor force who completed four or more years of college education had increased from 7.9 percent to 12.6 percent.

Two important reasons for the increase in the number of years of schooling are the strenuous efforts to prevent school dropouts and the demand for more advanced education to meet the needs of a far more complex society. Another reason for this gain is the inclusion of vocational training in the curriculum.

The expansion in higher education has been even more dramatic. College enrollment increased from 2.2 million in 1950 to 7.4 million in 1970. Projected enrollment for 1980 is over 11 million, almost two thirds of all 18-to-21-year-olds, compared to about 40 percent in 1960 and 4 percent in 1900.

Additional demands have been made on education as retraining programs and other adult education programs have become more important. It is too early to determine what the trend will be in these areas, but it seems likely that adult education will demand more and more of our resources.

Changes in Quality

The third reason for the increase in cost of education is the improvement being made in the quality of education. Education has changed not merely in the size of enrollment and length of study but also in the character and quality of the education offered. The successful launching of the Soviet Union's first satellite, Sputnik I, caused American educators to reexamine their curriculums and to consider new teaching methods. Greater emphasis on mathematics and science—and more recently on foreign languages, economics, and sociology—has required new kinds of facilities, better teacher preparation, and new instructional materials. Laboratories for teaching of languages and swimming pools for physical education are becoming common. Equipment that was once seen only in colleges is being brought into high school science laboratories. Specialists and consultants who were at one time considered an extravagance are now included as part of the educational staff without question as to their contribution. Few people doubt that the quality of our education today is better than it has been in the past. Continuing improvement, however, becomes an added expense.

Redirecting Our Resources

The fourth reason for the increasing costs of education relates to the market mechanism, illustrated by our computer in Chapter 1. To meet the growing costs, we have had to redirect our resources. Our computer has had to send out signals to attract new resources and redirect old ones, particularly human resources, to meet our changing needs. Since 1950 we have had to replace more than 125,000 teachers annually in the public elementary and high schools, besides meeting an existing shortage of from 50,000 to 100,000 teachers. The need for college teachers—about 32,000 new ones each year—was even more acute.

The demand for these human resources was extremely difficult to meet. You will recall that the mobility of labor is greatest among unskilled workers, and that it is more difficult to increase the supply of workers who have greater skill and training. A minimum of four years beyond high school is required to train a teacher, and a fifth year is being demanded in many school systems, particularly at the secondary level. At the college teaching level, training is more likely to require seven to ten years beyond high school. With a somewhat inelastic supply curve and a greatly increased demand curve, how did we attract additional teachers? The teacher shortage was understandable when we consider the number of overcrowded classrooms with overworked instructors who were paid salaries about equal to the average earnings of employees in all manufacturing industries, and less than workers in mining and transportation.

While the market mechanism lagged in response to a greater demand for teachers than supply, it did take hold. Salaries for teachers increased 294 percent from 1950 to 1969 while all wages for private nonagricultural workers rose 216 percent for the same period.

The problem at the college level was even more acute with department chairmen chasing after qualified candidates and frequently settling for less than they should have. The supply curve is even more inelastic for college professors than for public school teachers because of the time and demands of getting the Ph.D. In addition, the opportunities for employment in government and industry made these highly trained people extremely mobile. As above, the market mechanism reacted and salaries of college professors increased dramatically.

Between 1969 and 1971, depending upon the region and the discipline, the teacher shortage disappeared. New York City and other high salary scale areas found they had large waiting lists of qualified teachers. Department chairmen in most colleges now found qualified candidates chasing after them. Had the market mechanism done its job?

It would be easy for the economists to respond with a simple *yes*. However, a closer look into this period reveals several factors that may be important. The 1960's were a time of rising militancy for teachers, including a unionlike posture taken by the National Education Association in bargaining, a rise in membership in the American Federation of Teachers, and strike action in several cities. You will recall the effect of union action on increasing wages in Chapter 6. Does that explain the behavior of the market here?

A very different influence having little to do with economics that may be responsible for increasing the number of teachers at all levels was the influence of the draft. Many young men went into teaching or continued with their studies at the graduate level to avoid going into service. Enrollment in graduate school increased over 31 percent from fall 1965 to fall 1968. During the same period enrollment in education as a graduate field of study increased 43 percent. How does this distort the market?

There is also the sharp growth of funds, primarily federal, that has made graduate education possible for many more people. Programs were established to convert liberal arts majors to teachers frequently giving them subsidies to do so. Others wanted to get their Ph.D to go into the lucrative space program. When cutbacks were made in NASA in 1970 the college teaching market became flooded in physics, engineering, and mathematics. Here we have to take into account what subsidies can do to the supply side of the market as well as a change in citizen priorities. How does this latter compare to a switch in consumer preference?

The need for additional classrooms and equipment has been almost as great as the need for human resources. Greater flexibility commonly exists for meeting these needs because the supply curve for construction and equipment is far more elastic than for human skills. It is easy to switch from the construction of office buildings to the construction of schools so long as the public is willing to pay.

In the years from 1957–1958 to 1969–1970 the national expenditures for public education have increased by 214 percent per pupil. Even more significant is the increase in the portion of our national income spent for education. From 1950 to 1969 expenditures for public schools rose from less than 3 percent of national income to 4.3 percent. The increase for all education, particularly higher education, was even greater. As a result we are now allocating more of our total resources for education than ever before.

Why the Need for More Education?

The need for more years of education is a matter for both individual and national concern. From the individual's standpoint more education means, with few exceptions, higher income. From the national standpoint more education means meeting our shortage of human resources and increasing our economic growth.

Differences in Income and the Demand for Labor

Statistics show that the average college graduate earns annually almost three times as much as the person who did not finish elementary school, and about 80 percent more than the one who finished high school. Unemployment rates for high school dropouts are far greater than for graduates.

The Department of Labor has warned young people that they will face increasing competition in the job market, and that education is one of the best ways to prepare for this. The projection for job opportunities to mid-1970 indicates the greatest need to be for new semiprofessional and technical workers, a somewhat lesser need for white-collar workers, an almost equal need for skilled blue-collar workers, very little need for new unskilled and semiskilled workers, and a declining need for farmers and farm laborers. Clearly, education, income, and the demand for labor are all related.

Education and Economic Growth

Many economists believe that the most important single factor for economic growth in a mature industrial economy such as our own is education. The American worker is the most highly trained and best educated in the world, and he is also the most productive. Our business management is also foremost. The new knowledge and techniques of business should be developed and employed increasingly to benefit our entire nation. New production techniques can produce an abundance beyond man's highest hopes. It may well be possible to eliminate poverty and satisfy the basic needs of all our people in the not-so-distant future.

We have seen that all resources exist in limited supply. However, the resource that is scarcest of all is brainpower. To lose the fruits of even one creative mind can cost the nation dearly not only in terms of money but also in terms of lives, suffering, and failure to provide the inspiration of happiness and beauty. To allow the talents of a potential Albert Einstein, a Marian Anderson, a William Faulkner, a Henry Ford, a Pablo Casals, or a Jonas Salk to go undeveloped is to deprive all of us of a better life. Can there be a better investment than in "human capital"?

Footing the Bill

With the cost of education rising at a faster rate than our GNP, the problem of obtaining the necessary revenue is a major one. It involves directing more of our resources into education, perhaps at the expense of some other part of our economy, and making better use of the resources we already have.

Changes in Traditional Financing Methods

American education has traditionally been financed by local government, largely through the real property tax. Of the $2.1 billion received for public elementary and secondary schools in 1930, $1.7 billion was provided by local governments, $353 million by state governments, and slightly more than $7 million by the federal government. By 1970–1971 the pattern had changed greatly. Of the $42.5 billion received in revenue for public elementary as well as secondary schools, $23.5 billion came from local governments, $15.7 billion came from state governments, and $3.2 billion came from the federal government. Although local governments continued to supply most of the revenue, the role of the state and federal governments has increased tremendously. State budgets and the federal budget for 1970–1971 show that this trend is continuing at an accelerated rate, with current sources being 55 percent local, 37 percent state, and 8 percent federal.

Causes of the Change

Local school districts do not have the broad taxing power that the state and national governments have. Until recently almost all school revenue came from taxes on real estate. These taxes appear to be proportional, but they are, in reality, regressive. Many public administrators and public finance specialists are of the opinion that real estate taxes cannot be pushed much higher. In response to these opinions and to the pressure of real estate lobbies, state governments have been turning to the sales tax for additional revenue to use for educational purposes.

Even more significant has been the growing tendency of the states to increase their revenue by higher taxes—primarily income and sales taxes—and to return funds to the local school districts on a per student basis. The federal government, whose tax structure is the most progressive, appears to be following the lead of the states. Since our tax resources are greatest at the federal level, federal aid to education is expected to increase most rapidly.

Federal Aid to Education

Tradition has placed control of our school system at the local level. Few people would deny the need for financial aid from the federal government, but they fear that with aid will come control. The preference for local control is based on the argument that those who are closest to a situation are in the best position to make decisions. It permits diversity, experimentation, and adjustment to particular needs. However, all school districts and all states obviously do not have equal ability to pay for good education. When President Johnson introduced his education bill, he pointed out that federal assistance was needed to bring the full benefit of education to regions where the return from state and local taxes cannot support an adequate system of education.

New York state spends almost three times as much per pupil as does Mississippi and with less effort because incomes are so much higher in New York. The Elementary and Secondary Education Act of 1965 tries to help correct this imbalance. Over half the money appropriated under this law goes to public school districts serving the economically needy.

By providing aid to economically depressed areas, grants for supplementary educational materials and centers of instruction, and scholarships to needy students, the federal education law bypasses the controversy over aid to local schools.

Conflict over Aid to Parochial Schools

On both the state and national levels there has been a continuing controversy over direct aid to parochial schools. The opponents of such aid declare that it would violate our constitutional provision for the separation of church and state. It might also encourage the development of additional private schools and result in a dual system of education. The proponents argue that parochial school students are entitled to the rights and privileges of citizens at government expense. They point out that in 1970, 12 percent of our student population below college, nearly 5.5 million students, attended parochial schools. If these parochial school pupils were to be enrolled in the public schools, the tax bill for education would be considerably higher. At present, certain educational materials are provided; in addition, some states are supplying transportation and lunches.

Changes in Higher Education

The changing patterns of education are even more pronounced in higher education than at elementary and secondary levels. One significant trend is the increase of enrollment in public institutions. In 1950 more than one half of all college students attended private institutions. Today this enrollment is about 25 percent, and the projection for 1980 is even lower. This decline is matched by a corresponding increase in the number of students attending state and locally supported colleges and universities.

Increasing costs are another important trend in higher education. In 1942 the estimated yearly costs for a student in a private college were about $1,150, and at a public college about $850. Today most private institutions cost over $3,200 and the public institutions over $2,000. The projections for 1975 raise the figure to above $4,000 for private and above $3,000 for public colleges. In addition, tuition pays for only a portion of the cost of higher education. With few exceptions college students are being subsidized by money received from all levels of government and from endowment funds provided by individuals and corporations.

There is ample evidence to show that the investment made in higher education pays excellent dividends. California led the way by committing itself to providing extensive opportunities for higher education for all its young people. Some people attribute much of its economic growth to this support. Today other states are following California's example. However, as in the support of elementary and secondary levels of education, the poorer states are at a disadvantage.

Federal Aid to Higher Education

In 1960 federal aid to higher education was relatively insignificant. In contrast, aid in 1970 was $5.4 billion. Unfortunately for the poorer states, this money is not used to equalize educational facilities. Indeed, a complaint against the existing program is that the allocation of funds is widening the gap of inequality. Critics protest that most of the money to support research is going to those schools that already have the best facilities. One answer to this objection is that the results of research and the continued betterment of already superior institutions benefit higher education throughout the nation.

Help for the Individual Student

Aid for students attending private colleges and universities comes essentially from endowments and gifts. Some public help is available for students in both public and private colleges, but mainly in the former. There is a great variation among colleges in the percentage of the total cost that is paid by tuition. In many schools it is less than 20 percent, but the expense may still be prohibitive for many students.

There are three items of cost that the student must consider as part of the expense of attending college: (1) the tuition, (2) his living expenses, and (3) the money he could have earned if he were working rather than attending school (opportunity costs). This can mean a total potential expenditure of from $7,000 to $10,000 per year. If this expenditure is looked upon as an investment in human capital, the returns in the form of increased income for the individual and increased production for the society are well worth it. However, for the individual student and his family, the immediate actual expense, even though less than the potential, may present an insurmountable obstacle.

There are many sources that the individual student can turn to for financial assistance; in addition there are ways in which the student can reduce the cost. For the student of high ability there are scholarships offered by the school and by private donors. Some of these scholarships include living expenses as well as tuition, although rarely do they cover the entire cost. The number of scholarships available has been increasing at an accelerated rate. At the very best private institutions more than half the students are receiving some aid, and few students who do well academically are forced to leave for financial reasons.

Many state governments, as well as the federal government, have set up scholarship funds, and the number of these and the amount of money appropriated for them have increased each year. In addition, state and federal governments have set aside funds and given their own credit support to programs of student loans. These loans are long term with low interest rates, and actually act as a subsidy for the student.

Several bills have been introduced into Congress to allow tax credits to people who are paying for higher education. This would allow the taxpayer to deduct a considerable amount of the cost of higher education from his personal income tax.

Most students earn some money during summer vacations; some work for several hours a week during the school term. Many colleges provide assistance to students in finding jobs. A number of students meet their expenses by working in the college library or laboratories. A few schools have developed programs that divide the academic year so that students work at jobs related to their area of study as a regular part of their training. The use of such programs is likely to be expanded.

More Efficient Use of Our Resources

Complaints are frequently heard about the inefficient use of existing educational resources. Agriculture and industry have increased their output per worker, but what has been done in education?

Greater Use of Plant Facilities

Some schools operate their expensive plants on an all-year-round basis, claiming a saving of between 20 and 33 percent by this full utilization. The use of a trimester or quarter system and the addition of summer sessions are the most frequent methods. In addition to dollar savings, this system provides added opportunities and room for more students.

The year-round use of school facilities has disadvantages as well as benefits. An extension of the school year provides almost no saving on teacher salaries because the additional workload requires additional pay. Critics claim that such a program may reduce the quality of education because teachers frequently use their vacation time for advanced study, travel, and preparation for improving their classes. The number of teachers taking graduate training in the summer has led to improvement in their skills and knowledge that could not have taken place with an all-year-round program. The installation of air-conditioning equipment and the additional wear on the school plant may lower the expected savings. The increasing use of schools for adult education and as community centers has already increased the number of hours that buildings are in use. Critics add that many students cannot attend school on a year-round basis because they depend on summer earnings to continue their education.

Faced with increasing enrollment and mounting costs, schools must continue to search for ways to obtain the maximum use of their facilities. Experiments in utilizing school plants will undoubtedly continue. No conclusions on the quality of education or on the savings obtained from year-round use of facilities are yet available.

Savings from Improved Technology and Better Use of Staff

In the last 10 years, education has seen a host of innovations designed to improve the quality of learning and to increase teacher effectiveness. Teaching machines, team teaching, educational television, and audio-visual aids are used increasingly to enable teachers to work with more students and at the same time to carry on better individual instruction. In college introductory and survey courses, it is common practice for a major professor to lecture to a class of several hundred students. Once a week these large classes break up into smaller sections supervised by instructors and graduate students for discussions and quizzes. The same practice is now carried out on a larger scale by closed-circuit television.

Teachers' aides are being employed in increasing numbers to do many routine classroom tasks, freeing the teacher to concentrate on the highly skilled job of teaching. Although there is little doubt that these new techniques help reduce some of the costs, controversy exists concerning their effect on the quality of education. The problems associated with increased enrollment must not be allowed to result in a loss of personal attention and guidance to the student. Meeting quantitative needs without sacrificing quality, at a time when taxpayers are protesting, remains a major problem in our nation's educational system.

Part F
Some Projections for the 1970's

In our study of economics we have learned how to use many tools. With them we have analyzed our past economic developments and have applied them to our present problems. Before closing our exposition we would like to take a look into the future. Considering the number of variables that can throw any projection off target, it must be considered dangerous business and it would be ill-advised to consider this projection better than an educated guess. Nevertheless, if man seeks to control his environment, he must plan ahead to satisfy his needs best. To do so requires an understanding of what we know and, even more important, what we do not know. Most important of all is to recognize when projections are wrong and provide for the new direction.

Population

Nearly 30 million people may be added to the total U.S. population by 1980, giving us a figure of about 235 million by the end of the 1970's. Furthermore, there will be shifts in our population that should bring profound changes in the American pattern of living. Young adults (people in their 20's and 30's) will dominate, for they will increase by about 34 percent while all other age groups will increase by only 6 percent. This group is likely to spend heavily for housing, autos, clothing, and recreation. They will have a better education than their elders and will probably demand a greater say in political, economic, and social affairs. Total births will rise, despite the trend toward smaller families. This is because the number of women in peak child-bearing years (20 to 29) will rise by nearly 40 percent. Marriages will hit record levels. Indeed, President Nixon sees a need for 100 completely new cities of over 100,000 people, and 10 new cities of over 1 million within the next 20 years. Another "baby boom" will occur later in the 1970's, but the teenage population will level off and children of primary school age may decline in numbers. The teacher shortage now appears to have ended. College enrollments should rise from the current 7.9 million to 12 million. The number of people over 60 will increase by about 18 percent, as compared with a rise of less than 1 percent for the middle-aged (40 to 59 years of age). This will create a demand for more medical care, nursing homes, social security benefits, and retirement homes. The movement to the suburbs will continue, and many small towns will become cities. There will be a need for more shopping centers, housing, commercial structures, and plants in the suburbs, and serious problems will arise as more public utilities and public transportation are required. Large cities will grow slowly or may actually lose people, while small and medium-sized cities will probably add population rapidly. The fastest growth will occur in the West and the South. Altogether, over 22 million housing units will have to be built at a cost (not including land) of over $63 billion.

Jobs and the Labor Force

The labor force by 1980 will total about 100 million workers. Nearly 22,000 different types of occupations will exist—an increase of some 6,000 over the 1965 figure. White-collar jobs will account for over half of all employment by 1980, as compared with 47 percent in 1968. Employment in services will rise by over 50 percent. Blue-collar employment (which includes craftsmen, operatives, and laborers) will increase by only 13 percent. Proprietors, officials, and managers as a group will increase by about 20 percent. Professional and technical jobs will experience the fastest growth of all, but only 20 percent of all occupations will require a college degree. There will be a decline in employment in mining (over 10 percent) and agriculture (over 20 percent). Demand will be heavy for systems analysts, computer programmers and operators, engineers, recreation workers, office machine operators, business machine servicemen, and paramedical specialists. Women will play an increasingly important role in the labor force. The number of women workers in 1980 will be double that of 1950. Of the 41 million increase in the labor supply in the 1970's, nearly 6 million will be women. About 43 percent of America's women will be in the labor force in 1980, and they will account for about 37 percent of the total labor force. The black labor force will reach 12 million; they will increase their numbers at a rate 50 percent faster than whites. (This is because of a more rapid increase in Negroes of working age.) The economic situation of the Negro worker is expected to improve. The labor force of 1980 will have higher educational qualifications—70 percent of all adult workers will have completed four or more years of high school as compared with 60 percent in 1968. One of every six workers (age 25 and over) will have completed four years of college, as compared with only one in seven in 1968.

The Cities

During the 1960's the 100 largest metropolitan areas in the U.S. grew by over 13 percent, while growth for the country as a whole was about 11.4 percent. By 1970, some 57 percent of the population resided in the big urban areas. Each month brings a population increase equivalent to a city of the size of Toledo, Ohio, and each year we add the equivalent of a city as large as Philadelphia. During the next two decades the New York metropolitan region will add about 6 million people, and the Los Angeles and San Francisco areas will double in size. The growth of Washington, D.C., will be over 800,000—or like adding Baltimore to the current Washington area—and Baltimore will add over 700,000 to its region in the next 20 years. Between now and the year 2000 we shall have to build as much as the nation has previously built since the arrival of the first white man on this continent. Most of this will be in urban areas. Entirely new cities will spring up, perhaps like Columbia, Maryland, which was started in 1966. (Planning began in 1963; construction in 1966. Columbia had a population of 10,000 in 1971, and is expected to grow to 100,000 when fully developed by 1980.)

Cities will continue to face serious problems. Many businesses have been moving out of cities because of high living costs, taxes, high rents, high wage rates, poor transportation, congestion, the deterioration of schools and other public services, lack of adequate space, obsolete facilities, crime, social unrest, and pollution. Between 1965 and 1970 state and local taxes rose by 70 percent, but the number of city government workers increased 32 percent in the 1960's and the total payroll rose 118 percent. The cities must employ more policemen, teachers, firemen, sanitation workers, public health workers, and clerical personnel to meet growing public needs. Most city employees are service workers whose productivity does not increase much, but who must be paid more as living costs rise, as unions of public employees make greater demands, and as wages in the private sector rise. Meanwhile, city treasuries are pinched by eroding tax bases as middle-income people and businesses move out and as taxpayer opposition mounts.

Industry

The office, computing, and accounting machines industry will probably grow at an extremely high rate in the 1970's, continuing to be the most rapidly growing industry. Other fast-growing industries will be communications, plastics, synthetic materials, electronic components and supplies, photocopying equipment, and optical supplies. High growth rates will be recorded in gas, water, electric, and sanitary services; rubber and plastic products; business services; air conditioning; service industry machines; and radio, TV, and communications equipment. New construction should increase, bringing a rise in the growth of the industries that supply construction materials (such as building materials and construction machinery). The electrical machinery and supplies industry will expand. Increases in trucking, air cargo, and air travel will bring faster growth in transportation as a whole, but the National Railroad Passenger Corporation (AMTRAK), a quasi-government agency established by Congress in late 1970, will have to come to the rescue of intercity passenger railways. The number of passenger trains will dwindle from 376 to 150.

Technology and Productivity

The use of computers will double by 1980. Big business, government, and banking will increase their use of computers, and even small businesses will now be able to lease computer time from service centers. The use of delicate sensory instruments for such things as measuring data and controlling temperature will expand greatly. The amount of labor needed per unit of output will decline in many factory operations because of increased use of automatic loading and unloading devices, automatic lubricators, and the like. This will increase productivity in many industries. Improved communications can be realized through faster copying machines, videotape recorders, communications satellites, data transmission by telephone, and new devices for speeding the mail. Metal-cutting and metal-forming tools will improve, causing substantial savings in labor per unit of output. There will be new developments in power generation and the transporting of energy. Better air-traffic control systems will be designed, more powerful diesel-electric locomotives will haul specialized cars with increased capacity, and the capacity of trucks will increase because of more powerful engines and the use of lightweight metals to construct them. The biggest productivity increase (about 5.9 percent a year) will occur in agriculture, a factor that will lead to a continuing decline in agricultural employment. Productivity in manufacturing, transportation, trade, finance, insurance, and real estate is expected to increase at a rate of 2.8 percent a year. In mining, communications, and public utilities, output per man-hour will increase faster than in other nonagricultural industries. In construction and services, on the other hand, the projected increases will be lower than the average. (Generally, these are *labor-intensive* industries; hence, technological change has a smaller impact on productivity.)

The Gross National Product

The GNP should reach $1.4 trillion (in 1968 dollars) by 1980. *Personal consumption expenditures* will continue to account for a largest part of the GNP, reaching about $900 billion in 1980. The major subcategories of consumer spending are durable goods, nondurable goods, and services. The proportion accounted for by durables and services will be higher. The increasing number of new families will result in greater purchases of such durables as furniture and household equipment. Higher spending for services will be accounted for by medical care, recreation, and private education. Assuming a drop in defense spending, government's share of the GNP will decline slightly. Nevertheless, the total nondefense purchases of the federal, state, and local governments combined will increase by over three fourths. Housing, social welfare, community development, and educational improvements should account for growing federal expenditures. State and local governments will spend heavily on education, environmental control, highways, urban renewal, and health. *Business investment* will probably show a slight increase in the proportionate share of GNP, accounting for about 15.5 percent of the 1980 economy. Expenditures on plant and equipment should account for about two thirds of all gross private domestic investment. New housing expenditures will probably double in value by 1980, and inventories will be more than twice the value of the 1968 level. Finally, *net foreign purchases* of goods and services should see a fivefold increase by 1980.

Conclusion

If these projections are close to the mark, there is cause for optimism. Nevertheless, there will be problems. As the 1970's began, a gap of at least 5 percent separated the actual output of the U.S. economy and its potential output. Unemployment reached its highest rate in nine years, but inflation continued to erode the value of the dollar. Some sectors of the economy may grow much more rapidly than others, and some segments of the population may not share in the nation's growing affluence. Rising crime rates, pollution, urban congestion and blight, inadequate housing, discrimination against minority groups, and a host of other problems will challenge the economist, other social scientists, the politician, and the average citizen for years to come.

REVIEW: THE HIGHLIGHTS OF THE CHAPTER

1. Three segments of our economy do not seem to be sharing equally in the prosperity of our times—farmers, small businessmen, and the aged.
2. The "farm problem" is generally associated with the low income received by farmers in contrast to others. This leads us to the question of what our farm policy should be.
3. The technological revolution on the farm has changed farming from a way of life to a business. Small farms are disappearing. Output per worker has increased so that 4 percent of our working force provides more food than we now need. Fewer than 10 percent of our nation's farms supply one half the sales of farm products.
4. The inelastic demand for farm products is largely responsible for the fact that farmers' incomes are not so stable as other workers' incomes and prices of agricultural products are less stable than those of other commodities. A small change in supply brings about a major change in price. Getting farmers to cut down on their individual production runs into the problem of the fallacy of composition.
5. Other causes of the farmers' economic problems stem from the increasing costs of the "middleman," the excessive number of farmers, the competitiveness of the market, and the weather.
6. The farmer has been offered many kinds of aid, but the major solutions have

been aimed at raising farm prices as a means of raising his income. Most solutions have been based on the concept of parity, equating the purchasing power of the farmer with that of others. Reducing supply in order to raise prices has been tried by controlling acreage and by soil conservation. Other solutions suggested are increasing the demand, the price differential plan, dumping on foreign markets, retraining farmers, and a return to the free market.

7. Evidence shows that the number of business failures has been increasing and that small business prospers less than big business. The major reasons for business failures are managerial incompetence and insufficient capital.
8. Small business has an important role to play in the economy. There are more businesses that start each year than fail. Small business is a proving ground for ideas and resources. It increases competition; it is more flexible and mobile, allowing it to adjust to changes and special demands; and it is associated with our democratic ideals.
9. To help small business solve its problems, Congress set up the Small Business Administration. This agency provides information on running a business, helps in financing, makes loans for disaster relief, and aids in obtaining government contracts.
10. Other aids to small business come in the form of lower tax rates; local, state, and regional development corporations; trade associations; and buying cooperatives.
11. The number and percentage of our total population over 65 has been increasing very rapidly, so that today one person out of every eleven is in this age category. Statistics show this group to be far below the national average in income and liquid assets.
12. Our nation's change from an agricultural society to an urban industrial society has created social, emotional, and financial problems for the elderly.
13. Our Social Security program has transferred financial responsibility for the elderly from the individual to the society as a whole. Protection is now provided through pensions, survivors' benefits, hospital and nursing care, and unemployment grants. Payments for most of these are made by employer and employee.
14. Some aids to the aged include private pension plans, aid in employment and housing, and development of leisure-time centers. Suggestions for improving our Social Security laws and property taxes offer additional hope for many.
15. The increasing urbanization of the U.S. is aggravating such problems as traffic congestion, air and water pollution, and overcrowded housing.
16. Haphazard growth of urban areas, inadequate transportation systems, loss of certain industries, the changing composition of the population, the fragmentation of governmental authority, and lack of regional planning are creating economic problems for many metropolitan areas.
17. In each of the segments of the society that have been considered here, you have been concerned with problems of values as well as problems of economics. As citizens who have the benefit of some understanding of economic analysis, you have a special obligation to arrive at answers and to work to see them adopted.
18. The increased costs of education are due to a population increase, a demand for more years of education, and changes in the quality of education. To meet them, we must prepare to redirect some of our resources.

19. Meeting the demand for teachers was difficult because of the somewhat inelastic supply and the greatly increased need. Material requirements can be fulfilled more easily because the supply curve for them is more elastic.
20. People with more education have better opportunities for getting jobs and keeping them, and they tend to earn higher incomes.
21. Education is one of the most important factors in economic growth, particularly in a mature economy.
22. In the past, education has been financed primarily by local governments through real estate taxes. State and federal financing are playing an ever-increasing role because these governments have broader taxing powers.
23. Federal aid to education helps equalize educational opportunities. Controversy over federal aid arises because control of education is traditionally local and because aid to parochial schools raises the question of separation of church and state.
24. The cost of higher education to the individual and to the nation has increased faster than that of elementary and secondary education. There are many ways in which college students can obtain aid in meeting higher costs.
25. Attempts to increase efficiency in education have resulted in greater use of the school plant and the use of new teaching equipment and new methods of instruction.
26. Projections into the 1970's indicate that there is some reason for optimism, but little hope that the problems which social scientists are studying now will go away.

IN CONCLUSION: SOME AIDS TO UNDERSTANDING

Terms for Review

inelastic demand
middleman costs
flexible price support
fixed costs
chamber of commerce
pensions
subsidy
parity
acreage control
soil bank program
unemployment insurance
mandatory retirement
urban place
metropolitan area
standard metropolitan statistical area
standard consolidated area
megalopolis
spatial force
situational force
regional share concept
model cities program
regional planning
"human capital"
trimester system

Names to Know

Federal Farm Board
Rural Electrification Administration
Commodity Credit Corporation
Small Business Administration
Morrill Act
Baker v. *Carr*
Social Security Act
Medicare
Elementary and Secondary Education Act

Questions for Review

1. Explain the meaning of the following statements:
   (a) "Modern technology and chemistry have changed agriculture from a way of life to a business."
   (b) "In the last hundred years the number of farmers has declined from 50 percent of our labor force to 4 percent, but the total output of our farms has continued to accelerate."
   (c) "For the American farmer the last hundred years have brought many periods of unstable prices and incomes."
2. One justification for giving special aid to the farmer is that many of his problems are unique.
   (a) What are some of the causes of the problems of the farmer that are different from the causes of the problems of other producers?
   (b) Describe some of the solutions which have been tried to solve the farmer's problems.
3. Explain what is meant by the idea "The paradox for the farmer is that plenty may cause poverty."
4. Programs to help the farmer have focused on raising either income or the prices of farm products. Describe the methods used by the government and the farmer to reduce production and to raise the price level.
5. One of the continuing debates of our economy concerns the relative merits of small business and big business.
   (a) What is the definition of "small business"?
   (b) If you were starting your own small business, what problems would you face?
   (c) What has the government done to help small business?
   (d) Why could it be said, "Managerial skill, research, and a strong bank balance might have prevented many failures"?
6. We may question whether small business is the backbone of our economy, but we cannot question the need for its services.
   (a) Draw up a balance sheet of the advantages and the disadvantages of both a small business and a large business.
   (b) Explain why a very small percentage of our business organizations employ the largest percentage of workers.
7. In the past 30 years we have begun to develop a system based on collective responsibility for care of the aged.
   (a) What public plans are now in effect to care for the elderly?
   (b) Evaluate the merits of these plans, using criteria for social, economic, and ethical value judgments.
   (c) Why will this problem become inceasingly important in the future?
8. Explain the ways in which urban areas are categorized and defined. What economic factors are relevant to these definitions?
   What are some of the economic problems faced by metropolitan areas? How might these problems be solved?
9. Identify the many factors which have led to the great increase in educational costs in the last 25 years and explain the significance of each.

10. Explain in detail how the market and other circumstances increased our supply of teachers. Development of human resources is of benefit to both the individual and the nation.
    (a) What are the practical advantages to the individual which come from increased education?
    (b) Why could it be said that the nation is richer when its population is well educated?
    (c) How is education financed in the United States? What changes, if any, should be made in this system (or systems)?

Additional Questions and Problems

1. What are the arguments for and against government aid to marginal farmers? What sort of aid might bring about more efficient allocation of our productive resources? What measures might result in less efficiency?
2. Tell what is meant by each of these quotations:
   (a) "In the United States big business is the backbone of the total production, whereas small business supplies the specialization, the innovation, and the experimentation."
   (b) "Small businesses cast many ballots."
   (c) "Small business is the training ground for big business."
3. Two widely differing attitudes toward the problem of the aged are represented here. Discuss the merits of each point of view.
   (a) "We must establish new goals and new values in attempting to solve the problems of the aged."
   (b) "The individual is coddled by not being forced to provide for his later years. The hard worker and the thrifty individual are thus forced to take on the burden."
4. What are the economic characteristics of your region? Is it prone to any of the economic problems in this chapter?
5. How can local, state, and federal governments cooperate to solve urban economic problems?
6. Officials of some private schools, parochial schools, and private colleges are asking for public funds. Set forth the arguments both for and against their requests.

SELECTED READINGS

An Adaptive Program for Agriculture. New York: Committee for Economic Development, 1962.

Carlson, Valdeman. *Economic Security in the United States.* New York: McGraw-Hill Book Co., 1962.

Chinitz, Benjamin, ed. *City and Suburb: The Economics of Metropolitan Growth.* Englewood Cliffs, N.J.: Prentice-Hall, 1964.

Danière, André. *Higher Education in the American Economy.* New York: Random House, 1964.

Gordon, Mitchell. *Sick Cities: Psychology and Pathology of American Urban Life.* New York: The Macmillan Company, 1963. (Also available in paperback edition: Penguin Books, Baltimore, 1964.)

Hamilton, David. *A Primer on the Economics of Poverty.* New York: Random House, 1968.

Harris, Seymour E. *More Resources for Education.* New York: Harper and Row, 1960.

Higbee, Edward. *Farms and Farmers in an Urban Age.* New York: The Twentieth Century Fund, 1963.

Houthoukker, Hendrik S. *Economic Policy for the Farm Sector.* Washington, D.C.: American Enterprise Institute, 1967.

Keyserling, Leon H. *Agriculture and the Public Interest.* Washington, D.C.: Conference on Economic Progress, 1965.

The Mandate. Washington, D.C.: National Federation of Independent Business. Published periodically.

Miller, Herman P. *Rich Man, Poor Man.* New York: Thomas Y. Crowell Co., 1970.

Schultz, Theodore W. *The Economic Value of Education.* New York: Columbia University Press, 1963.

———. *Transforming Traditional Agriculture.* New Haven: Yale University Press, 1964.

Silk, Leonard S. *The Research Revolution: Brains and Economic Growth.* New York: McGraw-Hill Book Co., c 1960.

Stigler, George J. "The Case Against Big Business." *Fortune,* May 1952 (p. 123).

Weaver, Robert C. *Dilemmas of Urban America.* New York: Atheneum, 1967.

Will, Robert E. and Harold G. Vatter, eds. *Poverty in Affluence.* New York: Harcourt, Brace & World, 1965.

GLOSSARY OF ECONOMIC TERMS

Most of the terms appearing in this glossary are to be found in the text. For a more extensive treatment of any term concisely defined here, turn to the index to find the location of the term in the text.

ability-to-pay principle: justification for taxing people with larger incomes a greater percentage of their income, based on the principle of diminishing marginal utility.

absolute advantage: an advantage that one nation may have over another in trade by being able to produce a good more efficiently (at less cost).

acceleration principle: the principle that a change in sales at the consumer level will bring about a greater change in sales of producer goods.

acceptability: a characteristic of money that results in individuals and businesses accepting it as a medium of exchange in a wide market.

acreage quota: the amount of land a farmer may plant and still receive benefits from government price-support programs.

administered price: a price set under conditions of imperfect competition where the individual firm has some degree of control.

administrative budget: the expected receipts and expenditures of a government, as asked for by the administrative branch. It does not include money in public trust funds. (*Cf.* cash budget.)

ad valorem taxes: tax applied to the value of that which is being taxed, particularly imports.

agency shop: a situation in which all employees in a particular bargaining unit are required to pay union dues even though they may not wish to join the union.

aggregate demand: total spending in the economy; the sum of personal consumption expenditures, business investment, and government spending.

alternative costs: *See* opportunity costs.

antitrust: of an act or a policy designed to curb monopolistic tendencies or power.

arbitration: a method of settling a labor dispute in which both parties agree to accept the decision of a third party.

assessment: for taxation purposes the official valuation of property or income.

asset: anything of value that is owned.

automatic stabilizer: a tool used to compensate for changes in the business cycle without requiring action by a public official.

automation: use of machines to replace human labor in a continuous operation of production; usually involves a feedback system.

avoidance: a legal way to reduce tax payments.

balance of payments: a statement listing all financial transactions that a nation and its people have with all other nations.

balance sheet: an itemized statement of a business showing its assets, liabilities, and net worth on a given date.

bank reserves: the amount of money a bank holds in order to meet the requirements of the Federal Reserve Bank or of a law, or the demands of its depositors. In addition to these reserves, Federal Reserve Banks hold secondary reserves in the form of securities that can be easily converted into money.

base period: a time in the past used to measure changes. It is used to measure price index.

benefit principle of taxation: justification for taxing according to the benefits received from government by the taxpayer.

bill of exchange: a written claim for foreign currency. The same as a foreign exchange check.

black capitalism: a move to increase ownership of business among blacks as a means of increasing their participation in the economy.

blacklist: a list of workers, usually union organizers, circulated by employers and designed to prevent those on the list from getting jobs.

black separatism: the movement to have the black community resolve their problems internally through developing their pride and skills for self-determination and self-help. Its advocates oppose integration as being costly and not working.

bond: a security representing indebtedness, frequently issued in $1,000 denominations, and bearing a fixed rate of interest. Both governments and business firms issue bonds.

boycott: generally, a collective decision by one group to force action by another group. Usually used in connection with a union urging its members and others not to buy from an employer in order to force the latter to yield to its demands.

break-even point: the point at which total revenue and total expenditures equal each other.

budget: a plan of expected revenues and expenditures for a specific period of time.

business cycle: the expansion and contraction of the level of business activity at more or less regular intervals.

capital: a man-made instrument of production; a factor of production used in furthering the production process.

capital consumption: capital that is consumed in the process of production. The depreciation of capital that is subtracted from GNP to give NNP.

capital good: a good used in the production of other goods rather than to satisfy a human want directly. Same as producer good.

capitalism: an economic system in which the means of production are owned and controlled by private individuals with a minimum of government interference. Allocation of resources is determined by the market mechanism.

cash budget: total cash receipts and expenditures of a government, including those of public trust funds, such as social security. (*Cf.* administrative budget.)

check-off: an agreement between an employer and a union by which the former deducts union dues from the employees' paychecks and turns them over to the union.

closed shop: a firm in which only workers who are already union members will be hired.

collateral: something of value pledged by a borrower to secure a loan.

collective bargaining: a method of reaching an agreement in which representatives of employers and employees discuss proposed changes in the terms of the labor contract.

combination: a situation in which individuals or firms get together to influence market conditions. The most common types of industrial combinations in the United States have been pools, trusts, holding companies, mergers, and consolidations.

commercial bank: a financial institution whose primary function is to receive demand deposits and extend short-term loans to business firms.

common stock: the capital of a corporation, divided into shares which usually entitle the owners to voting rights and, if voted by the board of directors, dividends. (*Cf.* preferred stock.)

communism: an economic system in which, in theory all goods are owned collectively and in which payment of income is according to need. The term is used to describe the economy of the Soviet Union and of those nations that have similar ideologies. In practice the individual is given little freedom in determining the *What, How,* and *For Whom.*

company union: an organization of employees largely under the control of management and unaffiliated with any national or international union.

comparative advantage: the principle which explains that all nations will benefit if each concentrates its efforts on producing and exporting goods in which it has the greatest relative efficiency and on importing goods in which it has the least relative efficiency.

compensatory countercyclical policy: a program or plan designed to reverse the direction of the business cycle when it is believed that it is becoming inflationary or deflationary.

competition: a situation in which two or more parties seek to gain an advantage over the other(s). In classical capitalism it protects the consumer by assuring efficiency of production.

compulsory arbitration: enforced settlement of a dispute, as between management and a union, by law or by some government agency. It is practiced in New Zealand and Australia, but is generally frowned upon in this country.

conciliation: encouraging the settlement of a labor-management dispute by the use of a third party, who encourages discussion that will lead to a peaceful settlement.

conglomeration: a merger involving unrelated industries.

conspicuous consumption: the purchase and use of goods and services primarily for the purpose of enhancing one's social prestige rather than for satisfaction of material needs.

consumer cooperative: an association of consumers organized to purchase goods and services for its members. Profits are distributed to members on the basis of their purchases.

consumer good: an economic good used directly

rade: trade among nations in which all pol- estrictions that may impede its flow are nated.

om of contract: the principle that, in the ction of goods and services, individuals the right to enter into agreements resulting oduction. Such agreements must be within ramework of the law and may not be con- cies against society.

benefits: items that increase real income re not included in the basic wage, such as benefits. Fringe benefits are often included or contracts.

mployment: a condition of the economy in there is sufficient aggregate demand to oy all those who wish to work and are fied to do so. In the United States it is ently considered the condition of the econ- when the unemployment rate is less than cent.

ional distribution: payment—wages, rent, est, and profit—to the factors of production ding to their contribution.

al property tax: a tax on the assessed value operty; it is computed as a percentage of . Specific types of property may be exempt.

al sales tax: a tax on most goods collected time of their sale. Food and medicine are ently exempt.

ax: a tax on the value of property trans- primarily to avoid payment of inheritance state taxes.

ertificate: in the United States, formerly, a icate issued by the government that was mable in gold. Gold certificates are now by the Treasury and are held by the Fed- Reserve Banks as evidence of their gold ngs; these are used as part of their reserves t their deposits and Federal Reserve notes.

exchange standard: a method by which ries which have little gold may hold cur- s of other countries that are exchangeable old, such as Bolivia holding United States s.

par rate of exchange: the use of a gold ard, with fixed relative values of particular ncies, as a means of facilitating currency nge. Used primarily by the United States estern European nations before the Great ssion.

gold standard: a system in which the monetary unit is expressed in terms of gold. The government buys and sells gold freely at a fixed price.

good: when defined broadly, anything that people desire. Narrowly defined, it excludes nontangible items, which are called services.

Gresham's law: when two kinds of money are used in a country, the cheaper money will drive the relatively higher-valued money out of circulation.

gross: total amount before any deductions.

gross national debt: total indebtedness of the national government, including the debts owed by one governmental agency to another governmental agency. *Net debt* refers only to government obligations to the public.

gross national income: GNP stated as income rather than as production.

gross national product: the total retail market value of all goods and services produced in a nation during a given period, usually a year.

gross savings: the sum of capital consumption (depreciation), corporation savings, and personal savings.

guaranteed annual wage: the minimum yearly payment that an employer agrees to make to a worker. The employer agrees to employ the worker for a minimum number of weeks each year and to supplement his unemployment insurance benefits if he is laid off because of insufficient demand.

holding company: a corporation which is organized primarily to hold stock in one or more other corporations for the purpose of control.

homogeneous: a characteristic of money which refers to the fact that all similar units have similar value.

homogeneous product: a product in which all units are alike and which is therefore most suitable for achieving or maintaining pure competition. A market with homogeneous products is in contrast to the product differentiation usually found under monopolistic competition.

horizontal combination: a combination formed when two or more organizations producing the same goods or performing the same services merge.

imperfect competition: any market condition which differs from pure competition.

to satisfy human wants rather than for resale or to further production.

consumer price index: a measurement of the cost of living prepared by the U.S. Bureau of Labor Statistics.

consumer sovereignty: a central idea of the classical model that production should be determined by the market's response to consumer demand.

consumption: the utilization of goods and services to satisfy human wants.

contract: an agreement between two or more parties recognized and enforceable by law.

contraction: a decline of economic activity in the business cycle.

copyright: an exclusive right given to artists, authors, and musicians, or to their designated agents, by government to reproduce, publish, or sell what they have created.

corporate income tax: a slightly progressive tax levied on the taxable income of corporations.

corporation: an artificial person before the law; it is chartered by the state government, which allows it such powers as the right to issue stocks and bonds and to have perpetual life. The owners have only limited liability.

correspondent bank: a commercial bank that performs services for other commercial banks.

cost-push inflation: a rise in the price level that originates on the cost (or supply) side rather than because of excess demand. It usually occurs when economic groups try to increase their relative share of the national income.

countercyclical: reversing the direction of the business cycle.

countervailing power: the tendency of one economic group having monopolistic power to balance another group having monopolistic power, as in the case of a monopolistic producer and a monopolistic buyer.

craft union: a union of workers having the same or similar skills, such as electricians or plumbers. It is sometimes called a trade or horizontal union. (*Cf.* industrial union.)

credit: purchasing or borrowing with the promise to pay at some later date.

creditor nation: a nation whose citizens, businesses, and government owe less to foreign creditors than foreign debtors owe to them.

credit union: a cooperative savings and loan association.

cumulative preferred stock: stock with a stated dividend that must be paid before common stockholders receive their dividends. If not paid, the amount accumulates.

currency: that part of the money supply, in the form of coins and paper bills, that is issued by the government or its agent (central bank).

customs union: an agreement between nations to eliminate duties on goods traded between them and to have a common external tariff applicable to all nonmembers.

debenture bonds: long-term promissory notes issued by a corporation and backed only by the good faith of the corporation.

debtor nation: a nation whose citizens, businesses, and government owe more to foreign creditors than foreign debtors owe to them.

decreasing costs: costs which decline per unit as production increases.

deficit financing: the condition in which government expenditures exceed government revenues, the difference being made up by borrowing. In the United States it is frequently planned by the national government to increase aggregate demand.

deflation: a decline in the general price level; it results in an increase in the purchasing power of money.

demand: the quantity of goods or services that buyers are willing to purchase at various prices at a given time.

demand deposit: a deposit on account in a commercial bank upon which checks can be written and money withdrawn without any advance notice. Demand deposits make up the largest part of our money supply.

demand-pull inflation: a rise in the price level caused by too much money pursuing too few goods. The demand for goods is greater than the ability to supply them.

depreciation: reduction in the value of capital goods because of the wear and tear on them in producing other goods. Also called "capital consumption."

depression: the period in the business cycle when most measurements of economic activity are at their lowest. Characterized by low production, low prices, and high unemployment.

derivative deposits: those deposits that come into being as a result of people's borrowing from a bank.

devaluation: a decrease in the value of the unit of money (dollars, pounds, francs, etc.) in relation to gold or other currencies.

dictatorship of proletariat: according to Karl Marx and his followers, that stage in the evolution of society that follows the overthrow of capitalism, when representatives of the working class assume complete power.

diminishing marginal utility: the gradual decline in consumer satisfaction that each additional unit of consumption of a particular good or service gives.

diminishing returns, law of: when additional units of one factor of production are added to a constant quantity of other factors, eventually each additional unit added will yield less than the preceding unit.

discount: interest that is paid in advance.

discount store: a company that sells goods at less than standard list price.

discretionary policy: monetary and fiscal policy requiring action by an individual or a government agency and designed to compensate for the business cycle.

discretionary stabilizer: an economic tool, used to counter the direction of the business cycle, that requires action or decision making on the part of some authority.

disposable income: the amount of income individuals have left to spend and save. Personal income minus personal taxes.

distribution: the marketing or merchandising of commodities. *See also* functional distribution.

dividend: the return to shareholders from their ownership in corporate stock. It is paid from profits.

divisibility: a characteristic of money that allows it to be stated and used in fractions or multiples of the unit of money.

dollar shortage: foreign nations' lack of enough dollars to buy from the United States. Caused by a steady favorable balance of payments for the United States.

domestic system: production that takes place in the home rather than at the factory. Characteristic of production before the impact of the Industrial Revolution.

double counting: in determining GNP by the income method, the taking into account more than once of the value added to products.

dumping: selling goods to other countries below cost in order to get rid of surpluses or to destroy foreign competition.

durability: a characteristic of money that permits it to be used over a long period of time or to be replaced inexpensively.

economic freedom: the principle that individuals have mobility in the economy in that they are guaranteed the right to choose their own jobs, to buy and sell property, and to enter into or dissolve a business.

economic good: a good that is relatively scarce and requires effort to obtain; broadly defined, it includes services as well as physical goods.

economic growth: increase in real per capita income.

economic indicator: a measurement of one or several parts of the economy which is useful for evaluating the entire economy and predicting its course. It may be leading, coincident, or lagging, depending on its relation to the economy as a whole.

economic profit: profit remaining after explicit and implicit costs are paid. Sometimes called pure profit.

economic rent: the surplus paid in excess of what each resource would receive singularly as shown on a supply schedule.

economic system: the way society organizes itself through its institutions and its guiding principles and values in answering the central and related economic questions.

economic value: the value placed on a good because of its utility and scarcity.

economics: that branch of the social sciences that concerns itself with the production, distribution, and consumption of goods and services.

elastic demand: when a small change in price will result in a relatively greater change in the quantity people will buy, the demand for the product is said to be elastic.

elastic supply: when a small change in price will result in a relatively greater change in the quantity offered for sale, the supply of the product is said to be elastic.

emerging nation: a country which is poor and is only beginning to develop its economic potential. Usually refers to nations which have only recently been given their independence.

enterprise: that factor of production which is responsible for initiating production and organizing the other factors of production. It assumes the risk and receives as its payment profit.

entrepreneur: one who assumes the responsibility of enterprise. Management has taken over many of the functions of the entrepreneur.

equation of exchange: an equation that shows the relationship between the supply of money, prices, and business activity. It is stated as $MV = PT$, where M represents the supply of money, V its velocity, P the price level, and T the number of transactions.

equilibrium: in economic theory, a condition which, once it is achieved, will continue unless one of the variables is changed or unless the changing of one variable is not offset by an equal change in another variable. Examples include: the intersection of supply and demand, the point at which aggregate demand $(C + I + G)$ crosses the 45° line, the point at which investment equals savings, and the point at which marginal cost equals marginal revenue.

escalator clause: a provision in a contract to permit changes in payment to fluctuate with changes in the general price level. Most frequently used in connection with wage payments.

escape clause: a provision to allow the United States Tariff Commission to appeal to the President to nullify a trade agreement if the Commission finds that the trade agreement may hurt a domestic industry.

estate tax: a tax placed on the value of an inherited estate.

evasion: an illegal method of reducing tax payments.

excess profits tax: a tax on business firms in addition to the normal business tax. In the United States it is levied on profits above what the law designates as normal and is usually used during wartime.

excess reserves: bank reserves that are greater than those required by the Federal Reserve.

exchange rate: the price that one nation must pay to exchange its currency for another nation's currency.

exchange value: the value placed on a good or service based on the amount of other goods and services it may be exchanged for.

excise tax: a tax placed on a good or service at the time of its sale.

expansion: that phase of
ing which activity is in
by increasing employme

explicit costs: costs tha
firm, such as wages, ren

external cost: where the
of pollution is outside
example, waste dumped
for by the people in the f

factors of production: t
sary for the production
Most economists list fo
and enterprise. The ter
frequently used for lan
often used for enterprise.

Family Assistance Plan:
posal for providing pub
families with children.
income for all families a
come of the working poor

fascism: a politicoecono
mits private ownership
ized decision making a
and is politically a dicta

favorable balance of trad
a nation's total value of e
value of imports.

featherbedding: the emp
ers than are needed for
placing limitations on t
according to provisions
contract.

fiat money: money which
backing and circulates b
ment.

fiscal policy: planned cou
ary matters by the gove
fluence economic activity.

fixed cost: cost that does
volume of production.

foreign exchange: the pro
involving foreign curren
against another country.

franchise: granting by go
the right to have a monop
for a particular service.

free goods: those goods
that they can be had wit
air.

free
icy
elimi
freed
prod
have
in p
the
spira
fring
but
sick
in la
full
whic
empl
quali
frequ
omy
4 per
funct
inter
acco

gene
of p
value
gene
at th
frequ
gift
ferre
and e
gold
certi
redee
issue
eral
holdi
again
gold
coun
renci
for g
dolla
gold-
stand
curre
excha
and
Depr

to satisfy human wants rather than for resale or to further production.

consumer price index: a measurement of the cost of living prepared by the U.S. Bureau of Labor Statistics.

consumer sovereignty: a central idea of the classical model that production should be determined by the market's response to consumer demand.

consumption: the utilization of goods and services to satisfy human wants.

contract: an agreement between two or more parties recognized and enforceable by law.

contraction: a decline of economic activity in the business cycle.

copyright: an exclusive right given to artists, authors, and musicians, or to their designated agents, by government to reproduce, publish, or sell what they have created.

corporate income tax: a slightly progressive tax levied on the taxable income of corporations.

corporation: an artificial person before the law; it is chartered by the state government, which allows it such powers as the right to issue stocks and bonds and to have perpetual life. The owners have only limited liability.

correspondent bank: a commercial bank that performs services for other commercial banks.

cost-push inflation: a rise in the price level that originates on the cost (or supply) side rather than because of excess demand. It usually occurs when economic groups try to increase their relative share of the national income.

countercyclical: reversing the direction of the business cycle.

countervailing power: the tendency of one economic group having monopolistic power to balance another group having monopolistic power, as in the case of a monopolistic producer and a monopolistic buyer.

craft union: a union of workers having the same or similar skills, such as electricians or plumbers. It is sometimes called a trade or horizontal union. (*Cf.* industrial union.)

credit: purchasing or borrowing with the promise to pay at some later date.

creditor nation: a nation whose citizens, businesses, and government owe less to foreign creditors than foreign debtors owe to them.

credit union: a cooperative savings and loan association.

cumulative preferred stock: stock with a stated dividend that must be paid before common stockholders receive their dividends. If not paid, the amount accumulates.

currency: that part of the money supply, in the form of coins and paper bills, that is issued by the government or its agent (central bank).

customs union: an agreement between nations to eliminate duties on goods traded between them and to have a common external tariff applicable to all nonmembers.

debenture bonds: long-term promissory notes issued by a corporation and backed only by the good faith of the corporation.

debtor nation: a nation whose citizens, businesses, and government owe more to foreign creditors than foreign debtors owe to them.

decreasing costs: costs which decline per unit as production increases.

deficit financing: the condition in which government expenditures exceed government revenues, the difference being made up by borrowing. In the United States it is frequently planned by the national government to increase aggregate demand.

deflation: a decline in the general price level; it results in an increase in the purchasing power of money.

demand: the quantity of goods or services that buyers are willing to purchase at various prices at a given time.

demand deposit: a deposit on account in a commercial bank upon which checks can be written and money withdrawn without any advance notice. Demand deposits make up the largest part of our money supply.

demand-pull inflation: a rise in the price level caused by too much money pursuing too few goods. The demand for goods is greater than the ability to supply them.

depreciation: reduction in the value of capital goods because of the wear and tear on them in producing other goods. Also called "capital consumption."

depression: the period in the business cycle when most measurements of economic activity are at their lowest. Characterized by low production, low prices, and high unemployment.

derivative deposits: those deposits that come into being as a result of people's borrowing from a bank.

devaluation: a decrease in the value of the unit of money (dollars, pounds, francs, etc.) in relation to gold or other currencies.

dictatorship of proletariat: according to Karl Marx and his followers, that stage in the evolution of society that follows the overthrow of capitalism, when representatives of the working class assume complete power.

diminishing marginal utility: the gradual decline in consumer satisfaction that each additional unit of consumption of a particular good or service gives.

diminishing returns, law of: when additional units of one factor of production are added to a constant quantity of other factors, eventually each additional unit added will yield less than the preceding unit.

discount: interest that is paid in advance.

discount store: a company that sells goods at less than standard list price.

discretionary policy: monetary and fiscal policy requiring action by an individual or a government agency and designed to compensate for the business cycle.

discretionary stabilizer: an economic tool, used to counter the direction of the business cycle, that requires action or decision making on the part of some authority.

disposable income: the amount of income individuals have left to spend and save. Personal income minus personal taxes.

distribution: the marketing or merchandising of commodities. *See also* functional distribution.

dividend: the return to shareholders from their ownership in corporate stock. It is paid from profits.

divisibility: a characteristic of money that allows it to be stated and used in fractions or multiples of the unit of money.

dollar shortage: foreign nations' lack of enough dollars to buy from the United States. Caused by a steady favorable balance of payments for the United States.

domestic system: production that takes place in the home rather than at the factory. Characteristic of production before the impact of the Industrial Revolution.

double counting: in determining GNP by the income method, the taking into account more than once of the value added to products.

dumping: selling goods to other countries below cost in order to get rid of surpluses or to destroy foreign competition.

durability: a characteristic of money that permits it to be used over a long period of time or to be replaced inexpensively.

economic freedom: the principle that individuals have mobility in the economy in that they are guaranteed the right to choose their own jobs, to buy and sell property, and to enter into or dissolve a business.

economic good: a good that is relatively scarce and requires effort to obtain; broadly defined, it includes services as well as physical goods.

economic growth: increase in real per capita income.

economic indicator: a measurement of one or several parts of the economy which is useful for evaluating the entire economy and predicting its course. It may be leading, coincident, or lagging, depending on its relation to the economy as a whole.

economic profit: profit remaining after explicit and implicit costs are paid. Sometimes called pure profit.

economic rent: the surplus paid in excess of what each resource would receive singularly as shown on a supply schedule.

economic system: the way society organizes itself through its institutions and its guiding principles and values in answering the central and related economic questions.

economic value: the value placed on a good because of its utility and scarcity.

economics: that branch of the social sciences that concerns itself with the production, distribution, and consumption of goods and services.

elastic demand: when a small change in price will result in a relatively greater change in the quantity people will buy, the demand for the product is said to be elastic.

elastic supply: when a small change in price will result in a relatively greater change in the quantity offered for sale, the supply of the product is said to be elastic.

emerging nation: a country which is poor and is only beginning to develop its economic potential. Usually refers to nations which have only recently been given their independence.

enterprise: that factor of production which is responsible for initiating production and organizing the other factors of production. It assumes the risk and receives as its payment profit.

entrepreneur: one who assumes the responsibility of enterprise. Management has taken over many of the functions of the entrepreneur.

equation of exchange: an equation that shows the relationship between the supply of money, prices, and business activity. It is stated as $MV = PT$, where M represents the supply of money, V its velocity, P the price level, and T the number of transactions.

equilibrium: in economic theory, a condition which, once it is achieved, will continue unless one of the variables is changed or unless the changing of one variable is not offset by an equal change in another variable. Examples include: the intersection of supply and demand, the point at which aggregate demand $(C + I + G)$ crosses the 45° line, the point at which investment equals savings, and the point at which marginal cost equals marginal revenue.

escalator clause: a provision in a contract to permit changes in payment to fluctuate with changes in the general price level. Most frequently used in connection with wage payments.

escape clause: a provision to allow the United States Tariff Commission to appeal to the President to nullify a trade agreement if the Commission finds that the trade agreement may hurt a domestic industry.

estate tax: a tax placed on the value of an inherited estate.

evasion: an illegal method of reducing tax payments.

excess profits tax: a tax on business firms in addition to the normal business tax. In the United States it is levied on profits above what the law designates as normal and is usually used during wartime.

excess reserves: bank reserves that are greater than those required by the Federal Reserve.

exchange rate: the price that one nation must pay to exchange its currency for another nation's currency.

exchange value: the value placed on a good or service based on the amount of other goods and services it may be exchanged for.

excise tax: a tax placed on a good or service at the time of its sale.

expansion: that phase of the business cycle during which activity is increasing. Characterized by increasing employment and production.

explicit costs: costs that originate outside the firm, such as wages, rent, and interest.

external cost: where the cost or burden of cost of pollution is outside the individual firm, for example, waste dumped into streams and paid for by the people in the form of polluted streams.

factors of production: those ingredients necessary for the production of any good or service. Most economists list four: land, labor, capital, and enterprise. The term *natural resources* is frequently used for land, and *management* is often used for enterprise.

Family Assistance Plan: President Nixon's proposal for providing public assistance to needy families with children. It provides a minimum income for all families and supplements the income of the working poor.

fascism: a politicoeconomic system which permits private ownership but has highly centralized decision making about economic matters and is politically a dictatorship.

favorable balance of trade: a condition in which a nation's total value of exports exceeds its total value of imports.

featherbedding: the employment of more workers than are needed for efficient operation, or placing limitations on the output of workers, according to provisions in a labor-management contract.

fiat money: money which has no precious metal backing and circulates by order of the government.

fiscal policy: planned course of action on budgetary matters by the government designed to influence economic activity.

fixed cost: cost that does not fluctuate with the volume of production.

foreign exchange: the process of settling claims, involving foreign currency, that a country has against another country.

franchise: granting by government to a firm of the right to have a monopoly or partial monopoly for a particular service.

free goods: those goods which are so abundant that they can be had without cost, for example, air.

free trade: trade among nations in which all policy restrictions that may impede its flow are eliminated.

freedom of contract: the principle that, in the production of goods and services, individuals have the right to enter into agreements resulting in production. Such agreements must be within the framework of the law and may not be conspiracies against society.

fringe benefits: items that increase real income but are not included in the basic wage, such as sick benefits. Fringe benefits are often included in labor contracts.

full employment: a condition of the economy in which there is sufficient aggregate demand to employ all those who wish to work and are qualified to do so. In the United States it is frequently considered the condition of the economy when the unemployment rate is less than 4 percent.

functional distribution: payment—wages, rent, interest, and profit—to the factors of production according to their contribution.

general property tax: a tax on the assessed value of property; it is computed as a percentage of value. Specific types of property may be exempt.

general sales tax: a tax on most goods collected at the time of their sale. Food and medicine are frequently exempt.

gift tax: a tax on the value of property transferred primarily to avoid payment of inheritance and estate taxes.

gold certificate: in the United States, formerly, a certificate issued by the government that was redeemable in gold. Gold certificates are now issued by the Treasury and are held by the Federal Reserve Banks as evidence of their gold holdings; these are used as part of their reserves against their deposits and Federal Reserve notes.

gold exchange standard: a method by which countries which have little gold may hold currencies of other countries that are exchangeable for gold, such as Bolivia holding United States dollars.

gold-par rate of exchange: the use of a gold standard, with fixed relative values of particular currencies, as a means of facilitating currency exchange. Used primarily by the United States and western European nations before the Great Depression.

gold standard: a system in which the monetary unit is expressed in terms of gold. The government buys and sells gold freely at a fixed price.

good: when defined broadly, anything that people desire. Narrowly defined, it excludes nontangible items, which are called services.

Gresham's law: when two kinds of money are used in a country, the cheaper money will drive the relatively higher-valued money out of circulation.

gross: total amount before any deductions.

gross national debt: total indebtedness of the national government, including the debts owed by one governmental agency to another governmental agency. *Net debt* refers only to government obligations to the public.

gross national income: GNP stated as income rather than as production.

gross national product: the total retail market value of all goods and services produced in a nation during a given period, usually a year.

gross savings: the sum of capital consumption (depreciation), corporation savings, and personal savings.

guaranteed annual wage: the minimum yearly payment that an employer agrees to make to a worker. The employer agrees to employ the worker for a minimum number of weeks each year and to supplement his unemployment insurance benefits if he is laid off because of insufficient demand.

holding company: a corporation which is organized primarily to hold stock in one or more other corporations for the purpose of control.

homogeneous: a characteristic of money which refers to the fact that all similar units have similar value.

homogeneous product: a product in which all units are alike and which is therefore most suitable for achieving or maintaining pure competition. A market with homogeneous products is in contrast to the product differentiation usually found under monopolistic competition.

horizontal combination: a combination formed when two or more organizations producing the same goods or performing the same services merge.

imperfect competition: any market condition which differs from pure competition.

implicit costs: costs originating within the firm which are provided by the owner, such as time, money, or property.

import quota: a limit on the quantity of a product that may be imported during a specified period of time.

income tax: a tax on the net income of individuals or corporations, usually with progressive rates. The most important source of federal revenue.

index number: a measurement of relative change using statistical procedures.

industrial union: a labor union in which all workers in a particular industry, regardless of their jobs, are members. It is sometimes referred to as a vertical union.

industry-wide bargaining: collective bargaining in which one or several unions negotiate for a contract with virtually all the employers of an industry. In many instances a contract worked out with a particular employer sets the pattern for the entire industry.

inelastic demand: a condition in which the quantity of a product sold does not change, or changes very little, with a change in price.

inelastic supply: a condition in which the quantity of a product produced does not change, or changes very little, with a change in price.

inflation: an increase in the price level causing a decrease in the purchasing power of the monetary unit.

inheritance tax: a tax on those receiving shares of an estate.

injunction: a court order restraining an individual or a group from carrying on some kind of activity. Frequently used in connection with preventing or stopping a strike.

innovation: a new idea or method in the production process frequently involving the use of inventions in a practical way.

installment buying: acquiring goods or services by making either no down payment or a small down payment and afterwards making payments at regular intervals.

installment credit: a type of consumer credit involving periodic payments that allows the seller to repossess the article purchased if the buyer defaults on payment.

insurance: the financial operation whereby many people contribute to a fund from which those who sustain a loss are compensated.

interest: payment for the use of capital (loanable funds).

interlocking directorate: a condition in which one or more members of a board of directors of one company are also members of the boards of directors of other companies.

internal cost: where the cost or burden of the cost is within the individual firm. The expense of installing pollution (or waste) disposal units becomes part of the cost of production.

intrinsic value: the market value of the material in a thing, as the value of the metal in a coin.

inventory: goods in stock and usually available for sale.

investment: when applied to an individual or a firm, the purchase of assets which will produce income. When used in macroeconomics, it refers to capital formation and capital accumulation (capital goods produced plus inventory accumulation).

investment bank: a business that specializes in underwriting and selling new issues of stocks and bonds.

invisible exports and imports: financial transactions among nations involving services or such intangibles as shipping charges, insurance, tourist spending, and the transfer of loanable funds.

jurisdictional dispute: a conflict between rival unions as to which should have control over a given job or activity and be recognized by management.

labor: one of the factors of production involving human effort in the production process. Managerial activities are frequently considered a separate factor.

labor force: includes those over 14 years of age who are working, are looking for work, or are absent from work because of such things as labor disputes, illness, vacations, etc.

labor union: an organization of employees which acts in their behalf, particularly in connection with negotiating with management.

laissez-faire: a policy associated with the classical model of capitalism suggesting that the government should not interfere with the economy.

land: the factor of production from which goods originate; natural resources before man has worked on them.

law of increasing costs: the principle that, in a production situation, average total unit cost increases as the volume of a business increases. This principle is not universally applicable, since in some industries costs are constant and in others costs decrease as volume of business increases.

legal reserve: the percentage of deposits that member banks of the Federal Reserve System are required to keep either with the Federal Reserve Bank or in their vaults.

legal tender: a form of money which the government recognizes and creditors must legally accept as payment for debts.

liability: the debt of an individual or a firm that is owed to others. Does not include capital investment by owners (stock).

limited liability: the legal exemption of stockholders in a corporation from financial liability for the debts of the company beyond the amount they have invested.

limited life: a characteristic of a single proprietorship or partnership, in both of which the business ceases to exist upon the death of the owner (or one of the owners).

liquid assets: those assets that can easily be converted into cash, such as government bonds and other easily marketable securities.

liquidity preference: the preference that people and businesses have for holding their assets in cash rather than in a less liquid form.

lockout: closing of a business by an employer in order to put pressure on a union in a labor-management dispute. The employer's counterpart of a strike.

long run: in the case of a business, a sufficiently long period of time to permit the business to develop its capacity to produce. In the long run all costs become variable.

Lorenz curve: a measuring tool for plotting the degree of inequality in the distribution of income.

macroeconomics: the study of the economy as a whole rather than as individual economic units. Sometimes referred to as aggregate economics.

maintenance-of-membership shop: a situation in which workers who are members of a union must continue their membership for the duration of the contract.

management: the factor of production that is responsible for organizing and directing the other three factors. Some economists include management with labor or call this factor the entrepreneur depending on whether they are owners of the firm.

margin: in the purchase of securities, the amount of money that the buyer must deposit immediately with the broker. It is stated as a percentage of the total value of the securities.

marginal: yielding only enough value to cover the cost of production. May be used with land, labor, or a business.

marginal analysis: analysis of economic data by studying the results of the value added by an additional unit of one variable to another variable.

marginal cost: the additional cost for expanding output by one more unit.

marginal product: the additional product derived by adding one more unit (as an additional worker) of a factor of production.

marginal productivity wage theory: the principle that under competitive conditions the wages of all workers will be set by the productivity, measured in money, of the last worker hired.

marginal propensity to consume: the proportion of additional income that people spend.

marginal propensity to save: the proportion of additional income that people save.

marginal revenue: the additional revenue that a firm receives from the sale of one more unit. Under pure competition in the short run this is the same as the market price.

marginal revenue product: the additional revenue a firm receives by the addition of one more unit of a factor of production, such as an additional worker.

market: the place or situation in which buyers and sellers can meet for the purpose of exchange.

measure of value: that function of money which provides the standard for measuring the value of production, using the monetary unit as the common denominator (such as showing the value of apples and the value of candy bars in dollars).

mediation: a method of settling labor disputes in which a third party participates in a formal way in helping to bring about an agreement among the disputants. Plans offered by the mediator are not binding.

medium of exchange: the major function of money which facilitates the exchange of goods and services. Needed by an economy which has specialization of production.

mercantilism: an economic system most popular in the sixteenth, seventeenth, and eighteenth centuries which was characterized by a highly controlled market with numerous regulations designed to increase the flow of precious metals into the treasury of the "mother country." This system is usually considered a precursor of the classical model.

merger: the combining of two companies into one by the dissolution of one with the sale of assets to the other.

microeconomics: the study of the economic behavior of individual units in the economy, such as business firms.

military-industrial complex: the community of interests established between officials in the armed services and the defense industry. Alleged by its critics to work against the public interest.

minimum wage: the lowest wage that an employer can pay an employee as set by law. Usually expressed as an hourly rate.

mixed capitalism: an economic system in which the major portion of the instruments of production is owned and operated by private enterprise and the market mechanism is the major factor in determining the allocation of resources. However, a democratic government may provide for some ownership of, and control over, enterprise as well as assume considerable responsibility for the economic wellbeing of the nation.

model: a theory used by social scientists to analyze economic behavior. The closer the model is to the real world the more useful it is for analysis.

monetary policy: use of the tools of the Federal Reserve System in an attempt to achieve stable prices and full employment. The tools include changing interest rates and bank reserve ratios and, indirectly, the quantity of money for the purpose of modifying the business cycle.

money: a medium of exchange that is accepted by society. In the United States the term includes currency and demand deposits.

money wages: a term used to distinguish the number of dollars received by workers as contrasted with what those dollars will buy (purchasing power).

monopolistic competition: a market situation similar to pure competition but characterized by product differentiation and the effect that each firm's actions have on all other firms.

monopoly: a market situation in which there is only one seller of a product and there are no acceptable substitutes.

monopsony: a market situation in which there is only one buyer for a product.

multiplier: the reciprocal of the marginal propensity to save. This figure relates changes in investment and spending to changes in aggregate income.

national debt: the debt owed by the federal government. Does not include the debts of state and local governments or private debt.

national income: the total income payments made to the owners of the factors of production. Sometimes used to refer to gross or net national product.

nationalize: to take for government ownership, with or without compensation, a business or other property owned and operated privately.

natural monopoly: an industry in which competition would be costly and uneconomical.

natural resources: *See* land.

near-money: highly liquid assets other than money, such as time deposits and government securities.

negative incentives: charges, usually in the form of a tax, to discourage production or a level of production. Applied to discourage pollution.

negative income tax: a proposal of financial assistance to people with incomes below a certain minimum that would use the income tax principle except that the procedure would distribute rather than collect revenue.

net: that which is left after certain designated deductions are made from the gross amount.

net national product: gross national product minus capital consumption (depreciation).

net worth: total assets minus total liabilities. Recorded in the balance sheet of a firm.

oligopoly: a market situation characterized by only a few sellers of a product.

oligopsony: a market situation characterized by only a few buyers of a product.

open-market operations: the buying and selling of securities, primarily government securities, by the Federal Reserve System, usually to carry out a monetary policy.

open shop: a business which employs workers without reference to their membership in a union.

opportunity costs: what a factor of production could return if it were used in some other activity that society needed. The amount needed to get a factor of production away from some alternative use. Also called "alternative cost."

over-the-counter market: the market for securities sold by brokers outside organized stock exchanges. Over-the-counter securities are also called "unlisted."

parity: in the United States, as part of the farm policy, a plan designed to keep purchasing power of a unit of farm production (for example, a bushel of wheat) equal to the purchasing power of the units of production that a farmer buys in the same ratio as existed during some selected base period.

partnership: a form of business organization consisting of two or more individuals who share in the ownership and operation of the business according to a contractual arrangement. Liability is unlimited.

patent: an exclusive right, granted by the government, to make and sell inventions.

payroll tax: a tax on wages or salaries earned within the boundaries of a government, most frequently a city.

per capita output: GNP of a country divided by the country's population. Sometimes used to indicate the relative standard of living of a nation.

perfect competition: *See* pure competition.

peril point: the lowest figure at which a duty on imports can be set without threatening a domestic industry.

perpetual life: a characteristic of a corporation, in which the death of one or more owners does not automatically bring about an end to the business.

personal consumption expenditures: the money households spend for consumer goods. Disposable personal income minus savings equals personal consumption expenditures.

personal income: total money income received by individuals before the payment of personal taxes.

personal income tax: a tax on the income of individuals or families; it is usually progressive.

personal savings: the difference between disposable personal income and personal consumption expenditures.

picketing: a weapon of unions during a strike in which workers advertise their grievances by carrying signs and walking in lines in the neighborhood of a business, urging other workers not to work and customers not to buy.

piece rate: wages that are determined by the number of units produced or work done. This is contrasted with hourly wage rates, in which a fixed rate per hour is set.

portability: a characteristic of money that allows it to be carried easily.

poverty index: a sliding scale based on family size and location to determine what minimum income is needed for meeting acceptable family needs determined by the Department of Health, Education and Welfare.

preferential shop: a situation in which management agrees to hire union members so long as they are available.

preferred stock: that stock of a corporation that gives the owner preferential treatment in the payment of dividends and in the distribution of assets in the event the corporation is liquidated. Dividend rates are usually fixed. (*See also* common stock.)

price: the exchange value of goods and services stated in a monetary unit.

price index: a device for measuring the changing value of money over a given period of time or the average price of a number of selected commodities at a given time.

price level: the average of prices paid for goods and services in a given period.

primary deposits: those deposits made by people depositing cash in the bank.

private enterprise: organization of production in which business units are owned and operated by individuals who take risks and are motivated by the desire to make a profit. Contrasted with government or collective enterprise.

private property: property which an individual owns and over which he has the right to exercise reasonable control. Provides incentive for producing.

product differentiation: a condition in which a producer consciously tries to represent his product as different from similar products. Characteristic of monopolistic competition and some oligopolies.

production: any kind of activity which adds value to goods and services, including creation, transportation, and storage until used.

production function: use of the technical information that shows the amount of output that is capable of being performed by specific inputs (factors of production).

productivity: the output for a unit of a factor of production.

profit: payment to a business enterprise for the risks incurred. The amount left from total revenue after all costs are paid.

progressive tax: a tax in which the rate of payment increases as the tax base increases.

promissory note: a written statement agreeing to pay a certain sum of money to a specific person or firm at an indicated time.

propensity to consume: the proportion of income that people tend to spend at different levels of income.

propensity to save: the proportion of income that people tend to save at different levels of income.

proportional tax: a tax in which the rate of tax does not change with a change in the tax base.

prosperity: the uppermost phase of a business cycle.

protectionists: those who favor high tariffs and other restrictions on imports to the end that domestic goods will not have to compete with foreign goods.

protective tariff: a tax on imported goods designed to give domestic producers protection from price competition.

public utility: a business that provides essential services to the public and tends to be a natural monopoly. It must obtain a franchise from the government and is regulated by a government agency.

pure competition: a market situation in which there are a sufficient number of buyers and sellers acting independently and in which the product is a homogeneous one, so that the entry or exit of any one buyer or seller will not affect price.

pure profit: *See* economic profit.

quantity theory of money: the theory that the general price level will change in response to the money supply. Stated as the equation of exchange: $MV = PT$.

real wages: the amount of goods and services that can be bought with one's money wages. Useful for comparing changes in the standard of living by eliminating the influence of changes in the general price level. (*Cf.* money wages.)

recession: that phase of the business cycle that shows a downswing or contraction of the economy.

recovery: that period of the business cycle which follows a depression. Also known as an upswing or expansion.

recycling: converting waste products to usable material, usually to reduce pollution.

regressive tax: a tax in which the rate of payment decreases as the tax base increases.

rent: payment for the use of land. (*See also* economic rent.)

reserve ratio: the relationship of the amount of money that must be retained in a reserve account (reserve account with the Federal Reserve Bank plus vault cash) to the total demand deposits of a member bank.

retail price maintenance: the practice of permitting a manufacturer, under protection of state law, to set retail prices for his products. The laws are usually referred to as "fair-trade" laws.

revenue: the income of a government or business enterprise. When deductions are made, it is prefaced with the word *net.*

revenue sharing: a larger unit of government with greater taxing powers returning a portion of its revenue to a smaller unit of government.

revenue tariffs: duties placed on imports with the objective of raising revenues rather than protecting domestic industries. Such tariffs rarely discourage international trade.

sales tax: a tax placed on goods at the time of their purchase.

savings: that part of income that is not spent for consumer items.

savings bank: a financial institution specializing in small time deposits that are usually held for a considerable time.

savings and loan association: a financial institution owned by share purchasers (depositors) which specializes in long-term loans to finance real estate purchases.

seasonal fluctuations: regular and predictable changes in business activity caused by changes in the season, such as the increase in construction in the spring.

secondary boycott: action by a group of workers designed to bring pressure on a firm they have a disagreement with and involving the use of third parties not involved in the dispute, such as the refusal on the part of workers to handle goods coming from a plant that is being struck.

secondary reserves: assets that banks hold other than primary reserves that can be quickly converted into cash, such as government securities or commercial paper.

single proprietorship: the oldest and most common type of business organization, in which the business is owned by an individual.

single tax: a plan, proposed by Henry George, in which all income derived from land ownership would be taxed for the full amount, thereby eliminating the need to collect other taxes.

slowdown: a weapon of labor in which workers purposely reduce the speed at which they work, resulting in increased costs to the employer.

social cost: the price paid by people as a whole for the results of individual economic activities, such as pollution, imposed upon the public by industrial producers.

socialism: an economic system in which much or most of the means of production is owned and controlled collectively, usually by government, and in which central planning is substituted for the market in the allocation of resources.

soil bank: in the United States, a government farm program which pays farmers for withdrawing land from cultivation.

stability of value: a characteristic of money involving little change in what a unit will buy.

stabilizer: an economic tool used to reduce business fluctuations. It may be automatic, such as unemployment insurance, or discretionary, such as increasing or decreasing government spending.

standard allowable deduction: a rate (up to a maximum amount) that is applied to gross income and that may be deducted from gross income in determining taxable income. If it is used, no itemization of deductions is necessary.

standard metropolitan statistical area: a county or group of counties which contains at least one city of at least 50,000, or twin cities with a combined population of 50,000, the smaller of which must have at least 15,000 inhabitants.

standard of deferred payment: that function of money that expresses in terms of money the amount to be repaid.

standard of living: an evaluation of the way a family or group lives with reference to the consumer goods it has.

stock: ownership of a corporation, divided into shares and represented by certificates.

stockbroker: a middleman in the buying and selling of securities.

store of value: that function of money which allows the individual to accumulate wealth or purchasing power.

strike: a weapon of labor in which workers voluntarily stop working in order to bring pressure on the employer to meet their demands.

strikebreaker: a worker hired to replace a striking worker.

structural unemployment: unemployment caused primarily by change in consumer preferences, technology, lack of skills, and loss of markets.

submarginal: yielding less than enough to cover the cost of production. May be used with land, labor, or a business.

subsidy: government assistance to a program, an enterprise, or an industry in the form of a money payment that is generally made for the good of the general public. Farmers, the airlines, and the merchant marines have been subsidized at various times.

subsistence: a level of income necessary to maintain a minimum standard of living.

supply: the quantity of goods and services that sellers are willing to offer at various prices at a given time.

supramarginal: yielding more than the cost of production. Applicable to land, labor, or a business.

surplus value: in Marxian theory, the amount charged above the cost of labor. Other economic theory considers payments made to any of the factors of production, above what the market price would call for under competitive conditions, to be surplus.

tariff: a schedule of taxes on commodities imported or exported. In the United States only imported goods are affected.

tax: a compulsory charge upon individuals and businesses to pay for the cost of running a government and carrying out its policies. Designed to reallocate resources from the private to the public sector.

tax base: the commodity, income, or service on which a tax is levied; only that part of the value of an item which is taxed.

tax incidence: the business and/or individuals upon whom a tax finally comes to rest.

tax rate: a specified percentage of the value of a commodity, income, or service taxed.

taxable income: the amount of income remaining after subtracting all allowable deductions and exemptions and therefore subject to taxation.

technological unemployment: the displacement of workers caused by the introduction of labor-saving machinery.

technology: knowledge of the use of resources for more efficient production.

time deposit: an account in a bank on which (1) interest is usually paid, (2) the bank may legally withhold payment for a specified number of days, and (3) checks cannot be written. Sometimes called savings accounts.

token money: coins that circulate at a higher value than the market value of the commodity (metal) they are made of.

trade association: an organization of firms engaged in a common industry or business activity to promote their mutual interests.

trade-offs: the exchange of one benefit or value at the sacrifice or partial sacrifice of another. For example, to halt air pollution we pay a higher price for unleaded gasoline which helps us enjoy cleaner air.

trade union: *See* craft union.

transfer payment: money paid by one individual or institution (particularly government) to another without the rendering of services, such as social security payments.

trust: a form of business combination which became common in the 1890's in which stockholders exchange their voting shares for trust certificates for purposes of centralizing control of an entire industry in the hands of a few.

turnover tax: a form of sales tax commonly used in the Soviet Union.

underdeveloped country: technically, a nation which has realized little of its economic potential because of a lack of capital, technology, and skilled labor. More commonly it refers to countries with a relatively low per capita income.

underwrite: to guarantee to furnish a definite sum of money by a definite date to a business or government in return for securities, such as stocks and bonds.

unemployment: when referring to the economy as a whole, the difference between the number of persons in the labor force and the number of persons employed. Also refers to those who are able to work and are seeking work but cannot find jobs.

unemployment insurance: that part of our social security program that provides covered employees with insurance against the complete loss of income due to unemployment. Payment comes primarily from taxes paid by employers.

unfavorable balance of trade: the condition in which a nation's total value of imports exceeds its total value of exports.

union label: an emblem placed on a good signifying that it was made by union workers.

union shop: a business in which the employer is free to hire any worker provided that the worker is a union member or will become a union member after a specified period of time.

unit of account: the use of money as a measure or standard of value in an economy.

unlimited liability: a disadvantage of a single proprietorship and of a partnership making the owner or owners responsible (with no exclusion of their personal assets) for the firm's debts.

urban place: an area in which there are 2,500 inhabitants or more.

utility: the satisfaction that one obtains, or anticipates he will obtain, from the consumption, ownership, or use of a good or service.

variable cost: a cost that increases with increase in production.

velocity of circulation: the rate at which the supply of money is turned over (spent) for a given period of time, usually a year.

vertical combinations: a business organization that combines the various stages of production of a single finished good.

wages: the prices management pays for human effort.

wealth: the total value of economic goods.

welfare capitalism: a modified form of capitalism characterized by many social welfare programs, considerable government involvement in the economy, and legislation to provide a minimum standard of living for all citizens.

wildcat strike: a work stoppage that is not sanctioned by the union.

withholding tax: a tax deduction from wages and salaries by the employer. In the United States this method is applied to personal income and social security taxes to make payments more convenient.

working poor: marginal workers whose skills and total work time do not provide them with an income above the poverty index.

yellow-dog contract: a wage contract in which the worker agrees before he is hired not to join a union during his employment. Such contracts are no longer legal.

INDEX

1 2 3 4 5 6 7 8 9 10